CARIBBEAN SEA

The Bahamas
Havana
CUBA
Turks and
Caicos Islands
Cayman
Islands
JAMAICA
HAITI
Dominican
Republic
British
Virgin
Islands
Anguilla
Vieques
Saba Island
St. Lucia
Barbados
Trinidad

P9-CLD-167

Isla Margarita
Cartegena
VENEZUELA
GUYANA
Angel Falls
SURINAM
FRENCH GUIANA
COLOMBIA
Quito
ECUADOR
Amazon River
Galápagos Islands
BRAZIL
PERU
Cordillera Blanca
Manu National Park
Machu Picchu
Salvador
BOLIVIA
Nazca
La Paz
Chiquitos
Barretos
Salar de Uyuni
PARAGUAY
PACIFIC
OCEAN
Salta & Jujuy
Rio de Janeiro
Iguazú Falls
C H I L E
A R G E N T I N A
URUGUAY
Mendoza
Buenos Aires
Easter Island
ATLANTIC
OCEAN
Lake District
Península Valdés
Patagonia
Parque Nacional
Torres del Paine
Falkland
Islands
South Patagonian
Fjords

**SOUTH AMERICA
& THE CARIBBEAN**

WHERE TO GO WHEN
THE AMERICAS

NORTH, CENTRAL, SOUTH AMERICA,
& THE CARIBBEAN

WHERE TO GO WHEN
THE AMERICAS

NORTH, CENTRAL, SOUTH AMERICA, & THE CARIBBEAN

JOSEPH ROSENDO

CONSULTANT EDITOR

DK

LONDON, NEW YORK, MELBOURNE, MUNICH AND DELHI

DK LONDON
LIST MANAGER Christine Stroyan
PROJECT EDITOR Ros Walford
EDITORS Sadie Smith, Fay Franklin,
Jacky Jackson, Alexandra Farrell & Hugh Thompson

DESIGN MANAGER Mabel Chan
ART EDITOR Shahid Mahmood
DESIGNERS Steve Bere, Paul Jackson
& Marisa Renzullo
DTP DESIGNERS Natasha Lu & Jamie McNeill

PICTURE RESEARCH Ellen Root & Sarah Smithies
CARTOGRAPHY Casper Morris
& Ed Merritt from Merrit Cartographic
PRODUCTION CONTROLLER Shane Higgins
PROOFREADER Stewart Wild
INDEXER Helen Peters

DK DELHI
EDITORIAL MANAGER Aruna Ghose
DESIGN MANAGER Sunita Gahir
PROJECT DESIGNER Gouri Banerji
PROJECT EDITOR Shruti Singhi
PICTURE RESEARCH Taiyaba Khatoon
EDITOR Shalini Krishan
DESIGNER Pooja Badola
SENIOR DTP COORDINATOR Shailesh Sharma

QUADRUM SOLUTIONS PVT. LTD.
www.quadrumltd.com

— PUBLISHER Douglas Amrine

REPRODUCED BY Media Development Printing
PRINTED AND BOUND IN Singapore by Star Standard

First American Edition 2008
08 09 10 9 8 7 6 5 4 3 2 1

Published in the United States by Dorling Kindersley
Publishing, Inc., 375 Hudson Street, New York 10014

Copyright © 2008 Dorling Kindersley Limited, London
A Penguin Company

ISBN 978-0-7566-4094-1

www.traveldk.com

Every effort has been made to ensure that this book is as up-to-date as possible at the
time of going to press. Some details, however, such as telephone numbers, opening
hours, prices, and travel information are liable to change. The publishers cannot accept
responsibility for any consequences arising from the use of this book, nor for any
material on third-party websites, and cannot guarantee that any website address in this
book will be a suitable source of travel information. We value the views and
suggestions of our readers very highly. Please write to: Publisher, DK Travel Guides,
Dorling Kindersley, 80 Strand, London, WC2R 0RL, Great Britain.

COVER IMAGE: Monument Valley, Arizona/Utah, USA
TITLE PAGE IMAGE: Iguazú Falls, Argentina
HALF TITLE IMAGE: Horse and rider in the Calgary Exhibition
and Stampede, Canada
FOREWORD IMAGE: Manhattan, New York City

CONTENTS

FOREWORD

While working on WHERE TO GO WHEN – THE AMERICAS, DK Eyewitness Travel Guide's companion to the best-selling WHERE TO GO WHEN, I was struck not only by how many glorious places there are to visit, but also that after more than forty years of traveling I've barely scratched the surface of my own slice of the world.

Whereas WHERE TO GO WHEN encompassed the globe, WHERE TO GO WHEN – THE AMERICAS is packed full of exciting destinations throughout the Americas, which are as diverse, multicultural, wild, and exotic as the rest of the planet. From Tierra del Fuego on the tip of South America and polar-bear country in the far arctic reaches of North America to bustling Broadway and the sparkling, sun-blessed shores of the Caribbean isles, this continent is truly, to paraphrase Shakespeare, a brave new world that hath wondrous people and places in it.

WHERE TO GO WHEN – THE AMERICAS pays homage to the majesty and variety of the Americas. DK Eyewitness Travel has served up a delicious selection of opportunities in all countries, for all seasons and all tastes. This beautiful book helps us celebrate our continent in new and stimulating ways.

WHERE TO GO WHEN – THE AMERICAS inspires, encourages, instructs, and assists us on our quest to fulfill our travel dreams. Not only does it match the best time with the best experience in the best place, but it opens our senses and sensibilities to our neighbors, our neighborhood, and our true fellow Americans.

Books of this magnitude are often classified as "gift books," which really is an excellent description for this work because WHERE TO GO WHEN – THE AMERICAS wraps up the continent in a brilliantly illustrated, carefully researched, immensely informative, and entertainingly written package. And, once again, DK Eyewitness Travel Guides has created a vehicle that transports us instantly to other lands. Use this book as inspiration for your next wonderful adventure.

Happy Traveling!

JOSEPH ROSENDO

JANUARY

Where to Go: **January**

While January can offer nothing cheerier than a long hibernation in much of North America, the new year also offers crisp air, bright skies, and snowfall – perfect for skiing in the Rockies or for exploring the red-rock landscapes of the Southwest. Surf's up on the Hawaiian islands, which offer a balmy, sunny climate in January, and unlike many destinations in the Americas, don't suffer dramatic drops in temperature after dark. This is also a great time to venture out to the subtropical regions that get steamier as the year wears on. Florida is at its coolest and driest in January, while the levels of humidity in the stickier countries of South America are at their most comfortable. Below you will find all the destinations in this chapter as well as some extra suggestions to provide a little inspiration.

| FESTIVALS AND CULTURE | UNFORGETTABLE JOURNEYS | NATURAL WONDERS |

CARTAGENA Young dancers at a street festival

MAUI Tour group at the summit of Haleakalā volcano

CARLSBAD Speleotherms or rock formations within the Carlsbad Caverns

VALPARAÍSO
CHILE

South America's most historic Pacific seaport

Head south for midsummer in Chile's prettiest city, with twisting cobbled streets of brightly painted houses tumbling down to the sea.
www.vinayvalpo.com

CARTAGENA
COLOMBIA

A celebration of literature from every continent

When you've finished sightseeing, mingle with poets, authors, and playwrights at Colombia's annual Hay Literary Festival.
See pp16–17

MAUI
HAWAI'I, USA

A stunning road trip with beaches and waterfalls

Drive the scenic road to Hana on Hawai'i's second-largest island, stopping to admire beaches, falls, and forests along the way.
See pp26–7

THE CALIFORNIA MISSIONS TRAIL
CALIFORNIA, USA

Delve into California's history

The Missions Trail stretches for 620 miles (1,000 km), linking historic missions and pueblos from San Diego to Sonoma.
www.parks.ca.gov

> "The cave mouth swiftly swallows the trail, which drops into the darkness down a long series of sweeping switchbacks."

CARLSBAD CAVERNS NATIONAL PARK
NEW MEXICO, USA

Spectacular rock formations

Deep beneath a wilderness landscape hides a magical underworld of caverns and tunnels just waiting to be explored.
See pp28–9

SAINT PAUL WINTER CARNIVAL
MINNESOTA, USA

USA's oldest winter carnival

First staged in 1886, this carnival hosts wintry activities including curling, skating, snow sculpting, and a spectacular ice palace.
www.winter-carnival.com

> "Once past Ho'okipa, you feel as if you're leaving reality behind and entering some South Seas paradise."

MONUMENT VALLEY
UTAH, USA

Drive or hike through this iconic American landscape.

Instantly recognizable thanks to its sandstone towers, this surreal landscape is a great place to learn about Native American culture.
www.utah.com/monumentvalley

EVERGLADES NATIONAL PARK
FLORIDA, USA

A vast subtropical wilderness

Hike or boat through the mysterious mangrove swamps and lagoons, home to rare species including crocodiles, panthers, and manatees.
www.nps.gov/ever

LAS VEGAS
NEVADA, USA

Prepare for one long party

Themed hotels, sizzling shows, all-night shopping, casinos, and cocktails are available 24/7 at this fast-growing desert city.
See pp12–13

SAN MIGUEL DE ALLENDE
MEXICO

Laid-back arty retreat

This pretty colonial town has a thriving artistic community thanks to its perfect climate and photogenic streets.
www.sanmiguelguide.com

LAGO PATZCUARO
MEXICO

Traditional fishing, Mexican-style

On a boat trip across this lake, watch local fishermen working with their strange butterfly-shaped nets from tiny dug-out canoes.
www.patzcuarovacations.com

BIG BEND NATIONAL PARK
TEXAS, USA

Remote and majestic desert

One of the USA's wildest national parks, studded with cacti and pine-clad mountains, and bound by the majestic Rio Grande.
www.nps.gov/bibe

GLACIER PERITO MORENO
ARGENTINA

A magnificent glacier

This vast white mass ranks among Patagonia's prime tourist attractions, edging slowly forwards then splintering into huge chunks of ice.
www.inargentinatourism.com.ar

PATAGONIAN CRUISE
ARGENTINA

Take a voyage of discovery at the "end of the world"

Follow legendary seafarers through the Magellan Straits and Beagle Channel to see whales, elephant seals, icebergs, and mighty glaciers.
www.patagonia-travel.com

COSTA RICA
CENTRAL AMERICA

An exquisite pocket of natural beauty and coastal rainforest

Manuel Antonio National Park combines palm-fringed beaches with mangrove swamps and a forest ecosystem full of wildlife.
www.visitcostarica.com

Previous page: Coconut palms on a tropical beach at sunset, Maui, Hawai'i

Weather Watch

1 Hawai'i, USA In January, temperatures hover above 70°F (21°C) at sea level and the surf is far better than in summer. Rainfall varies significantly on each island.

2 Las Vegas, USA Though nights are cold – with potentially penetrating desert winds – the crisp, sunny days make this one of the most comfortable months to stroll along Vegas's world-famous Strip.

3 Jackson Hole, USA Dazzling blue skies and thick blankets of perfect white snow along the dramatic spine of the American Rockies create the ideal conditions for skiing and snowboarding.

4 Puerto Rico The sunshine, warm temperatures, low rainfall, and cloudless skies are a world away from the gloomy chill of much of the northern hemisphere. Swimming, snorkeling, and surfing are perfect at this time.

5 Colombia Humidity is at a comfortable level in January, one of the driest months. Snorkeling and swimming are pleasurable on the gorgeous islands, while in the capital, Cartagena, cool sea breezes temper the city's heat.

6 Chile January is peak tourist season in much of Chile, which is enjoying its summer. Lake District days are warm, but nights can get cool and rainfall is not unusual.

LUXURY AND ROMANCE

LAKE DISTRICT Yachts on Lago Villarrica

ACTIVE ADVENTURES

JACKSON HOLE Skiers at Teton Village Resort

FAMILY GETAWAYS

ORLANDO Disney cartoon characters come to life

THE LAKE DISTRICT
CHILE

Fairytale setting with lakes, thermal pools, and volcanoes

Relax in a riverside cabin and enjoy a thermal bath and pampering, or explore the virgin forests on horseback in this beautiful lakes region.

See pp24–5

MERIDA
VENEZUELA

A wonderful city flanked by two vast mountain ranges

Stay in romantic *posadas* outside the city, explore the Sierra Nevada by day, and relax in a luxurious spa before dinner.

www.steppestravel.co.uk

JACKSON HOLE
WYOMING, USA

This is big-thrill territory for skilful skiers

Top skiing opportunities with huge descents – and a small, friendly, and uncrowded town inhabited by real cowboys.

See pp20–21

"The valley is shrouded in fog but skiers above bask in blue skies, and the sensation is of skiing off the mountain and into the clouds."

SAN DIEGO
CALIFORNIA, USA

One of the west coast's top family destinations

Miles of beaches, plus plenty of child-friendly museums, parks, SeaWorld, the Birch Aquarium, and the world-famous San Diego zoo.

www.sandiego.org

ORLANDO
FLORIDA, USA

Every kid's dream vacation, but fun for all the family

Take the family to meet Mickey and his friends at Disney World, explore the other theme parks, and maybe even see a rocket launch.

See pp18–19

ATLANTA
GEORGIA, USA

Enjoy some Southern-style luxury and romance

Enjoy a break in one of the South's most dynamic cities, with a string of top hotels, cultural attractions, and cosmopolitan restaurants and bars.

www.atlanta.net

VALLE DE LA LUNA
CHILE

The lunar landscapes of San Pedro de Atacama

Trek through one of the driest places on earth, a high-altitude desert with salt lakes and weirdly shaped outcrops of stone and sand.

www.visitchile.com

FLORIDA PANHANDLE
FLORIDA, USA

Drive off on an old-fashioned family vacation

A road trip down the Florida Panhandle takes you through time-warped towns, and past alligator-filled swamps and beaches galore.

www.flphonline.com

VIEQUES
PUERTO RICO, CARIBBEAN

Laid-back islands washed by warm tropical seas

The pace of life is slow here, so just relax. Be active if you want, but even the wildlife, turtles, and manatees move slowly.

See pp22–3

MOUNTAIN PINE FOREST PRESERVE
BELIZE

Jungle walks and waterfalls

Trek or bike through this verdant forest preserve, with jungle-clad mountains, plentiful wildlife and the vertiginous Hidden Valley Falls.

www.travelbelize.org/mpr.html

MAMMOTH MOUNTAIN
CALIFORNIA, USA

Skiing and snowmobile drives

Get stuck into the white stuff at one of California's top wintersports destinations, based on the mighty slopes of Mammoth Mountain.

www.mammothmountain.com

MAYAN RIVIERA
MEXICO

Bask in the sun and explore fascinating ruins

Fantastic beaches, coral reefs, and Mayan ruins, plus family resorts with quiet forested walks and water rides make this a great destination.

See pp14–15

JAMAICA
CARIBBEAN

Savor the heady rum aromas and the hot rhythm of reggae

There's more to Jamaica than parties – try hiking in the Blue Mountains before soaking up the sun on a fabulous beach.

www.visitjamaica.com

WHALE WATCHING IN SAMANÁ
DOMINICAN REPUBLIC

Ultimate marine spectacle

Thousands of majestic whales home in on Samaná Bay to mate and calve, and engage in elaborate courting displays.

www.whalewatchsamana.de

KIAWAH ISLAND
SOUTH CAROLINA, USA

A delightful island resort that is relatively quiet in winter

The water is too cold to swim but the open spaces of the beach provide plenty of activities for kids and adults alike.

www.kiawahisland.org

GETTING THERE
See map p321, D4

Las Vegas is in southwest USA. International flights arrive into McCarran International Airport. Taxis run from the airport to the Strip.

GETTING AROUND
The best way to get around is by taxi, bus or the Monorail that connects many of the major hotels along the Strip.

WEATHER
In January, daytime temperatures average around 60ºF (16ºC) but can dip to 30ºF (-1ºC) in the evening.

ACCOMMODATIONS
The centrally located Tropicana Resort & Casino is good value for families and the budget-conscious; doubles from US$50; www.tropicanalv.com

Hard Rock Hotel and Casino, a mile east of the Strip, appeals to a younger crowd; doubles from US$129; www.hardrockhotel.com

Opulent Wynn Las Vegas is one of the most expensive resorts in the world; doubles can cost up to US$799; www.wynnlasvegas.com

EATING OUT
Casinos offer a dizzying choice. Buffets are good value, but vary in quality. For a view, head up to the Stratosphere's Top of the World (US$75). Caesars Palace's Cypress St. Marketplace (US$15) is good for a quick bite.

PRICE FOR TWO
US$550 per day including hotel, food, and entertainment.

FURTHER INFORMATION
www.visitlasvegas.com

Tying the Knot?

The pitfalls of a big night out in Vegas are like nowhere else in the world, as countless couples have discovered. With no blood tests or waiting periods required, all that's needed is the license fee (around US$55) and two people who are at least 18 years of age. About 120,000 couples a year get hitched in the many 24-hour chapels that line the Strip, making it the wedding capital of the world. It's a popular choice to have an Elvis impersonator present. If you're already married, don't feel left out – you can always renew your vows in style here.

Above (left to right): The slots at the Casino, Venetian Hotel; giant guitar sign of the Hard Rock Cafe; Ghostbar on the roof top of the Palms Casino Resort **Main:** Neon cowgirl at the Fremont Street Experience

SHOPPING AND SHOWS

AMERICA'S FOREMOST PLAYGROUND OFFERS SOMETHING for everyone to spend money on, regardless of your tastes. But why visit Las Vegas in January, when temperatures hit annual lows? That's a good reason right there – the heat that plagues the city throughout much of the year has eased, yet it's still warm. A city truly unlike any other, Las Vegas long ago shed its reputation as a destination primarily geared toward gamblers and sinners. Now, it has morphed into one of America's most multi-faceted – and fastest-growing – non-stop cities. The Fremont Street Experience, for instance, is a seven-block, open-air promenade that features the largest big-screen in the world, live entertainment, historic hotels, and unique shopping. Serious, late-night shoppers will be thrilled – where else can you wander a four-floor M&M candy superstore at 11pm? If the shops here don't satisfy, you can always head back to the Strip, where casinos like Wynn Las Vegas and the Venetian offer a wide array of high-end boutiques.

The city that never sleeps, Vegas bursts into action after dark when big-name performers fill the casino stages.

Commonly thought of as a high-roller's destination – after all, $100 show tickets, $50 blackjack tables and $10 drinks are the norm – Vegas offers several freebies that would warrant admission fees almost anywhere else. The Bellagio's fountain shows, held on an 8-acre (3-hectare) lake, are a sight to behold, as are the vivid and regular eruptions of the Mirage's 54-ft (16-m) volcano each night. Treasure Island's Sirens of TI show, with brave girls battling pirates, and the Flamingo Hotel's wildlife habitat are just two of the free family-friendly attractions.

The city that never sleeps, Vegas bursts into action after dark when big-name performers fill the casino stages and bars, and lounges throb with revelers. Celebs hit hot spots like the Palms and the Hard Rock, bringing a touch of LA or NYC glamour to the desert. Hungry? You can dine at a spectrum of eateries, from ballroom-sized buffets to elite places with international big-name chefs.

Inset: Gondolas on the Grand Canal, The Venetian Hotel and Casino.
Below (left and right): Mirage Hotel's nightly eruption; aerial view of Las Vegas.

HIGH-ROLLER'S DIARY

Always ablaze with colors and lights, this cocktail of luxury and lurid laughs makes Las Vegas one of the world's glam fests, with a vast choice of over-the-top experiences to try. Not a gambler? – the theme hotels and casinos are still fun to explore. In January you can see the city's best at a cool, leisurely pace in three days.

Three Days in Vegas

Explore the Strip, working your way from ancient Egypt to New York, and from Polynesia to Venice as you take in the magnificence of the mega-hotels. Later, head downtown to the Fremont Street Experience, a haven of under-cover entertainment and shopping. Or you could catch a steamy burlesque performance at Mandalay Place's Forty Deuce club. Finish the night, at any hour, by hitting Mr. Lucky's 24/7 Café, the Hard Rock's cool all-night coffee shop.

DAY 1

For a spot of morning-after self-indulgence, head to the Venetian's TAO, a spa that's an offshoot of a New York hot spot by the same name, which sports a 16-ft (5-m) Buddha and a faux beach to desport yourself upon. Move on to Caesars Palace, where you can almost believe you're in Italy, and grab a bite at one of the numerous dining options. Keep the party going by spotting a celeb at Pure, which is owned by, among others, Andre Agassi, Steffi Graf, and Celine Dion.

DAY 2

Up for some action? Take a Red Rock Canyon tour, or if this is just too real, slip into the Red Rock Casino Resort, located off the Strip, with its "adventure spa" where guests can try rock climbing or rafting trips. If all the gambling and imbibing has left you in need of a detox, head to Bathhouse Spa at THEhotel, where you relax in a eucalyptus steam room, sauna, and more. Cap your weekend with a picturesque toast to the city at the Palms' Ghostbar, where night owls enjoy breathtaking views from the club's "ghost deck," some 55 floors above the hotel pool.

DAY 3

Dos and Don'ts

✓ Try to secure show tickets well in advance. Many shows sell out, so check your desired show's website ahead of your trip to Vegas.

✗ Don't stray too far from the Strip late at night. With several popular casinos and resorts located well off the Strip, it's wise to take taxis whenever possible.

✓ Wear a watch. Clocks are hard to find in casinos, especially anywhere near the gaming floors.

✗ Don't bother bringing a car to the city. While most of the casinos offer plenty of free parking, traffic on and near the Strip can be troublesome at all hours.

FEB

MAR

APR

MAY

JUN

JUL

AUG

SEP

OCT

NOV

DEC

Below: Diners grabbing a bite at dusk, Caesars Palace

GETTING THERE See map p323, I5
The Mayan Riviera is a strip of coastline with offshore islands running 100 miles (161 km) south of Cancún on the Yucatán Peninsula. The international airport is at Cancún. Most resorts are within 2 hours' drive of Cancún.

GETTING AROUND
Regular fast buses link the major centers of the Mayan Riviera. Tours to the main sites are easy to arrange. Cars can be rented at the airport, in Cancún, and other major towns.

WEATHER
January is warm with average daytime temperatures of 82°F (28°C). It is frequently sunny, with only about 9 days' rain per month.

ACCOMMODATIONS
Crown Paradise Club, Cancún, is a large beachfront resort with pools and a water park; family rooms from US$300; www.crownparadise.com

Avalon Grand, Cancún, has simple rooms, two pools and a kids' club; family rooms from US$164; www.avalongrandcancun.com

Xpu-Ha Palace resort, Playa del Carmen, is a beach-front resort for families set in tropical gardens; family rooms from US$312; www.xpuha-palace.com

EATING OUT
Mexican standards – *quesadillas* and *burritos*, beans and rice – are staples, with seafood.

PRICE FOR A FAMILY OF FOUR
US$520 per day including hotels, food, car rental and fuel, tour, and entrance fees.

FURTHER INFORMATION
www.visitmexico.com

MAYAN RIVIERA FUN

Main: Tulúm and its beaches

OWDER-SOFT BEACHES FRINGE THE EASTERN COAST of Mexico's Yucatán peninsula, which is washed by an aquamarine Atlantic mellowed by a barrier reef and studded with little coral islands. Mayan temples built to worship the God of the Dawn sit sentinel on cliffs – poised to catch the rays of the rising sun. And at their backs lie vast stretches of rainforest, dotted with towering temples and broken by Mayan villages and little colonial towns.

Until the 1980s few tourists visited this area but then came Cancún – a purpose-built tourist city straddling a 10-mile (16-km) spit of gorgeous sand backed by a salt-water lagoon. As Cancún's popularity grew it spawned little towns to the south such as Playa del Carmen, Akumal, and Tulúm. Resorts and adventure parks were built and the coast was promoted as the Mayan Riviera. Today, the

Calendar Stone

The end of the world has been given a date. At least that is according to the Mayan Calendar. Over 1,000 years ago Mayan astronomers invented a system of solar, lunar, and astral calendars which they used to mark agricultural seasons and ritual events. The most complex of these was the Long Count. It began with the mythological creation of the current universe on August 11, 3114 BC and ends with demonic disorder before a new one is created – on December 21, 2012.

Left: Indian dancer in full costume

Right (left to right): A boat trip on the lagoon; water sports for the kids at Cancún; underwater cross off Isla Mujeres; Playa del Carmen beach

Mayan Riviera's combination of exotic but gentle nature, large hotels, and theme parks makes it a winner for families. The ocean here doesn't crash, it laps – so swimming off the beaches and islands is usually good for children. Adventures are exciting but safe. In parks like Garrafón, Xel-Ha or Nizuc, the forest has been trimmed back to make way for paths that even the smallest feet can tread. And there is a wide range of adrenaline-fuelled children's rides and water slides, snorkeling facilities, and tame tropical wildlife. With their lush Disney-style backdrops, the Mayan temples at rainforest-shrouded Cobá or the cliff-top ruins at Tulúm have a wide appeal. And there are plenty of animals – dolphins to swim with, sightings of wild parrots, monkeys, and macaws in the forests, and sleepy iguanas basking in the sun. The clubs and babysitting services at large hotels ensure that you can take the kids but occasionally be free of them too – to go diving off the coral reefs, or trek through vast caves, or simply to share a romantic meal with a partner.

RIVIERA DIARY

A week in pleasantly warm January will give you a taste of the Mayan Riviera's beaches, reefs, temples, and theme parks. Ten days would allow for further excursions such as a trip to Chichén Itza in the Yucatán, or for taking a boat ride out to the lovely Isla Cozumel. For more on the Yucatán, *see pp70-1*.

A Week of Beaches and Ruins

JAN

DAY 1
Once you've settled into your hotel in Cancún, head for the beach to unwind. In the afternoon take an adrenaline ride through the waves on a banana raft, or enjoy a more sedate trip in a glass-bottomed boat.

DAY 2
Make an early start for Isla Mujeres – a tiny island fringed with fine white sand and lapped by gentle waves. Spend the afternoon swimming, snorkeling, and zip-lining in the El Garrafón nature park.

DAY 3
Whiz down helter-skelter water slides with the kids and swim with dolphins in the Nizuc Water Park. In the late afternoon, if you're not too exhausted, hire a baby-sitter then head out for a night on the town.

DAY 4
Drive south to Playa del Carmen, check in to a hotel and spend the day at the Xel-Ha theme park. This is set in original tropical forest and built around a series of glassy clear pools that offer great and safe coral reef snorkeling for kids.

DAY 5
Drive to the Mayan city of Tulúm, which looks out over the aquamarine Atlantic on a craggy honey-colored cliff-top above a series of coral coves. While away the afternoon on the beaches to the south of the ruins.

DAY 6
Take a tour into the wildlife reserve at Si'an Ka'an to see pristine rainforest and coastal wetlands; float down a crystal-clear river filled with fish and tiny baby crocs.

DAY 7
Drive to the ruins at Cobá and enjoy wandering the forest trails and climbing to the top of the vertiginous pyramids. Bring plenty of sunscreen and insect repellent. Return to Cancún for the flight home.

Dos and Don'ts

✓ Bring your own mask and snorkel from home. They'll fit better and you'll avoid the extortionate rental prices.

✗ Don't touch coral reefs or wear sun lotion in the water. Many of the Mayan Riviera's reefs have been damaged by tourism and over-fishing.

✓ Learn some Spanish and win Mexican friends.

✗ Don't take photographs of Mayan people without asking.

FEB

MAR

APR

MAY

JUN

JUL

AUG

SEP

OCT

NOV

DEC

Below: Xel-Ha Natural Park, safe for kids to enjoy snorkeling

CARIBBEAN SEA

CARTAGENA

VENEZUELA

PANAMA

PACIFIC
OCEAN

● Medellín

● Bogota

COLOMBIA

ECUADOR

PERU

BRAZIL

GETTING THERE   See map p325, D6
Located in northwest Colombia, Cartagena is served by Rafael Núñez International Airport, which is 2 miles (3 km) from the center. Cruise ship passengers arrive at Terminal Maritimo, just a short distance from the hotel district.

GETTING AROUND
Unmetered yellow taxis are a good way to get around the city, but be sure to fix a price beforehand. Buses are slow going, but much of the city can be explored on foot.

WEATHER
Daytime temperatures average 86–90°F (30–32°C); humidity high all year round. The driest months are from December to April.

ACCOMMODATIONS
The cheap and cheerful Hotel Behique has doubles from US$38; tel. (575) 664 3511

The comfortable Centro Hotel is within the old city walls; double rooms from US$100; www.centrohotelcartagena.com

For the charm of an old colonial home, try El Marques Boutique Hotel; doubles from US$300; www.elmarqueshotelboutique.com

EATING OUT
A good three-course meal with wine will cost around US$10 per head. Try smoked meatballs at the cozy Restaurante Pelikanos or beans-and-rice at La Bodeguita del Medio.

PRICE FOR TWO
US$170 per day including food, excursions, local transportation, and accommodation.

FURTHER INFORMATION
www.turismocartagena.com

Showbiz City

With its showbiz good looks and big-screen presence, Cartagena has enjoyed many film-star roles. It was the setting of the 2007 Hollywood adaptation of Gabriel García Marquez's powerful novel *Love in the Time of Cholera (above)*. The city's pretty plazas and bold, vivid colors formed the perfect backdrop to this allegorical love story. Visitors can go on movie-themed walking tours of the city to see where scenes from several blockbusters – including the 1969 thriller *Burn*, starring Marlon Brando, and the 1984 adventure film *Romancing the Stone* – were filmed.

Above (left to right): Music and dancing at one of Cartagena's many celebrations; young dancers at a street festival; marching youth band
Main: Local women in brightly colored dress balancing baskets of fruit on their heads

COLORFUL COLOMBIA

S OARING TEMPERATURES ADD A STEAMY CARIBBEAN HAZE to Cartagena's exquisite streetscape, a picture-perfect labyrinth of balconied colonial buildings in a dazzling array of bubble-gum hues. Blossom-clad shutters look out on neat plazas hemmed by a riddle of cobblestone backstreets where vendors ply giant red papayas and juicy mangos in the shade. Sizzling kerbside food stalls emit the heady aromas of Cartagena's buttery, deep-fried *arepas* (maize pancakes) and meat-filled *empanadas* (corn-flour turnovers), handicraft sellers and performers roam the streets, and strumming musicians serenade cappuccino-sipping tourists. This permanent state of festival is part of the city's unique historic character, which has experienced slavery, sainthood, and swashbuckling buccaneers.

Facing the Caribbean Sea to the northwest and with a sweeping bay to the south, this pretty sea port is a jewel-box of Spanish colonial ostentation, declared a UNESCO World Heritage Site in 1984. Its vibrant streets boast some fascinating monuments and stunning architectural sights, including

the resplendent bronze Monumento a la India Catalina, which honors the region's pre-colonial indigenous people, the Los Zapatos Viejos (The Old Shoes Monument), which pays homage to a satirical poem by Luis Carlos Lopez (1883–1950), and the ancient, cannon-flanked fortifications that dominate the city's handsome, sea-facing ramparts.

A year-round cultural calendar runs from the Feria Taurina (bullfighting), Festival Internacional de Música (classical music festival), and Festival Internacional de Cine (film festival), to the star-studded Hay Festival – a magnificent celebration of literature from across the globe and a major A-list draw. The week-long Independence Day celebrations paralyze the city with high-tempo street parades and marching bands. A cluster of sandy off-shore islands offer respite from the melee, with lobster cooked on open fires and hammocks slung from mud-and-thatch fishing huts – the perfect antidote to the non-stop revelry.

> Blossom-clad shutters look out on neat plazas hemmed by a riddle of cobblestone backstreets where vendors ply juicy mangos in the shade.

Inset: Decorative panels on the side of a *chiva* (bus)
Below (left and right): Elegant colonial architecture; aerial view of Centro Histórico

FESTIVAL DIARY

January plays host to a highlight in the world's literary calendar as Cartagena welcomes novelists, journalists, and screenwriters from all over Latin America – and beyond. The Hay Festival, a rich celebration of creative talent, runs to a hectic schedule, so be sure to make time to explore the city and take in the sights.

Three Days of Culture

JAN

Spend the day exploring the city's Centro Histórico, known as Calamari by the locals. Visit the historic Ciudad Amurallada (Walled City) and the charming neighborhoods of San Diego, La Matuna, Getsemaní, and Santo Domingo. Take in the stylish elegance of the Hotel Santa Clara, located in the former Convent of Saint Clara of Assisi (c.1600), on Calle del Torno at lunchtime, before heading to the Bocagrande tourist zone for a rum-fuelled *chiva* (open-side bus) jaunt. When the sun sets, soak up the buzz of energetic literati discussions in Cartagena's atmospheric bars and bistros.

DAY 1

Have breakfast on Plaza de Bolivar and spend the morning at the grand Teatro Heredia to hear some of the world's finest travel writers share tales of exotic far-off lands. Have a picnic lunch by the historic Convento de la Popa, perched atop a 450-ft (140-m) hill, then stroll along the cannon-topped crumbling stone ramparts, the oldest of which were built in the early 17th century to protect the city from invasion. Pick up Costeña dolls and colorful ceramics in the rock-hewn former dungeons of Las Bóvedas and the nearby souvenir markets.

DAY 2

Pack beachwear, sun hats, and snorkeling gear for a day out on the water. Cartagena's surrounding islands, the Archipiélago Nuestra Señora del Rosario, sit among the coral reefs and turquoise waters that make up the Parque Nacional Natural Corales del Rosario y San Bernardo. A nature-lover's paradise, the park is home to dozens of species of fish, seabirds, and molluscs. Most tour boats take in three or four islands, allowing you plenty of time on the beach. In the evening, join poets, playwrights, and authors for fascinating debates over rum cocktails.

DAY 3

Dos and Don'ts

⊗ Don't be tempted to use *mototaxis* – these traffic-beating motorbikes may be fast and dirt-cheap, but they are also highly dangerous.

✓ Be sure to try the local *dedos de queso* (deep-fried cheese sticks). Street vendors sell them around the Plaza de Bolivar.

⊗ Don't attempt to change any currency with black-market money-changers – any so-called "great deals" will almost certainly involve counterfeit notes and coins.

✓ Wear comfortable shoes for exploring the maze of streets.

FEB

MAR

APR

MAY

JUN

JUL

AUG

SEP

OCT

NOV

DEC

Below: The clear azure waters of an off-shore island

GETTING THERE
See map p317, G5

The Walt Disney World Resort® is about a 30-minute drive southwest of Orlando International Airport

GETTING AROUND
Car rental is widely available and inexpensive. In the resort a system of buses, monorails, and ferryboats connects the attractions.

WEATHER
January brings coolish, dryish weather, with daytime highs of around 72°F (22°C), dropping to around 50°F (10°C) at night.

ACCOMMODATIONS
AmeriSuites Orlando/Universal is a budget option, next to Universal Studios and minutes from Walt Disney World; family rooms from US$139; www.amerisuites.com

Disney's Fort Wilderness Campground has air-conditioned cabins or rustic tents; family cabins from US$159; www.disneyworld.com

Nickelodeon Family Suites by Holiday Inn is heaven for kids, with two pool complexes and live Nickelodeon entertainment; family rooms from US$189; www.nickhotel.com

EATING OUT
There are hundreds of choices for all budgets and tastes, from fast food to gourmet dining. Most places welcome families and offer a children's menu.

PRICE FOR A FAMILY OF FOUR
US$600 per day, including accommodation, food, admissions, and transportation.

FURTHER INFORMATION
www.orlandoinfo.com

One Man's Vision

Film producer, entrepreneur, and philanthropist Walt Disney (1901–66) said he wanted to enable people to "leave today and enter the world of yesterday, tomorrow, and fantasy." Walt Disney World®, his project to make this vision a reality, opened five years after his death. Walt would perhaps be most proud of EPCOT® (the Experimental Prototype Community of Tomorrow), which brings to life the "brighter tomorrow" of which he often spoke.

A MAGIC KINGDOM – AND MORE

A MODERN-DAY AMERICAN RITE OF PASSAGE, a family trip to Orlando has long been an ideal option for parents looking to get away with the kids in tow. Orlando's attractions present young and old with an assault on the senses, and a steady stream of opportunities to get up-close and personal with beloved cartoon characters, fairytale figures, and movie icons. A life-size Goofy or Spider-Man is always available for a photo opportunity, and million-dollar amusement rides put visitors right into the heart of the action. The Orlando area is a can't-miss reward for children of all ages, a place where one is as likely to hear "It's a Small World" as any contemporary radio hit. Such is the pull of Mickey Mouse and his pals that grown-ups turn into big kids and even jaded teenagers turn off their cell phones to reconnect with the favorites of their youth. The Magic Kingdom® continues to be the focal point of the whole

Main: Evening falls on Main Street USA, at Walt Disney World®

Above (top to bottom): Killer whale performance at SeaWorld®; family fun at Splash Mountain in the Magic Kingdom®

Bottom (left to right): Fireworks over Cinderella Castle in the Magic Kingdom; Spaceship Earth geodisic sphere at Epcot®; Disney cartoon characters come to life; moonrise over the vast Vehicle Assembly Building and Titan rocket at the Kennedy Space Center

region, with most visitors starting at Orlando's original Disney property. But today, tourists have more options than ever before. Besides EPCOT's futuristic and international wonders, there are also Disney Hollywood Studios® (formerly MGM Studios) and Disney's Animal Kingdom®, saving families trips to California and Africa, respectively. With numerous additional properties, such as the Typhoon Lagoon and Blizzard Beach water parks, "the mouse" – as some locals call the company – offers so much that most families don't bother leaving its friendly confines. That said, the Orlando area contains plenty more by way of great family-friendly experiences. Universal Orlando Resort® is a must for movie fans, and SeaWorld® Orlando offers the chance to get soaked by the splash of a killer whale. Kennedy Space Center is a magnet for youngsters curious about space exploration, and the nearby beaches are a surfers' paradise. Orlando's attractive Winter Park neighborhood is full of colorful galleries and cozy eateries. Ask any kid, though, and the focus of a trip to Orlando has to fall squarely on Walt Disney World®. It remains, to many, "the happiest place on earth."

THEME PARK DIARY

In a region with more than 50 million visitors a year, it's often impossible to escape the crowds. A winter visit, outside the main vacation periods, is ideal for families looking to enjoy multiple parks in a limited amount of time. Four days should be enough time to explore the area without getting park burnout.

Four Fun-Filled Days

JAN

Begin your trip at Magic Kingdom®, the original and still best-known of the parks. If it's a weekday, you may get to do the Pirates of the Caribbean ride more than once, a luxury most park visitors can't enjoy. Cap a full day at the park by snacking on mouse-shaped fries while watching the nightly fireworks display.

DAY 1

Head to EPCOT®, splitting time between Future World and the World Showcase, where your family can tour the world in less than a square mile. Grab dinner and a well-deserved nightcap at Downtown Disney, an outdoor complex of shops, restaurants, and nightclubs.

DAY 2

Take a break from all things Disney and visit the Kennedy Space Center for a fun, hands-on introduction to space exploration. If you're lucky you might see a rocket launch. Then take the kids to meet Shamu the killer whale at SeaWorld® Orlando, a marine theme park that features Kraken, the biggest rollercoaster in the Orlando area. Or spend the afternoon at the Universal Orlando Resort®, which contains two theme parks and a large shopping district (Universal City Walk).

DAY 3

If your kids are old enough to appreciate movies, visit Disney Hollywood Studios. Attractions range from sedate (peek in on working animation studios) to scary (the Rock 'n' Roller Coaster goes from 0–60mph/97kmph in 2.8 seconds). Younger kids may prefer Disney Animal Kingdom, which is a cross between a zoo and a theme park. There, you can take a jeep safari past lions, rhinos, and other African beasts, or a raft ride through a tropical rainforest.

DAY 4

Dos and Don'ts

✓ Study maps of the larger parks in advance, plotting a course through the grounds to cut down on lengthy walks.

✓ If you hate crowds, or are travelling with small children, consider visiting the parks on weekdays, when lines, parking and traffic are more manageable than on weekends.

✓ Bring sunscreen and bottled water, as both can be costly to purchase inside the parks.

✗ Don't overlook the Disney Parks' Fastpass machines for popular rides. You can reserve a time to come back later in the day, skipping lengthy lines.

FEB

MAR

APR

MAY

JUN

JUL

AUG

SEP

OCT

NOV

DEC

Below: *Liberty Belle* riverboat in the Magic Kingdom

GETTING THERE   See map p320, F5
The town of Jackson in northwest Wyoming is well-served by airlines, with connecting flights from Chicago, Dallas, Salt Lake City, and Denver, among others. The airport is 10 minutes from the town center.

GETTING AROUND
There are regular shuttle buses between the town and ski resort.

WEATHER
January temperatures rarely climb above freezing. The weather can be capricious – blue skies or monumental snowfall.

ACCOMMODATIONS
Alpine House Inn in Jackson Hole is a B&B owned by two former Olympians; doubles from US$120; www.alpinehouse.com

Teton Village Resort has apartments with kitchens; one-bedroom apartments from US$170; www.teton-village.com

Four Seasons is a luxury hotel at the Jackson Hole resort with ski-in-ski-out access; doubles from US$360; www.fourseasons.com

EATING OUT
Whatever your taste and budget, you'll find it here, from traditional barbecue to sushi and, of course, thick slabs of beef. A local favorite is Bubba's BBQ, from around US$16.

PRICE FOR TWO
US$400 per day, including accommodations, food, ski passes, trips, transportation, and admissions.

FURTHER INFORMATION
www.jacksonhole.com

Fur-Trapping Country
Jackson Hole got its name from the fur trappers who used to enter the valley by descending from the steep-sloped mountains that surround it, thus giving the impression that they were entering a hole. One of these mountains is the iconic Grand Teton, a craggy slab that dominates the town and its surroundings. The "Jackson" comes from one of the beaver trappers, David Edward Jackson, who used to hunt for the valuable skins here in the early 19th century – he was also one of the pioneers of the Oregon Trail.

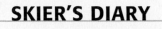

Above (left to right): Skiing at the Teton Village Resort in Jackson Hole; cowboy skier; Teton National Park
Main: Snowboarder soars over the wide open trails of Jackson Hole

DEEP-POWDER SNOWFIELDS

AMONG SKIERS, JACKSON HOLE IS LEGENDARY for its steep and challenging terrain, including Corbett's Couloir, a narrow plunge only for the foolhardy or Olympic contender. For the rest of us mere mortals, there are groomed trails (pistes) for effortless cruising, and deep-powder snowfields that leave skiers and snowboarders desperate to get back to them. Situated in the heart of the dramatic Tetons, Jackson Hole Mountain Resort is made up of two distinct mountains – Rendezvous and Apres Vous – which offer snow-seekers plentiful and varied opportunities.

Because of its relative isolation in the northwestern corner of Wyoming, the slopes here are rarely crowded, allowing skiers and boarders to feel as though they alone own the mountains. One of the most ethereal moments occurs during a temperature inversion, when the valley is shrouded in fog but skiers above bask in blue skies, and the sensation is of skiing off the mountain into the clouds. Away from the resort, the town of Jackson is a place of contrasts. Cowboys from the surrounding cattle ranches come here for country music in "honky tonk" bars, the wooden sidewalks clunk under their boots, and passers-by tip their cowboy hats and greet you with a "howdy." But here, too, are increasing numbers of classy galleries, up-scale boutiques, and toney restaurants.

> The valley is shrouded in fog but skiers above bask in blue skies, and the sensation is of skiing off the mountain into the clouds.

Beyond the groomed snowfields, residents and visitors alike continue to be enchanted by Yellowstone National Park, which lies on the town's doorstep. With its amazing concentration of geological and biological riches – 200 active geysers, at least 100 known waterfalls, 1,050 species of plants, and endangered species such as the gray wolf, grizzly bear, bald eagle, and lynx – it is no surprise that the park is crowded with visitors in warm-weather months. But it is in winter, when Yellowstone is a serene landscape of white, dotted by animals grazing in spots where geysers have melted the snow, that visitors are offered a memorable glimpse of a once wild land.

Inset: Cable car to the summit of Rendezvous Mountain
Below (left and right): Antler Arch in the town square; the Playhouse, Jackson

SKIER'S DIARY

January is a great time to visit Jackson Hole – both for the snow and for its scenic beauty. The weather is generally clear and sunny, but there can be periods of very heavy snowfall – the average each year is around 460 inches (1,170 cm). The slopes here are ideal for all levels of skier and snowboarder.

A Week on the Slopes

DAYS 1–2
Head to the slopes as soon as possible. Advanced skiers and boarders will enjoy the exciting, steep terrain of Rendezvous Mountain and for beginners there are gentle slopes at the base of Apres Vous Mountain. In the evenings, learn to two-step at the Million Dollar Cowboy Bar or catch a show at the Playhouse.

DAY 3
To get a glimpse of the area's wildlife, visit Yellowstone National Park, where you'll pass herds of buffalo and flocks of trumpeter swans. If you're lucky, you'll even see wolves. Watch the regular eruption of Old Faithful Geyser, that spouts steamy water some 100 ft (30 m) into the air several times an hour. Take a tour, drive the northern part of the park, or even cross-country ski your way around. Alternatively, take a dogsled tour through serene valley trails dotted with towering pines.

DAYS 4–5
Continue skiing and/or boarding on the many trails or take a guided heli-ski trip. For a little culture, visit the National Museum of Wildlife Art for stunning paintings, sculptures, and photographs. A horse-drawn sleigh ride is a great way to see the National Elk Refuge, the winter home of 8,000 of these stately creatures, who disappear back into the mountains when the snow melts.

DAYS 6–7
For a change of scenery, head to the other side of the Teton Pass for a day at Grand Targhee. If you are a better-than-average skier or boarder, take advantage of snowcat skiing or boarding on untracked powder which is not accessible by chairlift or hiking. Strap on a pair of snowshoes and take a walk in Grand Teton National Park, guided by a trained naturalist.

Dos and Don'ts

✓ Join the locals on Sunday evenings at The Stagecoach, a diner that turns into a "honky tonk" one night a week.

✗ Don't pack formal clothes, since this is a casual place more orientated to sports and leisure.

✓ Look at the arches anchoring each of the four corners of the town square, formed by thousands of intertwined elk antlers, all shed by the protected herd living just outside town.

✓ If the beauty of this region has entranced you, come back in late spring to explore it on horseback (see pp112–13). If you can't get to Yellowstone, wait for summer (see pp188–9).

JAN

DAYS 1–2

DAY 3

DAYS 4–5

DAYS 6–7

FEB

MAR

APR

MAY

JUN

JUL

AUG

SEP

OCT

NOV

DEC

Below: Million Dollar Cowboy Bar sign, Jackson

ATLANTIC
OCEAN

San Juan
PUERTO RICO   Culebra
VIEQUES

CARIBBEAN
SEA

GETTING THERE   See map p325, G4
Vieques has a small airstrip. Vieques Air-Link and Culebra Air connect San Juan to Vieques by air. Many people prefer to take the ferry from Fajardo for a 45-minute journey.

GETTING AROUND
Bus services are minimal, but taxis take you around for less than US$20. The island is small enough to bicycle around.

WEATHER
Though the weather is warm year round, January is the best month to visit with temperatures averaging 76°F (24°C).

ACCOMMODATIONS
For budget accommodation, try Bananas Guesthouse, on Esperanza Bay; doubles from US$65; www.bananasguesthouse.com

Sublime elegance is the hallmark at Inn on the Blue Horizon; doubles from US$125; www.innonthebluehorizon.com

Try chic W Retreat & Spa on Martineau Bay; doubles from US$300; www.starwood.com

EATING OUT
Local fare at simple restaurants should be about US$25 per day, but it costs more for a gourmet meal at Carambola, which has live jazz on Saturday nights.

PRICE FOR TWO
US$200–400 per day including accommodation, food, and transportation, depending on the accommodation.

FURTHER INFORMATION
www.viequestravelguide.com
www.gotopuertorico.com

An Eerie Glow

The nocturnal glow in Phosphorescent Bay is produced by dinoflagellates – bioluminescent micro-organisms called *Pyrodinium bahamense*. Dinoflagellates live in water with just the right tidal flow, temperature, and composition to provide the creatures with nutrients which induce a chemical reaction that results in a flash when agitated by movement, such as from passing fish, swimmers, or waves. The glow is best seen on moonless nights.

PEARLS IN A SAPPHIRE SEA

AFFECTIONATELY KNOWN AS THE SPANISH VIRGINS, Vieques and nearby Culebra are the largest isles in a mini-archipelago off the east coast of Puerto Rico. These pearls in a sapphire sea are edged by silky sands dissolving into waters of lapis lazuli. Far from the mainland crowds, life moves at a languid pace on laid-back Vieques, the perfect place to get stranded. Used for US Navy gunnery practise since World War II, the island was eventually abandoned by the Navy in 2003 after a 50-year pounding, leaving Vieques' wild horses and leatherback turtles in peace.

Although the eastern half of the isle is still off-limits, this beach maven's haven tempts with delightful guesthouses tucked into sandy coves fringed with coral reefs. The opening of the W hotel in 2008 suggests just how fashionable Vieques has become. The tiny main town, Isabela Segunda, clings

Main: The sun setting over a beach in Esperanza Bay

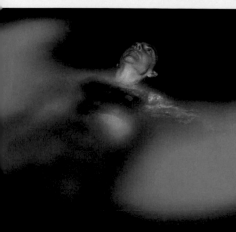

Left: A snorkeler holding aloft a starfish found in the waters off Vieques

Right (left and right): Faro de Punta lighthouse in Isabela Segunda; fishing boats moored in the clear waters of Esperanza Bay

to unpretentious ways – the main traffic comprises goats and locals on Paso Fino horses. The Faro Punta Mulas lighthouse and Fort Conde Mirasol, with its Vieques Art and History Museum featuring historical artifacts and nature displays, are worth a visit. On the south shore, the sleepy hamlet of Esperanza tantalizes with its teal-blue bay setting, great for snorkeling or simply snoozing the day away on the beach while being caressed by the tropical breeze.

Ecotourism is a major draw. Green hawksbill and leatherback turtles crawl ashore to nest on the sands, while manatees paddle in mangrove-fringed Laguna Kiani, part of the Vieques Wildlife Refuge. Laced with trails, it is perfect for hiking, mountain biking, or horse-back excursions. Kayaking on Phosphorescent Bay is best done at night, when slipping out of your kayak and into the waters triggers an explosion of bioluminescence, while if you glide on into the open ocean, you will discover a casket of gems such as a spectacular fringing reef. You may never want to leave.

Above: A cave at Vieques' Navio Beach

Below: Cheerful welcome sign greeting visitors to Vieques

ISLAND DIARY

January is the ideal time to visit Vieques as the weather is perfect – sunny and warm. The cloudless, dazzlingly deep blue skies make being outdoors a joy, and the isle's natural attributes beckon invitingly. Four days is adequate to take in the highlights at a leisurely pace, including a quick jaunt to nearby Culebra.

Four Days of Sun and Sand

JAN

DAY 1

After checking into your hotel in Vieques, go sightseeing to sleepy Isabela Segunda and visit the Faro Punta Mulas lighthouse and Fort Conde Mirasol, housing the Vieques Art and History Museum. Pick up some cheese and cold cuts at Chef Michael's Food Space for a picnic on nearby Bravos de Boston beach.

DAY 2

Head to Esperanza on the south shore to soak up the laidback tropical charm of this village. Stroll through Calle Flamboyán and drop in at the Vieques Conservation and Historical Trust museum to learn about local sealife, then meet the fish eye-to-eye as you snorkel in the bay. Linger over dinner and rum cocktails at Bananas.

DAY 3

Rent a bicycle or sign on for a guided cycling excursion along off-road trails in the rugged Vieques Wildlife Refuge. Then take a well-deserved break for relaxation at Green Beach and explore the mangroves at Laguna Kiani. At night glide across Phosphorescent Bay in a kayak and slip into the ink-black waters to spark a ghostlike green silhouette as you swim amid billions of twinkling dinoflagellates.

DAY 4

Take the ferry to nearby Culebra for a day lazing on Playa Flamingo, the most sensational beach in Puerto Rico. Surfers can ride the big waves while snorkelers can hike over to Playa Carlos Rosario, which has a fabulous offshore reef teeming with chromatic fish.

Dos and Don'ts

✓ Take plenty of mosquito repellent for exploring the mangroves.

✓ Time your visit to Phosphorescent Bay for a new moon, as the light of a full moon makes seeing the phosphorescence difficult.

✗ Don't overdo the rum cocktails! And drink plenty of water to avoid dehydration.

✓ Learn some Spanish. Although a large percentage of the population is English-speaking, Vieques is part of Spanish-speaking Puerto Rico.

FEB

MAR

APR

MAY

JUN

JUL

AUG

SEP

OCT

NOV

DEC

Below: Leatherback turtle nesting on the beach

GETTING THERE
See map p331, C3–4

International flights land at Santiago, the capital of Chile. From here a 75-minute flight south takes you to Temuco. Temuco's Aeropuerto Maquehue is a 4.5-mile (7-km) taxi ride from the city center.

GETTING AROUND
Buses are a good way of getting between major destinations, but a car is essential if you want to explore more freely.

WEATHER
Days are warm, with an average daytime temperature of 73°F (23°C). Rain is common.

ACCOMMODATIONS
Termas de Huife is a hot-spring resort, a 40-minute drive from Pucón, with doubles from US$260; www.termashuife.cl

The Hotel Atumalal near Pucón comes with a spa and views of Lago Villarrica; doubles from US$230; www.antumalal.com

Hotel Termas de Puyehue in the Puyehue National Park is a spa retreat with doubles from US$210; www.puyehue.cl

EATING OUT
Temuco's La Pampa restaurant, Pucón's La Maga, and Merlín in Puerto Varas serve delicious regional specialties. In coastal cities seafood reigns; try the shellfish at Club de Yates in Puerto Montt. Enjoy with Pisco Sour.

PRICE FOR TWO
US$300 per day, including luxury hotel and spa accommodation, food, car rental, and excursion costs.

FURTHER INFORMATION
www.sernatur.cl

The Mapuche People

The Lake District is the heartland of the Mapuche, who settled here in the 15th century. Ferocious warriors, they drove back the Inca Empire in the 1500s before embarking on 350 years of fierce resistance to Spanish rule. So ferocious were they that Spain ceded them territorial autonomy in 1641. The Mapuche became the only indigenous group in southern South America to resist colonization, their autonomy remaining intact until the 1870s, when the Chilean government ruthlessly put an end to all indigenous resistance in the region.

Above (left to right): Yachts on Lago Villarrica; view inside Volcán Villarrica
Main: Lago Llanquihue with Volcán Osorno in background

ANDEAN LAKESIDE LUXURY

WITH MIDNIGHT CLOSING IN, A TRAIL LEADS THROUGH LUSH FOREST to a secluded necklace of rock pools, where hot springs bubble and steam. The craggy peaks of Chile's Lake District, crowned by the smoldering Volcán Villarrica, tower over the burbling pools whose therapeutic waters beckon a nocturnal dip. Above, the southern hemisphere's night sky shimmers with stars. All around there is forest, through which gushing streams, heard but hidden from view, tumble. It's a midsummer night's dream – to lounge in thermal waters under the stars and red glow of volcanoes in Chile's enchanting Lake District.

A journey through this region, anchored in its north by the city of Temuco and in its south by Puerto Montt, brings with it the promise of balmy relaxation and the certainty of majestic lake and mountain scenery. The region takes its name from the many deep-blue lakes that spread across its entirety, forming part of a fairy-tale landscape that also features emerald forests, rolling green hills, thermal springs, and Andean peaks. A string of picturesque towns, dotted with the steeples of Bavarian churches built by the German communities that settled here in the 19th century, overlook the lakeshores and make for romantic stopovers. From the streets and plazas of these towns, paths lead to stunning beaches of black volcanic and fine white sands. For the energetic traveler, hikes and horseback rides reveal virgin forest where waterfalls tumble, crystalline rivers and streams cascade, and ancient woods of monkey-puzzle trees flourish. If you are feeling less energetic, you can enjoy a lake swim in warm, mineral-rich waters or a gentle road trip through stunning forest scenery to a luxury spa, where you can lounge in hot springs that bubble up from beneath the earth's crust. As you do so, beneath the gaze of volcanoes and forested peaks, the sensation is one of experiencing the earth at its most elemental.

> It's a midsummer night's dream – to lounge in thermal waters under the stars in Chile's enchanting Lake District.

Inset: The picturesque Volcán Villarrica at sunset
Below (left to right): Thermal hot springs; hotel spa; a monkey-puzzle tree

VOLCANIC DIARY

To really get to know Chile's Lake District you should factor in a journey of around ten days, starting at Temuco in the north and ending in Puerto Montt, the region's southern gateway. January is the height of the southern hemisphere summer, meaning long daylight hours and warm weather for your journey.

Ten Days Around the Lakes

JAN

DAY 1
Arrive in Temuco and browse the Mapuche handicrafts at its Mercado Municipal. Pick up a car and head for Conguillío National Park for millennia-old monkey-puzzle forests, lava fields, and views of Volcán Llaima.

DAYS 2–4
Head south to Pucón. Spend an afternoon horse-riding to the hidden El Claro waterfall. Later, under the gaze of Volcán Villarrica take a sunset stroll along lakeshores of black sand. Make the unforgettable hike to the summit of Volcán Villarrica to peer into its crater. At night, soothe aching limbs in bubbling hot springs. Next, spend a day at Lago Caburgua. Lounge on bleach-white beaches and swim in the lake's warm waters. Pass the night at a riverside cabin at Termas de Huife, where you can treat yourself to a thermal bath.

DAY 5
Drive to Valdivia along the stunning Seven Lakes Route. Wander Valdivia's Bavarian streets and its waterfront fish market, where sea lions bellow for scraps. End your day with a romantic riverside dinner.

DAYS 6–7
Continue onwards to the Termas de Puyehue in Puyehue National Park. Under the gaze of Volcán Osorno, indulge in 48 hours of therapeutic pampering.

DAYS 8–10
Make the short drive to Puerto Varas and walk the volcanic shores of Lago Llanquihue. Seek out the stunning Petrohue waterfall. Take to the skies on a light-aircraft excursion and drink in the breathtaking vistas of Volcán Osorno's crater and surrounding lakes. For your final day, head to Puerto Montt. Feast on seafood and browse the Mapuche wares at its famous market, before the return flight home.

Dos and Don'ts

✓ Watch out for stunning birdlife. Andean condors are easily sighted. Forests teem with species including Magellanic woodpeckers, parrots, hummingbirds, and kingfishers.

✗ Don't wear dark clothing on forest treks. It is a magnet for pesky, and very large, horseflies.

✓ Try the *quellén* – sweet wild strawberries that grow in abundance in this region in January.

✓ Bring waterproof clothing. Summer showers are common here.

Below: Bavarian style architecture in Puerto Varas

FEB

MAR

APR

MAY

JUN

JUL

AUG

SEP

OCT

NOV

DEC

Main: An old bridge on the Road to Hāna

THE WINDING ROAD TO HĀNA

THE LEGENDARY ROAD TO HĀNA WINDS FOR SOME 50 MILES (80 KM), threading its way through deep gorges, passing beneath towering waterfalls and above stunning black-sand beaches, and crossing more than 50 bridges. While it's not as perilous as the "I Survived the Road to Hāna" T-shirts might have you believe, it is essential to drive slowly and keep your eyes on the road. If you stay the night in Hāna you'll have more time to explore the area. However, the real point of the journey is not to see Hāna itself, but to enjoy the journey, which you can do as a long day trip from anywhere on Maui.

Almost all Hāna-bound drivers pass through the island capital, Kahului, but the road truly begins at the former plantation village of Pā'ia, now largely populated by surfers thanks to the proximity of the world's finest windsurfing beach at Ho'okipa. Once past that, you feel as if you're leaving reality

GETTING THERE　　　See map p322, H6
Maui's main airport receives non-stop flights from all over the western USA, as well as shuttles from Honolulu on O'ahu. There's also a daily ferry to Kahului from O'ahu.

GETTING AROUND
By far the best way to get around Maui is in a rental car, though Akina Aloha (www.akinatours.com) and Ekahi Tours (www.ekahi.com) run bus tours along the Road to Hāna.

WEATHER
Average daily temperatures in winter range from 78°F (26°C) down to 65°F (18°C).

ACCOMMODATIONS
The homely Mauian in west Maui offers seafront rooms at US$145; www.mauian.com

The Hyatt Regency Maui resort at Kā'anapali has ocean-view rooms starting at US$465; www.maui.hyatt.com

Plantation-style cottages at Hāna's Hotel Hāna-Maui cost US$475–1,075 per night; www.hotelhanamaui.com

EATING OUT
Maui's restaurants cover all cuisines and price ranges, ranging from sophisticated "Pacific Rim" nightspots in the resorts, where a meal for two can easily cost US$100, to simple diners where main dishes cost under US$10.

PRICE FOR TWO
US$605 per day including luxury hotel, car rental and gas, food, snorkel cruise to Molokini, and sunrise bike ride on Haleakalā.

FURTHER INFORMATION
www.visitmaui.com

Land of Volcanoes

Maui is a "volcanic doublet," formed by two overlapping volcanoes. The larger is dormant Haleakalā in the east, which stands over 10,000 ft (3,050 m) tall – high enough to force rain-bearing clouds to shed their water, resulting in the deeply weathered gorges with cloaks of velvet vegetation as seen on the Road to Hāna. Daily at dawn, tour parties are kitted out not far below the summit with bicycles and protective gear, and set off on the exhilarating ride back down to the ocean.

Left: African tulip tree in full bloom

Right (left to right): Waves crashing onto lava rocks at the Ke'anae Peninsula; black sand beach at Wai'ānapanapa, Wai'ānapanapa State Park

behind and entering some South Seas paradise. As the hillsides grow steeper, the road curves dramatically in and out of each successive gully. Rounding each cliff-top corner, you find yourself perched above the crashing waves; deep in the next recess, there's just time as you cross the slim valley bridge to glimpse another waterfall cascading down from the upper slopes of Haleakalā.

Among the many compelling sights along the way, be sure to stop and admire the white-opumod waves that crash unceasingly against rocky Ke'anae Peninsula; to marvel at the lava walls of the largest ancient temple in all Polynesia, in Kahanu Garden; to stroll on the black-sand beach at Wai'ānapanapa State Park; and to sample delicious fresh fruits or barbecued fish at a roadside stand. Many visitors barely pause at the sleepy village of Hāna, 50 miles (80 km) out from Kahului, but continue 10 miles (16 km) further on to 'Ohe'o Gulch, where you can bathe beneath breathtaking waterfalls or hike up into spellbinding rain forest.

MAUI DIARY

Most visitors come to Maui for breaks of a week or less, lured by its wonderful sandy beaches and turquoise waters. You should also make time to explore the island's spectacular tropical scenery. A road trip to Hāna – usually done as a day trip – is a great way to take in the many natural wonders of the island.

Five Days of Island Exploration

JAN

Fly into Kahului, and pick up a rental car or take a shuttle van to your hotel. Ideally you'll arrive in time to watch the sun set over the sea, and then enjoy a romantic dinner.

DAY 1

You'll want to spend your first full day on Maui on the beach, whether that's on the safe sandy strands near the main hotels, like Kā'anapali Beach in west Maui or Polo Beach in Wailea, or on some rougher and more remote spot like magnificent, wave-battered Big Beach near the island's southernmost point.

DAY 2

Now it's time to be a bit more active in the water, perhaps taking a snorkel cruise to the offshore islet of Molokini, or if you're an expert windsurfer, pitting yourself against the surf at fabled Ho'okipa Beach.

DAY 3

Set off early to drive the road to Hāna, pausing perhaps for breakfast in atmospheric little Pā'ia, and aiming for 'Ohe'o Gulch by early afternoon. Remember you can stop on the way back as well as on the way out.

DAY 4

Arrange to be picked up long before dawn, for a bus tour up to the 10,000-ft (3,050-m) summit of the volcano, Haleakalā. After enjoying stupendous views across the extraordinary moonscape, you're taken down to the lower limit of the national park, so you can freewheel back down again on a bicycle; you'll barely need to pedal on the 30-mile (50-km) ride to Pā'ia. There's still time for an afternoon on the beach before you catch the evening flight home.

DAY 5

Dos and Don'ts

☒ Don't take all your food and drink with you; it's more fun to stop at the fruit and snack stands along the way.

☑ Give way to oncoming traffic on the one-way bridges; it's customary for several vehicles to cross at a time in each direction.

☒ Don't stop too long or too often in the first few miles; there's a long day's driving ahead, and you'll risk missing out on the major beauty spots further along.

☒ Don't end up driving back after dark, when you can't appreciate the scenery.

☑ Ask the rangers at 'Ohe'o Gulch about current hiking, swimming, and driving conditions.

Above: Rainbow Eucalyptus tree

Below: Part of the coastline seen from the picturesque Road to Hāna

Below: Waterfall cascading into the Blue Pool near Kahanu Garden

FEB

MAR

APR

MAY

JUN

JUL

AUG

SEP

OCT

NOV

DEC

GETTING THERE See map p323, D2

Carlsbad Caverns National Park is in south-east New Mexico, 150 miles (240 km) northeast of El Paso and 300 miles (480 km) southeast of Albuquerque, at both of whose airports flights arrive from all over the USA.

GETTING AROUND

Driving is the only practical way to reach Carlsbad Caverns National Park.

WEATHER

The average daily high in January is 57°F (14°C), typically dropping to below freezing at night. Light snowfalls are possible. Conditions inside the caves hardly vary, at 56°F (13°C).

ACCOMMODATIONS

White's City, the cluster of buildings at the foot of the road up to the Park, has the mock-adobe Best Western Cavern Inn; doubles from US$72; www.whitescity.com

The Best Western Stevens Inn, in Carlsbad itself, 20 miles (32 km) northeast, is large and comfortable; doubles from US$97; www.stevensinn.com

EATING OUT

This part of New Mexico is not noted for its cuisine. The best you can expect at places like the Velvet Garter in White's City, or the Flume Room at the Stevens Inn in Carlsbad, is reasonable, standard American meat or fish dishes, with mains at US$12–20.

PRICE FOR TWO

US$225 per day including accommodation, food, car hire, and all admissions and tours.

FURTHER INFORMATION

www.nps.gov/cave

Creation of the Caverns

Carlsbad Caverns are set within the Guadalupe Mountain range – all that remains of the 400-mile (640-km) Capitan Reef that once lay on the bed of a primeval ocean. As the seas retreated, and the fossil-laden rocks emerged from the plains, sulphuric acid was released by microbes and oil deposits in the rocks, and it is this, rather than water erosion as in most limestone caves, that hollowed out the caverns. The formations within them, however – known as speleotherms – were created by running water, carrying minerals down through the ground.

Above (left to right): Towering stalagmites in Big Room cavern; the Witch's Finger; the delicate Doll's Theater
Main: The Lake of Clouds in Carlsbad's Lower Cave

CAVERNS AND CANYONS

WITH THEIR TOWERING STALAGMITES, TAPERING STALACTITES, dramatic curtains of translucent rock, and unpredictable swirls and flurries, the hundred-plus caverns of Carlsbad undoubtedly rank among the great natural wonders of the Americas. At the visitors' center, 7 miles (11 km) off the main highway, you're right above the centerpiece of the caverns. Lying 750 ft (230 m) below, the appropriately named Big Room can be accessed directly by elevator, but it's much more fun to walk down, through the equally literally named Natural Entrance. A paved trail from the visitors' center leads to the bat-guano-encrusted maw of the cave. Here, an amphitheater is laid out in tiers to accommodate the summer-evening "bat show" audience, but with a vast, gaping hole where you'd normally expect a stage. This cave mouth swiftly swallows the trail, which drops into darkness down a long series of sweeping switchbacks. It takes a while to acclimatize yourself to this empty, disorienting underground world, but any initial trepidation is dispelled after 15 minutes when you reach the first spectacular formations. Besides the features along the trail, you can peep into beautiful side caves like the King's Palace, filled with translucent "draperies" of limestone. Eventually you reach the Big Room – at 1,800 ft (550 m) long and 250 ft (76 m) high, the largest known "room" in any US cave system.

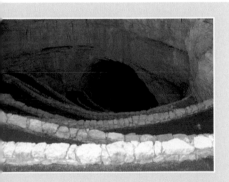

From here a separate loop trail meanders off to undulate around and among all sorts of stalactites, stalagmites, and countless other shapes of petrified rock. Though the rock itself is gray, the formations are stained and dyed by assorted red or brown minerals, and spot-lit in gentle pastels. Evocative, descriptive names include the Temple of the Sun, the Doll's Theater, and the Veiled Statue.

It's quite a shock to return to the sunlit world above, with its rugged "backcountry" landscape of canyons, cacti, and creosote bushes, and raptors such as eagles circling in the open skies above your head.

> The cave mouth swiftly swallows the trail, which drops into darkness down a long series of sweeping switchbacks.

Inset: Descent into the caverns from the Natural Entrance
Below (left and right): Flowering "walking stick" cactus; kit fox

UNDERGROUND DIARY

Carlsbad Caverns is not a place you just happen upon. If you've made the effort to get here, it's worth spending a few days, above and below ground. Stop off at once-lawless Lincoln, or the monochrome wonderland that is White Sands. Without the heat and crowds of the summer, the whole region takes on a timeless appeal.

A Long Weekend's Exploration

If you're coming from El Paso, Texas, up the long, lonely US-62/180, stop at Guadalupe Mountains National Park, to enjoy some great hiking in its lush canyons. If you're heading southeast from Albuquerque, pause instead at tiny Lincoln, little changed since it was home to Billy the Kid. Try to reach your hotel before sunset, by around 5:15pm – driving in the desert after dark is like being in a sensory deprivation tank.

Get up early to drive to the Park. That way, you can make your own way down to, and through, the Big Room. Then venture into the gloriously unnatural Underground Lunchroom for food and splendidly kitsch souvenirs. Later, join a guided tour of an otherwise inaccessible cave, such as the Hall of the White Giant – not for the nervous or infirm.

Take the 10am ranger-led tour of Slaughter Canyon Cave, 25 miles (40 km) southwest of the visitors' center. During the 2-hour tour, which is lit only by flashlights and headlamps, you'll see formations like the 89-ft (270-cm) Monarch, one of the tallest stalagmites in the world. If you hurry back to Carlsbad you'll have time for a trip to the Living Desert State Park, just northwest of town, for a close-up introduction to regional flora and fauna, from cute kit foxes to rather more menacing mountain lions and black bears.

Wherever you're heading back to, drive via southern New Mexico's greatest above-ground attraction: the dazzling gypsum dunes of White Sands National Monument, where the shifting, sculpted sands are punctuated only by the occasional solitary yucca.

Dos and Don'ts

 ✗ Don't expect to see the caverns' large bat population in January; they migrate south to Mexico every winter.

 ✓ Wear sturdy walking shoes in the caverns; even the most-used trails can be rough, slippery, and, of course, poorly lit.

 ✗ Don't visit the Hall of the White Giant or Spider Cave if you suffer from vertigo or claustrophobia.

 ✓ Drop in at the Million Dollar Museum in White's City, at the end of the road leading up to the park, to see its utterly undiscriminating collection of old Western junk.

Below: Horseback trek at White Sands National Monument

JAN
FRI
SAT
SUN
MON
FEB
MAR
APR
MAY
JUN
JUL
AUG
SEP
OCT
NOV
DEC

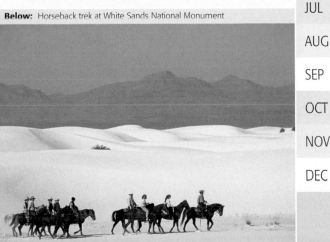

FEBRUARY

Where to Go: February

Conditions are still chilly in much of North America – though the snow makes a great winter wonderland of eastern Canada and New England. Balmier temperatures and warm seas greet you as you head south into Florida, where Miami is a sizzling destination. Mexico is temperate in February, while Central America is enjoying a dry season that allows you access to forested regions that are prohibitively drenched during the wetter months. The Caribbean, too, is delightfully dry, cooled by trade winds. The farther toward the Equator you venture, the steamier things get – perfect weather conditions for the sybaritic pre-Lenten carnival celebrated with style in Brazil. Below you will find all the destinations in this chapter as well as some extra suggestions to provide a little inspiration.

FESTIVALS AND CULTURE

TRINIDAD Colorful participant in the King and Queen of Carnival contest

UNFORGETTABLE JOURNEYS

INTER-AMERICAN HIGHWAY Kayaking in the Sea of Cortez

NATURAL WONDERS

PANAMA A keel-billed toucan

TRINIDAD
CARIBBEAN

It's Carnival time – the West Indies' biggest party

Join in with the revelers for three days of outrageous costumes, music, and, dance. And, stay on to discover more of Trinidad's rich culture.
See pp48–9

NEW ORLEANS MARDI GRAS
LOUISIANA, USA

Visit the birthplace of jazz

A riotous three-week festival with parades, parties, and street carousing accompanied by the city's best live musicians.
www.mardigrasneworleans.com

INTER-AMERICAN HIGHWAY
CENTRAL AMERICA

A country-hopping adventure

This beautiful epic journey has something for everyone as it takes you past mountains, beaches, jungles, and volcanoes.
See pp46–7

> "Panama is an emerald fantasia encompassing the Darién rain forests and the mist-shrouded cloud forests of Volcán Barú."

PANAMA
CENTRAL AMERICA

A fully feathered paradise for birders

Panama is now the top American destination for birding – look out for rainbow-colored toucans, macaws, and humming birds.
See pp42–43

GUANAJUATO
MEXICO

See colonial-Spanish Mexico at its finest

One of the oldest cities in the Americas, Guanajuato preserves a vast array of colonial architecture, including almost 40 churches.
www.guanajuatocapital.com

> "One minute you're winding through mile-high mountains, then the next you're plunging into lush valleys cloaked in subaqueous green."

DRIVING THE CARRETERA AUSTRAL
SOUTHERN CHILE

A road trip to remember

Traverse 1,000 km of unspoilt countryside, running between fjords, glaciers, rain forest, and snow-capped mountains.
www.experiencechile.org

PAINTED CANYON
NORTH DAKOTA, USA

An outlandish landscape

Hike through this bizarrely colored gorge in Theodore Roosevelt National Park, with its amazing hues of green, blue, red, and white.
www.nps.gov/thro

HARP SEAL SPOTTING
ILES DE LA MADELEINE, CANADA

New life on the archipelago

The remote archipelago in the middle of the Gulf of St. Lawrence offers a wonderful chance to see new-born harp seals.
www.tourismeilesdelamadeleine.com

HAVANA
CUBA, CARIBBEAN

Discover the culture capital of the Caribbean

While Cuba's vibrant arts scene pulses to an Afro-Latin beat, sip a mojito in Hemingway's favorite bar and enjoy Habanero life.
See pp38–9

LAGO DE NICARAGUA
NICARAGUA

A majestic lake crossing

Take a boat across the beautiful Lago de Nicaragua out to the dramatic Isla de Ometepe, topped by a pair of towering volcanoes.
www.world66.com/centralamericathecaribbean

RIDING THE ALTIPLANO TRAIN
PUNO–CUSCO BY RAIL, PERU

A "highly" scenic train ride

Travel across the altiplano in the Peruvian Andes on the highest railway line in the Americas.
www.perurail.com/Pages/cusco_puno1.htm

RIO PLÁTANO BIOSPHERE RESERVE
LA MOSQUITIA, HONDURAS

Honduras's Mosquito Coast

One of the finest rain forests in the Americas, and home to myriad plant and animal species.
www.unep-wcmc.org/sites/wh/rioplata.html

SALVADOR
BRAZIL

Salvador's "carnaval" is a joyous bacchanalian revel

This is a carnival where you take part in the parades instead of watching – and the music and partying is second to none.
See pp50–51

GRAN SABANA
VENEZUELA

One of South America's best-kept secrets

Hike through the beautiful uplands of Venezuela's Gran Sabana, the inspiration for Conan Doyle's *The Lost World*.
www.lagransabana.com/english

SEA OF CORTEZ
MEXICO

Swim with sealions and manta rays

Go sea kayaking in the incredibly rich wildlife environment of this scenic gulf coast and islands – see whales, dolphins, and sea birds.
www.loretobay.com

Previous page: Colorful local vegetable market, Guatemala

Weather Watch

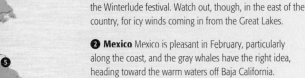

① Ottawa, Canada Snow is at its most luxuriant in Canada in February – great for skiers and skaters, and for the Winterlude festival. Watch out, though, in the east of the country, for icy winds coming in from the Great Lakes.

② Mexico Mexico is pleasant in February, particularly along the coast, and the gray whales have the right idea, heading toward the warm waters off Baja California.

③ Panama Panama, with its micro-climates, can surprise when it comes to weather. February, however, is reliably dry throughout most of the country – though the tropical forests of the Darién can see heavy rain at any time of year.

④ Miami, Florida With its tropical climate, Florida is more than comfortable enough in February that hiking in the Everglades is as much of an option as basking on the trendy beaches.

⑤ Trinidad Trinidad's temperatures are higher than in its neighboring Caribbean Islands, and February sees less rain and lower humidity than in the wet season (May–Dec).

⑥ Brazil Steamy Salvador, on the country's northeastern coast, is about to enter its rainy season, but conditions are still hot, sunny, and dry enough to make visiting for carnival a bone-warming delight.

LUXURY AND ROMANCE

MIAMI An Art Deco-style lifeguard hut, South Beach

PORT ANTONIO
JAMAICA, CARIBBEAN

One of the Caribbean's most luxurious hideaways

Once described as "the most exquisite port on earth," Port Antonio has great beaches, lagoons, and jungle-shrouded mountains.
www.portantoniojamaica.com

EATING AT HOLETOWN
BARBADOS, CARIBBEAN

Romantic dining in the oldest town in Barbados

Enjoy a delicious meal in the atmospheric setting of Holetown, while watching the sun dip into the Caribbean.
www.barbados.org/htown.htm

HOT SPRINGS NATIONAL PARK RESORT
ARKANSAS, USA

A time to unwind

Enjoy the friendly atmosphere of this appealing resort and relax in a bath of natural hot springs spa water.
www.hotsprings.org

MIAMI
FLORIDA, USA

Soak up the city's romantic Art Deco style

With a pulsating nightlife, laidback beach lifestyle, and quirky architecture, Miami offers a plethora of hedonistic delights.
See pp40–1

"Sizzling, sultry Miami has it all: miles of sunny beach by day, pulsing nightlife, fine dining, and trendy shopping."

US VIRGIN ISLANDS
CARIBBEAN

Beaches, forests, and Danish architecture

Ride the vertiginous Skyride in St. Thomas or check out the beaches and forests of St. John, or the old Danish settlements of St. Croix.
www.usvi.net/usvi

ACTIVE ADVENTURES

BAJA PENINSULA Diving among pork fish

LAKES REGION
NEW HAMPSHIRE, USA

Scenic snow-based activities for adrenalin-junkies

Under clear skies amid snowy mountains, there are plenty of adventures and trails to try, and also quiet, quaint towns to explore.
See pp44–5

CLIMBING BLUE MOUNTAIN PEAK
JAMAICA, CARIBBEAN

Conquer a Caribbean peak

Escape the coastal heat with a hike up the idyllic Blue Mountains.
www.jamaicans.com/tourist/thebluemountains.shtml

SPORTS FISHING
COSTA RICA

Some of the world's best deep-sea sports-fishing

Fishing expeditions off both the Pacific and Caribbean coasts, with marlin, dorado, wahoo, tuna, and snook aplenty all year around.
www.fishcostarica.com

DOG SLEDDING
ALASKA

Spectacular sub-Arctic tundra

Explore some of North America's most remote and beautiful wilderness, home to bald and golden eagles, wolves, caribou, moose, otters, lynx, and more.
www.alaskadogsledding.com

BAJA CALIFORNIA SUR
MEXICO

Whale watching in Los Cabos

Unwind on one of the many beaches or take part in an adventure sport in this beautiful Mexican destination.
See pp36–7

FAMILY GETAWAYS

OTTAWA Children enjoying the snow during Winterlude

"A snow playground in Jacques Cartier Park rings with the joyful squeals of kids flinging themselves downhill on snow slides."

OTTAWA
ONTARIO, CANADA

Snowy family fun

Winterlude festival is on this month and the city comes alive with all sorts of activities. Skate, ski, toboggan, and then warm up with hearty food and hot toddies.
See pp34–5

DOMINICAN REPUBLIC
CARIBBEAN

Island fun and games

There are plenty of energetic activities to be had on this family-friendly island, including snorkeling and horseriding.
www.godominicanrepublic.com

GULF SHORES
ALABAMA, USA

Popular Gulf of Mexico family hideaway

The white-sand beach is the main attraction, but there are also plenty of activities on offer too, including feeding alligators.
www.gulfshores.com

VANCOUVER
BRITISH COLUMBIA, CANADA

Something for all the family in the west coast capital

A plethora of city sights to take in, and a temperate climate, which means you can enjoy the beautiful countryside at any time.
www.tourismvancouver.com

FLORIDA KEYS
FLORIDA, USA

A beautiful and tropical getaway in the States

This strip of islands, improbably joined by the highway, allows for water sports galore, fine weather, and an interesting counter culture.
www.fla-keys.com

GETTING THERE   See map p314, E6

Ottawa is situated in the Canadian province of Ontario, around 280 miles (450 km) northeast of Toronto. The international airport is 20 minutes from downtown by cab.

GETTING AROUND

Ottawa is a pedestrian-friendly city, and the downtown core is well-served by city buses. In February, skating on the frozen Rideau Canal is both unique and practical.

WEATHER

At 16°F (−9°C), Ottawa's average daytime temperatures in February are brisk, while the nights are usually colder.

ACCOMMODATIONS

Premiere Executive Suites offer two-bedroom apartments from US$136 per night; in their upmarket locations, smaller apartments start at US141$; www.premieresuites.com

Hotel Indigo has one-room suites from US$140; www.ottawadowntownhotel.com

Westin Ottawa offers doubles from US$180; www.starwoodhotels.com

EATING OUT

In Ottawa, expect to pay about US$25 per head at most family restaurants. For elegant, dining, try Wilfrid's at the Fairmont Château Laurier (US$65 per head for three courses).

PRICE FOR A FAMILY OF FOUR

US$640 per day, including lodging, food, travel, sightseeing, shopping, and ski lifts.

FURTHER INFORMATION

www.ottawatourism.ca
www.ontariotravel.net

The World's Longest Rink

Stretching 125 miles (202 km) from Ottawa to Kingston, the Rideau Canal – a UNESCO World Heritage Site – was built as a safe route for military ships sailing from Kingston to Montréal. After the War of 1812, the British feared that the St. Lawrence River, a natural supply route, was prone to American attack. Yet, the canal was not used for military purposes. In 1970, its 5-mile (8-km) section winding through downtown Ottawa was groomed for skating. In 2005, the *Guinness Book of World Records* named it the world's longest skating rink.

Inset: Façade of the Canadian Museum of Civilization

Left (left and right): The cityscape at dusk; grand interior of the House of Commons

Right (left to right): One of the many snow sculptures made during Winterlude; an intricate ice sculpture at Confederation Park; visitors enjoying the ice slide at Jacques Cartier Park

Main: Children making the most of the snow in Ottawa during Winterlude

WINTER WONDERLAND

SPACIOUS PARKS, EXCELLENT MUSEUMS, AND HISTORIC SITES GALORE – the culturally versatile and vibrant city of Ottawa has more than its fair share to entertain families at any time of year, but it's in February when Canada's capital city truly shines. The flavor of Ottawa stays festive, with the advent of Winterlude, featuring ice and snow sculptures, icy slides, and skating. The Rideau Canal springs to life with brightly clothed skaters, while the seasonal snow playground across the Ottawa River in Jacques Cartier Park rings from morning to dusk with the shouts and squeals of children flinging themselves downhill on snow slides. Keen hockey fans fill pubs across the city, cheering on the Senators in the hopes that this will be the year they bring home the coveted Stanley Cup.

February is also an excellent time to discover the city's museums and sights. If you have an airplane buff in your family, fly by the Canada Aviation Museum, home to more than 130 vintage aircraft. Nearby, the RCMP

A snow playground in Jacques Cartier Park rings with the joyful squeals of kids flinging themselves downhill on snow slides.

WINTERLUDE DIARY

Winter in Ottawa is all about enjoying the snow and ice. During Winterlude (the first three weekends of February) you'll need at least one long weekend to enjoy the city's attractions. The nation's capital is also home to over half-a-dozen national museums – great places to warm up between skiing and skating expeditions.

Four Frosty Days in Ottawa

Admire the glittering ice sculptures in Confederation Park, then tour the Neo-Gothic Parliament buildings. After lunch, take a cab to the Canadian Museum of Science and Technology, where vintage steam locomotives are family favorites. In the evening, catch an outdoor concert – be sure to dress warmly.

DAY 1

Mornings are the best time to rent skates and head to the Rideau Canal, just after the ice has had its overnight grooming. Skate to the Bank Street Bridge and then return your skates before you stop for shopping and a pub lunch either in Old Ottawa South or the Glebe. Walk along the Canal to Dows Lake, where you can take a jingling sleigh ride. Before heading back downtown, warm up with a cup of hot cider.

DAY 2

Walk or skate to the Canadian Museum of Nature, home to kid-pleasing dinosaurs.

Fuel up with a long and leisurely Sunday brunch before hitting the bustling Byward Market to browse for local crafts and maple syrup. Cap the day with a play or concert at the National Arts Centre.

DAY 3

Rent a car and head for the Gatineau Hills, across the river in Québec, for a day of gentle downhill skiing at Camp Fortune. In the evening, cheer on the National Hockey League's (NHL) Ottawa Senators in the Kanata, or West End.

DAY 4

Dos and Don'ts

✓ Ask your Parliament Hill guide to point out the faces lurking in the corners of elaborately carved ceilings. These carvings were done by the artists to immortalize themselves.

✗ When skating on the Rideau Canal, don't check your boots in at the kiosk. Carry them so you can change if you get tired.

✓ Buy hot packs for your boots and mittens from a local store.

✓ If you're skating with children, head to the Rideau Canal early to rent one of the popular sleds.

✗ Don't miss out on "beavertails," Ottawa's characteristic deep-fried pastries you can buy from huts along the Rideau Canal.

Below: Douglas DC-3 on display at the Canada Aviation Museum

Musical Ride Centre offers an inside peek at Canada's famous equine spectacle performed by the renowned Mounties – you can also see the stables and practice ring, discover how horses are named and raised, and pick up some Mountie memorabilia. Across the river, the Canadian Museum of Civilization draws families with exhibitions focusing on Canadian and world history, and nature-themed movies on a huge IMAX screen. The building is also home to the Canadian Children's Museum, a hands-on place where kids can clamber aboard an elaborately decorated bus from Pakistan or try their hand at traditional crafts such as soapstone carving.

One of the great pleasures of winter in Ottawa is settling down to a leisurely restaurant meal. As snow drifts down outside, any eatery with a working fireplace will have it stoked with logs and glowing to ward off the chill. Menus offer rich, hearty fare from a wealth of culinary traditions, particularly French-Canadian. Adults and kids alike will enjoy thick slices of *tourtière* (meat pie), but *tarte au sucre* (sugar pie) might be a tad too sweet for calorie- and cavity-conscious grown-ups. Do make sure that your kids stick to a small serving, or you may be in for a long, sleepless night!

JAN

FEB

MAR

APR

MAY

JUN

JUL

AUG

SEP

OCT

NOV

DEC

GETTING THERE   See map p323, C4
Los Cabos International Airport is about 30 miles (48 km) from Cabo San Lucas and 8 miles (13 km) from San José del Cabo.

GETTING AROUND
It's easy to stroll around downtown Cabo San Lucas and San José del Cabo. Organized tours, taxis, public transportation, and rental cars and bikes are also available.

WEATHER
February temperatures average 80°F (27°C); but can drop to 60°F (16°C) in the evening. Sunscreen is recommended year-round.

ACCOMMODATIONS
Baja Bungalows in Cabo Pulmo Village offers solar-powered rooms with doubles from US$75; www.bajabungalows.com

Meals and drinks are included at Best Western Posada Real, San José del Cabo; doubles from US$202; www.bestwestern.com

On a beachfront location, Fiesta Americana Grand Los Cabos has doubles from US$392; www.fiestaamericana.com

EATING OUT
Allow US$10–15 pp for breakfast and lunch, and US$15–25 pp for dinner at most Los Cabos restaurants. Regional Mexican fare and fresh seafood are musts to try.

PRICE FOR TWO
US$800 per day including accommodation, food, and cost of all activities and excursions.

FURTHER INFORMATION:
www.visitloscabos.org

A Fragile Environment

The Sea of Cortez has one of the most pristine eco-systems on earth. Although development and economic exploitation poses threats to it, the Mexican government has initiated some safeguards. One such example is Cabo Pulmo National Marine Park, a 5-mile (8 km) stretch between southernmost Los Frailes and Pulmo Point on the East Cape. Home to three living reefs, including North America's only hard coral reef, this treasure of rich biodiversity contains hundreds of species of flora and fauna.

LOS CABOS ADVENTURES

POISED AT THE TIP OF MEXICO'S BAJA CALIFORNIA PENINSULA, which stretches nearly 1,061 miles (1,708 km) from the United States border and is almost geographically separated from the Mexican mainland, stunningly scenic Los Cabos offers an abundance of activities on both land and sea. Postcard-perfect Finisterra (Land's End) is widely recognized for its eye-popping, naturally sculpted rock formations, including El Arco (The Arch) with its basking sea lion colony, and Los Frailes (The Friars). Even more characteristic of the area is the contrast of rugged mountain ranges above startling cactus deserts that merge into white-sand beaches. Formerly a sleepy off-the-map fishing locale, much of the region has skyrocketed into a

Humpback whales, dolphins, sea lions, sea turtles, manta rays, and hundreds of marine-life species may be your companions at this teeming coral reef.

celebrity haven and party zone. Collectively known as Los Cabos, the area comprises the tourist hub of Cabo San Lucas – a cruise port famed for its nightlife – on the Pacific side and the tranquil, traditional Mexican town of San José del Cabo, which nuzzles the Sea of Cortez (Gulf of California). In between these two sharply contrasting communities is the 20-mile (32-km) "corridor" with luxurious resorts and championship golf courses set atop rocky cliffs.

Los Cabos' appeal is not unwarranted. Although many tourists are content to hole up in their resort, Los Cabos is also a magnet for adventurers seeking a wide range of experiences. World-class sport-fishing for blue marlin is hugely popular, and during the gray whale migration season of mid-December through February, visitors flock to see these majestic mammals literally pop out of the sea. For closer viewing, you can join an excursion in a range of craft from high-speed inflatable Zodiacs to reach-out-and-touch-them small panga boats.

Along the shore near San José del Cabo, an estuary offers peaceful respite to approximately 200 native and migratory bird species, including egrets and brown pelicans. Protected and pristine, Cabo Pulmo National Marine Park on the Sea of Cortez offers superior scuba-diving and snorkeling. Humpback whales, dolphins, sea lions, turtles, manta rays, and hundreds of marine-life species may be your companions at this teeming coral reef.

Main: Gray whale breaching
Below (left and right): El Arco, Cabo San Lucas; horseback riding, Cabo San Lucas
Inset: Diver surrounded by a shoal of pork fish in the Sea of Cortez

WHALE DIARY

With warm temperatures and low humidity, February is a splendid month for a multitude of active adventures in this region, whether on land or in the water. Better still, it's prime time for viewing the gray whales which migrate each year from the cold waters of the Bering Sea to the bath-tub warm Pacific.

Four Days at Sea

Get your bearings on a sea-kayak ride in the blue Sea of Cortez, paddling to Finisterra where the calm sea meets the crashing surf of the Pacific Ocean with its much-photographed, nature-sculpted rock formations: El Arco and Los Frailes. Relax and soak up the sun at popular Playa del Amor (Lovers' Beach). Then explore or snorkel the Gulf's more secluded bays and coves, as well as the peaceful estuary near San José del Cabo, home to approximately 200 species of birds and other wildlife.

Sign up for an all-day snorkeling or scuba-diving excursion to the Cabo Pulmo Marine Park, about 60 miles (97 km) north of Los Cabos, on the Sea of Cortez. Surrounded by desert and mountains, the park features a living coral reef and is a haven to hundreds of varieties of marine life and passing manta rays, sea turtles, sea lions, dolphins, and humpback whales.

Pick and choose your favorite activities or try something new. Take a sport-fishing excursion (the striped marlin and yellowfin tuna are usually biting this time of year), go parasailing above El Arco for an eagle-eye view, board a high-speed or easy-going vessel for a close-up visit to the gray and humpback whales, or pump adrenaline with an off-road safari through rural desert. If you are in need of something more relaxing after all the excitement this region has to offer, opt for a scenic horseback ride along one of Cabo San Lucas' beautiful beaches. Guided scenic rides are the best option, as the "cowboys" leading the tours point out local flora and fauna along the way.

Dos and Don'ts

✓ Although English is widely spoken in the area, learn a few pleasantries (hello, please, thank you, etc.) in Spanish.

✓ Taxi fares can be quite expensive in Los Cabos; negotiate with drivers before getting in the car.

✓ Check first before jumping into the waters of remote beaches; many have dangerous rip currents.

✓ Try to plan your trip before or after the weekend, when you'll have fewer crowds to contend with.

✗ Don't drive after dark in Mexico, and don't drive at all without the requisite automobile insurance (non-Mexican policies are not valid).

Below: Inquisitive gray whale approaching a tour boat

JAN

FEB

DAY 1

DAY 2

DAYS 3–4

MAR

APR

MAY

JUN

JUL

AUG

SEP

OCT

NOV

DEC

GETTING THERE   See map p325, B2

Several airlines serve Havana from Canada and Europe, and many fly from Central America. Charter flights link Havana to certain US cities for licensed US travelers (see www.treas.gov).

GETTING AROUND

Old Havana is made for walking. Tourist taxis serve the city and are hailed outside hotels. Avoid buses and Cocotaxis. Chauffeur-driven classic autos cost around US$16 per hour from GranCar (www.cuba.cu/turismo/panatrans).

WEATHER

February is usually dry, sunny, warm, and not too humid, with a daytime average of 75°F (24°C). Pack a jacket for evenings.

ACCOMMODATIONS

Many private room rentals are available; doubles from US$30; www.cubaparticular.com

Hotel Raquel is an Art Nouveau gem; doubles from US$100; www.hotelraquel-cuba.com

Hotel Nacional de Cuba is a 1930s classic with gardens overlooking the seafront; doubles from US$185; www.hotelnacionaldecuba.com

Hotel Parque Central offers modern comforts; doubles from US$220; www.nh-hotels.cu

EATING OUT

Cusine is not a Havana highlight, but there are some very good restaurants. You can dine well for around US$15.

PRICE FOR TWO

US$280 per day including accommodation, food, transportation, and admissions.

FURTHER INFORMATION

www.dtcuba.com

CULTURAL KALEIDOSCOPE

Cuba's capital city, Havana, exudes exoticism and eccentricity. With its slightly surreal blend of colonialism and Communism, it is steeped, too, in an almost tangible 1950s, pre-revolutionary charm that is simply irresistible. Teeming with creativity and spontaneity, the city can rightly claim to be the cultural capital of the Caribbean. It's also a showcase of spectacular architecture. At its core, Habana Vieja (Old Havana) has been named a UNESCO World Heritage Site, with its 18th-century palaces, founded on the wealth brought by treasure fleets en route to Spain. Later, vast riches from sugar and slavery funded a new wave of lavish edifices, and cobbled plazas were enclosed by elegant confections in stone. In the 20th century, modern Havana was imbued with effusive Art Deco, Beaux Arts, and Modernist designs with a tropical twist. A restoration project, now in its third decade and

Cuban Cabaret

Sexy Las Vegas-style cabarets (*espectáculos*) have been a part of Cuban culture since the sizzling 1930s heyday of Havana. Even the Communist revolution didn't put a damper on these erotically charged shows featuring troupes of long-legged *mulattas* in skimpy, sensational outfits. Every town has at least one. The best of all is the Tropicana, which opened in Havana on New Year's Eve 1939, featured acts such as Carmen Miranda and Nat "King" Cole and his trio (*above*), and still packs in the crowds for a night of "Paradise Under the Stars."

Main: The Tropicana's famous *mulatta* showgirls in action

Left: La Bodeguita del Medio bar

Right (left to right): Havana's colorful balconied buildings; locals passing the time with a game of dominoes; everyone seems to enjoy the huge Havana cigars

Right panel (top to bottom): Market stalls in front of the San Cristobál cathedral in Plaza de la Catedral; classic American autos of a bygone era

centered on four ancient plazas, continues to transform historic buildings into hotels, restaurants, and eclectic museums that range from the grandiose Museo de la Revolución to the esoteric – such as the delightful Museo de Naipes (Museum of Playing Cards), on Plaza Vieja.

Havana's arts scene is the envy of Latin America. Cuba's fine literary tradition is written into the very soul of Plaza de Armas, where visitors and locals browse the outdoor used-book market, and bars such as El Floridita and La Bodeguita del Medio seem haunted by the spirit of Ernest Hemingway. The time-worn streets are lined with galleries. Music and dance, from sentimental *son* to sizzling salsa, are the pulsating undercurrents to Cuban life. High culture is epitomized by the world-class Ballet de Cuba but, for sheer entertainment, check out the sensational cabarets – a throwback to the days when Havana was something of a sin city. Many of the venues have hardly changed since the 1950s, offering a glimpse of a lost era, and drawing first-time visitors back for more.

HABAÑERO DIARY

February is an ideal month to visit Cuba, when humidity is at its lowest and walking Havana's streets in mild temperatures under cloudless skies is sheer bliss. In five days you'll have time to get a real flavor of *habañero* culture. And, even if you're not here at Mardi Gras time, you're likely to come across lively local festivals.

Five Days of Cuban Culture

DAY 1
Explore the heart of Habana Vieja, focusing on Plaza de la Catedral and Plaza de Armas. Break for a *mojito* (rum, lime, sugar, and mint) cocktail and lunch at the bustling, atmospheric La Bodeguita del Medio.

DAY 2
Today it's southern Habana Vieja, starting in and around Plaza Vieja. Take a look into the churches here and pause at the birthplace of Cuba's premier national hero, José Martí. In the evening, you could enjoy a choral concert at Iglesia y Convento de San Francisco.

DAY 3
From Parque Central, head for the Museo de Bellas Artes (Fine Arts Museum), the Museo de la Revolución, and the Capitolio. Visit the Partagás factory to see cigars being made, then stroll the Prado (Paseo de Martí) and Malecón, the seafront promenade that teems with locals at sunset. Dine at La Guarida before an evening dance performance at the spectacular Gran Teatro.

DAY 4
Hire a classic American auto and tour modern Havana, visiting the Hotel Nacional, Cemeterio Colón, and Plaza de la Revolución, including the Museo de José Martí. Lunch at El Aljibe, then cross the harbor to tour the El Morro and Cabaña fortresses. Dine at a *paladar* (private restaurant), such as Hurón Azul, before heading off to the Jazz Café to see some of Cuba's top musicians in action.

DAY 5
Pay homage to American author Ernest Hemingway with a trip to Finca Vigía, his former home, and Cojímar, the setting for *The Old Man and the Sea*. Lunch at his favorite restaurant, La Terraza. Continue to Playas del Este to relax on the beach. Head back to the city center in time for a sensational finale at the Tropicana nightclub.

Dos and Don'ts

☑ Travel with perfect-condition cash notes to convert into Cuban pesos (CUCs). Be aware of the 11 percent tax added to all credit card payments

☒ Never buy cigars from a street vendor. Use government shops, and keep the receipt for customs.

☒ Don't carry any items of value when out in the streets. Take extra care of your camera, as snatch-and-grab is common.

☑ Consider a stay with a local family in a *casa particular* (private room rental), to get a feel for Cuban life.

Below: The view along the Malecón at sunset

JAN
FEB
MAR
APR
MAY
JUN
JUL
AUG
SEP
OCT
NOV
DEC

GETTING THERE See map p317, G7
Located at the southern tip of Florida, Miami is served by most major airlines; rental cars are available at the airport.

GETTING AROUND
A car is essential to get to the various city neighborhoods, but once you arrive, each area is easy to explore on foot.

WEATHER
February average highs of 78°F (24°C) and lows of 60°F (16°C).

ACCOMMODATIONS
For a truly romantic Miami Beach option, try The Hotel; doubles from US$259; www.thehotelofsouthbeach.com

In Coconut Grove, the Mayfair Hotel & Spa boutique hotel has doubles starting at US$289; www.mayfairhotelandspa.com

One of Miami's top hotels, the Ritz-Carlton offers doubles at a whopping US$500 per night; www.ritzcarlton.com

EATING OUT
Joe's Stone Crab is a South Beach institution, worth the wait in line. Chef Allen's in Aventura shows off the talents of top-rated chef Allen Susser. Downtown, Machy's is the place for French-influenced New American cuisine, whilst Tu Tu Tango in Coconut Grove is a firm favorite among locals and tourists alike.

PRICE FOR TWO
Miami is an expensive city. Allow at least US$500 per day for hotels, food, and car rental.

FURTHER INFORMATION
www.gmcvb.com

Sea of Waving Grass
Everglades National Park, a UNESCO World Heritage Site, is the largest subtropical wilderness in the USA. This sea of waving grass and wetlands is home to all manner of bird and animal life, including crocodiles, manatees, and egrets. A vast expanse of roughly 1.5 million acres (606,500 ha), the park offers solo hiking, or ranger-led tours, as well as air-boat tours and tram tours along a 15-mile (24-km) loop in the heart of the section known as the "River of Grass." Note that protection against biting insects is vital when visiting the Everglades.

Above (left to right): An Art Deco-style lifeguard hut, South Beach; Villa Vizcaya; sign for Calle Ocho, Little Havana
Main: The Colony Hotel in the heart of the Art Deco district

MIAMI BEACH DELIGHTS

SULTRY, SIZZLING MIAMI HAS IT ALL: miles of sunny beach by day, pulsing nightlife, fine dining, trendy shopping, an exciting arts scene, and a vibrant cultural life. While there is a bustling commercial downtown, for many visitors Miami means Miami Beach. South Beach (the southernmost part of Miami Beach) is home to the city's unique interpretation of the Art Deco style, where hotels and other buildings constructed in the 1920s and 30s are decked out in funky pastels, bearing distinctively Floridian motifs such as flamingos and sunbursts. For many visitors, however, the Deco buildings are simply a backdrop for a hedonistic playground: days are for sleeping or relaxing on the beach; nights for serious partying. Fun-filled South Beach has a vibrant gay community, and for those who love to party, a legendary club scene offering a myriad options for dancing the night away. Miami Beach is also an active arts conclave, home to the well-regarded Miami Ballet and to two museums, the Bass Museum of Art and the Wolfsonian. Beginning in the 1960s, an influx of Cubans fleeing Castro's regime swelled the city's population and gave Miami a unique Latin flavor and international air. A visit to vibrant Little Havana, with its authentic Cuban restaurants, is a must. It is enjoyable for its atmosphere and streetlife, with salsa beats pounding out from every other shop, as much as it is for its sights.

> For many visitors the Deco buildings are simply a backdrop for a hedonistic playground: days are for sleeping.

The scene shifts, however, in Coral Gables, a neighborhood of lush greenery and fine Mediterranean-style homes. Shoppers flock here for the boutiques and specialty stores along the "Miracle Mile" and the galleries, which showcase the best in Latin American art. Coconut Grove is yet another scene – young, bohemian, and fun – with lots of off-beat shops to explore. The Coconut Grove Arts Festival held every February is one of the nation's premier outdoor fine Arts Festivals, attracting hundreds of top artists and craftsmen.

Inset: Decoration on the Netherlands Hotel, South Beach
Below (left and right): The luxurious Biltmore hotel; Bayside Marketplace

PLEASURE DIARY

Getting to know Miami means exploring its diverse neighborhoods and five days should allow time for a rich sampling of the city's offerings. February is perfect, with wonderful warm sunshine. Feel free to forget sightseeing when you prefer to spend time basking on the city's many glorious miles of beach.

Five Luxurious Days

Start with a morning walk in South Beach to admire the Art Deco architecture along Ocean Drive, followed by a long, romantic lunch and some shopping on Lincoln Road. Afterwards, visit the Bass Museum on Park Avenue. Take a nap in preparation for some late-night clubbing.

Admire the gleaming skyscrapers downtown and browse the shops at the Bayside Marketplace on Biscayne Bay. After a Cuban lunch on Calle Ocho in Little Havana, explore the open-air markets and cigar and music shops reflecting Cuban culture. Later in the afternoon, visit the museum and gardens of Miami's most famous mansion, Villa Vizcaya, on South Miami Avenue.

Today's the day for funky shops and avant-garde clothing stores amidst the tropical foliage of Coconut Grove. Have lunch in an outdoor café, and visit the Barnacle State Historic Site, a bay-front mansion and the former home of naval architect and early settler Ralph Middleton Munroe.

Coral Gables, developed in the 1920s, offers lush landscaping, vintage Spanish-style homes and romantic plazas with flowing fountains. Enjoy the exclusive shops and galleries and have lunch at the Biltmore, the luxurious 1920s classic hotel. Treat yourself to a blissful afternoon relaxing on the beach.

Take the hour drive to the Everglades and say hello to the alligators and egrets. Renting a canoe and following clearly marked, easy-to-navigate canoe trails is a great way for a close-up look at the wildlife.

Dos and Don'ts

✓ Visit Miami on Sunday to Thursday to get a better deal on hotels; weekend hotel rates are much higher.

✗ Don't bother going to a South Beach club early in the evening. The real action begins after midnight.

✓ Take a guided tour of the Art Deco district, offered by the Miami Design Preservation League on Wednesday, Saturday and Sunday at 10:30am. Self-guided tours are also available at the Art Deco Welcome Center at Ocean Front Auditorium, 1001 Ocean Drive.

✗ Don't forget a sun hat. That tropical sun is hot, hot, hot!

JAN
FEB
DAY 1
DAY 2
DAY 3
DAY 4
DAY 5
MAR
APR
MAY
JUN
JUL
AUG
SEP
OCT
NOV
DEC

Below: Restaurants lining Lincoln Road

FEBRUARY

GETTING THERE
See map p324, H6
Panama lies at the southern end of the Central American isthmus. Flights land at Tocumén International Airport outside Panama City. Boca del Toro and Boquete are served by flights from Costa Rica.

GETTING AROUND
Tocumén International Airport is a 20-minute taxi ride away from downtown; Air Panama and Aeroperlas offer domestic flights, while buses ply across the country. Guided birding tours are the best for maximizing your time.

WEATHER
The weather in February varies by region. Darién can get rain all year, and temperatures vary with elevation, from about 90°F (32°C) to 50°F (10°C) in the high mountains.

ACCOMMODATIONS
Canopy Tower Ecolodge in Parque Nacional Soberanía is dedicated to birding; doubles from US$135; www.canopytower.com

Boquete's Coffee Estate Inn has doubles from US$130; www.coffeeestateinn.com

In the heart of Parque Nacional Darién, Cana Field Station serves birders; air-hotel deals start at US$700; www.anconexpeditions.com

EATING OUT
Panama has both cosmopolitan restaurants and eateries selling local fare. Boquete's Palo Alto Restaurante specializes in fresh trout.

PRICE FOR TWO
US$130 per day with accommodation, food, admissions, a guide, and transportation.

FURTHER INFORMATION
www.anconexpeditions.com

Main: A blue-and-gold macaw alongside a group of scarlet macaws

Quetzal Country

Many bird watchers visit Panama simply to spot the resplendent trogon, or quetzal – they're more numerous here than anywhere else in Central America. These denizens of the cloud forest were once worshiped by the ancient Maya for their iridescent green plumage. In springtime, the males woo their prospective mates by showing off their long tail plumes in swooping displays. Birders should listen for the quetzal's distinctive high-pitched, two-note whistle.

WINGED PANAMA

Engulfed in a thousand shades of green, Panama is an emerald fantasia encompassing the Darién rain forests and the mist-shrouded cloud forests of Volcán Barú – home to the resplendent quetzal. An ecological crossroads between two continents and two oceans, this Lilliputian tropical land is Brobdingnagian when it comes to birds. Over 1,000 species inhabit ten distinct ecological zones, from coastal mangroves to dry deciduous forests.

A number of Panamanian tour companies specialize in birding, so there are plenty of competent guides with eagle eyes and an encyclopedic knowledge of bird habits and habitats. With such wild extremes of terrain and microclimates, the country never fails in its promise of phenomenal birding – over a quarter of the nation is protected as national parks, whose range and quantity of birdlife is guaranteed to put a smile on any ornithologist's face. Coastal mudflats draw shorebirds in scores, their long bills jabbing at tasty morsels. Pick! Pick! Pick! The

Left (left to right): A keel-billed toucan; the rufous-crested coquette at the Canopy Lodge; the mist-shrouded Darién forest; tourists exploring the rain forest by aerial tram

Below: A hummingbird perching on a red heliconia

Inset: A watchful harpy eagle in Parque Nacional Soberanía

Massive harpy eagles sail overhead, talons at the ready, their hungry eyes scanning the forest canopy for sloths and monkeys.

BIRDER'S DIARY

Blessed with terrains spanning from right by the shoreline to high-altitude cloud forests, Panama boasts an astonishingly profuse bird population. February – the peak of dry season – is the best time to visit, when several migratory species are present. You'll need at least ten days to cover the best of the diverse ecosystems.

Ten Days in Avian Paradise

Arrive in Panama and meet your guide before heading to Parque Nacional Soberanía and settling in at the world-famous Canopy Tower hotel, dedicated to birders. Spend the afternoon spotting scores of species from the rooftop observatory, as well as seeing eye to eye with monkeys that cavort in the treetops.

DAY 1

After a morning hike in the rain forest, drive farther afield for some more bird watching in the area. The next day, drive on to Azuero, famous for its coastal wetland reserves. Expect to see spoonbills, stilts, boat-billed herons, and other shorebirds.

DAYS 2–3

Head to Boquete, situated in the cool highlands, either via air or an eight-hour road trip. A gateway to Volcán Barú, the aptly-named Sendero Los Quetzales (The Quetzal Trail) virtually guarantees quetzal sightings.

Take a break of sorts from birding to enjoy hiking or white-water rafting around Boquete, and then visit a coffee farm. You're still likely to find birds all around.

DAYS 4–6

Fly to Cana Field Station in Darién National Park with Ancón Expeditions. Few places in the world rival Cana for birding. Macaws, toucans, and hawk eagles can be seen as you hike the Boca de Cupe Trail.

Spend another day exploring the Mine Trail – great curassow and crested guan are commonly seen here.

DAYS 7–9

Return to Panama City, and if there's time, visit the Parque Natural Metropolitano and tick the species you see here off your list before your departure flight.

DAY 10

Dos and Don'ts

⊗ Don't forget to bring a strong insect repellent to keep away "chiggers" – parasitic mites that are plentiful in the tropics.

✓ Hire a professional guide. You'll see far more birds in their company.

⊗ Don't wear bright clothing. Birds are more easily seen when humans blend into the landscape.

✓ Do carry a good pair of binoculars as well as a tripod for your camera.

JAN

FEB

MAR

APR

MAY

JUN

JUL

AUG

SEP

OCT

NOV

DEC

Below: Sunlight pouring through the branches of trees in the rain forest

wetlands are flush with fulvous whistling ducks and other waterfowl, many of them migrating between the Americas, and the cloud forests ring to the bell-like clang of the three-wattled bellbird. Pelicans, frigate birds, and boobies roost on the islands off the Azuero Peninsula and the thick rain forests reverberate with the squawks, whistles, and coos of their own unique avian fauna. Antbirds are easily seen as they scavenge for insects and lizards flushed out by columns of army ants, while chestnut-mandibled and keel-billed toucans are a dime a dozen. Parrots barrel past in jet-fighter formation: Panama boasts as many as 18 species, from the diminutive Panama Amazon to six species of giant macaw. Meanwhile, the massive harpy eagle – the national bird – sails overhead, talons at the ready, its hungry eyes scanning the forest canopy for sloths and monkeys.

Panama is the ultimate pilgrimage for birders keen to spot the Holy Grail of neotropical birds – the quetzal. This emerald jewel of the cloud forest is more abundant here than anywhere else in Central America. It's no wonder, then, that birders flock to this paradise like migrating macaws.

GETTING THERE
See map p316, H4

The Lakes Region is about 55 miles (88 km) north of the Manchester, New Hampshire regional airport and about 100 miles (160 km) north of Boston's Logan Int. Airport.

GETTING AROUND
Most scenic towns in the Lakes Region are compact and walkable, but public transportation between towns is patchy; a car is essential.

WEATHER
With temperatures averaging around 35°F (1°C) and moderate snowfalls, February is a perfect time for winter sports fans.

ACCOMMODATIONS
Comfort Inn & Suites, Lincoln, is 3 miles (5 km) from Loon Mountain skiing; doubles from US$120; www.comfortinnloon.com

Franconia Inn, a skiing base with breathtaking views of Franconia Notch; packages available from US$224; doubles from US$230; www.franconiainn.com

The Manor on Golden Pond, on Squam Lake in Holderness, offers fireplace rooms from US$250; www.manorongoldenpond.com

EATING OUT
Apart from hotel restaurants, visitors face a surprising number of dining options. Mame's (US$35), in Meredith, serves upscale bistro fare in a building that dates to 1825.

PRICE FOR TWO
US$320 per day including hotel, food, and entertainment.

FURTHER INFORMATION
www.skinh.com

Dog Days of Winter

If visiting the region in early February, a trip to the Laconia World Championship Sled Dog Derby is a must. First held in 1929, the race's primary course, 18 miles (29 km) long, traverses the area's numerous lakes, and snakes through the woods. Competitors primarily come from the USA and Canada, with a few Europeans making their way over. Several secondary competitions are held as well, including a 6-mile (9-km), six-dog race and a junior-level three-dog race. The event is good for families, as kids can get close to the action.

Above (left to right): Skiers on the flat; a climber in the White Mountains; a snowboarder takes off **Main:** Downhill thrills on Loon Mountain

SNOWY ADVENTURES

PRISTINE MOUNTAIN TRAILS, FRESHWATER STREAMS, CRYSTAL CLEAR SKIES: the Lakes Region's abundant natural beauty is a wonder to behold any time of year. Some prefer it during the holidays, when festive sleigh rides provide thrills for the whole family. Others enjoy the autumn months for world-class leaf color amid breathtaking scenery. But for winter sports fanatics, from downhill speed skiers to cross-country walkers, February is the perfect time for a visit.

The region's numerous mountains hold top-notch downhill and cross-country trails for skiers of all levels. Nature-lovers can ditch the skis in favor of snowshoes and head out on lengthy walks, stopping to appreciate excellent bird-watching opportunities. Thrill-seekers can speed down luge runs, while the less adventurous can hop on inner tubes to glide down groomed hills. The list of available snow-based activities, including snowmobiling and ice fishing, just goes on and on. Located in central New Hampshire, the Lakes Region comprises a trio of large freshwater lakes.

Lake Winnipesaukee, the state's largest one (and the sixth largest natural lake in the USA), contains more than 250 islands and almost 300 miles (482 km) of shoreline. Winnisquam and Squam Lakes, while not as famous, each possess plenty of natural features and tend to be less-traversed than their better-known neighbor.

Quaint towns – the kind that New England is renowned for – line the lakes, and when it comes to town-to-town travel, personal pleasure boats are just as popular as cars. For decades, visitors of all kinds have appreciated the peace and quiet offered to them by towns such as Wolfeboro and Meredith, virtues also recognized by thousands of Bostonians and New Yorkers who have second homes hereabouts. Old-fashioned general stores and inviting art galleries add to the area's attractions. Aspen it is not, but any drive through the Lakes Region, with its many covered bridges, is truly a scenic one.

> The list of available snow-based activities, including snowmobiling and ice fishing, just goes on and on.

Inset: Cannon Mountain cable car, Franconia
Below (left and right): Mill Falls, Meredith; Lake Winnipesaukee at sunset

JAN
FEB
DAY 1
DAY 2
DAY 3
MAR
APR
MAY
JUN
JUL
AUG
SEP
OCT
NOV
DEC

WINTERTIME DIARY

The ideal depth of snow in the Lakes Region in winter is never guaranteed. However, if timed right, February visitors can enjoy the year's best skiing conditions. And, if there's no snow on the ground, there are still plenty of outdoor activities to enjoy, and several quaint and historic towns waiting to be discovered.

Three Days of Outdoor Thrills

Start things off in Wolfeboro, which despite billing itself as the "oldest summer resort in America," is still a fine place to visit in winter. Soak up Main Street's small-town feel before enjoying a picnic, weather permitting, on the Lake Winnipesaukee docks. Then head north to Loon Mountain for an afternoon of skiing or snowboarding. If the conditions aren't good, there's an indoor climbing wall and mountain biking trails. Stick around for the après-ski scene and share stories of near-misses with fellow snowbirds.

Drive to Franconia, where Cannon Mountain's 80-passenger cable car provides breathtaking views of the region. Take an intense hike through the White Mountain National Forest, being sure not to deviate from the paths for fear of getting lost in the wild. If the weather's too much to handle, escape the elements by popping into the New England Ski Museum. Finish the day with a meal in Laconia, the largest town in the Lakes Region. The city's main attraction, Weirs Beach, is mostly shuttered in the winter, but is still worth a look.

Give your body a rest and sleep in before heading to Gilford, site of Gunstock Mountain. Here, the activities range from the easy – enjoy the thrill of speeding down the state's longest tubing run – to the challenging – snowshoe or cross-country ski on 30 miles (48 km) of groomed terrain. Trek to Holderness, the largest town on Squam Lake, to appreciate the natural beauty that inspired the movie *On Golden Pond*. Finish your weekend with a quiet dinner in the quaint town of Meredith.

Dos and Don'ts

- ✓ Carry a cell phone at all times, especially when driving or engaging in any activities off the beaten track or alone.
- ✗ Don't be too fashionable. To avoid frostbite or hypothermia, wear the right gear. Cover all body parts, especially the head, ears, toes, and fingers.
- ✓ When pursuing outdoor activities, get hold of a good map, as not all trails (hiking or cross-country skiing) are signposted.
- ✓ Bring comfortable footwear, as the compact town centers lend themselves to lots of on-foot exploration.

Below: Hikers enjoying the view, the White Mountains

GETTING THERE See map p323, C2, and p324
Rental cars cannot cross national borders. If you don't have a car, fly to Tucson, Arizona, 60 miles (97 km) north of Nogales, and buy one. The journey is 4,000 miles (6,500 km).

GETTING AROUND
The road can be bad so use a four-wheel-drive vehicle. There is public transport along the route, but it is not always reliable.

WEATHER
The highway passes through diverse climates and terrains. Go in February, the dry season, as parts are impassible in the wet season.

ACCOMMODATIONS
The graciously modern Hotel Playa Mazatlán in Mazatlán, Mexico, offers doubles from US$106; www.playamazatlan.com

Hostal de la Noria, a restored colonial mansion in Oaxaca, Mexico, offers doubles from US$160; www.hotel-lanoria-oaxaca.com

Hotel Posada de Don Rodrigo has old-world charm in Antigua, Guatemala; doubles from US$100; www.posadadedonrodrigo.com

Hostal Casa De Campo Country Inn is a cozy hostelry east of Panama City; doubles from US$75; www.panamacasadecampo.com

EATING OUT
Avoid street food, but try *gallo pinto* – rice, black beans, chicken or pork, and plantains.

PRICE FOR TWO
US$165–215 per day including food, fuel, accommodation, and visas.

FURTHER INFORMATION
www.rocinantestravels.com

End of the Road

The Inter-American Highway dead-ends at Yaviza, south of Panama City, near the largest tract of pristine rain forest in Central America. This "Darién Gap" is a notoriously inhospitable world of swamps and jungle within the 2,236 sq mile (5,791 sq km) Parque Nacional Darién. Panama is resisting calls to extend the highway, fearing ecological disaster: since the completion of the road to Yaviza, much of the rain forest in the region has disppeared.

Main: The Inter-American Highway stretching southwards past the New Millennium Panama Canal Bridge

THE CALL OF THE OPEN ROAD

A DRIVE FOR THE ADVENTUROUS, the Inter-American Highway offers one of the most extraordinary car trips in the world. Unfurling through Mexico, Guatemala, El Salvador, Honduras, Nicaragua, Costa Rica, and into Panama, the journey conjures up a whirligig of astonishing landscapes and colorful drama.

For the first leg of your drive, begin in Nogales, on the Arizona border, and take Highway 15 south along the palm-fringed beaches of Mexico's Pacific coast. Then, head into the highlands for Mexico City, where you pick up the "official" Inter-American Highway, and Oaxaca, known for its spring-like climate, colonial architecture, and chromatic fiestas. Crucible of ancient cultures, Guatemala astounds with its temple ruins and blazingly colored Mayan dress while neighboring El Salvador welcomes visitors with smiling faces and volcanic landscapes of surreal allure. Next up, Honduras is lent vibrancy by its celebrations, such as the February Feast of Our Lady of Suyapa, in

Left (left to right): Painted terra-cotta figurines in Nogales, Mexico; boats at harbor on Mexico's Pacific Coast; colonial-era doorway in Mazatlán, Mexico; Guatemalan women in traditional handwoven dresses

Below: Howler monkeys in Costa Rica's verdant rain forests

Inset: Kayaking in the Sea of Cortez

DRIVER'S DIARY

February guarantees you plenty of glorious sunshine, although you'll likely face rain at some stage. A month allows enough time to drive the highway's full length without rushing, as the region is well worth exploring, offering vibrant culture, serene beaches, enigmatic Mayan ruins, and rain forests teeming with life.

A Month in Central America

Leave Nogales for Guaymas, on the Sea of Cortéz. After a night by the shore, it's onward to Mazatlán via the Highway 15 toll road. Then over the mountains to Guadalajara, with time to savor this flavorful city.

DAYS 1–5

Continue to Mexico City. Linger a day, and next day turn south for Oaxaca, a World Heritage Site steeped in colonial atmosphere. You'll probably want spend a day sightseeing in this lovely city.

DAYS 6–9

Descend the rugged Sierra Madre del Sur mountains and follow the Pacific Coast highway via Tapachula to Guatemala City, with time to take in festivals and Mayan culture, before continuing to San Salvador.

DAYS 10–13

Head east for Choluteca, in the extreme south of Honduras. Crossing into Nicaragua, you can bypass the capital city as you head on the mostly flat highway to the Costa Rican border at Peñas Blancas.

DAYS 14–17

The ruler-straight Inter-American Highway slices through savanna country before climbing into the volcanic highlands, then snaking down to San Ysidro de General. Two days is a minimum for a side-journey to Volcán Arenal, and you may well choose to spend several more days exploring Nicoya (see pp288–9).

DAYS 18–24

Crossing into Panama, take the short diversion to picturesque Boquete, a bird watcher's paradise (see pp42–3). Then the fast-paced highway delivers you east via Panama City to the Darién region, where the tarmac turns to dirt well before the end of the road.

DAYS 25–30

Dos and Don'ts

✓ Buy a set of accurate maps and do not drive at night.

✗ Don't rent a car for the journey as rental cars cannot cross national borders. You will have to own your vehicle.

✓ Carry plenty of essential spare parts, plus a spare can of gasoline, and an emergency kit in case of breakdown.

✗ Plan ahead, and check the conditions down the road during your journey. Get Temporary Vehicle Import Permits and visas for each country in advance (except US and Canadian citizens).

✓ Plan for the possibility of being turned back by the military in Darién as foreigners are not always allowed as far as Yaviza.

JAN
FEB
MAR
APR
MAY
JUN
JUL
AUG
SEP
OCT
NOV
DEC

> One minute you're winding through mile-high mountains, then the next you're plunging into lush valleys cloaked in subaqueous greens.

Below: Rivers of fire on the magnificent Volcán Arenal at night

Tegucigalpa. Slow down through Nicaragua to soak in the yesteryear pace of Granada. And Costa Rica? This country delivers on its fame for wildlife, from howler monkeys to scarlet macaws.

One minute you're winding through mile-high mountains, then the next you're plunging into lush valleys cloaked in subaqueous greens. It's not a race, so take time for inviting detours: to the base of the Copper Canyon in Mexico, the Cobán ruins in Guatemala, Volcán Arenal in Costa Rica, perhaps even a boat ride on the Panama Canal. The highway is paved the entire way before withering down to a dirt track in the rain forests of Panama's Darién Gap – an impassable 55-mile (89 km) swathe of dense jungle separating Central and South America. Yaviza, a vaguely menacing frontier town, is worth the visit only to boast that you made it to the end.

Punctures and border delays are part of the equation. Localized flares-ups, bandito activity, landslides, or flooding may necessitate changes of route. Unpredictability is part of the adventure, but the lasting impressions are entirely positive on this journey to the center of the earth.

Above (left and right): Local reveler dancing to the Parade of the Bands; competitor in the King and Queen of Carnival contest

GETTING THERE See map p325, I6
Trinidad's Piarco International Airport is 20 miles (30 km) from Port of Spain. Authorized taxis have fixed fares to various island destinations (about US$20 to Port of Spain).

GETTING AROUND
Car rental is available at the airport or can be arranged by your hotel. Buses and route taxis follow scheduled routes and are cheap. Taxis can be used for short trips or day-long tours.

WEATHER
Trinidad is always sunny and warm, but now is the driest time of year. Temperatures are around 83°F (29°C) by day, 65°F (18°C) at night.

ACCOMMODATIONS
The intimate Maracas Bay Hotel is on the island's most beautiful beach; doubles from US$69; www.maracasbay.com

Kapok Hotel in St. Clair has rooftop dining and it's an easy walk to downtown Port of Spain; doubles from US$181; www.kapokhotel.com

The luxurious Trinidad Hilton is built on a hill, with fantastic views; doubles from US$319; www.hiltoncaribbean.com/trinidad

EATING OUT
Dining options range from beach stall snacks at less than US$5 to fine international dining. The island's Indian heritage is evident in the food, with many vegetarian options.

PRICE FOR TWO
US$350 per day including accommodation, food, taxis, and admissions.

FURTHER INFORMATION
www.gotrinidadandtobago.com

The Steel Drum or Pan

Steel drums, which are at the heart of the Carnival, originated in Port of Spain about 60 years ago. They were originally carried on a neck-strap – hence the Pan Around the Neck Festival that precedes Carnival in early February. Plantation-owners banned African drums because they thought their slaves used them to send messages. The slaves improvized with gourds, stretched goatskins and whatever else was at hand. The steel pan is the latest example of this ingenuity.

CARIBBEAN CARNIVAL

THE MELLIFLUOUS SOUNDS OF CALYPSO WERE BORN IN TRINIDAD. Lilting tunes, pulsating rhythms, and heartfelt lyrics form the soundtrack to life here, rising and falling on the warm island breeze every day of the year. This native beat is at its very best during Carnival week. This is the biggest party in the West Indies, when thousands of people descend on the island for five hedonistic days, transforming the dusty streets and picturesque beaches into a riot of color, sound, and motion.

Introduced by French settlers in the late 18th century, over the years Carnival has become an unashamedly exuberant celebration of freedom, and today's revelers swarm the capital city, Port of Spain, and party with unbridled energy. Thronged with fantastically costumed partygoers in ornate masks and gleaming jewels, who dance and drink long into the night, the streets of the historic Savannah district are lined with performers, arts and crafts stalls, and sizzling barbecues, while the tuneful, metallic sounds of steel bands playing calypso, soca, and limbo music fill the air. It is sensory overload. Keep your strength up with street food, such as *roti* (a flatbread rolled with curried chicken or pork); "doubles" (two fried flatbreads filled with curried beans); and *pholourie* (fried split-pea flour balls with sweet chutney sauce). "Shark and bake" stands offer highly seasoned, mouthwatering shark dishes.

J'Ouvert, one of Carnival's main parades, begins before dawn. Dominated by soca music it is attended by increasingly mud- and paint-slathered revelers, most of whom are still going from the night before. The highlight, however, is the Parade of the Bands, which takes place on the last day, when the bands, some with 200 or more pan drummers, parade through the streets accompanied by their splendidly costumed supporters. It's an unforgettable sight. To be named Calypso Monarch, or top steel band, is one of the island's greatest honors, and adds a competitive edge to the intoxicating atmosphere.

As well as the main attractions of Carnival, there are hundreds of other smaller events taking place, including fringe musical performances, competitions, and bustling markets. All you need is the stamina to keep on partying.

Main: "Moko Jumbie" stilt-walkers in procession before the Parade of the Bands
Below (left and right): The beach at Maracas Bay; Queen's Royal College, in Port of Spain's historic Savannah district

CALYPSO DIARY

Port of Spain boasts the biggest, best, and brashest carnival in the Caribbean, held just before Lent. The official event lasts five days but the must-see parades are on the Monday and Tuesday. Spend the first day acclimatizing, then join in the party on days two and three. You'll be recovering for the last two days!

JAN

FEB

Five Sensational Days

Start *Dimanche Gras* (Fat Sunday) by relaxing on Maracas beach, then head for the center of Port of Spain to get caught up in the Carnival atmosphere. Relish great street snacks, cooked in front of you, and enjoy the loud, loud music. Then get an early night.

SUN

Wake up early because the first J'Ouvert (pronounced "jou-vay") revelers are on the streets well before dawn wearing *ole mas* (old costumes) or rags and daubing themselves (and each other) with mud and paint. As the day progresses and the music gets louder everyone, including you, should be dancing, eating, and drinking.

MON

Get up early again and head for Savannah, along with hundreds of thousands of other revelers. First, the fabulously costumed marchers make their way through the streets, accompanied by deafening, foot-tapping music. Then comes the Parade of the Bands itself, with tens of thousands of enthusiastic musicians and their supporters. Dance until the music stops.

TUE

Have a lie-in, then visit the splendid National Museum and Art Gallery to learn more about the island's rich past. In the evening enjoy a moonlit dinner by the sea.

WED

Spend the day seeing the real Trinidad at the ASA Wright Nature Center on the Spring Hill Estate, a 90-minute drive from Port of Spain. While sipping a cold drink on the center's veranda, and without walking a step, you can see an amazing number of exotic birds including 18 types of hummingbird.

THU

Dos and Don'ts

☑ Join in the celebrations. It may by noisy and tumultuous but it is all in fun and everyone is there to have a good time.

☒ Don't carry your passport, wear expensive jewelry, or flash large sums of money, and don't stray off the main thoroughfares.

☑ Take taxis or shuttle buses to and from the celebrations, especially late at night.

☑ Try the street snacks – they are safe and very tasty.

☒ Don't forget they drive on the left here – take extra care when crossing the street or if driving a rental car.

MAR

APR

MAY

JUN

JUL

AUG

Below: White-necked Jacobin hummingbird at ASA Wright Nature Center

SEP

OCT

NOV

DEC

GETTING THERE
See map p328, H7

Salvador lies on Brazil's northeastern coast. The international airport, Deputado Luis Eduardo Magalhães, is 21 miles (34 km) north of the city. Taxis from the airport to Pelourinho are around US$30, the bus is US$2.50.

GETTING AROUND
Taxis are recommended in the evening for safety, during the day visitors can get around on foot quite easily.

WEATHER
During Carnival expect hot, sunny days with a maximum temperature around 86°F (30°C).

ACCOMMODATIONS
For Carnival, you should reserve your hotel accommodation 3–6 months in advance, and there is usually a minimum stay of 5 nights.

Salvador Ibis, Rio Vermelho, is a budget option; doubles from US$40; www.accorhotels.com.br

Pousada do Pilar is a beautifully restored heritage building in Pelourinho; doubles from US$80; www.pousadadopilar.com

Monte Pascoal Praia hotel sits on Barra beach; doubles from US$120; www.montepascoal.com.br

EATING OUT
Local cuisine focuses on seafood, often served in *moqueca* stews, with coconut milk, spices and palm oil. A large meal will cost around US$18.

PRICE FOR TWO
US$200–250 per day, including accommodations, food, and admissions.

FURTHER INFORMATION
www.centraldocarnacal.com.br

The Room of Miracles

Salvador's symbolic church, Nosso Senhor do Bonfim, is famous for its power to perform miracles. Inside, in the *Sala dos Milagres* (Room of Miracles), grateful worshipers have hung replica heads, limbs, and organs to give thanks for miracles performed curing their afflicted body parts. The ostensibly Catholic church is also frequented by followers of the Afro-Brazilian religion *Candomblé*, which combines seemingly unreconcilable elements of Catholic worship with African spiritualist traditions.

Main: Celebrating Carnival in style, hundreds of thousands of partygoers dance in the streets
Above (top to bottom): Historic upper town of Pelourinho; woman in traditional Bahian dress; endless sandy coastline of Bahia

CARNIVAL!

Forget the feathers and floats and girls in tiny bikinis, and forget all notions of being a merely passive observer. The Salvador Carnival (Carnaval to the locals) is all about participation. Two million revelers flock to the Bahian capital to celebrate in an extravagant week-long street party. Hundreds of musicians, many of them Brazil's biggest names, perform musical marathons, singing and dancing for many hours, night after day after night.

Each band, or *bloco*, performs on a massive sound truck called a *trio elétrico*, a stage and multigigawatt monster sound system combined. Pied-piper like, the performers are followed by supporters, often dressed in specially co-ordinated outfits, and an excited crowd dancing in a musical frenzy as the truck slowly wends its way through narrow streets. Behind, in front and all around the *trios*, hundreds of thousands of people gather for the sheer fun of it – to drink, sing, and dance, to kiss a perfect stranger, make instant friends, and the next day do it all over again.

Above: Elaborate gilded interior of Igreja São Francisco Salvador da Bahia

Below: Costumed dancer representing the God of Medicine in a ritual *Candomblé* dance.

SALVADOR DIARY

Carnival is a last wild celebration before the 40 days of Lenten abstinence. The dates change every year due to the lunar cycle, but Carnival always takes place in February or early March. If you stay for the full five days you'll be able to join in the fun but relax and rest as well.

The Biggest Party in the World

Explore the historic Pelourinho quarter, the Afro-Brazilian museum, and the Convent of São Francisco.

Early in the evening, locals and musicians will start to gather for the more traditional *blocos* which parade through the narrow streets from about 7pm to 2am.

Save your energies for a full evening of Carnival and spend a leisurely day at one of the ocean beaches such as Stella Maris or Flamengo.

Enjoy a late lunch of *moqueca* to fuel up. In the evening, grab your *abadá* (the t-shirt that admits you to a *bloco*), and get dancing.

Enjoy some of the traditional sights around downtown. Starting with the Bonfim church then stop in at the Mercado Modelo for some fine souvenir shopping.

Head over to the nearby Solar do Unhão. This restored 18th-century sugar mill and mansion now houses Salvador's Museum of Modern Art. Come sundown, you still have your *abadá*, so go and dance again.

Spend a day on the water by taking a schooner tour of the islands around the Baía de Todos os Santos.

Around 5pm head to the Barra Lighthouse to catch the sunset and secure yourself a good spot to watch the evening's *trios* as they parade past.

On the last night of Carnival don't miss the "Meeting of the Trios," a final musical get-together which takes place in the small hours of the morning of Ash Wednesday at the Praça Castro Alves.

Dos and Don'ts

☑ Wear comfortable shoes, shorts, or a skirt with a pocket and a light t-shirt. Leave your valuables at home and carry only enough cash for the day.

☒ Don't procrastinate. Those visiting Salvador for Carnival should book their flights and hotels at least three months ahead of time, if not more, as they fill up quickly.

☑ See as many different *blocos* as possible. Even if you buy an *abadá* for one *bloco* or *trio*, you can still mix and match to experience a number of others.

☒ Don't sleep in too late if you want to do some sightseeing. The easiest time to get around before the crowds gather is between 10am and 2pm.

Below: Pawpaws, pineapples, and bananas hanging from a street stall

JAN

FEB

FRI

SAT

SUN

MON

TUE

MAR

APR

MAY

JUN

JUL

AUG

SEP

OCT

NOV

DEC

If you want, you can buy an *abadá* (a t-shirt-cum-ticket) that allows access to a large roped-off area immediately behind the stage truck. Dozens of rope-carriers hold the rope ensuring that the cordon stays intact as the throng moves through the streets. Or you can opt to be a *pipoca* (a popcorn) and bop around in the slightly more unruly crowd on the fringes of the roped-off area.

As well as the big names of Brazilian music that perform regularly at Carnival, including Daniela Mercury, Gilberto Gil, and Carlinhos Brown, there are dozens more traditional, community-based *blocos*. The Afro-Brazilian *bloco* Ilê Ayê kicks off Carnival with a Candomblé ceremony the night before the parade. The Filhos de Gandhi (Sons of Gandhi) are a popular all-male *bloco*, who parade dressed in white Gandhi robes to the sound of African Afoxé drumming.

On Shrove Tuesday, the very last night of Carnival when most of the rest of Brazil is already sleeping, Carnival in Salvador comes to a dramatic close with the "Meeting of the Trios." In the early hours of Ash Wednesday morning, all the *blocos* that are still parading head to Praça Castro Alves and join together for a last joint concert, one that ends just as the sun rises over Salvador.

MARCH

Where to Go: March

The third week in March brings the spring equinox to the northern hemisphere, and spring has certainly sprung in the United States. Historic Boston, beginning to warm up after a long winter, offers beer-soaked fun for St. Patrick's Day, while the southern states, and the deserts of the west, are coming into bloom. The bulk of Canada, on the other hand, has barely begun to thaw – indeed, the west of the country offers the best skiing at this time of year. Sun-seekers may want to head south to Central America, the Caribbean islands, or Mexico, to make the most of those countries' dry seasons before summer descends in all its sticky glory. Below you will find all the destinations in this chapter as well as some extra suggestions to provide a little inspiration.

FESTIVALS AND CULTURE

BOSTON Irish dancers in colorful costumes

UNFORGETTABLE JOURNEYS

NATCHEZ TRACE The formal gardens at Monmouth plantation

NATURAL WONDERS

ANZA-BORREGO DESERT STATE PARK Spectacular vista at Font's Point

BOSTON
MASSACHUSETTS, USA

Irish eyes are smiling at the St. Patrick's Day celebrations

This historic city turns shamrock green for the day, with parades, music, and dance to honor Ireland's patron saint. Even the beer is green!
See pp62–3

CALLE OCHO
MIAMI, FLORIDA, USA

The USA's biggest street party and Hispanic festival

Drawing over a million visitors every March, Miami's huge street party features plenty of Cuban rum, Caribbean food, and salsa galore.
www.calle8.com

NATCHEZ TRACE
MISSISSIPPI, USA

Historic mansions and a warm Southern welcome

Take a leisurely drive up this ancient trail that features lush scenery, antebellum plantation houses, and Civil War memories.
See pp68–9

PICO DUARTE
DOMINICAN REPUBLIC

Climb the Caribbean's highest peak

Hike up Pico Duarte, the tallest mountain in the Caribbean, set amid the pine and cloud forests of the Cordillera Central.
www.godominicanrepublic.com

> "Anza-Borrego contains enough twisting canyons and washes for a lifetime of exploring."

ANZA-BORREGO DESERT STATE PARK
CALIFORNIA, USA

A terrific floral kaleidoscope

Ride or hike into the desert and appreciate the tenacity of the flora and fauna – bobcats, mountain goats, and of course wildflowers.
See pp58–9

ANTIGUA
GUATEMALA

A joyful celebration of Semana Santa in a pretty colonial city

Carpets of petals cover the streets for processions of religious statues carried by the joyful locals. Enjoy, too, the colonial architecture.
www.visitguatemala.com

> "To visit Natchez and the Trace is to be surrounded by Southern hospitality and a slower pace of life."

ISLAS BALLESTAS
PISCO, PERU

Explore the abundant marine life of the Peruvian Pacific

Take the boat out to this small cluster of islands, the "Galapagos of Peru," which teems with sea lions, penguins, and myriad birds.
www.peru.info

JOSHUA TREE NATIONAL PARK
CALIFORNIA, USA

Unearthly desert landscapes

One of the west coast's most memorable national parks, with a boulder-strewn desert dotted with weirdly shaped Joshua trees.
www.nps.gov/jotr

MEXICO CITY
MEXICO

Join the party in the city where the drumbeat never stops

From ancient ruins to world-class art, Mexico City has it all. Explore its cultural delights, then party at a fiesta in the Zócalo.
See pp60–61

SAN FRANCISCO
CALIFORNIA, USA

California's most cultured city

San Francisco has exceptional museums and performing arts venues, as well as an appealing café culture established by writers and artists in the 1950s.
www.onlyinsanfrancisco.com

ISLA FERNANDO DE NORONHA
BRAZIL

Isolated tropical islands

Enjoy the small-scale tourism on these volcanic islands and go diving to explore the unique marine ecosystem.
www.noronha.com.br

PARQUE NACIONAL TORTUGUERO
COSTA RICA

A top turtle-watching spot

Watch magnificent hawksbill, green, and leatherback turtles haul themselves out of the sea to lay their eggs on this beautiful beach.
www.costarica-nationalparks.com

PEDRA AZUL
ESPÍRITO SANTO, BRAZIL

Brazil's remarkable, multi-colored mountain

A bare finger of rock almost half a mile high, Pedra Azul is famous for its surreal color changes at dawn and dusk.
www.pedraazul.com.br

ROUTE 66
USA

"Go west" may be a cliché but some clichés are worth doing

The urge to travel west is ingrained in the psyche of the USA – historically this has been a trip of promise and it still delivers on that.
www.historic66.com

GREAT SMOKY MOUNTAINS NATIONAL PARK
TENNESSEE/N. CAROLINA, USA

Great for wildlife and hiking

This stretch of the Appalachian Mountains is lovely in March, when the hills are clothed in flowers.
www.nps.gov/grsm

Weather Watch

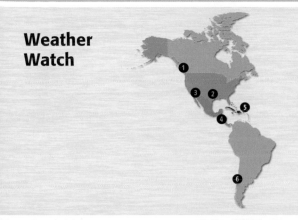

1 Whistler, Canada With the snow deep and powdery, and the temperatures higher than earlier in the ski season, March in Whistler is a Winter Wonderland – in springtime!

2 Mississippi, USA The Deep South is idyllic in March – magnolias and camellias burst into flower, days are warm but not too hot and, though there may be showers, the sleepy, moisture-heavy summer seems a distant prospect.

3 Anza-Borrego Desert, USA South-central California is clear and dry in March, with comfortable temperatures – though these do drop considerably after dark. In the Anza-Borrego desert the wildflowers are resplendent.

4 Guatemala Much of Guatemala is still dry, with the exception of the rainforests and some stretches of the Caribbean coast. Antigua afternoons are mild and balmy and nights are pleasantly mild.

5 British Virgin Islands With a tropical climate cooled by welcome trade winds, the British Virgin Islands hover at around 80°F (27°C) year-round. March is sunny and delightful, heralding the imminent end of the dry season.

6 Chile Long skinny Chile's weather ranges from sub-tropical to sub-polar. Patagonia is reaching the end of its summer, with some rain and wind, but pleasantly high temperatures.

LUXURY AND ROMANCE

BRITISH VIRGIN ISLANDS Secluded bays, perfect for overnight mooring

BRITISH VIRGIN ISLANDS
CARIBBEAN

A tropical island cruise

The pace of life is slow, the water clear, and the sand soft. An island paradise, with calypso, cocktails, and spicy seafood in the evenings.
See pp64–5

XOCHIMILCO
MEXICO CITY, MEXICO

Latin America's answer to Venice

Take a ride around the romantic canals of Xochimilco in a colorful *trajinera* boat whilst being serenaded by roving mariachi bands.
www.visitmexico.com

"Eat, sail, snorkel, swim – in the British Virgin Islands, you'll spend much of your time in stress-free indulgence."

ECO-LODGES IN PANAMA
PANAMA

An emerging destination

Choose from rain forest lodges like The Canopy Tower to beach properties like Punta Caracol Acqua Lodge, suspended on stilts above a coral reef.
www.eco-tropicalresorts.com

PRIVATE ISLANDS
CARIBBEAN

Rent your very own tropical paradise

Indulge your wildest film-star fantasies and rent a private Caribbean island – for as little as US$500 a week.
www.privateislandsonline.com

CAYO DISTRICT
BELIZE

Caribbean luxury, eco-style

The largest and arguably the most beautiful district in Belize, with jungle-covered mountains, and a string of captivating eco-lodges.
www.belizex.com/cayo.htm

ACTIVE ADVENTURES

PATAGONIA Bringing in a lake fish at the end of the day

PATAGONIA
CHILE AND ARGENTINA

Andean mountain lakes, leaping with salmon and trout

A fly-fisher's paradise – days spent by, on, or in crystal-clear water; evenings in a cozy lodge in the company of fellow anglers.
See pp72–3

CABARETE
DOMINICAN REPUBLIC

Perfect wind and waves on the island's north coast

One of the Americas' top water sports destinations, and self-proclaimed world kite-boarding capital. An excellent spot for surfing.
www.godominicanrepublic.com

WHISTLER
BRITISH COLUMBIA, CANADA

Heli-ski through perfect deep powder snow

Whistler's two huge and scenic mountains provide unforgettable skiing and snowboarding, and a lively and fun après-ski, too.
See pp56–7

NEW RIVER GORGE
WEST VIRGINIA

White-water rafting amid scenic mountains

Raft down the foaming waters of New River Gorge, a dramatic, thousand-feet deep fissure in the West Virginia Mountains.
www.nps.gov/neri

HONDURAS
CENTRAL AMERICA

Adventures and unspoiled natural beauty

Ride the whitewater in river canyons, dive the world's second-biggest reef, and explore untouched jungles in this amazing country.
See pp66–7

FAMILY GETAWAYS

YUCATÁN Snake head at the Warriors' Temple, Chichén Itza

"On the days of the vernal equinox, thousands gather at Chichén Itza to watch as the shadows form an undulating serpent of light and dark."

YUCATÁN
MEXICO

The Mayan snake-god makes his spectacular appearance

Explore the remains of two mighty empires – Mayan pyramids and pretty Spanish towns – whose legacy lives on in the local culture.
See pp70–71

PUERTO ESCONDIDO
MEXICO

Surf, sand, and sunsets on the Mexican Pacific

On the southern Pacific coast, this popular resort boasts excellent beaches, outstanding surf, and a laid-back ambience.
www.puertoescondidoinfo.com

THE AMAZON
ECUADOR

Wonderful rain forest adventures

Ecuador's Amazonian lowlands are relatively easy to reach and can be explored from a rain forest ecolodge.
www.sachalodge.com

CLEARWATER BEACH
FLORIDA, USA

Beaches, boat trips, and dolphin spotting

Dazzling white sands, a pleasantly small-town feel, and great water-based activities make this an ever-popular family holiday destination.
www.clearwaterbeach.com

FOSSIL RIM
TEXAS, USA

Overnight in this vast safari park near Fort Worth

This extraordinary park brings the sights, sounds, and smells of Africa to you. Plus, you're not far from lots of rodeo and sports action.
www.fossilrim.com

GETTING THERE
See map p313, C6

Whistler is in western Canada, in British Columbia. International flights arrive into Vancouver airport, 75 miles (120 km) from the resort. A shuttle bus transports visitors from the airport and downtown Vancouver to Whistler. Car rental is also available.

GETTING AROUND
A free village shuttle bus provides transportation from hotels to the ski lifts, and runs every 10 to 12 minutes during the day.

WEATHER
Whistler's daytime temperatures average 36°F (2°C) in March, but it is colder on the mountain.

ACCOMMODATIONS
Glacier's Reach has a number of apartments with full kitchens; one-bedroom apartments from US$170; www.resortquest.com

Executive Inn has chalet-style rooms; doubles from US$180; www.executiveinnwhistler.com

Fairmont Château Whistler, with complete luxury and ski-in-ski-out facilities; double from US$340; www.fairmont.com/whistler

EATING OUT
A mid-range three-course meal in Whistler costs under US$40 a head. For a treat, try the seafood and other stylish west coast fare at Araxi, or the award-winning Bearfoot Bistro.

PRICE FOR TWO
US$440–540 per day for accommodation, food, equipment, ski-passes, and entertainment. Heli-skiing is an additional US$600 per person.

FURTHER INFORMATION
www.tourismwhistler.com

Olympic Whistler

Whistler's Olympic dream has taken nearly 40 years to happen. The resort was developed in the 1960s, with the hopes of landing the 1968 Winter Games. But the Rocky Mountain resort of Banff submitted Canada's bid for the 1968 and 1972 games, and Whistler's 1976 bid came to naught when the Summer Games were awarded to Montreal. In 2010, Whistler will share the honor with Vancouver, hosting the downhill and cross-country ski races, as well as ski-jumping, luge, and bobsleigh events.

Above (left to right): Skiers and snowboarders at top of a ridge; dog sledding through the Whistler woods; skier at speed going over a bump
Main: Snowboarder performing a cliff jump above the ski lift at Whistler

WHISTLER WONDERLAND

I T'S ALL ABOUT THE GREAT OUTDOORS – winter in Whistler. If you can't climb up it, race down it, stride through it or suspend yourself from it, most visitors aren't interested. Everyone, from toddlers to octogenarians, is clad head-to-toe in bright Gore-Tex and carries ski poles or snowshoes.

This pretty resort village of around 10,000 permanent residents is cradled in one of the most scenic spots on Canada's west coast. The Whistler and Blackcomb mountains – with a combined total of 38 lifts, more than 200 ski runs, 13 sq miles (34 sq km) of skiable terrain, and one of North America's longest lift-serviced vertical descents – dominate the landscape. Quiet trails through thick forests of fragrant pine and cedar beckon alluringly to cross-country skiers and snowshoers. The icy surface of the frozen Green Lake seems purpose-made for ice skating. And then there's the heli-skiing. Whistler is a prime center for this extreme activity with a superb choice of pristine deep-powder runs that are only accessible by helicopter. When you've been the first to ski an almost vertical slope of feet-thick unpacked powder, or carved smooth, floating turns through fresh snow as it sprays up around your ears, then you know you've really skied the mountain. And then you're hooked – normal skiing or snowboarding will never be the same again.

There are few winter sports that someone here hasn't tried, from ice climbing to snow tubing. And a bit of snow and wind doesn't deter daredevils from other year-round activities like ziplining or bungee jumping.

Whistler is a surprisingly cosmopolitan place, with a lot to offer even those with no interest in hurtling headfirst down mountains. With the award-winning Bearfoot Bistro restaurant cellar holding 2,100 labels, and shops selling Cuban cigars and French lingerie, the town has evolved far beyond its backcountry roots – but it remains at its most charming when under a blanket of snow.

> When you've been the first to ski an almost vertical slope of feet thick unpacked powder…then you know you've really skied the mountain.

Inset: A bit of Whistler nightlife at Dusty's Bar and BBQ
Below (left to right): Above the clouds – ski lift at Whistler; cross-country skiing through the delightful countryside; cabins set in the mountain forest

DEEP POWDER DIARY

Whistler has one of the longest snow seasons in North America, and March is a great time to visit because temperatures are mild but snow is still plentiful. Because of the excellent conditions, rooms sell out quickly, so book ahead. Ski fanatics could easily spend two weeks here, but others will probably find five days ideal.

Five Days on the Pistes

After arriving from Vancouver, grab lunch at a mountainside restaurant and unpack. Spend the afternoon soaring over the tree-tops on a zipline tour, or strap on your skis and hit the slopes. In the evening, enjoy illuminated night-time snowboarding (early March, Thu–Sat only).

If you're a beginner or feeling a little rusty, brush up your skills with a lesson at the Whistler Blackcomb Ski and Snowboard School, then spend the rest of the day on the mountain. Afterwards, ease those aching muscles with a massage at one of the resort's spas and maybe a drink or two in one of the local bars.

Strap on some goggles and go snowmobiling along forested mountain trails, or spend a more leisurely day strolling through the village to shop for artwork, jewelry, and other luxury goods—there are more than 200 shops in the resort. In the evening, take a horse-drawn sleigh ride around Green Lake, followed by an indulgent fondue dinner.

For a truly memorable experience, blaze your own track through the waist-deep, unmarked virgin powder of Whistler's spectacular backcountry on an exciting heli-skiing excursion. Finish the day with a dinner at one of Whistler's excellent restaurants.

Explore the beautiful Whistler countryside beyond the ski resort by trying your hand at cross-country skiing or learning to mush a team of Alaska racing huskies along a snowy wilderness route.

Dos and Don'ts

✓ Buy a Fresh Tracks ticket, which will let you ski in pristine powder at sunrise, before the crowds arrive.

✓ Try skate-skiing, which combines elements of inline skating and cross-country skiing. Lessons are available at Lost Lake.

✓ Save money by booking self-catering accommodations – the village has a great selection of apartments.

✗ Don't think that you aren't good enough to heli-ski. If you can ski down a blue run you can do it – and you will never forget the experience (get a DVD of the trip made too).

JAN
FEB
MAR
DAY 1
DAY 2
DAY 3
DAY 4
DAY 5
APR
MAY
JUN
JUL
AUG
SEP
OCT
NOV
DEC

GETTING THERE   See map p321, D5-6

GETTING THERE   See map p321, D5-6
A 2-hour drive east from San Diego and south from Palm Springs, this park straddles the Peninsular Mountains near Mexico. It is accessed via Highway 78 from Palm Springs or by S22 off I-8 from San Diego. International flights serve both San Diego and Palm Springs.

GETTING AROUND
The park is best explored on foot or mountain bike via trails that begin at the Visitor Center.

WEATHER
March has clear skies, minimal rainfall, and temperatures of about 84°F (29°C).

ACCOMMODATIONS
Borrego Palm Canyon Campground has showers, toilets, RV and tent sites; US$15–29 per vehicle; www.reserveamerica.com

Palm Canyon Resort in Borrego Springs has a casual ambience straight out of a Western movie and offers doubles from US$70; www.palmcanyonresort.com

The luxurious Borrego Springs Resort & Country Club has comfortable doubles from US$130; www.borregospringsresort.com

EATING OUT
Campers should be self-sufficient; there are no shops in the park. The Western-style Big Horn Steakhouse (from US$10) and Hog Trough Café & Saloon (from US$2), are both at Palm Canyon Resort in Borrego Springs.

PRICE FOR TWO
US$175 per day including accommodation, food, travel, and parking; US$60 if camping.

FURTHER INFORMATION
www.theabf.org

The Desert Tortoise

California's endangered state reptile clings to existence in the southwestern desert, where it eats flowers and cacti. It can go a year without water as the shell reduces evaporation and it excretes a semi-solid acidic paste instead of urine. The desert tortoise digs burrows to avoid the midday heat and takes 15 years to reach sexual maturity. All the hatchlings in a single nest will be of the same sex, which is determined by the nest's temperature.

DESERT ABUNDANCE

FAMED FOR ITS SPECTACULAR WILDFLOWERS, California's largest state park sprawls over 938 sq miles (2,430 sq km) of desert and mountain terrain riven by canyons and graced by fan-palm oases. Bighorn sheep (*borregos*) roam the purple-hued mountains, giving the park its name. Anza-Borrego brims with the glories of nature, drawing visitors who appreciate the rugged outdoors.

This geological wonderland at the southern end of the Santa Rosa Mountains is laced with more than 110 miles (177 km) of hiking, riding, and mountain biking trails, while its more challenging dirt tracks appeal to off-roaders. The park, with an elevation range from just above sea level to 6,193 ft (1,888 m), contains enough twisting canyons and washes for a lifetime of exploring. Most trails weave through steep-sided canyons, following streambeds that succor cottonwoods, sycamores, willows, and

Main: Bright spring flowers on the rocky landscape of Anza-Borrego

Left (left and right): Bighorn sheep, or *borrego*, atop a rock; venomous rattlesnake warning unwary hikers with its loud tail

Right: Spectacular vista across the hills and desert from Font's Point

native fan-palms. Mineral springs draw desert critters – bobcats, kit foxes, mule deer, coyotes, and even mountain lions may be spotted. Burrowing owls lurk in the oases, while quails and roadrunners scurry across the sand, and desert tortoise and lizards chomp on cacti. Rattlesnakes are also common, so keep a wary eye on the trail.

The Native American Cahuilla lived in the canyons for millennia. Their legacy can be seen in bedrock mortars, pictographs, and petroglyphs painted and etched on to stone. The Visitor Center does a fine job of honoring the culture and portraying distinct micro-habitats of flora and fauna.

Spring is peak season for visitation as baby blue eyes, goldfields, creamcups, and California poppies emblazon the landscape in fiery colors. The exact timing of the wildflower bloom varies according to the winter rains, but timely downpours will see the desert floor transform almost overnight. However, be warned – they can disappear as quickly, too, so be sure to check ahead.

Above: Towering fan-palms at a shady oasis

Below: Tourists exploring the park on horseback

NATURALIST'S DIARY

Anza-Borrego is huge, and the numerous trails and dirt roads provide access to a range of terrains and ecosystems. Two days are sufficient to experience a good sampling of trails, with a chance to see wildlife, spectacular springtime blooms, and one of the most spectacular scenic vista points of southern California.

Two Desert Days

Start at the Visitor Center near Borrego Springs to get your bearings and learn about the flora, fauna, and the ancient Native American culture of the area. View the slide show and explore the cactus garden before setting out along the easy, 2-mile (3-km) long Borrego Palm Canyon Trail. Note the Indian grinding rocks and delight in the shade of the fan-palm oasis at the end of the trail.

Later, drive down County Road S22 to Culp Valley to admire the medley of wildflowers along Old Culp Valley Road. Hike the scenic Grapevine Canyon Trail, with stops at Angelina and Stuart Springs.

Visit Vern Whittaker Horse Camp for a horseback ride alongside the stream running through Coyote Canyon, which is a mecca for wildlife. For a chance to spot wild horses and bighorn sheep, hikers can follow the trail on foot for 18 miles (29 km).

In the afternoon, drive along sandy Old Kane Springs Road to Harper Canyon, also known as "Cactus Garden." Keep an eye out, too, for slow-growing desert ironwood trees. Then visit Fish Creek for its unusual formations, twisting canyons, and eerie caves.

The next stop is sunset at Font's Point, where the stark and dramatic desert landscape exhibits millions of years of geologic history. Admire the 360-degree vista and look among the rocks for embedded fossils.

Dos and Don'ts

✓ Stay on the trails, as the ecosystem is delicate and wandering off them can do lasting damage.

✗ Don't pick the wildflowers – it is strictly forbidden.

✓ Always carry plenty of water when venturing into the desert.

✗ Picking up a desert tortoise is illegal. Instead, report any sick or injured tortoises you come across to the Joshua Tree Tortoise Rescue; tel. (760) 369 1235.

✓ Check on the wildflower situation before you go by calling the Spring Wildflower Hotline; tel. (760) 767 4684 or visiting www.desertusa.com/wildflo/ca.html.

Below: Hiker eyeing a Native American pictogram

JAN

FEB

MAR

DAY 1

DAY 2

APR

MAY

JUN

JUL

AUG

SEP

OCT

NOV

DEC

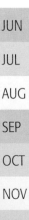

GETTING THERE   See map p323, F5

GETTING THERE
International flights arrive in Mexico City at Aeropuerto Internacional Benito Juárez, which is about 20 minutes to an hour from the city center by taxi depending on traffic.

GETTING AROUND
Traffic is horrendous in Mexico City, with limited parking. The safest and most reliable mode of transportation is to use a taxi arranged for you by your hotel.

WEATHER
In March, Mexico City enjoys warm, sunny days with an average high of 75°F (24°C) and an average night-time low of 46°F (8°C).

ACCOMMODATIONS
Hotel Park Villa has a lovely garden restaurant; doubles from US$84; www.whotels.com

Luxurious Casa Vieja is an elegant hacienda; suites from US$360; www.casavieja.com

Four Seasons has a serene courtyard; doubles from US$430; www.fourseasons.com/mexico

EATING OUT
In Mexico City, you will find cuisine from every region of the country, as well as dishes from South America and Europe. Try entrées featuring *mole*, a spicy sauce with a bit of chocolate, or tender marinated beef – *arrachera*. Hacienda de los Morales is a 16th-century hacienda serving Mexican and international cuisine; tel. (055) 5283 30 54.

PRICE FOR TWO
US$330–600 per day.

FURTHER INFORMATION
www.mexicocity.com.mx

Catedral Metropolitana

The largest and most important cathedral in the western hemisphere presents an impressive display of architectural styles, with an ornate Spanish Baroque façade and Neo-Classical dome. Begun in 1525, Catedral Metropolitana was built with rubble from the adjacent ruins of the Aztec Templo Mayor, which was destroyed following the Spanish conquest of 1513. Designed and constructed in stages, it took 240 years to complete.

Above (left to right): Teotihuacán; Tlaloc (rain god) amphora at Templo Mayor; Coyoacán
Main: Street performer in the Zócalo

AN AZTEC TREASURE

ANCIENT YET MODERN, MEXICO CITY PULSATES WITH LIFE AND CULTURE, serving up a veritable feast of history, art, music, and cuisine. Once known as Tenochtitlán by the Aztecs who founded their city in a giant volcanic caldera in 1325, this is North America's oldest city and one of the world's largest. The city's stunning contrasts can both delight and assault the senses. Narrow streets bustle with traffic and pedestrians, the spicy aroma of cooking food mingles with exhaust fumes. Elegant towers of glass and steel rise above ornate Spanish colonial *palacios* and ancient Aztec ruins. A maze of colorful market stalls stands alongside elegant shops filled with high-end fashions and jewelry, and everywhere the harmonies of church bells and street musicians compete with the shrill whistles of police directing traffic.

The cobblestone streets in the historic area present an impressive variety of boutiques, restaurants, and galleries housed in elaborate colonial mansions, exceptional museums, Baroque churches, and lush

> The plaza throngs with crowds that surround spectacularly dressed dancers as they stomp and chant to a rhythmic drumbeat.

urban parks. At the heart of the city, the vast open Zócalo is the gathering place for social and political events. On festival days, the plaza throngs with crowds that surround spectacularly dressed dancers as they stomp and chant to a rhythmic drumbeat. Overseeing the mayhem are some of the city's iconic structures: the magnificent Catedral Metropolitana, the Aztec ruins of the Templo Mayor, and the Palacio Nacional where Diego Rivera's mural *Epic of the Mexican People* tells the story of Mexico. Away from the Zócalo, organ-grinders play sweet, sad songs below the golden dome of the spectacular Palacio de Bellas Artes and in neighboring Alameda Central. The Paseo de la Reforma is lined with shimmering skyscrapers, embassies, galleries, hotels, and marble and gold monuments, while a few miles down the Paseo lies the green expanse of Chapultepec Park and the hilltop Castillo, which has commanding views of this splendid and constantly surprising city.

Inset: Catedral Metropolitana in the Zócalo
Below (left and right): Mexico City skyline; colorful boats in Xochimilco

SPANISH CITY DIARY

The city is warm and sunny in late March and the delicate violet-colored blossoms of the jacaranda trees are beautiful. Five days is enough time to see the highlights in the central historic area, visit charming Coyoacán and San Ángel, see fabulous museums and ancient ruins, enjoy fine dining, and attend evening performances.

Five Days of Cultural Delights

Explore the wonderful collection of Mexican and pre-Hispanic art and culture at the Museo Nacional de Antropologia. Visit the opulent Castillo de Chapultepec or Museo de Arte Moderno, with oils by the great Mexican muralists. Take a taxi along Paseo de la Reforma past the golden El Ángel (Winged Victory).

In Centro Histórico tour the sights surrounding the Zócalo, starting with Templo Mayor. Enter Palacio Nacional and admire Diego Rivera's brilliant murals. Explore Catedral Metropolitana's glittering altars and fabulous artworks. Have dinner overlooking the Zócalo and watch the Mexican honor guard lower the giant Mexican flag.

Tour the stunning white marble Palacio de Bellas Artes, then stroll through lovely Alameda Central, and visit the nearby museums. See Mexican masterpieces at Museo Nacional de Arte, decorative arts at Museo Franz Mayer, and Mexican folk art at Museo de Arte Popular.

Hire a car and driver and head to Teotihuacán, the incredible ruins of Mesoamerica's cultural and commercial center. Climb the Pyramid of the Sun, and walk along the Avenue of the Dead to the Quetzalpapalotl Palace Complex. Ascend the Pyramid of the Moon for panoramic views of the complex.

Take a taxi a few miles south of the center to lovely San Ángel and Coyoacán. Visit Bazar Sábado, a Saturday-only fine arts and crafts market, and the Museo Casa Estudio Diego Rivera y Frida Kahlo. Then head out to Xochimilco, 12 miles (20 km) southeast of the center, for a colorful canal trip on a flower-decked boat.

Dos and Don'ts

- ✓ For reasons of personal safety, behave and dress conservatively as you explore the city.

- ✗ Don't tempt pickpockets by wearing expensive jewelry or displaying wealth in public places.

- ✓ Visit Templo Mayor as early as you can in the morning, when it is easier to see the details of the carvings on the ruins and before the sun gets too hot.

- ✗ Don't hail a taxi from the street. It is a much better idea to ask your hotel to phone for a taxi for you.

JAN
FEB
MAR
TUE
WED
THU
FRI
SAT
APR
MAY
JUN
JUL
AUG
SEP
OCT
NOV
DEC

Below: Monument El Ángel on the Paseo de la Reforma

CANADA

USA

BOSTON

Washington, D.C.

Los Angeles

MEXICO

GETTING THERE See map p316, H4
Boston's Logan International Airport is about 3 miles (5 km) from South Boston.

GETTING AROUND
Boston's extensive public transportation system (MBTA) means there's no need for a car. South Boston is on the red subway line.

WEATHER
March sees about 4 in (10 cm) of rain. Daytime highs average 45°F (7°C), and it may drop below freezing at night.

ACCOMMODATIONS
The Boston Park Plaza Hotel is an affordable hotel in the heart of the city; doubles from US$159; www.bostonparkplaza.com

The Seaport Hotel is on Boston Harbor (ask for a room with a view); doubles from US$199; www.seaportboston.com

Nine Zero is a cutting-edge boutique hotel, located on bustling Tremont Street; doubles from US$239; www.ninezero.com

EATING OUT
At Boston's countless Irish pubs, St. Patrick's Day visitors won't have to look too hard for staples like shepherd's pie, or corned beef and cabbage. Legal Sea Foods has locations throughout the city, and is a good place to try classic New England fish dishes such as Boston baked scrod and seafood chowder.

PRICE FOR TWO
US$450 per day including accommodation, food, admissions, and local transportation.

FURTHER INFORMATION
www.bostonusa.com

A Touch of the Irish

Among Boston's many Irish bars are a number of authentic ones whose fittings and staff hail from the Emerald Isle. To feel at home, non-Irish types should brush up on their Celtic folklore. Tir na nÓg, a term you'll often see here, is the Irish equivalent of Olympus or Valhalla. Leprechauns are Ireland's national race of pixies, who guard the country's ancient treasure. If someone calls you Saint Brigit, that's a compliment, as she was renowned for her beauty and generosity. And Saint Patrick is the patron saint who drove the snakes out of Ireland.

Brogues as thick as Guinness can be heard in every pub, and the sounds of fiddles and penny whistles lilt through the streets.

SouthBostonOnline

Above: Leprechaun in the parade
Main: Crowds lining the streets to watch the parade pass by

THE EMERALD CITY

ANYONE WITH IRISH BLOOD IN THEIR VEINS WILL ENJOY A TRIP TO BOSTON, regardless of the time of year. But in the days surrounding March 17, New England's largest city really rolls out the bright green welcome mat as a wide array of events, festivals, and parades are held in celebration of St. Patrick's Day, Ireland's national holiday. Around half a million visitors come each year just to join in the party. Brogues as thick as Guinness can be heard in every pub; the sounds of fiddles and penny whistles lilt through the streets; and tipsy revelers walk (or crawl) from one bar to the next. The Irish Porter flows freely, and there's nothing odd about seeing someone tip back a pint of lager colored green in honor of the holiday. The area's performing arts centers showcase Irish-themed shows, from traditional Celtic dance troupes to big-name touring acts such as the Chieftains and Ronan Tynan, while satellite towns host lively St. Patrick's celebrations of their own, most notably Scituate, Worcester, and Holyoke.

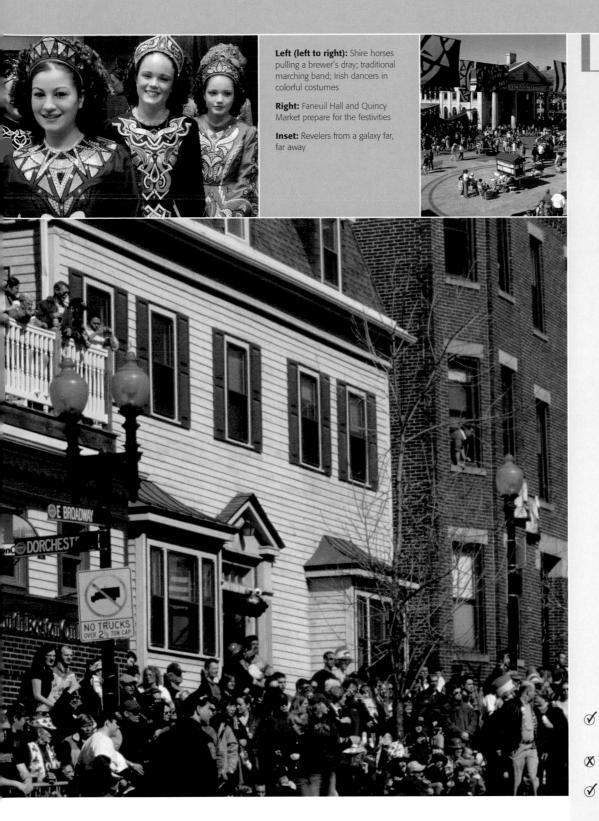

Left (left to right): Shire horses pulling a brewer's dray; traditional marching band; Irish dancers in colorful costumes

Right: Faneuil Hall and Quincy Market prepare for the festivities

Inset: Revelers from a galaxy far, far away

SHAMROCK DIARY

With its large Irish-American community, Boston stakes a claim as the best place in the USA to celebrate St. Patrick's Day. Much of the focus falls on South Boston, where Irish immigrants first settled, but everywhere gets into the Celtic spirit, with many non-Irish restaurants putting up decorations and serving green beer.

Three Days of Gaelic Revels

Dive straight in by donning a "Kiss me, I'm Irish" button and heading out on the town. The bars surrounding Faneuil Hall will be jammed – duck into the Purple Shamrock or the Black Rose for a pint or two. Since you are in Boston, stroll along a section of the nearby Freedom Trail for a spot of history, then tuck into Yankee pot roast, Indian pudding, or another Boston classic at Durgin Park, one of the city's oldest restaurants.

Start your day with a leisurely walk along Boston's Irish Heritage Trail, a 3-mile (5-km) self-guided walking tour that includes 16 different sites of Irish cultural, historical, and political significance (pick up a free trail map at a Visitor Information Center). Learn about the city's most famous native son at the John F. Kennedy Presidential Library and Museum, including details of his connection to his ancestral homeland. Cap your night in Somerville with some authentic Irish fare and free live music at the Burren pub.

Rise early and head to South Boston to stake out a spot along the parade route. Buy some green carnations to hand out to your favorite parade participants, and stay warm with a coffee or whiskey from one of the many bars and pubs. After the parade, while the crowds disperse, enjoy a relaxed pint at Amrhein's, a cozy hangout with the oldest hand-carved bar in the USA.

Continue the celebrations back downtown at Jose McIntyre's, Boston's only Irish-Mexican cantina. It's also the only place where you can have a margarita with your fish and chips and no one will think you're crazy.

Dos and Don'ts

☑ Be responsible when drinking. Use the excellent public transportation system and respect police officers, an extra contingent of whom work the holiday to keep the peace.

☒ Don't confuse South Boston with the South End, a different neighborhood known for its vibrant arts and dining scenes.

☑ The weather in March is notoriously fickle. Even if skies are clear, they could open up at any time, so dress for all eventualities, including comfortable, weatherproof shoes.

☒ Don't depend on credit cards, as many of the old-style pubs don't take plastic.

Below: Leprechauns performing an Irish reel

Everything culminates on the Sunday closest to the holiday, when South Boston ("Southie," as locals call it) hosts one of the world's largest St. Patrick's Day parades, and revelers in their hundreds of thousands descend upon this working-class neighborhood to celebrate all things Gaelic. Firemen, step-dancers, and pipe bands come from all over the country – and from Ireland as well – to march in the parade, and a spirit of celebration and goodwill fills the air. Family gatherings spill out of the neighborhood's numerous rowhouses, and the area's wide assortment of bars are packed to the gills. (In recent years the city has taken great pains to make it a family-friendly event, with public drinking strictly prohibited, keeping rowdy types off the streets and in the pubs.) But Southie's bars aren't the only ones that are packed, as the city's students, some 200,000-plus of them, use the weekend as an excuse to put on their green gear and let loose.

Anyone looking for a quiet, relaxed time, in which to discover one of America's greatest cities, won't stand a chance with all the excitement and commotion that the holiday brings, but everyone who loves a good time will be in heaven – an emerald one!

JAN

FEB

MAR

FRI

SAT

SUN

APR

MAY

JUN

JUL

AUG

SEP

OCT

NOV

DEC

GETTING THERE   See map p325, G4
The BVIs are a small group of isles lying east of Puerto Rico and the US Virgin Islands. The main airport is on Tortola. Flights from North America and Europe connect via Puerto Rico, St. Thomas, Antigua, St. Kitts, or St. Maarten.

GETTING AROUND
Sailing is the best way to see the islands. Ashore, you can walk, but explore farther afield by cab.

WEATHER
The climate is tempered by sea breezes ideal for sailing. Temperatures in spring average 82°F (28°C). Rainfall is seasonal, with February and March being the driest months.

ACCOMMODATIONS
Nanny Cay Marina and Hotel has a waterfront garden setting near the capital, Road Town; doubles from US$100; www.nannycay.com

On Tortola, Sugar Mill Hotel nestles into the hillside and offers fine dining; doubles from US$240; www.sugarmillhotel.com

A seven-day, live-aboard charter costs around US$1,100–2,500 per head, including meals.

EATING OUT
All yachts are stocked with food, but it's fun to eat at waterfront restaurants serving fresh seafood, conch gumbo, and grilled lobster.

PRICE FOR TWO
A seven-day cruise with food and transportation costs US$300–750 a day. Tips to the crew average 10–20 percent of the fee.

FURTHER INFORMATION
www.bvitourism.com
www.moorings.com

Wreck of the *Rhone*

The BVIs' most celebrated dive site is the R.M.S. *Rhone*, which sank in a hurricane in 1867. One of the world's first iron-hulled ships, it split in two and came to rest at depths of up to 20–80 ft (6–24 m) just west of Salt Island. Protected in the BVIs' only marine national park, it is now emblazoned with corals. Marine turtles swim in and out, and moray eels and barracudas peer out at divers. The wreck starred in the 1977 film, *The Deep*.

Above (left and right): Secluded island bays, perfect for overnight mooring; setting off for an unforgettable experience

TURQUOISE PARADISE

CARESSED BY CONSTANT WARM BREEZES AND TURQUOISE WATER, and with an abundance of pristine secluded harbors, the British Virgin Islands (BVIs) are a sailor's paradise, promising both adventure and leisure. When it comes to sailing the Caribbean, there is no more appropriate a place than the BVIs and no better way than by yacht charter – the ideal choice for exploring these exquisite and exciting isles at your own pace.

Vacationing aboard a crewed yacht is like staying in an exclusive villa with well-trained staff to cater to your every whim. Eat, sail, snorkel, and swim – that's likely to be your daily pattern, and with a crew of two or more – from skipper to cook – you'll spend much of your time sipping cocktails and sunning in stress-free indulgence. You'll pass the days sailing indolently from isle to isle, but be sure to anchor in time for happy hours at the islands' many fun-filled beach bars.

The BVIs comprise the main islands of Tortola, Virgin Gorda, Anegada, and Jost Van Dyke, along with more than 50 smaller islands and cays – many of them tiny uninhabited islets. While your skipper can recommend the best itinerary, the best thing about a BVI yacht charter is that you're free to explore the destination as you choose – there's nothing quite like a sense of absolute freedom to go "gunkholing" (island hopping) between the prettiest harbors and secluded beaches. You should definitely not miss out on the Baths on Virgin Gorda; these sculpted boulders form grottoes and arches ideal for snorkeling in crystal-clear waters. Another must-see is Jost Van Dyke, a relaxed barefoot paradise of just 200 inhabitants clinging to traditional island culture. Here, for a break from the mariner's life, take to the forested hills before sipping a well-earned Carib beer or heady rum cocktail at Ali Baba's or Foxy's beach bar, while getting seriously mellow to calypso rhythms.

After a chillout session, it's time for some action – adventure loafing *is* the main raison d'etre of a Caribbean sailing vacation. Charter yachts always carry snorkeling and fishing gear, while bigger boats often feature a dinghy, scuba gear, and even jet skis. That said, you're likely to find contentment merely lazing on deck with a rum swizzle in hand and without a care in the world, as you race along with the warm, scented wind in your sails.

Main: Yachts anchored in the turquoise waters of an idyllic bay
Below (left and right): Foxy's Bar – the perfect place to chill out; inside the Baths on Virgin Gorda

YACHT CHARTER DIARY

While cruising in the British Virgin Islands is a year-round affair, March is the ideal time for sailing here, when the weather is at its finest. It's possible to cruise the main islands in five days, but most sailing charters are for seven or ten days, and you may want an additional day or two for exploring Tortola.

A Week of Sailing in the BVIs

Fly into Road Town and take some time out to explore the islands' charming and somnolent capital city before boarding your yacht. Then set sail for Cooper Island to snorkel and dine.

Sail to Virgin Gorda, stopping at the Baths for a swim around the rock formations. Later, anchor at the Dogs to snorkel. Continue to North Sound for water sports and an island tour.

Cruise to Marina Cay or Trellis Bay, home to stunning coral reefs ideal for snorkeling and diving. Shop at Trellis Bay market and Aragon Studios, or try your hand at windsurfing or sea-kayaking. Then, catch a dinghy to the long sandy beach along Cane Garden Bay. Take a dip or simply lounge under the sun before dining on the freshest seafood at a waterside restaurant. The rum distillery is another attraction you can visit.

Sail over to Jost Van Dyke, stopping en route at the white-rimmed Sandy Cay for a spot of beachcombing and a botanical tour. Next. anchor at Great Harbour and savor cool cocktails and a hearty meal at Foxy's, a quintessential island beach bar.

Today, head over to Norman Island to explore the Caves, a popular snorkeling site. Anchor in the Bight – the largest anchorage on Norman Island – and dine aboard the Willie Thornton floating restaurant, fondly known as the Willie T.

Finally, return to Road Town for your flight back home.

Dos and Don'ts

- ✗ Don't forget to book well in advance, as March is the most popular cruising season.
- ✓ Take the opportunity to learn sailing. Your skipper will be happy to teach you the basics.
- ✓ Study what's included in packages when comparing different charter companies.
- ✗ Don't forget to budget a gratuity for the crew.
- ✓ Do a little background reading beforehand so you can select the places you'd like to visit.

Below: Typical mural painted on a wall along Ridge Road, Tortola

JAN

FEB

MAR

DAY 1

DAYS 2–3

DAYS 4–5

DAY 6

DAYS 7–8

APR

MAY

JUN

JUL

AUG

SEP

OCT

NOV

DEC

GETTING THERE   See map p324, D2, D3
Arrive either at Villeda Morales International Airport, 7 miles (11 km) from San Pedro Sula, or at Golosón International Airport, 4 miles (6 km) from La Ceiba.

GETTING AROUND
You can reach Roatán by air from La Ceiba. Otherwise, rent a car to get around, as rates are reasonable, although taxis are also good value and mountain bikes readily available.

WEATHER
You can expect sunshine, with cool breezes to temper the humidity, and little rainfall. The average temperature is 81°F (27°C).

ACCOMMODATIONS
The Jungle River Lodge at Río Cangrejal has rooms from US$30; www.jungleriverlodge.com

Posada Arco Iris in Roatán offers simple but clean doubles with ocean views from US$60; www.roatanposada.com

The Lodge at Pico Bonito has great facilities; cabins are US$220; www.picobonito.com

D&D Brewery, Los Naranjos, has cabins from US$31; www.dd-brewery.com

EATING OUT
Try *sopa de caracol*, conch stew with vegetables, spices, and coconut milk. Inland, look out for *anafre*, a fondue-like dish, made with refried beans, cheese, and sausage.

PRICE FOR TWO
US$245 per day includes accommodation, food, local travel, and activity charges.

FURTHER INFORMATION
www.letsgohonduras.com

Catarata de Pulhapanzak

This beautiful waterfall is 11 miles (18 km) from Lago de Yojoa, near San Buenaventura village. A guide will lead you down a slippery path into chest-high water, then through the rolling 141-ft (43-m) high cascade to a cave under the falls. Bring goggles and a change of clothes, as you will end up wet through. If you don't feel up to the challenge, admire the waterfall from the park through its veil of shimmering mist, often with rainbows forming in the sunlight. There are ponds for swimming and you can picnic or eat in the rustic-style restaurant.

Unmissable photo-ops await in the transparent waters of the Blue Channel where fish play hide and seek in azure waters.

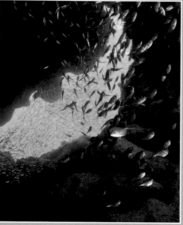

Main: Spine-tingling passage through the rapids of Río Cangrejal

RAPIDS, REEFS, RAIN FORESTS

THE RAFT HEADS TOWARDS THE NEXT RAPID, a spine-tingling Class IV. Spray drifts across the front of the boat as it twists and turns in the current, buffeted by glistening boulders. You recall your training earlier in the day and row with all the strength you can muster. The boat gathers speed, hits the rapid with a sickening bump, tilts alarmingly, then hangs in the air before plunging into a torrent of swirling water. For sheer adrenaline rush, nothing beats white-water rafting, and Honduras' Río Cangrejal ranks among the top places in the world to enjoy this exhilarating sport. To appreciate the spectacular beauty of the Cangrejal Valley at a more leisurely pace, rent a mountain bike, or cross the river by zipline as a curtain-raiser to the canopy tour of the Pico Bonito rain forest.

From here the pristine, white-sand beaches of the Bay Islands are no more than a 30-minute flight away. Roatán, the largest and most popular island, offers a full range of water sports, from waterskiing and

Inset: Glass sweeper fish in an underwater cave

Left (left to right): Swimming with dolphins at Anthony's Key Resort; sea kayaking in the Bay Islands' blue waters; up close and personal with a southern manta ray; riding a zip wire through the rain forest canopy in Pico Bonito Natural Park

Right: Exploring the mysterious world beneath Roatán's reefs

WATER SPORTS DIARY

Honduras offers excellent opportunities for all sorts of water sports. Río Cangrejal is the ideal jumping-off point for an adventure holiday. You'll need three days to try out the activities on offer, before moving on to Roatán's reefs. Finally, peaceful Lago de Yojoa is a perfect antidote to the activity of the Bay Islands.

Ten Adrenaline-Fueled Days

Test your nerves on the Class III–V white-water rapids of the Río Cangrejal. Later, explore the Pico Bonito Natural Park by walking the Zacate River trail. Cool off in swimming holes en route and look out for wildlife. Start your second day with a swim in the natural pools below Jungle River Lodge, before joining the High Wire Canopy Tour of Pico Bonito, the only one in Honduras. Spend a day exploring the stunning Río Cangrejal Valley and its scenic villages by mountain bike.

Fly to Roatán from La Ceiba and spend the rest of the day swimming or snorkeling in Half Moon Bay. Diving conditions should be perfect, so take your pick from the huge variety of diving and snorkeling expeditions to the Barrier Reef over the next two days. On your last day in Roatán, explore the clear waters of the Caribbean by sea kayak, then swim with dolphins at Anthony's Key Resort.

Take an early flight back to La Ceiba, then drive to Lago de Yojoa, arriving at Agua Azul restaurant where you can bird watch while you eat. Drive to D&D microbrewery for the night and ask for a tour of the Orchid Garden. Spend the next day hiking in Cerro Azul Meámbar National Park, enjoying the stunning scenery and cloud forest. Finally, hire a guide for the Taulubé caves where fruit bats lurk among 6-ft (2-m) high stalactites and stalagmites, and take in the fabulous Catarata de Pulhapanzak on your way back.

Dos and Don'ts

✓ Remember to bring your Open Water Diver Certification card to Roatán. Consult www.scuba.about.com for details.

✗ Don't forget to check the baggage restrictions for the internal flight to Roatán and pack accordingly.

✓ Take plenty of cash, as credit cards are not widely accepted.

✓ Bring baby oil as it is an effective deterrent against sandflies.

✗ Don't buy conch shells, black coral jewelry, dried seahorses, and other environmentally harmful products.

✓ Carry binoculars with you, as there are nearly 400 bird species around Lago de Yojoa alone.

Below: Rock formation on dolomite base in the Taulubé caves

JAN

FEB

MAR

DAYS 1–3

DAYS 4–7

DAYS 8–10

APR

MAY

JUN

JUL

AUG

SEP

OCT

NOV

DEC

wakeboarding, to sea kayaking and deep-sea fishing. But it is Roatán's proximity to the longest barrier reef in the western hemisphere that attracts divers and snorkelers from around the world. There are nearly 40 sites to choose from, all within striking distance of the shore. Drift dive through mysterious underwater canyons and ravines in search of 6-ft (2-m) high barrel sponges, squat on the sea bed to watch reef sharks feeding, or visit the barnacled hulks of the *Odyssey* or *El Aguila*. Unmissable photo-ops await snorkelers in the transparent waters of Blue Channel, where tangs, damselfish, barracuda, and snapper play hide-and-seek in azure waters.

Return to the mainland and head south to the forested slopes of Cerro Azul Meámbar (6,700 ft/2,042 m) for jaw-dropping views of Lago de Yojoa, Honduras' largest inland lake. Fishing and bird watching expeditions start from its reed-fringed shores, while those in search of more physically demanding challenges should look no further than the Taulubé caves or the spectacular Pulhapanzak waterfall, where the heart-in-mouth scramble across the cliff face could turn out to be the highlight of the trip.

GETTING THERE See map p317, B4
Natchez is 90 miles (145 km) north of Baton Rouge's national airport, and 170 miles (275 km) from New Orleans' international airport. Car rental is available at both.

GETTING AROUND
Natchez is pleasant to explore on foot. The Trace is lovely for hiking, biking, and horseback riding, but a car is needed for longer trips.

WEATHER
Temperatures average a high of 70°F (21°C) and lows of 50°F (10°C) in March, with a high possibility of rain.

ACCOMMODATIONS
The Natchez Eola Hotel marries Southern charm with modern amenities; doubles from US$141; www.natchezeola.com

In Natchez or Clinton, try the reliable Hampton Inn and Suites; doubles from US$99; www.hamptoninn.com

The 1904 Neo-Classical Tuscan Columns in Port Gibson features a player piano; doubles from US$85; www.pianohousebb.com

EATING OUT
You'll find plenty of traditional southern food such as fried chicken, turnip greens, and corn bread, as well as fine dining in grand style at mansions like Stanton Hall.

PRICE FOR TWO
Allow around US$280 per day to include accommodation, food, car rental, admission fees, and entertainment.

FURTHER INFORMATION
www.visitnatchez.com

Skirting the Issue

On the Natchez Trace, the sight of Southern Belles in sweeping hoop skirts soon becomes commonplace. In the 19th century, such skirts were de rigueur here, and now they're as much a symbol of the region as steamboats. Brutal to wear during the sweltering summer months, the multi-hooped petticoats are fitted over a bustle framework to keep their shape. Along with whalebone corsets, they are worn with pride by tour guides and re-enactors who take great pains, literally, to keep the South's rich history alive. Hoop skirts are part of the fabric of the region.

Above (left to right): Twilight over the Natchez Trace; paddle-steamer riverboat on the Mississippi; swampland forest walk on the Trace
Main: Magnificent Stanton Hall, a picture-book antebellum mansion

THE BEAUTIFUL SOUTH

TO CAPTURE THE ESSENCE OF THE AMERICAN SOUTH IN A SINGLE JOURNEY is a romantic dream for many travelers. With its natural beauty and rich history, the Natchez Trace is a perfect introduction to one of America's most breathtaking regions. Springtime, when the sweet smell of magnolias fills the air, is the ideal time to visit, avoiding summer's humidity. The Natchez Trace is a 444-mile (715-km) scenic parkway that follows an old trail trekked by traders heading back to Nashville, Tennessee from the port of Natchez, Mississippi. It links a series of towns and cities in Mississippi, Alabama, and Tennessee, each with its own charm. The region lends itself to leisurely drives, and traffic is never an issue, with strict speed limits and no trucks allowed on the Trace.

Natchez itself makes an ideal base from which to explore a stretch of the Trace. The town has more antebellum (pre-Civil War) houses than any other in the USA, but there is far more to Natchez than mansions and magnolias. The town is named for the native Natchez tribe, and their Grand Village offers a glimpse into the lives of the region's first settlers. Natchez-Under-the-Hill is today a genteel dockside leisure district yet, in its 19th-century heyday, it was the most notorious landing on the Mississippi, teeming with gamblers and outlaws. The Natchez Museum of Afro-American History and Culture chronicles the experiences of Natchez's freed slaves in the wake of the Civil War.

Where ever you go, you will be greeted by friendly Southerners who strive to keep the history and culture of this region alive. To visit Natchez and the Trace is to be surrounded by Southern hospitality and a slower pace of life, as warm and easy as spring breezes off the Mississippi River. But it's those antebellum mansions – architectural wonders, regardless of their historical significance – that are the stars of Natchez, and you take a step back in time when you step through their magnificent portals.

To visit Natchez and the Trace is to be surrounded by Southern hospitality and a slower pace of life...

Inset: "Spring Pilgrimage" performance by a gospel choir
Below (left and right): Spectacular formal gardens of Monmouth; octagonal mansion of Longwood

ANTEBELLUM DIARY

For the Natchez "Spring Pilgrimage," over 25 antebellum mansions, some of them private homes, open their doors to the public. Guides wear period costume, and gospel choirs perform plantation songs. With Natchez as your base, five days allows you to discover the many facets of this historic region at a leisurely pace.

Five Days on the Trace

Begin your visit with a day of plantation tours, including Melrose, the most intact antebellum estate in the USA; Monmouth, with its striking formal garden; quirky octagonal Longwood; Dunleith, whose colonnade encircles the house; and palatial Stanton Hall. End the day with dinner, drinks, and music at Bowie's Tavern.

Start with brunch at Café LaSalle at the Eola Hotel. Natchez-Under-the-Hill is well worth a visit for its shops, restaurants, and paddle-steamer riverboat trips. Call in at the Under-the-Hill Saloon for a lively happy hour, then enjoy an evening carriage ride around downtown.

Set off up the Trace. Worth a visit on your way are Emerald Bluff, a vast Natchez ceremonial mound; the Ruins of Windsor, eerie remnants of the largest antebellum mansion in Mississippi; and the Bullen Creek Trail forest walk. End the day in Port Gibson, the town Ulysses S. Grant found "too beautiful to burn."

Just outside Port Gibson is Sunken Trace, a moss-draped section of the original Trace. Magnum Mound is an ancient burial ground, and nearby Grindstone Ford marked the beginning of the Choctaw Nation. Visit antebellum Raymond, with its Confederate Cemetery and Civil War battle site, on your way to Clinton.

Explore the Clinton Nature Center, with trails through the lush native canopy and a butterfly garden bursting with color. Walk in the tracks of Andrew Jackson and John James Audubon at the Primitive Campsite exhibit. Allow a little time to see the beautiful brick streets of Clinton's Olde Towne before heading back to Natchez.

Dos and Don'ts

- ✓ Take advantage of guided tours; they really bring the history of the region to life.
- ✓ When driving the Trace, be aware of the many recreational cyclists and horseback riders who share the route with you.
- ✓ Make sure to allow enough time for plenty of stops along the Trace. You'll constantly see things that catch your eye.
- ✗ Don't forget comfortable footwear; Natchez is highly walkable and you'll want practical shoes for any trails you explore as well.

JAN

FEB

MAR

DAY 1

DAY 2

DAY 3

DAY 4

DAY 5

APR

MAY

JUN

JUL

AUG

SEP

OCT

NOV

DEC

Below: Ruins of Windsor

GETTING THERE   See map p323, I5

GETTING THERE
The Yucatán is most easily reached via Cancún, which has flights from many parts of North America and Europe, or Mérida, which has air links with several North American cities.

GETTING AROUND
The best way to get around the peninsula is to drive. There is a choice of car rental agencies in Cancún and Mérida.

WEATHER
In March, daytime temperatures in Mérida range from 70°F to 90°F (21°C to 32°C). Days are hot and dry while nights are cooler.

ACCOMMODATIONS
Hacienda Chichén, Pisté, is a converted hacienda close to the ruins; family rooms from US$160; www.haciendachichen.com

Hotel Dolores Alba, Mérida, is a popular, friendly hotel; family rooms from US$55; www.doloresalba.com

Hacienda Uxmal is a luxurious hotel next to Uxmal ruins; family rooms from US$150; www.mayaland.com

EATING OUT
Yucatecan cooking is a fusion of European techniques and Yucatec Mayan traditions and ingredients. Try refreshing lime soup and *pollo pibil* – chicken marinated in *achiote* (annatto), spices, and orange juice, then baked in banana leaves.

PRICE FOR A FAMILY OF FOUR
US$480 per day, including accommodation, food, entrance fees, car rental, and fuel.

FURTHER INFORMATION
www.mayayucatan.com.mx

The Maize People

You will see corn or maize on sale all over the Yucatán as plain cobs, ground into flour and shaped into tortillas, even sweetened with sugar, turned into a thick cream, and put into donuts and cakes. Maize has been cultivated in the Mayan world for so many thousands of years that it has become an inseparable part of Mayan culture, and to many Maya, it is the very stuff of creation. Maize Gods appear in the temples, and according to the most sacred of Mayan books, the *Popul Vuh*, man was molded from maize by the Maize God Hun-Nal-Ye.

THE MAYAN HEARTLAND

MEXICO'S YUCATÁN PENINSULA juts into the clear waters of the Caribbean just south of the Tropic of Cancer. It is most famous for the beaches that run like a sliver of mother-of-pearl near Cancún, but these are not the true jewels in its crown – the forest that swathes the peninsula is replete with ruined cities built by a civilization that began before the Romans and ended in the Renaissance. Many are still unexcavated, but others have been stripped of trees and vines to reveal the ornately carved temples, civic plazas, sports courts, and palaces that were the headquarters of the Mayan city states.

On the days of the vernal equinox, thousands gather at Chichén Itza to watch as the shadows cast down the great central pyramid form an undulating serpent of light and dark. This extends from the top of the temple, down the central stairway, to the gaping, fanged mouth of the snake-god Kukulcán. At

Main: Snake head detail from the Warriors' Temple in Chichén Itza

Uxmal and the nearby Puuc sites, pyramids and plazas are adorned with an elegant filigree of carved stone masks, geometric shapes, and sculpted animals. Wandering through the ancient Mayan cities gives a fascinating sense of a remote civilization, from its strange rituals to the details of everyday life.

These cities may be in ruins, but the Maya themselves are alive and well. From the sides of temples, they proffer woven hammocks and bright *huipil* shirts, and their friendliness and unhurried manner give a special tone and charm to Yucatecan life. Restored Spanish haciendas make wonderfully peaceful places to stay. The natural world is unique too: the limestone of the region is riddled with vast caverns, and underground rivers burst through in sapphire caves and waterholes called cenotes (sinkholes), which are unmissable places to swim. There is wilderness as well, from the flamingo-filled lagoons near the coastal village of Celestún to rain forests farther south. No matter how long you spend in the Yucatán, there is always more to see.

Above (top to bottom): A cenote, at Chichén Itza; the Temple of the Magician, allegedly built in a single night, in Uxmal

Bottom panel (left to right): Gracious portico of a traditional hacienda in Mérida; colorfully crowded vehicle in Mérida; jade burial mask from the Fuerte de San Miguel Museum in Campeche; view of the magnificent Five Floors Temple among the ruins at Edzná; bell tower at the Monastery of San Antonio de Padua in colonial Izamal

SPRING EQUINOX DIARY

The best way to see the Yucatán is to hire a car in Cancún and hop between the colonial towns that dot the peninsula. These towns can be used as bases for visits to the Mayan ruins and other sites. Ten days, starting on the vernal equinox (March 20–21), is enough time to experience the magic of this timeless world.

Ten Days in an Ancient World

Drive to Chichén Itza, stopping to swim in the Dzitnup cenote near Valladolid. Stay at a hotel close to the ruins.

Reach the ruins around 8am, before the crowds, and stay all day, positioning yourself so that you can see the serpent shadow on the stairs in the afternoon.

Head for Mérida, stopping at the charming colonial town and monastery at Izamal.

Wander around Plaza Mayor and the amazing market in Mérida, then on to the Anthropology Museum at Paseo de Montejo. Have dinner on a beautiful colonial patio.

Visit the flamingo preserve at Celestún, and after the tour relax on the long white beach before returning to Mérida.

Drive to Uxmal and visit the ruins there and at the small Mayan cities in the Puuc Hills – Kabah, Sayil, Labná, and the awesome caves at Loltún, a spellbinder for kids.

Take the inland road south from Uxmal to Campeche, passing remote villages and stopping at the unusual Mayan ruins of Edzná on the way.

In Campeche, explore the old town enclosed in walls built to keep out pirates. Take a cab to Fuerte de San Miguel Museum to see Mayan jade funeral masks.

Make an early start. Drive north past Mérida to the beach at Progreso and watch the sunset. Stay in Mérida.

Return to Cancún. Stop for lunch at Valladolid and visit the small but superb Mayan ruin nearby at Ek-Balam.

Dos and Don'ts

✓ Learn some Spanish since English is rarely spoken away from the coast.

✗ Don't drive at night.

✓ Book early to get a room near Chichén Itza around the equinox dates – they are in big demand.

✗ Don't take pictures of Mayan people without asking for their permission first.

✓ Carry plenty of water and wear a hat as the sun is fierce.

Below: Caribbean flamingos in a lagoon near Celestún

JAN
FEB
MAR
20th
21st
22nd
23rd
24th
25th
26th
27th
28th
29th
APR
MAY
JUN
JUL
AUG
SEP
OCT
NOV
DEC

You might find yourself fishing a small spring creek, in waters so clear you can be up to your waist and still read the labels on your waders.

GETTING THERE   See map p331, C4
From the international airport at the Chilean capital, Santiago, there are connecting flights to San Carlos de Bariloche, for the Alto Puelo area; Balmaceda for the Aisén region; and Neuquén. Your hosts will meet you and take you to your accommodation.

GETTING AROUND
Guides will accompany you on fishing trips.

WEATHER
March sees very little rainfall, with daytime temperatures of around 75–90°F (24–32°C).

ACCOMMODATIONS
Prices are per person, double occupancy, for 6 nights and 7 days' fishing, all inclusive.

Alto Puelo Lodge, in the Rio Puelo region, has three lodges in spectacular locations; from US$5,200; www.argentinachileflyfishing.com

Heart of Patagonia Lodge, in the Aisén area, is just 10 miles (16 km) from the Pacific; from US$4,250; www.heartofpatagonia.com

Jorge Trucco's Patagonia Outfitters, in the Neuquén area, has ten large, rustic lodges in beautiful settings on four watersheds; from US$3,500; www.jorgetrucco.com

EATING OUT
Fishing lodges serve three hearty meals a day plus snacks, using regional staples like Chilean sea bass, beef, lamb, and chicken. Excellent Chilean and Argentinian wine is included.

PRICE FOR TWO
Around US$1,200 per day, all inclusive.

FURTHER INFORMATION
www.interpatagonia.com

One That Didn't Get Away

Every region has its fish story. This one tells of one of Argentina's original fly fishermen, José Evaristo Anchorena, "El Bebé," who popularized Patagonia in the USA through his friendship with noted American anglers. While he was happy for Yankees to fish his rivers, he didn't show them all the best spots. One he kept secret was a pool on the Rio Chimehuín where, in 1961, he hooked a huge brown trout that fought ferociously, speeding from one side of the river to the other for a full hour. The fish weighed in at 24 lb (11 kg), a record that stands to this day.

Main: Casting a line in a spectacular Patagonian lake setting

REELING IN THE ANDES

Though the vast, broad plains of Patagonia are mostly semi-arid *pampas* rangeland, higher up in the foothills of the Andes the cool precipitation off the Pacific and the meltwater from glacial ice and snow give rise to hundreds of cold mountain lakes, and thousands of rivers, great and small, running down to the ocean. Fast-moving, clear, and cold, these rivers are much akin to those of Scotland or the American eastern seaboard, while the mountain landscape beyond owes more to Montana, or the high, cold slopes of the Himalayas.

It was in the early decades of the 20th century that American and European sports fishermen had the idea of introducing the fighting fish of the northern hemisphere into Patagonia's lakes and streams. With an assured food supply – and a lack of any natural predators – the brook, brown, and rainbow trout, steelhead, chinook, and Atlantic salmon all thrived in their new southern home, often reaching sizes never heard of in their native northern waters.

ANGLER'S DIARY

Fly-fishing lodges straddle the border between Argentina and Chile, and usually offer a mimimum one-week stay. In March the rivers are getting shallower, making the trout easier to hook, so it's an ideal month for the novice. This diary focuses on one region, but the overall experience is common to all three destinations.

A Week of Fly-Fishing Thrills

From San Carlos de Bariloche airport, it's a short car ride over the border into Chile, and then a transfer by jet boat across Alto Puelo Lake to your lodge. Take a deep breath of the mountain air and marvel at the stunning scenery. Chat with your fellow guests about the angling pleasures to come, over a delicious dinner and some excellent local wine (but don't forget, you'll want to make an early start in the morning!).

DAY 1

Lake Puelo winds between fir-clad hills, and offers scores of fish-friendly nooks and crannies. Rainbow and brown trout are the prime species here, and your guide knows just where to set a fly to tease them out of hiding. You can easily spend two days fishing here.

DAYS 2–3

Puelo River offers rapids and whirlpools, small feeder streams, quiet green banks, rushing waterfalls and crystal-clear turquoise water. Try drift-fishing, or dry-land cast from the banks. The guide will point out the most promising places to try over a couple of days.

DAYS 4–5

Chinook and Atlantic salmon were introduced into the Puelo system in the 1990s. For your last day on the water, re-tie those flies, take counsel with your guide and set out on the Puelo in search of salmon. Toast your success (or drown your sorrows) with fine Chilean wine accompanying a gourmet last supper.

DAY 6

Rise early, enjoy the dawn and a last hearty breakfast, then bid farewell to mountains, lake, and fish. Hop in the jet boat and zoom off across the still, turquoise surface of Lake Puelo on the way back to Bariloche.

DAY 7

Inset: Angler's equipment

Left (left to right): Alto Puelo gorge; wade-fishing near the rapids; bringing in a tired lake fish at the end of the day; selecting the perfect fly for the task

Right: Drift-fishing for steelhead

Dos and Don'ts

- ✓ Practise catch-and-release, mandatory now in both Argentina and Chile. And remember – go barbless.

- ✓ Sample the superb local wines. Cool Chilean whites go well with a streamside lunch, while the richer Argentinian reds are perfect with dinner.

- ✗ Don't forget that most lodges offer fly-fishing lessons, plus a range of non-fishing activities such as nature treks and boat trips, for loved ones not devoted to the sport.

APR

MAY

JUN

JUL

AUG

SEP

OCT

NOV

DEC

Where the fish lead, the fishermen have followed. The varied terrain of the Andes provides a different type of water for every taste and skill level: small, shallow streams; riffled creeks; fast rivers with impressive rapids; and vast, long lakes that snake between the mountains, the water clear and cold, shimmering a lovely translucent blue when the sun shines, as it does most days in Patagonia. One day you might find yourself wade-fishing a small spring creek, in water so clear you can be up to your waist and still read the labels on your waders. On another you could be drifting through lush, impenetrable temperate rainforest, snow-capped mountains looming on the near horizon.

There are huge trout here, in abundance, but they don't give themselves up to just anyone. Professional guides will advise on choice of fly, and offer tips on where to cast your line. Once the bait is taken, the real contest begins. The fish here fight the line all the way, as much above the water as below it. They swirl, dance, leap, and tail-walk, trying everything to throw the hook. Only through true skill will you have the pleasure of easing the net below that tired fish, removing the barbless hook from its mouth and saying "thank you," as it swims away back to its lair.

Below: Typical wood-built Patagonian fishing lodge

APRIL

Where to Go: April

April is a beautiful month to be in the USA – the northern states are settling in to a sunny spring, while the South has yet to get hot and steamy. In Louisiana, visitors can comfortably enjoy outdoor food, music, and culture at the lively Festival International de Louisiane, while the old town of Charleston and the South Carolina Lowcountry are highly picturesque at this time. Central

America is approaching the end of its dry season. Belize remains pretty sultry year-round; some countries, like Panama, show signs of getting very hot. In Brazil, summer is drawing to a close, which means temperatures are more comfortable and the heavy rains are easing. Below you will find all the destinations in this chapter as well as some extra suggestions to provide inspiration.

FESTIVALS AND CULTURE

EASTER ISLAND Ancient *moai* statue, carved from volcanic rock

UNFORGETTABLE JOURNEYS

BLUE RIDGE PARKWAY The winding Linn Cove Viaduct

NATURAL WONDERS

IGUAZÚ FALLS A footbridge overlooking the mighty cataract

EASTER ISLAND
CHILE

Remote home to one of the wonders of the world

This is one of the most isolated places on earth, with its huge, brooding, enigmatic sculptures, called *moai*.
See pp90–91

TOONIK TYME, IQALIT
NUNAVUT, CANADA

Week-long celebration of Inuit life

Marking the end of the long Arctic winter, this festival showcases Inuit skills and traditions – anything from throat singing to building an igloo.
www.tooniktyme.com

BLUE RIDGE PARKWAY
NORTH CAROLINA, USA

A jaw-dropping scenic drive

This celebrated driveway winds through mist-shrouded hills and great National Parks, revealing American heritage along the way.
See pp92–3

HIKING THE APPALACHIAN TRAIL
EASTERN USA

A great walking challenge

Tackle this legendary long-distance wilderness trek, stretching for 2,000 miles (3,218 km) from Georgia to Maine.
www.appalachiantrail.org

IGUAZÚ FALLS
ARGENTINA AND BRAZIL

The largest waterfalls in the world

The thundering Iguazú Falls boil away on the border of Argentina and Brazil. Brace yourself and stare down the Devils' Throat.
See pp82–3

LAYFAYETTE
LOUISIANA, USA

Lafayette street festival

Cajun, Creole, and Acadian rhythms, to feed the soul at the Festival International de Louisiane – and there is great food to keep you jumping too.
See pp98–9

"The streets of Lafayette come alive with a montage of performers and everyone dances with everyone."

BOAT TRIPS TO ISLA DE LA PLATA
ECUADOR

The alternative Galapagos

This island just off the coast of Ecuador is home to marine birds, sea lions, dolphins, manta rays, and humpback whales.
www.ecuador-travel.net

LOS GLACIARES NATIONAL PARK
ARGENTINA

Sub-Antarctic wilderness

Los Glaciares is home to almost 50 glaciers, fed by the giant Andean ice-cap, which slither into iceberg-dotted lakes.
www.losglaciares.com

VOLCÁN ARENAL
COSTA RICA

Spectacular volcano in the heart of Central America

One of the world's ten most active volcanoes, producing glowing lava flows, huge ash columns, and booming explosions.
www.arenal.net

LEXINGTON
VIRGINIA, USA

Historic 19th-century Virginian town

Set amid the undulating Shenandoah Valley, this appealing town has an old-world atmosphere and plenty of Civil War memorabilia
www.lexingtonvirginia.com

HELLS CANYON
IDAHO AND OREGON, USA

Tackle some of the West's most challenging white water

Raft down the Snake River as it twists and turns through the dramatic Hells Canyon, the deepest river gorge in the USA.
www.fs.fed.us/hellscanyon

GALÁPAGOS ISLANDS
ECUADOR

A group of volcanic islands with unique flora and fauna

April is the best month to see the legendary giant tortoises, as well as sea turtles, baby sea lions, and island flowers.
See pp86–7

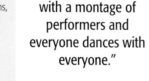

LOS ANGELES
CALIFORNIA, USA

More than just filmstars and freeways

The USA's mightiest metropolis is home to numerous attractions, from Art Deco landmarks to the superb collections of the Getty Center.
www.la.com

CABOT TRAIL
CANADA

This Cape Breton drive is wild, rugged, and beautiful

This route follows Cape Breton's northern shore before climbing to a high plateau. See fish eagles, moose, and pods of whales.
www.cabottrail.com

COLCA CANYON
PERU

The world's deepest canyon

Twice as deep as the Grand Canyon, the Colca Canyon boasts stunning natural scenery, along with condors and vicuñas, and beautiful old churches.
www.peru.info

Previous page: A shoal of razor surgeon fish, Galápagos Islands

Weather Watch

❶ North Carolina, USA April is a lovely time to drive the Blue Ridge Parkway. Temperatures in North Carolina are cold at high altitudes and conditions can change at a moment's notice – you might even see snow.

❷ Louisiana, USA Springtime in the south is mild and slightly humid, with cooler evenings. Sweet-smelling magnolia, jasmine, and camellias erupt throughout city gardens.

❸ Belize Belize is on the cusp of its rainy and dry seasons – in the north and by the sea, especially, days are still dry and sunny. Although humidity is high, cooling breezes keep temperatures from being stifling.

❹ Iguazú Falls, Argentina The falls are at their most impressive in April, as the water levels are high after the summer rains. Temperatures are cooling down.

❺ Galápagos Islands The rainy season is ending in the Galapagos Islands, off Ecuador, which means lower humidity, appealing temperatures of around 82°F (28°C), and brilliantly green, lush landscapes.

❻ Easter Island Though officially part of Chile, Easter Island is almost 2,500 miles (4,023 km) from the mainland and has its own climate. April is mild, if somewhat wet, with dazzling sunshine and cooling breezes.

LUXURY AND ROMANCE

TURKS AND CAICOS ISLANDS Snorkeling at Grace Bay, Providenciales

TURKS AND CAICOS ISLANDS
CARIBBEAN

Sun-bleached coral islands

Escape to these tiny islands for chilled-out days on the white-sand beaches, excellent diving among coral reefs, and luxurious pampering.
See pp84–5

"The isles and cays of the Turks and Caicos are fringed by snow-white sands and waters of startling electric blues."

CAPE MAY
NEW JERSEY, USA

The USA's most historic seaside resort

The historic town of Cape May has been famous for its invigorating sea breezes and genteel atmosphere since the 18th century.
www.capemay.com

PUERTO VALLARTA
MEXICO

Playground of legendary lovers Liz Taylor and Richard Burton

PV, as the locals call it, still retains an aura of Hollywood glitz but you can find delightful beaches away from the bright lights.
www.visitpuertovallarta.com

SCOTTSDALE
ARIZONA, USA

The place to live the Arizonan high-life

Nicknamed "The Beverly Hills of The Desert," Scottsdale is one of the liveliest and most affluent small cities in the West.
www.scottsdaleaz.gov

SANTA YNEZ VALLEY
CALIFORNIA, USA

Idyllic rural escape in the heart of Santa Barbara's wine country

Choose from over 70 world-class wineries, as well as a seductive array of romantic inns, top-notch restaurants, and tempting shops.,
www.syvva.com

ACTIVE ADVENTURES

SABA ISLAND Hikers in the verdant rain forest

SABA ISLAND
CARIBBEAN

The ideal spot for exploration on land and by sea

Saba is one large volcano cloaked in thick rain forest. It is fantastic for hiking, and diving in a lava-formed coral marine park.
See pp94–5

DIVING IN THE BOCAS DEL TORO
PANAMA

Remote archipelago

Plunge into the tropical waters surrounding these beautiful islands, home to abundant marine life and superb coral reefs.
www.bocas.com

URUGUAY
SOUTH AMERICA

Discover South America's hidden gem

From fun in the sun on Atlantic beaches to time in the saddle as a gaucho, this tiny country has many facets to discover.
See pp96–7

BUCKSKIN GULCH
UTAH, USA

Hike through the world's longest slot canyon

A challenging trek through the dramatic Buckskin Gulch, navigating tiny gorges between towering sandstone walls.
www.americansouthwest.net

SOUTHERN COASTAL ISLANDS
BELIZE

A fantastic waterworld

Swim with dolphins, dive, and maybe spot a whale shark. Or go on a rain forest hike if you fancy a break from the sea.
See pp88–9

FAMILY GETAWAYS

BRANSON The terrifying "Wildfire" ride at Silver Dollar City

BRANSON
MISSOURI, USA

Amusement parks in a gorgeous setting

Rides, shows, music, festivals, and all-round fun – this scenic Ozarks resort is a vacation paradise that's as lively or as laid-back as you like.
See pp80–81

NATIONAL CHERRY BLOSSOM FESTIVAL
WASHINGTON, D.C., USA

Spring festivities

This festival started in celebration of the gift of 3,000 cherry trees from Tokyo in 1912.
www.nationalcherryblossom festival.org

"The expansive beaches of the Lowcountry are an invitation to run, cycle, and generally let off steam."

LOWCOUNTRY
SOUTH CAROLINA, USA

More than springtime blooms and manners from heaven

There's a genteel air about these historic coastal towns, but beyond lie wild marshes and wide beaches that are perfect for exploring.
See pp78–9

ST. KITTS AND NEVIS
CARIBBEAN

Have some big family fun on these two small islands

Ride the sugar train, explore Brimstone Hill Fortress, walk through the rain forest, go snorkeling, or laze on the beach.
www.stkittstourism.kn

HILL COUNTRY
TEXAS, USA

Texas, German-style

This region boasts a distinctly German flavor, especially in historic Fredericksburg, and offers unspoilt scenery, lake swimming, hill views, and plentiful campsites.
www.hill-country-visitor.com

SOUTHERN CHARM

L IKE THE GRAND SOUTHERN BELLE SHE IS, the gracious seaside city of Charleston, South Carolina, is at her best in springtime, when her streets and historic gardens explode in a riot of blooming hues. The city's renowned house and garden tours open the doors to a hidden world of grandeur that set the stage for the lavish lifestyle of the antebellum South. Stroll along the cobblestone streets through one of the South's oldest and best preserved historic districts, where graceful mansions and carefully tended homes stand close together along narrow streets. Flowering vines curve around doorways that lead to secluded gardens and courtyards – the soft sea air is rich with the scent of magnolia and jasmine blossoms, and azaleas, rhododendrons, hostas, and columbine add beauty to the already elegant buildings they adorn. Along the Ashley River, outside Charleston, stand the remains of great plantations that once produced unbelievable wealth from harvests of indigo and rice. Many plantations displayed their wealth through grand gardens, and one of the greatest was at

GETTING THERE See map p317, G3
Charleston and Beaufort are on South Carolina's coast, with Charleston International Airport 15 miles (24 km) west of the city.

GETTING AROUND
Travel beyond the Charleston Historic District requires a car. Within it, walk, take a taxi, or use the Downtown Area Shuttle (DASH).

WEATHER
Spring in the Lowcountry has moderate humidity and mostly sunny weather. The daytime average is 76°F (24°C), with night temperatures dropping to 56°F (13°C).

ACCOMMODATIONS
Best Western King Charles Inn is a family favorite near the Historic District, Charleston; rooms from US$170; www.kingcharlesinn.com

Charleston Place offers an excellent location in Charleston and upscale family rooms from US$380; www.charlestonplace.com

Rhett House Inn is a gracious antebellum plantation home in Beaufort; family rooms from US$190; www.rhetthouseinn.com

EATING OUT
Many eateries offer family dining from US$9–16. Barbeque, fried chicken with grits (corn porridge) and hushpuppies (cornmeal fritters), and seafood are all local favorites.

PRICE FOR A FAMILY OF FOUR
US$648 per day for accommodation, food, local travel, and admission charges.

FURTHER INFORMATION
www.charlestoncvb.com
www.beaufortsc.org

Below (top and bottom): A cherub amid a bed of flowers at Magnolia Plantation; the grand spiral staircase at Nathaniel Russell House

Gullah Culture

When the Civil War ended, the sea islands of this area became a haven for newly freed slaves who flocked here to live in peace, creating the unique Gullah culture. St. Helena Island, between Beaufort and Hunting Island State Park, is home to a large population of the self-sufficient Gullah people. Here too is Penn Center, which began in 1862 as the first school for freed slaves. Today, the Gullahs are known for their farming, fishing, and fine crafts, including intricately woven sea-grass baskets.

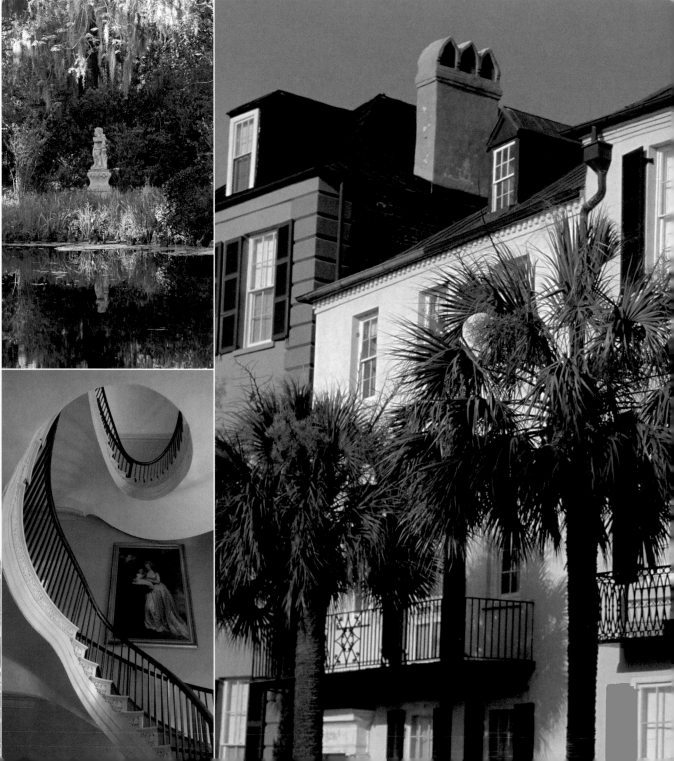

Magnolia Plantation, started in the 1830s as a gift for John Grimke Drayton's young bride. Each succeeding generation expanded the gardens in a natural style, and today visitors can explore the rambling paths through 50 acres (20 ha) of trees, shrubs, and flowers which gradually blend into the natural beauty of the Ashley River marshes. In contrast, the formal gardens of the nearby Middleton Plantation were carefully planned in the European style, incorporating geometric patterns, Greek-inspired statues, and terraced expanses of lawn leading down to the river.

Farther south along the coast, the town of Beaufort is a gem renowned for its elegant antebellum mansions and waterfront. If all this well-tended polite charm gets too much, just beyond the town lie the fertile tidal marshes of St. Helena Island, best explored by kayak – it's a teeming nursery of life where tall grasses shelter a rich abundance of shrimp, crab, and young fish, which in turn attract dolphins. A little farther on, Hunting Island State Park preserves a vast area of tidal marsh, lagoon, and maritime forest, and its expansive white-sand beaches are an invitation to run, cycle, and generally let off steam.

Above (top to bottom): Kayaks in open water near the tall grass marshes; cannon at Fort Sumter

Main: Early 19th-century town houses lining Charleston's elegant streets

Below: Undersea wonders at Charleston Aquarium

LOWCOUNTRY DIARY

Early April is the height of spring in Charleston. The area's rivers were once highways transporting cotton, rice, and indigo, and wealthy plantation owners had town homes, many of which are now open for tours. Allow six days to explore Charleston and Beaufort, the Atlantic beaches, and Lowcountry marshes.

Six Days of Heritage

DAY 1
Take a carriage ride down historic Charleston's cobblestone streets and hear local antebellum histories. Tour the 1808 Nathaniel Russell House and the antique-filled 1825 Edmondston-Alston House.

DAY 2
Gaze into the Great Ocean Tank at the Charleston Aquarium to see a 200 lb (90 kg) loggerhead turtle swimming with other marine life, including sharks and pufferfish. Take a 30-minute boat trip across Charleston Harbor to Fort Sumter National Monument, where the Civil War began on April 12, 1861.

DAY 3
Visit the legendary aircraft carrier, U.S.S. *Yorktown,* and other famous ships and aircraft at Patriots Point Naval and Maritime Museum. Then spend the afternoon building sand castles and sunning on Sullivan's Island.

DAY 4
Drive the Ashley River Road National Scenic Byway, canopied by moss-draped oaks, and explore the gardens at Magnolia and Middleton Plantations. Stop at Charles Towne Landing, the Carolinas' first European settlement, and visit the native Carolina animal zoo.

DAY 5
Explore the Lowcountry near Beaufort. Kayak through salt marshes and watch for bottlenose dolphins. Return to antebellum Beaufort, and browse the boutiques and galleries along Bay and Carteret Streets.

DAY 6
Drive to Hunting Island State Park and walk through the maritime forest's sandy trails. Climb the Lighthouse for sweeping views and then enjoy the beautiful beaches for the rest of the day.

Dos and Don'ts

✓ Wear comfortable shoes and explore the historic streets of Charleston and Beaufort on foot to glimpse private gardens, visit old churches, and admire the antebellum architecture.

✓ Stroll through Charleston's White Point Gardens beneath the huge live oak trees and let the kids climb on the cannons.

✗ Don't forget to spend time relaxing on a bench-swing in the Beaufort Waterfront Park for a magnificent view of the boats.

✓ Children of all ages love exploring the pathways that wind through Magnolia Plantation, discovering arched bridges over ponds and hidden nooks with garden statues.

Below: Carriage ride past antebellum mansions in Charleston's East Battery

JAN
FEB
MAR
APR
MAY
JUN
JUL
AUG
SEP
OCT
NOV
DEC

Above (left and right): Branson country and western club; Table Rock Lake at sunset

GETTING THERE
See map p317, B1

Springfield-Branson National Airport is the arrival point for several domestic carriers that provide direct or connecting flights from most major US cities. Branson is 43 miles (70 km) south.

GETTING AROUND
Rental cars are the best option for getting to and around Branson. Because the Strip is relatively compact, many attractions are within walking distance of one another. Taxis are also available.

WEATHER
April highs can reach 68°F (20°C), with night-time lows around 45°F (7°C). Rain and an occasional thunderstorm are quite possible.

ACCOMMODATIONS
Grand Country Inn has its own free water park (indoor section open all year); family rooms from US$80; www.grandcountry.com

Howard Johnson Hotel has a pool and is close to the Strip; doubles with two rollaway beds from US$86; www.hojobranson.com

Still Waters Condominium Resort is on Table Rock Lake; one-bedroom condo from US$119; www.stillwatersresort.com

EATING OUT
Try Ozark specialties such as barbecue, cornbread, catfish, and handmade fudge. A restaurant dinner might cost US$15–25. Dinner theaters will be at least twice that.

PRICE FOR A FAMILY OF FOUR
US$475 per day, including accommodation, food, and suggested rides and shows.

FURTHER INFORMATION
www.explorebranson.com

Marvelous Marvel Cave

Marvel Cave was discovered in the 1500s by Osage Indians, who dubbed it "The Devil's Den" and made it a forbidden place. In the 19th century, explorers renamed it Marble Cave (in fact the rock is lime-stone). It has been open as a tourist attraction since 1894, and well deserves its current name. It's not for everyone, though – the descent is via about 600 stairs, and some passages are low and narrow. A cable tram returns visitors to the surface.

OZARKS ADVENTURES

FOR A FUN-FILLED BREAK, head for the hills of Branson. Nestled in the enchanting Ozark mountains, this family friendly vacation paradise is surrounded by rolling green hills, tranquil lakes, and – come the warmth of springtime – blooming forsythia, dogwoods, and wildflowers. The region is buzzing at this time of year, not just with the spectacle of nature returning to life, but also with festivals celebrating music, heritage, crafts, and food.

Once a sleepy little backwoods village, where the local folk took their young 'uns to favorite fishing holes, Branson has grown into a world-renowned mega-resort with lavish Las Vegas-style entertainment, thrilling amusement parks, abundant outdoor activities, and an impressive selection of accommodation and dining options. More than 50 live-performance theaters host everything from spectacular Broadway-type productions to toe-tapping, knee-slapping, twangy bluegrass and country music shows. Nearly all of this is on or around the 5-mile (8-km) stretch referred to as "the Strip" or "Country 78."

High on the list of family favorites is 1880s-mining-town-themed Silver Dollar City, with thrill rides, live shows, and demonstrations of pioneer handicrafts. Descending nearly 500 ft (152 m) beneath the theme park, Marvel Cave was a popular attraction before Branson's rise to fame. A National Natural Landmark, the cave is filled with glittering rock formations.

Dolly Parton's Dixie Stampede is another big hit, an action-packed extravaganza that includes stunt horse-riding, pyrotechnics, comedy, music, and other exuberant enter-tainment. The four-course dinner feast is especially enjoyable, with chowder, whole chickens, buttered corn on the cob, baked potatoes, and other goodies all to be slurped or eaten with your hands (silverware supplied upon request).

Plenty more activities await families: a scenic railway ride through the Ozark foothills; narrated sightseeing tours aboard World War II-inspired amphibious "duck" vehicles; and a lively lunch or dinner show on the elegant *Showboat Branson Belle*, an 1880s-style paddle-wheeler that plies the waters of Table Rock Lake. And, for a more peaceful interlude, you could always grab some poles and seek out a secluded fishing hole.

Main: Silver Dollar City "Wildfire" ride
Below (left and right): "American Plunge" ride at Silver City; Dolly Parton's Dixie Stampede

DOWN HOME DIARY

Early spring is ideal for a fun-filled family adventure in the Missouri Ozarks. Some attractions may still be closed (water parks, for example), but you'll avoid the summer crowds, and two top music festivals are in full swing. Four days is just right to enjoy some lively shows, revel in amusements galore, and take a trip out of town.

Four Days of Rip-Roarin' Fun

Dive headlong into your adventure with a narrated sightseeing tour on a "Ride the Ducks" amphibious vehicle. Choose from land or lake tours, or take one of each. Then get on over to Dolly Parton's Dixie Stampede for an evening of fabulous fun and a four-course dinner feast that kids of any age will love to eat with their hands.

Spend the entire day at Silver Dollar City, about 9 miles (14 km) from the Strip. Among 30 rides and attractions is the giant swing that blasts sky-high out of barn doors and will fit the whole family (minimum height 48 in). View demonstrations of pioneer handicrafts including woodcarving, basket-weaving, blacksmithing, and candy-making, and try your hand at some. Take a tour of Marvel Cave and its beautiful "cathedral" cavern. Included in the price of admission are music and comedy shows and festivals. You'll be there during the month-long World-Fest, heralded as America's largest international cultural festival.

Head over to the five-day BransonFest (usually Tue–Sat, second week of April, venue changes yearly), which offers daily shows with top-name performers, and also showcases regional culture, history, art, and food. In the evening, climb aboard the *Showboat Branson Belle* for the dinner-show cruise.

Chug through the lovely Ozarks on a narrated journey into local lore on the Branson Scenic Railway. End the day with one more family show – try "The Haygoods," featuring eight siblings singing in *a cappella* harmony.

Dos and Don'ts

☑ Explore the local antique shops that purvey traditional handmade quilts and other regional collectibles.

☒ Before casting your line, don't forget to check that you're in possession of any requisite fishing license.

☑ Be aware that there can be considerable traffic congestion along the Strip. Park and walk whenever possible, to save time and alleviate stress.

☑ Come prepared for changeable weather: bring rain gear, hats, sunglasses, and – no matter what the weather forecast predicts – sturdy footwear.

Below: Branson Scenic Railway in the Ozarks foothills

JAN
FEB
MAR
APR
DAY 1
DAY 2
DAY 3
DAY 4
MAY
JUN
JUL
AUG
SEP
OCT
NOV
DEC

GETTING THERE   See map p330, F6

Straddling the border of Argentina and Brazil, the Iguazú Falls stretch across a precipice for nearly 2 miles (3 km). Flights land at Puerto Iguazú, via Buenos Aires in Argentina and at Foz do Iguaçu via Sao Paulo in Brazil.

GETTING AROUND

The best way to discover the falls is on foot. Extensive networks of walkways edge the cataracts on both sides of the border.

WEATHER

In April, the average temperature range is 63–82°F (17–28°C). This is the rainy season, when humidity and water levels are high.

ACCOMMODATIONS

In Puerto Iguazú, Hotel Esturión offers suites with river and rain forest vistas; doubles from US$125; www.hotelesturion.com

The Sheraton Iguazú Resort and Spa is the only hotel within the Iguazú National Park on the Argentinian side of the falls; doubles from US$300; www.starwoodhotels.com

In Brazil, try Hotel Das Cataratas; doubles from US$350; www.hoteldascataratas.com

EATING OUT

Specialties in Argentina include tropical river fish such as *surubí*. In Brazil, fish, rice, beans, and fried bananas are tropical staples.

PRICE FOR TWO

Around US$350 per day, including accommodation, food, tours, and admissions.

FURTHER INFORMATION

www.iguazuargentina.com
www.cataratasdoiguacu.com.br

Wildlife of the Paranaense

Home to some 450 species of birds and 80 varieties of mammal, the Paranaense rain forest around the Iguazú Falls is a treasure trove of exotic fauna. Most visible are the raccoon-like coatimundis (*above*) and vibrant butterflies. Capuchin monkeys chatter and scream, and iguanas and caiman lounge beside streams. Swifts nest on rock faces, darting in and out of the vapor kicked up by the falls. Predatory kites circle the sky and treetops come alive with colorful birds. However, feline forest dwellers, such as the puma and jaguar, keep a low profile.

> This great wonder of the natural world is shared between Argentina and Brazil and derives its name from the native Guaraní word for "big waters."

Main: The mighty Iguazú Falls, drawing over a million spectators each year
Above: Iguacú River and the Devil's Throat – the crowning jewel of the Iguazú Falls

GREAT CASCADES

S NAKING WESTWARDS FROM SOUTHERN BRAZIL for hundreds of miles, the Iguaçu River grows in size as it collects the water from over 30 rivers on its way to the Argentinian border. Here, the river, swollen to bursting point, widens and slows as if gathering itself for what is coming. Suddenly, the ground just falls away, forcing the river to plunge hundreds of feet in over 250 separate churning waterfalls, forming the planet's widest span of falling water.

This is the mighty Iguazú Falls, higher than Niagara and wider than the Victoria Falls. This great wonder of the world is shared between Argentina and Brazil and faces another country, Paraguay, and derives its name from the native Guaraní word for "big waters." Never was a name so apt.

The surrounding Iguazú National Park, a lush subtropical rain forest, forms a perfect green frame for the waterfalls, laced with trails of red earth – pathways into an enchanted kingdom of squalling toucans, screaming

Left (left to right): Thirsty butterfly atop a lantana floret; winding footbridge at the Iguazú Falls on the Argentinian side; the vast Itaipú – one of the biggest power plants on the planet; speedboats near the foot of the cascades

Inset: Characteristically colorful toucan at Parque das Aves in Foz do Iguaçu, Brazil

DEVIL'S THROAT DIARY

The falls are at their dramatic best during the April rains. For the full experience, take in the views from both sides of the border. With Argentina's Puerto Iguazú as your base, drink in the falls, explore the forest, and enjoy adventure activities. You could also take a city break to Rio (*see pp302–3*) or Buenos Aires (*see pp238–9*).

Three Days at the Cataracts

Arrive early to the Argentinian side of the falls and begin your adventure with a jungle hike, spotting toucans and other tropical birds as you go.

Drink in the views from the Upper Circuit, as cascade upon cascade tumbles into the Lower Iguazú River.

After lunch, experience the falls from close quarters, along the Lower Circuit.

Later, hop on a boat to San Martín Island for stunning vistas of the San Martín cataract. Follow this with a powerboat ride to the foot of the towering waterfall.

DAY 1

Still on the Argentinian side, ride the eco-train through the forest before trekking to the lip of the legendary Garganta del Diablo waterfall – the mightiest of them all – and feel the jaw-dropping power of this cataract.

In the afternoon, take a gentle boat ride along the Upper Iguazú River drifting past gallery forests rich in birdlife. Alternatively, to be more energetic, hike the quiet Macuco Trail to spot capuchin monkeys and tropical birds. At the trail's end, cool off beneath the beautiful Salto Arrechea waterfall.

DAY 2

Cross to the Brazilian side and head to the gigantic Itaipú hydroelectric dam – among the largest projects of its kind in the world.

Returning to nature, walk to the foot of the Garganta, which comprises 14 individual cataracts, and marvel at the panoramic vistas along the way.

Visit a tropical bird sanctuary before returning to Argentina for your flight home.

DAY 3

Dos and Don'ts

☑ Bring mosquito repellent, a plastic bag for your camera, and proper rain gear – you're going to get soaked.

☒ Don't forget that United States and Canadian citizens must obtain a Brazilian visa before traveling to Brazil.

☑ Check to see if your trip coincides with monthly full-moon walks to the Garganta del Diablo – the views are worth it.

☒ Don't start out on the lovely Macuco Trail too late into the afternoon – the return trek will take roughly 3 hours.

☑ Arrive early at the falls to avoid large crowds.

Below: Passengers on the unique eco-train ride to Devil's Throat

JAN

FEB

MAR

APR

MAY

JUN

JUL

AUG

SEP

OCT

NOV

DEC

capuchin monkeys, and butterflies of kaleidoscopic colors. But it's the falls that are the star attraction, and visitors can walk far out across the churning surface of the river on a network of carefully constructed walkways, right up to the cataracts that tumble down like cascading veils into a frothing maelstrom of bubbling foam, spray, and water. Vapor clouds billow upwards from the crashing torrents, drenching skin and creating huge rainbows that arch across the falls. Up close this awesome spectacle almost overpowers the senses. Rich color abounds – the glistening falls, the emerald rain forest, and the soupy mud-brown river – while the thunderous roar of the water is deafening and a refreshing spray soaks you to the skin.

A sense of experiencing the planet at its most primordial and powerful heightens at the Garganta del Diablo (Devil's Throat). At 262 ft (80 m) it is the biggest of all Iguazú's cataracts. Standing above the Garganta, you see why it has been a source of legend for the Guaraní for millennia, as its torrents rage furiously over rocks and mist rises above the cataract's rim. Looking into the abyss that swirls at its core, the sensation is of peering into the very heart of the earth.

ATLANTIC
OCEAN

Providenciales
**GRAND
TURK**
BAHAMAS | Caicos
Islands
Turks
Islands

HAITI | DOMINICAN
REPUBLIC

GETTING THERE   See map p325, E3
There are daily international flights to
Providenciales (Provo) and Grand Turk from
Florida, New York, and Nassau; and weekly from
London. Private charter planes link the isles.

GETTING AROUND
Provo has tourist charter buses and taxis; cars,
scooters, and bicycles can be rented. Minivans
act as communal taxis on Grand Turk and
smaller isles, but Cockburn Town is walkable.

WEATHER
Temperatures are perfect in April, averaging
84°F (29°C) in the daytime. Rainfall is minimal.

ACCOMMODATIONS
Provo has dozens of fine hotels to choose
from. Options on most other islands are
limited.

The Tuscany has a magnificent beach front
with doubles costing from US$525;
www.thetuscanyresort.com

Bermudian-style architecture and a pool at
the Caribbean Paradise Inn; doubles from
US$135; www.caribbean-paradise-inn.com

Historic colonial Grand Turk Inn, Grand Turk:
doubles from US$250; www.grandturkinn.com

EATING OUT
There are local eateries in Provo town, and
hotel restaurants serve international fare.

PRICE FOR TWO
US$400–695 per day including hotel,
food, and sightseeing. Round trip to
Grand Turk US$135.

FURTHER INFORMATION
www.turksandcaicostourism.com

The National Dish

Local islanders love to eat the queen conch
(pronounced "konk"), a giant marine snail that is
easily identified by its gnarly, spiral shell with a
lustrous pink inside. Feeding on seabed larvae, the
conch grows to over 12 in (30 cm) long. The mollusk's
sweet, slightly rubbery white meat is considered a
delicacy and is eaten raw in conch salad, or made
into fritters, chowders, gumbo, and it even makes a
good burger. However, the conch has been over-
exploited and sadly it is now in short supply.

ROMANTIC ISLAND ESCAPE

IF YOU ARE LOOKING FOR IDYLLIC ISLANDS THAT ARE PRISTINE, uncrowded, and made for a relaxing
hedonistic escape, look no farther. Part of the British West Indies, the Crown colony of Turks and
Caicos (pronounced "kaykos") Islands are all this and more. Specks in the vast Atlantic Ocean
southeast of the Bahamas and north of Hispaniola, they sit atop a marine plateau ringed by the third
largest coral reef system on earth. The Columbus Passage, the deep channel between Grand Turk and
the rest of the islands, is a main route of migrating humpback whales, manta rays, turtles, and
dolphins. Add exceptional wall diving and excellent visibility, and it's understandable why divers are
delirious about the diving here. Ashore, these quaintly named isles and cays are fringed by snow-
white sands and startling electric blue waters.

Providenciales, or Provo as it is known locally, is the westernmost and most developed isle. It has
a plethora of ritzy resorts centered on Grace Bay Beach, a gentle 12-mile (19-km) scimitar of sand

**Below (top to
bottom):** Sea
anemone on the coral
reef; a massage on
the beach at Parrot
Cay; Cockburn Town
house, Grand Turk

that's ranked as one of the world's most beautiful beaches. Pure luxury and pleasure are on offer here. Choose your daily dose of fun from waterskiing, wake-boarding and parasailing or a relaxing pamper in a sumptuous spa. Or you can be whisked to sea on a sunset cruise after a round at the championship course at Provo Golf Club. At night, there's the eerie thrill of glowworms.

The lusher larger isles – Middle, North, and East Caicos – are a wildlife photographer's dream, boasting fantastic birds in wetlands easily accessed by a splendid trail system. South Caicos is where the turquoise flats of Belle Sound boil with bone fish and briny salt ponds draw flocks of rose-pink flamingos and local and migrating rare birds.

Grand Turk, the sleepy political and historical capital island, is all colonial wood-and-stone clapboard houses cloaked in crimson bougainvillea. Donkeys plod the dusty streets but you can saddle up on fine local steeds to splash through the waves. Old-world inns here prove picture-postcard perfect places for romantic candlelit suppers. On neighboring Salt Cay, you'll see ospreys atop old wooden windmills, and in early April divers can swim out to commune with whales.

BLISSED-OUT DIARY

Fringed by frost-white sands and waters of blue perfection, the Turks and Caicos Islands are ideal in April. Most of the best attractions are found on and around Providenciales and Grand Turk. You'll find six days is plenty of time to sample the best of these superb isles, with a trip to Salt Cay to see the humpback whales.

Six Days of Sun and Sea

DAY 1
Arriving in Provo, rest up at your hotel on Grace Bay or on a nearby cay. Head for the beach and take the occasional dip in the ocean. In the evening enjoy a romantic candlelit dinner alfresco, perhaps at the upscale Anacoana Restaurant, at the Grace Bay Club.

DAY 2
Take a sightseeing jaunt around Provo, including the Conch Farm and lovely Sapodilla Bay. Later, enjoy a beach cruise, stopping off at Iguana Cay for a spot of snorkeling. End the day with a relaxing spa treatment and a cocktail as the sun goes down.

DAY 3
Hit the heights by parasailing at Grace Bay. Then either laze the day away on its long stretch of sensational sands or go out for a scuba dive or snorkel. Alternatively, you might like to spend the afternoon playing golf or take a sport-fishing trip.

DAY 4
Fly to Grand Turk and pass the morning exploring Cockburn Town on foot, being sure to visit the Turks and Caicos National Museum. Savor a meal here and take in a rake 'n' scrape band at the Salt Raker Inn.

DAY 5
Jump onto a ferry or boat ride to Salt Cay for whale-watching (the entire herd of humpbacks passes through here), and to see sleepy Balfour Town. Visit the Salt Ponds to spot the local and migrating birds such as ospreys, pelicans, boobies, and flamingos.

DAY 6
Return to Provo by charter flight. Have one last swim before setting off for your return trip home.

Dos and Don'ts

☑ Be sure to shuffle your feet through the sand when wading in the shallows. Stingrays often hide beneath the surface and can lash out with their barbed tails if stepped on.

☒ Don't take home conch shells as souvenirs – they may be seized by Customs.

☑ Use plenty of sunscreen, as the sun is intense and can burn you even through a T-shirt.

☒ Don't be tempted to eat the local delicacy, conch, as it is now an endangered species.

JAN
FEB
MAR
APR
DAY 1
DAY 2
DAY 3
DAY 4
DAY 5
DAY 6
MAY
JUN
JUL
AUG
SEP
OCT
NOV
DEC

Main: One of the many inlets on Grand Turk

Above (top to bottom): Horseback riding on Grand Turk; sunset sailing trip on a catamaran

Below: Reggae band, Lovey and the Lively Stones, performing on Provo Island

Below: Snorkeling with sea stars along Grace Bay Beach, Providenciales

GETTING THERE See map p327, A6

GETTING THERE
The islands of the Galápagos archipelago straddle the Equator, 600 miles (1,000 km) off the coast of Ecuador, South America. International flights go to Quito and Guayaquil in Ecuador, then take a flight to a domestic airport in Santa Cruz.

GETTING AROUND
Small cruise ships and charter boats offer organized excursions around the islands.

WEATHER
Pleasantly warm with temperatures averaging 81°F (27°C). Feb–Apr are the rainiest months, when the islands are at their most verdant.

ACCOMMODATIONS
Hotel Galápagos, Santa Cruz, has sea views; doubles from US$70; www.hotelgalapagos.com

Nemo is a sleek catamaran for 12 passengers; from US$1,830 (per person) for 8 days; www.galapagosinformation.com

Cachalote I is a charming schooner carrying 16 passengers; from US$2,050 (per person) for 8 days; www.galapagostraveler.com

Galápagos Explorer II, a luxury cruise yacht, carries100 passengers; from $3,180 (per person) for 7 days; www.galapagosexplorer.com

EATING OUT
Seafood is a specialty, try the amazing ceviche. Avoid lobsters, due to their over-fishing. Catered meals are included on boat charters.

PRICE FOR TWO
US$450—750 per day including accommodation, food, cruise, and entrance fee to the islands.

FURTHER INFORMATION
www.galapagos.org

The Origin of Species

When naturalist Charles Darwin visited the Galápagos in 1835, he noted how each of the 13 islands had a unique species of finch. Darwin speculated that they were all descended from one mainland species and isolation had encouraged the origin of individual species adapted to their unique environments. In 1859, using evidence he collected in the Galápagos, Darwin upset the established view of creation with the publication of his evolutionary theory in *The Origin of Species*.

Above (left to right): Galápagos tortoise resting; colorful Sally Lightfoot crab, San Cristobal Island; blue-footed booby displaying
Main: Brown pelican plunging to catch a mullet

FAR SIDE OF THE WORLD

No one has ever suggested that the Galápagos Islands are a tropical paradise. One could hardly imagine a more forlorn piece of earth. Darwin called them "the gardens of Hell." In these volcanic islands, the youngest – those farthest west – are still rising from the sea, the product of a "hot spot" hundreds of miles below the ocean floor. The older isles – about five million years old – are softly worn down, in contrast to the newer, more rugged isles. Even the coconut palm, the supreme emblem of the Pacific, is missing. Yet people come back from these islands speaking of marvels and exotic encounters: the islands' namesake (*Galápagos* is Spanish for tortoise), the giant tortoise, heaving its 610-lb (275-kg) weight up the beach, sea lions that let you lie down beside their newborn pups, and Galápagos hawks that land on your head.

The islands, which owe their unique quality to their isolation, were set aside as a national park in 1959. Visits are strictly regulated and a licensed naturalist guide accompanies each cruise boat to enforce the park rules and educate tourists on the unique ecology, geology, flora, and fauna of this fascinating and fragile archipelago.

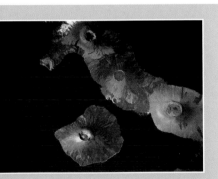

> Everywhere, lava lizards dart back and forth and iguanas lie torpid on shoreline lava floes like prehistoric flotsam washed ashore.

Huge manta rays glide shadow-like under the boat while bottlenose dolphins break the water's surface beside you. On Floreana and Jervis islands, go ashore to watch flamingoes wading in pink-tinged, oozy mud. You can dive with hammerhead sharks off Bartolomé Island or snorkel with penguins off Fernandina. Everywhere, lava lizards dart back and forth, iguanas lie torpid on shoreline lava floes like prehistoric flotsam washed ashore, marine turtles' eggs are hatching, and female frigate birds wheel overhead as their mates proudly puff up their vermilion chests. You don't need to be interested in evolutionary theory to be thrilled by these islands, where 90 percent of the reptiles, 80 percent of the land birds, and 40 percent of the plants are unique.

Inset: Satellite image showing the craters on the islands of Isabela and Fernandina
Below (left to right): Isolated cove on Bartolomé island; diving among a school of striped salema; watchful marine iguana

NATURALIST'S DIARY

The Galápagos are unique in offering spectacular eye-to-eye encounters with wildlife: most of the animals and birds show no fear of humans. The islands are best explored on an organized cruise, departing from Puerto Ayora, Santa Cruz. It's worth adding a few days for exploring Quito and the Andean town of Otavalo.

Nine Days Exploring the Islands

Visit the Charles Darwin Research Station in Puerto Ayora to view the giant tortoise breeding program.

DAY 1

Explore the verdant Santa Cruz highlands, keeping a look-out for its giant tortoises.

DAY 2

Depart by boat for Española (Hood). Commune with marine iguanas, sea lions on sandy beaches, and colonies of albatrosses and blue-footed boobies.

On nearby Floreana, watch flamingoes and snorkel with marina turtles and sharks at Devil's Crown. Leave your mail in the "Post Office Barrel."

DAYS 3–4

Hike through the misty highlands of Isabela and swim with sea lions and Galápagos penguins at Tagus Cove.

Look for dolphins and whales in the Bolivar Channel. On Fernandina, photograph cormorants and hike to the summit of a spectacular crater.

After the long haul to Genovesa (Tower), anchor in spectacular Darwin Bay for fabulous birding plus a chance to snorkel with Galápagos fur seals.

DAYS 5–8

Next stop—Bartolomé for a hike to the summit of Pinnacle Rock and panoramic views. Continue to South Plaza, to see the enormous sea lion colony.

Go snorkeling at Santa Fe. Look out for its land iguanas and prickly pear cacti.

DAY 9

Return to Santa Cruz to begin your homeward journey.

Dos and Don'ts

✓ Stay on the trails. The ecosystem is delicate and wandering off the trails can do lasting damage.

✗ Don't touch the creatures – it is strictly forbidden.

✓ Travel by small boat (fewer than 20 passengers is ideal), which offers a more intimate experience.

✗ Don't overdo it if you fly in to Quito on your first day – you may need some time to adjust to the 9,350-ft (2,850-m) altitude.

JAN
FEB
MAR
APR
MAY
JUN
JUL
AUG
SEP
OCT
NOV
DEC

Be amazed by the innumerable species of marine life, from nurse sharks, barracudas, and moray eels to technicolor reef fish.

GETTING THERE
See map p324, C2

Belize is one of the smallest countries in Central America. Flights land at Phillip Goldson International Airport (30-minutes drive from Belize City's center), and Tropic Air and Maya Island Air run services from the domestic terminal to the airstrip at Placencia.

GETTING AROUND
Placencia is easily negotiated on foot. Golf carts, scooters, and bicycles are popular modes of transport and can be rented easily.

WEATHER
April is one of the sunniest months in Belize, and although the high humidity levels are tempered by cooling breezes, the temperature still averages 86°F (30°C).

ACCOMMODATIONS
The Inn at Robert's Grove is a luxury beach resort with water sports facilities; beach-view rooms from US$215; www.robertsgrove.com

Long Caye Adventure Lodge has solar-powered lighting and activity packages from US$250 a night; www.slickrock.com/glv.htm

A good alternative to Long Caye is Atoll Island Lodge; US$65 per night; www.glovers.com.bz

EATING OUT
Belizean cooking is Caribbean with Creole and Garifuna (Black African) influences, and fresh fish and seafood are widely available.

PRICE FOR TWO
Around US$550 per day with food, local transportation, accommodation, and activities.

FURTHER INFORMATION
www.travelbelize.org
www.placencia.com

Main: Scuba diver observing a school of French grunts
Above: Fisherman at Queen's Cay

Gentle Giants

Originally land creatures, manatees began evolving some 50 million years ago and now thrive in warm, shallow coastal waters, lagoons, and river estuaries. These large sea mammals, weighing up to 1,000 lbs (454 kg), are related to elephants and are similarly long-lived, with a life expectancy of about 50–60 years. While they're endangered, there are said to be up to 1,000 manatees in Belizean waters, the densest population in Central and South America. Nite Wind tours at Placencia Dock organizes responsibly led manatee-watching expeditions.

CARIBBEAN SPLASH

A CORAL ISLAND, SHADED BY COCONUT PALMS and fringed with beaches of virgin white sands; exotic thatched-roof cabins from where you can enjoy a stunning sunset as you feast on succulent barbecued fish you may have had a hand in catching; a day spent honing your snorkeling or scuba-diving skills, testing your mettle in a sea kayak, learning the art of fly-fishing, or trying your hand at windsurfing or kite boarding. These are some of the pleasures awaiting you on Glover's Reef, a World Heritage-protected, marine atoll some 45 miles (72 km) from mainland Belize. Glover's forms part of the world's second longest barrier reef, one of the most biologically diverse habitats on earth. Diving and snorkeling enthusiasts never cease to be amazed by the seemingly inexhaustible range of pinnacles, sinkholes, and swim-throughs, the variety of hard and soft corals, and the innumerable species of marine life, from nurse sharks, barracudas, and moray eels to multicolored reef fish. Placencia, the nearest resort

Left (left to right): Shaded palm-tree oasis on South Water Cay Beach; canoe trip down the Rio Grande's green banks; tourists exploring underwater caves in the forest; visitors on the Stann Creek forest trail in the Jaguar Reserve

Inset: Atlantic nurse shark with attendant parasitic remora

JAN

FEB

MAR

APR

DAY 1

DAY 2

DAY 3

DAY 4

DAYS 5–8

MAY

JUN

JUL

AUG

SEP

OCT

NOV

DEC

ATOLL DIARY

With ideal weather and good diving conditions, April is the best time to visit Belize, especially if you're counting on seeing whale sharks. Placencia is within reach of scenic inland vistas and although it is a busy time of year, you wouldn't know it on Glover's Reef, where peace and quiet is guaranteed.

Eight Days of Aquatic Action

From Placencia, take a boat excursion to Laughing Bird Caye and enjoy reef diving, or snorkel if you prefer. On the way back, take to the waves again, this time to swim with bottle-nosed dolphins.

In the morning, join a whale-shark expedition to Gladden Spit Marine Reserve. Spend the rest of the day sea kayaking on Placencia Lagoon, looking out for manatees and unusual bird species.

Belize has more to offer than just beaches and marine life, so sign up for an excursion to the mainland. Cockscomb Basin Wildlife Sanctuary and Jaguar Reserve enjoys a superb setting in the rain forest beneath the rugged Maya Mountains. The action-packed trip includes tubing, waterfall swimming, and a hike into the forest to see tapirs, howler monkeys, bush dogs, and armadillos.

Travel by boat from Placencia to Glover's Reef and check in at Long Caye Adventure Lodge or Atoll Island Lodge. Spend the rest of the day soaking up the fabulous surroundings.

Enjoy four days of exhilarating water-based activities. Whatever your level of experience, make the most of what's on offer by trying out as many different sports as possible. Glover's Reef has some of the best sea kayaking in the world and there will be opportunities to visit famous dive sites, including the Blue Hole (see pp106–7). You will also learn about the reef's unique ecosystem and become familiar with the local flora and fauna.

Dos and Don'ts

✓ Visit the Placencia Tourism Center for local information.

✗ Don't forget to check the baggage allowance for domestic flights and pack accordingly.

✓ Keep US$40 handy to pay departure tax.

✗ Don't join a dive-boat tour that returns to port after 5pm, when snappers spawn – this is when whale sharks feed.

✓ Bring binoculars for manatee- and bird-watching expeditions.

✗ Don't forget to book accommodation well in advance.

Below: Sea kayakers on the barrier reef

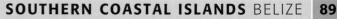

to the reef, lies about 45 minutes away by boat and is an easygoing yet active fishing village with lots to offer adventure-seekers. Rent a canoe and comb the lagoon for sightings of the elusive manatee, which feeds on the grass beds, or train your binoculars on the white egrets, boobies, and pelicans that nest in the contorted white branches of mangrove trees.

Other activities include island hopping on a 14-ft (4-m) ketch or swimming with bottle-nosed dolphins along the route taken centuries ago by pirates searching for Spanish gold. For the experience of a lifetime head out to Gladden Spit Marine Reserve for an encounter with a whale shark. Up to 60 ft (18 m) long and weighing around 12 tons, these behemoths of the deep are attracted to Belize's coastal waters by the billions of eggs released into the sea by the hordes of snapper that come here to spawn. The best time to see them is three or four days before and after the full and new moons. Marine explorer Jacques Cousteau saw whale sharks only twice in his lifetime, but you may get lucky, going by record sightings in recent years – even if you don't, one thing's for certain – by the end of your trip, you'll feel closer to nature than ever before.

Above: *Moai* statue, carved out of volcanic rock

GETTING THERE   See map p331, A8
Easter Island, one of the most isolated places on earth, lies 2,400 miles (3,800 km) west of the Chilean mainland. Cruise lines do call at the island, but Chilean airline LAN offers the only scheduled flights, via Santiago or Tahiti.

GETTING AROUND
Rent a four-wheel-drive car or mountain bike, get a taxi, or ride horses like the locals. Some walking is required to reach many *moai* sites.

WEATHER
Average temperatures vary from 65 to 76°F (18 to 24°C). April has about 15 rainy days.

ACCOMMODATIONS
Hotel O'tai is conveniently located on a main street in Hanga Roa, near shops and bars, with doubles from US$124; www.hotelotai.com

Hotel Taha Tai, a 10-minute walk from central Hanga Roa, has spacious if somewhat plain doubles from US$135; www.hotel-tahatai.co.cl

Posada de Mike Rapu offers chic oceanfront luxury, 4 miles (6 km) from Hanga Roa; from US$598 (with meals, bar, transfers, and tours); www.explora.com/rapa-nui_thehotel.php

EATING OUT
Jardin del Mau (US$20) serves decent seafood and pasta. La Taverne du Pêcheur (US$50) offers French-influenced fare, while Te Moana (US$15) has everything from burgers to curries.

PRICE FOR TWO
US$300 per day, including accommodation, food, transportation, and admission charges.

FURTHER INFORMATION
www.visitchile.org

SILENT GIANTS

Ask your friends what they know about Easter Island, and they will almost certainly mention the huge, brooding statues known as *moai*. Almost 900 *moai* pepper this unlikely outpost of civilization, a small chunk of volcanic rock in the South Pacific some 1,250 miles (2,000 km) from Pitcairn Island, the nearest inhabited place. Why did the native inhabitants, the Rapanui, carve these *moai*? How did they move them from the quarry, high on the slopes of an extinct volcano, to locations miles away? And why were all the *moai* toppled? Definite answers are few, but a number of experts believe the statues represented the ancestors of the island's clans, and that clans pulled down each other's *moai* during a 17th-century war for control of the island's diminishing resources (all the *moai* now standing have been re-erected in modern times). There is less agreement about how the Rapanui moved these huge statues – the largest one that was transported weighs 82 tons – across the island. Sleds, log rollers, and other mechanisms have all been suggested, but no one knows for sure.

The mystery just adds to the allure of this utterly idiosyncratic place. Until its airport opened in 1967, Easter Island was extremely difficult to reach. Even now, it's a five-and-a-half-hour flight from Santiago, Chile. As a result, it's one of the few places on earth where you can almost completely escape the background noise of modern global culture. There are no chain stores or traffic lights; neither are there any malls, condos, cell phones, or billboards. Locals on horseback trot down dirt streets in Hanga Roa, the only town on the island. Shopkeepers and bartenders have time to chat, and no one cares about the latest Hollywood scandal. At night, the sky is spangled with impossibly bright stars – after all, Hanga Roa creates only the faintest amount of light pollution.

Many people dream of visiting Easter Island, but only about 40,000 arrive annually. Since April falls between high and low seasons, you may find yourself contemplating a *moai*, gazing across an ancient crater, or strolling along a beach without another human being in sight. As crying seabirds and the ceaseless wind create the only sounds, and salt-scented air fills your lungs, you may truly feel you've arrived at the end of the world.

Main: *Moai* on Anakena Beach, sporting red scoria topknots
Below (left and right): Traditional dancers showcasing Polynesian culture; horseback riders at Ahu Tahai near Hanga Roa

Where is Everyone?

The indigenous Rapanui once lived all over Easter Island, but civil warfare and lack of resources had devastated the population by the 18th century. Another blow came in 1862, when slave raiders captured 1,000 Rapanui. Only 15 returned, bringing smallpox with them. By the 1870s, just over 100 Rapanui were left. Foreigners later forcibly moved them to Hanga Roa and ran the rest of the island as a sheep farm, until Chile ended the lease in 1953. Most lands outside town are now national parks, but some have been returned to the Rapanui.

ISLAND DIARY

April is a great time to visit Easter Island – the summer crowds of January and February are gone, but the winter chill hasn't set in yet. Surfers, hikers, and scuba divers might enjoy a longer stay, but for most visitors three days are sufficient to see the *moai* and get a taste of the island's unique Polynesian culture.

Three Days in Mid-Ocean

Visit the Father Sebastián Englert Anthropological Museum to learn about the island's history. Explanatory panels are in Spanish, so buy an English guidebook in the museum boutique. Return to town for a casual seafood lunch, then spend the afternoon browsing through small souvenir shops, the colorful artisans' market, and the outdoor municipal market. As dusk approaches, head to Ahu Tahai, near the museum. Bring your camera and tripod to capture the seven *moai* silhouetted against the spectacular sunset.

Since the island's archeological sites can be hard to find and few have interpretive panels, sign up for an all-day guided tour (English-speaking guides are plentiful and lunch is usually included). Make sure the tour features the Rano Raraku quarry, where *moai* in various states of completion stud the hillsides like lost soldiers from a different planet. Other popular stops include Rano Kau (a volcanic crater lake), the Orongo village archeological site, and the 15 *moai* at Ahu Tongariki. Finish the day with the touristy, yet immensely enjoyable, Polynesian dance and music show at the Hanga Roa Hotel.

Sporty types can book a horseback tour, indulge in some heart-thumping mountain biking along the hilly south coast, tackle the hiking trail from the museum to Orongo village, surf challenging waves, or scuba dive in the crystal-clear (if somewhat fish-free) waters. If all that sounds exhausting, simply pack a picnic and head to Anakena Beach for a relaxing afternoon.

Dos and Don'ts

☑ Bring lots of cash, in Chilean *pesos* or US dollars. Many businesses don't accept credit cards, or charge a premium if they do.

☒ Don't step on *ahus*, the stone bases supporting the *moai*. The Rapanui consider it sacrilegious to walk on or near them.

☑ Wear lots of sunblock since constant breezes make it easy to forget how powerful the sun is.

☒ Don't forget to bring an umbrella and jacket, in case of rain.

☑ Book rooms well in advance, as hotels often sell out.

MAY

JUN

JUL

AUG

SEP

OCT

NOV

DEC

Below: View from Orongo village along the eastern rim of Rano Kau

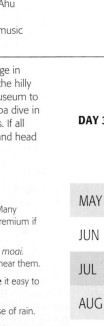

GETTING THERE　　　See map p317, G1
Fly into Roanoke Regional Airport in Virginia and fly out from McGhee Tyson International Airport in Knoxville, Tennessee.

GETTING AROUND
Rent a car that is comfortable to drive for long stretches and on mountain curves. The parkway speed limit is 45 mph (72kph).

WEATHER
Late April is warm in the lower slopes, but can sometimes reach near freezing at high altitudes. Be ready for all kinds of weather.

ACCOMMODATIONS
The Inn at Ragged Gardens in Blowing Rock has rooms with baths and fireplaces from US$170; www.ragged-gardens.com

The luxurious Inn on Biltmore Estate is near the Biltmore Estate Winery; doubles start at US$290 and two-night packages include admission to the Estate; www.biltmore.com

The rustic Fryemont Inn overlooking Bryson City and Great Smoky Mountains National Park offers double rooms from US$133; www.fryemontinn.com

EATING OUT
Try eclectic Metro! in downtown Roanoke (US$19). Blowing Rock's Speckled Trout & Oyster Bar serves fresh local trout and seafood (US$15), while Café on the Square (US$18) in Asheville has an outdoor patio.

PRICE FOR TWO
US$445 per day including accommodation, food, local travel, and admission charges.

FURTHER INFORMATION
www.blueridgeparkway.org

RIDING THE RIDGE

TRACING A SERPENTINE PATH FOR 469 miles (755 km), the Blue Ridge Parkway is one of America's most celebrated scenic highways. Built purely for the pleasure of driving, the road features gentle curves and frequent overlooks presenting views of sensually rounded, blue-misted hills. Hawks glide above, while historic farmlands lie nestled in forested valleys below. In April, the mountains explode in a palette of pinks, reds, and violets as wild rhododendron and mountain laurel bloom, lining the parkway with brilliant hues for miles. The woodlands wear a thousand shades of newborn green, while the delicate blooms of dogwood, redbud, iris, and trillium color the landscape.

Main: Scenic vista of misty hills from the Blue Ridge Parkway

A National Park itself, the parkway connects two others, beginning in Virginia's Shenandoah National Park and ending at the Great Smoky Mountains National Park. There are numerous

The Missing Link

All but 7 miles (11 km) of the 469-mile (755-km) long Blue Ridge Parkway were built between 1935 and 1967, but the remaining section took another 20 years. The engineering challenge of building an environmentally sensitive road at an elevation of 4,100 ft (1,250 m) around one of the region's oldest mountains resulted in the graceful sweep of the Linn Cove Viaduct. Assembled on site, the 1,243-ft (379-m) long viaduct was built in 153 segments, each weighing 50 tons.

Left (left to right): Peaceful Mabry Watermill; bright azaleas lining the parkway in spring

Right (left to right): Great Smoky Mountain Railroad; south façade of the magnificent Biltmore mansion

attractions along the way, such as Mabry Watermill, with its lovely millpond, or the elegant mansion of 19th-century denim millionaire, Moses H. Cone, which he willed to the Park Service for all to enjoy. Groomed carriage roads offer amazing views as they wind past mountain lakes and meadows. You'll want to explore the famed Folk Art Center, which showcases fine quilts, pottery, carvings, and crafts from the distinguished artisans of the Southern Highland Craft Guild.

Nestled in the mountains along the parkway, the artistic town of Asheville, renowned for its colorful residents, creative lifestyle, and galleries, deserves a longer stay. George Washington Vanderbilt built his famed Biltmore Estate here in 1895, with grounds by noted landscape architect Frederick Law Olmsted. Today it is one of the most visited historic sites in the USA.

The parkway ends at the Great Smoky Mountains National Park, 45 miles (72 km) from Knoxville, famed for its misty mountain vistas and for Cades Cove, with its hand-hewn farms.

OPEN-ROAD DIARY

The Blue Ridge Parkway is lightly traveled at this time of year, and while some of the smaller visitor facilities may be closed, the long stretches of open road without traffic are fun to drive on, as well as offering stunning scenic views and outstanding roadside beauty.

Seven Days on the Road

DAY 1
Enter the parkway at Roanoke and head south, stopping at Mabry Mill. Exit at Blowing Rock, where winds blow from the river gorge 3,000 ft (915 m) below. Explore the town, dine, and stay the night.

DAY 2
Visit the Moses H. Cone Memorial Park. Marvel at Linn Cove Viaduct, and walk to pretty Linville Falls. Lunch at Little Switzerland before exploring the wild area near Craggy Gardens. Do stop at the Folk Art Center for locally produced crafts before exiting at Asheville.

DAY 3
Take a break from driving and spend the day exploring Asheville. Visit the Biltmore Estate and tour the mansion, gardens, and winery, and enjoy the shops and restaurants in Historic Biltmore Village. Downtown offers the Thomas Wolfe Memorial State Historic Site, Grove Arcade, walking tours, and galleries.

DAYS 4–5
Back on the parkway, continue to the Pisgah Inn and, for a great view, hike to the ridge top where the Vanderbilt Hunting Lodge once stood. The Devil's Courthouse Trail also leads to grand vistas or you can take the self-guided nature trail at the parkway's highest point of 6,047 ft (1,843 m).

When the parkway ends, head into Cherokee to see the Museum of the Cherokee Indian and the native Qualla Arts and Crafts Shop. Then drive to Bryson City for the Great Smoky Mountain Railroad Depot.

DAYS 6–7
Spend a day or two in the Great Smoky Mountains National Park, and take an auto tour, or explore the great outdoors on horseback. Highlights include Cades Cove Loop, with its fascinating pioneer history.

Dos and Don'ts

- ✓ Consider extending the trip, starting at the north end of Shenandoah National Park.
- ✗ Don't exceed the speed limit (45mph/72 kph) and adjust your speed to suit the conditions on the parkway.
- ✗ Don't hesitate to stop and explore whenever you spot something interesting along the way.
- ✓ Travel on the US 52 highway to Andy Griffiths' hometown, Mount Airy, the inspiration for his classic 1960s comedy.

Below: Carefully preserved mansion in the Moses H. Cone Memorial Park

JAN
FEB
MAR
APR
MAY
JUN
JUL
AUG
SEP
OCT
NOV
DEC

GETTING THERE   See map p325, H4

Saba Island is situated 25 miles (40 km) from St. Maarten. Several major airlines fly to St. Maarten to connect with Winair, which operates at least five flights a day to the island's only airport – Juancho E. Yrausquin.

GETTING AROUND

Saba covers just 5 sq miles (12 sq km). Most people hike; "The Road" is just 10 miles (16 km) long, but car rental is also available.

WEATHER

Daytime temperatures in April average 84°F (29°C), cooling to around 79°F (26°C) overnight. While there may be the odd afternoon shower, rain is more likely at night.

ACCOMMODATIONS

Ecolodge Rendez-Vous in Windwardside offers solar-powered cottages; doubles at US$65–85; www.ecolodge-saba.com

Windwardside's Cottage Club has doubles from US$105 a night; www.cottage-club.com

On a mountain ridge near Hell's Gate, The Gate House offers superb views; doubles from US$125; www.sabagatehouse.com

EATING OUT

The Gate House Café offers French and Creole cuisine at US$40–45 per head.

Be sure to try the Red-Curry-Coconut Shrimp at Rainforest Restaurant (US$30 per head).

PRICE FOR TWO

US$390 per day, including accommodation, food, taxi fares, and diving excursions.

FURTHER INFORMATION

www.sabatourism.com

The Impossible Road

The dusty, shabby appearance of Saba's only road belies its fascinating origins. At the beginning of the 20th century, the islanders decided to build a road running through Saba's four villages – Hell's Gate, Windwardside, St. John's, and The Bottom – but authorities insisted that its construction would be impossible, thanks to the island's steep and rugged terrain. Tenacious local Josephus Lambert Hassell learned engineering through a mail-order course, and in 1938, rallied some islanders and began work on the road. Five years later, it was completed.

Above (left and right): Taking the plunge into the depths of Saba Island's waters; longsnout sea horse brightening up the sea bed
Main: Diver exploring the colorful coral life in the clear waters off Saba, one of the best dive locations in the world

CARIBBEAN ADVENTURE

MOUNT SCENERY, A MAGNIFICENT VOLCANO that last erupted 5,000 years ago, stands over the Caribbean island of Saba like a giant sentinel, watching over the untouched, forest-clad mountains, quaint villages, and pristine turquoise waters of the sun-drenched paradise below. Here, dramatic terrain, untamed beauty, and abundant wildlife coax you out of doors and into the very heart of a dazzlingly picturesque and idyllic land.

If you're a nature enthusiast, bird watcher, diver, or climber, Saba Island is the place to be. Luxurious swathes of rain forest thrive in the island's fertile soils, a legacy of the rivers of lava that once flowed from its volcano. A hike through this dense vegetation from the village of Windwardside and up the steep incline to Mount Scenery is a grueling 90-minute climb, but the rewards are spectacular. You'll come across weird and wonderful tropical plants, mahogany trees, mosses, and bromeliads, as well as vividly colored butterflies and countless birds – Saba is a refuge for 87 different species and is home to the Caribbean's largest population of red-billed tropic birds.

Saba's volcanic heritage also shaped its underwater landscape. The steep sides of the volcano that formed Saba's mountainous interior extend beneath the sea's calm surface, plummeting to depths of 1,000 ft (305 m). As you descend into the waters, a mystical world opens up before your eyes – shimmering fish and graceful reef sharks dance around coral gardens, through channels carved out millions of years ago by fuming streams of lava.

Although hiking and diving are popular activities, there are other ways to enjoy the great outdoors. Boulder- and rock-climbing opportunities are plentiful, historic ruins dot the island, and charming villages uphold traditional ways of life. So leave your worries behind and enjoy the Saba experience.

> As you descend a mystical world opens up before your eyes – shimmering fish and graceful reef sharks dance around coral gardens.

Inset: The color-changing coney fish in its red phase
Below (left to right): Clean and green Saba – a haven for nature lovers; The Bottom, one of Saba's four delightful villages

WATERWORLD DIARY

The tiny island of Saba had no airport until 1963 and no pier until 1972, so few travelers visited the island. Those who did, found an unspoiled paradise. While Saba now boasts modern facilities, little else has changed. As such, it's ideal for nature and activity enthusiasts, especially in April, when the weather is delightful.

Five Days in a Diver's Paradise

DAY 1
Familiarize yourself with the island and its four quaint villages – Hell's Gate, Windwardside, St. John's, and The Bottom – which is where all the evening action takes place. Take a walk to one of the villages and then stroll back along the road to enjoy the views.

DAY 2
Go for an early-morning dive to explore spectacular underwater lava tunnels and reefs. Prepare yourself for a shark encounter if you're planning to dive off Shark Shoals. Then, take a long walk into the forests with a guide. Guides are not compulsory on some walks, but it is worth hiring one for at least one hike, because you are likely to get much more out of it.

DAY 3
Devote your entire day to diving. Begin with another morning dive at Tedran Reef, a steep coral-encrusted wall popular with barracuda. Then rest, sunbathe, or swim before experiencing an unforgettable nocturnal dive at Tent Reef, one of the most sought-after diving spots in Saba.

DAY 4
After all that diving, take some time out to relax or sleep. Then explore the shops in the villages – be sure to buy some famous Saba lace, painstakingly created by the women of Saba, using unique needlecraft techniques. In the afternoon, snorkel in the shallower waters of Torrens Point, popularly known as Saba's "nursery."

DAY 5
Refrain from any more diving if you are flying out the next day. Instead, try your hand at something different but as exciting – Saba offers some of the finest rock climbing with degrees of difficulty to suit everyone.

Dos and Don'ts

- ✗ Don't forget to bring your dive certification.
- ✓ Scale the 800 steps carved into the stone from Ladder Bay to The Bottom. Until the late 20th century, nearly everything landing on Saba had to be carried up these steps.
- ✗ Don't forget to bring suitable footwear and binoculars if you are interested in hiking and birding.
- ✓ Sample the island's lobsters at a village restaurant.

JAN
FEB
MAR
APR
MAY
JUN
JUL
AUG
SEP
OCT
NOV
DEC

Below: Luxurious holiday resort on Saba

Take the less-traveled route and ride horseback along isolated beaches, across sand dunes and through palm groves.

GETTING THERE
See map p330, E9
Carrasco International Airport is 9 miles (14 km) east of Montevideo center. From Buenos Aires, a ferry service operates across the River Plate to the Montevideo docks (US$65–75).

GETTING AROUND
Reliable bus services run in Montevideo and throughout Uruguay. Taxis are plentiful and affordable. Car rental is available at the airport and in town (from US$50 per day).

WEATHER
Temperatures range from a nighttime low of 52°F (11°C) to 75°F (24°C) during the day.

ACCOMMODATIONS
In the heart of Montevideo's old center is the Edwardian-style Hotel Plaza Fuerte; doubles from US$65; www.plazafuerte.com.uy

In Punta del Este, Hotel Remanso is near the beach but has a rooftop pool too; doubles from US$85; www.hotelremanso.com.uy

Estancia La Sirena Marinas del Rio Negro at Mercedes is a charming, historic working ranch; doubles from US$200 inclusive of full board and activities; www.lasirena.com.uy

EATING OUT
People eat late and eat meat – lots of it – usually in *parrilladas* (grill rooms). *Asado* (barbecue) is a favorite. Non-meat options include *tortilla española* (Spanish omelet). You can eat well for under US$10.

PRICE FOR TWO
US$200 per day including accommodation, food, taxis, car hire and gas, and activities.

FURTHER INFORMATION
www.visit-uruguay.com

Home on the Range
Uruguay has beautiful beaches and a cosmopolitan capital, but it also has a booming "*estancia* tourism" market. There's nothing to compare with riding herd on a range that's the size of a small state. The *gauchos* here are all but born in the saddle, and are considered among the finest horsemen in the world. Several of these working ranches date from the early 19th century and are magnificent inside and out. Many welcome visitors, whether or not you're handy with a lasso.

Inset: Landmark Palcio Sa building in Montevideo's historic central plaza

Left (left to right): Color del Sacramento lighthouse; dramatic "fingers" sculpture on Punta del Este beach; sunset over Punta del Este

Right (left to right): *Gauchos* rounding up wild horses; ruined mission of Calera de las Huérfanas

Main: Uruguay's beautiful native *criollo* horses

PLAYAS AND PAMPAS

Uruguay, AT ROUGHLY THE SIZE OF OKLAHOMA, may be small by South American standards, but its manageable size is what endears it to so many travelers. You can do it all here. Where else can you wake up on a sprawling *estancia* (ranch) straight out of a Western movie set and still make it to the glittering sands of some of the world's most popular beaches that same afternoon? Or have breakfast near the silent ruins of a former Jesuit mission and dinner in the cosmopolitan whirl of the capital? Take the less-traveled route and ride horseback along isolated beaches, across sand dunes, and through palm groves. Drive the coast roads, stopping to revel in the sun and surf, and sign on at a working ranch where you'll be able to ride with the *gauchos* (cowboys) and even help with cattle drives. The country's beautiful *playas* (beaches) hardly need an introduction: names like Piriápolis, La Barra, La Paloma, and, above all, Punta del Este are famous for their heady combination of beautiful views, weather, and people.

GAUCHO DIARY

April is fall in Uruguay, but you won't need more than a light jacket for the evenings. It can be humid inland, but ocean breezes keep things very pleasant on the coast. This is the perfect time to visit: the high season has ended and even the beaches are less busy. Five days will give you time to appreciate Uruguay's many facets.

Five Days of Discoveries

Check into your hotel in Montevideo and spend some time in the fascinating Old City. The portside market, pedestrianized Calle Sarandí, and the grand Teatro Solís are must-sees within easy reach of each other.

DAY 1

Head out early to Punta del Este, 83 miles (130 km) east along the scenic coastal road. It's quieter at this time of year, but there's still plenty to do, from hang gliding and horseback riding to tennis and golf, all with ocean views. Take a tour on the *Muriel*, a century-old yacht. Later on, you can explore the town's museums and shops and, later still, its many nightclubs and cafés.

DAY 2

Continue east to La Barra and La Paloma to revel in the seaside solitude, or head back towards Montevideo and then west to your *estancia*. Pause at Nueva Helvecia, Colonia del Sacramento, Conchillas, and Calera de las Huérfanas, arriving at Mercedes before nightfall.

DAY 3

Spend the day with the *gauchos*, or you could birdwatch, fish, swim, or water-ski. It's worth a visit to Mercedes, "the city of flowers," and the nearby historic settlements of Fray Bentos (where you can cross into Argentina) and Soriano. A meal cooked *parrillada*-style, under the stars back at the ranch, is the perfect end to your day.

DAY 4

Take the inland route back to Montevideo. Stop along the way in the picturesque towns of Palmitas and Cardona. You'll be back in time for an evening stroll along the riverside *ramblas* (boulevards) and a show at the planetarium before dinner in the Pocitos district.

DAY 5

Dos and Don'ts

✓ Rent a car for trips out of Montevideo. In the city, buses or taxis are fine, but you'll need your own transport for travel along the coast and to the *estancia*.

✗ Don't be surprised if you are charged for bread in restaurants. It's the norm here, as is having at least one beef dish at every meal.

✓ Remember that three currencies circulate freely: the *peso uruguayo*, *peso argentino*, and the US dollar. Brazilian *reais* are not widely accepted.

✗ Don't expect to cross freely into Argentina. You need to show your passport before you can purchase a ferry ticket.

JAN

FEB

MAR

APR

MAY

JUN

JUL

AUG

SEP

OCT

NOV

DEC

Below: Fishing boats on Montevideo's waterfront

If you're more inclined to watch the waves than the people, there are also dozens of lesser-known places towards the frontier with Brazil, ideally suited to a get-away-from-it-all vacation. You'll find plenty of empty sands, and a piece of seaside paradise to claim as your own.

When you're ready to trade in your beach sandals and sunscreen for boots and a cowboy hat, the famous *estancias* to the west will be happy to take you in – and to put you to work riding herd, if you're willing. Along the way are abandoned Jesuit missions such as Calera de las Huérfanas, and Portuguese fortresses like the delightful Colonia del Sacramento, a UNESCO World Heritage Site. Conchillas is a former British mining town while Nueva Helvecia was a Swiss settlement that is now best-known for its cheese. Half-hidden in the hazy distance of the green *pampas* are the great ranches, some the size of small countries.

As well as basking on the beach and taking to the trail, be prepared to succumb to the charms of the capital itself, lovely Montevideo, a little gem of a city nestled between the two contrasting sides of one of South America's most fascinating destinations.

GETTING THERE
See map p318, H4

Lafayette is in Southern Louisiana, 35 miles (56 km) from the Gulf of Mexico, 50 miles (80 km) west of Baton Rouge, and 129 miles (208 km) west of New Orleans. Fly into either one of the three destinations and rent a car.

GETTING AROUND

Lafayette has a free shuttle service from the festival parking area into downtown. You'll need to rent a car or taxi to visit nearby attractions.

WEATHER

April is warm and humid, with an average daytime temperature of 80°F (27°C).

ACCOMMODATIONS

Holiday Inn Lafayette-Central is a recently renovated hotel with doubles from US$95; www.holidayinn.com

Conveniently located, Hilton Lafayette & Towers offers doubles from US$150; www.hilton.com

The Juliet Boutique Hotel offers elegance in a historic downtown Lafayette building; doubles from US$240; www.juliethotel.com

EATING OUT

Cajun and Creole cuisine is spicy; seafood and sausage dishes often feature a rich, dark roux sauce, while okra, sweet potatoes, squashes, beans, corn, or rice are part of most meals. Many restaurants serve well-priced food at special festival stands.

PRICE FOR A FAMILY OF FOUR

US$380 per day including accommodation, food, local travel, car rental, and boat tour.

FURTHER INFORMATION

www.lafayettetravel.com
www.festivalinternational.com

Acadian Heritage

The French-speaking Catholics of Acadie (Nova Scotia, Canada) were expelled in 1755, a story later popularized in the epic poem, *Evangeline* (1847). Eventually, the Acadians came to Louisiana, settling around the town now called Lafayette. The skilled farmers blended hard work, thrift, and religion with a love for music, dance, and humor. Over time, they came to be called Cajuns. Today, Cajun culture is infused with elements of Caribbean, African, Creole, Hispanic, and Native American customs.

Main: Musicians at the festival
Above (top to bottom): John Magnie of The Subdues entertaining crowds with the accordion; amusing antics of costumed paraders

BAYOU RHYTHMS

DANCE, DANCE, DANCE! IT DOESN'T MATTER IF YOU DON'T KNOW THE STEPS, just grab a partner and move your body to the heart-pounding, foot-stomping, and soul-satisfying music that fills the streets of Lafayette for five whole days every April. It's a time when the streets come alive with a montage of performers and everyone dances with everyone – young with old, rich with poor, and neighbors with neighbors. Savor the rhythms of Cajun waltzes, zydeco bands, and Creole fiddling and give in to the emotions evoked by Canadian folk songs and heart-wrenching Acadian tales of lost love and homeless wanderers.

With performers from every corner of the French-speaking world, Festival International de Louisiane is a celebration of *joie de vivre*. Bop to the beat of African drums, listen to Caribbean chants, laugh at Parisian cabaret, and join in the fun with street performers – simply surrender to the festive fervor. With six sound stages,

Above (top to bottom): Hard at work on the zydeco rubboard; crowds at a daytime performance

Below: Boiled crawfish – a local delicacy

FESTIVE CAJUN DIARY

Warm days, cool evenings, and colorful blooms in late April set the stage for the five-day Festival International de Louisiane. The open-air extravaganza of French-influenced music, dance, and art draws performers from all over the world. The streets are filled with performers and spontaneous good times.

Five Days of Music and Dance

Head out to the Acadian Cultural Center and stop at the Vermilionville Heritage and Folklife Park for a boat tour on Bayou Vermilion.

Attend the festival's opening party at Blue Moon Saloon and dance the night away.

DAY 1

Visit the Dutch Romanesque St. John Cathedral in downtown Lafayette and view the museum's collection of 18th-century Baroque Neapolitan crèches, with authentically dressed miniature characters.

Join the fun at the opening ceremonies and visit the Festival Artwalk.

DAY 2

Drive out to Rookery Road at Lake Martin for a look at Louisiana's nesting aquatic birds, including great blue herons, snowy egrets, and roseate spoonbills.

Eat fried catfish topped with seafood *étouffée* and sweet beignets for lunch before taking in the afternoon's performances – you need to keep your energy levels up.

DAY 3

Start your day at Café Des Amis in Breaux Bridge with a zydeco breakfast, featuring live Creole folk music.

Dance from afternoon to evening and enjoy street performances as you stroll from one stage to another.

DAY 4

Attend the outdoor French Mass at the Community Coffee Scène Héritage on Sunday morning. Then, dance to the varied music at the Official Festival's International Jam at Grant Street Dancehall.

DAY 5

Dos and Don'ts

☑ Wear comfortable shoes, casual clothing, and carry your cash and credit cards safely so you can dance with abandon.

☒ Don't just stand there, dance – even if you're not familiar with the steps.

☑ Eat at the festival; it's a great way to sample many of the local restaurants' best dishes at reasonable prices. Head to food stands well ahead of meal times to minimize your waiting time.

☑ Make hotel reservations well ahead of time, especially if you want to stay within walking distance of the festival.

JAN
FEB
MAR
APR
MAY
JUN
JUL
AUG
SEP
OCT
NOV
DEC

designated dance floors, and spontaneous street dancing, you'll work up a mammoth appetite in no time. And to top it off, there's the heady world of Cajun cuisine. Savory scents of local fare seasoned with Tabasco sauce and cayenne peppers fill the warm spring air. Shrimp jambalaya, crawfish *étouffée*, Cajun sausage, and spicy rice and beans are but a few of the dishes that blend French class with Caribbean sass. For dessert, sample flaky French pastries, rich beignets rolled in powdered sugar, and Louisiana bread pudding that simply melts in the mouth.

The festival also serves up a generous helping of the arts, from colorful Cajun- and Creole-inspired artworks and cinema, theater, and dance acts to fun-filled activities for children. When your feet refuse to dance any more and you're filled up with good food and wine, explore beyond Lafayette's festive streets. Escape to the countryside, where the rivers and marshes teem with a dazzling array of water birds. Take a boat trip on the bayou at Vermilionville for a glimpse of Cajun history and visit the Cultural Center to learn more about Cajun culture. Then, follow the irresistible rhythmic beat of the music back to the festival and dance the night away.

Below: Dancers bringing alive the wild and passionate mood of the festival

MAY

Where to Go: May

Summer is just around the corner in North America – even chilly Canadians and Americans from Alaska can get out and enjoy the sunshine. Mountain regions are less snowy and more accessible for non-skiiers, though things get dramatically colder at higher elevations. The Southern states are abundant with magnolia, but sunshine and bright skies are tempered by the odd rainstorm.

It's not quite hot enough to swim in the Atlantic, but beach holidays are possible. Central America is heading into its wet season and the Caribbean islands are facing a thunderstorm or two. May is a good time to head for the Amazon which is a little less wet than earlier in the year. Below, you will find all the destinations in this chapter, and some extra suggestions to provide a little inspiration.

FESTIVALS AND CULTURE

MEMPHIS Musician playing on Beale Street

UNFORGETTABLE JOURNEYS

AMAZON RIVER Canoeists paddling upriver

NATURAL WONDERS

AMBERGRIS CAYE Blue-crowned motmots eating their prey

MEMPHIS
TENNESSEE, USA

Sing the blues at the Memphis in May festival

This sleepy Southern city comes alive in May, with a month-long festival of blues, soul, roots, and jazz music, and a sizzling barbeque-cooking contest.
See pp104–5

ST. LOUIS
MISSOURI, USA

One of the South's most cultured cities

St. Louis has many cultural attractions, including the superb St. Louis Art Museum, and the historic towns of Ste. Genevieve and St. Charles are nearby.
www.explorestlouis.com

AMAZON RIVER
BRAZIL

The water teems with wildlife in the world's largest river

Take a slow cruise within Brazil's interior and float lazily in the Amazon, see pink river dolphins, and listen to opera in the jungle.
See pp114–15

TREKKING IN THE SIERRA MAESTRA
CUBA

Cuba's loftiest mountain range

Trek through cloudforests to Pico Turquino, the island's highest mountain at the heart of the rugged Sierra Maestra.
www.dtcuba.com

"Stretching as far as the eye can see is a scattering of tree-shrouded islands enclosing sapphire lagoons."

AMBERGRIS CAYE
BELIZE

Quiet island paradise with diving sites galore

Belize is still relatively undeveloped, beautiful, and friendly, and the sea life is extraordinary on the world's second-largest coral reef system.
See pp106–7

TORONTO
ONTARIO, CANADA

This lakeside culture capital has something for everyone

From blockbuster musicals to Shakespeare, from modern buildings to Victorian Gothic, and from wine to baseball – Toronto has it all.
See pp118–19

"It's easy to while away a vacation in Toronto, feasting on paella, grooving to Peruvian folk music, and watching a festival parade."

WHITEWATER RAFTING IN COSTA RICA
CENTRAL AMERICA

White water and rare wildlife

Costa Rica boasts some of the best rafting in Central America; there's a good chance of spotting crocs, too.
www.infocostarica.com/sports

CRATERS OF THE MOON NATIONAL MONUMENT
IDAHO, USA

Surreal petrified lava

This eerie landscape has vast expanses of solidified lava dotted with cinder cones and craters.
www.nps.gov/crmo

DENVER
COLORADO, USA

Urbane city in the shadow of the Rockies

The region's most cosmopolitan city, Denver has cultural diversions and a surfeit of museums, including the stunning Denver Art Museum.
www.denver.org

CRUISING DOWN THE COLUMBIA RIVER
OREGON, USA

An unforgettable river journey

Take a sternwheeler ride through the spectacular Columbia River Gorge in the footsteps of legendary explorers Lewis and Clark.
www.sternwheeler.com

ANDROMEDA BOTANICAL GARDENS
BARBADOS, CARIBBEAN

The Caribbean's finest gardens

These coastal gardens feature arboreal curiosities, such as a Panama hat tree, a shaving brush tree, and a majestic old bearded fig.
www.barbados.org/androm.htm

MOUNT ST. HELENS
WASHINGTON STATE, USA

Scene of a devastating volcanic eruption in 1980

Its top blown off by the force of the explosion, this volcano is a monument to the natural power of the earth at its most destructive.
www.fs.fed.us/gpnf/mshnvm

ST. LUCIA
CARIBBEAN

The island gets hot and steamy – it's not just the weather

St. Lucia hosts one of the world's best jazz festivals – and when the music is over, there's stunning scenery and fascinating history to discover.
See pp122–3

INSIDE PASSAGE
ALASKA, USA

Take a bracing sea voyage to this remote US state

Cruise the network of fjords that line Alaska's southeastern shore that harbor ice cliffs, misty mountains, and hardy sea mammals.
See pp110–11

YOSEMITE NATIONAL PARK
CALIFORNIA, USA

Mountain spectacle

One of America's most celebrated national parks, enclosing the Yosemite Valley, walled by mile-high cliffs of sheer bare granite.
www.nps.gov/yose

Weather Watch

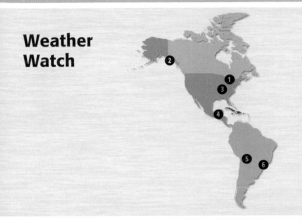

❶ Toronto, Canada May might start off cool, but the snowfall that characterizes the winter months drops dramatically, and by the end of the month it's warm enough to spend a lot of time outside.

❷ Alaska, USA This is the ideal time to get out on the water in this remote state. Long hours of sunlight, warm to hot daytime temperatures, and less rain than later in the year. Nights are very cold, however.

❸ Tennessee, USA The steamy Southern summer is just around the corner. Temperatures hover around 75–78°F (24–26°C) with sunshine and the odd storm.

❹ Belize May in Belize is hot and gets rainier as the month progresses. It is always steamy but is cooled by delicious sea breezes on the coast, and sea visibility is excellent.

❺ Bolivia Winter is approaching in Bolivia. La Paz, the world's highest capital, is dry and warm, with cool evenings. Temperatures are higher at lower altitudes, while the lush rainforest is entering its dry season.

❻ Brazil The Amazon Basin stays hot and chokingly humid year-round, but May is one of the less rainy months. Brazil's east coast is wet, while in the northeast, a very hot, dry period is beginning.

LUXURY AND ROMANCE

NEW YORK CITY View of Manhattan

ACTIVE ADVENTURES

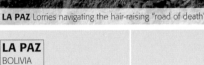

LA PAZ Lorries navigating the hair-raising "road of death"

FAMILY GETAWAYS

CODY Fishing in a lake below the Grand Teton mountain range

NEW YORK CITY
NEW YORK STATE, USA

The perfect long-weekend break for city-lovers

Where better for a romantic holiday than the city that's played backdrop to some of the greatest movie love stories?
See pp116–17

VANCOUVER ISLAND
BRITISH COLUMBIA, CANADA

Wine tasting and whale watching

Explore historic Victoria city, then enjoy a heady blend of wine and fine food, and myriad outdoor activities amid imposing scenery.
www.vancouverisland.travel

LA PAZ
BOLIVIA

A high-altitude holiday that will take your breath away

The world's highest capital is a gateway to action adventures, vibrant cultures, and spectacular Lake Titicaca.
See pp108–9

> "Trail rides, cattle-drives, and roping are all part of the fun, along with flyfishing, canoeing, and campfire singalongs."

CODY
WYOMING, USA

Saddle up for a taste of the cowboy life

Cattle trails and campfire sing-alongs are just part of the fun on a dude ranch set in the spectacular Rocky Mountains.
See pp112–13

SAVANNAH
GEORGIA, USA

Open beaches, flower gardens, grand mansions, and mystery

The pretty city presents a picture-postcard façade while in the background simmers seductive jazz, spicy food, and steamy stories.
See pp120–21

SURFING AT BATHSHEBA
BARBADOS, CARIBBEAN

Top surfing destination

Known as the "soup bowl," Bathsheba receives a steady supply of big Atlantic rollers year-round.
www.barbados.org/bathsheb

BIRDING IN COSTA RICA
CENTRAL AMERICA

Your chance to spot a quetzal

One of the world's top ornithological destinations, Costa Rica is visited by almost 900 species.
www.birdwatchingcostarica.com

LAKESHORE
MINNESOTA, USA

Take time out at an old-fashioned lake-side camp

There's plenty for adults to do including fishing and golf – or just resting. And kids will love being in the great outdoors.
www.lostlake.com

BELIZE
CENTRAL AMERICA

Affordable tropical destination for kids and adults

A great place for adventurous families interested in Mayans, local culture, marine parks, jungle adventures, and shady hammocks.
www.belizenet.com

THE BEACHES, TORONTO
ONTARIO, CANADA

Chic downtown Toronto

A stylish district on the banks of Lake Ontario, awash with beautiful houses, cool bars, trendy shops, and a string of appealing beaches.
www.beachestoronto.com

BAFFIN ISLAND
NUNAVUT, CANADA

Arctic adventures in Canada's far north

Hike and kayak through one of the America's final frontiers: a wintry wonderland of ice floes, northern lights, and polar bears.
www.baffinisland.ca

SEAWORLD, SAN ANTONIO
TEXAS, USA

Amazing marine theme park

The Texas arm of this popular USA theme park chain offers maritime encounters with orcas, dolphins, sharks, and sea lions.
www.seaworld.com

OUTER BANKS
NORTH CAROLINA, USA

Unspoiled barrier islands with wildlife and fabulous beaches

Explore these superb shores and dunes, historic sites, and romantic inns during the early summer before the heat and crowds arrive.
See pp124–5

CHESAPEAKE BAY
MARYLAND, USA

The largest estuary in the USA

The peaceful waters of Chesapeake Bay make for superb marine adventures, including sailing, fishing, and crabbing.
www.baydreaming.com

SANIBEL AND THE CAPTIVA ISLANDS
FLORIDA, USA

Diminutive Florida islands

These small islands boast miles of sandy beaches and outdoor activities, from fishing and birding to boating and snorkeling.
www.sanibel-captiva.org

GETTING THERE See map p317, C2

Flights land at Memphis International Airport, 12 miles (19 km) south of downtown. Greyhound buses and trains stop in downtown. Drivers can approach the city on the I-40 (east–west) or I-55 (north–south).

GETTING AROUND

Downtown Memphis is a pleasure to walk around, with a useful trolley route along the Mississippi. You will need a car or taxi to reach outlying attractions including Graceland.

WEATHER

The steamy Southern summer is approaching, but May is more appealing with an average daily temperature of 75–79ºF (24–26ºC).

ACCOMMODATIONS

The best value downtown is at the Sleep Inn at Court Square, facing the Mississippi; doubles from US$90; www.choicehotels.com

Elvis Presley's Heartbreak Hotel, next to Graceland, is the top choice for Elvis fans; doubles from US$110; www.elvis.com

The Peabody is elegant and historic; doubles from US$200; www.peabodymemphis.com

EATING OUT

The Arcade offers homecooking from US$5 in an iconic diner building, while Four Way Grill near the Stax museum serves hearty soul food. Try the Corky's chain for dry ribs.

PRICE FOR TWO

US$230 per day including accommodation, food, transport, and entrance fees.

FURTHER INFORMATION

www.memphisinmay.org

Graceland

In 1957, 22-year-old Memphis boy Elvis Presley, fresh from recording *Heartbreak Hotel*, spent $100,000 on a stone-clad mansion where he lived for the rest of his life. Graceland is surprisingly small and, despite the shag carpet lining the walls of the Jungle Room, not as tacky as you might expect. Audio tours provide snippets from Elvis's daughter, Lisa Marie, and snatches of his songs. In the garden are the graves of "the King" and his family, along with his airplanes and cars, witty movie montages, and boutiques selling Elvis coffee beans.

SHAKE THE BLUES AWAY

MEMPHIS IS A MAGICAL CITY; UNIQUELY AMERICAN and unlike anywhere else in the world. Set in an evocative spot on the mighty Mississippi River, this is the place that brought us blues, soul, and rock'n'roll, the place that homeboy Elvis Presley could never quite leave, and the place tormented by the memory of Martin Luther King's assassination in 1968. A fairly poor Southern city, built on cotton and relatively untouched by the sanitizing effects of modernization, Memphis has a dreamy appeal. Sitting in faded, red-boothed diners where Elvis once ate, chatting to the chef who served Isaac Hayes his specials, or being measured for a suit by Mr Lansky, the man who kitted out The King himself, you could imagine yourself in a timewarp. But it's not a place preserved in aspic. The Reverend Al Green may still sing sweet soul music at his gospel church, but he's likely to be clutching a skinny cappuccino. Old blues men still

Main: The Blues City Café on Beale Street after dark

Left: The Memphis skyline and boats on the Mississippi River

Right (left to right): Dishing up at the World Championship BBQ cooking contest; Rock'n'Soul Museum sign; street musician Rudy Williams blowing his trumpet on Beale Street

Right panel (top to bottom): Elvis snow globes at Graceland; the Stax Museum of American Soul Music

play urban juke joints unchanged for 50 years, but their audience is joined today by pierced punk girls selecting Carl Perkins and Otis Redding on the jukebox.

The city's seductive mix of retro charm, edgy hip, and sleepy Southern eccentricity is rolled into one during the Memphis in May festival, which is held over the course of the month. The festivities kick off with the Beale Street Music Festival on the riverfront, with stages hosting acts as different as Bobby "Blue" Bland and Gov't Mule. Lovers of blues, soul, and southern roots music rub shoulders, clink beer cans, and dance until their feet are sore. Mid-month, the World Championship Barbecue Cooking Contest begins and foodies descend on the city. Memphians are passionate about their BBQ, and this paean to the pleasures of pork is the place to join them. The Sunset Symphony rounds off the festival at the end of the month, drawing thousands who come to picnic and party to the rousing harmonies of the Memphis Symphony Orchestra as a dazzling firework display blazes in the twilight.

MAY FESTIVAL DIARY

On a visit to Memphis in May, you should spend at least a few days in the city, focusing your trip around the music festival (held over a weekend early in the month) or the cooking contest in mid-May. Both events are spread over three days. The following diary has you in the city during the music festival.

Six Days of Musical Magic

DAY 1
Wander the streets of downtown, checking out Beale Street, where blues was born, and watching the river traffic on the Mississippi. The glossy Rock'n'Soul Museum gives a fascinating overview of the city's musical heritage, while tiny Sun Studio, where young Elvis recorded his first disc, offers evocative tours.

DAY 2
Rise early and head out to Graceland, which warrants a whole day. In the evening, stroll along Beale Street, where the music bars will be hopping with everything from blues to bluegrass.

DAY 3
The lively Stax Museum of American Soul Music, housed in the eponymous (now defunct) recording studio, tells the story of the only place in the 1960s Deep South where blacks and whites could make music together. In the afternoon, head to Tom Lee Park by the river for the first afternoon of the music festival.

DAY 4
The funky coffee bars and thrift stores of the Cooper-Young district, Midtown, are buzzing on weekend mornings – hang out here for a while before heading back to the music festival in the afternoon.

DAY 5
Sunday is church day: soul singer Al Green's Full Gospel Tabernacle holds services open to all, where the man himself makes regular appearances. Spiritually edified, head back to the festival for the final line-up.

DAY 6
Built around the old Lorraine Motel, where Dr Martin Luther King was assassinated in 1968, the National Civil Rights Museum tells the painful story of the struggle for desegregation in the South. It's an unmissable stop on any Memphis itinerary.

Dos and Don'ts

☑ Take a Mississippi sternwheeler tour. There's no better way to experience the river at close hand.

☒ Don't wander too far away from the main streets of downtown at night. Memphis is becoming safer, but it still has its problems and tourists can be seen as fair game.

☑ Forget about diets. This is a city that adores its food fattening and rib-sticking. Hunker down and join in.

☒ Don't go thinking you won't come home besotted by Elvis.

Below: A steamboat drifting along the lazy Mississippi River

JAN

FEB

MAR

APR

MAY

DAY 1

DAY 2

DAY 3

DAY 4

DAY 5

DAY 6

JUN

JUL

AUG

SEP

OCT

NOV

DEC

TREASURE ISLAND

Tʜᴇ ᴠɪᴇᴡ ɪꜱ ʙʀᴇᴀᴛʜᴛᴀᴋɪɴɢ as the light aircraft wings across the green hinterland of Belize City and crosses the coast towards the glittering expanses of the Caribbean. Stretching as far as the eye can see is a scattering of tree-shrouded islands enclosing sapphire lagoons fringed with dazzling white sand. These are the cayes, formed over thousands of years as salt-tolerant mangroves took root in the unusually shallow waters, trapping fragments of coral and river silt. The topography constantly changes as new islands form and others are eroded by storms, hurricanes, and human intervention.

The largest and most northerly caye, Ambergris, is a magnet for divers, snorkelers, and water sports enthusiasts. The major draw is the Barrier Reef, the longest in the western hemisphere and undeniably a natural wonder. It appears as an uninterrupted line of breaking surf, dividing the

GETTING THERE   See map p324, C2
International flights arrive at Phillip Goldson International Airport, 11 miles (17 km) northwest of Belize City. From there, Tropic Air and Maya Island Air fly on to San Pedro, the only town on Ambergris Caye.

GETTING AROUND
San Pedro is easily negotiable on foot though golf carts and bicycles can be hired. Water taxis are used to get around Ambergris Caye.

WEATHER
May is hot and sunny, with late afternoon showers, but breezes temper the humidity. The average temperature is 81°F (27°C).

ACCOMMODATIONS
Ruby's doubles have a fan and a balcony with a sea view for US$40; book in advance; www.ambergriscaye.com/rubys

Sun Breeze Beach Hotel offers doubles with views of the pool for US$165; www.sunbreezehotel.com

Ramon's Village has thatched cabanas with access to a sandy beach for US$250; www.ramons.com

EATING OUT
A wide variety of fresh seafood is available, but other local specialties include chicken stew cooked in coconut milk, with pepper sauce. Meals are usually served with beans, rice, plantains, and potato salad.

PRICE FOR TWO
US$320 per day including accommodation, food, local travel, and admission charges.

FURTHER INFORMATION
www.ambergriscaye.com

Above: Lighthouse Reef Atoll basking in the bright sunshine of the Caribbean

Below (top to bottom): Juvenile Morelet's crocodile, with its characteristic yellow color; *Pomacanthus paru*, the French angelfish, commonly found in shallow reefs

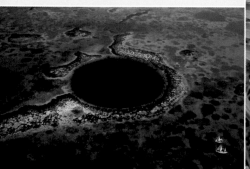

The Blue Hole

Located 40 miles (64 km) southeast of Ambergris Caye at the center of Lighthouse Reef Atoll, the Blue Hole did not even appear on Admiralty navigation charts when legendary diver Jacques Cousteau measured its dimensions in 1972. Now, UNESCO has added the Hole to its World Heritage List and the site draws more than 20,000 divers a year. While the Blue Hole, at 1,000 ft (305 m) across and 450 ft (137 m) deep, is not for the inexperienced, the perimeter teems with coral, fish, sea urchins, and giant green anemones. It is great for snorkeling.

Main: Elegant pair of foureye butterflyfish – they mate for life – looking for food on a coral reef near Ambergris Caye

Right (left to right): Iconic Handprint Cave, a relic of Mayan Pre-Columbian civilization; scuba divers silhouetted against the crystal blue water; diver admiring colorful sponges

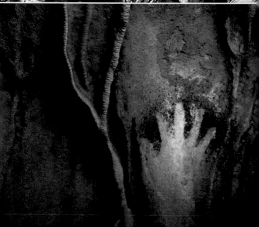

JAN

FEB

MAR

APR

MAY

turquoise coastal waters from the lapis lazuli of the deepening sea. The best introduction to the reef is the Hol Chan Marine Reserve – prepare to be amazed at the shoals of iridescent fish darting among coral canyons, spurs, and ridges. This section of the reef is home to an astonishing variety of marine life from nurse sharks, stingrays, and moray eels to molluscs, tunicates, and sea anemones. Another jaw-dropping attraction is the Blue Hole, a seemingly bottomless limestone karst sinkhole. A third of the way down are stalactites and stalagmites, reminders of the Hole's cavernous origins. They protrude from the walls at a 12-degree angle, the result of a gigantic earthquake millions of years ago which set Lighthouse Reef Atoll at a tilt.

While diving and snorkeling top the activities list, Ambergris also offers fishing, parasailing, sailboarding, and bird watching. Afterwards, relax at one of San Pedro's oceanside restaurants, with barbecued fish so fresh you might have seen them swimming in the sea just a little earlier.

DIVING DIARY

There are more than 35 diving and snorkeling sites off Ambergris Caye and the coastal islands are a short flight away (*see pp88–9*). Underwater visibility is excellent around the Barrier Reef (about 100 ft/30 m), the sea is warm, and the skies are sunny. Visiting in May means missing the expensive seasonal peaks.

Five Days of Marine Life

Join a half-day excursion to Hol Chan Marine Reserve, which includes a swim in Shark Ray Alley, where you can touch nurse sharks and stingrays. After lunch, snorkel off the beach at Ramon's Village, then take a romantic sunset cruise on the "No Rush" catamaran.

DAY 1

Spend the day diving and snorkeling off Lighthouse Reef Atoll, around the famous Blue Hole. In the evening, travel by water taxi to the north end of the island for dinner at Mambos, one of Belize's finest and most exclusive restaurants.

DAY 2

Take a boat to Swallow Caye Wildlife Sanctuary, east of Belize City, where you will see the endangered West Indian manatee in its natural habitat. Enjoy the snorkeling stops on the way and have a tasty barbecue lunch on the beach.

DAY 3

Try a new sport – kitesurfing or windsurfing off the shores of San Pedro. After lunch, visit the island's latest attraction, the Butterfly Jungle Gardens, where you can see 25 butterfly species amid flowering plants.

DAY 4

Take binoculars for the full-day excursion by boat and minivan to Lamanai. While traveling down the New River, your guide will point out herons, jabiru storks, ospreys, and even a crocodile or two. Later, hike from Lamanai Outpost Lodge into the rain forest to see Mayan ruins in a fabulous natural setting.

DAY 5

Dos and Don'ts

✓ Bring plenty of mosquito repellent. While breezes usually keep these pests at bay, they can be a nuisance when the wind drops. Check that your hotel rooms have netting.

✗ Don't forget to check the current baggage allowance with Tropic Air/Maya Island Air before departure.

✓ Remember to bring an underwater camera for diving and snorkeling expeditions.

✓ Before setting out for Hol Chan Marine Reserve, call in at the excellent interactive Visitor Center (open 9am–5pm daily) for information and brochures about Belize's marine habitats.

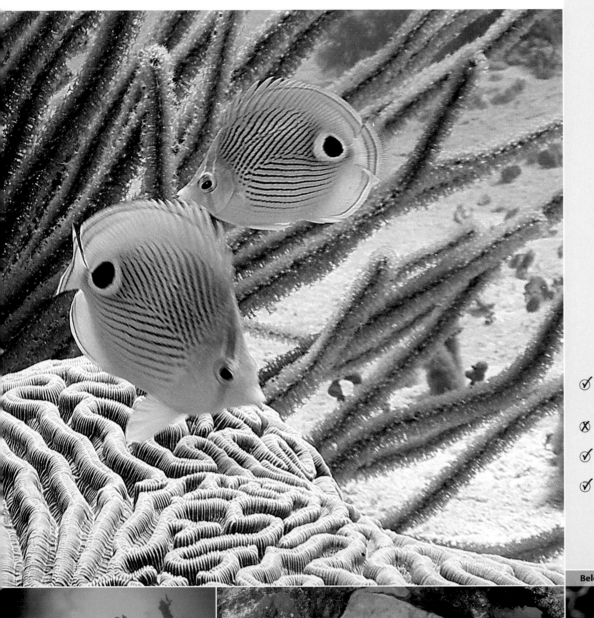

Below: Blue-crowned motmots with a catch of tropical butterflies

JUN

JUL

AUG

SEP

OCT

NOV

DEC

GETTING THERE See map p330, B3
El Alto International Airport is 6 miles (10 km) from La Paz city center.

GETTING AROUND
In La Paz, taxis and *trufis* (collective taxis) show their destination in the front window. *Micros* (buses) run from La Paz to all destinations.

WEATHER
In May, La Paz is usually dry, with a daytime average of 60°F (16°C); 38°F (3°C) at night. In the Yungas, conditions are more tropical.

ACCOMMODATIONS
In La Paz, Hotel Rosario is a charming, colonial-style guesthouse; doubles from US$47; www.hotelrosario.com

La Cúpula in Copacabana, built in Moorish style, overlooks Lago Titicaca; doubles from US$22; www.hotelcupula.com

Sol y Luna, in Corioco, is an ecolodge; doubles from US$20 (two nights minimum, payment in *bolivianos* only); www.solyluna-bolivia.com

In Sorata, the Residencial Sorata is a historic mansion of faded grandeur; doubles from US$12; resorata@ceibo.entelnet.bo

EATING OUT
La Paz's best eateries are in the Sopocachi district and the Zona Sur. In villages, hotels double as restaurants.

PRICE FOR TWO
US$180 per day including accommodation, food, admissions, trips, and local transportation.

FURTHER INFORMATION
www.boliviaweb.com

High Fashion, Andes-Style

A bowler hat, layers of petticoats, and multicolored *aguayos* (woolen wraps) are sartorial trademarks of every *chola*. The climate may explain the petticoats, and an *aguayo* is ideal for carrying everything from babies to produce – but bowler hats? The stories vary of their adoption by (or imposition on) the women of La Paz in colonial times, but today *cholas* wear a bowler as a sign of pride in their heritage. Most come from the last European bowler-maker, in Italy.

ON TOP OF THE WORLD

For even the most seasoned traveler, a visit to La Paz is not one that will be forgotten. For a start, you arrive at one of the world's highest airports, more than 2.5 miles (4 km) above sea level. And the view is staggering, with phenomenal vistas of the encircling mountains and, above all, the sight of triple-peaked Illimani, with its snow-capped summit ignited a blazing orange by the sun.

La Paz is an adventure in itself. The city is a vast, colorful open-air market. Every square inch of street space is taken up by *cholas* (indigenous women of Aymara or Quechua descent) selling an endless array of unique handicrafts, clothing, food, and drink – everything you could ever need and much more. But it's the nearby Yungas and Lago Titicaca regions that really lure the adventure traveler. The Andes offer innumerable hikes along millennia-old Inca trails to beautiful hamlets such as Sorata and Takesi.

Main: View over bustling La Paz, the highest capital city in the world

Left (left and right): Coroico's colonial church and main square; hair-raising El Camino de la Muerte ("the Road of Death"), winding its way through the Yungas from La Paz to Coroico

Right: Totora-reed boat moored at Copacabana on Lago Titicaca

Tiahuanaco, capital of a lost empire which predated even the Incas, is just two hours away toward beautiful Lago Titicaca. Colonial Copacabana is a gateway to the lake's many treasures, such as the mysterious Isla del Sol (Island of the Sun), said to hide the entrance to an ancient underwater city. The lost-in-time Yungas villages of Coroico, Chulumani, and Yanacachi are reached through pristine rainforest, and hiking or canoeing is a delight in the heady, flower-scented lowland air.

You could happily spend your entire trip exploring at a snail's pace, but this part of Bolivia is home to the country's best, most adrenaline-filled experiences, and many of the region's larger towns offer exhilarating outings. Some folks might choose to hurtle down the world's highest ski run or one of the planet's most dangerous roads. For the more upwardly mobile there's the chance to tackle some of the tallest and most challenging peaks in the western hemisphere. Or why not take to the air and paraglide above virgin rainforest? On an Andean adventure, the sky's the limit.

Above: Stone carving on the entrance façade of Iglesia de San Francisco, La Paz

Below: Mountain hut on Chacaltaya, site of the world's highest ski run

ANDEAN DIARY

May is an ideal time to visit La Paz and the surrounding region, as the weather is pleasant and mild. At 2 miles (3,200 m) above the ocean, any strenuous activity will leave you a bit out of sorts initially, but a day of rest is generally all you'll need before you embark on a full week of unforgettable high-altitude adventures.

Eight Days Above the Clouds

Spend the first day acclimatizing with the help of *yerbe mate* tea, prized by the locals for its restorative powers.

The next day, take the bus to Lago Titicaca, stopping on route for a tour of the ceremonial center of Tiahuanaco. Continue to the tradition-steeped lakeside town of Copacabana. In the evening, try local trout for dinner.

Take a day tour to Isla del Sol and spend the day exploring the ruins. The waters of the Fuente del Inca spring are said to be rejuvenating. Isla de la Luna (Island of the Moon) is a short boat-ride away.

Head for Sorata, the starting point for many awesome treks, from short jaunts to Cerro Istipata or San Pedro Caves, to the outrageously hard, Inca-era Mapiri Trail. Go east for the world's most dramatic and dangerous mountain bike descent, the Yungas road, to Coroico. Cool off in its waterfalls and pools before climbing sacred Cerro Uchumachi or exploring on horseback.

The pretty villages of Chulumani, Ocabaya, Chicaloma, and Yanakachi are in prime hiking and bird-watching country. Chicaloma is famous for *saya* music and dance. In Yanakachi you could volunteer a few hours' help at the Fundación Pueblo orphanage.

Return to La Paz via Calaco to to see the eerie landscape of Valle de la Luna (Moon Valley). Back in La Paz, take in a *peña* – a Bolivian folk music program. The next day, stroll the main thoroughfare, the Prado; explore the old city, the museums, and churches; and don't miss the unique *mercado de hechicería* (witches' market).

Dos and Don'ts

⊗ Don't over-exert yourself in the first few days. A debilitating case of *soroche* (mountain sickness) could ruin your trip.

✓ Ask politely before photographing local people, especially *cholas*, who are often vehemently camera-shy.

⊗ Don't frequent money changers (*cambistas*) on street corners. If you must use their services (such as on a Sunday, when everything is closed), bring a calculator and have your bills handed to you one by one.

✓ Don't eat fruit or vegetables bought from an open-air vendor without washing them first.

Below: The stunning peaks of Illimani mountain

JAN

FEB

MAR

APR

MAY

DAYS 1–2

DAY 3

DAYS 4–5

DAY 6

DAYS 7–8

JUN

JUL

AUG

SEP

OCT

NOV

DEC

GETTING THERE See map p313, C6

GETTING THERE
Large cruise ships depart from Vancouver (British Columbia), Canada, and many cruise companies will provide a transfer from Vancouver International Airport to your ship. You can also fly to Juneau, Alaska, and join a small cruise ship.

GETTING AROUND
Vancouver International Airport is a 20-minute taxi ride from the city center. A new airport rapid transit line is scheduled for completion in time for the 2010 Winter Games.

WEATHER
The cruising season runs from mid-April to September. May is the driest month. Days are very long and generally warm at 62–80°F (17°C–27°C), but bring a sweater as nights are cool at 59–66°F (15°C–19°C).

ACCOMMODATIONS
Celebrity Cruises; doubles from US$900 per person for 7 days; www.celebritycruises.com

Carnival Cruise Lines has ocean view doubles from US$1,200 per person; www.carnival.com

Luxury on the Holland America Line; doubles from US$1,500 per person for 7 days; www.hollandamerica.com

EATING OUT
Meals are included on the Inside Passage ships. On shore excursions, try an open-fire salmon bake for about US$35 per person.

PRICE FOR TWO
US$460 per day including cruise, shore excursions, dining, and tips.

FURTHER INFORMATION
www.cruising.org

Klondike Gold Rush

The now tiny hamlet of Skagway reached its peak in 1898, at the height of the Klondike gold rush. Skagway was the gateway town where miners assembled their gear and supplies before trekking up over the Chilkoot pass into Canada. The Canadian authorities didn't try to prevent the countless foreigners from entering, but the Mounties did insist that each miner bring one full ton of supplies, enough to keep himself alive for a year. Every pound of that ton the miners carried on their backs up the icy steps of the Chilkoot pass.

Above (left to right): Sockeye salmon swimming upriver to spawn; bear catching migrating sockeye salmon; tail of a humpback whale
Main: Sunset in Stephens Passage, just outside Juneau

VOYAGE OF DISCOVERY

CAPTAIN JAMES COOK DID NOT BELIEVE IN THE EXISTENCE of an Inside Passage. Rumours of such a route, he supposed, were the work of Russians and Spaniards, spread with the purpose of confounding sensible English seamen. Sailing north to the edge of the Bering Sea in the 1770s, Cook kept steadfastly to the dangerous outer shore rather than venture into the network of channels that fringe Alaska's southeast shores.

It was not until a generation later that Cook's protégé George Vancouver charted a navigable course through this fractal coastline. He did not think much of the landscape, declaring it "useless." His senior lieutenants thought otherwise – they were younger men whose souls had been touched by the Romantic movement then sweeping Europe, whose spirits yearned for wild, untamed places where God and nature could commune, places they considered to be sublime. Sublime this coastline undoubtedly is. The product of a slow collision between tectonic plates,

followed by four successive epochs of glaciation, the geography of the Inside Passage coastline has been sculpted on a scale to impress. Mountains rise steeply out of deep icy waters and soar 3,300 ft (1,000 m) above sea level, with headwaters lost in a crown of cloud and mist.

The region's channels, fjords, estuaries, and sea currents support an assortment of animal species. The cool currents give rise to an array of sealife including herring, salmon, porpoise, sea lions, and sea otters, along with orca, humpback, and grey whales. Along the shore, the rocks are thick with sea stars, geoducks, and abalone, while grizzly and black bears feast at the river mouths in spring.

Although the Inside Passage has a vulnerable ecosystem, with some wildlife under threat of extinction, man's tread here has been relatively light – the fjords, forests, and salmon remain for visitors to experience, in all their sublime beauty.

> Mountains rise out of deep icy waters, and soar above sea level with headwaters lost in a crown of cloud and mist.

Inset: *Galaxy* cruise ship in Glacier Bay National Park
Below (left and right): A ski plane; Creek Street, Ketchikan

NATURE-LOVER'S DIARY

May offers gloriously long days for cruising Alaska's Inside Passage. Large cruise ships sail from Vancouver to Juneau and Skagway, then back down past Ketchikan and Misty Fjords in a period of seven days. For those with more time, Vancouver merits an extra night's stay (see p156–7).

Seven Days in the Fjords

DAY 1 Departing Vancouver, find your sea legs the first full day at sea. Today's highlight is a visit to Tracy Arm, an L-shaped fjord with the dual ice cliffs of the Sawyer glacier lying hidden at the end.

DAY 2 From Juneau, Alaska's state capital, set out in search of humpbacks on Stephens Passage, or take a helicopter or ski plane up to the Mendenhall glacier and explore by dog sled. End the day with an Alaska salmon bake – freshly caught wild salmon grilled over an alderwood fire.

DAY 3 Sample the colorful history of Skagway by strolling the boardwalks and poking your nose into the saloons preserved as part of the Klondike Gold Rush National Historic Park. Take the fast ferry to Haines and explore the Chilkat Bald Eagle Preserve, an estuary habitat rich with wildlife, including moose and American bald eagles.

DAY 4 On day four, the ship noses into the Glacier Bay National Park. This 62-mile (100-km) long fjord has a dozen tidewater glaciers whose tall blue cliffs of ice regularly calve off icebergs, which crash into the ocean sending spray hundreds of feet into the air.

DAY 5 The cruise proceeds to Ketchikan, the gateway to the extraordinary Misty Fjords National Monument, which can be visited by fast boat or floatplane.

DAYS 6–7 The last full day of the voyage is spent entirely at sea. As the ship approaches Johnstone Strait near the north end of Vancouver Island, look out for orca whales feeding on salmon and rubbing their bodies along the shoreline in a small bay called Robson Bight.

Dos and Don'ts

☑ Keep your eyes peeled for wildlife. There are good chances of spotting an amazing array of land and sea mammals.

☒ Don't forget to bring a light waterproof jacket, as rain is never more than a day away. A Gore-Tex® jacket comes in handy after sunset, when the temperature drops a good 50°F (28°C).

☑ Give the captain of your prospective cruise line the third degree before you set sail. It's the best way to avoid disappointment.

☑ Feast on salmon. There are four different species on the west coast: chinook (or king), spring, chum, and sockeye.

Below: Sheets of ice crashing into the water, Glacier Bay National Park

JAN
FEB
MAR
APR
MAY
JUN
JUL
AUG
SEP
OCT
NOV
DEC

ROCKY MOUNTAIN HIGHS

O KAY, DUDES, SADDLE UP! COWBOYS, ROUNDUPS, RIDING HERD... the ways of the West have been romanticized in scores of movies and novels, and now, with a swagger to make John Wayne and Annie Oakley proud, you're about to pull on your spurs and experience the cowboy culture for yourself on a guest or "dude" ranch – named for city folks who fancy a taste of life on the frontier. Since you're not really a cowpoke, you'll have it pretty easy. No bunkhouse for you. Instead, accommodations will probably be a beautifully appointed log cabin. As for the food – beans, beans, and more beans? No way. Expect the biggest and tastiest meals you've ever tucked into, with three squares a day. Dusty after a day on the range? Well, hop into the hot tub. Trail rides, cattle-drives, and roping are all part of the fun, along with fly-fishing, bird- and wildlife-watching, canoeing, and campfire sing-alongs.

GETTING THERE   See map p320, G4
The closest major airport is in Salt Lake City, 275 miles (440 km) southwest of Jackson, with connecting flights to Cody and Jackson.

GETTING AROUND
Car rental is widely available.

WEATHER
Daytime highs average 65°F (18°C), with nighttime lows around 35°F (2°C). It gets cooler the higher up you go.

ACCOMMODATIONS
Many ranches do not open until mid- or late May. Prices per night for two adults and two children include meals and activities.

Bill Cody Ranch is in the Wapiti Valley; from US$560 (discounts for kids under 11); www.billcodyranch.com

Flat Creek Ranch is in Jackson Hole; from US$825; www.flatcreekranch.com

Spotted Horse Ranch is on the Hoback River in Jackson Hole; from US$1,140 (kids under four stay free, those aged four to five stay half-price); www.spottedhorseranch.com

EATING OUT
Dude ranch meals are hearty and usually excellent. Expect home-baked breads and lots of meat. Many ranches offer chuck-wagon suppers, and packed lunches for outings.

PRICE FOR A FAMILY OF FOUR
US$750–1,000 per day, depending on the ranch you choose, including lodgings, food, car rental and gas, activities, and admissions.

FURTHER INFORMATION
www.duderanch.org

The Call of the Wild

The Rocky Mountain wolf was once close to extinction but has made a big comeback since the first packs were re-introduced to Yellowstone National Park in 1997. It is estimated that some 1,300 wolves now roam the Northern Rockies, in packs that can cover up to 70 miles (110 km) a day. Ranchers argue that wolves kill their livestock, while environmentalists counter that these predators cull unfit members of herds of elk, bison, deer, and moose. For now, the wolves are here to stay, and hearing their distinctive howl is part of the thrill of being in these wilds.

Main: Tack room of a dude ranch

Left (left to right): Family fun feeding the livestock; looking for wildlife on a Grand Teton National Park walking trail

Right: Horses grazing in lush pastures at Jackson Hole

Right panel (top to bottom): Horseback riding against a backdrop of Grand Teton peaks; fishing at sunset near Snake River; boots lined up ready for dude-ranch guests

Also included is some of the most beautiful scenery in the world. The northwest corner of Wyoming is a spectacularly scenic place for a ranch vacation. This parcel of the northern Rocky Mountains stretches from the frontier town of Cody, Wyoming, west through Yellowstone and north and south in a grand sweep that takes in the magnificent valley known as Jackson Hole as well as the Grand Teton and Yellowstone National Parks. As you explore the surrounding country, or go about your ranch chores (and these probably won't be more strenuous than saddling your mount or helping feed the livestock) your eyes will constantly be drawn to a snowy mountain peak, a crystal-clear creek darting through a meadow, or bison wandering through an upland valley. (If you choose to spend more time in Yellowstone National Park or Jackson Hole, and you should, *see pages 188–9 and 20–1.*) Dudes, tenderfoots, city slickers, greenhorns – whatever visitors who choose to spend time on a ranch in these beautiful landscapes might be called, they are in for the times of their lives.

RANCH HAND'S DIARY

In May, the high passes have just been cleared of snow, and most of the three million annual visitors have not yet arrived. Many ranches accept guests for short periods in spring, allowing you to divide your time between two gorgeous places, the Wapiti Valley near Yellowstone and the Grand Teton–Jackson Hole region.

A Week on the Trail

DAY 1 Settle in to your ranch in the Wapiti Valley, near Cody, then take a ride through pine forests along the north fork of the Shoshone River, where rushing waters cut through volcanic cliffs.

DAY 2 After a morning on the ranch, maybe trying your hand at roping a steer, drive into Cody to see the Buffalo Bill Historical Center, devoted to Western artifacts, and Trail Town, where cabins and other buildings evoke frontier life.

DAY 3 Join the ranch hands on a guided hike or ride along the buttes and forested valleys of Washakie Wilderness.

DAY 4 Drive the Beartooth Highway, one the most scenic routes in America and, at 10,947 ft (3,339 m), one of the highest. Then head south through Yellowstone and Grand Teton National Parks to a ranch at Jackson. Keep an eye out for bears, bison, and other wildlife.

DAY 5 Take a guided hike across mountain meadows, with Grand Teton peaks filling the horizon. Or head into Jackson for a visit to the National Museum of Wildlife Art. For a panoramic view of the mountains, ride the chairlift to the summit of Snow King Mountain.

DAY 6 Explore the mountain wilderness on a trail ride. Your guides may take you to a glacial lake where you can fish and canoe. Or take a float trip down the Snake River.

DAY 7 Follow the Wind River valley into Dubois, surrounded by multi-hued badlands. Hike the Badlands Interpretive Trail, and drop into the National Bighorn Sheep Center. Return to the ranch in time for an evening ride to watch the sun setting over the snow-capped peaks.

Dos and Don'ts

☑ Bring binoculars for close-up views of wildlife and scenery.

☒ Don't feed wild animals.

☑ Keep your distance – at least 100 yards or meters – from bears.

☒ Don't hike into backcountry without leaving word of your plans with a responsible person.

☑ Keep an eye out for sudden changes in the weather.

Below: Entrance to Cody's Buffalo Bill Historical Center

JAN
FEB
MAR
APR
MAY
JUN
JUL
AUG
SEP
OCT
NOV
DEC

GETTING THERE   **See map p328, A4**
River cruises depart Manaus, the capital of Amazonas state. Eduardo Gomes international airport is 10 miles (17 km) from the downtown river terminal.

GETTING AROUND
Downtown Manaus is a bustling commercial and pedestrian zone, easily covered on foot. For longer distances or after dark, take a taxi. Iberostar (www.iberostar.com.br) offers Amazon cruises on large ships, while Viverde (www.viverde.com.br) runs riverboat trips.

WEATHER
It is hot year-round in the Amazon, normally 86–96°F (30–36°C), with almost 100 percent humidity. By May, the wet season has ended.

ACCOMMODATIONS
Basic lodging at Mango Guest House; doubles from US$75; www.naturesafaris.com.br

Luxurious Tropical Manaus has colonial-style decor and three vast pools; doubles from US$200; www.tropicalhotel.com.br

Across the river from Manaus is Amazon Tiwa Amazonas Ecoresort, a jungle lodge; packages for doubles from US$380; www.tiwa.com.br

EATING OUT
Try Amazonian fruits, such as nutritious *açaí* served crushed and frozen, and *cupuaçu* ice cream. Sample local dishes at Choupana from around US$25; tel. (92) 3635 3878.

PRICE FOR TWO
US$3,150 including a five-day Iberostar cruise, airport transfers, and tips.

FURTHER INFORMATION
www.amazonastur.am.gov.br

THE WORLD'S BIGGEST RIVER

Downstream of Manaus, two tributaries come together to form the mighty Amazon River. The Rio Negro is dark, with the color and acidic tannic taste of cold black tea, while the Rio Solimões, in contrast, is a light milky brown, like warm *café com leite*. Curiously, their waters meet but do not join. Instead, they travel on side by side for miles, hardly interacting. The two broad currents stream along together side by side, with little swirls and eddies developing where they join. Differences in velocity and alkalinity, and the weight of suspended matter between the two rivers, prevent their mixing. Enter this water and you can float with your feet in the milky Solimões and your head in the cool dark Rio Negro. A few miles farther on, the differences dissolve and finally the two rivers merge. The Portuguese name for this bizarre and beautiful phenomenon is *encontro das*

Opera in the Jungle

The striking dome-topped Teatro Amazonas is the centerpiece of the restored historic central square in Manaus. This opera house was erected over a century ago in 1896, at the height of a rubber boom that had made the entire Amazon region rich. A guided tour of the theater reveals a lobby of Italian marble and parquet floors of rich tropical hardwood, plus a mural in the ballroom depicting scenes from the first Brazilian opera performed here – the tale of an Indian princess and her doomed love for a Portuguese explorer.

Main: The meeting of the waters at the confluence of the Rio Negro and Rio Solimões

Left: Freshwater fish for sale at the Mercado Adolpho Lisboa

Right (left to right): Colorful riverboats moored at the jetty on the Manaus waterfront; canoe paddling through a flooded forest on the Rio Negro

aguas – the meeting of the waters. River cruises usually save it for journey's end, by which time visitors have developed some of the expertise and vocabulary required for exploring a region where the river can rise or fall over 39 ft (12 m) in a single season and where vast forest lands get flooded and become lakes, then swamps, then dry land again. As part of a cruise, you may find yourself paddling through forests where the water reaches the highest branches, called either *varzea*, if they border the Solimões and its tributaries, or *igapó*, if they border the Rio Negro. You will paddle past *igarapés*, countless tiny channels that lead in through the trees, and meet *caboclos* – the river people who spend their days in canoes, who eat piranha fish and *jacaré* (caiman), and who make their homes on high stilts to stay above the floodwaters. When you leave the Amazon, you will almost certainly feel *saudade* – nostalgic longing for a magical place that you might never have the opportunity to see again.

Above: A pair of gold-and-blue macaws

Below (top and bottom): Squirrel monkey; pink Amazon river dolphin

RIVER CRUISE DIARY

The rainy season is over by May, but the Negro and Solimões rivers are still near their highest, which makes this the best time to explore the flooded areas. Cruises depart weekly and provide an introduction to some of the astonishing sights and sounds along the world's largest river.

Five Days on the Amazon

Visit the Teatro Amazonas in Manaus, the luxurious opera house and concert hall built over a century ago in the heart of the jungle. Then head down to the river port to board the *IB Grand Amazon* and set sail for your first night out on the water.

DAY 1

Trek through the *igarapés* to Novo Airão, where with luck you can see small bright-pink Amazon river dolphins. You might also spot alligators submerged in the water. While away the afternoon fishing with a hook and line for piranha at Lago Araçari, but watch out for their razor-sharp teeth.

DAY 2

Rise early to catch the sun coming up over a small side tributary called the Rio Padaurí, known for its birdlife. Black cormorants, tiger herons, and tall white egrets are common sightings. Travel through the flooded forest around Igarapé Aturiá on a photo safari. Look out for squirrel monkeys, toucans, and gold-and-blue macaws along the way. Back on the boat, watch the sun go down to a soundtrack of soothing classical music or just the noises of the jungle.

DAY 3

Travel up Rio Cuieiras to visit the *caboclo* stilt-house community at Cambebas and learn how they process the poisonous mandioc root into staple carbohydrates. This is also a good place to pick up local handicrafts. Relax in the afternoon and just enjoy being here.

DAY 4

Rise early to experience the meeting of the waters. Afterwards sip champagne over breakfast, then sail back upstream to Manaus.

DAY 5

Dos and Don'ts

✓ Bring mosquito repellent and cover up in the evenings – mosquitoes are most likely to bite in the hour after sunset.

✗ Don't pass up a chance to visit the Mercado Adolpho Lisboa, the old wrought-iron market hall in the center of town.

✓ Pick up a cotton hammock in one of the chandlery shops near the riverboat terminal. It will make a fine souvenir.

✗ Don't skip the natural history lectures aboard the IB *Grand Amazon*. They are fun and extremely informative.

Below: A row of wooden *caboclo* stilt-houses

JAN
FEB
MAR
APR
MAY
JUN
JUL
AUG
SEP
OCT
NOV
DEC

CANADA

USA

NEW YORK CITY
Washington, D.C.

Los Angeles

MEXICO

GETTING THERE See map p316, G5
LaGuardia domestic airport is 20 minutes
from midtown by taxi. Newark and JFK
international airports are linked to the city
by rail and bus (allow an hour by road).

GETTING AROUND
Walking is the best way to explore Manhattan
but subways, buses and taxis are plentiful.

WEATHER
May is very pleasant and fairly dry, with highs of
around 75°F (24°C) and lows of 55°F (13°C).

ACCOMMODATIONS
The Comfort Inn Midtown is conveniently
located close to Times Square; doubles from
US$300; www.applecorehotels.com

The Library is among the most charming of
the city's many new, small luxury hotels;
doubles from US$379; www.libraryhotel.com

Classic elegance reigns at the Waldorf-Astoria,
the ultimate "grand hotel"; doubles from
US$430; waldorfastoria.hilton.com

EATING OUT
Expect to pay US$15–20 for a sandwich and
drink at Katz's and other classic New York
delis, at least US$50 a person at a hip eatery
like Spice Market in the Meatpacking District,
and upwards of US$125 each at Chanterelle
and other temples of gastronomy.

PRICE FOR TWO
Around US$500–850 per day, depending on
hotel and restaurant choices, including all
entertainment, admissions, and transportations.

FURTHER INFORMATION
www.nycvisit.com

Hit the Heights

The Empire State Building, perhaps the world's favorite
skyscraper, took shape above the skyline in just a
little more than a year, with some 3,400 laborers
constructing on average four floors a day. Inaugurated
on May 1, 1931, it remained the tallest building in
the world for the next 40 years. Its spire was originally
intended as a mooring mast for airships. More than
114 million visitors have admired the spectacular
views from the 86th-floor observation deck, the
scene of romantic rendezvous in such films as *An
Affair to Remember* and *Sleepless in Seattle*.

Above (left to right): Leafy Central Park; Metropolitan Museum of Art façade; *Prometheus* statue at Rockefeller Center
Main: Manhattan's bustling bar scene

WE'LL HAVE MANHATTAN

THE BUSIEST AND MOST BUZZING CITY IN AMERICA, one of the world's great hubs of commerce and culture, also happens to be one of the most appealing, even romantic, places on earth. It's partly the physical charms of the city, which are considerable. The soaring skyscrapers of stone and glass are majestic, the lawns and trees of Central Park are all the more welcoming, surrounded as they are by concrete, and the style for which the city sets the standard is in evidence in chic shops and on the streets. More than physical appeal, though, New York generates a jittery thrill – it may sound corny, but you could say that being in this city feels a little like falling in love. Part of the thrill of being in New York is feeling that something exciting, important, incredible seems to be happening all around you. Strolling though neon-lit Times Square or past Carnegie Hall, you can't help but sense that you are surrounded by legends, and walking down the narrow canyons of Wall Street you are aware that momentous decisions are being made in the eyrie-like offices above you.

Adding to the city's charms is a sense of familiarity. The streets and landmarks appear in so many films and photographs, clubs and restaurants are mentioned so often in gossip columns and celebrity interviews, that first-time visitors will come upon sights they've seen and heard of time and again. Even New Yorkers can be taken aback at just how much there is to see and do in their city, and the scene is ever changing. Downtown is flourishing, with new hotels, shops, and restaurants. Slaughterhouses in the Meatpacking District are being transformed into hip night spots. Beautifully landscaped walkways, in full bloom at this time of year, now line the banks of the Hudson River. So come and enjoy this intoxicating city for a few days. Go to the theater, dine well, dance into the wee hours, stroll the leafy streets of the West Village or Upper West Side. To paraphrase the song, be a part of it – the energy that makes the "city that never sleeps" eternally enticing.

> It may sound corny, but you could say that being in this city feels a little like falling in love.

Inset: Iconic New York yellow cab at night
Below (left and right): Manhattan from the air; shoppers in SoHo

BIG APPLE DIARY

A long springtime weekend in New York is the perfect time to indulge yourself and your loved one. Savor urbane delights like a Broadway show, sip on a Manhattan cocktail at twilight, stroll hand-in-hand through Central Park, and fall under the spell of a hard-edged city that can be the most romantic place on earth.

Four Perfect Days

Arrive Thursday in time for a show, with pre-theater cocktails at the King Cole Bar, the Algonquin, or any other one of the city's classic watering holes. Have a late-night supper at Joe Allen's or another Broadway haunt, where the star you just saw on stage may be sitting at the next table.

Fifth Avenue is the epicenter of New York luxury: treat yourselves at Saks', Cartier's or Tiffany's. Take the time to admire the lofty spires of St. Patrick's Cathedral and the Art Deco towers of Rockefeller Center. Sample some classic New York street food, such as hot dogs or pretzels, for lunch. Later, ascend to the observation platform of the Empire State Building. In the early evening, hail a horse-drawn carriage for a ride through Central Park to the Metropolitan Museum of Art. The strains of a string quartet float through the galleries and the views of the park and city from the Roof Garden are sumptuous.

Enjoy a leisurely Saturday: walk through Greenwich Village, gallery hop in Chelsea, shop in SoHo, lunch in Paris – that is, the city's ultra-Parisian bistro, Balthazar. Later, head to the Meatpacking District for a star-studded dinner and the cool club scene.

Brunch on the lakeside terrace of the Boathouse Café in Central Park, then slip into a gondola for a glide across the waters. If you have time, visit the Museum of Modern Art before a matinee or afternoon concert. To end your visit in spectacular style, enjoy a pre-departure cocktail at the Rise Bar atop the Ritz-Carlton, Battery Park City, with its stunning harbor views.

Dos and Don'ts

- ✓ Make reservations for hot shows and cool restaurants well in advance to avoid disappointments.
- ✗ Don't be afraid to join New Yorkers underground on the excellent subway system.
- ✓ Buy inexpensive one-day Fun Passes for unlimited rides on buses or the subway.
- ✗ Don't confine your visit to midtown; there's so much more to discover in the city's many neighborhoods.
- ✓ Bring a comfortable pair of walking shoes.

Below: Bright lights of Broadway

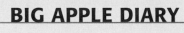

JAN
FEB
MAR
APR
MAY
THU
FRI
SAT
SUN
JUN
JUL
AUG
SEP
OCT
NOV
DEC

THE WORLD IN ONE CITY

S TEP INTO TORONTO'S ST. LAWRENCE MARKET and it's hard to figure out what to do first. Sample New Zealand manuka honey or Pakistani sea salt? Pick up some Chinese "forbidden" rice or Argentinean chorizo? Or simply wander the busy aisles of this Victorian market building in a happy daze, inhaling the mouthwatering aromas of fresh bagels and apple fritters? The dilemmas presented by a visit to the St. Lawrence Market mirror the bewildering range of choices available to you when visiting Toronto itself. What was once a restrained, WASP-y bastion is today one of the world's most cosmopolitan cities – more than half of Toronto's adult population was born outside of Canada. As a result, it's easy to while away your vacation feasting on paella and dim sum, grooving to Peruvian folk musicians and bhangra dance beats, and watching the latest festive parade wind its way through the city streets.

GETTING THERE   See map p316, E4

Lester B. Pearson International Airport is 16 miles (26 km) from downtown Toronto. Outside of rush hour, it's about 25 minutes by taxi or an hour by Airport Express shuttle.

GETTING AROUND

Walk, use public transportation, or hail a taxi downtown, and cycle along the lakefront. A car is only needed for trips out of town (but Stratford can also be reached direct by rail).

WEATHER

May is generally mild and almost summery. Temperatures are 45–63°F (7°–17°C). The lakeside is usually cooler than downtown.

ACCOMMODATIONS

The Days Hotel and Conference Centre is good value for a downtown location; doubles from US$90; www.daysinn.com

The Holiday Inn on King is within walking distance of theaters, concert halls, and sports stadia; doubles from US$200; www.hiok.com

The Hazelton Hotel in posh Yorkville offers celebrity style, with matching prices; doubles from US$650; www.thehazeltonhotel.com

EATING OUT

Meals from just about every world cuisine are available for US$15–20 each. Expect to pay at least US$70 per person at gourmet hotspots.

PRICE FOR TWO

Allow around US$550 per day including accommodation, food, local transportation, a day's car rental and gas, admissions, and theater and Jays tickets.

FURTHER INFORMATION

www.torontotourism.com

Main: The Michael Lee-Chin Crystal, the bold, futuristic new extension to the Royal Ontario Museum

Impressive Impresario

When the late Ed Mirvish saved Toronto's Beaux Arts Royal Alexandra Theatre from the wrecker's ball in 1962, locals were skeptical. The theater and the stretch of King Street on which it stood were derelict, and Toronto's theater scene was moribund. But the man who'd made his fortune with a kitsch discount store called Honest Ed's revived the Royal Alex and built the 2,000-seat Broadway showcase Princess of Wales Theatre nearby. Today, King Street is known as the Entertainment District, and Toronto is the third-largest live theater center in the English-speaking world.

Above left (top to bottom): Francesco Pirelli's *Monument to Multiculturalism* (1985) on Front Street; quirky shops and stalls of the Kensington Market; a pair of Cabbagetown's ornate Victorian villas

Left: Ward Island, viewed from the top of the CN Tower

Bottom (left to right): Blue Jays pitcher Roy Halladay; Toronto skyline, with the CN Tower and the Rogers Centre clearly visible

Enticing as Toronto's multicultural vibe is, it's just one reason culture buffs love the place. Toronto offers a huge range of exhibitions, concerts, and cultural festivals. Travelers with a classical bent head to the Canadian Opera Company or the Toronto Symphony Orchestra. Fans of cutting-edge drama buy tickets to the Soulpepper or Tarragon theatres, while more traditional theatergoers make the trip out to delightful Stratford for Shakespearian and modern classics.

The city also has many distinctive, pedestrian-friendly neighborhoods to discover. Cabbagetown is known for its many well-preserved Victorian houses; Queen Street West is where Goth kids mix with fashionistas; the restored Distillery District is a former industrial complex that's now a cultural and leisure hub; and clotheshorses spend their time prowling the quirky boutiques surrounding the Kensington Market. Even the Business District yields treats. Hop on a "Red Rocket" – the city's iconic streetcar – to "New" City Hall. It won raves for its futuristic design when it opened in 1965, of the sort now lavished on Daniel Libeskind's Crystal extension to the Royal Ontario Museum.

COSMOPOLITAN DIARY

Winter weather in Toronto features far too many damp, grey, cold days. So when May rolls around, the locals can't wait to get outside. Sidewalks sprout café tables, street theater abounds, and just about every weekend offers an outdoor festival or two. Five days lets you sample the city's buzzing scene and head out of town as well.

Five Days in a Culture Capital

DAY 1
View the city from the observation deck of the CN Tower, until 2007 the world's tallest freestanding structure at 1,815 ft (553 m) tall. Then take in a Blue Jays baseball game at the Rogers Centre (formerly called the Skydome for its fully retracting roof). If it's early May, end the day with a tasting at Santé, the international wine festival.

DAY 2
Spend the morning – or the day – perusing everything from Egyptian mummies to modern art at the Royal Ontario Museum (ROM). To clear your head and empty your wallet, browse the luxury boutiques on nearby Bloor Street. Dine beneath the indoor vertical garden at Sassafraz, a stylish Yorkville restaurant.

DAY 3
Take the 15-minute ferry ride from Harbourfront to Ward's Island, the farthest east of the three Toronto Islands. It's worth renting a bike and cycling the trails that link the islands, stopping for lunch on the secluded, shady patio of the Rectory Café. Back at Harbourfront, a waterfront arts and retail complex, you might come across a literary reading or art exhibition.

DAY 4
Head out to Stratford, a picturesque small city 2 hours' drive southwest of Toronto, to enjoy a performance at the renowned Stratford Shakespeare Festival.

DAY 5
For your last day, explore one of Toronto's vibrant ethnic neighborhoods. You could fuel up with moussaka in Greektown or cannoli in Little Italy; or shop for silks in the Gerard India Bazaar. Later, visit Casa Loma, the faux-medieval 1914 "castle" whose construction bankrupted its millionaire owner. End your visit with a blockbuster musical at the Royal Alex or Princess of Wales Theatre.

Dos and Don'ts

✓ Explore the PATH system, a strange but useful web of underground corridors linking many downtown buildings.

✗ Don't be afraid to walk across a lane of traffic to reach a waiting streetcar. Look carefully, but most locals are used to this somewhat hair-raising system and will stop.

✓ Go for afternoon tea at the Fairmont Royal York or Le Méridien King Edward Hotel, where it feels like the sun hasn't completely set on the British Empire.

✗ Don't forget to pronounce the city's name "Traw-na" if you want to sound like a local.

Below: A classic Toronto "Red Rocket" streetcar

JAN
FEB
MAR
APR
MAY
DAY 1
DAY 2
DAY 3
DAY 4
DAY 5
JUN
JUL
AUG
SEP
OCT
NOV
DEC

GETTING THERE See map p317, G4
Fly into Savannah International Airport, 11 miles (18 km) from the Historic District. The Golden Isles are 80 miles (129 km) south of Savannah, along the Atlantic Coast.

GETTING AROUND
Plan on walking, taking a tour, or using the hop-on trolley to explore Old Savannah. Rent a car for trips beyond the Historic District.

WEATHER
May has average daytime highs of 84°F (29°C) and nighttime lows of 61°F (16°C). Expect occasional showers, high humidity, and mostly sunny skies.

ACCOMMODATIONS
Catherine Ward House Inn, an elegant hotel with 250 years of history, has rooms from US$160; www.catherinewardhouseinn.com

Romantic Gastonian, near Forsyth Park, has rooms from US$225; www.gastonian.com

Jekyll Island Club Hotel is a classic historic resort hotel, with rooms from US$240; www.jekyllclub.com

EATING OUT
From home-style restaurants to fine dining, there is a lot to choose from in Savannah. Try the romantic 45 South for contemporary cuisine (US$40), or enjoy an elaborate meal in a fine old mansion, at Elizabeth (US$50).

PRICE FOR TWO
US$580 per day including accommodation, food, local travel, and admissions.

FURTHER INFORMATION
www.savannahvisit.com

Garden of Good and Evil

John Berendt mingled in Savannah's high society for eight years, as well as among drag queens, voodoo witches, and various eccentrics. In 1994, he wrote *Midnight in the Garden of Good and Evil*, about a scandalous murder and a mysterious ritual in Bonaventure Cemetery. Detested by many locals for sensationalizing their gracious city, the book is a fictionalized exposé of Savannah's wealthy. A tour points out major locations, such as the cemetery.

ANTEBELLUM ELEGANCE

ROMANTIC AS A SULTRY SOUTHERN BELLE and as eccentric as a Southern grande dame, Old Savannah is at her seductive best in spring when the perfume of magnolias fills the air and the gardens are awash with color. The city's cobblestone streets, shaded by moss-draped oak trees, are laid out in a grid with 22 beautiful green squares, each decorated with ornate fountains and statues.

A stroll along the charming streets, accompanied by the clip-clop of horse-drawn carriages, leads past elegant antebellum mansions displaying regal white columns, and restored late 19th-century town homes, trimmed with scrolled ironwork balconies. Here, too, are hidden gardens where azaleas bloom, elaborate Gothic churches, and fine Federal and Regency-style mansions, decorated with handsome antiques. The sweet sounds of jazz, the alluring scent of roasting pecans, and the *Waving Girl* statue

Main: Forsyth Park Fountain, shaded by live oak trees

Left (left and right): Horseback riding along the beach on Cumberland Island; historic stern-wheeler berthed on the Savannah River

Right: Balconies with elegant wrought-iron scrollwork at Marshall House, Savannah's oldest hotel

welcome visitors to promenade along the Savannah River. Shops in the historic brick-built warehouses display gifts and clothing, while galleries offer regional art and finely crafted jewelry, and the mouthwatering aromas of seafood and Southern fried chicken lure in hungry diners.

South of Savannah, the Golden Isles have warm sand beaches bordered by dunes and salt marshes filled with majestic herons and white-plumed egrets. These barrier islands along Georgia's Atlantic Coast were once the exclusive resorts of the vacationing wealthy. Today, most of Cumberland Island is protected as a National Seashore, where only 300 visitors each day can savor the fresh salt air and enjoy the pristine beaches. Here, vistas include grazing wild horses, sea turtle tracks on sandy beaches, and hundreds of bird species soaring on the sea breezes. On nearby Jekyll Island, wander past grand old mansions in the historic Millionaires Village and then head over to Driftwood Beach to walk hand-in-hand down the beach as the sun slowly sets into the sea.

OLD SAVANNAH DIARY

May is a wonderful time to visit Savannah and the Golden Isles. The weather is warm, flowers are in bloom, and the streets and island beaches are not yet inundated with summer visitors. Two days in gracious Savannah, followed by three days in the islands to enjoy the solitude, are the perfect getaway.

Five Days in the Old South

DAY 1
Take a horse-drawn carriage tour through Old Savannah and then stroll along the shady streets to explore Forsyth Park and the beautiful squares on your own. Tour some of the historic homes, notably Davenport House, Telfair's Owens-Thomas House, and the Green-Meldrim House. Visit the Cathedral of St. John the Baptist and the First African Baptist Church. After dinner, walk along the riverfront and indulge yourself at a chocolate shop or a tavern.

DAY 2
Take a riverboat cruise aboard a 19th-century stern-wheeler for views of the bustling harbor, historic cotton warehouses, and the *Waving Girl* statue. Head over to the City Market for lunch and shopping, and then explore the Isle of Hope's antebellum community, Old Fort Jackson, or visit Bonaventure Cemetery. Take an early-evening ghost tour of haunted Savannah, and then dine at a fine restaurant.

DAY 3
Drive to Jekyll Island and rent bicycles to explore the historic town and cottages there, before heading to the beach for an afternoon of sun and sand. End the day with dinner at the famous Jekyll Island Club Hotel.

DAY 4
Take the morning boat out to Cumberland Island National Seashore to explore the white-sand beaches and shady woodlands of magnolia, oak, and pine, where herds of wild horses roam.

DAY 5
Drive to St. Simons Island to visit the lighthouse and Fort Frederica National Monument. Have lunch there before heading to the airport for your flight back home.

Dos and Don'ts

✓ Wear comfortable walking shoes and explore the tree-lined streets and squares of Old Savannah by foot.

✗ Don't forget to pack for the beach, as well as for fine dining in Savannah, where it is traditional to dress for dinner.

✓ Read or watch *Midnight in the Garden of Good and Evil*; it conveys Savannah's air of mystery and romance.

✗ Don't forget to reserve rooms and car rentals in advance.

✓ Check for city-sponsored concerts, and take a blanket to sit on the lawn of Forsyth Park, for an evening of music.

JAN
FEB
MAR
APR
MAY
JUN
JUL
AUG
SEP
OCT
NOV
DEC

Above: *Waving Girl* statue, of Savannah native Florence Martus (1869–1943), who greeted every ship entering and leaving harbor for 44 years

Below: Inviting verandah retreat at the Jekyll Island Club Hotel

Below: Languid street-corner café on a summer's day

GETTING THERE   See map p325, I5

GETTING THERE

Hewanorra, the main international airport, is in the south of the island, 40 miles (64 km) from the capital, Castries. The smaller George Charles Airport at Vigie is north of Castries. Flights come in from major hubs in the USA, and Toronto and Montreal in Canada.

GETTING AROUND

Taxis and minibuses are cheap, but rent a car to explore the island. If using taxis, fix the price and currency before setting off.

WEATHER

St. Lucia has great weather year-round: in May, daytime temperatures are about 85°F (29°C). Warm rains fall mainly between May and October.

ACCOMMODATIONS

The charming Village Inn and Spa at Rodney Bay offers total relaxation; doubles from US$125 a night; www.villageinnandspa.com

The chic Discovery at Marigot Bay is beside the island's prettiest bay; doubles from US$280; www.discoverystlucia.com

Sandals Grande St. Lucian Spa and Beach Resort is luxurious; doubles from US$500; www.sandals.com/main/grande/gl-home.cfm

EATING OUT

Enjoy seafood at Jacques in Castries for about US$25, or savor local dishes at JJ's Paradise at Marigot Bay from US$20 a head.

PRICE FOR TWO

US$400–500 per day for accommodation, food, transportation, and tickets.

FURTHER INFORMATION

www.stlucia.org

St. Lucia's "Pyramids"

The 2,619-ft (798-m) Gros Piton and the 2,461-ft (750-m) Petit Piton, St. Lucia's "pyramids," are the island's most spectacular landmarks. These volcanic pinnacles rising out of the sea dominate the southwestern landscape. From a distance, they appear to be side by side but on a closer look, you can see just how far apart they are. The Pitons, their summits covered by tropical rain forests, stand on either side of Soufrière Bay. Hire a guide to explore them – it is worth the visit and makes for an unforgettable day trip.

Main: Crowds enjoying the Jazz Festival on Pigeon Island

JAZZ IT UP!

S T. LUCIA IN MAY MEANS ONE THING – JAZZ. The long, balmy evenings are filled with the sweet scent of rum and the sensual sounds of jazz wafting on the breeze through open doorways. Up-and-coming stars entertain picnicking families, talented locals perform impromptu skits on side streets, and world-class musicians give sell-out concerts in dramatic settings. For 10 days each year this island paradise in the Lesser Antilles, known for its beaches and rainforest, comes alive with blues and ragtime at one of the world's greatest jazz festivals.

Initially held in the capital city of Castries, the main event moved to Pigeon Island, a handsome outcrop of land to the north of St. Lucia, accessed by a white-sand causeway. Fringe performances and scores of other live events take place day and night in the island's towns and villages. Soak up the atmosphere at sunset performances on the pier at Pointe Seraphine, on the Vigie Peninsula, or while having lunch at Derek Walcott Square in central

Left (left to right): Colorful heliconias in the Diamond Botanical Gardens in Soufrière; the bustle of Castries market; a man climbing a palm tree on Soufrière beach against a backdrop of the Pitons; boats moored at Marigot Bay

Below: Lou Rawls performing at the festival

Inset: George Benson and Al Jarreau

The long, balmy evenings are filled with the sweet scent of rum and the sensual sounds of jazz wafting on the breeze through open doorways.

JAZZ DIARY

Beautiful St. Lucia in the eastern Caribbean is renowned for its stunning beaches, towering Pitons, and tropical vegetation. In May, the silence of its long, warm days is broken by the strains of world-class jazz. A six-day trip gives you enough time to hear great live music and explore the island's other treasures.

Six Days on a Music Trail

Relax and get your bearings. Then stroll around Castries. Visit the Point Seraphine shopping center by the cruise terminal and buy some great duty-free gifts. Make your way back to the city center and enjoy some free jazz in the square.

Head over to Pigeon Island for the world-renowned Jazz Festival. Make sure you have tickets – these grant admission only and do not guarantee seating. Take a blanket to sit on and a small cooler for drinks. You can also buy food and drink from numerous vendors.

In between listening to talented performers, take the time to explore Pigeon Island's National Park. Check out the old buildings, some of which used to be part of the largest British forts in the Caribbean.

Spend a day exploring Castries. Visit the bustling and colorful market and enjoy more jazz – there are scores of free events staged in the capital during the festival.

Head down the west coast to Soufrière, the place where the French first settled on St. Lucia (there used to be a guillotine in the town square). Visit the Soufrière volcanic area, but stick to the paths. Then explore the nearby Diamond Estate botanical gardens and take a dip in the mineral springs.

Enjoy your last day relaxing at the Marigot Bay beach, one of the most beautiful beaches in the Caribbean – the perfect way to end your stay.

Dos and Don'ts

✓ Enjoy as many jazz events as you can pack into your schedule, especially the free ones.

✓ Wear a sun hat if sitting outside during the day; the sun can be blistering.

✓ Relish the local food specialties such as conch (often called *lambi*), roti, and coconut fritters.

✗ Don't drink too much alcohol in the hot sun, because if you pass out, you'll miss all that great jazz – and maybe get badly burnt.

JAN
FEB
MAR
APR
MAY
DAY 1
DAY 2
DAY 3
DAY 4
DAY 5
DAY 6
JUN
JUL
AUG
SEP
OCT
NOV
DEC

Castries. Relax to the soothing sounds of soul at afternoon gigs in the Fond d'Or Heritage Park on the east coast, or at midnight in the southern towns of Laborie, Soufrière, and Vieux Fort. A carnival-like atmosphere descends on the island – children dress up, dance, and sing at open-air concerts and fans cheer as their musical heroes roll out their favorite tunes. There are also arts and crafts displays, fashion shows, culinary events, and street theater, all allowing visitors to experience the island's cultural life. It is noisy and crowded but, above all, it is friendly.

This musical extravaganza might be the main draw, but there is a lot more to see. Attractions include historic colonial buildings in Castries, Soufrière, and on Pigeon Island, working cocoa and sugar plantations, a volcanic area with bubbling pools, fabulous beaches, and world-class scuba diving among other water sports. And of course the unforgettable Pitons, enormous rocks dominating the island's west coast. Together with the St. Lucia Jazz Festival, these magnificent sights will call you back to the island year after year.

Below: Ruined fortifications in Pigeon Island National Park

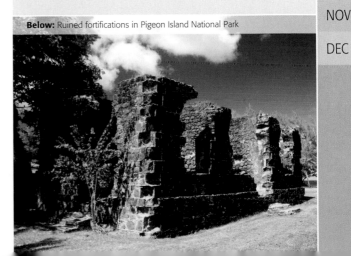

GETTING THERE   See map p317, I2
Located in North Carolina, the closest airport is at Norfolk, 90 miles (145 km) to the north.

GETTING AROUND
Local ferries and a car are the only ways to get around on the Outer Banks.

WEATHER
The average May daytime temperature is 76°F (23°C) and nights are 60°F (15°C).

ACCOMMODATIONS
The 88-room Sanderling Resort & Spa, on the beach in Duck, is the most luxurious Outer Banks lodging; doubles from US$179; www.thesanderling.com

Near the glorious National Seashore beaches of Hatteras Island, the cozy 12-room Inn on Pamlico Sound in Buxton promises breakfast in bed or on your private deck; doubles from US$120; www.innonpamlicosound.com

The Captain's Landing hotel on Ocracoke Island has a private suite with a balcony overlooking the charming harbor; doubles from US$110; www.thecaptainslanding.com

EATING OUT
Try elegant Elizabeth's Café, Duck, for fine country dining (US$60). In Kitty Hawk, High Cotton serves up chicken 'n ribs (US$20); and Owen's Restaurant, Nags Head, features Maine lobster and aged prime beef.

PRICE FOR TWO
US$350 per day including accommodation, food, and car rental.

FURTHER INFORMATION
www.outerbanks.org

A BEACH AND WILDLIFE HEAVEN

THE OUTER BANKS IS A BEACH-LOVER'S DELIGHT comprising 100 miles (160 km) of unspoiled coastline across a chain of barrier islands. It is full of fascinating discoveries too: with hideaways where wildlife and birds abound, prize fishing grounds, and colorful historic sites such as Roanoke Island.

The developed communities of Nags Head, Kill Devil Hills and Kitty Hawk in the center of Bodie Island are known for their mammoth sand dunes, formed by shifting winds. One of them was used by the Wright Brothers for their historic flight. The Wright Brothers National Memorial and Jockey Ridge State Park are two popular stops here. To the north is Duck, the most upscale island community. Beyond are a 7,000-acre (2,832-ha) Audubon preserve and the red-brick Corolla Lighthouse, which is one of a series of lighthouses along the Outer Banks dating from the 1870s.

The Lost Settlers

Roanoke Island, between the mainland and the Outer Banks, has a fascinating history. Fort Raleigh National Historic Site marks the place where the British under Sir Walter Raleigh established a colony over 400 years ago. It was the birthplace of Virginia Dare, the first English child born in the New World. But the 116 men, women, and children of the settlement disappeared without explanation. Their story is recreated in the outdoor pageant "The Lost Colony" presented each summer in Manteo. Lovely Elizabethan Gardens have been planted here in memory of the lost settlers.

Main: The famous Cape Hatteras Lighthouse

Left (left to right): Ocracoke Island rum cocktails; Chicamacomico Lifesaving Station

Right (left to right): Sanderling Inn; Currituck Wild Horse Sanctuary

Right panel (top to bottom): Hang-gliders and kite-flyers at Jockeys Ridge State Park, Nags Head; sailboats in Ocracoke harbor, Ocracoke Island

The Outer Banks begins to the south, past Bodie Lighthouse and the busy marina and sport fishing center at Oregon Inlet. Across the inlet is Hatteras Island, with its protected National Seashore since 1953, which stretches for 72 miles (115 km), and is home to the Pea Island National Wildlife Refuge. Built in 1870, the much-photographed Cape Hatteras Lighthouse warns ships away from the perils of Diamond Shoals, known as the "Graveyard of the Atlantic." A few surviving early US lifesaving stations serve to remind visitors that more than 600 ships sank here.

A 40-minute ferry ride takes you to Ocracoke Island, the most romantic outpost of the Outer Banks. Its deep inlet made it suitable early on as a port for ocean-going vessels and it has been a town since 1735. The secluded location also made it a favorite haunt of the infamous pirate Blackbeard, who was killed hereabouts and whose treasure, some believe, remains buried on the island. Return ferries are frequent but you may never want to leave.

BEACHCOMBER'S DIARY

These unspoiled islands tucked between the Atlantic Ocean and Pamlico Sound boast 120-mile (193-km) strands of golden sand. Stay in a romantic inn in May, an ideal time before the summer crowds and heat arrive. While the ocean may be too chilly for swimming, days are warm enough for beachcombing.

Five Days at the Seashore

Your first day is probably best spent relaxing and savoring the wonderful sand and sea. Whether you choose a single base with day trips or plan to tour, there is a lot to see and do here on the Outer Banks.

Head for Kill Devil Hills and the Wright Brothers National Memorial to see a replica of Orville and Wilbur Wright's flying machine. At Jockey Ridge State Park in neighboring Nags Head, check out the hang gliders soaring from the highest natural sand dune in the eastern USA, one of several in the area that can reach 140 ft (43 m). Join kids of all ages who love climbing and sliding down these huge sand piles. Then drive across Roanoke Sound to Manteo and explore Fort Raleigh National Historic Site, which is the site of Sir Walter Raleigh's lost colony.

Follow N.C. Route 12 north to the town of Duck for the area's most upscale shops. Farther on, past the Audubon preserve, is the red-brick Currituck Beach Lighthouse in Corolla, built in 1875.

Cross the inlet south to Hatteras, and you're in the heart of the National Seashore with 70 miles (112 km) of pristine beach. For many, this is what the Outer Banks are all about. View the birds, wildlife, and wildflowers at Pea Island National Wildlife refuge. Join the photographers snapping the 208-ft (63-m) Cape Hatteras Lighthouse, the country's tallest.

Board the car ferry to picturesque, unspoiled Ocracoke Island, and spend your last day exploring the historic village and savoring the white sands that are a beach-lover's dream.

Dos and Don'ts

✗ Don't miss a visit to Ocracoke's British Cemetery, the burial ground of four British sailors, casualties of a German submarine in 1942.

✓ Look for Currituck Wild Horse Sanctuary near Corolla. It protects the few remaining descendants of mustangs brought by the first Spanish settlers in 1583.

✓ Check out the Roanoke Island Festival in May with events celebrating the first English settlement in America.

✓ From mid-April you can climb up Cape Hatteras Lighthouse.

Below: Natural shoreline at Cape Hatteras National Seashore

JAN

FEB

MAR

APR

MAY

DAY 1

DAY 2

DAY 3

DAY 4

DAY 5

JUN

JUL

AUG

SEP

OCT

NOV

DEC

JUNE

Where to Go: June

Summer has arrived in the northern hemisphere. Canada is warming up nicely, although showers are likely in the south. Throughout North America the tourist season is gearing up, but the summer hordes have yet to descend. In the USA, the Southwestern deserts are glorious, with manageable temperatures at higher elevations, while the Rocky Mountains are resplendent with colorful wildflowers.

Even Chicago, famously cold in winter, is mild enough to allow some outdoor living. While much of Central America is drenched in daily downpours, June brings the winter solstice to the southern hemisphere, celebrated in Cusco, Peru with a spectacular Inca festival. Below you will find all the destinations in this chapter as well as some extra suggestions to provide a little inspiration.

FESTIVALS AND CULTURE

CHICAGO Band playing at Buddy Guy's Blues Club

UNFORGETTABLE JOURNEYS

GREAT RIVER ROAD The lazy Mississippi

NATURAL WONDERS

NIAGARA FALLS Horseshoe Falls lit up at night

CHICAGO
ILLINOIS, USA

Try Chicago's four-day Festival for a celebration of Blues Music

Tune into this amazing event, but when you need a break, explore this huge and interesting city, and enjoy shopping, museums, and visual arts.
See pp130–31

CUENCA
ECUADOR

Colonial gem in Ecuador's southern sierra

Explore this atmospheric city of Spanish churches, whitewashed houses, cobblestone streets, and spacious squares.
www.cuenca.com.ec

GREAT RIVER ROAD
MIDWEST, USA

Follow the Mississippi River on this Midwestern drive

Take this scenic drive along the Upper Mississippi River past riverboats, ancient Indian burial mounds, and pioneer log cabins.
See pp134–5

JEFFERSON NATIONAL FOREST
VIRGINIA, USA

On the Appalachian Trail

The west-central Virginia section of the trail passes through some outstanding displays of azaleas and rhododendrons in this month.
www.appalachiantrail.org

NIAGARA FALLS
CANADA AND USA

A thundering wonder of the natural world

The Falls cast a magic spell over honeymooners and daredevils alike. Embrace adventure and sail right up to this awesome cataract.
See pp132–3

INTI RAYMI
CUSCO, PERU

Traditional Andean winter solstice festival

Traditional celebrations in honor of the Sun God, Wiracocha, held in the stunning Inca ruins at Sacsayhuamán, just outside Cusco.
www.cusco.net

"Riverboats, ancient Indian burial mounds, and pioneer cabins are among the highlights of the Great River Road."

PANTANAL
BRAZIL

The world's largest freshwater wetlands

The animals here are far more visible than in the rainforest – see giant otters, tapirs, caiman, herds of capybara, and many birds.
www.braziltourism.org

GETTYSBURG NATIONAL MILITARY PARK
PENNSYLVANIA, USA

Historic battlefield and cemetery

Explore the site of the Civil War's most devastating battle, with sobering mementos of the encounter which cost 51,000 lives.
www.nps.gov/gett

CHIQUITOS
BOLIVIA

A beautiful untouched region with historic churches

Follow the trail to the Jesuit mission towns and find a forgotten world in their glorious 17th-century churches and musical people.
See pp148–9

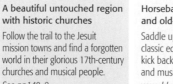

BLUEGRASS COUNTRY
KENTUCKY, USA

Horseback riding, wine tasting and old-time bluegrass music

Saddle up for a ride through classic equestrian country, then kick back in the local wineries and music venues.
www.bluegrasskentucky.com

MACHU PICCHU
PERU

A fantastic feat of construction on the side of a mountain

It's a strenuous high-altitude hike through the mountains, but the glorious views of this ancient city make the effort worthwhile.
See pp140–41

AVENUE OF THE VOLCANOES
ECUADOR

Fire and smoke in the Andes

Lining the highway south of Quito, this majestic line of snowcapped volcanic peaks is one of Ecuador's most unforgettable sights.
www.ecuador.us/volcano.htm

KODIAK ISLAND
ALASKA, USA

As the salmon run they attract the famously large bears

As well as huge bears you'll see moose with their calves, foxes, seals, and maybe orcas – and an astonishing amount of birdlife.
www.kodiakisland.org

FINGER LAKES
NEW YORK STATE, USA

Shimmering lakes and wine tours

Tour the vineyards set along the shores of eleven slender ice-blue lakes, fed by waterfalls that cut through dramatic gorges.
See pp146–7

YUKON
CANADA

Midsummer in Canada's wild north

June is a memorable time to visit the pristine Yukon region, its great stretches of sub-arctic wilderness bathed in the midnight sun.
www.travelyukon.com

Weather Watch

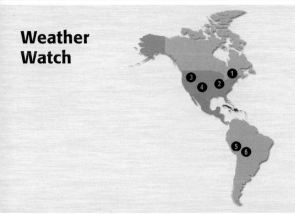

❶ **Montréal, Canada** Montreal is mild and sunny in June, and humidity not too much of a problem. You are likely to need an umbrella, but not for long.

❷ **Chicago, USA** The Midwest's so-called "windy city" is delightful this month, with warm temperatures and pleasant breezes wafting off Lake Michigan. It will no doubt rain, but you should plan on packing your summer gear.

❸ **Idaho, USA** With daytime highs around 60°F (16°C), the Rocky Mountain state of Idaho is an outdoor paradise in June, offering perfect conditions for fishing, swimming, rafting, and hiking.

❹ **Colorado, USA** The cool 7,000-ft (2,133 m) plateau of Mesa Verde can provide welcome relief from the hotter desert plains below. Days are warm and sunny.

❺ **Peru** June is a good time to visit Peru, and perfect for walking. Cusco, starting point for the four-day Inca Trail, is dry and sunny and relatively cool. Temperatures, and humidity, increase as you approach the ruins of Macchu Picchu.

❻ **Bolivia** January is mid-winter in Bolivia. The Amazon lowlands are enjoying a dry season, although humidity is high. Weather in the altiplano, on the other hand, is cool and crisp.

LUXURY AND ROMANCE

BERMUDA Turquoise sea and soft white sand at Elbow Beach

BERMUDA
NORTH ATLANTIC

The perfect tropical island getaway for two

Laze on coral sands, swim in turquoise waters, watch a spectacular sunset, and dine by candlelight under the stars – who could ask for more?
See pp144–5

"Enjoy romantic picnics in the warm island breeze, and sip rum punch while watching the vermilion beauty of a Bermudan sunset."

CUSCO
PERU

Be charmed by Peru's most romantic city

Ancient Inca monuments and magnificent scenery, best appreciated during a stay at the Monasterio, voted the best hotel in South America.
www.cuscoperu.com

WAIKĪKĪ
HAWAI'I, USA

Hawai'i at its brashest, glitziest, and most hedonistic

Pose on the beach, shop till you drop then chill out in one of Waikiki's string of mouthwatering restaurants and bars.
www.waikiki.com

CHARLEVOIX
QUÉBEC, CANADA

Luxury and romance in rural Québec

This beautiful region combines superb scenery and outdoor attractions, and offers great boutique shopping and fine dining.
www.charlevoix.worldweb.com

CHARLESTON
SOUTH CAROLINA, USA

One of North America's most alluring cities

The most quintessentially southern city in the USA has a tropical ambience and rambling old streets of historic villas.
www.charleston.com

ACTIVE ADVENTURES

STANLEY Casting a line for trout in a waterfall

STANLEY
IDAHO, USA

Fantastic fly-fishing in clear mountain lakes

Outdoors activities abound in Idaho, from fly-fishing to white-water rafting, in a heavenly, snow-capped mountain setting.
See pp138–9

"Fly-fishers can hike into the wilderness or just find a stretch of crystal clear water into which to cast a line."

GLACIER NATIONAL PARK
MONTANA, USA

Superb Alpine hiking

Over 700 miles (1,125 km) of trails wind through pristine forests and alpine meadows, and between small glaciers and rugged peaks.
www.nps.gov/glac

DAYTONA BEACH
FLORIDA, USA

Learn to surf at a summer camp on Daytona Beach

Florida is underrated as a surf destination, and while there aren't awesome waves in summer, they should be perfect for learners.
www.surfline.com

VOYAGEURS NATIONAL PARK
MINNESOTA, USA

A watery wilderness

Hop in a boat and lose yourself in Voyageurs' maze of unspoilt lakes and islands, home to eagles, moose, and bear.
www.nps.gov/voya

TRANS-APOLOBAMBA TREK
BOLIVIA

Challenging five day trek

Bolivia's finest hike takes you deep into the Cordillera Apolobamba, surrounded by dramatic mountain scenery.
www.bolivianmountains.com

FAMILY GETAWAYS

MESA VERDE NATIONAL PARK Guided tour at Balcony House

MESA VERDE NATIONAL PARK
COLORADO, USA

Ancient cliff dwellings

Take a trip to the land of the Puebloan people preserved in Mesa Verde National Park, with 4,000 known archeological sites.
See pp136–7

CUSTER COUNTRY
MONTANA, USA

Follow in the footsteps of the controversial colonel

Scout out some of the historic sites associated with Custer, or enjoy the popular annual Battle of Little Big Horn reenactment.
www.custer.visitmt.com

MYRTLE BEACH
SOUTH CAROLINA, USA

Seaside family fun in South Carolina

The cheerful Atlantic resort of Myrtle Beach offers something for all the family, from diving to paintballing, plus miles of sandy beach.
www.myrtlebeach.com

MONTRÉAL
QUÉBEC, CANADA

French-speaking city where the Old World meets the New

Tour the city from a horse-drawn carriage, see Cathédrale Notre-Dame, practise your French, and don't miss the fireworks.
See pp142–3

BOSTON
MASSACHUSETTS, USA

Relaxed family fun in a historic city

Glide across a lagoon on a Swan Boat in Boston Public Garden and come face to face with sharks at the New England Aquarium.
www.bostonusa.com

GETTING THERE   See map p314, E6
Chicago sits at the edge of Lake Michigan. Most international traffic arrives at O'Hare Airport, 20 miles (32 km) northwest of the city center.

GETTING AROUND
Chicago's elevated railroad ("The El") is an easy way to get around. Rail and bus stops are within walking distance of the Blues Festival, as are public parking garages.

WEATHER
June brings pleasant temperatures, with an average daytime high of 81°F (27°C), dropping to 60°F (15°C) at night.

ACCOMMODATIONS
The Tremont Chicago, north of Michigan Ave (The Magnificent Mile), is a good base; doubles from US$219; www.tremontchicago.com

The Palmer House Hilton, in the heart of the Chicago Loop, a walk from Grant Park; family rooms from US$349; www.hilton.com

Dating from 1920, Drake Hotel is a Chicago classic; doubles from US$349; www.thedrakehotel.com

EATING OUT
From cheap fast-food favorites to stylish, high-end cuisine – Chicago has it. For a colorful intro to Chicago-style deep dish pizza, head to Gino's East (US$15).

PRICE FOR TWO
US$420 per day including accommodation, food, and entertainment.

FURTHER INFORMATION
www.choosechicago.com

Talkin' 'Bout the Blues

An offshoot of the Mississippi Delta Blues of the 1920s, Chicago Blues evolved after the "Great Migration" of poor African-American workers from the south to northern industrial cities such as Chicago. While the Delta Blues leaned heavily on guitar and harmonica, Chicago Blues used drums, piano, and bass. Chicago Blues musicians have included Buddy Guy, Earl Hooker, and Muddy Waters (below).

BIG, FUNKY BLUES FESTIVAL

IF YOU'RE A SERIOUS FAN OF THE BLUES, there's no better place to be than at the Chicago Blues Festival. You'll think you're in heaven watching dozens of big-name performers, including a living legend or two. If new to the Blues scene, it's the perfect opportunity to immerse yourself in the sights and sounds that comprise its rich history. Considered by some to be the country's largest free music festival, Chicago Blues is held in the sprawling Grant Park, the city's so-called "front yard." Since its inception in 1984, the event has evolved into a four-day, six-stage monster. Each year, the festival hosts both top-tier acts and up-and-comers, and past performers have included B.B. King, Buddy Guy, and Stevie Ray Vaughan. It is also the nation's largest celebration of past Blues greats, with many big names recognized each year. Highlights have included the centennials of Louis Jordan and

Main: One of the six stages at the Chicago Blues Festival

Tommy McClennan. Hardcore fans arrive early to stake out their spots in front of the larger stages, while casual types hang in the back and munch on signature Chicago treats such as Italian beef sandwiches, spicy sausages, and loaded hot dogs; it's the reason why the Festival is also fun for all ages with its concession stands and music-themed attractions. Even after the festival closes, the action continues into the night, as revelers fill the city's numerous music clubs from the cavernous House of Blues to hole-in-the-wall dive bars and the city resounds to impromptu jam sessions.

Chicago's climate can be an unforgiving one, but June offers one of the surest bets – neither bitterly cold nor horribly humid – and its citizens find time to relax as kids are finishing school, sidewalk cafés are opening up, and they begin to spill out onto Lake Michigan's many beaches. Truly an international and populist gathering, attendees come from all over the globe and artists from as far as Australia and Japan.

Top: Field Museum, Museum Campus

Above: Underneath Kapoor's *Cloudgate* sculpture ("the Bean")

Below: Crown Fountain in Millennium Park

Left (left to right): Buddy Guy (left) live at the Chicago Blues Festival 2005; Buddy Guy's Blues Club

Right: Impressionist art at the Chicago Art Institute

FESTIVAL DIARY

One of the world's best music events, the Chicago Blues Festival runs from Thursday through Sunday, with key acts throughout, but only true fans attend all four days. The grounds open at 11am daily, with performances running until 9:30pm. Consider alternating days at the festival with days exploring the city.

Five Days in the Windy City

Visit the festival site, walking the grounds and checking out vantage points from which to enjoy the sounds. Take a break and visit the nearby Art Institute of Chicago, known for having one of the country's foremost collections of Impressionist and American art.

Spend the day strolling along the Magnificent Mile, one of the world's great shopping streets. Stop to enjoy famous Chicago-style deep dish pizza at one of the originators – Pizzeria Due or Pizzeria Uno. Then, walk off the calories by exploring Water Tower Place, the city's premier upscale shopping mall.

Just before entering the festival, stop by Buckingham Fountain — to some, the symbol of the city — and snap postcard-worthy photos. Post-festival, immerse yourself even further in the Blues by catching a late-night set at a top venue like Buddy Guy's (where the owner makes frequent appearances) or at B.L.U.E.S.

Start the day with a filling brunch at a down-home eatery like Stanley's or Sweet Maple Café, before heading on to the Museum Campus, where you'll find three of the city's most popular museums — the Shedd Aquarium, the Field Museum of Natural History, and the Adler Planetarium. Walk through Millennium Park's architectural wonders before tuning into the festival one last time.

Enjoy Navy Pier's many attractions, without the weekend crowds, before raising a parting glass to the Windy City at the Signature Room, on the 95th floor of the Hancock Tower, while drinking in the fabulous views.

Dos and Don'ts

✓ Bring a camera to Millennium Park's *Cloudgate*, Anish Kapoor's reflective, bean-shaped sculpture. Below, be inspired by the optical vortex with dozens of reflections.

✗ Don't ask for ketchup on your hot dog. Many locals consider it a taboo, and some stands, despite offering many toppings (from banana peppers to dill pickle spears), will refuse.

✓ Try to catch a game at Wrigley Field. Dating back to 1914, it's the country's second-oldest ballpark still in use. Even if you can't get tickets, head to the surrounding neighborhood (Wrigleyville) and soak up the atmosphere.

Below: Buckingham Fountain

JAN
FEB
MAR
APR
MAY
JUN
DAY 1
DAY 2
DAY 3
DAY 4
DAY 5
JUL
AUG
SEP
OCT
NOV
DEC

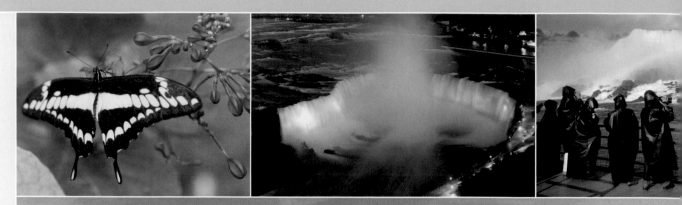

GETTING THERE
See map p314, D7

Part of the border between Ontario, Canada, and New York State, USA, the Niagara Falls are 80 miles (129 km) by road from Toronto and 21 miles (34 km) from Buffalo. The nearest airports are in Toronto and Buffalo, with a small one in Hamilton, Ontario.

GETTING AROUND

You can reach Niagara by train or bus, but public transport in the area is limited. A bus plies between central attractions in summer, but you'll need a car to reach most wineries.

WEATHER

June is mild, with an average temperature range of 57–76°F (14–25°C). Rain is possible, so carry a jacket and umbrella.

ACCOMMODATIONS

Marriott Niagara Falls Fallsview Hotel & Spa in Ontario has superb views; doubles from US$169; www.niagarafallsmarriott.com

Queen's Landing in Niagara-on-the-Lake overlooks Lake Ontario; doubles from US$225; www.vintage-hotels.com

Red Coach Inn in New York State has doubles from US$89; www.redcoach.com

EATING OUT

The towns around Niagara have inexpensive chain eateries and upscale bistros. Wherever you eat, don't miss the local strawberries.

PRICE FOR TWO

US$425 per day including accommodation, food, transportation, and admissions.

FURTHER INFORMATION

www.tourismniagara.com (Canadian side)
www.niagara-usa.com (American side)

Roll Out the Barrel

The Niagara Falls have exerted a hypnotic power over generations of daredevils. In 1859, the Great Charles Blondin strolled over the gorge (above) on a tightrope, inspiring his rival, The Great Farini. The two eventually carted across a stove, a washing machine, and a washerwoman in a bizarre contest of one-upmanship. Some 40 years later, Annie Taylor became the first to go over Horseshoe Falls in a barrel. Later, others made the trip in everything from a rubber ball to a diving bell. Police now levy fines on those who try to repeat Annie's feat.

Main: The mighty Niagara Falls thundering in full force as the *Maid of the Mist* heads closer

THE WONDERS OF NIAGARA

BACK IN 1842, CHARLES DICKENS WROTE OF THE NIAGARA FALLS, "When I felt how near to my Creator I was standing, the first effect, and the enduring one – instant and lasting – of the tremendous spectacle, was peace." Peace may not be your first impression when you visit the Niagara Falls today, as you try to drown out the tourist hubbub that roils around like a human whirlpool, particularly on the Canadian side. Instead, the entire experience can be either lively or overwhelming, depending on your fondness for the sugary scent of cotton candy and the clanging of slot machines. But just take a moment to tune out the background noise and focus on the inimitable thunder of 150,000 gallons (568,000 liters) of water hurtling over the Niagara Escarpment every second – that's not something you experience every day. It's a primal noise that rarely fails to stun visitors, no matter how jaded, cynical, or cosmopolitan they may be – the thrill never seems to die out.

Left (left to right): Swallowtail butterfly on a colorful flower at the Butterfly Conservatory Gardens; Horseshoe Falls lit up at night; tourists at the Niagara Falls

Right: A sidewalk in Niagara-on-the-Lake, a quaint, 19th-century small town in Ontario

WILD WATER DIARY

It began with the falls: the torrent that missionary Louis Hennepin called "a vast and prodigious cadence of water" when he first saw it in 1678. Today, there's so much more to see in the area. June – when attractions open, the weather is lovely, and the holiday crowds have yet to descend – is the perfect time to enjoy it.

Four Days at the Falls

After arriving in Niagara Falls, Ontario, head straight for the falls – the best views are from the Canadian side. Next, hop aboard the *Maid of the Mist*, a tour boat that cruises so near the falls you'll come away soaked. Then see the falls from the inside out on the cliff-hugging walkway known as Journey Behind the Falls. At dusk, see the cataract illuminated with multicolored lights.

Cross over to the American side on the Peace Bridge to enjoy a challenging hike along some 15 miles (23 km) of trails bordering the falls and river. For a simpler walk with stunning views, try the rim path in Niagara Falls State Park. After dinner, drive to Earl W. Brydges Artpark for an outdoor concert before crossing back to Canada.

Cycle or take a 10-minute drive along the Niagara Parkway to the Butterfly Conservatory, an enclosed tropical jungle home to more than 2,000 butterflies. Then visit Niagara-on-the-Lake, a town so picturesque it seems like a stage set. Browse for gifts in the myriad shops and take in a play at the Shaw Festival.

Tour the vineyards west of Niagara Falls, home to more than 60 wineries. Take the self-guided tour at Inniskillin, one of the largest vineyard companies, and get a taste of a family-run establishment at Marynissen. Indulge in a leisurely tasting dinner at On the Twenty, one of Canada's most renowned restaurants. Remember – don't drink and drive.

Dos and Don'ts

- ✓ Try Niagara icewine: a rich, honey-sweet way to end a meal.
- ✗ Don't drive on the busy streets near the falls. Hop on the People Mover shuttle bus instead.
- ✓ Be patient if you're crossing the Canada–US border, as security is stringent and delays are common. Bring a passport or other authorized travel document (*see also p324*).
- ✓ Bring a raincoat, even if it's sunny. The mist can drench you.
- ✗ Don't hesitate to check out at least one spectacularly tacky wax museum on Clifton Hill. It's part of the experience.

JAN
FEB
MAR
APR
MAY
JUN
DAY 1
DAY 2
DAY 3
DAY 4
JUL
AUG
SEP
OCT
NOV
DEC

Of course, there's more to Niagara Falls than just the falls. There's the indefatigable honeymoon industry – check into a room with a heart-shaped whirlpool bath, if you must. Then there's the quaint elegance of Niagara-on-the-Lake, where genteel day-trippers from Toronto and Buffalo enjoy witty plays by George Bernard Shaw and his contemporaries at the Shaw Festival. There are flowerbeds banked with thousands of roses at the Niagara Parks Botanical Gardens, classical music concerts in winery vineyards, hiking and cycling trails, and a somewhat strange yet enjoyable sideshow of wax museums and souvenir shops lining Clifton Hill.

That being said, it all comes back to three cataracts – the immense Horseshoe Falls, the curtain-like American Falls, and the comparatively narrow Bridal Veil Falls. Other sights come and go, eventually yielding their place to the next trendy destination, but the falls maintain a constant hold on the traveler's psyche. Every self-respecting vagabond should see the Niagara Falls at least once, despite – or perhaps because of – the cotton candy, the casinos, and the cacophony.

Below: The American and Horseshoe Falls as seen from New York State

GETTING THERE   See map p319, E3–F4

GETTING THERE
Arrive by car or fly to the International airport at Minneapolis-St. Paul, Minnesota. There's a regional airport at Dubuque, Iowa.

GETTING AROUND
A car is the only way to travel the Great River Road, marked by green Pilot's Wheel signs.

WEATHER
June is one of the best times to travel with daytime temperatures of 55–80°F (13–27°C).

ACCOMMODATIONS
St. Paul's sleek Crowne Plaza Riverfront sits on a bluff overlooking the Mississippi; doubles from US$149; www.ichotelsgroup.com

The Historic Trempealeau Hotel faces the river; rooms with shared bath from US$45; motel rooms US$55–65; suites US$100–120.

Charming 19th-century homes-turned-bed-and-breakfast inns in Galena are US$75–150; www.bedandbreakfast.com/galena-illinois

In Dubuque, stay overnight on a vintage steamboat, the *William M. Black*; US$98 for two people; www.mississippirivermuseum.com

EATING OUT
The Historic Trempealeau Hotel is a classic, with a river view. In Galena, The Generals' Restaurant has historic charm, and Fried Green Tomatoes serves Italian food in an 1838 store that belonged to Ulysses S. Grant's father.

PRICE FOR TWO
Allow about US$325 per day for lodging, food and car rental; entrance fees extra.

FURTHER INFORMATION
www.experiencemississippiriver.com

Frontier Trading

Trappers, explorers, and Native Americans once gathered to barter goods in Prairie du Chien, where the Wisconsin and Mississippi rivers meet. Now, for three days in mid-June each year, a sea of white tents serves as home for over 600 latter-day traders at the Prairie Villa Rendezvous. Dressed like mountain men, pioneer women or buckskin-clad Indian braves, they cook over open fires and compete in events. The selling or swapping of frontier-era wares such as furs, pipes, powder horns, pouches, moccasins, carvings, and Indian jewelry is all part of the fun.

Inset: Portrait of first lady Julia Dent Grant in the home of Ulysses S. Grant in Galena, Illinois

Left: Entrance to a quaint shop in historic Galena, Illinois

Right (left to right): Galena Main Street shopping district; towboat pushing barges down the Mississippi; Mississippi viewed from Great River Bluffs State Park, Winona; view of the Mississippi from an observation point, near Genoa, Wisconsin

Main: Old-style paddle-steamer moored on the river in Wisconsin

MIDWEST RAMBLES

The great river road was established in 1938 as a national parkway along the Mississippi. For 270 scenic miles (435 km) the Upper Mississippi River section of the Great River Road parallels the river through four Midwestern states, beginning in St. Paul, Minnesota, and ending in Dubuque, Iowa. There is a great deal to discover in this section of the river road: riverboats, ancient Indian burial mounds, frontier-style events, and pioneer log cabins are among the highlights. Quaint villages with fine examples of the ornate architectural style born in the heyday of river travel reveal the region's history. Small river towns also have a nostalgic story to share. One such is Galena, Illinois which, with its spired churches and brick mansions on terraces up a steep hillside, still looks much as it did when Ulysses S. Grant was a clerk in his father's leather shop here before the Civil War. The Mississippi River undoubtedly played a crucial role in 19th-century America; it has been called the country's first

Riverboats, ancient Indian burial mounds, frontier-style events, and pioneer log cabins are among the highlights.

RIVERBANK DIARY

Five days is just long enough to do justice to one of the most scenic drives in the USA. The Great River Road along the Upper Mississippi River winds over hills, along towering bluffs, and through old river towns. June is one of the best times to travel in the Midwest, as the summer heat has yet to set in.

Five Days by the Mississippi

Visit the Mississippi River Visitor Center in St. Paul, then proceed on the east bank of the river into Pepin, Wisconsin to see a replica of the pioneer log cabin birthplace of Laura Ingalls Wilder, author of *Little House on the Prairie*. Lake Pepin, formed by dams on the river, is a paradise for boaters and wildlife watchers. Drive on to spend the night in Trempealeau.

In Trempealeau there's a well-preserved 1890s Main Street and Perrot State Park, with 500-ft (152-m) river bluff panoramas. The observation platform here is the first opportunity for a good look at the Mississippi's amazing lock system. On to La Crosse, a thriving small city with plenty of history, plus the world's largest six-pack, standing near the visitable Heileman Brewery.

Next stop, Prairie du Chien, for the Prairie Villa Rendezvous *(see box)* and the Villa Louis Historic Site, a celebrated restored Victorian mansion. Prime river views and hiking trails can be found at Wyalusing State Park, 10 miles (16 km) to the south. Enjoy more views and a picturesque main street at Pikes Peak State Park in McGregor, Iowa. Turn north for Iowa's Effigy Mounds National Monument, with its 191 prehistoric Indian burial mounds estimated to be 2,500 years old.

Drive east across the river and south to Galena, Illinois, where many of the buildings are on the National Register of Historic Places. It makes for a wonderful stop with Victorian architecture, shopping for antiques, and the retirement home of President Ulysses S. Grant to enjoy. Finally, cross the river to Dubuque, the oldest city in Iowa, and visit the National Mississippi Riverboat Museum.

Dos and Don'ts

✓ Read Mark Twain's *Life on the Mississippi* to relive the colorful past when the Mississippi River was noted for the number of bandits that raided its islands and shores.

✓ Bring your bike. The Great River Bicycle Trail out of Trempealeau travels for 24 miles (38 km) through the prairies and backwaters of the upper Mississippi River valley.

✗ Don't forget your binoculars. An impressive array of North American bird life can be seen along the river. The Audubon Society's Great River Birding Trail parallels both sides of the Mississippi River. See www.greatriverbirding.org

Below: The modest log-cabin home of Laura Ingalls Wilder

JAN
FEB
MAR
APR
MAY
JUN
DAY 1
DAY 2
DAY 3
DAYS 4–5
JUL
AUG
SEP
OCT
NOV
DEC

Interstate, a great transportation artery for commerce through ten states on the western frontier. It still provides drinking water for millions, is a playground, a shipping lane, and a boundary between states. The river scenery is also dramatic in places. The glaciers that drifted and flattened most of the Midwest missed this area, leaving intact the steep banks cut by the river so that limestone bluffs rise more than 500 ft (152 m) above the river.

This National Scenic Byway also gives you a good view of the river's system of locks and dams. Some 29 have been built between Minneapolis and Granite City, Illinois alone, turning the river into a virtual stairway. The great and colorful steamboat era, roughly 1830 to 1870, has today given way to faster modern practises – enormous barges are pushed by towboats. One little towboat can push as many as 15 barges full of heavy grain, gravel, or chemicals – a load equivalent to a 3-mile- (4-km-) long train or a line of semi-trailer trucks 34 miles (54 km) long.

Dubuque, the final stop of this trip, offers fascinating river lore at the National Mississippi River Museum and Aquarium, and the chance to try your luck at a riverboat-turned-casino.

GETTING THERE   See map p321, G4
Mesa Verde National Park, on US Highway 160 in southwestern Colorado, is a 1-hour drive east from Cortez or a 90-minute drive west from Durango. Rent a car at either airport.

GETTING AROUND
A car is essential to get to Mesa Verde. Half-day bus tours are available but a car is still needed afterwards to get around the park.

WEATHER
At an altitude of 7000-ft (2,133-m), expect warm days – 75–85°F (24–29°C) – and cool nights – average 55°F (12°C).

ACCOMMODATIONS
Reserve ahead for the Far View Lodge, the only hotel in the park. Rooms with private bath, balcony, US$118–148; family packages from $339; www.visitmesaverde.com

Tent and RV sites are found at the Morefield campground south of the park entrance, from US$20 per night. Equipment provided.

Outside the park, Durango is a colorful Old-West town. Rates at Best Western Durango Inn and Suites, a pleasant motel, begin at US$155; www.bestwestern.com

EATING OUT
The Metate Room Restaurant in Far View Lodge serves gourmet local cuisine; its Terrace Restaurant has a casual buffet.

PRICE FOR A FAMILY OF FOUR
From US$284 per day including hotel, food, and car rental. Half-day bus tours add US$176.

FURTHER INFORMATION
www.nps.gov/meve

The Cliff Palace

Great skill was needed to create the cliff dwellings, some of which have survived by being protected by the overhanging cliff and need little supportive maintenance. Discovered in 1888 by two local ranchers, the largest site, the Cliff Palace, is a veritable apartment block with 150 rooms, housing anywhere from 100 to 150 people and includes 21 *kivas*, rooms used for religious rituals. A subterranean room remained at 50°F (10°C) all year round, making it comfortable in the summer, with only a small fire needed in the winter.

Main: The Cliff Palace, an astonishing architectural feat

LAND OF THE PUEBLO PEOPLE

THE 700-YEAR-OLD PUEBLO HOMES OF MESA VERDE, stacked into alcoves in the canyon walls, never fail to amaze. Constructed during the Great Pueblo period around AD 1200, the cliff dwellings were beautifully designed communal houses that blended with the environment, displaying highly sophisticated architectural know-how. The builders were the Anasazi, the earliest inhabitants of the American Southwest, who evolved from nomadic hunters to an agricultural people and constructed these complex villages in multi-level pueblo style. They lived at Mesa Verde, which means "green table" in Spanish, from AD 500 to 1300.

Mesa Verde National Park preserves this spectacular ancient site, and also offers many opportunities for families to explore the ruins. The park contains over 4,000 known archeological sites including cliff dwellings, *kivas* (pit houses used for worship), masonry towers, and farming structures. The best preserved site, Spruce Tree House, had

Left (left to right): Guided tour with a park ranger at Balcony House; doorway in Far View House; a thistle flower; mesa (table) tops at Mesa Verde National Park

Right: Interior of a room accessed by ladder in Spruce Tree House

Inset: Petroglyphs carved by ancient inhabitants, found at Petroglyph Point

Those who love to climb and explore ancient ruins – both adults and children alike – will find this an exciting visit.

MESA VERDE DIARY

Exploring America's best-preserved pueblo ruins, the cliff dwellings of the ancient Anasazi people, is a learning adventure for all ages, whether you're on ranger-led tours or on your own. It takes two to three days to fully appreciate Mesa Verde, and sunny days in June, before the summer heat and crowds arrive, are ideal.

Three Days Exploring Ruins

First stop is the Visitor Center for information, for an orientation to the park and to reserve tours. Sign on for the half-day afternoon tour. If time allows, take a drive along the Mesa Top loop road to get an overview of the park. The evening campfire talks at 9pm in front of Spruce Tree House are free, interesting, and fun. Don't forget to bring a flashlight.

While you are fresh in the morning, begin at the Chapin Mesa Museum for more in-depth information about the Anasazi. Then take the Cliff Palace loop road drive, ending with the guided tour of the Cliff Palace, a highlight of Mesa Verde. Come back at 5pm for the free, easy 1-mile (2-km) Far View Sites Walk with a ranger who describes life on the mesa top.

Take your pick: tour the self-guided Spruce Tree House, but remember there is a 100-ft (30-m) descent (and ascent!), or drive out to the Wetherill Mesa to see mesa-top sites and views of cliff dwellings. A guided tour of the Long House here is available.

Another option is to take a hike on the nearly 3-mile (5-km) loop trail to Petroglyph Point along the edge of the plateau. Here, there's a panel where you can see petroglyphs, the delightful picture drawings and symbols carved into rock by ancient dwellers. The trail also provides awesome canyon views.

Dos and Don'ts

✗ Don't underestimate the drive from the entrance to the park headquarters. This narrow twisting 15-mile (25-km) mountain road can take an hour.

✓ Read descriptions of the various sites carefully before attempting them. Some require extensive climbing and hiking that may be too much for young children – not to mention their parents.

✗ Don't overdo it on the first day at Mesa Verde; it takes time to acclimatize to the altitude at 7,000 ft (2,133 m).

✓ Sign up the kids for the free Junior Ranger program. Pick up activity sheets for ages 4–12 at the Visitor Center.

JAN
FEB
MAR
APR
MAY
JUN
DAY 1
DAY 2
DAY 3
JUL
AUG
SEP
OCT
NOV
DEC

130 rooms and was home to 60 to 80 people. There are several ways to explore Mesa Verde: the National Park Service offers a half-day ranger-guided bus tour to the best sites, with short hikes and many vantage points for photos. Or you can drive the 6-mile (9-km) loop road, with short paved trails, that covers 12 sites and gives an overview of the park. You can only enter the alcove cliff-dwelling sites on guided tours but many other sites and trails are open. Those who love to climb and explore ancient ruins – both adults and children alike – will find this an exciting visit.

Mesa Verde grew to an estimated population of 2,500, but the Anasazi lived in their cliff dwellings for less than a century. Why they abandoned these homes is not known. Theories range from drought that dried up the food supply to enemy attack. But contrary to popular belief, the Ancestral Pueblo people of Mesa Verde did not die out. They migrated south and today's Pueblo people in settlements such as Taos and Santo Domingo in New Mexico, and at the Hopi reservation in Arizona, are their descendants.

Below: Spruce Tree House at night

GETTING THERE
See map p320, E4

The closest major airport is Boise, 130 miles (210 km) southwest of Stanley. Some regional airlines also fly to Hailey's Friedman airport, about 80 miles (128 km) south of Stanley.

GETTING AROUND

A car is needed; four-wheel-drive is best for unpaved wilderness roads. Rental is available at both airports.

WEATHER

Expect daytime highs of around 65°F (18°C) dropping to around 35°F (2°C) at night.

ACCOMMODATIONS

Salmon River Lodge has rustic but pleasant rooms on the banks of the Salmon River; doubles from US$70 (US$80 with a kitchen); www.mywildidaho.com

Redfish Lake Lodge has lakeside cabins and motel-style units; doubles from US$70, cabins from US$150; www.redfishlake.com

Mountain Village Resort has hot springs on site; doubles from US$85; www.mountainvillage.com

EATING OUT

Stanley offers plenty of burgers and sandwiches at places like the Bridge Street Café. For fancier fare, the rustic dining room at Redfish Lake Lodge serves Idaho trout, prime rib, and other local fare. Sun Valley has some fine restaurants.

PRICE FOR TWO

About US$400 per day, including lodging, food, car rental and gas, two guided trips, and white-water rafting.

FURTHER INFORMATION

www.stanleycc.org

The Stanley Gold Rush

In the 1820s, fur trappers discovered huge colonies of beavers on the banks of the Salmon River and the surrounding streams and lakes. Pelts were highly prized but gold, discovered in the 1860s, was even more valuable. Prospectors poured in by the thousand, among them John Stanley, a Civil War veteran. He stayed just long enough to give the town and the Stanley Basin their names. By the 1890s most of the others had also moved on to the Yukon's Klondike and other gold fields. All that now remains of the Gold Rush days are a few abandoned shacks.

Above (left to right): Jagged Sawtooth mountain peaks; angler's equipment; fishing for trout in a waterfall
Main: Fly-fishing the clear waters of the Salmon River

CAST A LINE IN PARADISE

Y OU CAN'T MISS THEM. MOUNTAIN PEAKS, DOZENS OF THEM, many rising more than 10,000 ft (3,000 m) and forming a great wall of snow and granite. There's not much else here, just bracingly fresh air, a cobalt-blue sky and all those soaring peaks and craggy spires, capped with a blanket of white long into the summer. Fishing fans who are lucky enough to find themselves in Stanley, in the midst of the Sawtooth National Recreation Area in central Idaho, would have every right to think they'd died and gone to heaven. More than 300 alpine lakes, brimming with trout, are nestled in these mountains, and the Salmon River, one of the finest trout and steelhead (ocean-going trout) streams in the country, darts through the wide valley known as the Stanley Basin.

Native Americans have lived off the bounty of the Sawtooth waters for thousands of years, and some of the first white men to fish the Salmon were none other than Lewis and Clark. The explorers came upon the river in 1805. They thought it might be a passage to the Pacific Ocean but, finding it impossible to navigate, nonetheless delighted in the fish they plucked out of the rushing waters. Most modern-day explorers get no farther than the popular resort of Sun Valley. Stanley itself is a frontier town of less than 100 residents, 70 miles (112 km) farther north. Blessedly off the beaten path, it's accessible only through vertigo-inducing mountain passes and scenic river-valley trails. Stanley records Idaho's coldest winter temperatures, but with the summer thaw come fishers, hikers, white-water rafters, and other outdoors enthusiasts to enjoy the largest tract of wilderness in the United States.

Fly-fishers in pursuit of steelhead can hike into the wilderness on well-maintained trails, float down the Salmon River on guided trips, or just find a stretch of crystal-clear water into which to cast a line. Wherever you choose to do so in this high mountain heaven, you won't be able to keep your eyes off the glorious peaks that surround you.

Fly-fishers can hike into the wilderness, float down the Salmon River, or just find a stretch of crystal-clear water into which to cast a line.

Inset: Trophy brown trout
Below (left and right): Riding a lakeside trail; sundown over Red Fish Lake

ANGLER'S DIARY

By June, wildflowers are blooming in the mountain meadows where elk herds feed, and the steelhead are running. Most trails and roads have been cleared of snow but the high peaks are still picturesquely white-capped. You can get a good taste of this ruggedly beautiful region in a week, and fish a range of excellent waters.

A Week of Fly-Fishing

DAYS 1–2
Grab your gear and familiarize yourself with Valley Creek, Stanley Lake, and other excellent fishing spots around Stanley. During your explorations, step into the Stanley Museum, housed in a ranger's cabin from the 1930s.

DAY 3
Experience the Salmon River on a float trip with a fishing guide, or on a white-water rafting trip – especially exciting during the high waters of the June runoff.

DAY 4
Pack a lunch and hike into the wilderness to fish in Sawtooth Lake, where Mount Regan is reflected in the clear waters (the round trip is about 10 miles/16 km). Or hike along any of the creeks flowing into Redfish Lake.

DAY 5
Drive over 8,700-ft (2,650-m) Galena Summit for sweeping views of the Sawtooth peaks. Galena Lodge is a great place for lunch, and the nearby Lake Trails provide relatively easy access to the angling waters of Baker Lake and Norton Lakes. For a dose of civilization, continue into bustling Sun Valley for dinner, but make the return trip before nightfall or stay over.

DAY 6
Sign on for another day with a fishing guide, either on the Salmon River or in the high mountain lakes. Alternatively, arrange a horseback trip deep into the wilderness.

DAY 7
Follow Route 75 along the Salmon River, stopping to cast a line every now and then, and to soak in the riverside hot springs. If you make it as far as Sunbeam, you could explore the nearby ghost town of Custer.

Dos and Don'ts

✓ Bring swimwear. You'll need it in some hot springs but you may also be tempted to brave a plunge into the icy waters of a mountain lake.

✓ Stop in at Stanley's Rod and Gun Club Saloon for a drink.

✓ If you're in Sun Valley on Saturday night, catch the Sun Valley Ice Show.

✗ Don't leave trash behind on your wilderness treks.

✓ Bring a sweater and jacket for cold nights.

Below: White-water rafting on the Salmon River

GETTING THERE
See map p327, D5

Machu Picchu is located around 50 miles (80 km) northwest of Cusco. The flight from Lima International Airport to Cusco takes 2 hours.

GETTING AROUND
It takes around 4 hours to get to Aguas Calientes from Cusco by train; the price varies according to the standard of train. The Inca Trail is a 3–4 day hike from just outside Cusco.

WEATHER
June in Cusco is dry and sunny. The altitude keeps temperatures cool at around 55°F (13°C), dropping at night. Machu Picchu and Aguas Calientes have a wet and humid climate with average temperatures of 64°F (18°C).

ACCOMMODATIONS
El Monasterio is a sumptuous converted monastery in Cusco; doubles from US$495; www.monasterio.orient-express.com

The Machu Picchu Inn in Aguas Calientes is at the foot of the Inca ruins; doubles from US$445; www.peruhotels.com

The Sanctuary Lodge is at the ruins; doubles from US$795; machupicchu.orient-express.com

EATING OUT
Typical Peruvian cuisine usually consists of rice and beans served with a meat. Guinea pig, or *cui*, is a specialty as is the local grain, quinoa.

PRICE FOR TWO
US$690–800 per day including accommodation, food, internal flights, local transportation, and admission to Machu Picchu.

FURTHER INFORMATION
www.machupicchu.org

Inti Raymi

On the day of the winter solstice, the ancient Incas honored their Sun God. They sacrificed a llama to ensure a plentiful harvest in the coming year. The festival was suppressed by the invading Spaniards as a pagan ritual but today it has been revived and is one of the most spectacular of its kind in South America. On June 24, thousands descend on Cusco for the week-long celebrations to mark the Festival of the Sun. There are street parties, live music and shows, and a procession to the Inca fortress of Sacsayhuamán, above the town.

Breathtaking views of the mountain draped in a shroud of morning mist… one of the world's most iconic sights – Machu Picchu.

Main: Ruins at Machu Picchu rising majestically out of the clouds

CITY IN THE CLOUDS

SET ON A RIDGE ABOVE THE ROARING URUBAMBA RIVER, this ancient Inca citadel is one of the most evocative sights in South America. The small fortress city sits majestically in a saddle between two mountain peaks in the subtropical Andean foothills, surrounded by dense vegetation and often shrouded in mist. The extraordinary stonework is a testament to the incredible skills of Inca stonemasons more than 600 years ago – vast gray granite blocks fitted together so exactly that a knife blade cannot be slipped between their joints. Invisible from below, and entirely self-contained, Machu Picchu was not found by the Spanish Conquistadors who were wreaking havoc throughout the continent in the 16th century. The ruins were forgotten, and it was an American archeologist, Hiram Bingham, who stumbled upon them in 1911. Short hikes from the site give some sense of its extraordinary position. A perilous ascent up Wayna Picchu, the small peak beyond the city, offers dizzying views.

Inset: Llama with traditional tasseled decoration

Left (left to right): People at a colorful Pisac market; detail of the incredible stonemasonry skills of the Incas at Sacsayhuamán; Cusco at night; train winding its way through the fertile Sacred Valley

Right: Steep steps on the Inca Trail

PERUVIAN DIARY

Peru is incredibly diverse, with a long coastal stretch, dense Amazon jungle, colonial cities, and Andean splendor. To make the most of Machu Picchu and the Cusco region, a week is the bare minimum, as you'll need some time to acclimatize to Cusco's rarefied air and to explore the ruins at your own pace.

A Week on the Inca Trail

JAN

FEB

MAR

APR

MAY

JUN

DAY 1
Most flights into Lima arrive in the evening so rest and prepare yourself for your onward journey.

DAY 2
Try to get a window seat for some fabulous views of the Andes on the Lima to Cusco flight. Take it easy on your first day at altitude, by wandering around the cobbled streets of Cusco, enjoying its lively markets.

DAY 3
Make a visit to Pisac in the Sacred Valley which has some extensive ruins as well as a wonderful textile market on Tuesdays, Thursdays, and Sundays.

DAY 4
Take the Vistadome train to Aguas Calientes. The glass roofs of the Vistadome carriage allow you to enjoy the views of mountains and waterfalls. From Aguas Calientes it's a short bus trip to Machu Picchu. Stay over on-site or stay in Aguas Calientes and get the first bus up next day.

DAY 5
The ruins look magical in the sunrise and skies are often clearer in the morning than in the afternoon. Take some time to wander by yourself, before the tour groups arrive. Take the afternoon train back to Cusco.

DAY 6
Spend the day in Cusco, relaxing in one of its many cafés and watching the world go by. There are also numerous active excursions available from the town, such as rafting on the Urubamba River, and some excellent downhill cycling.

DAY 7
Fly back to Lima and do a last bit of souvenir shopping before heading homewards.

Dos and Don'ts

☑ Request a window seat on your flight to Cusco for a good view of the spectacular Andean scenery.

☒ Don't overdo it on your first day at altitude in Cusco. Avoid fatty foods, alcohol, and any strenuous activity. Keep hydrated and drink coca tea, a local remedy for sickness.

☑ Book early if you intend to walk the Inca Trail. New laws have restricted the number of people allowed on the trail at one time, and in peak season it can be booked up around three months in advance.

☒ Don't miss out on the local textiles. Beautiful hand-woven shawls are available in the markets at Pisac and in Cusco.

JUL

AUG

SEP

OCT

NOV

DEC

Below: Traditional Andean fabric found in local markets

Machu Picchu is four hours by train from Cusco, a bustling and atmospheric colonial city, bursting with color. Cobbled streets, busy markets filled with rainbow-hued textiles, museums, and cafés make it a wonderful place to spend a few days relaxing and acclimatizing to the effects of the altitude and people-watching the ebb and flow of the visiting crowds. However, if you are keen to explore further, there are plenty of day trips to explore the small market towns nearby.

Later, a spectacular rail journey will wind its way through the fertile Sacred Valley, the breadbasket of the Inca civilization where corn, fruit, and vegetables grow in abundance, with sheer mountain walls on either side, taking you to Aguas Calientes, a small, ramshackle town that is a base for travelers exploring the site. Aside from the train, the ruins are accessible only by foot, and the Inca Trail is a spectacular three-to-four-day trek to the ancient site. Hikers pass through the regimented Inca terracing, a huge diversity of lush vegetation, and breathtaking views of the mountain draped in a shroud of morning mist, and eventually arrive at daybreak to be greeted by one of the world's most iconic sights – Machu Picchu.

GETTING THERE

See map p314, E6

Montréal, on the shore of the St. Lawrence River in the province of Québec, is around 314 miles (505 km) from Toronto. Trudeau International Airport is around 30 minutes from downtown by cab.

GETTING AROUND

Don't bother with a car unless you're doing a day trip out of town, as the city's subway (Métro) and bus services are excellent.

WEATHER

Montréal is sunny and warm in June, with an average daytime temperature of 68°F (20°C). Showers are common but short.

ACCOMMODATIONS

Check into the historic Auberge Bonaparte lodge in Old Town; doubles from US$145; www.bonaparte.ca

Candlewood Suites has well-priced suites a few blocks east of downtown; doubles from US$160; www.cwsmontreal.com

Le Saint-Sulpice is a sleek boutique hotel in Old Montréal; one-bedroom suites with sofa bed start at US$245; www.lesaintsulpice.com

EATING OUT

Montréalers love to eat, which makes the city a haven for foodies. You can dine well for US$50 per head, while family-style fare is easy to find at US$20 per person. Be sure to try Montréal's special smoked meat.

PRICE FOR A FAMILY OF FOUR

US$550–600 a day, with accommodation, food, travel, admissions, and sightseeing.

FURTHER INFORMATION

www.tourisme-montreal.org

A History of Fun

With its Ferris wheel, tot-friendly carousel, and gravity-defying roller coasters, La Ronde may look like any other fun park. Yet, it holds a unique place in Canadian history. Opened in 1967 – Canada's centennial year – as the amusement section of Canada's first World's Fair, La Ronde attracted millions and remained open until 2:30am every day. Ask most Canadian baby boomers if they went to La Ronde in 1967 – or if they just dreamed of it – and you're likely to get a misty-eyed smile.

Main: Stunning interior of the 19th-century Notre-Dame Basilica
Above (top to bottom): Inside Berri-UQAM Métro station; puffins at the Biodôme; Montréal Museum of Archaeology and History by night

SOPHISTICATED CITY

ACCORDING TO AN OLD CANADIAN JOKE, you only *exist* in Toronto, while you truly *live* in Montréal. Although just a good-humored quip, it definitely captures something of the essence of the largest French-speaking city outside France. With its hugely popular jazz and comedy festivals, wide-ranging array of restaurants, thriving arts scene, and lively bars, Montréal crackles with an energy that's quite electrifying.

With a versatility to be proud of, Montréal is a city that suits every sensibility. Besides being a haven for grown-up pleasures, the city excels at entertaining families. The Montréal Biodôme, inside the velodrome originally built for the 1976 Summer Olympics, recreates five distinct ecosystems from North, Central, and South America, and houses macaws, penguins, lynx, and other creatures in their "natural" habitats, all year round. Affiliated institutions include a botanical garden, planetarium, and "insectarium" – the latter being a hit with bug-loving kids.

JAN

FEB

MAR

APR

MAY

JUN

FRANCOPHILE'S DIARY

June is the perfect time to visit Montréal, before the heat gets too sultry and the crowds too large. If you dislike crowds, avoid the end of the month, when the city practically shuts down for the International Jazz Festival. Picnic on Mont Royal, stroll the streets of Old Montréal, and soak up the city's laid-back vibe.

Four Days of *Joie de Vivre*

Explore atmospheric Old Montréal (Vieux-Montréal) on a horse-drawn *calèche* ride. Coax the kids into visiting the Notre-Dame Basilica, definitely the city's most stunning church. Then head to the huge family restaurant at the Centre des Sciences de Montréal for lunch with a river view, before visiting the center's interactive exhibits and IMAX theater.

DAY 1

Spend the day getting dizzy on the rides at La Ronde, the amusement park. Stick around for an evening display of "pyromusical arts" – fireworks synchronized to music – at the Montréal Fireworks Festival, an annual spectacle that kicks off in mid-June.

DAY 2

Rent bikes in Old Port and cycle along Canal Lachine to Atwater Market to buy baguettes, cheese, fruits, and other treats. Ride back to the Old Port to return the bikes. Then take a cab to Mont Royal, the "mountain" (more of a big hill) that dominates the city and is topped with a landmark cross. Enjoy a picnic in the park on the slopes, while away the afternoon shopping in the nearby Plateau Mont-Royal, or try one of the neighborhood's chic restaurants for dinner.

DAY 3

Today, it's all about animals. Visit the Biodôme to see creatures from the Americas, and the Montréal Insectarium for your fill of creepy critters. If you still feel up to a carnivorous dinner, head to a deli for smoked meat sandwiches on rye (vegetarians can opt for cream cheese on a famously chewy bagel).

DAY 4

Dos and Don'ts

✘ Don't refer to the city's airport as Trudeau. It was renamed in 2004 but most locals still call it Dorval.

✓ Dine fashionably late. Unless you have small children in tow, showing up for dinner at a restaurant before 7pm confirms that you're a tourist.

✘ Don't be alarmed if store clerks address you in French. Say *"Je suis désolé, je ne parle pas français"* ("I'm sorry, I don't speak French"), and locals will usually do their best to help you out, as many of them are bilingual.

✓ Broach politics if you must, but be prepared for a long, and possibly testy, conversation.

JUL

AUG

SEP

OCT

NOV

DEC

Top: Vibrant display of color at the Montréal Fireworks Festival

Above: Horse-drawn carriage *(calèche)* rides in the city – a popular tourist attraction

Below: Mouthwatering Montréal-style bagels at St-Viateur Café

For many families, the cobblestone streets and 18th-century buildings of Old Montréal are like a living history museum. Linger over *moules frites* (mussels and fries) in one of the pretty cafés lining Place Jacques Cartier. Poke your nose into any shop or hotel in the area and you'll likely discover intriguing evidence of times past: a pressed tin ceiling, an enormous stone fireplace, or some 300-year-old chinaware dug up during a renovation. To visit an actual historical museum, stop by the Pointe-à-Callière, the Montréal Museum of Archaeology and History, in the same neighborhood, or the McCord Museum of Canadian History on Rue Sherbrooke.

Even below street level, Montréal has an unmistakable verve. Underground City, a 19-mile (30-km) network of subterranean corridors, was created around the Métro system and is home to shops, restaurants, hotels, and entertainment venues. It also contains some of North America's most distinctive subway stations, designed by leading architects. And because the carriages roll on rubber wheels, stations don't vibrate with ear-splitting screeches each time a train pulls in. Sophisticated, practical, and just a bit unusual – Montréal's stations *are* the city in a nutshell.

Below: Cafés lining a sidewalk in Old Montréal

Bermuda
● HAMILTON

ATLANTIC OCEAN

GETTING THERE   See map p325, F1
Bermuda's international airport is 10 miles (16 km) east of Hamilton. Taxi or minibus are the only ways to reach your hotel.

GETTING AROUND
There is no car rental available on the island. Public transport is by taxi, bus, and ferry. Scooter and bicycle rental is widely available.

WEATHER
June is humid, with an average high of 81°F (27°C), dropping only to 71°F (22°C) at night. Short tropical downpours are common.

ACCOMMODATIONS
The Fairmont Hamilton Princess is a luxury resort combining classic European chic with Bermudian style and atmosphere; doubles from US$229; www.fairmont.com/Hamilton

Bermuda's most casual resort is 9 Beaches, on the western tip of Bermuda. Some cabanas are built over the water; doubles from US$270; www.9beaches.com

The Reefs is an elegant, charming resort on the south coast overlooking Christian Bay, with its own private beach; doubles from US$425; www.thereefs.com

EATING OUT
Bermuda's food is typically Caribbean, with tropical fruits and vegetables, seafood, and spicy seasonings. Traditional dishes and top-range international cuisine are both available.

PRICE FOR TWO
US$540 per day including accommodation, food, admissions and local transportation.

FURTHER INFORMATION
www.bermudatourism.com

Precious Rainwater

Rainfall has for centuries been the island's main source of drinking water. From the stepped roofs of buildings it is funneled to underground storage tanks. The roof tiles are arranged so that the water is channeled along a series of hairpin-bend gullies to the downpipes. Bermudan roofs are painted white and kept spotlessly clean in order not to contaminate the water. Large hotels and other facilities have increasingly installed their own desalination plants and, in times of drought, it is no longer necessary to ship in water, as used to be the case.

> Enjoy romantic picnics in the warm island breeze, and sip rum punch while watching the vermilion beauty of a Bermudan sunset.

Inset: Bird of Paradise flowers in the Botanical Gardens

Left (top to bottom): Cruise ship docking in Hamilton at sunset; Commonwealth War Memorial in King Square, St. George

Left: Anglican Cathedral of the Most Holy Trinity, built in 1897, in Hamilton

Right (left to right): spectacular views from the Port Royal golf course; beautiful Elbow Beach

Main: Typically colorful, white-roofed Bermudan houses in Hamilton

CORAL SANDS, SAPPHIRE SEAS

I T'S LITTLE WONDER THAT BERMUDA IS SUCH A DRAW FOR SWEETHEARTS and honeymooners from around the world. Not only does this charming archipelago have some of the most stylish and elegant island resorts, year-round sunshine, and abundant natural charms, but it is also surrounded by thousands of miles of clear, swirling Atlantic waters, lending it the intoxicating air of some mystical land perched at the edge of the world.

Bermuda is made up of seven main islands and hundreds of smaller ones, some not much more than large rocks. They are home to ultra-modern sophistication – exclusive spa hotels, world-class golf, and fine dining – as well as historic buildings that have remained untouched for centuries, and unspoilt beaches. Horseshoe Bay, a crescent-shaped expanse of glorious pink sand lapped by sapphire waters, is considered by many to be the most beautiful of all. Anywhere on the islands you will always be able to find a secluded spot in which to while away long, lazy days

JAN

FEB

MAR

APR

MAY

JUN

DAY 1

DAY 2

DAY 3

DAY 4

JUL

AUG

SEP

OCT

NOV

DEC

BERMUDA DIARY

Bermuda is a near-perfect destination for a romantic getaway. There are beautiful beaches and turquoise seas, and intimate waterside restaurants for dining under the stars. June is an ideal month because it is not too hot, and four days is long enough to unwind, spend quality time together and still have time to explore the island.

Four Days of Tropical Romance

Relax and spend the day sunning on the beach and swimming in the warm, clear waters. Sit at the water's edge and let a stingray nibble at your toes. Then enjoy a side-by-side massage in the resort spa. A daily ritual should be watching the sunset together with a cocktail on your balcony, before dressing up for a romantic dinner at one of the many waterside restaurants.

Hire a two-seater scooter and set off to explore the eastern side of the main island. Take the South Shore Road to the Botanical Gardens with its splendid display of more than 1,000 different plants and trees. Continue east to St. George, a UNESCO World Heritage Site with strong British links, for a tour and a late lunch, then return along the northern coast, stopping off at the amazing Crystal and Fantasy Caves.

Get those scooters out again and head west along the south coast. Take your swimming gear as there are many fabulous beaches along this coast, including lovely Elbow Beach and Horseshoe Bay, both with spectacular pink sands. If you can tear yourself away, you could visit the historic mansions in Paget or continue to the northern tip of the island for a tour of the historic Royal Naval Dockyard.

Shop for gifts and souvenirs in historic Hamilton, but get your shopping out of the way by lunchtime. Spend the afternoon back on the beach, swimming and soaking up the sun before enjoying the the last spectacular sunset and alfresco dinner of your stay.

Dos and Don'ts

- ✓ The sun is fierce here. Be sure to use a high-factor sun cream, and wear a hat and sunglasses.

- ✗ Don't forget that they drive on the left here. Take especial care if you hire a scooter, and when you cross the road.

- ✓ Remember the rules of safe scootering – never speed, brake early, and take corners slowly. And, however tempting it might be to feel the wind in your hair, a crash helmet is obligatory and could be a lifesaver.

- ✗ Don't leave unattended items on the beach when you go for a swim.

basking on coral sands or in the dappled shade of a palm tree, enjoy romantic picnics in the warm island breeze, and sip rum punch while watching the vermilion beauty of a Bermudan sunset.

For an exhilarating change, you could take to the water for world-class scuba diving, kayaking, and sailing. Back on dry land, a gentle horseback ride along secluded, mangrove-lined shores is an unforgettable experience. A speedier option is to hop on a scooter and take a spin around the islands. Hamilton is one of the world's smallest, but busiest, ports. There is excellent shopping here, with top-name designer boutiques and art galleries lining the streets. Old-fashioned horse-drawn carriages are a romantic way to see the sights, such as the Royal Naval Dockyard in Sandys Parish, which was established in 1809 to defend Britain's interests in the region against Napoleon. The late-17th-century Verdmont Museum on Collector's Hill contains fine antiques made from island cedar and mahogany, and Waterville is a splendid Georgian home located in the parish of Paget. At either, you'll be transported back 200 years. But wherever you go and whatever you do, these jewelled islands, the ultimate in romantic getaways, won't fail to dazzle and delight.

Below: Spectacular rock formations in the Crystal Caves

See map p316, F4

GETTING THERE

The Finger Lakes lie just south of Lake Ontario. The closest international airport is Rochester, 30 miles (48 km) northwest of Canandaigua.

GETTING AROUND

A car is needed for touring the lakes.

WEATHER

June days are mostly sunny, with an average temperature of 68°F (20°C).

ACCOMMODATIONS

The Acorn Inn is an elegant bed and breakfast in Canandaigua; doubles from US$148; www.acorninnbb.com

The Inn at Glenora Wine Cellars, near Watkins Glen, is on winery grounds; doubles from US$159; www.glenora.com

1890s Greek-Revival Hillcrest Manor is a good choice in Corning; doubles from US$145; www.corninghillcrestmanor.com

Taughannock Farms Inn overlooks Cayuga Lake, near Ithaca; doubles from US$80; www.t-farms.com

EATING OUT

The Taste of New York Lounge at Canandaigua's Wine & Culinary Center is excellent. Ithaca's Moosewood is internationally famous for creative vegetarian fare and for its cookbooks.

PRICE FOR TWO

US$350 per day, including accommodation, food, car rental and gas, and admissions. Day tours, visiting several wineries, with chauffeured transportation and dinner, begin at US$270.

FURTHER INFORMATION

www.fingerlakes.org

Rochester

Situated on Lake Ontario, Rochester is where the Finger Lakes meet the Great Lakes. It boasts one of the few major urban waterfalls, tumbling 96 ft (29 m) into the Genesee River, in the High Falls Historic District. Rochester gained fame as the home of George Eastman, the father of popular photography, and of the Eastman Kodak Company. Eastman House (above) is the oldest museum of photography in the world. Different but no less appealing is the Strong National Museum of Play, with the world's largest toy collection as well as lots of hands-on exhibits.

Above (left to right): Corning Museum of Glass; bison sculpture, Rockwell Museum of Art; historic boathouses on Canandaigua Lake
Main: Rainbow Falls in Watkins Glen State Park

WATER AND WINE

THE LONG, NARROW, GLACIER-CARVED, ICE-BLUE Finger Lakes are natural wonders surrounded by gorges brimming over with more than 1,000 waterfalls. The 11 lakes range from 3 to 40 miles (5 to 65 km) in length, yet some are as little as 600 yards (550 m) wide. Native American tradition has it that they were made by the fingers of Great Spirit as he blessed the land. They are beautifully framed by gentle hills of vineyards and farmland. Watkins Glen is a jewel, with its stunning gorge and a series of 19 waterfalls. Rainbow Falls was called a "poem of nature" by Mark Twain in 1871, and remains so today, with its rippling swirls of rock, shimmering waters, and the misty greens of ferns and moss. Walking trails wind through the glen, including one that leads behind the roaring 60-ft (18-m) drop of Central Cascade. An even more spectacular one, with a drop of some 215 ft (65.5 m) – making it the highest cascade in the eastern USA – is in Taughannock State Park, north of Ithaca. Even the Cornell University campus in Ithaca boasts gorges, as well as striking Triphammer Falls.

The lakes temper the climate, resulting in perfect conditions for the cultivation of wine grapes. This accounts for one of the largest areas of vineyards in the USA, with over 100 wineries, most offering tasting opportunities. Many run tours for visitors, and some have restaurants with splendid lake views. With conditions similar to northern Europe, the region is best known for Rieslings and other German-style wines, but in recent years the varieties of wine being made have expanded. Five wine trails, named for the lakes they border, make for delightful touring.

There are other delights tucked into these rural hills. The Corning Museum of Glass contains one of the most comprehensive collections of historic and art glass in the world, and the Rockwell Museum, also in Corning, has the best collection of western American art in the eastern USA. The region also offers hiking and biking trails, fishing, water-sports, golf, and other outdoor pleasures galore.

Called a "poem of nature" by Mark Twain in 1871, it remains so today, with its rippling swirls of rock and shimmering waters.

Inset: 1940s postcard from the Finger Lakes
Below (left and right): Triphammer Falls; Taughannock Cascade

CASCADE DIARY

June is a sparkling month, when waterfalls fed with melted winter snow are at their splashiest, and vineyards are beginning to thrive. Spend a week touring the lakes, sampling the wines, tasting the local cuisine, and exploring the spectacular gorges, delightful trails, and inviting towns of this region.

A Week of Lakeland Trails

DAY 1
On arrival at Canandaigua, visit the New York Wine & Culinary Center for their 2-hour introduction to the region's wines, and lunch. Take a paddle-wheeler cruise on the lake, go hiking or biking on Ontario Pathway trails, or spend the afternoon browsing the many galleries and antiques shops on Main Street.

DAYS 2–3
Drive east to Geneva and south to Watkins Glen, visiting some of the 21 vineyards on the Seneca Lake Wine Trail on the way – Hermann Wiener and Glenora in Dundee are recommended stops. The next day, follow the gorge path winding over and under the waterfalls at Watkins Glen State Park. The park also offers swimming and fishing. Drive to Hammondsport.

DAY 4
At Hammondsport, visit Pleasant Valley, the region's oldest winery, as well as that of Dr Konstantin Frank, who pioneered quality German-style wines. Have lunch at Bully Hill, known for its colorful wine labels and its fascinating wine museum.

DAY 5
Drive to Corning. Watch glassblowers in action at the world-class Museum of Glass. The Rockwell Museum of Western Art is also well worth a visit.

DAYS 6–7
End the week in Ithaca, home to Cornell University. This cosmopolitan small town on the south shore of Cayuga Lake, between two stunning gorges, gives easy access to beautiful hiking and biking trails, as well as some 15 wineries lining the Cayuga Wine Trail. Spend your last afternoon enjoying a leisurely drive back to Canandaigua or Rochester.

Dos and Don'ts

☑ Consider taking one of the many guided winery tours if you want to do any serious wine tasting. Leave the car behind.

☑ Think about a detour to Seneca Falls, at the top of Cayuga Lake, if you have an interest in Women's Rights. The Women's Rights National Historic Park tells the story of the first ever Women's Rights Convention, held here in 1848.

☒ Don't forget that you need a license if you wish to fish, except for on Free Fishing Days during the last full weekend in June.

Below: Keuka Lake at twilight, viewed from vineyards near Hammondsport

JAN
FEB
MAR
APR
MAY
JUN
JUL
AUG
SEP
OCT
NOV
DEC

GETTING THERE   See map p327, G7
The gateway to the Jesuit mission churches of Chiquitos is Bolivia's modern city Santa Cruz. The international airport is a 10-mile (16-km), US$10 taxi ride from the center.

GETTING AROUND
The Jesuit missions circuit is a semicircular, 615-mile (990-km) journey from Santa Cruz to San José and back. Roads are variable in quality, so you'll need to rent a Jeep or similar.

WEATHER
In Bolivia's eastern lowlands, June is the midwinter dry season, with temperatures around 81–91°F (27–33°C), high humidity, and occasional thunderstorms.

ACCOMMODATIONS
Santa Cruz: Los Tabijos Hotel is a large, full service hotel with gardens and pool; doubles from US$175; www.lostajiboshotel.com

Concepción: Gran Hotel Concepción is an old-style hacienda hotel with a garden and pool, located opposite the church; doubles from US$30; tel: (591) 3 964 30 31.

San José: Hotel La Casona is a rustic, Old World-style hotel close to the main square; doubles US$10; tel: (591) 3 972 22 85.

EATING OUT
Lowland Bolivian cooking is simple, hearty fare of beans and rice dishes augmented by chicken or barbecued beef.

PRICE FOR TWO
US$255 per day including accommodation in a double room, car rental, gas, and food.

FURTHER INFORMATION
www.chiquitania.com

Dedicated Restorer
The fact that the Jesuit missions of Chiquitos continue to exist is thanks largely to the efforts of one man, the Swiss-born Jesuit architect Hans Roth. Roth arrived in San Rafael in 1972 at the age of 38 with a return air ticket and a six-month mandate to save that one church from collapse. He never returned home, choosing instead to dedicate the next 27 years of his life to restoring Chiquitos' churches. Roth's efforts were recognized in 1990, when UNESCO declared six of these churches World Heritage Sites.

Main: Elaborate decoration on the façade of the mission church of San Miguel de Velasco

A FORGOTTEN WORLD

THE MASSIVE *TEMPLOS* (JESUIT CHURCHES) OF CHIQUITOS AREN'T RUINS, NOR MUSEUMS, but rather offer a glimpse into a vanished way of life; living monuments to a brief but glorious moment in history when peoples of the old world and the new lived together in peace and harmony, sharing worldly goods, celebrating the works of a single god. Though this early utopia disappeared in less than a century, some of its unworldly aura still clings to the impressive buildings. In 1576 the Spanish colonial authorities permitted the Jesuits to set up missions throughout the Viceroyalty of Peru; 11 years later the Order reached Santa Cruz. It was largely a way of establishing Spanish sovereignty in the face of constant encroachment by slave-raiding expeditions from Portuguese Brazil. The Jesuits' first mission was built at San Javier, followed in quick succession by San Rafael, San José de Chiquitos, Concepción, San Miguel de Velasco, and Santa Ana. Each settlement, governed by a *cabildo* (council of chiefs) and a pair of

JAN
FEB
MAR
APR
MAY
JUN
DAY 1
DAY 2
DAY 3
DAY 4
DAY 5
JUL
AUG
SEP
OCT
NOV
DEC

Left (left to right): Bolivian children at play at the mission church at Santa Ana; Mass in progress at San Rafael de Velasco; baptistry of San Miguel de Velasco; exterior of the mission church at San José de Chiquitos; a Bolivian instrument-maker constructing a violin

Below: Decorated baptistry of the Jesuit mission at San Javier

Inset: Angel decoration on the façade of the Jesuit mission at Concepción

Living monuments to a brief but glorious moment in history.

BOLIVIAN DIARY

It takes at least five days to comfortably make the road trip through some of Bolivia's fascinating Chiquitos Jesuit mission towns. June is the start of the region's winter dry season and is the perfect time to travel, as the roads are usually dry and during the day the temperature is pleasant.

Five Days on the Mission Trail

Rent a 4WD in Santa Cruz and take Highway 10 north some 140 miles (225 km) on good paved roads to San Javier. Enter and marvel at the extraordinary church, begun in 1749. In the complex of mission buildings nearby, don't miss the Museo Misiones de Chiquitos (Museum of the Chiquitos Missions), which covers the history of the church and the region.

The second stop, Concepción, is an easy 50 miles (80 km) or so on paved roads, with beautiful scenery on the way. The cathedral complex here is arguably the most impressive in the region, so take your time exploring it. Concepción is also a good place to shop for art and crafts – the craftsman who work restoring the cathedral sell their pieces in workshops nearby.

San Miguel de Velasco lies another 120 miles (200 km) or so along hard-packed dirt roads from Concepción. It was once a mining center, and over 1 ton of gold was said to have gone into decorating the rich Baroque interior and altar. After admiring the extravagance, stroll the streets of this isolated and authentic old colonial town.

San José is just over 120 miles (200 km) farther on. Unlike the other churches, the edifice in San José is built of stone and adobe, which gives it a look and ambience like no other.

Retrace your steps to Santa Cruz. Try to get back to Santa Cruz in time for an elegant dinner – you've certainly earned it.

Dos and Don'ts

✓ Enjoy the scenery on the drive. In addition to the mission churches, the region has some of the loveliest verdant scenery in Bolivia.

✗ Don't forget to top up your gas tank in Concepción, as gas stations become rare from that point onwards.

✗ Don't drive at night. There are no lights on the roads, service stations close generally by 9pm, and cattle and livestock may be by or on the roadside.

✓ Roads are quiet but watch out for logging trucks on the back roads. These monsters move fast and their drivers often think they own the road. Give them a very wide berth.

Below: The Museo Misiones de Chiquitos (Mission Museum) at San Javier

Jesuit priests, was designed to be self-sufficient, with property held in common and communal activity – whether music, craft or art – dedicated to the worship of God. At the center of each community they built a church. These are extraordinary structures, reflecting the Jesuits' ideals in their simple but massive shape and magnificent decoration. The wooden frame of tropical hardwood beams and columns supported a sloping roof large enough to shelter all 2,800 souls of a typical mission at once. Between the columns, mud and straw adobe was used to make walls, which were then covered with gesso and decorated with the intricate filigree of Iberian Baroque.

In 1767, the dream ended abruptly when the Jesuits were expelled by the Spanish and many churches destroyed. In Chiquitos, after nearly 150 years of control by the local church, in 1931 the Franciscan order took over the mission churches and were left in peace. Six of the original churches survived in quiet decay until the last quarter of the 20th century, when they were rediscovered and restored to their former glory by Hans Roth, a former Jesuit himself.

Where to Go: July

The tourist season is in full swing in North America, and while you're spoilt for choice for places to enjoy summer fun, inland destinations can be hot and humid so it's wise to head for the coast. However, this is also the time to take a leisurely tour of the vacation retreats of New England or to get active among the natural wonders of the Pacific Northwest. Canada, bathed in long hours of daylight, reveals its natural splendors at this time of year. The remotest islands are accessible, offering endless scope for outdoor adventure. In the Dominican Republic, meanwhile, even the tropical Caribbean heat can't stop the city of Santo Domingo from dancing till it drops. Below you will find all the destinations in this chapter as well as some extra suggestions to provide a little inspiration.

FESTIVALS AND CULTURE

VANCOUVER Shakespeare play performed at Bard on the Beach festival

UNFORGETTABLE JOURNEYS

SALAR DE UYUNI Cacti and the other-worldly salt plains

NATURAL WONDERS

SAN JUAN ISLANDS Orca breaching far out of the water

VANCOUVER
BRITISH COLUMBIA, CANADA

A month of summer festivals in a spectacular setting

While away the long summer days in Vancouver, where outdoor festivals offer folk, pop, and classical music, theater, and a huge firework display.
See pp156–7

NEW HAVEN
CONNECTICUT, USA

Historic home of Yale University

The USA's prettiest university town, centered on the delicate spires and cobbled courtyards of Yale's neo-Gothic collegiate buildings.
www.cityofnewhaven.com

NEWPORT
RHODE ISLAND, USA

A charming coastal area with culture and outdoor fun

Sailing enthusiasts love this part of New England for the regattas in Newport and there's nautical history by the bucketful in Mystic Seaport.
See pp174–5

MONTRÉAL COMEDY FESTIVAL
QUÉBEC, CANADA

Massive comedy event

Montréal's long-running "Just For Laughs" festival showcases established and emerging comedy acts in both English and French.
www.hahaha.com

DOMINICAN REPUBLIC
CARIBBEAN

Tropical Fiesta de Merengue

Join the hip-swaying locals dancing in the streets to a Caribbean beat, but save time to enjoy beaches, rain forests, and historical treasures too.
See pp176–7

SALAR DE UYUNI
BOLIVIA

Traverse world's highest and largest salt lake

The incredible 4WD tour across this salty plateau includes amazing sunsets, mountain vistas, clear blue skies, and deep red sunsets.
See pp158–9

QUTTINIRPAAQ NATIONAL PARK
NUNAVUT, CANADA

A glaciated polar desert

Go hiking, skiing, or dog-sledding across the icy tundra of Nunavut, located inside the Arctic Circle at the northernmost tip of Canada.
www.pc.gc.ca

AVALON PENINSULA
NEWFOUNDLAND, CANADA

Drive the most easterly corner of north America

Tour this isolated peninsula where small villages share the rocky cliffs with seabirds, the boggy tundra with caribou, and the sea with whales.
See pp172–3

THE ALCAN HIGHWAY
ALASKA, USA–CANADA

Drive the remarkable Alaska–Canada Highway

Almost 1,400 miles (2,250 km) long, this highway is a spectacular engineering feat and a truly challenging roadtrip.
www.alcan-highway.com

DRIVING THE CASCADE LOOP
WASHINGTON STATE, USA

Forests and volcanic peaks

This 400-mile (644-km) round trip through the Cascade Mountains shows the pine-clad wilderness of northwestern USA at its finest.
www.cascadeloop.com

> "Thousands of golden-headed gannets cover the sea stack, rising and filling the blue sky with a whirlwind motion."

SAN JUAN ISLANDS
WASHINGTON STATE, USA

A nature-lover's paradise, teeming with wildlife

Over 100 islands washed by the nutrient-rich Pacific waters and sparsely inhabited are perfect for seabirds, fish, and orca whales.
See pp166–7

JASPER NATIONAL PARK
ALBERTA, CANADA

Mountain wilderness

The largest park in the Canadian Rockies is home to the awesome Columbia Icefields, as well as grizzly bears, wolves, moose, and caribou.
www.jaspernationalpark.com

KLUANE NATIONAL PARK
YUKON, CANADA

Glaciers and lofty peaks

Home to Mount Logan, Canada's highest mountain, and a wild landscape of immense icefields and the mighty Kaskawulsh Glacier.
www.pc.gc.ca

LAKE TAHOE
CALIFORNIA AND NEVADA, USA

One of America's highest, longest, and deepest lakes

This sprawling, pine-fringed lake on the California–Nevada borders offers excellent hiking, plus beaches in summer and skiing in winter.
www.tahoe.com

BOUNDARY WATERS
MINNESOTA, USA

The ideal place to find your own wild wonderland

A vast area of pristine forest with hundreds of canoe routes through island-studded, crystal-clear, fish-filled water.
www.bwcaw.org

Weather Watch

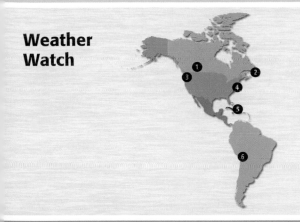

1 Calgary, Canada Lying between the foothills of the Canadian Rockies and the prairies, Calgary is sunny and warm for most of the month. It's less stormy than earlier in the summer, but showers and cool nights should be expected.

2 Newfoundland, Canada Sub-Arctic Newfoundland, the weather-beaten, easternmost part of North America, is at its best in summer. Though rain is still likely, this is a wonderful month to explore the island.

3 Washington State, USA Washington's enchanting San Juan islands are popular in July, when sunshine and warm temperatures offer perfect conditions for outdoor activities.

4 Washington, D.C., USA Where better to celebrate July 4 – Independence Day – than in Washington, D.C.? The nation's capital gets hot and humid in summer, but there are many excellent air-conditioned museums to cool off in.

5 Dominican Republic The Caribbean wet season isn't too dramatic here, with rain every few days. It is sunny and hot, of course, with temperatures of 70–95°F (21–35°C).

6 Bolivia Though Bolivia is in the midst of a chilly winter, and can get very cold at night, the volcanoes, lakes, and hot springs of the southern highlands amply reward exploration with bright sunshine, blue skies, and crystal-clear air.

LUXURY AND ROMANCE

CAPE COD Rose-covered cottage on Nantucket Island

CAPE COD
MASSACHUSETTS, USA

Golden beaches, quiet islands, and charming villages

Quaint clapboard cottages, historic inns, fabulous fresh seafood to eat on the beach at sunset – this is a perfect romantic escape.
See pp170–71

"Shingled houses and cottages surround old churches, and fishing fleets return with oysters, mussels, and lobsters."

CARMEL VALLEY
CALIFORNIA, USA

A sun-soaked sylvan land of plenty

Close to the Monterey Peninsula, this valley offers a blend of award-winning wineries, world-class golf links, hotels, and fine-dining.
www.carmelvalleychamber.com

TALL PINE LODGES
MANITOBA, CANADA

Hide away in this wonderful forested sanctuary

Choose an activity – from hiking, cycling, or riding to tennis, fishing, canoeing – then wind down in your own private Jacuzzi.
www.tallpinelodges.com

POCONO MOUNTAINS
PENNSYLVANIA, USA

Rural playground

Idyllic mountain scenery makes this a year-round retreat, with quaint country inns, restaurants, shops, and a host of outdoor activities.
www.800poconos.com

VIEUX-MONTRÉAL
QUÉBEC, CANADA

A haven of Gallic charm in Canada's second-largest city

The only French-speaking city in the Americas, Montréal offers some of Canada's finest dining and an array of places to drink, shop, and sleep.
www.tourisme-montreal.org

ACTIVE ADVENTURES

CORDILLERA BLANCA Stunning high-mountain landscape

CORDILLERA BLANCA
PERU

One of the world's most spectacular mountain ranges

The terrain is so high you'll need to acclimatize before you can even think about trekking among the glacial lakes and snowy peaks.
See pp164–5

SKIING IN THE CHILEAN ANDES
SANTIAGO, CHILE

South America's best pistes

Tear down the slopes in one of the resorts around Santiago, enjoying the region's famed "champagne snow."
www.chileanski.com

GWAII HAANAS NATIONAL PARK
BRITISH COLUMBIA, CANADA

Adventures at sea

Kayak through the fertile waters of Gwaii Haanas in the Queen Charlotte Islands, and you may even spot bears and sea lions.
See pp160–61

CERRO RICO MINES, POTOSÍ
BOLIVIA

Colonial-era silver mine

Plunge into the bowels of the earth where vast seams of silver once made Potosí the most valuable city in the entire Spanish empire.
www.enjoybolivia.com

BIRDING IN WITLESS BAY
NEWFOUNDLAND, CANADA

Seabird wonderland

The four islands of Witless Bay Ecological Reserve are home to North America's largest Atlantic puffin colony.
www.env.gov.nl.ca/parks

FAMILY GETAWAYS

PENNSYLVANIA DUTCH COUNTRY Amish family enjoying a sugary feast

PENNSYLVANIA DUTCH COUNTRY
PENNYSYLVANIA, USA

Wholesome family fun

Tour the back roads of Pennsylvania to see how the Amish live, and visit working farms and country estates.
See pp162–3

OKLAHOMA
USA

Take a break in the Sooner State

Explore Oklahoma City's zoo, kayak the Mount Fork River, and learn about the state's Native American culture and history.
www.travelok.com

"Washington's National Mall is filled with a colorful array of musicians, performers, artists, storytellers, cooks, and craftsmen."

WASHINGTON, D.C.
USA

Celebrate the July 4th in style in the nation's capital

This elegantly laid out city is filled with world-class museums and historical monuments – all lit up by fireworks on Independence Day.
See pp154–5

WASKESIU LAKE
SASKATCHEWAN, CANADA

Versatile family destination

In the heart of the Prince Albert National Park, Waskesiu Lake offers the chance to hang out on sunny lakeside beaches or plunge into the wilderness to hike and spot wildlife.
www.waskesiulake.ca

CALGARY
ALBERTA, CANADA

Action-packed rodeo and the flavor of the Wild West

The drama and skills on display at the Calgary Stampede are best appreciated live and up-close – fun and excitement for the family.
See pp168–9

GETTING THERE   See map p316, F6

GETTING THERE
Washington, D.C., is served by two international airports: Dulles and Baltimore-Washington. Taxis, metro rail, and buses connect to the city center.

GETTING AROUND
The Metro is a great way to get around, with five lines serving downtown D.C. Metrobuses are another quick and cheap mode of transport.

WEATHER
Washington can be hot and humid in summer, with average temperatures of 88°F (31°C).

ACCOMMODATIONS
Holiday Inn Capitol Hill is great for families, with a pool and free children's meals; family rooms from US$170; www.holiday-inn.com

Embassy Suites is a spacious hotel between the White House and the Capitol; family rooms from US$275; www.embassysuites.com

Hotel Palomar is a stylish boutique hotel; family rooms from US$379; www.hotelpalomar-dc.com

EATING OUT
The dining scene is eclectic, from traditional restaurants serving classic American and international dishes to a vast number of ethnic restaurants. Children will be happy with the wide range of diners, burger and chili joints, and pizza parlors. Maryland seafood and superior steaks will suit the grown-ups.

PRICE FOR A FAMILY OF FOUR
US$500 per day including accommodations, food, entrance charges, and local travel.

FURTHER INFORMATION
www.washington.org

Smithsonian Institution

Despite never visiting the USA, James Smithson, a British scientist, left his entire fortune to found the Smithsonian Institution in Washington, upon his death in 1829. He would surely be amazed to see that his bequest has grown into the world's largest museum organization and a highlight for every visitor to Washington. The Smithsonian oversees 16 D.C. museums, including the very popular Air and Space Museum, plus the National Zoo and six research centers. All are free and open daily, and the holdings include art, history, and natural science.

FOLKLIFE AND FIREWORKS

A HANDSOME CITY BUILT TO HUMAN SCALE, Washington, D.C. never fails to delight visitors. The highest points of the skyline will always be the gleaming Capitol dome and the slim shaft of the Washington Memorial, a profile that has been carefully protected by law. Standing at either end of the long lawns of the National Mall, they are part of the brilliant city plan of Frenchman Pierre-Charles L'Enfant. Inspired by Paris, L'Enfant envisioned the city's wide avenues radiating from scenic squares and circles, adorned by sculptures and fountains, a design unique in America.

The only difficulty in Washington is deciding what to do first. The museums alone could fill days on end, and then there are the stately buildings of government – the US Capitol and the Supreme Court – which can be explored by guided visit. Even the President's home, the White House, may be toured.

Main: Red, white, and blue balloons float in front of the Capitol

Left: Performers playing Jazz at Blues Alley

Right (left to right): Studying the Vietnam Veterans' Memorial; elegant building façades in Georgetown; crowds at the Smithsonian Folklife Festival; colonial military demonstration at the Independence Day celebrations

Right panel (top and bottom): Interior of the National Archives; fireworks celebrating Independence Day with the Capitol in the foreground

July sees the city at its vibrant best, with two of its most important events taking place in close succession. The first, the Smithsonian Folklife Festival, celebrates cultural heritage and is an entirely free, open-air event. During the two weeks of the festival, the National Mall is filled with a colorful array of musicians, performers, artists, storytellers, cooks, and craftspeople, creating an energetic celebration. This coincides with Independence Day on July 4th, when a real electricity descends on the city, as fireworks explode over the striking Washington Monument.

Even when the heady excitement of these festival days has died down, there is still much to be enchanted by, from a ride on a mule-drawn barge on the C&O canal and watching elephant training in the National Zoo, to the exciting hands-on National Museum of Natural History and puppet shows in the Discovery Theater. There is nothing stuffy about this well-ordered, historic city – beneath its austere surface you will find a very modern heart.

Above: International Spy Museum in the Penn Quarter

BIRTHDAY DIARY

The two-week Smithsonian Folklife Festival takes place at the beginning of July each year. Over a million visitors flock to the National Mall, which is filled with music, entertainment, crafts, and food. The Independence Day festivities of July 4th always fall during this festival period, bringing a real vibrancy to the city.

Four Days in America's Capital

Head straight to the National Mall to enjoy the festival – watch the artisans at work, enjoy the wares in the food tent, dance to the lively music, and browse the craft stalls. When you've had your fill, stroll down to the Tidal Basin to see the moving memorials to America's famous presidents – Thomas Jefferson, Abraham Lincoln, and Franklin D. Roosevelt, and have a look at the abstract Vietnam Veterans' Memorial.

Spend a day visiting some of the city's excellent museums. Start in the National Museum of Natural History for dinosaurs, an insect zoo, and a living coral reef. Afterwards, choose from the National Gallery of Art, one of America's most important museums, or the popular National Air and Space Museum. In the evening, head to Georgetown for jazz at Blues Alley.

If you can face more museums, head for the Penn Quarter, home to the International Spy Museum, the Shakespeare Theater, the Smithsonian American Art Museum, and National Portrait Gallery. Otherwise, head to the Chesapeake and Ohio Canal (C&O) for a ride in a mule-driven canal clipper, or to the Discovery Theater for a puppet show. End the day watching the spectacular fireworks over the city as it celebrates Independence Day.

See the pandas at the National Zoo, the fish at the National Aquarium, or the famous bonsai at the National Arboretum. Take a cruise on the Potomac or a tour across the river to Mount Vernon Estate, the home and gardens of George Washington.

Dos and Don'ts

☑ Get an insider's view of D.C. on a walking tour through Embassy Row, Georgetown, and other interesting neighborhoods (www.washingtonwalks.com), or consider a guided cycling tour of the sites (www.bikethesites.com).

☒ Don't overlook the city's sporting heroes – Washington Redskins' merchandise makes great souvenirs of the town.

☑ Be aware of the 14.5 percent tax levied on hotels in the city, which will be added to the bill at the end of your stay, on top of the room rate.

JAN
FEB
MAR
APR
MAY
JUN
JUL
2nd
3rd
4th
5th
AUG
SEP
OCT
NOV
DEC

GETTING THERE   See map p313, C6
The third-largest city in Canada, Vancouver is served by international and domestic flights. Vancouver International Airport is about 9 miles (14 km) from the city center.

GETTING AROUND
Downtown Vancouver is walkable and has a vast network of cycle paths. Ferries cross to North Vancouver and to the southern suburbs. An east-west rapid transit line takes you from downtown to the suburbs.

WEATHER
Vancouver in July gets 295 hours of sunshine and only 40mm of rain. Average daytime temperatures are around 75°F (24°C).

ACCOMMODATIONS
Barclay House has doubles from US$150; www.barclayhouse.com

A waterfront hotel near theaters and galleries, Granville Island Hotel; doubles from US$250; www.granvilleislandhotel.com

Pan Pacific Hotel Vancouver in the Canada Place cruise ship terminal has doubles from US$450; www.panpacific.com

EATING OUT
Raincity Grill serves delicious local cuisine and British Columbia wine by the glass for about US$60 per person. For top-quality seafood, try C restaurant (US$90 per person).

PRICE FOR TWO
US$450 per day including accommodation, travel, meals, festival tickets, and sightseeing.

FURTHER INFORMATION
www.tourismvancouver.com

Local Wineries

Culinary culture has grown by leaps and bounds in Vancouver over the past decade, and nothing shows this better than the development of high-quality British Columbia wines. There are now some 135 wineries in the province. Sumac Ridge and Mission Hill are two of the better-known quality vineyards. Look for B.C. whites – especially Gewürztraminer, and that local specialty, ice wine. Many of Vancouver's restaurants have local vintages available by the glass.

Above (left to right): Planetarium; totem pole; *inuksuk*, an Inuit directional marker, overlooking English Bay at sunset
Main: Stilt-walker at Jericho Park Folk Festival

Above: View of the North Shore

CULTURAL DELIGHTS

VANCOUVER IS ONE OF THE MOST NATURALLY SPECTACULAR CITIES in the world, and at barely 100 years old it is also one of the youngest. Like many young towns, it is still establishing itself as a cultural hub but its arts scene is beginning to thrive and it is also a magnet for lovers of the outdoors. During the high summer month of July, the city hums with a series of festivals that simultaneously celebrate Vancouver's history as a meeting point of East and West, and its wealth of culture, both outdoor and in.

The first such festival is Bard on the Beach, a summer-long celebration of Shakespeare, with a pair of the Bard's plays performed every night in July in an enormous open tent set on the waterfront overlooking English Bay. As the evening's performance wears on, the sun sinks slowly behind the mountains of the North Shore, until the last red rays have vanished. On the third weekend in July, some 30,000 music lovers head to the sandy beaches of Spanish Banks for a three-day festival of folk, acoustic, Indian classical, Hong Kong pop, and hip hop known as the Vancouver Folk Music Festival. Performances take place on two stages set at opposite ends of a green swath of land overlooking the beach, ocean, and mountains beyond.

Finally, over the last two weeks of July, Vancouver hosts perhaps the perfect combination of popular culture and art – the HSBC Celebration of Light. Every third evening hundreds of thousands of spectators flock to the city's long undulating waterfront to watch a stunning fireworks display that explodes over the waters of English Bay, set off in time to the simultaneous stereo broadcast of classical symphony music. This annual fireworks festival is an ongoing work of art that is a perfect match for the breathtaking beauty of Vancouver's dramatic surroundings.

Hundreds of thousands of spectators flock to the city's waterfront to watch a stunning firework display

Inset: Fireworks exploding over English Bay
Below (left and right): A band playing outdoors at Vancouver Folk Music Festival; actors performing in *Love's Labour's Lost* at the Bard on the Beach festival

SUMMER DIARY

Vancouver's stunning outdoor setting is at its best in July, when there is barely a drop of rain and the sunset and glimmering twilight last until well past 10pm. Three days is ample opportunity to sample the city's natural delights, culinary and cultural offerings, and festival entertainment.

Three Days of Festivities

Rent a bicycle and set out along the Stanley Park seawall, the thin black ribbon that loops around the tract of rainforest at the city's heart. The cycle ride offers glimpses of totem poles, towering Douglas Fir, and bald eagles circling over the bay. On a July evening, you can watch Shakespeare played out beneath a large tent overlooking English Bay.

Walk to the hip new high-rise community of Yaletown – a good place for a latte and a biscotti – and take a little blue ferry across False Creek to Granville Island, a vast covered market packed with regional delicacies, such as smoked salmon and ice wine. In the afternoon, head out to the beachfront at Spanish Banks for the Vancouver Folk Music Festival.

Cross the Lion's Gate Bridge to North Vancouver and take the tram 3,300 ft (1,000 m) up to the lookout atop Grouse Mountain. From your perch on the eyrie, you can gaze out over the whole of British Columbia's Lower Mainland – the long blue arm of Burrard Inlet, the slow proud Fraser River, teeming with homecoming sockeye salmon, and the rounded white volcanic dome of Mount Baker in the south. Come sundown, on three magical evenings in July, walk down to the waterline to see the sky explode with fireworks, to the sound of a classical symphony.

Dos and Don'ts

✓ Head for the beach at Sunset Beach, Kitsilano Point, Spanish Banks just before sunset and watch the sun going down behind the mountains at English Bay.

✗ Don't forget a sweater or light coat to wear after sunset. Vancouver evenings are always cool, even in summer.

✓ Sample Vancouver's restaurants, which rival larger culinary centers, such as San Francisco, in the quality of their ingredients and preparation, while prices retain the modesty of a smaller city.

✗ Don't forget to stock up on that local staple, wild salmon, either fresh or smoked.

JAN
FEB
MAR
APR
MAY
JUN
JUL
DAY 1
DAY 2
DAY 3
AUG
SEP
OCT
NOV
DEC

GETTING THERE   See map p330, C4
Access to the Salar de Uyuni is via the town of Uyuni, located on the eastern edge of the salt pan. Uyuni is a 5-hour bus journey away from Potosí, which can be reached via a 12-hour bus journey from La Paz. Alternatively, air-hop from La Paz to Sucre and take a bus from Sucre to Uyuni.

GETTING AROUND
The only way to explore the salt flats is by 4-wheel drive. Several agencies in Uyuni offer expeditions to the flats.

WEATHER
Winter is chilly in the Bolivian highlands. Daytime temperatures reach 54°F (12°C), but drop to 14°F (−10°C) at night. The skies are a clear crystalline blue.

ACCOMMODATIONS
Basic lodge-style accommodations are included in all guided tours into the Salar.

Uyuni's Los Girasoles Hotel offers clean accommodation; doubles from US$25.

Hotel Toñito in Uyuni is good; doubles from $30; www.bolivianexpeditions.com

EATING OUT
Basic meals are included on all tours. In Uyuni, the Minuteman restaurant offers pizzas and espresso.

PRICE FOR TWO
US$130 per day for two nights' accommodation in Uyuni, meals, entry fees, and a three-day tour into the Salar.

FURTHER INFORMATION
www.uyuni.com.bo

A WHITE WILDERNESS

I<small>T'S A TRIP FOR THOSE NOT AFRAID TO ROUGH IT</small>, for those on the lookout for something extraordinary and otherworldly. A horizon-to-horizon expanse of pure, blinding white, the vast high plain known as the Salar de Uyuni is the world's largest salt pan, 25 times greater in size than its more famous cousin in Bonneville, Utah. It is so out of the ordinary, it fully justifies the sobriquet of surreal. Not for nothing is one small corner of the Salar nicknamed the Salvador Dali desert.

Located in the highlands of southern Bolivia, the Salar is all that's left of a vast prehistoric lake that once lapped at the flanks of the High Andes. When Lake Minchin dried, it left behind a salt flat 4,650 sq miles (12,000 sq km) in area, containing some 10 billion tonnes of salt. Periodically, when the rains fall or the snow melts on the Andes, the Salar fills with a thin film of water, turning into a

Salt of the Earth

Salt forms the literal bedrock of the economy in the tiny pueblo of Colchani, a 12-mile (20-km) flight from Uyuni. The villagers, all members of the Colchani salt cooperative, extract blocks of nearly pure salt from the Colchani reserve, processing them for sale and export. Salt cutters live on the salt pan five days at time, sleep in tiny salt igloo domes, and rise each morning to hack out vast hunks of rock-hard salt and shape them into transportable blocks. Chewing coca to ward off fatigue, each man cuts, shapes, and stacks some 500 blocks a day.

Main: A jeep drives along a stretch of the flooded salt pan, Salar de Uyuni

Left: Red algae on Laguna Colorada

Right (left to right): Andean Altiplano flamingos; a steam train graveyard at Uyuni

Right panel (top to bottom): Room at the Luna Salada Lodge Hotel built with salt; the Arbol de Piedra ("Tree of Stone") in the Uyuni highlands; an abandoned kiln on Laguna Colorada; tourists at the Sol de Mañana geysers

vast mirror that appears to dissolve into the blue sky. And in the midst of this salt sea stands Incahuasi Island, a tiny outcrop of rock and productive soil, where cacti grow up to 33 ft (10 m) high and rabbits nibble on the brown grass. The now-extinct volcanic cone of Mount Licancabur rises high at the southern margins of the Salar. Close to its lower slopes are the near-scalding hot springs of Laguna Challviri which, coupled with the cold snow melt, provide a sublime outdoor soak. From here, a short rattling trip over stony ground leads to Laguna Colorada, the "Colored Lake," where an infestation of red algae has resulted in a rich assortment of birdlife including three species of South American flamingos: the Chilean, the Andean, and the James flamingo.

Your last stop on this spectacular tour is the Sol de Mañana, or Morning Sun, where geysers spew forth in the morning air, hot mud bubbles up from the earth, and where every morning the sun rises in a glorious fantasia of reds over the salty white plain.

Above: Cacti in Salar de Uyuni

JAN

FEB

MAR

APR

MAY

JUN

JUL

SALT PAN DIARY

The high-altitude Salar de Uyuni is at its driest and clearest in the midwinter month of July. Four days is enough time to explore the salt flats, geysers and hot springs, high volcanoes, and the colorful lakes full of flamingos. The itinerary below is typical of the tours offered by agencies in the region.

Four Days in Empty Space

The journey, in a 4WD, starts with a stopover at the train cemetery, where dozens of abandoned engines and carriages rust beneath a deep blue sky. The tour then skirts the edge of the Salar to Colchani, where villagers dig out salt with pick and shovel and leave it in piles to dry in the sun. From here, the expedition heads due west into the unrelieved blinding whiteness of the salt plain. The first stop is the Luna Salada Lodge Hotel, which has walls, chairs, and beds made entirely of salt. Then it's off to Isla Incahuasi, a surreal outpost of cacti, grassy hills, and small brown viscacha rabbits, surrounded by a sea of salt.

DAY 1

On day two, the expedition heads for the Siloli desert, with its extraordinary stone formations including the Arbol de Piedra ("Tree of Stone"), and the tiny lakes Hedionda, Chiar Kota, and Ramaditas, colored cobalt blue, royal purple, and emerald. Day's end finds the tour at a simple lodge by the Laguna Colorada, a vast lake colored red with algae, rich food for the thousands of bright-hued flamingos.

DAY 2

An early morning departure brings the tour to Sol de Mañana, where bubbling springs and geysers fill the morning air with hot steam. From this otherworldly locale, the expedition moves to the Laguna Challviri hot springs for a refreshing soak. The expedition then climbs the wind-swept slopes of Licancabur volcano.

DAY 3

The 4WD re-enters the Salar for a leisurely day's exploration on the way back to the town of Uyuni.

DAY 4

Dos and Don'ts

☑ Remember to carry lots of water. The high altitude and strong sun dries you out quickly

☒ Don't forget a sleeping bag and bring lots of warm clothes. There's little heat out on the salt flats, and the winter temperature at night is chilly.

☑ Take a couple of days to acclimatize to the altitude. Tours into the Salar de Uyuni start at 11,480 ft (3,500 m) and rise to 14,760 ft (4,500 m).

☑ Take your bathing suit for a soak in the hot springs.

AUG

SEP

OCT

NOV

DEC

GETTING THERE See map p313, B5

Air Canada offers flights from Vancouver to the Haida-Gwaii Queen Charlotte Islands, from where you must take local transport. Daily ferries ply between Prince Rupert, on the Canadian mainland, and the islands. Access to Gwaii Haanas National Park Reserve is via floatplane, boat, or kayak.

GETTING AROUND

While on tour, you'll paddle a fair distance in your kayak, but the mothership – your base – will help. To get around the islands, hop on a taxi, seaplane, or ferry.

WEATHER

Haida Gwaii is at its best in July, with over 16 hours of sunlight and a temperature range of 57–63°F (14–17°C).

ACCOMMODATIONS

Kayak tours where you spend nights aboard a mothership offer adventure, activity, and comfort. For most tours, arrive the day before and stay overnight.

Archipelago Ventures offers six-day tours from US$2,200; www.tourhaidagwaii.com

Sea Raven Motel has doubles from US$2,400; www.searaven.com

EATING OUT

You don't come to Haida Gwaii for the food. Mothership tours usually include hearty fare.

PRICE FOR TWO

Around US$850 per day for a six-day tour plus overnight stay, a meal, and souvenirs.

FURTHER INFORMATION

www.haidagwaiitourism.ca
www.queencharlottekayaking.com

The Spirit of Haida Gwaii

Taking pride of place at Vancouver International Airport's departure lounge, *The Spirit of Haida Gwaii* is a gigantic jade sculpture by Haida artist, Bill Reid. The 18-ft (6-m) long canoe is filled with creatures from Haida mythology. Raven, the trickster, holds the steering oar while Grizzly Bear sits in the bow, his back shielding the others from the waves. Bear Mother looks ahead – she has cubs to care for. In the center is Kilstlaai, a shaman dressed in a Haida cloak and holding a staff carved with the Seabear, Raven, and Killer Whale.

Above (left and right): Ancient Haida mortuary poles at the UNESCO World Heritage Site in Sgang Gwaay, kayakers next to the mothership
Main: Starfish and sea urchins beneath a tide pool

Above: Soaking in a natural hot-spring pool at the preserve

HOME OF THE HAIDA

MAGIC ABOUNDS IN GWAII HAANAS, the "Place of Wonders" in the Haida tongue, and no other name suits this enchanting forested archipelago more aptly. Amazing adventures and incredible sights greet you when you visit this hidden jewel, known to Haida natives as Haida Gwaii, the Islands of the People. As you paddle your tiny kayak through the calm waters or simply dawdle along a rocky shore, you'll suddenly spot a black bear loping along or a sea lion popping his head out of the water to give you a curious stare. Drifting in the shallows on a slackening tide, you'll glance into the clear water below and find a multihued garden of marine life – orange anemones, purple sea stars, and multicolored nudibranchs – carpeting the seabed.

Along the way, you'll find yourself spellbound by the natural beauty of Gwaii Haanas: hot springs, spruce-clad mountains, spy-hopping whales, nesting puffins and auklets, salmon-munching black bears, and scavenging bald eagles. The works of man, too, are here. In now-abandoned settlements such as Nan Sdins and Sgang Gwaay, small groves of tall, intricately carved cedar poles display totems that declare a clan's lineage or tell the story of a prominent chief or family. Such is the power and artistry of these totems that UNESCO declared them a World Heritage Site as far back as 1981.

There are, of course, disadvantages to a kayak – they're slow, precarious, and lack shower facilities. But in the enchanting land of Haida Gwaii, there's a simple solution – a mothership and kayak combo, blending the grace of a kayak with the comforts of a larger ship. Each morning, you set out to explore a different bay or channel. At lunch or at day's end, when you tire, the mothership picks you up so you can refuel with a meal and shower. It then motors along in search of yet another spot for the next day, where you can discover more of the magic that lies in store in the Place of Wonders.

Glance into the clear water and find a multihued garden of marine life – anemones, sea stars, and nudibranchs – carpeting the seabed.

Inset: Starfish of every color in Gwaii Haanas
Below (left and right): A family of Steller sea lions; painted paddles at Skidegate

KAYAKER'S DIARY

Often referred to as the Galapagos of Canada, Gwaii Haanas National Park Reserve – on the southern tip of the Queen Charlotte Islands – is a majestic, species-rich archipelago of some 130 islands teeming with diverse wildlife. July offers warm temperatures and sunshine-filled evenings.

Six Days in the Wilds

Be up early to make your way to the seaplane dock in Queen Charlotte City by 7am. A half-hour flight over remarkable territory brings you to the northern limit of Gwaii Haanas National Park Reserve, where you'll board the mothership. The first stop is a hike and a visit to Taanoo, a Haida winter village. — **DAY 1**

A short paddle takes you to Hot Springs Island and a chance for a morning snack. A midday journey aboard the mothership traverses Juan Perez Sound, leaving enough time for a paddle in North Burnaby Strait. — **DAY 2**

At the bottom end of Burnaby Strait, Burnaby Narrows boasts one of the richest concentrations of marine life anywhere on the Pacific Coast. Drift and paddle your way over anemones, sea stars, and other intertidal creatures. When the tide rises, the kayaks, along with the ship, sneak through the narrows into Skincuttle, the inlet where the mothership spends the night. — **DAY 3**

Skincuttle is rich in wildlife and you're likely to spot tufted puffins, rhinoceros auklets, storm petrels, sooty shearwaters, and humpback, orca, and minke whales. — **DAY 4**

Paddle the tidal pools of the Gordon Islands, explore the natural caves, or walk on a black-sand beach. — **DAY 5**

Marvel at the houses and totem poles at Sgaang Gwaay and Nan Sdins. Stay overnight at Rose Harbour, an old whaling station near the southern tip of Gwaii Haanas. Early next morning, take the incredible 45-minute flight across the length of Gwaii Haanas back to Queen Charlotte City. — **DAY 6**

Dos and Don'ts

✓ Pack your things in a flexible bag you can cram into awkward spaces on a boat. Pack light, but bring clothes to cover every eventuality – fleece pants, a warm hat, shorts and T-shirts, shoes that like water, and a swimsuit for Hot Springs Cove.

✓ Bring your own alcoholic drinks if you're fond of a nip in the evening.

✗ Don't forget your saltwater fishing license if you're keen on trying your luck with a line.

✓ Carry a dry bag to store your camera in while you paddle.

JAN
FEB
MAR
APR
MAY
JUN
JUL
AUG
SEP
OCT
NOV
DEC

GETTING THERE   See map p316, F5
Wilmington is served by Philadelphia International Airport. Brandywine Valley is located just outside Wilmington while Lancaster County, or the Pennsylvania Dutch Country, is within 2 hours' drive.

GETTING AROUND
A car is essential to properly tour the picturesque back roads of the region.

WEATHER
July in Pennsylvania tends to be hot and humid with highs averaging 85°F (29°C). Come prepared with light and airy clothing.

ACCOMMODATIONS
The Wilmington Quality Inn is minutes from downtown Wilmington; family rooms from US$120; www.brandywinesbest.com

The Brandywine River Hotel is a cozy hotel in the heart of Brandywine Valley; family rooms from US$129; www.brandywineriverhotel.com

The Amish View Inn in Lancaster County is surrounded by farmland; family rooms from US$169; www.amishviewinn.com

EATING OUT
The home-made food of the Pennsylvania Dutch is delicious, Germanic, and copious. Don't miss the Amish-style feast at Plain and Fancy Farm (US$18 adults/US$10 kids).

PRICE FOR A FAMILY OF FOUR
US$400–450 per day including accommodation, entertainment, and food, but not car rental.

FURTHER INFORMATION
www.thebrandywine.com
www.padutchcountry.com

Shoo-Fly Pie

One Amish treat the family will surely enjoy in the Pennsylvania Dutch Country is the intriguingly named Shoo-Fly Pie. This sweet, sticky dessert is made of molasses with a crumb topping. The more-traditional "wet-bottom" pie features layers of molasses underneath the crumb topping while the "dry-bottom" pie is mixed together in a more cake-like form. The gooey molasses are so sweet that flies must be constantly shoo-ed away.

Turning off main roads, one quickly sees that horse-drawn buggies outnumber cars, while a typical resident's place of work is a field.

Main: Young Amish boys at a horse auction

PENNSYLVANIA PASTORAL

CAN YOU SURVIVE FOR THREE DAYS WITHOUT A PHONE? It is good to occasionally take a break from modern technology and see that it is possible to live without the Internet, cars, and the latest popular fashions. A visit to the small towns of southeastern Pennsylvania proves that people can and do live without much of modern society's trappings, and visitors can experience this unique culture first-hand.

Driving through a patchwork of farmland and rolling hills in Lancaster County, one encounters quaint villages where residents revel in barn-raisings and community gatherings. Turning off main roads, you will quickly see that horse-drawn buggies outnumber cars, while a typical resident's place of work is actually a field or farm. Women dressed in bonnets and aprons sell jams at roadside stalls while men with long beards work horse-drawn ploughs. This is no film set – Lancaster County is home to the Amish and other "plain" religious groups known collectively as

Above An exhilarating ride at Dutch Wonderland theme park

JAN

FEB

MAR

APR

MAY

JUN

TOURING DIARY

A trip to southeastern Pennsylvania offers a multifaceted long weekend of fun with plenty of educational opportunities. The region is at its seasonal best in July when outdoor events are hosted, crops are at their height, and fruits such as apricots and peaches are ripe for picking.

JUL

A Weekend in the Country

Enjoy one final day of city life in Wilmington, Delaware. Head to Trolley Square or the riverfront area and hang out at the shops, restaurants, and outdoor cafés.

DAY 1

From Wilmington head out to the surrounding Brandywine Valley. This scenic area contains a wealth of historic mansions and gardens. Take a tour of Rockwood Mansion, a 19th-century English-style country estate which hosts a Victorian ice cream festival in July. Alternatively, take a trip to Linvilla Orchards working farm which offers the opportunity to meet farm animals and pick fruit. For an evening treat check the dates of the Longwood Gardens Fireworks and Fountains; a renowned extravaganza set in beautifully landscaped gardens.

DAY 2

Drive northwest and deep into the Pennsylvania Dutch Country. Stop by Cherry Crest Adventure Farm to navigate the Amazing Maize Maze, then head to Plain and Fancy Farm to experience the Amish way of life. The farm offers horse-drawn buggy rides and a 2-hour "Amish Experience" farmland tour. Finish the day with an Amish feast: a vast communal meal of ham, fried chicken, sausages, and filling desserts.

DAY 3

In Strasburg, explore more of Lancaster County on the Strasburg Railroad. The restored Victorian steam train offers a great view of the countryside. Later, take the kids to the Dutch Wonderland amusement park, which has rides and a water play area for cooling off. On your way back to Wilmington, visit New Castle – a colonial town featuring charming inns, shops, pubs, and restaurants.

DAY 4

Inset: Detail of an Amish quilt

Left (left to right): Firework display at Longwood Gardens; renovated historic buildings in Market Square, Wilmington; Strasburg Railroad steam train; an Amish couple in a horse-drawn buggy

Right: Enjoying a ride through a corn field at the Cherry Crest Adventure Farm

Dos and Don'ts

AUG

☑ Come prepared with maps and a specific itinerary. With so much to see and many winding country roads, you'll want to know exactly where you're going to stay on track.

SEP

☒ Don't be too intrusive. The Amish are friendly but private people and prefer not to be questioned or photographed.

OCT

☑ Watch out for horse-drawn buggies. Drive slowly on the back roads and respect the buggy drivers you encounter.

NOV

DEC

the Pennsylvania Dutch. Recognizable by their plain, dark attire, the Amish are the strictest sect, shunning electricity, telephones, and cars – or any device connecting them to the outside world. Driving along winding back roads, characterful villages with names such as Paradise and Bird-in-Hand offer different and fascinating insights into the Amish way of life. Families can take a buggy ride to see what life is like in the slow lane. Delicious home-made jams and baked goods can be sampled while you watch as handmade pretzels being twisted into shape. Visit working farms where cows are milked and butter is churned using age-old methods. Above all, experience the joy of a communal, pass-the-plate smorgasbord typical of the Amish.

Nearby, Brandywine Valley offers equally breathtaking scenery as well as a wealth of historical attractions. The area is peppered with small towns, each with a rich colonial history. In between, remarkable mansions and estates built by early American industrialists are now open to the public and host family-friendly events in the summer. For Fourth of July celebrations look no further than Longwood Gardens' spectacular fountains and fireworks display.

GETTING THERE   See map p327, B4
Treks into the Cordillera Blanca depart from Huaraz, 261 miles (420 km) north of Lima, a 7-hour drive away.

GETTING AROUND
Tour operators organize transport for treks and guides are compulsory. Huaraz is manageable on foot but taxis are ubiquitous.

WEATHER
In July, average daytime temperatures in Huaraz are around 70°F (20°C). On a trek, temperatures vary from 47°F (8°C) to 70°F (20°C), but can be freezing in the passes.

ACCOMMODATIONS
Cordillera Blanca Hiking offers alpine ascents and guided treks from US$60 per day, with equipment; www.cordillerablancahiking.com

Pony Expeditions has a similar range of camping tours, plus mountain biking, from US$60 per day; www.ponyexpeditions.com

Hotel Colomba, a converted hacienda set in gardens on the river opposite the Huaraz town center, has simple double rooms from US$60; www.huarazhotel.com

EATING OUT
Food on the treks will be plentiful but basic campfire fare. In Huaraz, restaurants include Creperie Patrick and Café Andino, a popular meeting place with good lunches and coffee.

PRICE FOR TWO
US$100 per day including accommodation, food, local transport, and trekking charges.

FURTHER INFORMATION
www.peru.info

Peru's First Empire

Between 1000 BC and 500 BC, the Chavín people created the first great urban culture in South America. Despite the long duration of their empire, little is known about them, as few remains have survived. What we do know comes mostly from the scant remaining Chavín art. This is unique and beautiful, comprising series of interlocking patterns that seem abstract, but on closer inspection reveal religious images – notably a shamanic jaguar god.

THE WHITE RANGE

THE CORDILLERA BLANCA IN TROPICAL PERU is a breathtaking mountain range – the Andes seem to jostle each other here, forming a dramatic series of folds whose jagged tips are cloaked in ermine-white snow, while lower down, the indigo-hued forests and golden Alpine grasslands are studded with a myriad jewel-like lakes. At its heart lies Huascarán National Park – a UNESCO World Biosphere Reserve whose 27 icy peaks over 16,400-ft (5,000-m) glisten brightly against the deep-blue sky.

Archeological sites litter the region, crumbling on the sides of windy mountains, and freeze-dried mummies have been found on some of the highest summits. At the 1,300-year old temple fortress of Chavín de Huantar, stone heads watch over a filigree of intricately carved walls and tunnels – the only surviving architectural testament to an empire which covered nearly half of northern Peru. The

Main: Trekkers at Lake Cullicocha in the Cordillera Blanca

Left: Viscacha, an alpine rodent closely related to the chinchilla

Right (left to right): Spectacular scenery from the edge of a glacier-fed lake; tents pitched for the night; mountaineering ascent in the Huascarán National Park

descendents of the Chavín people still live here in villages accessible only by foot or hoof, where Quechua, the ancient native language, is more commonly heard than Spanish. This life of growing quinoa (an indigenous cereal) and tending livestock has changed little since the 16th century.

Wildlife is abundant too, as spectacled bears roam the cloud forests in search of food, while llama-like vicuñas and viscachas nibble on the high slopes. Pumas hunt white-tailed deer in the mountain grasslands, and the air is thick with hundreds of species of rare and endangered birds, from huge soaring condors to tiny, flitting, emerald and iridescent-blue humming birds.

The only way to get to the heart of the Cordillera Blanca is on foot, and as treks involve long, steep stretches and overnight camping, walkers need to be active and adventurous. But the Cordillera Blanca's gain far outweighs its pain – the pure mountain air, magnificent views, and spectacular beauty more than compensate for the occasionally strenuous ascents and descents.

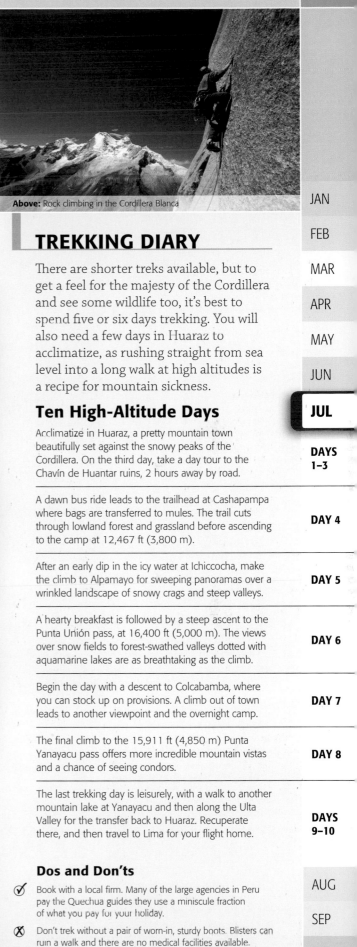

Above: Rock climbing in the Cordillera Blanca

Above (top and bottom): Icy peak of Alpamayo in sunset colors; hiking through alpine grasslands overlooked by snowy crags

TREKKING DIARY

There are shorter treks available, but to get a feel for the majesty of the Cordillera and see some wildlife too, it's best to spend five or six days trekking. You will also need a few days in Huaraz to acclimatize, as rushing straight from sea level into a long walk at high altitudes is a recipe for mountain sickness.

Ten High-Altitude Days

DAYS 1–3 Acclimatize in Huaraz, a pretty mountain town beautifully set against the snowy peaks of the Cordillera. On the third day, take a day tour to the Chavín de Huantar ruins, 2 hours away by road.

DAY 4 A dawn bus ride leads to the trailhead at Cashapampa where bags are transferred to mules. The trail cuts through lowland forest and grassland before ascending to the camp at 12,467 ft (3,800 m).

DAY 5 After an early dip in the icy water at Ichiccocha, make the climb to Alpamayo for sweeping panoramas over a wrinkled landscape of snowy crags and steep valleys.

DAY 6 A hearty breakfast is followed by a steep ascent to the Punta Unión pass, at 16,400 ft (5,000 m). The views over snow fields to forest-swathed valleys dotted with aquamarine lakes are as breathtaking as the climb.

DAY 7 Begin the day with a descent to Colcabamba, where you can stock up on provisions. A climb out of town leads to another viewpoint and the overnight camp.

DAY 8 The final climb to the 15,911 ft (4,850 m) Punta Yanayacu pass offers more incredible mountain vistas and a chance of seeing condors.

DAYS 9–10 The last trekking day is leisurely, with a walk to another mountain lake at Yanayacu and then along the Ulta Valley for the transfer back to Huaraz. Recuperate there, and then travel to Lima for your flight home.

Dos and Don'ts

✓ Book with a local firm. Many of the large agencies in Peru pay the Quechua guides they use a miniscule fraction of what you pay for your holiday.

✗ Don't trek without a pair of worn-in, sturdy boots. Blisters can ruin a walk and there are no medical facilities available.

✗ Don't leave for a trek without adequate supplies – warm clothes, plenty of sun cream, rain gear, a water bottle, Kendal mint cake or energy bars, a plastic bag to carry out all your rubbish, a sense of humor, and lots of resilience.

✓ Expect to tip the porters about 10 percent of your total tour cost at the end of the trek.

JAN
FEB
MAR
APR
MAY
JUN
JUL
AUG
SEP
OCT
NOV
DEC

GETTING THERE See map p320, B2
Anacortes is the mainland terminus for the Washington State Ferry service to the San Juan Islands. The Airporter shuttle connects it with Sea-Tac International Airport and Seattle.

GETTING AROUND
Ferries stop at San Juan, Lopez, Shaw, and Orcas Islands, where cars, bikes, motor scooters, and taxis can be rented. Public buses run on San Juan and Orcas Islands.

WEATHER
Expect sunny skies, with highs of around 75°F (24°C) and lows of about 55°F (13°C).

ACCOMMODATIONS
Lopez Farm Cottages, set in pastureland and orchards outside Lopez Village, are US$170 per night; www.lopezfarmcottages.com

Rosario Resort is a cliff-top mansion with modern annexes on Orcas Island; from US$225 per night; www.rosarioresort.com

Tower House is a Queen Anne-style bed and breakfast in Friday Harbor with rooms from US$165 per night; www.san-juan-island.com

EATING OUT
Fresh shellfish and salmon with locally grown vegetables are sure bets on any menu. Top dining rooms in Rosario Resort and Roche Harbor serve innovative Northwest cuisine, while simpler restaurants abound.

PRICE FOR TWO
US$400 per day including food, local travel, accommodation, and activities.

FURTHER INFORMATION
www.guidetosanjuans.com

Orca Country

Orca whales are the stars of the show in the San Juans. These 25-ft (8-m) long creatures live in the cool waters of the Puget Sound in groups, or pods, of five or more, headed by females. They feed on the fish, squid, porpoises, dolphins, and other animals that thrive in the area. Orcas can sometimes be seen breaching and even sliding on to the shore to scare seals into the water and into the jaws of the rest of the pod. Maneuvers like this earned the orca its traditional name "killer whale."

Main: Flock of Bonaparte's Gulls above the Puget Sound

PACIFIC PARADISE

A FIRST-TIME VISITOR WHO BOARDS A FERRY IN ANACORTES and glides into the San Juan archipelago may well have the sensation of entering an enchanted land. Here, in a maze of inlets and channels, more than 170 islands and islets emerge from the blue waters of the northern Puget Sound. Hillsides forested in old-growth Douglas fir rise from the shores, and the soaring snow-capped peaks of the Olympic Peninsula tower in the distance. Porpoises scythe through the water, while sea lions and seals sun themselves on the rocks, and ospreys and bald eagles glide overhead, scanning the water for fish.

The presence of so much natural beauty is spectacular enough, but then something utterly remarkable happens – the calm waters erupt in a spout, fins cut the surface, a huge, shiny, arched, black mass rises out of the water, flashing a white underside. For half a second it hangs above the water, and then with a splash, it's gone. Another

Above: Picturesque lighthouse at Lime Kiln Point

Top: Cyclists relishing the winding coastal roads of San Juan Island

Above: Branches of the indigenous Douglas fir tree found all over the region

Below: Obstruction Pass in the San Juan Islands with Mount Baker in the distance

Bottom: Crimson anemone in the clear waters of a tidal pool

ARCHIPELAGO DIARY

July is a lively month in the islands. The weather is excellent, and all activities are in full swing. In five days, you can enjoy the sights on the three major islands. To get the most out of your time, do not bring a car – the wait to drive on to a ferry can be 3 hours or even longer, but foot passengers can just walk aboard.

Five Days of Island Hopping

DAY 1
Make the 45-minute crossing to Lopez Island, often called "Slopez" for its easygoing lifestyle. Rent a bike and cycle on roads that roll over gentle hills, stopping at Shark Reef Park to explore the many tidal pools.

DAY 2
Continue on to Orcas Island by ferry and rent a car or a moped at Orcas Village. One of your first stops should be the 2,400-ft (732-m) high summit of Mount Constitution in Moran State Park for spectacular views over the islands and the mountains of the nearby Olympic Peninsula. Hike the 3-mile (5-km) long trail around Cascade Lake, also in Moran State Park, and end the day with a sunset sail from Deer Harbor, keeping a lookout for wildlife and whales.

DAY 3
Have your hotel pack a lunch and climb into a kayak for a full-day tour of the island's inlets and other nearby islets. Enjoy a cocktail and dinner with live entertainment at historic Rosario Resort in the evening.

DAY 4
Move on to San Juan Island and explore the lively waterfront of Friday Harbor. Visit the Whale Museum to learn about the orca whales that live in the waters surrounding the island. You may sight some of them from the beach at Lime Kiln Point State Park. Board a fishing charter and try your hand at landing a salmon.

DAY 5
Hike through San Juan Island National Historical Park, which commemorates the presence of 19th-century American and British troops on the island, to the top of Mount Young. Take an afternoon whale-watching cruise from Friday Harbor before leaving the islands.

Dos and Don'ts

✓ Bring binoculars for close-up views of whales, eagles, seals, and other wildlife. Don't forget the video camera to capture the orcas in motion.

✗ Don't leave trash behind on your hikes and kayak excursions.

✓ Pack lightly and only bring as much as you can comfortably handle. You'll be moving around quite a bit.

✓ Bring a pair of rubber shoes with you for walking on pebbly beaches or wading through water.

JAN

FEB

MAR

APR

MAY

JUN

JUL

AUG

SEP

OCT

NOV

DEC

leap, another splash... a pod of the resident orca whales is feeding. Seeing these magnificent creatures encapsulates the magic of these islands, where every experience is memorable – viewing the landscape of sea, forests, and mountains from the top of Mount Constitution on Orcas Island; scouting the tidal pools on the Lopez Island beaches for agates, seahorses, and anemones; or just enjoying a glass of wine on a terrace overlooking seaside villages that hug the forested coasts.

These settings are the backdrop for as many outdoor adventures as an enthusiast can squeeze into a day. Kayaking is the preferred way to cut through the calm waters and explore the scores of inlets that etch the islands. More than 30 miles (48 km) of hiking paths lace Moran State Park, and the rolling landscapes of Lopez Island are especially appealing to cyclists, while scuba divers investigate undersea kelp forests and caverns brimming with octopuses and other marine life. Even if you aspire to nothing more active than a whale-watching cruise, the orcas never fail to make an appearance. As common as these sightings are, seeing an orca is always a thrill, and in the same way, these lovely islands grow more enchanting the better a visitor gets to know them.

WILD-WEST STAMPEDE

I T'S THE LONGEST EIGHT SECONDS IN THE WORLD—an eternity ticking by, as a cowboy grips with hand and knees and heart to the bull or the horse that's twisting and turning beneath him, doing everything in its power to buck him off. It's grit and it's gumption and it's the Calgary Stampede – ten action-packed days when every second counts, whether it is the eight-second qualifying bell in bull-, saddle bronc-, and bareback-busting; the race against the clock in tie-down roping, steer-wrestling, and barrel-racing; or the world-famous chuckwagon teams, emblazoned with colorful advertisements, thundering around the racetrack that's aptly known as the half-mile of hell.

They call the Stampede the greatest outdoor show on earth, and for good reason. It tempts the world's best cowboys and cowgirls to Calgary for the richest prize money in professional rodeo – and then it rolls out the red carpet for them, and for those who come to share in the action. In this most western of western cities, Stampede means that it's time to throw on hats and boots and offer a warm

Main: Chuckwagon racing at the Calgary Stampede

GETTING THERE
See map p313, E6
Calgary's international airport is on the northeast edge of town, 20 minutes from the city center.

GETTING AROUND
Calgary's Light Rail Transit system, called the C-Train, has two stops at Stampede Park, and is a handy alternative to driving from your hotel.

WEATHER
Afternoon temperatures can hit 86°F (30°C) in July, but the average is closer to 75°F (24°C). Afternoon thunder showers are possible.

ACCOMMODATIONS
The Best Western Suites Downtown has suites with kitchenettes or full kitchens; from US$270; www.bestwestern.com

The Kensington Riverside Inn is just minutes from downtown and offers free parking; junior suites from US$499; www.kensingtonriversideinn.com

The Fairmont Palliser Hotel is a historic hotel built in 1914 and restored to its original glory; family rooms from US$500; www.fairmont.com

EATING OUT
You'll find great meals available for around US$15–25 per person. Try the 1886 Buffalo Café in downtown's Eau Claire Market for hearty breakfasts and stroll downtown to Stephen Avenue for pubs, bistros, and fine restaurants.

PRICE FOR A FAMILY OF FOUR
US$700–1,000 per day including accommodation, food, local transportation, and admission charges.

FURTHER INFORMATION
www.tourismcalgary.com

Head-Smashed-In Jump

A designated UNESCO World Heritage Site, Head-Smashed-In is the best preserved buffalo jump known. The native tribes, collectively known as the Blackfoot, were experts in the behavior of buffalo. By predicting the movement of the herds, they were able to hunt the beasts by running them over the precipice in great numbers. The animals were then carved up and the flesh dried for the coming months. There are still many buffalo skeletons and marked trails to be seen, and a superb interpretive center gives the site historical and cultural context.

Top: Competing in a rodeo at the Stampede

Above: Enjoying a fairground ride at dusk

Below: Bar U Ranch National Historic Site

welcome. But it's more than that – it is a celebration of the pioneer spirit and ranching history that helped to found this part of the world, a living legacy of the days when herding on horseback was the only way to make a livelihood.

You can feel the energy as soon as you enter Stampede Park, on the edge of downtown and bordered by the Elbow River. A neon-trimmed fair lines the grounds, with gravity-defying rides for cowboys and non-cowboys alike. The Stampede Casino kicks into full gear, providing a high-end cousin to the bar-room poker of the old west. Cattle and horses vie for blue ribbons in agricultural competitions, while the Indian Village showcases the culture of the region's five First Nations peoples, including arts, crafts, and dancing. At the appropriately named Saddledome Stadium, and throughout the grounds, top music artists boost the excitement and noise.

You'll find the main events at the Grandstand where the itinerary goes almost as quickly as the wagons: rodeo in the afternoon and chuckwagon races in the early evening, followed by a high-energy musical show and topped off with fireworks. Prepare your best "yee-haw!" – you'll need it.

Above: Aerial view of the Calgary Stampede's grounds

JAN

FEB

MAR

APR

MAY

JUN

JUL

RODEO DIARY

Prepare to spend two days fully immersing yourself in the excitement of the Stampede. Then take some time to explore the rest of this interesting city – its historic and elegant sandstone buildings, pioneering western heritage, thriving arts scene, and Olympic legacy. Calgary is also a gateway to four UNESCO World Heritage Sites.

A Week of Pioneer Spirit

DAYS 1–2
Orient yourself with a trip up the Calgary Tower. Then hit the Stampede for the casino, midway, agricultural shows, Indian Village, and, of course, the rodeo and chuckwagon events, plus the Grandstand show.

DAY 3
Visit the Heritage Park Historical Village, on the edge of the sailboat-dotted Glenmore Reservoir, southwest of downtown. You'll find pioneer-era buildings, a steam locomotive, and even a paddlewheeler.

DAY 4
There's plenty in town for the kids to enjoy – Glenbow Museum is a must-see for its permanent exhibits dedicated to the Blackfoot and other First Nations peoples. For thrills, try Canada Olympic Park, with its Skyline zipline ride, mountain-bike park, and luge rides.

DAY 5
Just east of downtown, Fort Calgary re-creates the late-1800s home of the North West Mounted Police, while nearby Calgary Zoo has wildlife from Canada to Africa.

DAY 6
Visit Spruce Meadows in the city's southwest – consistently named the world's best outdoor show-jumping venue. From there, it's a quick trot down the Cowboy Trail to the Bar U Ranch National Historic Site.

DAY 7
Leave the city behind to appreciate the dramatic Alberta scenery – head to the mountain towns of Banff and Lake Louise, and then on to Jasper, past the ancient glaciers of the Columbia Icefield. Or day-trip 90 minutes northeast to the renowned Royal Tyrrell Museum and the land of the dinosaurs in Drumheller, or head two hours south to the ancient cliff-site hunting ground at Head-Smashed-In Buffalo Jump.

AUG

SEP

OCT

NOV

DEC

Dos and Don'ts

✓ There's plenty of entertainment for adults too. At night, Calgary becomes the city that doesn't sleep while the Stampede's in town – try Stampede Park.

✗ Don't delay in booking your accommodations – hotels in and around Calgary start to fill up as much as a year in advance for the 10 days of Stampede. The best rates and rooms go to those who make early reservations.

✓ Follow the cowboy example and wear a hat (and sunscreen) to protect yourself from the strong summer sun. Mountain breezes can fool you into thinking it's cooler than it really is.

GETTING THERE
See map p316, H4–5

Cape Air links Boston with Provincetown and Martha's Vineyard, and Provincetown with Nantucket. You can fly from Nantucket to Martha's Vineyard, but the boat trip is lovely.

GETTING AROUND
Explore Provincetown and its surroundings by bike. On Nantucket, rent a car or hire taxis. A car is best for getting around Martha's Vineyard.

WEATHER
Expect plenty of sun, with highs reaching 80°F (27°C) and lows around 60°F (15°C).

ACCOMMODATIONS
The charming Crowne Pointe Inn, Provincetown, is a former sea captain's home; doubles from US$300; www.crownepointe.com

The Jared Coffin House is one of Nantucket's finest mansions; doubles from US$280; www.jaredcoffinhouse.com

The Charlotte Inn is Edgartown's oldest and most elegant hostelry; doubles from US$250; www.relaischateaux.com/charlotte

EATING OUT
Seafood is everywhere, including local treats like clam chowder and lobster rolls. An order of fried clams at a clam shack is about US$10. A lobster dinner will cost around US$50.

PRICE FOR TWO
US$600 including accommodation, food, tours, flight to Nantucket, boat to Martha's Vineyard, and 3 days' car rental and gas.

FURTHER INFORMATION
www.provincetown.com; www.nantucket.net; www.mvol.com

Beacons of Hope

Over the past 300 years, some 3,000 shipwrecks have been recorded off Cape Cod, Nantucket, and Martha's Vineyard. Lighthouses were built to guide ships, and today these beacons, such as the one at Race Point near Provincetown, are a favorite of visitors. The Old Harbor Life-Saving Station in Provincetown is the last remnant of the Lifesavers, a corps of rescuers who patroled the beaches during storms to scour the rough seas for shipwrecks, and braved the surf to save as many souls as they could.

Above (left to right): Wharf at Menemsha; brightly colored buoys; striking red clay cliffs at Aquinnah
Main: Cottage porch in Oak Bluffs

Above: Provincetown viewed from the top of Pilgrim Monument

OLD-STYLE CHARMS

L IGHTHOUSES RISE ABOVE WIDE BEACHES, CLIFFS, AND SWEEPING DUNES, and stands of birches and pines grow to the edges of ponds and marshes. From some vantage points, a shoreline pounded by rugged surf stretches as far as the eye can see; from others, bays and inlets follow the curve of the land. In the many historic towns and villages, shingled houses and cottages surround proud old churches, and ports are home to fishing fleets that return from the wild sea with catches of oysters, mussels, lobsters, and swordfish. Some of America's easternmost, most beautiful, and most beloved shorelines are those that fringe Cape Cod and the islands of Nantucket and Martha's Vineyard. America's earliest history was forged on these shores: Norse explorers noted Cape Cod as early as the 10th century, and pilgrims made first landfall near Provincetown, at the end of the Cape, on November 20, 1620. The tiny island of Nantucket, 30 miles (48 km) south of Cape Cod, was the world's largest whaling port for much of the 19th century, and Martha's Vineyard, just off the southern coast of Cape Cod, was settled in 1642. Provincetown, Nantucket town, and Edgartown on Martha's Vineyard are especially historic and beautiful, and in all of them, many fine old houses have been converted to luxurious and romantic inns.

Cape Cod and the Islands have been summer resorts since the late 19th century. Natural wonders, especially the hundreds of miles of unspoiled beaches, are the major draw, and swimming, sailing, and other outdoor activities are popular. These are also places to enjoy spectacular sunsets, leisurely dinners overlooking moonlit bays, and exploring shops on quaint lanes. Nantucket is an exclusive retreat for the wealthy, and Martha's Vineyard counts many famous politicians and other celebrities among its summer visitors. As the song says, "if you're fond of sand dunes and salty air, quaint little villages here and there," this far-flung corner of the country will capture your heart.

Shingled houses and cottages surround proud old churches, and fishing fleets return with oysters, mussels, lobsters.

Inset: Rose-covered cottage on Nantucket Island
Below (left and right): Commercial Street, Provincetown; Nantucket beach

SEASHORE DIARY

You could certainly spend over a week on Cape Cod and the Islands, but seven days allows you time to savor the best of these historic and enchanting land- and seascapes. A short flight from Provincetown to Nantucket and a pleasant sea journey from Nantucket to Martha's Vineyard make it easy to get from place to place.

A Week on the Cape

Settle into your hotel in Provincetown and get into the swing of things with some people-watching and window-shopping along Commercial Street. Rent a bike for an evening ride to Herring Cove to watch the sunset, then dine at a waterside restaurant.
DAY 1

Climb the 116 steps of the Pilgrim Monument for a great view, before hitting the beach at Race Point. Take a sunset sail aboard the schooner *Bay Lady II*.
DAY 2

Bike along the Province Lands Trail or hike across the breakwater to Long Point. After lunch, take a whale-watching cruise to the waters of Stellwagen Bank. Maybe end your day with a clam bake on the beach.
DAY 3

Fly from Provincetown to Nantucket. After settling into one of Nantucket town's historic inns, stroll the cobblestone streets and do some shopping for antiques and folk art along Centre Street.
DAY 4

Make a morning visit to charming Siasconset village and its excellent beach. In the afternoon, take a Nantucket Historical Association Guided Walking Tour, then watch the sunset at Madaket Beach.
DAY 5

Board the boat for Martha's Vineyard. Explore Edgartown, where you can stay in one of the many old inns, and take the ferry to Chappaquiddick for a walk through Cape Pogue Wildlife Refuge to the adjoining beach.
DAY 6

Spend a day exploring the rest of the island: Oak Bluffs, with its gingerbread cottages; the fishing village of Menemsha; and Aquinnah, with its spectacular cliffs.
DAY 7

Dos and Don'ts

✓ If hiking, take precautions against deer ticks, which carry Lyme Disease – tuck trousers into socks, use insect repellent, and check your skin after being outdoors.

✗ Don't walk on dune grass and other fragile plantings. If an area is cordoned off, don't cross the rope.

✓ When swimming or surfing be mindful of the dangerous undertow. Only swim where it is safe to do so – take advice on that from locals.

✓ Be sure to try all the fabulous local seafood specialties.

JAN
FEB
MAR
APR
MAY
JUN
JUL
AUG
SEP
OCT
NOV
DEC

CANADA

Vancouver

AVALON
PENINSULA

Ottawa

USA

GETTING THERE   See map p314, I5
Fly into St. John's International Airport, rent a car, and drive 4 miles (6.5 km) downtown.

GETTING AROUND
A car is needed for trips to seabird colonies, villages, and to venture beyond St. John's.

WEATHER
Average temperatures in July are 57°F (14°C) along the coast, with afternoon highs reaching 68°F (20°C) on sunny days. Expect periods of wet weather and chilly evenings.

ACCOMMODATIONS
The small Murray Premises Hotel near the wharf in St. John's provides highspeed Internet facilities; rooms from US$160; www.murraypremiseshotel.com

The Fairmont Newfoundland in St. John's offers fine dining; rooms from US$200; www.fairmont.com

Manning's Bird Island Resort offers clean accommodation; rooms from US$80; www.birdislandresort.com

EATING OUT
Cod cheeks, caribou stew, seal flipper pie, and Jigg's dinner (boiled vegetables and salted meat) are standard Newfoundland fare, with baked apple pie or steamed pudding for dessert.

PRICE FOR TWO
US$500–600 per day including accommodation, food, car rental and fuel, and admissions to the various sights.

FURTHER INFORMATION
www.newfoundlandlabrador.com
www.stjohns.ca

The Rock

Newfoundland, an island fondly known as The Rock by those who call it home, is a world apart. Fiercely independent, Newfies are fun-loving, hard-working folk. Their ancestors arrived by sea from Europe centuries ago to fish the icy Atlantic waters and, over the years, many chose to stay through the long winters rather than sail back to Europe. They speak a lilting form of English with traces of Elizabethan phrasing. Humor and toe-tapping music fill their evenings, helped along by the bottom-of-the-rum-barrel drink called Screech.

Thousands of
golden-headed gannets
cover the sea
stack rising offshore,
filling the blue
sky with a whirlwind
motion.

Inset: Gannets on Bird Rock in Cape St. Mary's Ecological Reserve

Left (left and right): The view from Cape Spear; caribou

Right (left to right): Cannon on Signal Hill, St. John's; an isolated house at Tors Cove; colorful façades of the houses in St. John's

Main: A brilliant summer sunrise over Cape Spear Lighthouse

ENDLESS HORIZONS

THE CACOPHONY OF TENS OF THOUSANDS of nesting seabirds is heard long before Bird Rock in Cape St. Mary's Ecological Reserve comes into view. The foot-worn path across the coastal barrens is lined with fields of mosses, lichens, and wild iris trimmed by sheep grazing in the meadow high above the sea. The path rises to the rocky edge of the cliff, leading into clouds of birds. Thousands of golden-headed gannets cover the sea stack, and rising and filling the blue sky with a whirlwind of motion. The mammoth rock is packed with nesting seabirds feeding chicks and preening mates jostling their neighbors. Periodically the gannets spread their wings to soar out to sea to fish. This then is the fantastic introduction to the winged wonders of Newfoundland's Avalon Peninsula.

The preserve is just one of the many natural delights along the narrow road that circles the Avalon Peninsula. The small villages that cling to the rocky shore are known as outports, and date from the 1600s. Most of the

Above: Pouch Cove, an outport on the Avalon Peninsula

JAN

FEB

MAR

APR

MAY

JUN

JUL

COASTAL ROAD DIARY

July is high season in St. John's and the Avalon Peninsula. Although there won't be huge crowds, rooms can still be hard to find, so book ahead. Four days is enough time to see the best of the area's natural wonders. If you have another day to explore, head over to Terra Nova National Park for a day of hiking.

Four Days on The Rock

Drive up Signal Hill in St. John's for the exceptional views. While you're up there, admire the stone Cabot Tower and explore the fascinating Johnson Geo Center. Then drive to Quidi Vidi Battery Historic Site. Head out next to Cape Spear Lighthouse, the most easterly point in North America. Return to St. John's and explore the boutique shops, churches, and waterfront. End your day with dinner and a pub visit for lively music and a bit of Screech.

DAY 1

Head south to Bay Bulls and take a boat trip to Witless Bay Ecological Reserve to watch the comical puffins, kittiwakes, mures, and graceful humpback whales in the icy waters. In the fishing village of Ferryland, visit the Colony of Avalon museum and watch archeologists search for artifacts from the 1620s.

DAY 2

Continue south through a remote plain of sub-Arctic tundra along the rocky coast. Explore the quaint fishing villages, watch for wild caribou near Trepassey, and stop at the observation platform in St. Vincent's to look for whales. Visit the Salmonier Nature Park to glimpse the animals and birds native to Newfoundland and Labrador. At Cape St. Mary's Ecological Reserve, walk along the footpath to see the seabird rookery.

DAY 3

Return to St. John's and visit the museum and art gallery at The Rooms. Then head to the Railway-Coastal Museum to learn about the trains and boats that supported Newfoundland's fishing villages before highways were built. At Pippy Park, the Memorial University Botanical Garden features native flora and butterflies. Wind up with dinner in the Historic area.

DAY 4

Dos and Don'ts

✓ Be sure to plan ahead for accommodation.

✗ Don't look for fancy rooms or restaurants outside of St. John's, but do expect warm hospitality.

✓ Ask for help when you need it; the local people are amazingly friendly and helpful when asked.

✓ Take along a box lunch and warm clothes when traveling beyond St. John's, as local restaurants can be far apart.

AUG

SEP

OCT

NOV

DEC

peninsula remains wild and remote, with vast open plains of sub-Arctic tundra where great herds of caribou graze. The cold blue waters of the Atlantic Ocean teem with capelin, providing a feast for whales and seabirds along the coast. Boats at Bay Bulls carry passengers into Witless Bay Ecological Reserve where they can watch humpback whales dive and resurface with a great whoosh, at times breaching far out of the depths with sheets of water streaming from their backs.

St. John's is one of the oldest settlements in North America, and the most easterly. From the top of Signal Hill the view stretches in all directions. The narrow rock-bounded entrance of St. John's Harbour has offered sanctuary to ships for four centuries, beginning with Basque fishermen who arrived in the 1500s to harvest cod for the European market. Surrounding the harbor, the characterful old town with its cobbled streets and colorful clapboard row houses buzzes with plenty of specialty shops and restaurants. At night the lilting strains of fiddles blend with the laughter drifting out of the pubs lined along historic Water Street that specialize in warming up cold travelers – just as they have for centuries.

See map p316, H5

GETTING THERE
Newport is 26 miles (42 km) from Providence's airport. Mystic is 49 miles (79 km) from Newport and 42 miles (68 km) from Providence. From Newport, ferries to Block Island take 2 hours.

GETTING AROUND
The towns are compact and walkable, but a car is essential for trips around the region.

WEATHER
July brings warm, humid conditions. Average temperatures hover around 80°F (26°C).

ACCOMMODATIONS
The Mystic Hilton is situated directly across from the Mystic Aquarium; doubles from US$249; www.hiltonmystic.com

Newport's secluded, upscale Castle Hill Inn & Resort is on a scenic, 40-acre peninsula; doubles from US$589; www.castlehillinn.com

The National Hotel is one of Block Island's largest hotels; doubles from US$229; www.blockislandhotels.com

EATING OUT
Try lobster at the summertime seafood shacks. Mystic Pizza (US$10), famous from the 1988 film, is popular for its cheap pies. In Newport, the Red Parrot (US$25) and Brick Alley Pub (US$25) are casual, lively eateries.

PRICE FOR TWO
US$500 per day including accommodation, entertainment, and food.

FURTHER INFORMATION
www.gonewport.com
www.mysticcountry.com

Architectural Opulence

Visitors to Rhode Island are often blown away by the splendor of its historic houses, most of which, built in the Gilded Age of the late-19th century, have been immaculately maintained and restored. Newport's famed Cliff Walk is an ideal starting point to admire the the mansions, and take in the view of the rugged coastline. Don't miss The Breakers (below), built for Cornelius Vanderbilt II in 1895 at a cost of $7 million (roughly $150 million today).

SAILING AND HISTORY

Main: A racing yacht at a sailing regatta, Newport, Rhode Island

THE THOUGHT OF A FEW DAYS BY OR ON THE SPARKLING SEA in New England is pure heaven for many people. And when it comes to a seaside retreat, there's no better place than America's sailing capital: Newport, Rhode Island. Throw in a concert or two at one of the country's largest classical music festivals, and you have the ingredients for a perfect summer weekend on many levels.

Newport has attracted a legion of admirers and is proud of its rich history. More than a century ago, wealthy families from all over the country chose this remote port as the place to build their summer homes. And what fabulous homes they were, with the likes of the Vanderbilts and Astors sinking millions into mansions that still impress. While he was President, John F. Kennedy spent his summers here, and countless dignitaries have come to watch the world's premier sailing

Above (top to bottom): Newport Bridge at dusk; the schooner *Adirondack* sailing past New York Yacht Club's Newport clubhouse; pianist Piotr Anderszewski performing at Marble House, Newport Music Festival

Bottom (left to right): Local lobster and clams at a clam bake; Block Island North Lighthouse; Newport Harbour, Rhode Island; beluga whale, Mystic Aquarium

regatta, the America's Cup. Today, the city provides visitors with plenty of sightseeing and nautical attractions, not to mention shopping and dining opportunities.

In keeping with the sailing theme, no trip to the area would be complete without a stop in Mystic, Connecticut's loveliest summertime haven. A must for history buffs as well as serious sailors, the town's old seaport provides a glimpse into America's nautical past. But if skiffs and schooners aren't your thing, Mystic still has plenty to offer including a nationally acclaimed aquarium (most notable for its beluga whales) and a picturesque downtown that's chock full of inviting galleries, shops, and restaurants.

For a quieter but no less scenic outing, visitors should take the ferry to Block Island, a small parcel of land off the Rhode Island coast whose year-round population only numbers in the hundreds. The island possesses many attractive hiking trails and historic Victorian buildings, yet manages to maintain a nostalgic, small-town ambience that's hard to beat.

Above: The harbor in Mystic Seaport

ISLAND DIARY

July is warm and a perfect time to visit one of southern New England's most charming destinations. Places such as Newport and Mystic can be explored with just one night's stay in each, as both have compact centers. Don't miss Block Island, a scenic getaway that's just a quick ferry ride from Newport.

A Seaside Weekend

Spend the day at Mystic Seaport, the nation's largest maritime museum. Sailors of all stripes will have to be peeled away from the extensive collection of historic ships to explore the main draw, a recreation of a 19th-century seaport. Enjoy a lobster lunch at an old standby such as Abbott's Lobster in the Rough or S&P Oyster Co. Take a stroll through Mystic's quaint downtown before tipping back a nightcap at a cozy pub – the Harp and Hound is a good one.

Head for Newport and take a brisk walk along the 3.5-mile (5.6-km) Cliff Walk, popping into a couple of breathtaking mansions along the way. Classical music enthusiasts can attend the Newport music festival held at the mansions in July. Sport fans shouldn't miss the International Tennis Hall of Fame, which is housed in an ornate casino that dates back to 1880. Wander along Thames Street to pick up some souvenirs or freshly made fudge before heading off on a sunset cocktail cruise around the harbor. Cap off the day with a gourmet seafood dinner at an upscale waterfront restaurant such as The Mooring or One Bellevue.

Hop on the ferry for the 2-hour ride to tiny Block Island. A quiet place, the island boasts natural treasures that include 17 miles (27 km) of beaches and 32 miles (51 km) of trails. After a hike along one of these trails, make for commercial Water Street and chow down on a lobster roll or fried clam basket at the Harbor Grill.

Dos and Don'ts

✓ You won't find a market on every corner, so be sure to have supplies of sunscreen and water with you at all times.

✗ Don't forget to double-check the Block Island ferry schedule. With no other means of making it back to the mainland, you don't want to miss the last ferry back.

✓ If you have rented a car, allow time for finding parking when in Newport. Public parking is scarce in summer. Private lots are dotted throughout the city, though many are expensive.

✗ Don't forget comfortable footwear, as the compact town centers lend themselves to lots of walking, with most exploration possible only on foot.

JAN
FEB
MAR
APR
MAY
JUN
JUL
DAY 1
DAY 2
DAY 3
AUG
SEP
OCT
NOV
DEC

GETTING THERE   See map p325, F4
Santo Domingo, Punta Cana, and Puerto Plata all have international airports.

GETTING AROUND
To explore, rent a car and get a good map. For day tours, take a taxi with a certified guide as a driver. Buses run between all major towns.

WEATHER
July temperatures can reach 86°F (30°C), only falling to 76°F (25°C) at night. Tropical rainstorms, short but heavy, are likely.

ACCOMMODATIONS
The beachside Puntacana Resort and Club, in Punta Cana has its own spa and golf course; doubles from US$176; www.puntacana.com

Hotel Santo Domingo is a centrally located luxury hotel close to the Malecón; doubles from US$179; www.hotelsantodomingo.com

The charming Casa Colonial Beach and Spa Resort in Puerto Plata is home to the acclaimed Lucia restaurant; doubles from US$260; www.casacolonialhotel.com

EATING OUT
Miro Gallery, in Cabarete, near Puerto Plata, displays the work of local artists and serves a wide range of contemporary dishes. Mesón de la Cava, set in a cavern in Santo Domingo, features live music. Santo Domingo's Museo de Jamón (Ham Museum) serves good tapas.

PRICE FOR TWO
US$350 per day, including accommodation, food, local transportation, and excursions.

FURTHER INFORMATION
www.godominicanrepublic.com

Caribbean Combo

Dominicans love to dance – the only thing they love more is the music that they dance to! Almost every community has its own *combo* (three-man band) to supply the pulsating, foot-tapping rhythms. Traditional instruments are the *tambora* (goat-skin drum), the accordion-like *melodeon*, and a *guira*, originally a gourd filled with stones or seeds but now often a washboard or cheese grater. Other home-made instruments, such as bamboo-cane flutes and seed-pod *marimbas*, may be added, as well as modern horns, strings, flutes, or a piano.

The dark rum flows liberally, sweet cigar smoke drifts on the breeze, and dancing is a way of life.

Main: Merengue dancers in action in a Santo Domingo restaurant

DANCING IN THE STREETS

THE SENSUAL BEAT OF MERENGUE MUSIC resonates through the very soul of the Dominican Republic. Its distinctive rhythms can be heard at all hours of the day and night, pumping out of cars, shops, and houses, drifting on the warm breeze over emerald-green treetops and across brilliant swathes of golden sand. This is a truly charismatic place, where the dark rum flows liberally, sweet cigar smoke drifts on the breeze, and dancing is a way of life.

The annual, carnival-like Fiesta de Merengue in July is a vibrant, full-on shindig lasting a full nine days. If you're lucky enough to be here at the time, you really have no option but to get up and join in. Thousands of people from all over the world cram onto El Malecón, the long road running parallel to the seafront in the old colonial capital of Santo Domingo, to move their hips to the music of top performers and up-and-coming stars. Merengue, salsa, Latin jazz, and *bachata* (a slower, guitar-based merengue) fill the air. Although this thoroughfare is the focal point of the

Above: Alcázar de Colón in Santo Domingo's historic center

FIESTA DIARY

The Dominican Republic, which shares the island of Hispaniola with Haiti, is a large country, full of contrasts. A week-long visit in July gives you the chance to learn about merengue, the national dance, at its lively Fiesta, but also to take time out and explore more of the many facets of this fascinating and beautiful land.

A Week of Merengue Magic

Explore your resort, and sign up for any tours you want to do. Enjoy your first sunset, then follow the sound of music to discover what merengue is all about.

The next day you could try some inshore scuba diving or snorkeling. The waters here are warm, clear, and teem with tropical fish. After dinner, hit the dance floor to put your merengue knowledge into action.

Take a guided day-long tour to Santo Domingo, the oldest extant city in the Americas. Spend the morning visiting its historic heart. The 15th-century Alcázar de Colón was home to Columbus's son, who became the city's first governor. After lunch, head for the Malecón to hear the merengue bands and watch the colorfully costumed dancers swirl and sway.

Spend a couple of days getting back to nature. Perhaps try "canyoning" with a guide along the Rio Jimenoa. You start at the headwaters and jump, splash, and swim your way back, ending by jumping through a waterfall into the lake below. Explore the stunning natural beauty of Jarabacoa national park – walk some of its well-marked trails to spot many exotic birds and plants.

Hire a taxi for a tour of the north coast. There are miles of fabulous beaches, and picturesque fishing villages. If you ask your driver where to stop for lunch you'll get to sample some great local cooking.

If you want to shop for souvenirs, be sure to try local handicrafts stores. At sunset, take a horse ride along the beach, then dance the night away for one last time.

Dos and Don'ts

✓ Join in the fun. In fact, once the music starts it is almost impossible not to get up and dance.

✗ Don't get too adventurous when exploring inland. Stick to main roads and remember to keep an eye on your fuel gauge. Gas stations are not common in the countryside, and even if you find one, it may have run out of fuel.

✓ Remember that many restaurants only take cash. Find out before you sit down to dine.

| JAN |
| FEB |
| MAR |
| APR |
| MAY |
| JUN |
| **JUL** |
| DAYS 1–2 |
| DAY 3 |
| DAYS 4–5 |
| DAY 6 |
| DAY 7 |
| AUG |
| SEP |
| OCT |
| NOV |
| DEC |

Inset: Merengue dancer in colorful traditional dress

Left (left to right): Locals join in the fun at the Fiesta; Diving amid the coral; typical north-coast beach of Las Terrenas; lush and rugged Cordillera Central national park, west of Santo Domingo

Right: Air-dried hams hanging from the rafters in the tapas bar of the Museo de Jamón

event, the revels spill over onto the beach, and into every bar, hotel, and restaurant in the area. The city almost bursts at the seams with colorful parades, arts and crafts displays, aromatic food stalls, spectacular fireworks, and constant dancing. It truly is the mother of all street parties.

If you can tear yourself away from the festivities, you'll find plenty of other ways to spend your time in this Caribbean paradise. There are magnificent national parks; untamed swamp and savanna; over 1,000 miles (1,600 km) of fabulous, palm-fringed beaches; and verdant tracts of rainforest offering unmissable opportunities for bird-watching, hiking, and ecotourism. In Santo Domingo, the magnificent old buildings include the first hospital, university, and cathedral in the Americas, built more than 500 years ago. Scores of other charming, historic buildings have been faithfully restored, and many now house cultural centers, galleries, museums, boutiques, and restaurants.

And if, as your vacation draws to a close, you simply can't stop your feet from tapping to that addictive beat, then you might just have to start planning your return, for the next, four-day long, merengue festival that takes place here in the fall.

Where to Go: **August**

Summer is in full swing in the northern hemisphere, with much of North America getting very hot. Ocean breezes keep things cooler along the coasts, while inland lakes and mountains offer their own refreshing respite. In the Rocky Mountains temperatures can plummet below freezing at night, though days will be gloriously sunny; Santa Fe is kept pleasant by its higher elevation. Even famously forbidding Newfoundland is a joy to explore at this time of year, when it is at its warmest. In the southern hemisphere, many of the South American countries offer good conditions, with rainfall and humidity at a manageable level, and daytime temperatures not prohibitively hot. Below you will find all the destinations in this chapter and some extra suggestions to provide further inspiration.

FESTIVALS AND CULTURE

BARRETOS A lively display by flag-waving cowboys

UNFORGETTABLE JOURNEYS

THE VIKING TRAIL The beautiful Tablelands, Gros Morne National Park

NATURAL WONDERS

YELLOWSTONE NATIONAL PARK Plains buffalo grazing in the park

BARRETOS
BRAZIL

Enjoy rodeo, Brazilian-style

Don your stetson and grab a ringside seat for Wild West action like bucking broncos and bull-riding, followed by evenings of sizzling steaks and samba.
See pp202–3

POTOSÍ
BOLIVIA

Marvel at the world's highest city

With an altitude of over 13,125 ft (4,000 m), Potosí is an atmospheric colonial city.
www.boliviaweb.com/cities/potosi.htm

THE VIKING TRAIL
NEWFOUNDLAND, CANADA

If exploring wild tundra landscapes with few people and roaming caribou appeals, take the Viking Trail across Newfoundland.
See pp192–3

DEVIL'S TOWER NATIONAL MONUMENT
WYOMING, USA

Surreal geological landmark

Hike around this soaring volcanic outcrop, whose rock walls tower above the Belle Fourche River.
www.nps.gov/deto

YELLOWSTONE NATIONAL PARK
WYOMING, USA

An American wilderness

Yellowstone National Park is a great place to see bears, wolves, eagles, elk, steamy geysers, and herds of great thundering bison.
See pp188–9

BURNING MAN
NEVADA, USA

A walk on the wild side with a flaming climax

The venue doesn't sound promising – the unhospitable Nevada desert – but there's no other festival like it elsewhere on the planet.
See pp204–5

WISCONSIN STATE FAIR
WISCONSIN, USA

All the fun of the fair

Feast on cream puffs, relax to live music, or jump on thrilling fairground rides at this annual extravaganza.
See pp182–3

DRIVE THE ICEFIELDS PARKWAY
ALBERTA, CANADA

Spectacular highway

Stretching 143 miles (230 km) between Jasper and Lake Louise, the Icefields Parkway traverses an unforgettably rugged landscape.
www.icefieldsparkway.ca

GLACIER BAY NATIONAL PARK
ALASKA, USA

Dramatic coastal wilderness

Cruise through the fjords of Glacier Bay, home to no fewer than 15 glaciers, including the spectacular Grand Pacific Glacier.
www.nps.gov/glba/

GRAN CHACO
PARAGUAY

Explore South America's final frontier

One of most sparsely inhabited areas on the continent, with endless miles of rolling savannah.
www.botany.si.edu/projects/cpd/sa/sa22.htm

HIKING THE GREAT DIVIDE TRAIL
BRITISH COLUMBIA, CANADA

An amazing trekking challenge

Tackle this epic trail, which snakes for around 750 miles (1,200 km) along the Continental Divide, traversing six national parks.
www.rmbooks.com/gdt/gdt.htm

MANU NATIONAL PARK
PERU

Wildlife in abundance

Visit one of the most important national parks in the world and see giant otters, caymans, and flocks of macaws.
See pp200–1

> "The park is so isolated in parts that several indigenous groups have never had contact with outsiders."

LEADVILLE
COLORADO, USA

Historic city with stunning scenery

Leadville boasts a historic center of old red-brick Victorian-era streets and breathtaking views of the surrounding mountain peaks.
www.leadville.com

LA PAZ TO COROICO BY ROAD
BOLIVIA

Heart-stopping highway

Travel the highway that descends 3,500 m (1,067 ft) in just 40 miles (64 km) through mountain scenery.
www.trekker.co.il/english/la_paz

MAMMOTH CAVE NATIONAL PARK
KENTUCKY, USA

World's longest cave system

An enormous subterranean wonderland full of majestic caverns and perplexing limestone labyrinths.
www.nps.gov/maca

Previous page: Butterflies sipping minerals from a riverbank, Manu National Park, Peru

Weather Watch

❶ **Québec, Canada** Summer has hit southeastern Canada. As ever, though, you should expect the unexpected, and be prepared for afternoon thunderstorms.

❷ **The Hamptons, USA** August is peak season in the swanky Hamptons and for very good reason – the beaches are by far at their best at this time of year, with warm waters and balmy ocean breezes.

❸ **Yellowstone National Park, USA** Long, warm days offer delightful conditions for exploring the surreal landscape of Yellowstone. Temperatures plummet at night, however, and there may be the odd afternoon storm.

❹ **Santa Fe, USA** At a higher elevation than the deserts to the south, New Mexico's loveliest city offers dazzling sunshine in August, along with crisp, starlit nights.

❺ **Ecuador** August is dry and pleasant in Ecuador; the coastal regions are hot, while temperatures in the Andean city of Quito are tempered by its altitude, with warm days and delightfully cool evenings.

❻ **Argentina** Much of Argentina is enjoying a warm winter. The northern regions are cooler and drier than during the rest of the year. Salta, at the foothills of the Andes, boasts sunny days, low humidity, and cold nights.

LUXURY AND ROMANCE

THE HAMPTONS The lighthouse in the hamlet of Montauk

MENDOCINO
CALIFORNIA, USA

A beautiful, tranquil slice of old America

This wonderfully preserved little town on the California coast has hotels full of charm, fine food, a laidback feel, and fabulous sunsets.
www.mendocino.com

THE HAMPTONS
NEW YORK STATE, USA

Manhattan society's favorite seaside escape

Here you can rub shoulders with the rich and famous or chill out in a charming colonial oceanside hideaway – the choice is yours.
See pp194–5

QUÉBEC CITY
QUÉBEC, CANADA

A sliver of old France in the New World

Old Québec combines the best of both worlds – the romance of the old world, with the excitement, comfort, and luxury of the new.
See pp186–7

SALTA & JUJUY
ARGENTINA

Colonial charm and colorful canyons

Enjoy the amazing colors of the Cafayete Ravine by day, and snuggle up by the fireside at night with the local red wine.
See pp190–1

MACKINAC ISLAND
MICHIGAN, USA

Idyllic and old-fashioned island charm

It's small, it's quiet, it's romantic and only horses and carriages and bikes are allowed on the island.
See pp196–7

ACTIVE ADVENTURES

DENALI NATIONAL PARK Hiker taking a break near Mt. McKinley

DENALI NATIONAL PARK
ALASKA, USA

The home of Mt. McKinley

A beautiful gem of a parkland, filled with moose, caribou, and bears, with North America's highest peak as its centerpiece.
See pp198–9

> "It's never really crowded here, unless you count the population of grizzlies, caribou, Dall sheep, wolves, and other wild inhabitants."

COLUMBIA RIVER
OREGON, USA

A gorgeous inland utopia for windsurfers

The gorge of the Columbia in Oregon creates unique conditions for windsurfing enthusiasts.
www.el.com/to/hoodriver

APOSTLE ISLANDS
WISCONSIN, USA

Island retreat on lovely Lake Superior

These 22 wonderfully windswept lakeshore islands offer outdoor enthusiasts a wide ride of excellent water sports.
www.nps.gov/apis

KAIETEUR FALLS
GUYANA

One of the world's most spectacular waterfalls

Hike around these majestic falls, which tumble for almost 755 ft (230 m) amidst a pristine landscape of tropical rain forest.
www.kaieteurpark.gov.gy

MOUNT COTOPAXI
ECUADOR

A breathtaking test for the adventurous cyclist

Explore the stunning region around Mount Cotopaxi by mountain bike.
www.ecuadorexplorer.com

FAMILY GETAWAYS

SANTA FE Hispanic dancers at El Rancho de las Golondrinas

> "Nestled in the Sangre de Cristo Mountains, the beautiful city of Santa Fe proudly calls itself "The City Different. "

SANTA FE
NEW MEXICO, USA

Colorful desert city

The unique blend of Native Pueblo, Spanish, and cowboy cultures are displayed throughout this city in its many museums and ancient monuments.
See pp184–5

PAWLEYS ISLAND
SOUTH CAROLINA, USA

One of the east coast's best kept secrets

Laidback family getaway with pristine beaches, excellent surf, and plenty of family activities ranging from biking to crabbing.
www.discoverpawleysisland.com

PRINCE EDWARD ISLAND
CANADA

Anne of Green Gables country

Cycle or drive through the pastoral countryside and visit Green Gables House, the inspiration for L.M. Montgomery's classic novel.
www.gov.pe.ca/lmm

LOS ANGELES
CALIFORNIA, USA

One of the USA's premier family destinations

Home to an unrivaled array of blockbuster attractions, including the world-famous Disneyland and the popular Universal Studios.
www.losangeles.com/attractions

BRYCE CANYON
UTAH, USA

Weird and wonderful scenery that never fails to fascinate

Famed for its bizarre stone pillars known as "hoodoos," this Utah canyon can be toured by car and then further explored on paths.
www.nps.gov/brca

GETTING THERE
See map p316, B4
The Wisconsin State Fair is held at the State Fair Park in West Allis, Milwaukee. Mitchell International Airport, 6 miles (10 km) from the city center, is linked to the city by Amtrak trains and shuttle and bus services.

GETTING AROUND
Milwaukee's bus system (Milwaukee County Transit System) is a good way to get to the fair. Park-and-ride shuttles also operate.

WEATHER
August temperatures average highs of 79°F (26°C) and lows of 62°F (17°C). It is the wettest month, but showers are short-lived.

ACCOMMODATIONS
For old-world charm try Knickerbocker on the Lake; doubles from US$139; www.knickerbockeronthelake.com

The upscale Ambassador Hotel is in the heart of downtown; doubles from US$149; www.ambassadormilwaukee.com

Hotel Metro is a luxurious boutique hotel; doubles from US$239; www.hotelmetro.com

EATING OUT
The fair has a vast range of food options, from traditional bratwurst to buffalo burritos. Outside the fair, go for a butter burger at Solley's Grille (US$10) or check out the French-inspired Lake Park Bistro (US$30) in leafy Lake Park.

PRICE FOR TWO
US$350 including accommodation, food, and entertainment.

FURTHER INFORMATION
www.wistatefair.com

Cream Puff Crazy

Appearing only during the 11 days of the fair, the legendary cream puff – a fluffy, calorie-laden delight – has been produced by a team of bakers and dairy farmers for more than 80 years. And what a team it is – more than 200 employees work all hours to produce the 50,000 cream puffs sold daily. Thousands of people line up, phone in, or drive through for the pastries, piled high with cream from Wisconsin's best dairy cows. An even sweeter treat is the Celebrity Cream Puff Eating Contest, featuring a slew of local celebrities eating giant puffs without using their hands.

Above (left to right): Biomes at Mitchell Park Conservatory; the ultra modern Milwaukee Art Museum
Main: Exciting funfair ride illuminated against the night sky, Wisconsin State Fair

Above: Boats docked on the Milwaukee River

ALL THE FUN OF THE FAIR

STRAINS OF LIVE MUSIC DRIFT ACROSS THE FAIRGROUND, mingling with the squeals of delighted children on Ferris wheels, the lively chatter of picnicking families, and the din of noisy farmyard animals. This cheerful, chaotic atmosphere fills the warm summer air at the annual Wisconsin State Fair – an 11-day extravaganza showcasing the very best of the state, from livestock events and horticultural displays to food stalls, homebrewery exhibitions, and open-air concerts.

A beloved summer ritual since 1851, the fair has grown to welcome more than 850,000 visitors annually. Today the range of events is breathtaking, but the focus is still Wisconsin's agricultural heritage. Watching a goat being milked or a calf being born is a favorite spectacle with kids and an eye-opener for anyone who wasn't brought up on a farm. Youngsters of all ages will also enjoy the interactive events. Sign up for the wacky "Moo-la-palooza" – a mooing contest – and you could walk off with US$1,000. From cup-stacking to Hula-Hooping, the spirit of honest competition is palpable.

> Strains of live music drift across the fairground, mingling with the squeals of delighted children on Ferris wheels.

The fair is also famed for the quality and variety of its food. Where else can you enjoy so much good-natured gluttony in one place? On average, more than 40 different "foods on a stick" are offered, 60,000 baked potatoes sold, and 350,000 cream puffs gobbled up. You could attend every day of the fair, eat three meals and countless snacks, and still not come close to trying even half the delicacies. Cream puffs, meat pies, root-beer flavored milk, and roasted corn-on-the-cob dripping with dairy-fresh butter – the choice is dizzying.

Besides eating your weight in cheese and watching livestock watch people, there are plenty of other diversions. Magicians and rock legends give sell-out shows; shoppers revel in an endless array of stalls, selling everything from model cars to jewelry; and dozens of rides keep thrill-seekers happy. The definitive populist event, this vibrant fair offers something for everyone, a fact to which generations of Wisconsinites and legions of out-of-towners can attest.

Inset: Sign atop a live reptile booth, Wisconsin State Fair
Below (left and right): Fair entertainer; prize cow competition; Miller Brewery

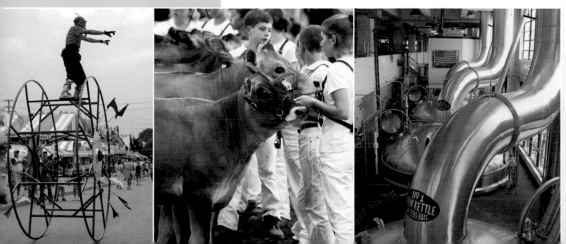

STATE FAIR DIARY

The fair runs for 11 days and nights, from 8am until midnight on weekends and 8am until 11pm on weekdays. Although exploring the fair could easily fill several days, be sure to make time to see the sights in historic Milwaukee, with its wealth of museums, vibrant arts scene, and old-world brewing traditions.

Three Days of Midwestern Fun

Head straight to the fair and hit the ground running. Check out the Midway for thrilling rides, then watch daredevils on bikes or chainsaw-wielding "Lumberjills" at the BMX Park. Stop by the horticulture building to see an amazing array of flowers and plants on display, or learn all about the circus at Circus World Museum. If it's hot, take a spin around the skating rink in the Petit Cool Zone. Be sure to snack along the way, then dance it all off at one of the evening shows.

Use this day to explore the sights in Milwaukee. Have a cooked breakfast such as "hoffel poffel" (scrambled eggs with potatoes, onions, salami, and cheese) at Jo's Café, or go for a healthy vegetarian option at the popular Beans & Barley. Walk off a few calories exploring the Milwaukee Art Museum, if you're feeling cultured, or the Harley-Davidson Museum, if you're feeling tough, or visit Mitchell Park Conservatory, which boasts a spectacular diversity of plantlife, from shrubs and cacti to tropical flora. Milwaukee is all about beer, so be sure to go on a tour of the Miller Brewery. Browse eclectic boutiques on Brady Street or in the hip, arty neighborhood of Riverwest before sampling the trendy nightlife in each.

Spend a day with the animals. The fair showcases the best of Wisconsin's animals – cows, pigs, sheep, horses, chickens, and more. Witness a live animal birth in the Birthing Barn, get up close and personal with the Budweiser Clydesdales, and cheer on a swine or two at one of five daily pig races. See champion animals and the petting zoo in the Ag Village, and then stand in line for a famous State Fair cream puff.

Dos and Don'ts

✗ Don't bother dieting. Foods at the fair run the gamut with the freshest of Wisconsin ingredients, none of which should be missed. Taste it all and walk off the calories later.

✓ Do be hands-on. The fair offers plenty of opportunities for you to participate.

✗ Don't forget your rain gear. Wisconsin's weather is notoriously temperamental, so it's best to be prepared.

JAN
FEB
MAR
APR
MAY
JUN
JUL
AUG
DAY 1
DAY 2
DAY 3
SEP
OCT
NOV
DEC

GETTING THERE
See map p318, B2

Santa Fe is in northern New Mexico, 65 miles (105 km) northeast of Albuquerque's international airport, where you can rent cars.

GETTING AROUND
Santa Fe is best enjoyed on foot, but a car is needed to explore beyond downtown.

WEATHER
In August, daytime temperatures average 83°F (28°C) and the weather is generally dry and sunny, although it can change rapidly to heavy rain. Nights and mornings are cooler, with a nighttime average of 54°F (12°C).

ACCOMMODATIONS
The Santa Fe Motel is close to the Plaza; rooms from US$150; www.santafemotel.com

Fort Marcy Hotel Suites are conveniently located modern condominiums with full kitchens; from US$350; www.fortmarcy.com

Inn of the Anasazi, near the Plaza, offers rich decor with a blend of Native, Latino, and Anglo styling; rooms from US$480; www.innoftheanasazi.com

EATING OUT
Creative, spicy Southwestern cuisine combines flavors found in Mexican and Native American dishes with unusual spices. Café Pasqualís (from US$22) has a festive atmosphere, while the Shed offers hearty cuisine with spicy chili sauces from US$10.

PRICE FOR A FAMILY OF FOUR
US$650 per day including accommodation, food, local travel, and admission charges.

FURTHER INFORMATION
www.santafe.org

Georgia O'Keeffe

Innovative and provocative, noted modernist master Georgia O'Keeffe was already renowned for her canvases depicting intricately detailed flowers in softly graded colors when she first visited Taos, New Mexico, in 1929. She fell in love with the blue skies and landscape and began painting the stark white animal skulls she found while exploring, often including a delicate flower. The Georgia O'Keeffe Museum in Santa Fe houses 1,100 of her works, the world's largest permanent collection of her art.

Main: Terra-cotta pottery display outside a typical Southwestern adobe building
Above (top to bottom): Ladder to Alcove House at Bandelier National Monument; colorful local artwork; desert-bleached skulls for sale

ADOBE OASIS

BATHED IN CLEAR HIGH-DESERT SUNLIGHT and nestled in the Sangre de Cristo Mountains, the beautiful city of Santa Fe proudly calls itself "The City Different." Here, traditions that go back hundreds of years honor the unique blend of Native Pueblo, Spanish, and Anglo cultures that are the foundation of this vibrantly creative city. Lining the streets are desert-hued adobe buildings with lovely walled garden courtyards, vivid blue-green doors, and styles derived from the traditional dwellings built by the Pueblo Natives long before the Spanish arrived.

Today, the fusion of these diverse cultures is expressed in the city's captivating collection of museums, art galleries, and restaurants. The Plaza is the heart of the city, and families will want to explore the Palace of the Governors, where Pueblo artisans offer exquisite natural turquoise and engraved silver jewelry under the portico, as they have for generations. Inside, the Wild West comes alive in a wealth of exhibits including authentic firearms,

Above: Colorful Hispanic dances at El Rancho de las Golondrinas

Above (top to bottom): Canyon Road gallery, showcasing vibrant art; sculptures outside the boutique shops of Canyon Road

Below: Sculpture of a Native American warrior at the entrance of the Museum of Indian Arts and Culture on Museum Hill

SOUTHWESTERN DIARY

The pleasantly warm days and cool nights of August are perfect for discovering the attractions of Santa Fe and for driving the scenic mountain roads to Bandelier National Monument. Four days allow enough time to see the highlights, visit the shops and art galleries, and enjoy the area's savory fusion cuisine.

Four Days of Fun and Culture

Explore the art galleries, museums, and churches near the Plaza. Learn Santa Fe's fascinating history at the Palace of the Governors, where displays depict cowboys, Indians, and life in the Wild West. Visit the famous Georgia O'Keeffe Museum, and admire the "Miraculous Staircase" in the Loretto Chapel.

Drive to Museum Hill to enjoy the colorful folk-art toys and miniature villages at the Museum of International Folk Art. The Museum of Indian Arts and Culture's multimedia exhibit "Here, Now, and Always" is a fun way to learn about Native American culture, while younger children will love the innovative displays and activities at the nearby Santa Fe Children's Museum.

Drive to El Rancho de las Golondrinas and explore this outdoor living history museum, where children can experience colonial life on a Spanish hacienda.

Stroll the length of Canyon Road and visit the sculpture courtyards, art galleries, and the intimate garden at El Zaguán. Then, head to the Santa Fe Southern Railway for a scenic trip through the desert in vintage rail cars.

Drive to Bandelier National Monument and walk through the canyon to explore ancestral Pueblo cliff dwellings and village ruins. In the afternoon, visit Los Alamos for the Science Museum, where interactive exhibits explain atomic power and tell the story of the Manhattan Project and the first atomic bombs.

Dos and Don'ts

☑ Remember to take it easy and drink plenty of water, as the air is thin at 7,000 ft (2,134 m) above sea level.

☒ Don't forget to make reservations far ahead and to check the Santa Fe Southern Railway schedule.

☑ Purchase the Museum of New Mexico's four-day passes to the Palace of the Governors, the Museum of Fine Arts, the Museum of International Folk Art, the Museum of Indian Arts and Culture, and the Museum of Spanish Colonial Art.

☒ If staying in Santa Fe over the weekend, don't miss the traditional Native American folktales and Wild West yarns at the Wheelwright Museum of the American Indian.

JAN
FEB
MAR
APR
MAY
JUN
JUL
AUG
DAY 1
DAY 2
DAY 3
DAY 4
SEP
OCT
NOV
DEC

a working printing press, and even a clock shot by Pancho Villa, the Mexican revolutionary general. Guided tours relate the dramatic story of how the Spanish built this adobe building in 1610, as a fortress in the wilderness, and how the Pueblo Indians battled them and drove them away from Santa Fe for 12 years. Children especially like the Bland Mud Wagon, a real stagecoach that looks like it just rolled out of a John Wayne movie.

The boutique shops and galleries surrounding the Plaza offer a dazzling array of brightly colored ceramics, hand-woven woolens, intricately tooled leather belts, and cowboy boots. Sparkling silver jewelry, earth-toned Southwest landscape paintings, and large whimsical sculptures are just a few of the offerings found in the hundreds of art galleries. Kids will be awed and enthralled by the exceptionally creative exhibits and hands-on play opportunities at the nearby Santa Fe Children's Museum. Parents with older children will want to visit the area's most popular museum, where the legendary paintings of Georgia O'Keeffe capture the unique beauty and ethereal light of New Mexico's sun-drenched desert landscape.

GETTING THERE   See map p314, E6
The Jean Lesage International Airport is 10 miles (16 km) from Québec City. A taxi costs about US$30. There is no shuttle or bus service.

GETTING AROUND
Major sites are easy to reach by foot or a taxi. To visit outlying sites, rent a car.

WEATHER
Average August temperatures are 55–73°F (13–23°C). Warmer days aren't unusual, particularly early in the month. Late afternoon thunderstorms are common.

ACCOMMODATIONS
With a great Upper Town location Auberge Saint-Louis offers small, basic rooms; doubles from US$69; www.aubergestlouis.ca

The Upper Town's castle-like Fairmont Le Château Frontenac is a city landmark; doubles from US$159; www.fairmont.com

Down the street, try the romantic Hotel Le Clos Saint-Louis; doubles from US$175; www.clossaintlouis.com

EATING OUT
Restaurants serve Québécois or French food as well as world cuisines. A meal for two costs about US$40 in a casual eatery and US$120 or more in an upscale restaurant.

PRICE FOR TWO
US$400–500 per day including food, accommodation, transportation, and sightseeing.

FURTHER INFORMATION
www.quebecregion.com

The Fall of New France

In 1759, at the height of the Seven Years' War, British forces commanded by Major-General James Wolfe scaled the cliffs below the Plains of Abraham outside the heavily defended Québec City walls. Lieutenant-General Louis-Joseph Montcalm, Marquis de Montcalm, made a call that changed the course of North American history: he met the attackers with a poorly trained militia. Both Wolfe (*above*) and Montcalm died, but the British captured the city, triggering a series of victories that led to New France passing under British control.

Above (left to right): A horse-drawn carriage saunters through an Old Québec street; colorful, flower-lined façades surround Place Royale
Main: A striking nighttime view of Fairmont Le Château Frontenac towering over Québec City

Above: A gift from France, Fontaine de Tourny lights up Parliament Hill

SHADES OF THE PAST

CROSSING THROUGH THE PORTE SAINT-LOUIS (St. Louis Gate) past the stone walls encircling Vieux-Québec (Old Québec) is like stepping into another world, one that is familiar and contemporary but also rooted in a colorful and extraordinary past. Bustling rue Saint-Louis is abloom with flower baskets and alive with the buzzing of animated conversations that drift from sidewalk cafés. Galleries sell Inuit soapstone sculptures and bold abstract prints. Some of the stores could be those of any busy street in any North American downtown... but then you notice the steep mansard roofs of the 18th-century homes, the silver spires spearing the sky, and a Victorian-era cannonball lodged in the roots of a tree.

The past, present, and future shift effortlessly in this magical city like layers of sheer, colorful scarves laid one atop the other. Sleek young professionals chatter on cell phones outside Grande Allée nightclubs as horse-drawn carriages clop by. Guests snuggle under cotton sheets to watch Hollywood movies on plasma televisions in hotel rooms forged from Victorian warehouses. Like the settlers who carved this city from the vast woods of New France, food lovers can dine on the region's famed duck, but these days, they can complement their meal with vintage wines from California and Australia, as well as from France.

> The past, present, and future shift effortlessly in this magical city like layers of sheer, colorful scarves laid one atop the other.

The city is a magnet for history buffs, who can easily spend a whole vacation touring restored mansions, visiting historic military sights, and exploring museums. But even for those who would do almost anything other than look at exhibits about long-ago battles, Québec City's four centuries of history give the place an alluring glow. Every crooked street seems to lead to a garlic-scented restaurant with a chalkboard menu; every ancient staircase seems to offer a different view of the wide St. Lawrence River; and with every new day, the city unravels a new layer of itself for the curious visitor.

Inset: The Royal 22e Regiment at attention outside the Citadelle
Below (left and right): A cruise liner lies in port in Lower Town; diners enjoy the fare served at a sidewalk café along Grande Allée

QUÉBÉCOIS DIARY

Few North American cities rival Québec for sheer historical charm. August is a perfect time to leave behind the modern world and allow the relaxed pace of this timeless city to envelop you. Four days will allow you to see the city's main sights, and also fit in a little shopping. For more on Québec *see pp282–3*.

Four Days Steeped in History

DAY 1
Start where the city itself began in 1608, Place Royale, a cobblestone square in Basse-Ville (Lower Town). Browse through boutiques on rue du Petit-Champlain. After lunch, visit the Musée de la Civilisation (Museum of Civilization) and hunt for antiques in the shops along rue Saint-Paul. Dine at renowned Laurie Raphaël, then enjoy a nightcap at Café du Monde, overlooking the river.

DAY 2
Stroll along the Terrasse Dufferin, a boardwalk along the cliffs in Haute-Ville (Upper Town). Visit the city's fortified walls and the Citadelle. Refresh yourself with a café au lait at Chez Temporel, then pose for a caricature at one of the artists' stalls on rue du Trésor. After dinner, tour the city by *calèche* (horse-drawn carriage) before visiting l'Emprise, the laidback jazz bar at the Hotel Clarendon.

DAY 3
Venture outside the city walls to Parc des Champs-de-Bataille (Battlefields Park). Learn about Québec's art history at the nearby Musée National des Beaux-Arts du Québec before heading to Grande Allée, a lively boulevard lined with shops and restaurants. In the evening, take a starlight cruise with Croisières AML on the St. Lawrence from Basse-Ville to the Île d'Orléans.

DAY 4
Sample the bountiful breakfast at the Fairmont Le Château Frontenac, then head to the west end of town for half a day of indulgent treatments at the Amerispa at Château Bonne Entente. Return to Haute-Ville for outstanding cuisine in the romantic solarium at Le Saint-Amour.

Dos and Don'ts

- ✓ If you have good knees, take the Escalier Casse-Cou (Break Neck Stairs) between Haute-Ville and Basse-Ville. But take the funicular back up — it's a steep trip.

- ✗ Don't drive within the city walls, unless your idea of a romantic getaway involves spending the whole weekend searching for a parking space.

- ✓ Dust off that high school French. While many tourism industry workers speak English, a well-timed *s'il vous plaît* (please) or *merci* (thank you) will often earn you a smile.

- ✓ Don't rush. Québec City is best savored at a relaxed pace.

JAN
FEB
MAR
APR
MAY
JUN
JUL
AUG
SEP
OCT
NOV
DEC

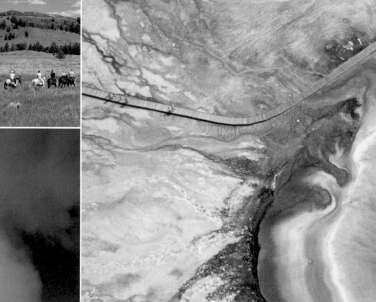

GETTING THERE
See map p320, F4

Yellowstone National Park is in the Rocky Mountain Range. It is mainly located in the state of Wyoming. The closest major international airport is in Salt Lake City, Utah.

GETTING AROUND
Cars can be rented at the airport for the 320-mile (515-km) drive to Yellowstone. There are small airports closer to the park, within a 1–2 hour drive. Regional airports are in Cody and Jackson, WY; Bozeman and Billings, MT; and Idaho Falls, ID. The West Yellowstone, MT, airport is only open from June to September.

WEATHER
August has daytime temperatures of up to 86°F (30°C) but it can drop below freezing at night. Thunderstorms are frequent.

ACCOMMODATIONS
All of the accommodations in the park are managed by Xanterra Parks and Resorts, with rooms in historic lodges, motels, and cottages. Old Faithful Inn, Mammoth Hot Springs Hotel, and Yellowstone Lake Hotel are popular choices; doubles from US$110; www.xanterra.com

Budget accommodations, from US$70 a night, may require sharing a bathroom.

EATING OUT
Restaurants range from elegant lodge dining to an Old West Cookout. There are many cafeterias and grills that also offer packed lunches.

PRICE FOR TWO
US$230–300 per day including accommodation, food, car rental and gas, and park admission.

FURTHER INFORMATION
www.nps.gov/yell/home.htm

Wonders of Yellowstone

Known as "Mi tsi a da zi," or "Rock Yellow River" to the Minnetaree tribe of Native Americans, the region's name was simplified by early fur trappers to Yellowstone. It took a major exploration by a forerunner of the U.S. Geological Survey in 1871 to introduce the world to the wonders of the park. Accompanying that expedition were photographer William H. Jackson and artist Thomas Moran. Their images helped convince President Grant to set aside the land as the world's first National Park in 1872.

Main: Aerial view of the Grand Prismatic Spring in Yellowstone – the spring is around 380 ft (120 m) in diameter

WHERE BUFFALO ROAM

T HE DUST RISES AS HEAVY HOOVES FALL, the older males stand guard, young calves stay close to their mother's side. Time comes to a standstill a sing a primeval scene that once had all but vanished from the planet, but is now slowly returning – North American buffalo or bison on the move. You wait till the herd disappears into the valley below, then continue on your way, forever changed by the sheer magnitude of the wild beauty of Yellowstone National Park.

More than half a million years ago, a gargantuan volcanic explosion blanketed western North America in ash and scooped out a vast caldera 50 miles by 30 miles wide (80 km by 50 km wide). Today that caldera, located just north of the spectacular Grand Teton Mountains, is green and lush with landscapes and ecosystems unique in the world. Stunning tableaus of green mountain meadows, wild rivers, azure lakes, and snow-capped peaks set the

Left (left to right): Majestic bull elk; plains buffalo grazing in the park; stripey Least chipmunk on a tree stump; signpost for the Continental Divide – the ridge of mountains that runs from Alaska in the north to Mexico in the south

Left panel (top and bottom): Visitors on a horseback tour through the park; Old Faithful geyser

Above: Canary Spring, named after the yellow algae growing at its edge

JAN

FEB

MAR

APR

MAY

JUN

JUL

WILDERNESS DIARY

August days are long and warm, with the chance to participate in ranger-led tours and activities. It is possible to see the park's highlights in four days. Try to escape the crowds and explore the spectacular wilderness. Guided fishing and boating trips, naturalist-led outings, photo-safaris, and overnight hikes are all available.

Four Days in the Parkland

AUG

Watch the spectacular eruption of Old Faithful, Yellowstone's most popular geyser, early in the morning when crowds are thin.

Stroll along the walkways at Upper Geyser Basin to see spouting geysers, steaming pools, and bubbling springs. Be sure to see the colorful Morning Glory Pool.

DAY 1

Drive, or if you are feeling energetic walk, along the 20-mile (32-km) Grand Canyon of the Yellowstone, stopping frequently for breathtaking views of the waterfalls and magnificent, coppery-orange canyon.

DAY 2

Visit lovely, marshy Hayden Valley in the early morning and watch for herds of bison. Elk, grizzly bears, wolves, bald eagles, and geese may also be seen from the road.

In the afternoon, join in one of the ranger-led daytime programs offering guided nature and history walks. There are also evening slide-shows and talks offered at a variety of locations throughout the park.

DAY 3

Drive the length of Lamar Valley, starting as the sun comes up, stopping frequently to look for bison, pronghorn antelope, bear, and wolves in the valley and along the gently rolling hills.

DAY 4

Dos and Don'ts

✓ Stop in visitors' centers for park maps and brochures, get the latest information on wildlife viewing, and peruse the exhibits on this incredible wilderness park.

✗ Don't try to see too much in one go – limit your exploration to one section of the park each day and take along a packed lunch or have meals close-by.

✓ Try to be outdoors at dawn when there are no crowds, getting out of the car often to walk, hike, take tours, and attend the ranger programs available at the park.

SEP

OCT

✗ Don't be caught out by the changeable weather; dress in layers as it may be below freezing at dawn and over 86°F (30°C) by mid-afternoon with a late-afternoon thunderstorm.

NOV

✓ Drive slowly, be patient, and watch closely everywhere you go. Sometimes animals can be seen very close to the road.

DEC

backdrop for an otherworldly landscape of 10,000 steaming fumaroles, geysers, bubbling mud pots, and psychedelically colored thermal springs (the color is caused by pigmented bacterial growth in the cooler water at the edge of the pool).

This huge park preserves one of the most intact ecosystems in the United States. August is an ideal time to visit because although tourists are present in large numbers, they tend to congregate in the popular areas, so discovering the real wilderness beauty of Yellowstone is as simple as getting off the beaten path anywhere in the park. A walk along the South Rim Trail east from busy Artist Point leads you up a brief, steep ascent that takes you far from the crowds and plunges you into a pristine world leaving civilization far behind. Following the gentle terrain of the canyon rim, the trail offers stunning views of the canyon, the Yellowstone River, and the cascading cataract of lower falls. A turn on the short Lily Pad Lake Trail takes you farther into the outback to the unspoiled splendor of the lily-covered lake where moose, bear, and elk roam freely and the vistas here are as wild and visually captivating as they were when the park was first discovered.

GETTING THERE See map p330, C6
Salta airport is a 2-hour flight from Buenos Aires. Taxis and shuttle buses run to the city center, 5 miles (8 km) away. San Salvador de Jujuy is 55 miles (88 km) north of Salta.

GETTING AROUND
Car hire is available at the airport and in town, with rates from about US$75 per day.

WEATHER
Days are clear and sunny with highs of 70°F (21°C), but evenings are chilly (42°F/5°C).

ACCOMMODATIONS
El Castillo is a romantic Italianate castle, 10 minutes' drive from central Salta; suites from US$125; www.hotelelcastillo.com.ar

Hotel Solar de la Plaza is a converted mansion near Salta city center; doubles from US$250; www.solardelaplaza.com.ar

Altos de la Viña is set on a hilltop 2 miles (3km) from Jujuy; suites from US$140; www.hotelaltodelavina.com.ar

EATING OUT
El Solar del Convento, a former Jesuit convent in Salta, serves *parilla* (charcoal grills) and *tamales*. Dinner for two around US$40.

Manos Jujeñas in Jujuy is great for regional specialties. Allow US$20 for a meal for two.

PRICE FOR TWO
US$250–350 per day including accommodation, food, car rental and gas, and all admissions.

FURTHER INFORMATION
www.welcomeargentina.com/salta
www.turismo.jujuy.gov.ar

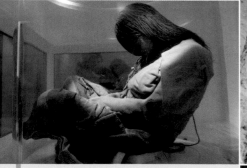

The Ice Maiden

La Doncella (The Maiden) was found in an icy pit at 23,000 ft (7,000 m), near the peak of the Andean volcano Llullaillaco. The 15-year-old and two younger children found with her were preserved by the sub-zero temperatures and low humidity. They are believed to have been sacrificed over 500 years ago in an Inca ritual to thank the gods for the corn harvest. She is now on display in a specially chilled chamber in Salta's Andean Archeological Museum. This angered some indigenous people, but had the blessing of Salta's own Quechua people.

ROMANTIC GLOW

There's something special about the light here in Salta. A physicist might try to explain it by the altitude of nearly 4,000 ft (1,200 m), or by the latitude, just south of the Tropic of Capricorn, or perhaps by the almost total absence of humidity in the air. An artist would simply note its qualities, how the rich, golden hue of the light gives a special glow to everything it illuminates. It may be for this alone that Argentines refer to this city as Salta La Linda – Salta the Beautiful. Needless to say, it's the perfect setting for a romantic break. At least a day in Salta could be spent just enjoying the sunshine, idly strolling the ancient cobbles, hand-in-hand beneath the orange trees on Plaza 9 de Julio, admiring the delightful colonial architecture, browsing for treasures in the myriad handicraft stores, and sampling local delicacies, such as the tasty little meat and cheese pastries known as *empanadas salteñas*.

Main: Spectacular colors of the Humahuaca Gorge

Left: Interior of the Basilica de Salta

Right (left to right): Church in Tilcara; seats in the shade at Cachi *pueblo*; young gaucho on horseback;

Right panel (top and center): Sunset over the salt flats of Salinas Grandes; canyon road near Cafayate

Nature-lovers will revel in the afternoon drive south to Cafayate, where the Salta sun shines on lush green valley-floor vineyards, sere desert foothills and highland plateaus, and soaring rock formations sculpted into natural works of art. In the Cafayate Ravine, the striated cliffs and water-slashed gulleys come in every conceivable color: terra-cotta and rust, slate green, chalky yellows, lemon, orange, and bonfire red. Some of these striking formations have evocative names, such as Garganta del Diablo (the Devil's Throat). Others are simply nameless things of beauty.

Back in the city, come nightfall, the temperature drops steeply and swiftly. Those looking for the warmth of human company can stroll the lively cafés, clubs and *bodegas* of bustling, bright Balcarce. For others, the nip in the air makes the Salta evening a time for snuggling by a fire, a time in which to warm your insides with a glass or two of local rich, strong red wine, while enjoying the glow from the *parilla*'s bed of coals, and the sparkle in your companion's eyes.

Above: Salta's leafy Plaza 9 de Julio

HIGH-COUNTRY DIARY

Five days is an ideal length of time to explore Salta and nearby Jujuy and take some drives through the high country around them. If you are here in the third week of August you can enjoy the events of Jujuy Week, but all month you are likely to come across events marking the festival of Pachamama, the Earth Mother.

Six Days in the Sunshine

DAY 1
Stroll Salta's colonial center, basking in the warm winter sunshine. Admire the terra-cotta façade of the Iglesia San Francisco and the ornate interior of the Basilica. Take the cable car almost 1,000 ft (300 m) up to the top of San Bernardo Hill, and enjoy the panoramic view of the Lerma Valley. At night, feast on traditional Argentinean barbecue, *parilla*.

DAY 2
Have breakfast in bed, enjoying the colonial ambience of your hotel. Later on, take a walk and perhaps stop to view the tapestries and colonial art in the Provincial Museum of Fine Arts. Visit the Andean Archeological Museum. In the evening, visit a *peña folclórica*, a folk tavern, and watch dancers perform the *zamba*.

DAY 3
Hire a car and take the scenic route south through the Calchaquíes Valley. Wander the square in the tiny traditional *pueblo* of Cachi. Scramble up the edges of the eroded red hills at Quebrada de las Flechas (Ravine of the Arrows) near Angostaco. Peer into the Devil's Throat gorge near the Quebrada del Río de las Conchas (Canyon of the River of Shells). Stop in at a winery such as San Pedro de Yacochuya, near Cafayate.

DAY 4
Make the short drive north to San Salvador de Jujuy Spend the day exploring its compact colonial heart.

DAYS 5–6
Drive the striking road north through the Humahuaca Gorge, up into the high, arid desert country, to the artists' colony of Tilcara and the spectacular salt flats of Salinas Grandes. Enjoy a last romantic night in Jujuy, before driving back down the valley to Salta.

Dos and Don'ts

✓ Try the wines. Argentinean vintages are inexpensive and of very high quality – the perfect accompaniment to a romantic fireside dinner. (See pp216–7)

✗ Don't overlook the Andean Archeological Museum, even if you're not normally a museum person. The wind-dried sacrificial mummies are astonishing.

✓ Bring plenty of cash for local art and crafts. Metalware, textiles, pottery, and other handicrafts are all very tempting.

✗ Don't forget to bring a warm sweater or fleece. The temperature drops dramatically when the sun goes down. But also bring sunscreen and a hat for the daytime.

JAN
FEB
MAR
APR
MAY
JUN
JUL
AUG
SEP
OCT
NOV
DEC

GETTING THERE   See map p314, H5
Newfoundland has two international airports,
St. John's and Gander Mountain, and a regional
airport, Deer Lake. Rent a car from here to get
to Gros Morne National Park, which is 20 miles
(32 km) away. A car ferry from North Sydney,
Nova Scotia, docks at Port aux Basques, 186
miles (300 km) from the park entrance.

GETTING AROUND
A car is required for the Viking Trail.

WEATHER
August is one of the warmest and driest
times to visit, with average daytime
temperatures of 61–77°F (16–25°C).

ACCOMMODATIONS
Red Mantle Lodge, Shoal Brook, offers hotel
style accommodation in the park; rooms from
US$120; www.redmantlelodge.ca

Neddies Harbour Inn, Norris Point, is a modern
waterfront inn in the heart of the park, with
rooms from US$175; www.theinn.ca

Tuckamore Lodge, Main Brook, offers luxury
accommodation with breakfast, from US$140;
dinner available; www.tuckamorelodge.com

EATING OUT
The best restaurants are in or near the Gros
Morne National Park. Smaller places have
reasonably priced simple fare, such as
chowders, cod cheeks, and seal flipper pie.

PRICE FOR TWO
US$630 per day including hotel, food,
car rental, gas, and admissions.

FURTHER INFORMATION
www.newfoundlandlabrador.com

Viking Village

In 1960, explorer Helge Ingstad was combing the
northeast coast of America for evidence of the
existence of the fabled Viking settlement recorded in
the saga of Leif Erikson, a Norse explorer (970–
1020 AD) who may have been the first European to
land in north America. After much searching, locals
told Ingstad of earth mounds near L'Anse aux
Meadows. In 1961, he returned with his archeologist
wife and uncovered an ember pit like one found in
Greenland at the house of Eric the Red. A full
excavation revealed a whole Viking village.

Above (left to right): Boat trip in Gros Morne National Park; large bull moose; kayaking fun
Main: Hiking in Gros Morne National Park

Above: Lobster Cove Lighthouse, Lobster Cove

WILD AND ROCKY COAST

THIS IS A STUNNING TRIP ALONG A NARROW SLIVER of highway carved through the spectacular tundra landscape. Known as the Viking Trail, the route follows the Great Northern Peninsula that stretches into the Atlantic Ocean toward Greenland. It takes you from the dramatic coastal mountains and fjords of Gros Morne National Park north along an unforgettably wild coastline to the remote northern tip of the island of Newfoundland, where Leif Erikson and a handful of Viking settlers landed a thousand years ago.

At the southern end of the Trail is Gros Morne National Park, treasured by geologists who come to study some of the world's oldest rocks, part of the earth's mantle that rose through the ocean floor as tectonic plates collided. The Long Range Mountains shelter beautiful sapphire-blue fjords while timeless fishing villages cling to tiny harbors along the boulder-strewn shoreline. L'Anse-aux-Meadows, at the northern end of the Viking Trail, is the oldest known European settlement in the western hemisphere. The landscape today is much as it must have been when the Vikings arrived, with coastal bogs and tuckamore forests of stunted white spruce and balsam fir twisted by the constant force of onshore winds. Reconstructions of the Viking longhouses built of sod stand on a grassy headland by the sea, and costumed enactors portray the self-reliant lifestyle of the mighty Viking seafarers who built their outpost here. Abandon the car and follow hiking trails that lead through arctic-alpine barrens in which caribou roam, past volcanic cliffs and sea stacks along a coast where minke whales can be seen feeding offshore. A boardwalk leads through coastal bog, where moose often graze, to Western Brook Pond and boat tours take passengers into this vast glacier-carved fjord where streams turn to misty cascades as they tumble down sheer rock walls 2,000 ft (609 m) above the water.

> Follow hiking trails that lead through arctic-alpine barrens in which caribou roam, past volcanic cliffs along the coast.

Inset: Viking enactors in the recreated village, L'Anse-aux-Meadows
Below (left and right): Exposed sedimentary rock; Tablelands, Gros Morne

NEWFOUNDLAND DIARY

August is the warmest and driest month of the year in Newfoundland, and although it is also the busiest, you will still find beaches and mountain vistas where you are the only ones enjoying them. August is also the best time to see wildlife in the National Park. Five days is all you need to enjoy the wild scenery.

Five Days on the Viking Trail

Explore Gros Morne National Park, stopping at the Visitors' Center and the Discovery Center to learn about the park's geology. Hike with a park geologist to the Tablelands – barren mountains formed when tectonic plates collided millions of years ago – and walk on the earth's mantle. Kayak on the blue waters of Trout River Pond for fascinating views of the Tablelands. There are fabulous sunsets from the Lobster Point Lighthouse.

Visit Bonne Bay Marine Station and watch marine life as seen by a real-time underwater camera. Drive to Western Brook Pond, walk through the wetlands on the boardwalk, and take the boat trip down the fjord beneath towering mountains. For an evening of comedy and drama, attend the Gros Morne Theatre Festival.

Head north along the coast and stop at the Arches to watch the waves crashing onshore. Stop at Port au Choix National Historic Site and learn about the area's earliest inhabitants, the Maritime Archaic people, who lived here 4,000 years ago.

Drive to L'Anse-aux-Meadows National Historic Site with its Viking enactors at the recreated village. The museum at this UNESCO World Heritage Site relates the discovery and excavation of the village. Visit nearby Norstead Village to see the recreation of the Viking ship that sailed from Greenland. In St. Anthony, the museum at Grenfell Historic Properties tells of the good Doctor Grenfell who tended those in remote outposts.

Return along the Viking Trail to Deer Lake Airport.

Dos and Don'ts

☑ Dress in layers and be prepared for cold, wet, and hot weather. Bring a camera and binoculars for watching wildlife.

☒ Don't forget to book accommodations well ahead of time as August is the busy season and there are a limited number of rooms available.

☒ Don't forget to check the schedule for Gros Morne Festival Theatre, Western Brook Pond boat trips and ranger-led activities as soon as you arrive. Make reservations at once.

☑ Look out for moose at dawn and dusk, drive slowly, and if you spot one, keep a safe distance.

JAN
FEB
MAR
APR
MAY
JUN
JUL
AUG
DAY 1
DAY 2
DAY 3
DAY 4
DAY 5
SEP
OCT
NOV
DEC

SOCIETY'S SEASIDE HIDEAWAY

GETTING THERE   See map p316, G5

GETTING THERE
From Manhattan, the Hampton Jitney, a bus service, operates frequently. The Long Island Railroad runs five times a day. Or rent a car at LaGuardia airport, and drive there (100 miles/160 km), avoiding Manhattan traffic.

GETTING AROUND
You will need a car. There are rental agencies in and around East Hampton.

WEATHER
Ocean breezes keep temperatures around 80°F (27°C), with nighttime average lows of 68°F (20°C). The sea temperature is warm.

ACCOMMODATIONS
Bassett House, a 19th-century farmhouse, offers 12 antiques-filled rooms; doubles from US$325; www.bassetthouseinn.com

1770 House has just six rooms, some with fireplaces, or a private carriage house, and a choice of casual or fine dining; doubles from US$495; www.1770house.com

Mill House Inn is a luxury bed-and-breakfast in an 18th-century East Hampton cottage; doubles from US$550; www.millhouseinn.com

EATING OUT
Many restaurants in East Hampton set the same high standard as the best in Manhattan, with prices to match. Seafood is a specialty.

PRICE FOR TWO
Around US$800 per day, depending on your choices of hotel and dining, including car rental and gas, admissions, and incidentals.

FURTHER INFORMATION
www.hamptons.com

A Pirate in the Hamptons

Of all the celebrities who have visited the Hamptons, Captain William Kidd is perhaps the most notorious. In 1792, he raided the *Queddagh Merchant*, one of the largest treasure ships on the high seas, off the coast of Madagascar. Rumor has it that he buried gold from his haul on the shores of Long Island, and he did indeed stash some booty at an estate on Shelter Island before sailing for Boston, where he was captured and sent to England for trial and execution.

Main: Beach with dunes, Southampton

S PEND ANY TIME AT ALL IN NEW YORK IN AUGUST and you'll hear the mantra all around you: "The Hamptons, the Hamptons." What folks are talking about are a string of villages at the east end of Long Island, the oceanside antidote to summer in the city, a vacation playground only a couple of hours away. Manhattanites refer to a visit to Southampton, Bridgehampton, East Hampton, Amangansett, Sag Harbor, Montauk, and their neighboring villages as "making the scene in the Hamptons." The "scene" is a reference to the lifestyles of the rich and famous who have beachside mansions here, to cocktail receptions and lawn parties, trendy clubs, and stellar restaurants. Sometimes, in fact, the social scene can be so overwhelming that the real appeal of the Hamptons, the stretches of white sand (some of the finest beaches in the United States) and the landmarks of a colonial past, can get lost in the fray.

Above (top to bottom): Mansion on Georgica Lane, East Hampton; Sag Harbor Whaling Museum

Left: East Hampton windmill

Right (left to right): Lighthouse at Montauk Point; Sag Harbour seafood restaurant; shops in central East Hampton

As the old story goes, a stranger asks someone on the street of East Hampton the way to the ocean, and the reply is, "What ocean?" The first people to discover the appeal of the Hamptons were Puritans, who sailed across Long Island Sound from settlements in Connecticut and Massachusetts to farm, fish, and hunt whales. Their houses and churches surround village greens and, at Montauk, the lighthouse commissioned by President George Washington in 1792 still stands atop a rocky promontory. Summertime visitors began to arrive in the 19th century, on the new Long Island Railroad, and the quaint villages soon became a playground for wealthy Northeasterners, whose lavish "cottages" still line the country lanes. These days, the Hamptons are among America's most charming seaside retreats. Colonial houses are now charming inns, windmills and church steeples are scenic markers for countryside walks, and large tracts of woods and farmlands remain. Where ever you are in the Hamptons, you are never far from a beach. And, gazing out to sea from any of them, the scene hasn't changed for centuries.

Above: Fishing at sunset in East Hampton

OCEANSIDE DIARY

August is by far the busiest month in the Hamptons. On weekends, traffic is often at a standstill and reservations at hotels and restaurants are as prized and hard to come by as a big win on the lottery. Plan a midweek visit, when the scene is tamer, and in three days you can discover the towns and beaches at a leisurely pace.

Three Days in the Hamptons

Arrive in East Hampton in time for lunch and a walk around town to see such colonial landmarks as the Osborne-Jackson House and Hook Mill. Drive out to the Pollack-Krasner House to see the paint-splattered studio where abstract expressionist Jackson Pollock created many of his masterpieces, then follow Georgica Road, passing lavish mansions, on your way to the beach for a walk and a late-afternoon swim.

Begin the day with a morning swim at Egypt Beach then explore the surrounding villages. In Southampton, another colonial-era town built around a green and pond, the Parrish Museum of Art houses an important collection of works by Fairfield Potter and other American artists. In Bridgehampton, Duck Walk vineyards offer tastings and tours. The best way to explore Montauk, at the far east end of Long Island and surrounded by water on three sides, is on the trolley that stops at the lighthouse and other sights. End the afternoon with a sunset cruise from Montauk harbor.

After a leisurely morning at the beach, drive across the peninsula to Sag Harbor, a quaint village with a colonial-era customs house, a 19th-century whalers' church, and a museum of whaling. From here you can board a ferry to Shelter Island for a walk through the woodlands and along the beaches of Mashomack Preserve. Return to Sag Harbor in time for a drink and a play at the acclaimed Bay Street Theater, then return to East Hampton for a late-night supper.

Dos and Don'ts

☑ Base yourselves at East Hampton. With its good selection of inns and restaurants, it's the most convenient place to stay.

☒ Don't forget to obtain a beach-parking permit (ask at your hotel) and obey the rules to the letter as fines are stiff.

☑ Take a break from Manhattan-style haute cuisine to enjoy a lobster roll or fish and chips.

☑ Pay attention to warning flags when swimming: white means it's safe to swim; blue advises caution; red means danger. No flag – no swimming.

JAN
FEB
MAR
APR
MAY
JUN
JUL
AUG
DAY 1
DAY 2
DAY 3
SEP
OCT
NOV
DEC

GETTING THERE　　　See map p319, H2

Mackinac Island lies in Lake Huron, where Michigan's Upper and Lower Peninsulas meet. Ferry services run from Mackinac City and St. Ignace. The closest airport is in Pellston, 35 miles (56 km) away.

GETTING AROUND

Cars are forbidden but the island is compact enough for most visitors to explore on foot. Bicycles can be rented, and horse-drawn carriages are popular as well.

WEATHER

August brings warm, pleasant conditions, with temperatures reaching about 75°F (24°C). Occasional thunderstorms can produce 3 in (7 cm) of rain for the month.

ACCOMMODATIONS

The Mission Point Resort offers old-world hospitality and stunning sunset views; doubles from US$184; www.missionpoint.com

The Lake View Hotel, the island's oldest (1858), is charming, Victorian-style; doubles from US$260; www.lake-view-hotel.com

The luxurious Grand Hotel has hosted many presidents; doubles from US$500; www. grandhotel.com

EATING OUT

Restaurants serve plenty of fresh fish and seafood from US$50.

PRICE FOR TWO

About US$500 per day including hotel, entertainment, and food.

FURTHER INFORMATION

www.mackinacisland.org

Fudging It

For well over a century, Mackinac Island has been acclaimed for its fudge, made the old-fashioned way using a marble slab (*above*). For true candy-lovers and chocoholics, there's no better time to indulge than during the official Fudge Festival, held every August. Events include bike tours, concerts and extreme kite-flying exhibitions. "Golden tickets" are randomly hidden in packages sold at fudge shops around the island, and those who discover one could win a vacation package for a future visit.

Main: The vast verandah of the Grand Hotel
Above (top to bottom): Marquette Park by the waterfront; a bike used as planter; a horse-drawn carriage with a uniformed driver

WHERE TIME STANDS STILL

WHATEVER YOUR DEFINITION OF "REST AND RECUPERATION," from a luxury spa service or gourmet meal to a quiet ride along untouched coastline, Mackinac Island is likely to provide it – and more. A tiny speck of land in Lake Huron in the upper reaches of Michigan, Mackinac (pronounced "mack-in-awe") has, for more than a century, provided a romantic, luxurious getaway spot. Today it has an approximate year-round population of 500 but draws almost one million visitors throughout the summer, attracting international crowds for its natural beauty and relaxed atmosphere. For some, it's the island's old-fashioned charm and refreshing resistance to certain modern annoyances, including a ban on cars, that appeal. For others, it's the bike- and horse-friendly environment.

A walk down historic Main Street, lined with Victorian-style storefronts, the aromas of freshly made fudge wafting throughout the island from its many fudge shops (especially during the Fudge Festival) invokes a feeling of

Top: Red Coat re-enactors, Fort Mackinac
Below: Victorian-style storefront display

Above: Round Island Lighthouse, the Straits of Mackinac

JAN
FEB
MAR
APR
MAY
JUN
JUL
AUG
SEP
OCT
NOV
DEC

MACKINAC DIARY

A weekend on Mackinac Island provides an idyllic escape – and August is the warmest month. The island has remained relatively unchanged over the years, with Victorian-style storefronts and buildings. You'll find a distinct Midwestern civility, and since no cars are allowed, the only traffic is on horseback, on foot or by bike.

Three Days of Car-Free Charm

DAY 1

Rent a bike to explore the far reaches of the island, using Lake Shore Road, a mostly flat, 8-mile (12-km) ring around Mackinac. (When veering off-road, be careful to navigate the series of hills and bluffs that have stalled many a novice cyclist.) Peruse Main Street's many shops, galleries, and eateries, and then enjoy an evening tour through the town center on a horse-drawn carriage. Finish your first night at the Chippewa Waterfront Hotel with a drink at the Pink Pony, an old-fashioned bar that has been slinging drinks since the 1930s.

DAY 2

Take a free tour of the Michigan Governor's summer residence, which dates back to 1902 and offers fantastic harbor views. Buy some fudge before stepping back in time with a visit to historic Fort Mackinac (recreated to suggest an 1880s atmosphere). Swing by St. Anne's Church to watch locals partake in a weekly square dancing hoe-down, then cap your night with a cocktail at the Mustang Lounge, a popular local watering hole housed in an 18th-century log cabin.

DAY 3

Go along to the historic Grand Hotel, where non-guests can dine at any of the six restaurants on site. Be sure to enjoy the view from the vast porch — at 660 ft (200 m) the longest in the world, according to the hotel. Finish your weekend with a romantic harbor cruise, passing by the Round Island and Old Mackinaw Point lighthouses while admiring a perfect sunset under the Mackinac Bridge.

Dos and Don'ts

✗ Don't ignore the general rules regarding the island's many horses. Don't touch a horse without its owner's permission, and don't ever approach a horse from behind.

✓ Consider renting a bike, the only means of transportation possible for those looking to explore all corners of the island.

✓ Bring comfortable footwear, as the island provides opportunities for lots of walking, with much exploration possible only on foot.

✗ Don't fail to sample the famous local fudge.

stepping back in time. Most visitors approach the island by ferry, and arrive at the docks to be greeted by porters from all the major hotels and resorts with horse-drawn taxis. Not only are the carriages ubiquitous throughout the island, but you can hire one to drive yourself and those looking to hop on horseback have several riding stables to choose from. Visitors who would like a more energetic ride opt for a bike, Mackinac's main mode of personal transport. You'll find standard two-wheelers are available for rental, as well as tandems, kids' bikes and covered models.

The town's compact size of less than five square blocks lends an unhurried vibe to most activities but if the shops, eateries, and historic hotels produce a sensory overload, visitors can always lose themselves in the island's natural wonders. Hiking and biking trails lead to fields of summer wildflowers such as wood lilies, hawkweeds, and buttercups, and to dramatic limestone formations. A popular resting place for migrating birds, the island can boast a dizzying array of visitors including cormorants, great blue herons, Canadian geese and loons – a thrill for amateur ornithologists. You might catch otters frolicking in the waters, while bats help keep mosquitoes at bay.

GETTING THERE
See map p322, F3

Visitors can get to the park entrance by car, tour bus, or the Alaska Railroad from Anchorage, which is 240 miles (386km) north of the park entrance) or Fairbanks, 125 miles (202 km) to the south.

GETTING AROUND
One road, accessible only by tour bus or pre-booked shuttle bus, penetrates the park itself. Private vehicles aren't permitted beyond the park entrance area from where free buses circulate between sites of interest.

WEATHER
In summer, Denali enjoys a relatively warm climate, with daytime temperatures up to 70°F (21°C). August sees some rain.

ACCOMMODATIONS
Denali Grizzly Bear Cabins offers good value doubles; US$185; www.denaligrizzlybear.com

Denali Crow's Nest has cozy log cabins overlooking Denali Village; doubles from US$199; www.denalicrowsnest.com

Inside the park itself, you can only camp in tents and recreational vehicles.

EATING OUT
The Perch, Mile 224 Parks Hwy, serves Alaska specialties (US$30). The Overlook Bar & Grill, Mile 238.5 Parks Hwy, benefits from nice views.

PRICE FOR TWO
Allow US$18 for camping (includes a US$4 reservation fee). Entrance into the park for a week costs US$20 per person.

FURTHER INFORMATION
www.reservedenali.com
www.nps.gov/dena

The Wolves of Denali

As one of the few places in the USA where wolves are protected from hunters, trappers, and disgruntled ranchers, the Denali National Park wilderness offers ideal conditions to study the complex social interactions within wild wolf packs. The first studies of Denali's wolves in the 1940s were carried out by dogsled and on foot. Today, researchers use satellite technology, which has revealed that disease, starvation, accidents, and territorial disputes – rather than humans – are the major causes of decimation of this shy species.

Above (left to right): Semi-aquatic North American beaver; camper in the wide open spaces of Mt. McKinley; a brace of Dall sheep grazing
Main: Lone bull moose on a ridge in front of Mt. McKinley

Below: Hiker and moose at Wonder Lake

PEAKS AND VIEWS

DENALI NATIONAL PARK, ALASKA'S MOST POPULAR DESTINATION, is renowned for its wildlife-viewing opportunities – the park's expanses of sub-Arctic tundra and alpine peaks practically guarantee memorable views and experiences. There may be a little summer congestion around the entrance and along its single wilderness road, but with 9,375 sq miles (24,281 sq km) it's never really crowded here, unless you count the population of grizzlies, caribou, moose, Dall sheep, wolves, and other inhabitants. This gem of the US National Park system has as its centerpiece North America's highest peak, the 20,320-ft (6,194-m) Mt. McKinley, which dominates the surrounding landscape. When the peak is visible, visitors are treated to more than 3 vertical miles (4.8 km) of rock and snow, but even when hidden behind banks of clouds – which is frequently the case – there's plenty to inspire visitors. In the summer, the tundra explodes with wildflowers and berries, while in late August and early September, it blazes with brilliant tawny browns, yellows, oranges, and reds.

Historically, this region was a hunting ground for the Native Athabascan peoples, but its relatively harsh climate prevented permanent settlement until gold was discovered at Kantishna in 1905, at which point even the conditions couldn't thwart starry-eyed fortune-seekers. Their reckless destruction of the landscape, however, inspired naturalist Charles Sheldon to successfully lobby Washington for its preservation, and Mt. McKinley National Park – later renamed Denali or "the Great One" in the Athabascan language – was created in 1917.

The Denali Park Road, which now provides the easiest access to the backcountry, traverses open tundra, boggy lowlands, braided glacial rivers, and colorful mountain passes to arrive at lovely Wonder Lake where, given fine clear weather, the landscape opens up providing the most breathtaking vistas and that perfect photo to impress the folks back home.

It's never really crowded here, unless you count the population of grizzlies, caribou, moose, Dall sheep, wolves, and other wild inhabitants.

Inset: A brilliantly colored blueberry bush
Below (left and right): Bear eating; bull caribou amid the blueberry bushes

DENALI DIARY

August is a warm and colorful month in which to visit this impressive park. Although you need to plan well for any adventures deep into the backcountry, a range of activities lies within easy reach of the park road. You'll need about four days to get the best out of Denali.

Four Days in the Wilderness

Spend the first day exploring the entrance area and hiking the several short trails. A particularly pleasant option follows a 2-hour loop past Horseshoe Lake, with a good chance of seeing moose. More energetic hikers can tackle the half-day climb up the trail to the summit of 3,425-ft (1044-m) Mt. Healy. **DAY 1**

Take the 6-hour shuttle bus trip to Wonder Lake, with excellent chances of seeing moose, caribou, and grizzlies along the way. Set up a tent at the Wonder Lake Campground and – if the weather cooperates – enjoy spectacular close-up views of Mt. McKinley. **DAY 2**

Hike and explore around Wonder Lake, tasting fresh blueberries, looking for beaver dams, and watching for bears, moose, caribou, and other wildlife. The very energetic may like to tackle a 14-mile (22-km) return hike along the road to the historic gold-mining district of Kantishna, which has a tiny summer population of around 135 people. **DAY 3**

Take an early shuttle bus back to the entrance area, perhaps stopping off for a short hike at any inviting spot that appeals along the way. A good choice would be Polychrome Pass, where the colorful terrain overlooks distant braided rivers. Finish off the Denali experience with a meal of Alaska salmon or other local specialty in Denali Village. **DAY 4**

Dos and Don'ts

✗ Don't underestimate the popularity of Denali in the summer. To avoid disappointment, book campgrounds and shuttle buses well in advance.

✓ Get the best of the park by riding the shuttle bus into it – Mt. McKinley isn't visible from the entrance area.

✗ Don't approach or feed any wildlife. Keep all your food inside a vehicle or a bear-proof container.

✓ Bring a tent, sleeping bag, camp stove, and food for overnight trips beyond the park entrance area.

✓ Bring plenty of mosquito repellent.

JAN FEB MAR APR MAY JUN JUL **AUG** SEP OCT NOV DEC

GETTING THERE   See map p327, D5
The closest international airport is at Lima. From there, Cusco is a 40-minute flight. A further 40-minute flight aboard a small twin-engined plane will get you to Boca Manu. Then a motorized canoe takes you on the 90-minute trip down the Madre de Dios River to the lodge.

GETTING AROUND
In Cusco you can explore on foot. In the Park all your trips, on land or water, will be with a guide.

WEATHER
This is the dry season, and Park temperatures can reach a humid 88°F (31°C), with lows of 64°F (18°C). In Cusco, daytime temperatures average 68°F (20°C) but drop sharply at night.

ACCOMMODATIONS
The Picoaga Hotel, in central Cusco, is in a charming colonial mansion; doubles from US$155; www.picoagahotel.com

The Manu Wildlife Center has accommodation in rustic cabins, with en-suite facilities; three-night, full-board packages, including the flight from Cusco, from US$1,090 per person; www.manu-wildlife-center.com

EATING OUT
Peruvian dishes include *arroz con pollo* (a spicy chicken and rice dish) and *lomo salteado* (fried beef with tomatoes, onions, and potatoes). Food will be provided when staying in the park.

PRICE FOR TWO
US$370–440 per day including accommodation in Cusco and in Manu National Park, food, and internal flights.

FURTHER INFORMATION
www.peruverde.com

Giant Otters
One of the world's most endangered species, the giant otters that are found in Manu National Park are actually quite ferocious animals—fending off jaguars and killing caymans that cross into their nesting territory. The park was made a UNESCO World Natural Heritage Site in 1987. This has helped in some ways to stave off the reduction in numbers of these otters over the years, maintaining the clean water and fish stocks that are essential for the survival of the species.

For sheer wilderness, it doesn't get much better than this.

Main: Group of red-and-green macaws taking off from a claylick in Manu National Park
Above: Overlooking the misty rain forest **Inset:** Tufted capuchin in an acrobatic pose
Top (left to right): Typical lodge accommodations; violet-fronted hummingbird; roots of palms in Manu National Park; steering through the Madre de Dios River

LAND OF THE GIANT OTTER

THE VIEW OVER MANU NATIONAL PARK from the small, twin-engine plane that takes you to Boca Manu is humbling. Nearly 3,125 sq miles (8,095 sq km) of dense lowland tropical jungle and misty cloud forest, sloping up into the Andes, stretch out around you, crisscrossed by the sludgy brown waters of the Manu and Madre de Dios rivers. Manu National Park is the largest tropical park in South America, and home to an extraordinary diversity of plant and wildlife. Found in this verdant jungle are more than 1,000 species of bird including the flamboyant, strutting Cock-of-the-Rock, 200 species of mammal, such as the giant otter, tapir, and majestic jaguar, and more than 15,000 species of plant. All of this is remarkably preserved in pristine condition due to the inaccessibility of the area and careful controls and monitoring of the numbers now allowed to visit. The park is so isolated in parts that several indigenous groups within have never had contact with outsiders.

Above: Manu River meandering through Manu National Park

PERUVIAN PARK DIARY

You will need at least three nights in Manu in order to fully experience all that the jungle has to offer. August is also an excellent time of year to visit the Andean region, so it's worth exploring the pretty colonial streets of Cusco. You could extend your trip with a visit to the Inca citadel of Machu Picchu (see pp140–41).

A Week in the Rainforest

Flights tend to arrive into Lima in the evening; if there's time, explore some of the capital's excellent museums.	**DAY 1**
Fly over the Andes to Cusco and spend the day exploring its churches and colorful markets.	**DAY 2**
A short flight by light aircraft will take you to Boca Manu, a small frontier town on the banks of the Manu River. From here a motorized canoe ploughs deep into the forest along the Madre de Dios River, to the Manu Wildlife Center. Settle into your cabin then, in the afternoon, explore the jungle in search of monkeys.	**DAY 3**
A pre-dawn start for the 25-minute boat trip to the macaw lick to see Amazon parrots and large macaws feasting on the clay. Later, climb the 110-ft (34-m) high platform over the rainforest canopy to observe the frantic dusk activity of the jungle fauna. Take a night hike to a tapir lick to watch them feed.	**DAY 4**
Head out onto the nearby Blanco Oxbow Lake in search of the resident giant otter family, and take a night-time boat trip on the Madre de Dios River, following the reclusive black caiman.	**DAY 5**
Emerging from the jungle by canoe at Boca Manu, take a flight back to Cusco and enjoy the dry air and laid-back atmosphere of this bustling town.	**DAY 6**
Fly back to Lima, or you could choose to extend your trip with a visit to the hidden Inca city at Machu Picchu.	**DAY 7**

Dos and Don'ts

✓ Make sure you take a good insect repellent and long-sleeved clothing. Mosquitoes here are large and persistent.

✗ Don't expect luxury. Accommodations here are basic, but you'll feel like you are in the heart of the jungle.

✓ Bring a good pair of binoculars. You may not get close enough to see some of the more elusive birds and mammals.

✓ Bring several changes of clothes for your time in the jungle — nothing dries in the humidity!

JAN
FEB
MAR
APR
MAY
JUN
JUL
AUG
SEP
OCT
NOV
DEC

No tourist or commercial activity is permitted inside the reserve, so your stay in Manu will be in a lodge, located just outside. These are rustic wooden structures surrounded by jungle, with screened cabins, limited or no electricity, and terraces equipped with hammocks that look out over the forest. The lodges provide the obligatory guides who are extremely well-informed and an invaluable aid in helping visitors to spot the more evasive jungle-dwellers and spectacular flora.

Hiking along forested trails in search of tapir, and following the faint footprints of the elusive jaguar, brings out the adventurer in visitors. On the river, the boat becomes a silent viewing platform as everyone waits with bated breath for the slick head of a rare giant otter to emerge from the water, or for a black cayman to catch the light as it slides from the bank and into the mud. Ploughing deeper into the preserve aboard a long, slender motor-canoe, the foliage becomes thicker, the humidity more intense, and the chattering of monkeys and birds and the steady hum of insects almost deafening. The scale and density of the jungle is breathtaking here. For sheer wilderness, it doesn't get much better than this.

RIDE 'EM COWBOY

I T BEGAN IN A BAR IN THE RANCH COUNTRY OF NORTHERN SÃO PAULO, in 1956, when a dozen wealthy young ranchers had the idea of staging a weekend display of bull carts, leather violins, and other items of traditional Brazilian cowboy culture. It has since grown into a ten-day high-stakes rodeo, with its own purpose-built stadium and extensive fairgrounds, an annual celebration of cowboy traditions that attracts over half a million visitors. The Barretos Festa do Peão Boiadeiro is the premier rodeo event in Brazil, and one of the major stops on the international rodeo circuit. Rodeo fans from north of the Rio Grande will recognize most of the competitive events on offer in the 35,000-seat stadium: bronco-riding (known as *sela americana* or "American saddle" in Brazil), steer-wrestling, bareback-riding, barrel-racing for the female competitors, and the incredible and dangerous spectacle of bull-riding.

GETTING THERE   See map p329, E3
Barretos lies 260 miles (420 km) northwest of São Paulo. There is a local airport 3 miles (5 km) from the city, and a larger regional airport in Ribeirão Preto, 75 miles (120 km) south of Barretos.

GETTING AROUND
The Parque do Peão, or rodeo ground, is just over a mile (2 km) from the city center. Taxis are plentiful but, on rodeo days, the roads fill up and traffic may be reduced to a crawl.

WEATHER
Days are normally sunny and hot, reaching 85°F (30°C). Nights are pleasantly warm.

ACCOMMODATIONS
Hotel Berrante Dourado is basic, clean, and comfy, with gardens and pool; doubles from US$45; www.hotelberrantedourado.com.br

Mabruk Barretos Apart is located in a small highrise in the city center; doubles from US$50; www.mabrukhotel.com.br

The Barretos Country Hotel is 2 miles (3 km) out of town, near the airport; doubles from US$75; www.barretoscountryhotel.com.br

EATING OUT
At the rodeo you will find all-you-can-eat barbecue for as little as US$12. Elsewhere an average meal for two will cost US$10–15.

PRICE FOR TWO
US$250 per day including accommodation, food, and taxis, plus tickets for the rodeo and evening concerts.

FURTHER INFO
www.independentes.com.br

Rodeo Queen

The very first *Rainha da Festa,* or Rodeo Queen, was picked by the group of ranchers who originated the Festa. From then on, the title was awarded to the Barretos girl who had sold the most tickets for the rodeo's charity raffle. In 1970, good works gave way to beauty, as young women from the city and region paraded in (often skimpy) cowgirl costumes, a process that went nationwide in the 1990s. Since 2002, however, the competition has returned to its regional roots, as a contest in beauty and elocution among the young women of Barretos.

Main: *Cutiano* competitor struggles to remain on his mount

Left: High-speed action in a barrel-racing event

Right (left to right): "Bull dogging" or steer-wrestling; display by flag-waving cowboys; young competitor on sheepback

Right panel (top to bottom): Entrance to a children's mini-stadium; rodeo clowns entertain during the bull riding competition; handcrafted saddle

More unusual – unique to Brazil, in fact – is the riding style called *cutiano*. In this terrifying event, the rider has to stay on a bucking horse with the aid of only two straps secured around the animal's girth. A stroll through the fairgrounds outside the stadium only reinforces the exotic nature of the Festa do Peão Boiadeiro, with its unique blend of American-style rodeo and Brazilian country culture. In the restaurants and on food stalls, *churrasco* – Brazilian barbecue – is everywhere but, unlike the American cookout, in Brazil the beef is held close to the coals and cooked quickly, the thin slices served up hot and juicy with more than a modicum of coarse barbecue salt. Given the superb quality of the meat, *churrasco* can't be anything but mouthwateringly delicious.

The evenings are purely Brazilian, with all-night parties on two stages, featuring Brazil's biggest artists playing everything from *sertaneja*, Brazilian-style country music, to *forró*, an upbeat country polka, as well as the ever-popular samba. Everyone dances, and everyone sports a cowboy hat.

Above: The spectacular horseshoe-shaped rodeo arena

FESTA DIARY

The Festa do Peão Boiadeiro in Barretos lasts a full ten days, but much of the first week is taken up with qualifying rounds for the various rodeo events. The final three days see the breathtakingly thrilling finals of all the competitive events, capped off every night by a big-name musical performance in the rodeo grounds.

Three Days of Thrills and Spills

Go straight to the big arena to see the action. The day features a full program of bronco-riding, calf-wrestling, barrel-riding and bucking bulls. Take time out to stroll the fairgrounds and sample Brazilian country cooking. Save some energy for the evening festivities on either of the fairground's two main stages.

DAY 1

Today offers more thrills in the main stadium. In between, stroll the craft and saddlery shops in the rodeo grounds. The leatherware in particular is of exceptional quality. If you are a rider you can buy a superb, handcrafted saddle at a fraction of the cost up north. Saturday's evening show is traditionally the biggest concert of the rodeo, with both main stages featuring top Brazilian artists playing pop, country, *forró* (like polka), and sometimes samba.

DAY 2

The last day of the rodeo is also the finals of the International Rodeo Competition. This is the day that the top riders from Brazil and around the world have been working towards since the Festa began. The rides are guaranteed to be wild, fast, and furious. In the evening, head for the town of Barretos and indulge in a blow-out meal of Brazilian *churrasco*, where the cuts of meat are grilled on skewers over a pit of glowing coals. Prime cuts include *picanha* (rump steak) and *maminha* (shoulder steak). If you're particularly hungry, look for a restaurant offering *rodizo* – all you can eat for a single, reasonable price.

DAY 3

Dos and Don'ts

☑ Book your accommodation early – hotels fill up months in advance of the rodeo dates.

☑ Try the traditional Brazilian cowboy food – dishes made with *carne seca* (jerk beef), fried manioc, and sweet corn meal cake for dessert.

☒ Don't forget your equine loved one's measurements. Brazilian saddles, bridles, and other riding gear offer top quality leather and workmanship.

☑ Buy and wear a big cowboy hat. Everyone else will be wearing one and, as long as you don't take photos, no one back home need ever know.

JAN
FEB
MAR
APR
MAY
JUN
JUL
AUG
SEP
OCT
NOV
DEC

GETTING THERE
See map p320, C6

Black Rock Desert is a vast, barren lake bed north of Reno, Nevada. Take the Interstate 80 east from Reno, and Hwy. 447 north 78 miles (126 km) to Gerlach, then Hwy. 34 for 11 miles (18 km) to Burning Man. Small private aircraft may land at the temporary Black Rock Airport with special permission.

GETTING AROUND
After parking your vehicles at your camp, you can get around Black Rock City solely on foot or bicycle – with the exception of mutated art cars. There is a daily bus between Black Rock City and nearby towns Gerlach and Empire.

WEATHER
Temperatures in Black Rock Desert can be extreme, exceeding 100°F (38°C) by day and falling to about 40°F (4°C) at night.

ACCOMMODATIONS
Bring your own tents or RVs. The nearest lodgings are 80 miles (129 km) away, but camping is part of the experience. Burning Man is a Leave No Trace event – bring all you need and take it away when you leave.

EATING OUT
Visitors must fend for themselves. Communal kitchens exist and you're encouraged to contribute to a gift economy. Center Camp Café sells coffee and Arctica sells ice – nothing else may be bought or sold.

PRICE FOR TWO
About US$80 per day including local travel, food, and admissions based on camping, if driving from San Francisco.

FURTHER INFORMATION
www.burningman.com

Legacy of The Man

"The Man" was born – and first died – on June 21, 1986, when Larry Harvey and Jerry James burned an 8-ft (2-m) tall wooden figure on Baker Beach in San Francisco, drawing many spectators. The Man grew larger and more elaborate each year, and a pulley system was eventually used to raise its arms. Stuffed with flammables, it ballooned to huge proportions, weighing over a ton. Today, its physical form is repeated each year. While there is no self-conscious symbolism to The Man or its death, its settings change to reflect the event's annual theme.

Main: A lively crowd at Center Camp Café, Burning Man Festival

THE BURNING MAN

THE REMOTE, BARREN, AND UTTERLY INHOSPITABLE Black Rock Desert is an unlikely venue for a near-mythical annual gathering dedicated to self-expression and self-reliance. This event is held the week before Labor Day, when close to 50,000 libertine people arrive, establish Black Rock City overnight, let their hair down however they choose, and vanish without a trace one week later.

A tradition born in 1986, when Larry Harvey and his friends torched an 8-ft (2-m) tall wooden man in San Francisco, the act eventually became a colorful and wacky annual ceremony – the Burning Man. Harvey's idea grew so popular that it ultimately moved to Black Rock Desert. Today's Burning Man takes its name from the ritualistic burning of "The Man," a 40-ft (12-m) tall wooden effigy, the centerpiece of Black Rock City, which is arranged, almost amphitheater-like, in a radial arc. Besides exuding a fun, unique, and out-of-this world appeal,

Left (left to right): The dramatic climax of Burning Man – the effigy, up in flames; *Angel of the Apocalypse* by the Flaming Lotus Girls (2005); self-expression in the form of a mutant vehicle; *Tea with Ken*

Right (top to bottom): Festival goers on Center Camp's "dance floor"; bold display of fire dancing at Burning Man; artistic creativity in action at Burning Man

Above: *The Belgian Waffle* by the Uchronians (2006)

DESERT DIARY

While the weather in August is erratic, nothing – neither rain nor heat – diminishes the spirits of participants. The event lasts a week, but you can miss the first day. Six days are enough, with two days to adjust to the sensory overload. The sensational climax – the burning of The Man – should not be missed.

Six Days in Black Rock City

DAY 1
Arrive at Burning Man and establish your lodging. Commune with neighbors and arrange to participate in your local theme camp.

DAYS 2–3
Dedicate your time to exploring Black Rock City, organized as two-thirds of a circle; you'll receive a map upon arrival. Admire art (decorated) vehicles and bicycles, the preferred mode of transportation for getting around the playa (ancient lake bed). People-watch at Center Camp: sooner or later, everyone passes through for coffee. Strip off and paint your body. At night, participate in fire dancing, a popular pastime on the playa.

DAY 4
Head to "The Temple," a traditional, two-story structure resurrected every year in a different form. Visit a theme camp such as Astral Head Wash for a shampoo and demolish a dolly or have a drink at the Barbie Death Camp and Wine Bistro.

DAY 5
If you haven't already, take in the massive sculptures and other art displays on the playa. At night, gather at the center of the playa for the main event – to watch the huge effigy go up in flames. Don't forget to bring electroluminescent (EL) wire: this must-have accessory can be used to make glowing light sculptures.

DAY 6
Pack up and prepare for a culture shock when you return to the real world. It's best to leave early the next day – despite the late-night partying – as the road out gets clogged with 20,000 vehicles leaving all at once.

Dos and Don'ts

✓ Bring plenty of warm clothing, a shelter, and essential supplies. You'll be turned away at the gate if you cannot demonstrate an ability to meet basic survival needs.

✗ Don't forget to fill up on gasoline before arriving; local gas stations get swamped after the event.

✓ If you plan to take professional or motion images, you'll need to register your camera or video camera in advance.

✓ Leave your dog at home. Dogs and other animals are not allowed at Burning Man.

✗ Don't exist on the communal generosity of others without also contributing yourself.

JAN
FEB
MAR
APR
MAY
JUN
JUL
AUG
SEP
OCT
NOV
DEC

the Burning Man is a test of self-sufficiency in harsh settings. Dust storms are typical, winds may whip away tents, and torrential rain can turn the playa into mud. There's also no room for commerciality; the sole vendor is a coffee shop in Center Camp, a tented area for civic activities.

Each year the event is themed, and theme camps are the interactive core, with art as a unifier. Great efforts are made to erect wildly original and innovative artworks in the desert, most of which are finally burned – a metaphorical purification of the artists' motives.

Nobody at Burning Man is a spectator, and many are exhibitionists, their bodies clad in paint and glitter. Consider it a surreal amalgam of Mardi Gras, Halloween bacchanal, and the Fourth of July, celebrated while "mutant vehicles" cruise around like throwbacks from a *Mad Max* movie.

A radical experiment in temporary community, Burning Man is based on a mind-altering freedom from social restrictions. The Nevada playa is an immense *tabula rasa* for people to live outside the realm of convention, a fantastical party where you can be who or what you want to be.

SEPTEMBER

Where to Go: **September**

Autumn is a glorious time to be in North America. The peak season crowds have thinned out, and most destinations take on a softer, more mellow complexion once the summer has faded. The east coast of the USA and Canada, and the higher elevations of the Southwestern states, are showing early signs of their rich fall colors. This is a fine time to enjoy the great outdoors, when the skies are still blue. The deserts of western USA are a little more forgiving this month than the rest of the year, and even San Francisco, famed for its climatic mood swings, is relatively settled in September. Meanwhile, in South America, spring is well on its way. Below you will find all the destinations in this chapter as well as some extra suggestions to provide a little inspiration.

FESTIVALS AND CULTURE

QUITO Tropical wildlife in the Mindo Nambillo Cloud Forest

UNFORGETTABLE JOURNEYS

BLACK HILLS Horseback riding on the Plains of South Dakota

NATURAL WONDERS

NAZCA The intricate spider-monkey design

QUITO
ECUADOR

Take a trip back in time to a 16th-century colonial capital

Splash in thermal baths, ascend volcanoes, admire giant butterflies in the cloud forest, and scare yourself silly on the Devil's Nose train.
See pp218–9

"A true Andean gem, Quito has two distinct but complementary facets, each with its own unforgettable sights and styles."

BLACK HILLS
SOUTH DAKOTA, USA

Remote frontier territory with spectacular landscapes

Mt. Rushmore and the Crazy Horse Memorial are dramatic man-made additions to the natural wonders of canyons and mountains here.
See pp228–9

ALGONQUIN PROVINCIAL PARK
ONTARIO, CANADA

Unforgettable parklands

Paddle a canoe around the park's myriad waterways, with over 2,400 lakes and miles of streams and rivers to explore.
www.algonquinpark.on.ca

NAZCA LINES
PERU

Vast, enigmatic drawings etched into the desert floor

Nothing can compare with seeing these ancient artworks for yourself – enjoy a gods'-eye view from a light aircraft.
See pp224–5

ISLA DEL SOL
BOLIVIA

Mystical cradle of the Inca civilization on Lake Titicaca

Hauntingly beautiful Isla del Sol was revered by the Incas as the birthplace of the sun and moon.
en.wikipedia.org/wiki/Isla_del_Sol

PENDLETON ROUND UP
OREGON, USA

Sharpen your spurs for rodeo

Steer-wrestling, Brahma bull-riding, and greased pig-catching are just some of the attractions on offer at this cowboy extravaganza.
www.pendletonroundup.com

ALOHA FESTIVALS
HAWAI'I, USA

A unique celebration of Hawaiian culture

Celebrated across the whole of Hawai'i, this is the islands' premier cultural event, with traditional music, dance, and history.
www.alohafestivals.com

VERMONT
NEW ENGLAND, USA

Catch the fall on a tour of the northeast back roads

The prime place to see all the colors of the New England fall: maple, beech, and ash frame picture-perfect clapboard villages.
www.travel-vermont.com

"No picture can prepare you for the mystery of these vast designs, etched into the dry, rocky desert of western Peru."

SEQUOIA NATIONAL PARK
CALIFORNIA, USA

The forest giants

Wander amidst an array of giant Californian redwoods, including the General Sherman, the largest tree on the planet.
www.nps.gov/seki

TIWANAKU, LA PAZ
BOLIVIA

Bolivia's most important archeological site

The capital boasts significant monumental stone ruins from the pre-Colombian civilization.
en.wikipedia.org/wiki/Tiwanaku

COAST TO COAST
CANADA

A legendary train ride east to west over the mountains

Canada's interior is a land of wide vistas so there's a lot of scenery to enjoy, but the mountains are the true highlight of the journey.
See pp226–7

PACIFIC RIM NATIONAL PARK
BRITISH COLUMBIA, CANADA

Vancouver Island delights

This beautiful park is home to a wealth of Native American cultural sites, long sandy beaches, and mature rain forest.
www.pc.gc.ca/pn-np/bc/pacificrim

BUMBERSHOOT, SEATTLE
WASHINGTON, USA

America's best pop-culture fest

Summer's over, but Seattle makes up for it with the USA's biggest new music and arts festival, hosting a range of international performers.
www.bumbershoot.org

IQUITOS
PERU

Unforgettable Amazon river journeys in Peru

Take a boat from Iquitos through Peru's lush lowland rainforests, some of the best preserved and least explored in the Amazon
www.biopark.org/iquitos.html

OZARK MOUNTAINS
MISSOURI, USA

Sylvan uplands in the heart of the USA

The Ozarks present a beguiling landscape of rocky peaks surrounded by rolling forest and crystal-clear lakes.
www.ozarkmtns.com

Previous page: Mesa Arch and canyon walls, Canyonlands National Park, Utah

Weather Watch

❶ Cape Breton, Canada This is as good as it gets, climate-wise, in Nova Scotia, with bright blue skies and fall landscapes more than compensating for cold temperatures.

❷ New York State, USA The harsh heat of the New York summer should start to abate in September, though expect some still very warm days with bright and sunny skies, and high humidity in the city of New York itself.

❸ South Dakota, USA The rugged Great Plains state enjoys pleasant conditions in September, with warm daytime highs and much cooler evenings. The sun can still be harsh during the day, however. Take sunscreen.

❹ San Francisco, USA September is warm and sunny. Rain is unlikely, and although those summer fogs have abated, you should still bring warm clothing just in case.

❺ Peru Though coastal regions can be misty in the Peruvian springtime, and Lima is often overcast, the southwestern coastal desert areas, including Nazca, are hotter and drier, with cold nights.

❻ Argentina Spring is an appealing time to visit Buenos Aires and the Andean foothills. The highlands around Mendoza are bright and cool, with warm daytime temperatures, dropping dramatically after dark.

LUXURY AND ROMANCE

MENDOZA Sycamore-lined road between the vineyards

MENDOZA
ARGENTINA

Wine tasting and breathtaking natural beauty

Charming, leafy Mendoza; great mountain views and a colonial mansion, set amid the vines, are all part of this Argentinian wine tour.

See pp216–7

SEDONA
ARIZONA, USA

Crystals, cameras, and canyons

This popular New Age, film and cultural center boasts a string of top restaurants and hotels, such as the Enchantment Resort.

www.visitsedona.com

TAOS
NEW MEXICO, USA

A town with a special mix of cultures and atmospheres

Wander through the historic pueblo and its art galleries and new age centers, or just chill out in the lovely hot springs.

www.taosvacationguide.com

SAN FRANCISCO
CALIFORNIA, USA

America's favorite city with a beautiful bayside location

San Francisco combines iconic landmarks with vibrant ethnic communities, bohemian neighborhoods and world-class art.

See pp212–3

"This west coast capital of sophistication has something for everyone, from fine art museums to casual dining."

COLONIA DE SACRAMENTO
URUGUAY

Take a step back in time

Explore the delightful winding streets and pretty Portuguese architecture of this riverside resort town.

whc.unesco.org/en/list/747

ACTIVE ADVENTURES

UTAH'S NATIONAL PARKLANDS A hiker in a narrow pass, Zion Canyon

UTAH'S NATIONAL PARKLANDS
USA

Surreal landscapes

A spectacular desert with a vast collection of amazing geographic features that provide great, if occasionally challenging, hiking.

See pp214–5

THE JOHN MUIR TRAIL
CALIFORNIA, USA

Unforgettable wilderness trek

Enjoy miles of prime hiking through some stunning national parks, starting at Yosemite and finishing at Mount Whitney.

johnmuirtrail.org

BANFF NATIONAL PARK
ALBERTA, CANADA

Canada's oldest national park

Encompassing a spectacular section of the Canadian Rockies, see glaciers, icefields, coniferous forest, and mirror-blue lakes here.

www.pc.gc.ca/banff

OLYMPIC NATIONAL PARK
WASHINGTON STATE, USA

Prime west-coast wilderness

Take a hike through this varied national park, with landscapes ranging from Pacific Ocean beaches to glaciated peaks.

www.nps.gov/olym

COLORADO
USA

Discover your inner cowboy on a dude ranch

Try a real outdoor adventure, learning how to really ride on a western ranch – and hike, fish, and go climbing and rafting, too.

www.coloradoranch.com

FAMILY GETAWAYS

PHILADELPHIA Carousel ride at Giggleberry Fair

PHILADELPHIA
PENNSYLVANIA, USA

Take a walk through a living history book

A sophisticated city that has plenty to offer families – as well as historical sights, it has sports, museums, and rides for the kids.

See pp220–1

THE THOUSAND ISLANDS
NEW YORK STATE, USA

Upstate New York family fun

The Thousand Islands region provides plenty of entertainment, ranging from balloon rides to white-water rafting.

www.1000islands.com

FUNDY ISLES
NEW BRUNSWICK, CANADA

Island-hopping far from the usual tourist routes

Kids will marvel at a close encounter with a humpback whale, and you can't help but laugh as comical puffins take flight.

See pp210–1

CAPE BRETON ISLAND
NOVA SCOTIA, CANADA

A wild island hideaway

Here are misty waterfalls, forests of fall colors, whales rising majestically beyond the waves, and fabulous seafood.

See pp222–3

LAKE GEORGE
NEW YORK STATE, USA

An inland sea in upstate New York

In the heart of the Adirondacks, this giant forest lake is ringed by campsites, fine hotels, and places to swim, hike, sail, and more.

www.visitlakegeorge.com

GETTING THERE
See map p314, G6

The Bay of Fundy separates New Brunswick from Nova Scotia. St. John's airport is around 50 miles (80 km) northeast of the Isles, with flights from Montréal and Toronto. Deer Island is reached by ferry from Letete. Campobello Island is linked by seasonal ferry to Deer Island and Eastport, and by road from Lubec. Grand Manan ferries run from Blacks Harbour.

GETTING AROUND

Car rental is available at the airport, and the ferries take vehicles. Some lodgings rent bikes.

WEATHER

September daytime temperatures average 66°F (19°C), but nights are cooler.

ACCOMMODATIONS

Campobello Island's Lupine Lodge offers log-walled rooms close to the ocean; family rooms from US$145; www.lupinelodge.com

In St. Andrews, Seaside Beach Resort offers self-contained waterside apartments; two-bed suites from US$125; www.seaside.nb.ca

Beach Front Cottages, on Grand Manan, are self-contained sea-view chalets; family units from US$120; www.beachfrontcottages.ca

EATING OUT

Fresh, locally caught lobster, scallops, and salmon are abundant on all three islands. Try seafood chowder sprinkled with dried dulse.

PRICE FOR A FAMILY OF FOUR

US$350–400 per day including car rental and gas, ferries, accommodation, food, and tours.

FURTHER INFORMATION

www.tourismnewbrunswick.ca

A Seaweed Feast

For many people, seaweed may not be as appetizing a prospect as seafood, but it forms an important part of the islands' economy. Dulse, a red-hued variety, is collected by hand at low tide, then sun-dried on the distinctive racks that dot the shoreline. Islanders tend to eat it freshly dried, as a snack, but it may be served fried, or added to salads and soups. While dulse is an acquired taste, it is filled with minerals and vitamins, and is found in health-food stores worldwide. Nori, used for sushi and sashimi, is now also being cultivated for export to Japan.

Main: Colorful Atlantic puffins on Machias Seal Island, in the Bay of Fundy

THE PULL OF THE TIDES

FAR OFF THE BEATEN TOURIST TRACK, and little-known outside of Atlantic Canada, the Fundy Isles draw outdoor-lovers searching for adventure beyond the ordinary. The three main populated islands – Deer, Campobello, and Grand Manan – each have their own personalities, but are linked by history and geology. The natural phenomenon of the world's highest tides dictates the pattern of life for residents and visitors alike, with ferry links to the outside world, islanders' working hours, and even simple pleasures like beachcombing totally dependent upon the tide.

Closest to the mainland is Deer Island. This is a peaceful fishing community, its shorelines dotted with herring weirs and lobster pounds. The most exciting thing going on here is Old Sow, the largest whirlpool in the western hemisphere at 250 ft (76 m) across. Campobello Island's road link to the USA has attracted many wealthy Americans to spend their summers here. The most famous was Franklin D. Roosevelt, whose family estate now forms the Roosevelt

Left (left to right): Harborside on Grand Manan; live lobster; herrings curing in an island smokery; Franklin D. Roosevelt's summer cottage on Campobello Island; meadows of lupins edge the Bay of Fundy

Below: Swallowtail Lighthouse at North Head on Grand Manan

Inset: Herring weir on Deer Island

Above: Spectacular results on a whale-watching trip

Bike rides through waterside meadows of lupins and wild roses; beachcombing on the shoreline for agate and amethyst…

ISLAND DIARY

September visitors to the Fundy Isles will encounter fewer crowds while still enjoying pleasant weather. This is also one of the best times of year for whale-watching. Four days is a good length of time to visit all three islands, even though, by virtue of the ferry routes, you must inevitably include a return to the mainland mid-trip.

Four Days on the Bay

DAY 1 Catch the ferry from Letete, New Brunswick, to Deer Island. Take a leisurely drive down the coast, through seaside villages dotted with art galleries and past impressive lobster pounds, to the island's southern extremity, Deer Island Point Park. With a bit of forward planning, you could time it right to view Old Sow. From the Point, it's a short ferry ride to Campobello Island.

DAY 2 Get up early to watch the sun rise over Herring Cove Provincial Park. Divide your day between here and Roosevelt Campobello International Park. Later, return to the mainland, by ferry or the road bridge, and spend the night in the mainland resort town of St. Andrews.

DAY 3 Drive to Black's Harbour and set off aboard a morning ferry for Grand Manan Island. The crossing takes 90 minutes. Allow a couple of hours to explore the island by road. After lunch, join a whale-watching trip into the Bay of Fundy, from which you can expect to see magnificent humpbacks in close proximity. In the evening, try to get an ocean-view table at the Compass Rose Restaurant for dinner.

DAY 4 Take a morning bird-watching boat trip. Puffins will steal the show but you may also spot playful seals in calmer waters. In the afternoon, take the time to explore wildflower meadows along the west coast and seek out gemstones along the beach at Red Point, before heading back to the ferry for the mainland.

Dos and Don'ts

✓ Accommodations are limited, so make reservations before traveling to the islands.

✗ Don't forget to carry a tide timetable with you.

✓ Be at Deer Island Point Park 3 hours before high tide to get the best view of Old Sow whirlpool.

✓ Sample the local scallops, which are renowned for their size and sweetness. And do give dulse a try!

JAN FEB MAR APR MAY JUN JUL AUG **SEP** OCT NOV DEC

Campobello International Park. His charming Arts and Crafts summer cottage is open to visitors, and the park offers lovely vistas and perfect picnic spots. Herring Cove Provincial Park is another favorite, with a long sandy beach, walking trails, and a golf course to keep all the family happy.

Grand Manan is the largest of the Fundy Isles. While its setting is blissfully peaceful, the extreme tides stir up nutrients from the ocean floor, which attract an amazing variety of marine life. Right and humpback whales are the species most often spotted, but finback and minke are also present. Late August through mid-September is considered the best time of year to view these magnificent creatures. Bird-watchers will be captivated by the hundreds of varieties recorded on the Isles, and no one can fail to be entertained by the comic appeal of the local puffins. The best way to view them is on a boat tour to Machias Seal Island. But there's much more to enjoy as well – bike rides through waterside meadows of lupins and wild roses; beachcombing on the shoreline of Red Point for agate and amethyst; or simply immersing yourself in island life and doing nothing much at all.

GETTING THERE   See map p321, A3
San Francisco is a major transportation hub on the Pacific Coast. Most flights arrive at San Francisco International Airport, 13 miles (20 km) south of the city center.

GETTING AROUND
Cable cars are an easy way to get to many downtown sites, while Muni buses and the BART light rail connect other parts. The street grids make driving easy, but parking can be difficult.

WEATHER
September is one of the warmest months, with bright sunny days, little fog, and an average high of 72°F (22°C).

ACCOMMODATIONS
Experience the beat-generation atmosphere at the historic Hotel Boheme; doubles from US$164; www.hotelboheme.com

The sumptuous Westin St. Francis is at the heart of downtown Union Square; doubles from US$219; www.westinstfrancis.com

The Clift Hotel combines traditional luxury and contemporary styling; doubles from US$375; www.clifthotel.com

EATING OUT
Book ahead at stylish Postrio, which serves celebrity chef Wolfgang Puck's fusion cuisine (US$55), or sample tantalizing French-Vietnamese fare at Le Colonial (US$35).

PRICE FOR TWO
US$185–265 per day includes food, local travel, accommodation, and admissions.

FURTHER INFORMATION
www.onlyinsanfrancisco.com

Golden Gate Bridge
An engineering marvel, the Golden Gate Bridge was the world's largest man-made structure when built in 1937. The vermilion bridge spanning the 2-mile (3.2-km) wide Golden Gate Straits was designed by Charles Ellis and Leon Moisseiff. Supported by two elegant 746-ft (227-m) tall piers, each suspension cable weighs 11,000 tons and contains 27,572 parallel wires that could circle the earth three times.

CITY BY THE BAY

WITH A SPECTACULAR WATERFRONT SETTING made more dramatic by the iconic Golden Gate Bridge, cosmopolitan San Francisco is a stylishly chic and bohemian city. This West Coast capital of sophistication has something for everyone, from fine art museums to casual dining. In fact, "The City" (it's never referred to as 'Frisco) is a culinary trove, with more restaurants per capita than any other place in North America.

San Francisco is a city of neighborhoods, each as distinct as a thumbprint: peoples from all over the world have stitched their cultural enclaves on to the city's quilt. Chinatown whisks you to the Orient with its giddy whirligig of scents, sights, and sounds, while the nearby North

> This West Coast capital of sophistication has something for everyone, from fine art museums to casual dining.

Beach exudes laid-back Italian charm. Haight-Ashbury is a must-visit for its offbeat reminders of the Flower Power era. Pacific Heights boasts astounding Beaux Arts mansions and Victorian gingerbread houses. The glittering skyscrapers of the Financial District rub shoulders with the fashionable department stores of Union Square, while Golden Gate Park offers plenty of outdoor pursuits as well as one of North America's foremost museums: the recently reinvented de Young. The SOMA district's Museum of Modern Art and Legion of Honor (replete with classics from Rembrandt to Rodin) are also guaranteed to satisfy culture vultures.

Despite its large size, it's easy to get your bearings. San Francisco – at the tip of a peninsula – is laid out in a rough grid, with glittering boulevards running west from the waterfront to the Pacific Ocean. While local neighborhoods are best explored on foot, San Francisco's 42 hills will have you huffing and puffing. Fortunately, the legendary cable cars, comfortable BART subway, and Muni bus system make getting around a cinch. To really feel like a local, take in an opera or the comedy cabaret, *Beach Blanket Babylon*. Hop on a ferry at Pier 39 for a cruise on the bay, being sure to step ashore on Alcatraz for a thrilling tour. Join the early risers practicing *tai chi* in Washington Square and jog along the windswept Marina. It soon becomes apparent why San Francisco is consistently rated as America's favorite city.

Main: Golden Gate Bridge against the San Francisco skyline
Below (left and right): Sailing past the historic island prison of Alcatraz; cable cars on California Street
Inset: Telling time in an age-old manner at the de Young Museum

Above: Revelers at a masked ball at the San Francisco Opera

CITY LIGHTS DIARY

Fall in San Francisco is the best time of year weather-wise, as the famously cold summer fogs clear and rainfall is rare. Brilliant sunny weather makes for enjoyable days exploring on foot, while the lush parks draw families and picnickers. Five days are just enough to savor the main sights and attractions.

Five Days of Urban Culture

Admire the incredible modern art at the San Francisco Museum of Modern Art in the SOMA district, then stroll around Union Square, where the main attractions are the fine boutiques and upscale department stores. In the evening, dine at Postrio before enjoying cocktails and the spectacular view from the Starlight Room.

DAY 1

Enjoy the atmosphere of Chinatown, with time to savor some of the local specialties. Then invigorate yourself with a cappuccino in North Beach for the climb to Coit Tower. Be sure to visit City Light Books and, in the evening, take in an opera or laugh tears at the longest-running music revue, *Beach Blanket Babylon*.

DAY 2

Ride the cable car to Nob Hill for great views. Visit Grace Cathedral and the Cable Car Museum, then continue to Ghiradelli Square. Walk the waterfront, visiting the U.S.S. *Pampanito* and Fisherman's Wharf. Then walk downhill to fun-filled Pier 39. Afterwards, board a ferry for a guided tour of Alcatraz.

DAY 3

Drive out to Golden Gate Park, which fills most of the day. Allow time for the spectacular de Young Museum and California Academy of Sciences. Then enjoy the serene beauty of the Japanese Tea Garden or admire the redwoods at the San Francisco Botanical Garden.

DAY 4

Dress warmly for a walk across the Golden Gate Bridge, not missing Fort Point National Historic Site. Spend the afternoon in awe of the art at the Palace of the Legion of Honor.

DAY 5

Dos and Don'ts

☑ Bring some cold-weather clothing so that you can easily add an extra layer. San Francisco can be bitterly cold if a rare late summer fog rolls in.

☑ Ride the famous cable cars and historic trams – a great way to get to know the city and enjoy a unique and integral aspect of San Francisco's heritage.

☒ Don't restrict yourself to one area. Explore the city's many neighborhoods, from North Beach and Chinatown to the Marina District.

JAN
FEB
MAR
APR
MAY
JUN
JUL
AUG
SEP
OCT
NOV
DEC

See map p321, E3–4, F3–4

GETTING THERE
The largest airports near southern Utah are in Las Vegas, (southwest of Zion Canyon), and Salt Lake City (northeast of Zion). Small airports near the towns of Moab and St. George get some regional flights.

GETTING AROUND
The practical way to reach and explore the parklands of southern Utah is by car; rentals are available in Las Vegas and Salt Lake City.

WEATHER
September has hot days and cooler nights. The average daytime high in Moab reaches 87°F (31°C), while the nighttime low is 51°F (11°C). Springdale is warmer. Rain is rare.

ACCOMMODATIONS
Springdale's El Rio Lodge is a welcoming mom'n'pop motel; doubles from US$69; www.elriolodge.com

The riverside Desert Pearl Inn in Springdale offers great views; rooms from US$150; www.desertpearl.com

Upscale Red Cliffs Lodge resort, northeast of Moab, offers horse riding and rafting; rooms from US$200; www.redcliffslodge.com

EATING OUT
Standard American fare comes cheap at US$12–15 for a full meal. For variety, try Springdale's Spotted Dog Café or the Desert Bistro in Moab (around US$25–30).

PRICE FOR TWO
$400 per day for accommodation, food, car rental, and admissions.

FURTHER INFORMATION
www.utah.com

Lake Powell

Perhaps southern Utah's most incongruous spectacle is the mighty body of water that lies at its heart. Created by the Glen Canyon Dam in 1963, Lake Powell took 17 years to fill. The price of its construction, apart from the US$300 million, was the drowning of idyllic Glen Canyon, hailed by the few river-runners who saw it as the finest of Utah's canyons. While none could mistake the lake as being natural, four million visitors descend here each year to cruise around its many buttes-turned-islands and explore its countless hidden recesses.

Main: A boat plying the waters of Lake Powell between unearthly rock formations
Above (top to bottom): The forests of Boulder Mountain putting on a display of color in the fall; Delicate Arch; a hiker crossing Zion River in Zion National Park; the gushing waters of Calf Creek Falls

ROCKY ADVENTURELAND

I F THE WORD "DESERT" SUGGESTS A FEATURELESS EXPANSE of windblown sand to you, the spectacular scenery of southern Utah will come as a revelation. From the surreal, incandescent hoodoos – bizarre rock formations – of Bryce Canyon to the awesome jigsaw-puzzle plateaus of Canyonlands stacked one atop the other toward the panoramic horizon, Utah's so-called "high country" is a wonderland of stunning beauty, where the bare bones of the earth lie eroded in a million peculiar formations perfect for exploration. While trails in the national parks provide immensely rewarding opportunities to hike into the wilderness, the whole place is on such a scale that to appreciate it in full will take many hours just driving through the prodigiously breathtaking landscape.

Zion Canyon makes for a deceptively gentle welcome, with lush meadows lining the valley floor beneath mighty walls of red sandstone. Head east from here to reach the fiery pinnacles of Bryce Canyon, then continue

Above: A hiker negotiating a narrow passage in Zion Canyon

ROCKBOUND DIARY

September is ideal for touring southern Utah; the edge is off the summer heat, the sun sets late enough to allow for long days outdoors, and the fall colors are spreading downward from the higher elevations. Each of the desert parks can hold your interest for days, so allow for over a week to get a real sense of them.

Nine Days on the Canyon Trail

A drive of a few hours on the I-15 Interstate from Las Vegas or Salt Lake City will bring you to Zion Canyon; camp here or check into a motel in Springdale.

DAY 1

For a memorable day's hiking in Zion Canyon, climb the West Rim Trail to perilous Angel's Landing, then stroll the Riverside Walk back on the canyon floor.

DAY 2

Drive east to Bryce Canyon and hike down into its maze of multi-hued, top-heavy sandstone pillars.

DAY 3

Continuing east through Grand Staircase-Escalante National Monument, hike to Calf Creek Falls, and be dazzled by the fall colors on Boulder Mountain.

DAY 4

Having spent a day exploring Capitol Reef National Park, drive on to the town of Green River.

DAY 5

Take a day trip from Green River: drive a dirt road south, then venture deep into the Horseshoe Canyon to see the ancient pictographs in the Great Gallery.

DAY 6

Head southeast from Green River to Moab, detouring to swoon at the sweeping views from the Island in the Sky District of Canyonlands National Park.

DAY 7

On a day trip into Arches National Park, hike up to Delicate Arch for excellent photo opportunities.

DAY 8

Drive south from Moab to the Needles District of Canyonlands for another day-long hike, threading between rock pillars to reach the confluence of the Green and Colorado rivers. From Moab, drive north to the I-70 to return to Las Vegas or Salt Lake City.

DAY 9

Dos and Don'ts

✓ Get up early; by the end of September, the sun sets at 7pm. For a full day on the road, you need to make an early start.

✗ Don't expect to spend your nights carousing; you can buy alcohol in Utah, but it's only served with restaurant meals.

✓ Make sure you have enough gas in your tank before you set off into the back country.

✓ Carry emergency supplies – especially enough water and a flashlight – when you're hiking or driving in the desert.

JAN
FEB
MAR
APR
MAY
JUN
JUL
AUG
SEP
OCT
NOV
DEC

into Utah's largest park, Grand Staircase-Escalante National Monument. Much of this vast expanse is accessible only to the hardiest of backpackers, but a trail setting off from beside Highway 12 leads to rainbow-hued Calf Creek Falls. The high slopes of Boulder Mountain beyond are a prime location to enjoy fall colors. Once past Capitol Reef, a jagged anticline that formed a fearsome natural barrier to Mormon settlers, you discover Utah at its most desolate, with stark mounds of gray clay towering over the highway. It's amazing to think that prehistoric peoples painted the eerie pictographs of remote Horseshoe Canyon here over a thousand years ago.

The funky outpost of Moab in southeast Utah, a haven for lycra-clad devotees of extreme sports, makes a great base for exploring the final two parks, Arches and Canyonlands. Arches, small enough to explore in a day, holds over 2,000 natural rock arches. This includes Utah's state symbol, Delicate Arch, a free-standing stone crescent that frames the La Sal Mountains. Largest of all Utah's parks is the vast Canyonlands, offering the opportunity to take in fabulous desert vistas in its Island in the Sky District, and explore sublime hiking trails in the Needles District.

GETTING THERE   See map p330, B8

GETTING THERE
There are daily flights to Mendoza from Buenos Aires and Santiago in Chile. The 5-mile (8-km) taxi trip from airport to city center takes around 15 minutes, and costs about US$8.

GETTING AROUND
Mendoza's city center is pleasant to explore on foot, but to reach the wineries you'll need a car. Automendoza (www.automendoza. com) rents a mid-size sedan with AC and unlimited mileage for about US$75 per day.

WEATHER
Mendoza's skies are usually clear and sunny. September's spring weather reaches highs of around 68°F (20°C), lows of 43°F (6°C).

ACCOMMODATIONS
Argentino Hotel offers luxury accommodation; doubles from US$95; www.argentino-hotel.com

Club Tapiz is a restored colonial villa with an elegant restaurant, on a working vineyard; doubles from US$150; www.tapiz.com.ar

Park Hyatt Mendoza is the premier hotel in town, with stylish, modern rooms; doubles from US$225; www.mendoza.park.hyatt.com

EATING OUT
1884, with a romantic setting and huge list of local wines, has mains from US$10. Azafran serves delicious food, with mains from US$5, amid the barrels of an historic wine shop.

PRICE FOR TWO
US$350 per day, including accommodation, food, tours, four days' car rental, and taxis.

FURTHER INFORMATION
www.turismo.mendoza.gov.ar

The Malbec Grape

Argentina's signature varietal is Malbec, a grape that originated in Hungary. It has long been cultivated in France, where it serves as one of the six grapes used in blending Bordeaux. A purple-black grape with a thin skin and plum-like taste, it needs lots of sun and heat, as well as a wide swing between day- and night-time temperatures. This has resulted in Malbec falling from favour in the old world, but Argentinean wineries have perfected its use, making intense wines with plum and cherry flavors, and a nose heavy in vanilla, which improve with ageing.

Above (left to right): Sycamore-lined road between the vineyards; decorative tilework in Plaza Espagna, Mendoza
Main: Mount Tupungato, towering over the vines of the Catena Zapata winery

Above: Maipu's relaxing, leafy central plaza

VINEYARDS AND VISTAS

H APPY IS THE MAN WITH A HOME IN MENDOZA, runs an old expression still heard at times in Argentina. Almost as happy are those who merely get to visit. It is a city of hot days and constant sunshine, kept cool at night by its high-altitude location. Mendoza breathes the crisp, dry air of the desert, yet is lush with greenery and flowing water, channeled into the city from the Andes snowmelt via ancient irrigation works and elegant canals. It is a city where one becomes accustomed to seeing beauty – not just in the people or the elegant monuments and plazas, but also in the glimpses of a snowy peak that one happens upon in the course of a Mendoza day.

These little droplets of loveliness become a torrent when you venture out into wine country, and yet still, somehow, they come as a surprise. You'll be cycling down a tree-lined lane near Maipu when the vista will open up to a view of snow-capped Mount Tupungato. Or, standing in a tasting room, trying to conjure the right wine-vocabulary word for the delicious red liquid swirling over your palate, you'll look up and be confronted by the looming snow-white ranks of the Andes. Or you'll be crossing the Uco valley, trying to fit in just one last winery, when you'll be dazzled by the sudden glow of sunset on the low golden hills that form the valley's walls.

The vineyards themselves are centuries old, but the opportunities to visit and taste – and indeed Argentinean wine as a thing of quality and beauty – are fairly new. Only in the last 15 years have the vintners of Mendoza learned to favor quality over quantity, and begun to win awards, particularly for their Malbec reds, and Torrontés and Semillon whites. With the success of tasting visits, many wineries have begun to establish small on-site inns, and even upscale spas. With its nearly 700 wineries, one could spend a lifetime exploring Mendoza's wine and landscapes. Unhappy is the man who, having once discovered Mendoza, finds he has to leave again.

> You'll be cycling down a tree-lined lane when the vista will open up to a view of snow-capped Mount Tupungato.

Inset: Corks from one of Mendoza's fine estates
Below (left and right): Harvesting Malbec grapes; cellar at Catena Zapata winery

TASTING DIARY

The spectacular high plains around Mendoza are the center of Argentina's wine country, home to hundreds of wineries large and small. Six days in the spring gives time to visit a representative sample of historic, traditional *bodegas* and modern wineries, traveling both with a guide and on your own, by car, by bike, and even on foot.

Six Days Amid the Vines

DAY 1 Arrive in Mendoza and check in to a luxurious hotel on the city's central square. Stroll the paths and pergolas of Plaza Independencia, then get into wine country mood with a long, leisurely lunch. Ask the sommelier for a light varietal like a Semillon or Torrontés. Save the hearty Malbec for dinner, to take off the evening chill.

DAY 2 Put yourself in the hands of the local experts and take a guided wine tour, such as the one offered by Trout and Wine (www.troutandwine.com).

DAY 3 Pick up a copy of *Caminos de las Bodegas*, a set of maps showing the location of most Mendoza wineries and available in most hotels. Rent a car and set out to explore on your own.

DAY 4 Move on from Mendoza to nearby Maipu, to the relaxed and charming setting of the hotel Club Tapiz. Dine that evening at its lovely Terruños Restaurant.

DAY 5 Set out to explore Maipu's local wineries by pedal power (www.bikesandwines.com). Maipu's roads are quiet, flat and tree-lined, and several wineries offer a gourmet luncheon – with wine of course.

DAY 6 Drive back to Mendoza, have a final wander round the city's quintet of formal central squares, and a last leisurely outdoor lunch, sampling some of the vintages you've come to love in the surrounding countryside.

Dos and Don'ts

☑ Check your country's restrictions on wine imports. At any Mendoza winery you'll be tempted to pick up a bottle or a case, which could cost you dearly in import duty.

☑ Talk to your restaurant sommelier, who can match a local wine perfectly to your meal and budget.

☒ Don't drink and drive. Consider hiring a local driver and car, at a cost of about US$15 per hour.

☑ Study the online wine map at www.winemapargentina.com before your trip, to help you get the best from your tour.

JAN
FEB
MAR
APR
MAY
JUN
JUL
AUG
SEP
OCT
NOV
DEC

GETTING THERE   See map p326, A6
Mariscal Sucre International Airport is 3 miles (5 km) north of Quito's Old City. Taxis from there are US$6, or US$5 to the New City.

GETTING AROUND
Use the excellent local bus system, although taxis are inexpensive and recommended at night. Children must ride in the back seat.

WEATHER
September is warm and sunny, ranging from a nighttime low of 53°F (12°C) to 75°F (24°C) in the afternoons.

ACCOMMODATIONS
Sol de Quito Museum Hotel is nearly that: a museum of Ecuadorian culture; rooms from US$55; www.soldequito.com

The tiny but beautiful Hotel de la Rábida is an elegant colonial-style hotel with doubles from US$63; www.hotelrabida.com

Hotel Relicario del Carmen, built in 1705, has locally handmade furniture. Rooms start at US$85 and extra rooms are discounted; www.hotelrelicariodelcarmen.com

EATING OUT
While traditional highland dishes reign, fish ceviche, and *fanesca* (fish stew) are also popular. Soups include *locro de papas* (potato and cheese) and *sancocho de yuca* (vegetables with manioc). Try *empanadas* or *humitas* (ground corn steamed in the husk).

PRICE FOR TWO
US$135–195 per day including accommodation, food, and local travel.

FURTHER INFORMATION
www.vivecuador.com

The Old City

Quito's Centro Histórico is so faithful to its colonial heritage that the entire district was declared a World Heritage Site by UNESCO in 1978, the first city ever to be so named. A walking tour is a must: turn down a narrow cobblestone street and instantly you're back in the 16th century. There is pristine colonial architecture and ambience at every turn, from courtyards with quiet fountains and centuries-old tilework, to churches and convents that have remained unchanged for nearly five centuries. If you have only one day in Quito, spend it here!

Main: Night view of the splendid cathedral in the Plaza de la Independencia, Old City

THE JEWEL OF THE ANDES

THE CONTINENT'S SECOND-HIGHEST CAPITAL CITY, QUITO is nestled in a narrow valley at the base of the Pichincha Volcano. A true Andean gem, the city has two distinct but complementary facets, each with its own unforgettable sights and style. To the north lie the modern suburbs of El Norte (New City), with their sleek avenues lined with impressive embassies and offices. Touted as Quito's main business and tourist area, you'll find most banks, businesses, hotels, upscale shops, and restaurants here. Farther south is the Centro Histórico (Old City), which forms the colonial center and has some of the finest views of the Andes. Many of the city's well-known festivals and cultural venues are located here and the area has a vibrant atmosphere. The district's narrow cobblestone streets are crammed with Baroque churches, pastel-colored houses, tranquil courtyards, and stunning architecture. It's easy to see why the Centro Histórico was named a World Heritage Site by UNESCO.

Above: Cotopaxi and Chimborazo volcanoes in Cotopaxi National Park

Above: Spectacular views atop the Nariz del Diablo (Devil's Nose) train

Below (top and bottom): Colorful toy toucans in Otavalo's market; hikers in search of tropical wildlife in the Mindo Nambillo cloud forest

JAN

FEB

MAR

APR

MAY

JUN

JUL

AUG

SEP

DAY 1

DAY 2

DAY 3

DAY 4

DAY 5

DAY 6

OCT

NOV

DEC

ECUADOREAN DIARY

Whether you're walking through the cobblestone streets of Quito's Old Town, or the majestic cloud forests of Mindo, September in the Andes is ideal, with little precipitation and plenty of sun – perfect for all outdoor activities. You'll want at least six days to do justice to Ecuador's many cultural delights.

Six Days in the Highlands

Spend your first day relaxing. Stop at a café in El Norte and visit the Parque El Arbolito and the Casa de Cultura, or the nearby Museo del Banco Central.

Take a walking tour of the Centro Histórico, starting with the Plaza Grande, and visit the Basilica de Voto Nacional with its gargoyles and clock tower with a café at the top. Hire a taxi to the summit of El Panecillo and end the day with a meal at a quaint restaurant in La Ronda.

Take the *teleférico* (cable car) to the top of Guagua Pichincha, an active volcano that overlooks Quito. In nearby La Mariscal, the tourist epicenter of Quito, take in a free *rondador* (pan pipes) concert and then head north to the market town of Otavalo.

A riot of color, Otavalo is the most impressive market extravaganza in South America. You'll want all morning to take it in. After lunch, head south to Riobamba.

Be up early for a ride on the roof of the infamous Devil's Nose train – it leaves at 7am. The final descent, at an angle that seems physically impossible, offers great views, if you can keep your eyes open. After returning to Quito, take a well-earned rest and admire the panoramic vistas of the Centro Histórico in the evening.

A trip to the Mitad del Mundo Equatorial Line Monument is in order. Nearby is the Bosque Protector Mindo-Nambillo. This cloud forest is an astonishing sub-tropical paradise with millions of butterflies, rare plants and flowers, tubing rivers, and well-maintained mountain biking trails.

Dos and Don'ts

✓ Rest easy for the first day. At more than 9,200 ft (2,805 m), you will need to acclimatize yourselves to the thinner air.

✗ Don't leave anything unaccompanied in a taxi or bus.

✓ Ask before photographing local people, even in Otavalo. While most will not object, some older merchants may.

✗ Don't forget that the US dollar is the legal currency in Ecuador. This applies not only to bills, but to coins as well.

✓ Carry your passports at all times and make a copy of it as well, just in case.

Quito thrives on this diversity. By night and on weekends, the Latin zest for life takes over, and El Norte springs to life in a riot of color and celebration. On Sundays, Quiteños and travelers alike flock to the Centro Histórico to hang out in its many parks and bistros.

Ecuador is small – and affordable – so visitors can see more than just the capital in a few days, without breaking the bank. Guided day trips and extended excursions to the Andean villages that ring the city, as well as to the area's many nature preserves, are popular. In particular, Ecuador's best-known national park is home to Cotopaxi, one of the world's highest active volcanoes, and shelters some of the continent's last remaining herds of wild horses. At the thermal baths of Papallacta, visitors can splash or soak in naturally heated pools varying in temperature from comfortable to boiling, and the Mindo Nambillo cloud forest's lush depths offer activities from tubing along quiet rivers to challenging rock climbs. The handicraft center of Otavalo, and the spectacular Nariz del Diablo (Devil's Nose) train ride – with its series of steep switchbacks which put most roller coasters to shame – are perennial favorites.

CANADA

USA   PHILADELPHIA
    Washington, D.C.
• Los Angeles

MEXICO

GETTING THERE   See map p316, F5
Philadelphia is accessible by car, bus, train, and air. The international airport is 7 miles (11 km) from Center City.

GETTING AROUND
Center City, the downtown core, is easy to get around on foot or by train. To reach out-lying sites, such as Gettysburg, you need a car.

WEATHER
September temperatures range from 58 to 78°F (14–26°C), and it's one of the sunniest and driest months of the year.

ACCOMMODATIONS
Family-friendly, the Holiday Inn Philadelphia is a short walk from historic sites and has a rooftop pool; from US$170 for a room with two doubles; www.hiphiladelphiahotel.com

The Gables B&B in the University City area, has a wraparound porch; from US$210 for two doubles with shared bath; www.gablesbb.com

The elegant Ritz-Carlton Philadelphia has valet parking, a spa, and flat-screen TVs; from US$359 for a room with two double beds; www.ritzcarlton.com

EATING OUT
You can't visit Philly without trying a cheesesteak at Pat's or Jim's (US$10). Family-style eateries abound at US$20 a head; expect to pay US$60 a head at fancier spots.

PRICE FOR A FAMILY OF FOUR
US$630 per head per day including attractions.

FURTHER INFORMATION
www.gophila.com

Benjamin Franklin

It seems everywhere you go in downtown Philadelphia you encounter the city's most famous son, Benjamin Franklin, whether it's in bronze (*above*) or as real-life impersonators. Contrary to popular belief, Franklin was never president of the USA. He did, however, manage an impressive number of achievements. He helped found Philadelphia's first hospital, subscription library, and volunteer fire brigade, as well as the University of Pennsylvania. He was one of the five men who drafted the Declaration of Independence. And, as many schoolchildren know, he dabbled a bit in kites and electricity.

Above (left to right): Carousel ride at Giggleberry Fair, Peddler's Village; fast action at a Flyers hockey game; Philadelphia Museum of Art
Main: Shark-spotting at the Adventure Aquarium

Above: Fresh flowers and food at Reading Terminal Market

A LEARNING EXPERIENCE

IF YOU TEND TO THINK THAT YOUR KIDS DON'T LIKE HISTORY, think again. Obviously, you haven't been to Philadelphia lately and seen youngsters shifting on their parents' shoulders to get a better glimpse of the Liberty Bell, or listening with rapt attention as a re-enactor in colonial costume explains some detail of 18th-century life – from the way early Americans cast their votes to the methods once used to make ice cream. You haven't heard kids begging their parents for a ride in one of Philly's horse-drawn carriages or to go on a lamp-lit ghost tour of Society Hill.

This compact city has more to offer than just a taste of American history, however. It provides endless scope for learning, but that's just the beginning. Philadelphia is also a sophisticated city that's awash with art and culture, sports, and fun attractions for all ages. Those who wouldn't be caught dead in an art gallery are happy to visit the steps at the Museum of Art, where Rocky ran in the movie, and can be captivated by the colorful murals that decorate walls across the city depicting everything from sports heroes to Noah's Ark.

The Adventure Aquarium in Camden gives budding naturalists a fascinating close-up of sharks, penguins, and crocodiles. And children who aren't certain that science is their thing often wake up to the thrill of experimentation at the Franklin Institute Science Museum where, among other things, they can walk through a giant model of a human heart.

Hungry youngsters? Stop by the lively Reading Terminal Market for picnic food – local cheeses, soft pretzels, the works – for lunch, or bring your feast aboard a sunset cruise along the Delaware River. Need open spaces? Head out to visit the world of the Amish in Lancaster County. Or get a taste of farm life at Fox Chase Farm, a 112-acre (45-hectare) farm in Fairmount Park. Don't forget to see historic Gettysburg – site of one of the most famous battles of the Civil War, and President Lincoln's address.

> A sophisticated city that's awash with art and culture, sports, and fun attractions for all the family.

Inset: Impressive and historic, the Liberty Bell and Independence Hall
Below (left and right): Amish man driving a buggy; Benjamin Franklin Parkway

JAN

FEB

MAR

APR

MAY

JUN

JUL

AUG

SEP

DAY 1

DAY 2

DAY 3

DAY 4

OCT

NOV

DEC

FAMILY FUN DIARY

September is the perfect time to visit this, the birthplace of the United States: the summer crowds have thinned and it is usually sunny and warm – with a bit of crispness late in the month. With its full program of arts, sports, and, as always, great food and shopping, you'll have a jam-packed four days.

Four days of Entertainment

Do the history bit first – take in Independence National Historical Park and visit Independence Hall (where the Declaration of Independence was adopted and the Constitution signed) and photograph the Liberty Bell. If you are hungry to know more, go to the nearby National Constitution Center. In the evening, loosen up by joining the cheering throngs at a Philadelphia Flyers pre-season hockey game.

If your children are seven or under, they'll love the interactive Please Touch Museum. If they're older and "been there, done that," go for the unusual – drop by the fascinating Eastern State Penitentiary, now a museum, to see gangster Al Capone's cell. For something quirky, visit Philadelphia's Magic Gardens, a unique house and courtyard covered in mosaics made from old plates, bottles, bicycle wheels, and more.

Get out of the city and explore some of the region's rolling countryside with a day trip to Peddler's Village in Bucks County. The attraction includes shops, restaurants, and a 10,000-sq ft (930-sq m) indoor entertainment complex with rides, called Giggleberry Fair.

Work off excess energy with a bike ride along Fairmount Park's network of scenic paths. After lunch, visit the Philadelphia Zoo – the nation's oldest – known for its success with animals that are reluctant to breed. Get a bird's-eye view from the Channel 6 Zooballoon, which ascends 400 ft (122 m) above the park. Then treat yourselves to rich sundaes and milkshakes at the Franklin Fountain, a re-creation of a Victorian shop.

Dos and Don'ts

☑ Catch some action at an exciting sports event while you're here – try a major league baseball, football or hockey game.

☑ Sample the local favorite snack – a Butterscotch Krimpet. Tastykake bakes up 3.5 million of these snack-sized cakes every week.

☒ Don't be too self-conscious to attempt Rocky Balboa's famous run up the front steps of the Philadelphia Museum of Art – few movie buffs can resist. For extra points, get your picture taken with the Rocky statue at the foot of the steps.

☑ Call the city "Philly" – even locals do.

GETTING THERE
See map p314, H6

International flights arrive at the Robert L. Stanfield airport, Halifax. Take a connector flight to Sydney on Cape Breton Island and rent a car. Baddeck is about 50 miles (80 km). The island is also linked by road to the Nova Scotia mainland via the Canso Causeway.

GETTING AROUND
A car is needed to explore the island.

WEATHER
Clear skies and sunshine are the norm in late September. Daytime temperatures may vary from 41°F (5°C) on the coast to 60°F (15°C) inland. At night it can drop to near freezing.

ACCOMMODATIONS
Inverary Resort is a lakeside family resort in Baddeck; family rooms from US$185; www.capebretonresorts.com

Duncreigan Country Inn, Mabou, is a charming modern waterside inn; family rooms from US$180; www.duncreigan.ca

Keltic Lodge at Ingonish has its own spa and great views; family rooms from US$300; www.kelticlodge.ca

EATING OUT
Local seafood is the highlight here. Rusty Anchor in Pleasant Bay serves chowder and seafood (platters from US$23) on the waterside patio. Baddeck has excellent restaurants.

PRICE FOR A FAMILY OF FOUR
US$535 per day, including accommodation, food, local travel, tours and admissions.

FURTHER INFORMATION
www.cbisland.com

Alexander Graham Bell

Bell (1847–1922), the inventor of the telephone, chose Baddeck for his summer estate, Beinn Bhreagh ("beautiful mountain"), claiming that Cape Breton out-rivaled many parts of the world in its simple beauty. The fascinating museum at the Alexander Graham Bell National Historic Site provides a glimpse into the life and legacy of this master innovator. His fascination with fields as diverse as aeronautics, agriculture and medical science produced numerous other inventions. A full scale model of his HD-4 hydrofoil craft is one of the highlights.

Main: Island handicrafts for sale at Neil's Harbour Point

WILD ISLAND BEAUTY

CAPE BRETON ISLAND IS ATLANTIC CANADA'S CRAGGY SURF-TOSSED SECRET. Every autumn a palette of rich reds, crimson-browns, and golden-yellows join the deep greens of spruce and fir as the nightly frost turns the forests and hillsides into vibrant masterpieces of great beauty. The bogs are rich with bright red cranberries and moose can often be seen grazing in the wetlands at dawn and dusk. The sunny, cloud-speckled skies are deep blue, and soaring gulls, seabirds and bald eagles often glide above the sea. The roads offer frequent pull-outs, where sweeping vistas include mountain ranges, barren headlands and glacial valleys. And out to sea, beyond the crashing waves, watch for the pods of humpback whales traveling along the coast. The best of Cape Breton Island's natural beauty is revealed along the spectacular highway known as the Cabot Trail. Carved into the rocky cliffs rising from the sea, the road twists ever higher as it traces the coastline through Cape Breton Highlands National Park and

Left (left to right): The winding road of the Cabot Trail; re-enacting the past at Fortress Louisbourg; Beulach Ban Falls; wild island moose; sighting on a whale-watching tour

Below: Red Shoe Pub in Mabou, with good food and live music most nights

Inset: Local folk art on display at Pleasant Bay

Above: Fall colors in the Highlands National Park

JAN

FEB

MAR

APR

MAY

JUN

JUL

AUG

SEP

Out to sea, beyond the crashing waves, watch for the pods of humpback whales.

TRAIL DIARY

Late September offers long sunny days and cold nights that turn the mountainsides into a tapestry of brilliant colors. The summer crowds are gone, attractions are still open, and the friendly islanders have time to chat. In five days you can explore tiny villages, country trails, and craft shops, and even go whale-watching.

Five Days of Discovery

Explore the art galleries and boutique shops in waterfront Baddeck. Allow several hours for the Alexander Graham Bell Museum.

DAY 1

Take the Cabot Trail, with views across Bras d'Or Lake and lovely Margaree Valley. Pause at the charming Margaree Salmon Museum, then turn south toward Inverness, stopping at Glendora Distillery for a tour and taste of single-malt whiskey. Continue to Mabou, where the island's best musicians play at the Red Shoe Pub.

DAY 2

Head north to Chéticamp via Joe's Scarecrows – a quirky collection of masked figures gathered in a field. Take a whale-watching tour, then visit the Elizabeth LeFort Gallery & Museum with its displays of traditional French-Acadian works of art in wool.

DAY 3

Stop at the visitors' center at Cape Breton Highlands National Park for a trail map. From here it's a superb drive to Ingonish via delightful Pleasant Bay. You could stop on route to hike the Skyline Trail in search of moose, or follow the short trail to Beulach Ban Falls and a 15-minute self-guided boardwalk route through the bog. Alternatively, take the spectacular (but unpaved) Meat Cove Road, with its fabulous ocean views.

DAY 4

Drive to St. Ann's and the Gaelic College of Arts & Crafts to see the Great Hall of the Clans. Then head south to tour the splendid Louisbourg Fortress, chat with costumed actors, and enjoy an 18th-century-style lunch. If there's time before you leave, take in a performance of Cape Breton music at the Louisbourg Playhouse.

DAY 5

Dos and Don'ts

☑ Drive the scenic Cabot Trail clockwise for the best views.

☒ A whale-watching tour can last 3 hours or more, so don't leave yourself short of time – and don't embark on it if you are a poor sailor and the sea is at all rough.

☒ Don't forget to pack your camera, binoculars, and sturdy walking shoes or hiking boots.

☑ When you are in Chéticamp, be sure to try the Acadian delicacy of Rappie (meat and potato) Pie

OCT

NOV

DEC

around the northern tip of the island. The National Park's unspoiled mountain wilderness of forests, lakes, and rivers supports a huge variety of wildlife. The best way to explore is to park the car and hike some of the two dozen trails. Brief self-guided boardwalk paths lead through the wetlands, while challenging trails lead upward to grand vistas of ocean headlands and hidden valleys. Here, too, are paths which lead to places where misty waterfalls stream down cliffsides, and rushing rivers teem with brook trout and Atlantic salmon.

Cape Breton Island was settled by French-speaking Acadians and later by Scots, who carved their homesteads into the rugged countryside. Tiny villages scattered along the coast surround protected inlets that offer shelter for fishing boats. The music-loving Cape Bretoners take pride in their heritage. Scottish children are once again learning Gaelic and, in towns like Chéticamp, you're likely to hear the lilting sounds of Acadian French. Whatever their heritage, the hardy residents greet visitors their island with the Gaelic *Ciad Mile Failte* – "one-hundred-thousand welcomes."

GETTING THERE   See map p327, C6
The Nazca Lines lie 14 miles (22 km) from Nazca town. Nazca is accessible only by road. Lima's international airport is 275 miles (440 km) away, a 6- to 8-hour trip.

GETTING AROUND
Tours to, and flights over, the Lines can be arranged at your hotel or at the airport.

WEATHER
Nazca is far enough from the coast to escape the sea mist. Daytime temperatures reach around 72°F (22°C). Nights are crisp.

ACCOMMODATIONS
The backpacker-orientated Hotel Alegria in central Nazca has rustic rooms and a pool; doubles from US$45; www.hotelalegria.net

Hacienda Majoro, in Nazca town, is a converted ranch house set in extensive gardens with a pool and Peruvian restaurant; doubles from US$80; www.hotelmajoro.com

The Maison Suisse at Nazca airport is the plushest hotel in town, with mock-European buildings set in gardens around a pool; doubles from US$100; www.aeroica.net

EATING OUT
Peruvian cuisine is strong on fish and poultry, served with rice or potatoes, and *quinoa* grain. Be sure to try *ceviche* (fish marinated in lemon juice) and roast *cuy* (guinea pig).

PRICE FOR TWO
US$250 per day including accommodation, food, bus from Lima, scenic flights, and tours.

FURTHER INFORMATION
www.peru.info/perueng.asp

Saviour of the Lines

German archeologist Maria Reiche (1903–88) was the first person to map Nazca from the air. Her theory, still widely believed today, was that the Lines were used as an astronomical observatory. Reiche was instrumental in protecting the figures from being destroyed by the Inter-American highway, and for securing their World Heritage Site status. She was buried at Nazca with full state honors.

ENIGMA IN THE DESERT

No PICTURE CAN PREPARE YOU FOR THE MYSTERY of these vast designs, etched into the dry, rocky desert of western Peru. From the air it seems as if the playthings of the gods have been thrown to earth and then gathered up by a gigantic hand, leaving only their imprints in the dust. There's a spider-monkey with a spiraling tail; a vast lizard, a llama, a whale, and a dog; and a whole aviary of birds, including a hummingbird 305 ft (93 m) long. They lie scattered on the ground alongside bizarre, abstract humanoid figures with tripod legs or four-fingered hands, and round-headed sentinels with staring, bush-baby eyes. Small wonder, then, that the Nazca Lines have inspired fantasists and fiction writers, from Erich von Däniken to Anthony Horowitz, who've suggested that the geoglyphs could be anything from alien landing sites to portals for malevolent demons.

Left: Aerial view of the intricate spider-monkey

Right (left and right): Nazca headdress on a mummified skull; Nazca vessel depicting a warrior

Main: Hummingbird viewed from the air

No one is quite sure who made the lines or why, but, as with many other artifacts of pre-Columbian America, they almost certainly have a ritual, shamanistic significance. Recent research has linked them with earlier drawings and glyphs by the Paracas people of Palpa. Symbols representing water and fertility found in Paracas drawings are repeated in the desert. There are records of shamanic walking rituals invoking the spirits of rain and fecundity, which would have been crucial elements of survival in this parched wilderness. Other archeologists, like Maria Reiche, have linked the drawings to a vast pre-Incan calendar, or to archetypal patterns repeated in traditional weavings.

The Nazca civilization left other remains in the area too, at the partially excavated and badly looted ceremonial site of Cahuachi, south of Nazca town, and at Chauchilla, to the west, where the pre-Columbian posts are thought to have been used for drying mummies prior to burial. But, once you have taken to the skies for a gods'-eye view of the Nazca Lines, it is these that you will have forever etched upon your memory in all their inexplicable splendor.

Above: Colorful woolen Quechua rug

LINE-GAZER'S DIARY

The Nazca Lines are so captivating that it's best to see them several times – from the air for a general overview, and then in more detail from the viewing platforms on the ground. Three days will give you plenty of time to view the lines, find out about Nazca culture and history, and even form your own theory about the lines.

Three Days of Desert Art

Head straight to the airport to book your flight with one of the various air taxi services. The earlier you do this, the better chance you have of getting the plane and time of your choice *(see below)*. After your flight, head into Nazca town and buy a copy of Dr. Reiche's book *Mystery on the Desert* to learn more about the lines. Adventurous gourmets should dine on roast *cuy* at La Carreta, to the accompaniment of live Andean music.

Take a tour to the Lines to see them in more detail from the observation platforms. Choose a tour that also takes in the Nazca burial sites at Chauchilla and Cahuachi. Stop for lunch and souvenir shopping at a local village where you'll see the Quechua people weaving vivid, intricate fabric. In the evening, sample delicious *ceviche* at La Taberna. Add your name to the thousands signed on the walls by previous visitors.

Spend the day visiting the Nazca museums. The Museo Didáctico Antonini preserves important burial remains. It also displays a scale model of the Lines, and has an ancient aqueduct running through its grounds. Take a taxi to the Museo Maria Reiche, which is in her former home, outside of town. Her tomb is in the garden. Visits include a short lecture on the Lines. In the evening, visit the Maria Reiche Planetarium (located in the Nazca Lines Hotel), which is devoted to Nazca astronomy.

Dos and Don'ts

✓ Take the bus from Lima, rather than drive yourself. The route through the desert is poorly signposted and not very scenic.

✓ Book your flight over the lines for around 2pm. Earlier or later, the sun is too harsh and the shadows too strong.

✓ Choose the smallest plane available, and ideally one with windows that open, for the best aerial photos.

✗ Don't pocket shards of pottery or artifacts from the desert. Persistent looting has scattered fragments everywhere. If you find any, hand them in to staff at the Museo Antonini.

JAN
FEB
MAR
APR
MAY
JUN
JUL
AUG
SEP
DAY 1
DAY 2
DAY 3
OCT
NOV
DEC

GETTING THERE   See map p312, H6
Halifax is a small waterfront city on Canada's east coast. The international airport is 14 miles (22 km) from the city center. There are also international flights to other major cities, including Vancouver, Toronto, Montréal, and Edmonton.

GETTING AROUND
You can travel across Canada both east- and westbound by train, beginning in Halifax or Vancouver, and between other towns and cities.

WEATHER
Daytime temperatures average 65°F (18°C) in Vancouver, 68°F (20°C) in Toronto.

ACCOMMODATIONS
The most economical way to travel is in Via Rail's Comfort class, with a partially reclining seat and a shared bathroom; www.viarail.ca

On the Rocky Mountaineer, choose from RedLeaf (economy) and GoldLeaf (luxury), staying overnight in hotels en route; www.rockymountaineer.com

The Royal Canadian Pacific trains through the Rockies offer pure luxury in vintage rail cars, with private cabins; www.cpr.ca

EATING OUT
Dining carriages serve meals featuring regional ingredients like salmon, beef, and local wines.

PRICE FOR TWO
Rail-only tickets between Toronto and Vancouver cost from US$1,100 for a 3-day journey. A 17-day rail vacation package (Halifax–Vancouver) costs from US$680 per day, including rail tickets, accommodation, local tours, meals, and taxes.

FURTHER INFORMATION
www.canadatourism.ca

The Spiral Tunnels

In the late 1800s, near the mountain town of Field in British Columbia, the "Big Hill" and its dangerous 4.5 percent gradient caused many a heart to race – and several runaway train engines. To solve the problem, engineers began building the Spiral Tunnels in 1907. Still in use today (both the *Rocky Mountaineer* and *Royal Canadian Pacific* routes include them), the tunnels corkscrew into Mount Ogden and Cathedral Mountain, essentially doubling back on themselves inside the mountains and allowing a much more gradual slope.

Main: Rocky Mountaineer travels alongside the Bow River through Alberta

RIDING THE RAILS

THE TWIN RIBBONS OF STEEL that stretch for thousands of miles across Canada have tales to tell of the travelers who have made history on this journey – Mounties and military men, royalty and roustabouts, pioneers and poets. More than a century ago, these rails united a nation still in its infancy, weaving together the threads of a landscape as varied as the people making their home within it. It's still an epic journey today, following the mighty St. Lawrence River to the granite outcroppings of the Canadian Shield; across the great prairie plains and through pine and spruce in the Rockies; emerging from west coast cedar rainforests to greet the Pacific Ocean.

Ride the rails from sea to sea and you'll glimpse the old stories, set against the rhythmic sway of the train. Lobster traps piled on eastern wharves, the train slowing to a stop at the Great Lakes to let a party of canoeists off, the grain harvest waiting in the fields as the sun silhouettes a first glimpse of the Rockies.

Above: Sunrise on Maligne Lake and Spirit Island in Jasper National Park

Above (left to right): Vintage Canadian Pacific poster; luxurious cabin interior on the Canadian Pacific; dining carriage on Via Rail; Union Station in Toronto; Rocky Mountaineer crossing the dramatic Stoney Creek Bridge; Peggy's Cove Lighthouse in Nova Scotia

Below: Entrance to one of the spiral tunnels in Yoho National Park, British Columbia

CROSS-COUNTRY DIARY

The train can transport you between Canada's east and west coasts in as little as five days, but this vast and varied country is worth a more in-depth experience – whether it's exploring the arts scene in Toronto, the dramatic Rocky Mountains, or the wave-washed shores of the Pacific and Atlantic coasts.

Two Weeks by Train

Fly into Halifax the day before the train departs to explore the historic wharves of the harbor, where tall ships often dock, and the rocky coast and dramatic lighthouse of Peggy's Cove, a nearby fishing village.	**DAY 1**
Overnight on Via Rail's *Ocean* service between Halifax and Montréal, traveling alongside Canada's windswept Atlantic coastline to the St. Lawrence River. Spend a night in Montréal to enjoy the boutiques and bistros of this cosmopolitan French-speaking city.	**DAYS 2–4**
Take the train to Toronto. Stroll the waterfront, hit the museums, or head to the theater district to enjoy Broadway shows. Then board Via Rail's *The Canadian* for the journey north of Lake Superior, a landscape known as the Canadian Shield.	**DAYS 5–6**
The Canadian then sweeps across prairie plains through Manitoba and Saskatchewan and on to Alberta, revealing the snow-capped Rocky Mountains. Take a self-drive or tour option between Jasper and Banff on the Icefields Parkway, past spectacular glaciers and through national parks. Alternatively, take another train on to Calgary, from where you can take the luxurious *Royal Canadian Pacific* to the Rocky Mountain resort of Banff.	**DAYS 7–9**
In Banff, join the *Rocky Mountaineer* for its two-day trip on the historic track through the Rockies into British Columbia's desert-like interior and on to lush Vancouver.	**DAYS 10–12**
Spend your last days in Vancouver on Stanley Park's waterfront, at the VanDusen Botanical Garden, or exploring in Gastown and Chinatown.	**DAYS 13–14**

Dos and Don'ts

✓ Take advantage of the friendly on-board atmosphere to strike up conversations with fellow travelers.

✓ Keep your eyes open for wildlife – deer and moose are often seen across the country, while elk and bears might be spotted in the Rockies.

✗ Don't underestimate distances in Canada: 3,915 miles (6,300 km) of railroad tracks join Halifax, Nova Scotia, with Vancouver, British Columbia.

There, among the saw-toothed peaks and climb-me-if-you-dare mountains, the stories reach their climax. They tell of the explorers who found the first routes through treacherous mountain passes, the engineers who mapped the rail line, the thousands of workers who laid down the tracks (and sometimes their lives) to build high, heart-in-mouth bridges and long tunnels into unforgiving rock. Once through the mountains, the stories blow with the tumbleweed of British Columbia's semi-arid interior, where iron and copper deposits paint the cliffs rusty red or blue-green – and, finally, they drift in the mist across Vancouver's harbor, where cruise ships and seaplanes launch from the Pacific shoreline.

Many travelers choose a small portion of the cross-Canada route, focussing on the east coast, for example, or charting a grand circle through the Rockies. But the intrepid can cross the entire nation by rail between Halifax and Vancouver. So settle back in your seat, relax, and let the scenes unfold outside your picture window. This trip is all about the journey.

JAN
FEB
MAR
APR
MAY
JUN
JUL
AUG
SEP
OCT
NOV
DEC

MIDWESTERN MAJESTY

GETTING THERE See map p319, B3

GETTING THERE
In the west of South Dakota, 400 miles (650 km) north of Denver and 600 miles (950 km) west of Minneapolis, Rapid City has a regional airport and is a fine hub from which to explore.

GETTING AROUND
Rent a car at the airport to access the area's many parks, monuments, and byways.

WEATHER
September is pleasant and dry, with average daytime highs of about 75°F (24°C) cooling down to about 45°F (7°C) at night.

ACCOMMODATIONS
Family-owned Sweetgrass Inn B&B is just out-side Rapid City at the foot of the Black Hills; doubles from US$115; www.sweetgrassinn.com

Hotel Alex Johnson, in the heart of Rapid City, was built in 1928 and is on the National Register of Historic Places; doubles from US$124; www.alexjohnson.com

Within Custer State Park is historic Sylvan Lake Lodge; cabins with full kitchen from US$125; www.custerresorts.com

EATING OUT
This is carnivore country; you'll find steak from locally reared cattle or buffalo on almost every menu (try Rapid City's Fireside Inn). Other local specialties include pheasant, trout, walleye (pike-perch), and pasties (meat pies).

PRICE FOR TWO
US$250 per day including accommodation, food, car rental and gas, and park admissions.

FURTHER INFORMATION
www.travelsd.com

Main: Native American of the Sioux tribe

H ERE, IN A REMOTE CORNER OF SOUTH DAKOTA, is where the grandeur of the Great Plains meets the rugged, spruce-covered Black Hills; where the history and culture of the great Sioux tribe sit alongside those of the American people. Dramatic doesn't begin to describe the terrain, which has been scoured and scraped by glaciers into hills, canyons, and prairie. It's a place of man-made as well as natural splendor. Overlooking a sylvan landscape of pine, spruce, birch, and aspen is Mount Rushmore, the epic, inspiring sculpture of American presidents George Washington, Thomas Jefferson, Theodore Roosevelt and Abraham Lincoln. In counterpoint, not far away in Custer, the Crazy Horse Memorial depicts the great Native American warrior astride his horse. Begun in 1948, when completed it will be the world's largest sculpture. Many Native Americans believe that it violates the sacredness of the land.

Icons in Stone

Designed in 1925 by sculptor Gutzon Borglum, Mount Rushmore is one of the most revered patriotic sites in the United States. Carved into a granite peak in Harney National Forest, the monument commemorates four iconic American presidents. For its construction, around 400 workers labored from 1927 to 1941, removing an astonishing 450,000 tons of rock. Not one life was lost during the work – remarkable, given the amount of dynamite used. Mount Rushmore is considered the largest work of art on earth, and welcomes more than two million visitors each year.

Left (left to right): Riding the range in Custer State park; Crazy Horse Memorial.

Right (left to right): Entrance to the Black Hills National Forest; rock formations in the Badlands National Park.

Right panel (top and bottom): Spires of Needles highway; Chinese red ring pheasant, the state bird

Driving is one of the great pleasures of visiting South Dakota, whether it's along the hypnotically beautiful Spearfish Canyon Byway, which roves through a picturesque narrow canyon, or the famous Needles Highway, a gorgeous stretch that winds sharply through forests of high trees and towering granite "needles" and plunges through tunnels blasted out of the living rock. In contrast to the lush vistas of the Black Hills, Badlands National Park is a surreal, Martian-esque landscape of towering red sun-baked rock formations that stretch over the arid landscape as far as the eye can see.

It's easy to believe that you've stepped back in time as you wander the lovingly restored streets of Deadwood, explore the trails of Custer State Park, and revel in the spectacle of the autumn Buffalo Roundup, a rollicking celebration where full-blooded Sioux mingle with cowboys and local merchants. In some ways you have – this is still wild, untamed territory, where the spirit of the frontier lives on, set against a backdrop of some of the nation's greatest natural wonders.

Above: Buffalo grazing the Dakota prairies

JAN

FEB

MAR

APR

MAY

JUN

JUL

AUG

SEP

BLACK HILLS DIARY

Comfortable weather, manageable crowds, and the lively annual Buffalo Roundup at the end of the month make September an ideal time to visit the Black Hills region. In three days you can see all the major sights, from Mount Rushmore to Badlands National Park, and still have time to watch the roundup at Custer State Park.

Three Days on the Frontier

Wake up early to beat the crowds to Mount Rushmore, with its four 60-ft (18-m) faces carved into the rockface at a height of 500 ft (150 m). Have lunch back in Rapid City, then take the scenic drive skirting the Black Hills northwest to the Spearfish Canyon National Scenic Byway, which offers stunning views of the surrounding mountains. Be sure to stop for a stroll through Deadwood, a preserved Old West town famous as the site of the murder of Wild Bill Hickok.

DAY 1

Take Route 44 about 60 miles (96 km) southeast of Rapid City to the breathtaking rock formations of Badlands National Park. Get your bearings at Ben Reifel Visitor Center, then head out to explore the park on the picturesque 5-mile (8-km) Castle Trail, a great spot for spotting wildlife such as buffalo, coyote, prairie dogs, buzzards, and chickadees.

DAY 2

Drive to Custer State Park, about 45 miles (73 km) southwest of Rapid City, via the Crazy Horse Memorial which is on your route. Hike the trails, check out the wildlife, and take part in the festivities at the park's annual Buffalo Roundup, when the thundering herd of nearly 1,500 beasts are expertly corraled by cowboys and cowgirls. After a chuckwagon lunch in the park, take in the astonishing spectacle of towering granite spires along the 14-mile (23 km) Needles Highway.

DAY 3

Dos and Don'ts

✓ Dress in layers – the weather in the Black Hills can be quite cool in the mornings and evenings, warm during the day.

✓ Check the dates of the Buffalo Roundup in advance – in some years it falls on the first weekend of October.

✓ Stay hydrated (be sure to bring your own water bottle when walking the trails in the various parks}, and wear sunblock; though the weather may not be overly hot, the sun can still be intense.

✗ Don't feed wildlife in the parks, and don't approach buffalo as they may charge at speed if threatened.

OCT

NOV

DEC

OCTOBER

Where to Go: **October**

Fall is bedding down nicely in North America. The colors are at their resplendent peak along the east coast – quite simply, there is no prettier time to vacation in New England. California, is warmer than the east, and the Pacific Northwest contrasts its golden fall foliage with wild beaches. Hiking conditions are perfect in the Southwest, while the big surf breaks have yet to arrive in Hawai'i, making it safer to swim. A lively festivals calendar takes advantage of fall's clemency; in Mexico, the days surrounding the Day of the Dead are unmissable. Canada's snowy northern wastes offer the chance to see polar bears, while in South America you can almost travel to the ends of the earth. Below you will find all the destinations in this chapter and some extra suggestions to provide inspiration.

FESTIVALS AND CULTURE

ALBUQUERQUE Preparations in Balloon Fiesta Park

UNFORGETTABLE JOURNEYS

OREGON The lighthouse at Haceta Head

NATURAL WONDERS

GRAND CANYON The awe-inspiring landscape of the canyon

ALBUQUERQUE
NEW MEXICO, USA

Blue skies filled with a graceful kaleidoscope of colors

Few sights can match the spectacle of 750 hot-air balloons all taking off at once in the desert at the Albuquerque Balloon Fiesta.
See pp242–3

FANTASY FEST
FLORIDA, USA

The world's biggest fancy-dress party in Key West

Locals and visitors take to the streets of Key West in costume, with parades, parties, and plenty of music and rum.
www.fantasyfest.net

OREGON COAST
OREGON, USA

A scenic drive along a stunning coastline

Drive along Highway 101 and take in the timeless landscapes of the Oregon coastline, with scenes of surf, sand, and rain forest.
See pp246–7

HIGHWAY 61
USA

Scenic journey around Lake Superior

Drive the magnificent stretch of Highway 61 from Duluth to the Canadian border, immortalized in song by local boy Bob Dylan.
www.visitduluth.com

GRAND CANYON
ARIZONA, USA

Explore the Grand Canyon by car and on a mule

To truly appreciate this huge fissure sculpted by the Colorado River, take mule trips and enlist on canyon hikes.
See pp240–1

CÍRIO DE NAZARÉ FESTIVAL
BRAZIL

A joyous religious celebration

The Círio de Nazaré honors the image of the Virgin Mary of Belém with parades and wild partying.
www.paratur.pa.gov.br/english/eng_cirio.asp

PATAGONIAN FJORDS
CHILE

Explore a fantastical icy world on a cruise liner

Wonder at astonishing glaciers and imagine yourself as an Antarctic explorer, heading to the end of the world.
See pp244–5

"In this magnificent natural theater, great vertical rock faces rise from the sea, and gushing waterfalls plunge into deep channels."

WHITESHELL PROVINCIAL PARK
MANITOBA, CANADA

Natural hideaway

Enjoy a spot of rejuvenation in this beautiful park, with its mix of unspoilt scenery and cozy inns, particularly beautiful during fall.
www.whiteshell.mb.ca

ANNAPOLIS
MARYLAND, USA

Historic state capital

Explore this time-warped little city on Chesapeake Bay, its captivating red-brick streets dotted with historic landmarks, including the venerable Maryland State House.
www.annapolis.com

NEW ENGLAND FALL
NEW ENGLAND, USA

North America's woodlands at their most spectacular

Take a road trip through New England in fall, when the forests turn a thousand brilliant shades of red, yellow, purple, and gold.
www.visitnewengland.com

IWOKRAMA RAINFOREST
GUYANA

Rain forest hike

Hike or boat through this remarkable rain forest in central Guyana, one of the world's best places to spot Jaguars.
www.iwokrama.org

THE LAURENTIANS
QUÉBEC, CANADA

Wilderness retreat in Québec

Hike or kayak in the rugged Laurentian mountains, which are clothed in dense tracts of maple forest and dotted with pretty hidden lakes and waterfalls.
www.laurentians.worldweb.com

BUENOS AIRES
ARGENTINA

European culture combined with Latin passion

Buenos Aires might be a great place to party, but it also has history, fabulous architecture, and the best steaks in the world.
See pp238–9

BIG SUR
CALIFORNIA, USA

Wild coastline drive between San Francisco and LA

Driving between these two great coastal cities you'll see some of America's finest wind- and wave-lashed coastlines and a lot more.
www.visitcalifornia.com

"No other place in Hawai'i so perfectly fulfils dreams of a pristine Polynesian paradise as this island."

KAUA'I
HAWAI'I, USA

A volcanic island with spectacular landscapes

Hike though tropical bird-filled jungles, snorkel fish-filled waters, and enjoy views over a wild and rugged Polynesian paradise.
See pp248–9

Weather Watch

❶ **Cape Churchill, Canada** Mid-fall in Canada's icy wilderness, when the polar bears migrate, is bitterly cold, with temperatures consistently well below freezing. Wind, rain, and sun conditions can change at a moment's notice.

❷ **Maine, USA** October is sunny and crisply cold, with the constant possibility of rain and wind. The best of the fall colors will be fading by the middle of the month.

❸ **Oregon, USA** Though winter is approaching on the wild, ocean-pounded coast of the Pacific Northwest, there is still sunshine to be had; temperatures can get as high as 60°F (16°C), but rain showers are practically a given.

❹ **Grand Canyon, USA** Arizona's Grand Canyon sees sunshine and the odd shower in October; the rim has warm daytime highs and cooler nighttime lows, with more extreme contrasts in the inner gorge.

❺ **Mexico** October is a lovely month to be in Mexico; the heat and the rains of summer are over. In Oaxaca in the Yucatán daytime temperatures stay reasonably high.

❻ **Chile** October brings long, bright (and practically ozone-layer free) days in the south of this skinny country, with high temperatures. Howling winds add drama, as do sudden changes in conditions.

LUXURY AND ROMANCE

MOUNT DESERT ISLAND Wooden bridge over the pond in Somesville

MOUNT DESERT ISLAND
MAINE, USA

Fall colors by day and fine seafood at sunset

Explore winding forest and waterside trails on this unspoiled and far-from-desert island retreat.
See pp236–7

ILHABELA
BRAZIL

Exquisite island just off the Brazilian coast

This stunning volcanic island is swathed in dense tropical foliage and studded with waterfalls and beautiful beaches.
www.ilhabela.org

CALIFORNIA WINE COUNTRY
CALIFORNIA, USA

A riot of fall colors

The rolling hills, quaint towns, and warm hospitality will make this a special holiday. As will, of course, the fine wines to be had here.
See pp250–1

BAHÍA CONCEPCIÓN
MEXICO

Beautiful beaches on the Sea of Cortez

This idyllic bay stretches for miles along the Bay of Cortez, with beautiful white-sand beaches.
www.baja.com/lugares/baja california/info_bahaiconcep.htm

COPACABANA PALACE, RIO
BRAZIL

Sumptuous Art Deco palace

One of Latin America's most memorable places to stay is located right on the world-famous Copacabana beach.
www.copacabanapalace.com.br

ACTIVE ADVENTURES

CAPE CHURCHILL Young male polar bears sparring

CAPE CHURCHILL
MANITOBA, CANADA

The undisputed polar bear capital of the world

Polar bears aplenty gather here to await the coming of the sea ice. Buggies will take you out onto the tundra for a close, safe encounter.
See pp234–5

BIG BEND NATIONAL PARK
TEXAS, USA

Rafting, Rio Grande style

Ride one of America's most famous rivers on a variety of rapids. Santa Elena canyon is the most common destination.
www.nps.gov/bibe

CLIMBING MOUNT WHITNEY
CALIFORNIA, USA

Conquer an amazing peak

Trek to the top of Mount Whitney, a challenging hike with superlative views from the summit.
www.nps.gov/seki/planyourvisit/whitney.htm

AQUÁRIO NATURAL
BRAZIL

Brazil's premier underwater wonderland in Bonito

Snorkel or dive amidst teeming shoals of tropical fish in the waters of this marine sanctuary.
www.amazonadventures.com/bonito.htm

GAULEY RIVER
WEST VIRGINIA, USA

Top white-water rafting destination

Raft down the free-flowing Gauley River, through scenic gorges and valleys, with several challenging class V+ rapids en route.
www.nps.gov/gari

FAMILY GETAWAYS

OAXACA Colorful sand picture

"In the gorgeous colonial city of Oaxaca, the celebrations are at their most vivid."

OAXACA
MEXICO

Kids will enjoy the macabre but joyous Day of The Dead

Feast on skulls and other ghoulish delights – chocolate of course – as Mexican families honor their dead with parties and celebration.
See pp252–3

CURAÇAO
CARIBBEAN

Dutch-style diminutive Caribbean island

Curaçao boasts plenty of kids' attractions including the Curaçao Seaquarium, Dolphin Academy, and an Ostrich Farm.
www.curacao.com

NAPLES
FLORIDA, USA

Holiday in Florida with a local flavor

Rent your own holiday home in this genuine Floridian town on the Gulf of Mexico coast, with sun-drenched beaches and calm waters.
www.naples-florida.com

SCOTTS BLUFF
NEBRASKA, USA

Family recreation on the Oregon Trail

The area around this famous Nebraskan landmark has loads of family activities, as well as Oregon Trail attractions.
www.visitscottsbluff.com

HALLOWEEN
NEW YORK CITY, USA

America's biggest Halloween celebrations

Join the crowds for the Big Apple's riotous Halloween party, with bands, parades, and people in spooky costumes.
www.halloween-nyc.com

GETTING THERE See map p313, H3
Churchill is not accessible by road. Calm Air flies daily from Winnipeg's international airport (www.calmair.com). Return fares start from US$1,000. The Muskeg Special train departs Winnipeg on Tuesday, Thursday, and Sunday. The journey time is about 36 hours, and return fares are around US$300.

GETTING AROUND
Everything in Churchill is within walking distance. Tundra vehicles take you to the bears.

WEATHER
Temperatures range from 40°F (5°C) to 5°F (-15°C), but a northerly windchill can make it feel much, much colder. Dress in layers.

ACCOMMODATIONS
To wake with the bears, Tundra Lodges are remote mobile bunkhouses, but are for tour groups only. There's a wide range of B&Bs.

Bear Country Inn is simple but cozy; doubles from US$140; bearcinn@mts.net

Polar Inn is warm and welcoming; doubles from US$195; www.polarinn.com

The Aurora Inn offers two-story apartments; doubles from US$235; www.aurora-inn.mb.ca

EATING OUT
Gypsy Bakery is a Churchill landmark serving northern delicacies like arctic char and caribou.

PRICE FOR TWO
Around US$1,800 per day, including return flights from Winnipeg, accommodation, food, and all tours, trips, and admissions.

FURTHER INFORMATION
www.polarbearalley.com

Prince of Wales Fort
Churchill was founded on the fur trade. In 1717, the Hudson's Bay Company built a trading post on the Churchill River, establishing ties with a nomadic tribe known as the Dené. In 1732, to solidify their grip on the area, they began work on a giant stone fortress, across the river from present-day Churchill. Hampered by the sub-arctic conditions, it was 40 years before Prince of Wales Fort was completed. Only ten years later, three French warships weighed anchor at the mouth of the Churchill River, and the under-manned post surrendered without firing a shot.

Confident and curious, bears walk right up to the vehicles, standing up and offering the chance to gaze deep into their eyes.

Main: Majestic adult polar bear taking his first steps of the winter out onto the frozen sea-ice of Hudson Bay

SEASON OF THE BEAR

POLAR BEAR CAPITAL OF THE WORLD – Churchill's nickname pretty much says it all. It's around 30 years since a local mechanic invented the first Tundra Buggy™, basically a big metal can on over-sized tires, and bounced out across the tundra in search of polar bears. Churchill now attracts visitors from all over the world for the first six weeks of winter, known locally as "bear season." It begins with a trickle of polar bears – and bear tourists. The bears, forced ashore three months previously by melting sea-ice, are hungry to hunt again for seals on frozen Hudson Bay. Churchill is the first place on the Bay where the sea freezes so, as each passing day grows colder and more ice builds, the trickle of bears becomes a flood. As they gather on the Cape, the human visitors follow, piling aboard lumbering tundra transports, eager to get up-close and personal with a polar bear. Confident and curious, bears walk right up to the vehicles, sometimes standing up and offering the chance to gaze deep into their brown and bloodshot eyes.

JAN
FEB
MAR
APR
MAY
JUN
JUL
AUG
SEP
OCT
DAY 1
DAY 2
DAY 3
DAY 4
DAY 5
NOV
DEC

Above: Bears and Buggy in a close encounter at sunset

POLAR BEAR DIARY

Polar bears can be spotted throughout October and early November, gathering along the coast and on Cape Churchill. By month's end, over 40 polar bears may be seen in one day. A trip to this far-flung outpost is bound to be costly but, after five days of wildlife encounters, you'll feel you've had a money-can't-buy experience.

Five Days in the Tundra

You're sure to want to get nose-to-nose with a polar bear as fast as possible! Head out on a tundra vehicle to the Churchill Wildlife Management Area in search of bears. This is by far the best way to see them in their natural environment.

A bus tour of the town and its environs explores the cultural and natural history of the "accessible Arctic." Learn about the fur trade and local history, and try to spot wildlife such as arctic foxes, arctic hares, and a strange, partridge-like bird called a ptarmigan.

Every day is different on the tundra. A second trip by tundra vehicle will give you just the right amount of "bear time." With luck you'll see a mother with her cubs (called coys), or watch young males in their ritual play-fight sparring.

Visit a northern trapping camp for a ride on a husky dog sled (or a training cart if there's no snow yet). Try some bannock, a Native-American flatbread, and hot chocolate before heading back to town. Later you could join a helicopter tour for an aerial view of Wapusk National Park of Canada and the forming sea-ice.

Spend your last day in town. The Eskimo Museum, one of North America's oldest and most extensive collections of Inuit sculpture and artifacts, is a true northern treasure. Visit the Parks Canada Visitor Centre for a glimpse inside a replica of a polar bear maternity den, and to learn more about Prince of Wales Fort and other historic sites in the area.

Dos and Don'ts

✓ Bring extra film, memory cards, and batteries. Polar bears eat up pictures and the cold eats up batteries.

✗ Don't expect the train to be on time! It often runs between 4 and 12 hours behind schedule.

✓ Be sure to get your passport stamped at the post office with Churchill's unique polar bear logo.

✓ Remember that group tours fill up a year in advance. Also, tour companies book almost all "bear season" hotel space at least a year ahead. Independent travelers can try checking for cancellations around midsummer.

Inset: Polar bear cub cleverly sheltering from the elements

Left (left to right): Young adult male bears play-fighting; team of husky sled-dogs; downtown Churchill; arctic fox, with its dense winter coat

Right: Arctic hare in white winter camouflage

Once the ice is stable they'll be gone but, at this time of year, bears are a constant presence around Churchill. "Polar Bear Alert" vehicles patrol the small town, and everyone has a bear-encounter story ready to tell, true or mostly true. You may even see a bear in the sky, as conservation officers perform a "bear lift," relocating a miscreant animal north along the coast by helicopter.

However, there is more to Churchill than polar bears. This northern outpost lies on the treeline, a transitional zone where the boreal forest gives way to barren tundra, and wildlife abounds. It's a place where a walk downtown may be accompanied by a red fox, and an arctic hare may hop past your restaurant window. It's a cultural meeting place too, in which three native cultures – the Cree, Dené, and Inuit – are linked by fur-trade history. Beaded mukluk boots sit alongside polar-bear T-shirts in gift stores. Roast caribou and poached arctic char vie with cheeseburgers on menus.

"Bear Season" can be crowded, chaotic, and cold. But there's something about Churchill, the place and the people, and something about being so incredibly close to wildlife in its natural habitat, that make this trip of a lifetime even more thrilling than you can possibly imagine.

GETTING THERE
See map p316, I3

Hancock County Airport is 12 miles (19 km) from Bar Harbor, with direct flights from Boston. Bangor International Airport is 50 miles (80 km) away, and has a shuttle service to Bar Harbor.

GETTING AROUND
Free Island Explorer Buses operate until mid-October, visiting major points of interest in the Park. A car offers more freedom to explore, and rental is available at both airports.

WEATHER
October is generally sunny and crisp, with highs around 58°F (14°C) and night-time lows of 38°F (3°C). It is often breezy, with rain always possible.

ACCOMMODATIONS
Bar Harbor Inn & Spa has a waterfront location within walking distance of shops and restaurants; doubles from US$190; www.barharborinn.com

Ullikana offers French country charm in a Tudor-style house at Bar Harbor; doubles from US$195; www.ullikana.com

The Claremont Hotel at Southwest Harbor is a historic shoreline resort; doubles from US$170; www.theclaremonthotel.com

EATING OUT
Maine is known for its excellent lobster, crab, and other seafood, as well as wild blueberry pie and cobbler. On the island, there's everything from fine dining options to ultra-casual eateries.

PRICE FOR TWO
US$500 per day, including accommodation, food, car rental and gas, and admissions.

FURTHER INFORMATION
www.barharborinfo.com

The Carriage Roads

In the early 1900s John D. Rockefeller Jr., a summer resident, decided to create a way for visitors to enjoy the island by horse-drawn carriage. He personally supervised the construction of over 45 miles (73 km) of Carriage Roads – delightful, gently-graded, winding crushed-stone lanes that afford wonderful views of sparkling water and tree-covered mountainsides. Today they are part of the Acadia National Park, a gift to the nation from Rockefeller.

FALL'S FIERY GRANDEUR

AN ISLAND OF MISTY MOUNTAINS, surrounded by miles of rugged coastline, Mount Desert is home to charmingly weathered New England villages nestled along deep coastal coves and fjord-like inlets. Over two-thirds of the island is preserved for all time as spectacular Acadia National Park. In fall, the island's woodlands explode with the finest crimsons, reds, and brilliant golds. Miles of groomed Carriage Roads, speckled with brilliantly hued leaves, meander through the woods, gently curving up the mountainsides to expose vistas of cerulean blue ponds below. Reveling in crisp fall air filled with the fragrance of the north woods, walkers, horseback riders, and cyclists follow these graceful paths across elegant stone bridges that span sparkling mountain streams. All roads eventually lead to Jordan Pond House, where afternoon tea and popovers on the lawn by the pond are an Acadia tradition.

Main: The still, clear waters of Eagle Lake

Above (top to bottom): Road through the Park; forest foliage on a Park trail; view over Cadillac Mountain

Bottom (left to right): Wooden bridge over the pond in Somesville; Bass Head Light; Bar Harbor restaurants; kayaking off Bar Harbor

Bar Harbor is the island's main town. Quaint and romantic, its seaside streets are lined with colorful shops, fine restaurants, and upscale galleries. Laughter and conversation fill the air as browsers admire Maine handicrafts, whimsical moose carvings, and warm woolen sweaters. Tour operators offer adventures for tomorrow's pleasure: a kayak trip along the coast; a boat ride to see whales and seals or catch lobsters; bicycle rental for exploring the Carriage Roads.

There are two things that you must do. First, take a leisurely drive along the scenic Park Loop Road through vibrant woodlands and along the stunning coastline. At Otter Point, climb down to the water's edge and savor the salt-laden breeze, crashing waves, and seagulls soaring overhead. Second, join the evening throngs at the summit of Cadillac Mountain, with panoramic vistas of the fiery woodlands and the island-dotted bay beyond. At sundown, visitors sit in quiet reverence, broken only by gentle applause as the sun dips below the horizon. Afterwards, relax in a cozy inn by a crackling fire, then snuggle under a goose-down comforter to the sound of waves rolling ashore.

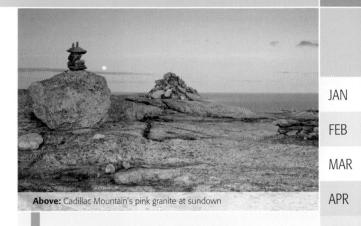

Above: Cadillac Mountain's pink granite at sundown

ISLANDER'S DIARY

The end of the first week of October is when fall foliage typically reaches its peak in Acadia National Park, but by mid-month many businesses will have closed for the season. Three days allows enough time to drive the scenic routes, discover the pretty villages, and also explore the Carriage Roads and hike or kayak for half a day.

Three Days in Acadia

Explore Acadia National Park by driving the Loop Road, stopping often for the views and to see Sand Beach, Thunder Hole, Otter Cliff, and Otter Cove. Head to Jordan Pond House and walk the Carriage Roads until mid-afternoon, and then enjoy popovers on the lawn at Jordan Pond House. Take a private horse-drawn carriage ride for two, and then drive to the top of Cadillac Mountain for the sunset. At Bar Harbor, have a romantic dinner at The Reading Room, which offers ocean-fresh seafood and continental cuisine.

DAY 1

Drive to Northeast Harbor and stroll the serene paths at the Asticou Azalea Garden, where autumn foliage forms a backdrop to the arched bridges, stone lanterns, and benches in the Japanese Garden. Continue into Northeast Harbor to visit the art galleries and shops, and have lunch. Follow the blue waters of Somes Sound into Somesville, where a lovely bridge arches across the pond and there's a great bookstore across the street. Continue on to Southwest Harbor and explore the shops and galleries before an early dinner at casually elegant Red Sky. Finally, drive out to Bass Head Light to watch the sun go down.

DAY 2

Take a hike in Acadia National Park, rent a bike in Bar Harbor and cycle round Eagle Lake, or join a kayak or boat trip run by one of the adventure shops in Bar Harbor. Later, head to Southwest Harbor for a relaxed lobster dinner on the deck at Beal's Lobster Pound, by the light of the setting sun.

DAY 3

Dos and Don'ts

✓ Reserve far in advance for the most luxurious rooms, as early October is one of the busiest times of the year.

✗ Don't bring fancy clothes, unless you like to dress up for dinner, as casual attire is standard everywhere.

✓ Walk or cycle along the Carriage Roads. Slow is best for appreciating the amazing stonework of the bridges, brilliant autumn foliage, and the many mountain and water views.

✗ Don't be surprised to hear the island's name pronounced "dessert" as well as "desert" – either is acceptable.

JAN

FEB

MAR

APR

MAY

JUN

JUL

AUG

SEP

OCT

NOV

DEC

GETTING THERE   See map p331, G2

GETTING THERE
International flights to Buenos Aires land at Ministro Pistarini Airport (known locally as Ezeiza), 35 miles (22 km) from downtown. The city is 45 minutes away by bus or taxi.

GETTING AROUND
Both the city's subway system and taxis are reliable, but the best way to explore Buenos Aires is on foot: distances are short and streets follow an easily navigable grid system.

WEATHER
October is springtime in Buenos Aires and the weather is great, with an average temperature range of 59–73°F (15–23°C).

ACCOMMODATIONS
The chic Home Hotel is located in the heart of Palermo Viejo; doubles from US$120; www.homebuenosaires.com

In San Telmo, the tango-inspired Mansión Dandi Royal offers doubles at US$130; www.mansiondandiroyal.com

The Hotel Emperador combines a central location with traditional elegance; doubles from US$220; www.hotelemperador.com.ar

EATING OUT
Steakhouses are ubiquitous in the city – try La Brigada for some juicy cuts. Palermo Viejo is the trendy dining zone, where restaurants serve modern Argentinian and fusion food.

PRICE FOR TWO
US$200–250 per day including food, local travel, accommodation, and admissions.

FURTHER INFORMATION
www.bue.gov.ar

City of the Dead

La Recoleta Cemetery has been the burial place of Argentina's elite since the 19th century. Presidents, generals, artists, and aristocracy lie interred here in mausoleums of granite and bronze adorned by marble sculptures of angels and crying mothers. Built tightly against each other, the tombs are visited via a labyrinth of streets and narrow passageways. The most famous resident here is Evita Perón, while the most beautiful tomb is said to be that of newspaper baron José C. Paz, crowned by allegorical sculptures of the immortal soul.

Above (left to right): Puerto Madero's modern waterfront; the glitzy façade of Galerios Pacifico; street performer in Dorrego Plaza, San Telmo
Main: Avenida 9 de Julio, one of the widest streets in the world

Above: Inside the lavish Teatro Colón

A SPIRITED CITY

Marble stairs snake up towards a 19th-century mansion, and in its lavishly cool interior, crystal chandeliers drip from a grand ceiling, antique smoked mirrors adorn wine-red walls, and luxurious velvet chaise longues sprawl across a mosaic floor. You weave through a crowd of hip, gorgeously dressed twenty- and thirty-somethings before reaching the bar and ordering cocktails from flirtatious staff. Welcome to Buenos Aires, South America's most intoxicating city.

In Argentina's beautiful capital, highlights come dizzyingly fast – the colorful houses of La Boca, built by Italian immigrants a century ago; the extraordinary La Recoleta Cemetery; the magnificent Teatro Colón opera house; and the iconic Obelisco. Wander the city and you might be forgiven for thinking you're in Europe, as you soak in tree-lined boulevards lined with *belle époque* mansions or wide avenues of French-style palaces and Parisian cupolas. In the central Tribunales lie great squares such as Plaza de Mayo, where Evita Perón once wooed the masses, while San Telmo is all about cobblestone streets, colonial façades, and whitewashed Spanish churches.

But peek beneath the city's European veneer and you'll discover the vibrancy of South America. It's in the electrifying atmosphere of its soccer stadiums, in the eroticism of the tango – the passionate dance that so embodies the Argentine psyche – and in the *porteños* (locals), who love leisurely lunches and hedonistic nights.

Most strikingly, Buenos Aires now has a flair for the chic and modern, which stands brashly against the city's backdrop of old-world grandeur. Find it in Palermo, home to the groundbreaking Museum of Modern Latin American Art (MALBA); in Puerto Madero, the slick new docklands complex; and in ultra-cool Palermo Viejo, with its hip stores, boutique hotels, and stylish bars. Once known as the Paris of South America, this wonderfully complex city is today more seductive than ever before.

In the central Tribunales lie great squares such as the Plaza de Mayo, where Evita Perón once wooed the masses.

Inset: Bronze plaques of Evita and Juan Perón at San Telmo's famous flea market
Below (left to right): Colorful Caminito Street; iconic figure in La Boca; Viva tango!

BUENOS AIRES DIARY

There is so much to see and do in Buenos Aires that you could stay for two weeks or more, but four days are sufficient to see the city's main sights, take in a tango show or a soccer game, and get a taste of its thriving nightlife. Remember that San Telmo is best visited on a Sunday, when its famous antiques fair takes place.

Four Days in the City of Tango

Spend the day in the downtown area, starting at Plaza de Mayo, and then walk along Avenida de Mayo to view the Plaza del Congreso and the Palacio del Congreso Nacional (National Congress) building.

After lunch, admire the monumental grandeur of Avenida 9 de Julio, and browse the shops on Florida, the main shopping street. In the evening, take a riverside stroll in Puerto Madero.

DAY 1

In La Recoleta, visit Evita Perón's tomb, view art at the National Museum of Fine Arts, and walk along Avenida Alvear, the city's most Parisian avenue. Later, stop for tea at the sumptuous Alvear Palace Hotel.

DAY 2

Discover the city's historical heart along the streets of San Telmo, with their crumbling mansions, Spanish churches, and antique shops. Stop at Plaza Dorrego for the antiques fair and join the tango dancers and buskers on Calle Dorrego.

In La Boca, browse Diego Maradona memorabilia on a stadium tour of La Bombonera, home to the Boca Juniors soccer team. Then it's back to San Telmo for dinner and a tango show.

DAY 3

Gorge on modern art at the MALBA and stroll the neighborhood's ornate parks and gardens. Wander the cobbled streets of Palermo Viejo, dipping in and out of designer shops. Stop for coffee at Plaza Serrano.

End your stay with a romantic dinner at one of Palermo Viejo's stylish restaurants.

DAY 4

Dos and Don'ts

✗ Don't think about dining early. Restaurants start getting pretty busy around 10pm.

✓ Take in the frenzied atmosphere of a local soccer match.

✗ Don't miss out on Malbec red wine – it's Argentina's best (see p216).

✓ Check out Night of the Museums (Noche de los Museos) – when over 100 of the city's museums, and many impressive private buildings, remain open for free all night.

JAN
FEB
MAR
APR
MAY
JUN
JUL
AUG
SEP
OCT
NOV
DEC

GETTING THERE   See map p321, E4
Las Vegas McCarran International Airport is served by a number of airlines, has car-rental agencies on site, and is conveniently located for a drive to the Grand Canyon.

GETTING AROUND
Once at the National Park, it is best to park your rented car and walk, or use the shuttle service or a taxi.

WEATHER
Sunny days with a chance of showers are normal for October. Expect average highs of 65°F (18°C) and lows of 36°F (2°C) on the South Rim, while the inner gorge has a high of 86°F (30°C) and a low of 58°F (14°C).

ACCOMMODATIONS
Designed in the 1930s, Bright Angel Lodge is centrally located, with doubles from US$86; www.grandcanyonlodges.com

Historic adobe hotel Thunderbird Lodge has doubles from US$112; www.tbirdlodge.com

El Tovar on the canyon rim offers rooms from US$186; www.grandcanyonlodges.com

EATING OUT
Meals are readily available at major hotels, with fine dining at El Tovar and family-style dining at Bright Angel Lodge. Prices vary, but good meals are available at all budget levels.

PRICE FOR TWO
About US$490 per day, including lodging, food, local travel, admission, and activities.

FURTHER INFORMATION
www.nps.gov/grca
www.nps.gov/cach

Desert View Watchtower

Inspired by the Ancestral Puebloans' ancient towers that can still be seen at Hovenweep, Wupatkti, and Mesa Verde, legendary architect Mary Ann Colter captured the essence of the past in the design of the Watchtower, which opened in 1933. On the edge of the canyon at Desert View, the four-story tower was designed to harmonize with the setting and provide exceptional views from the top floor. Inside, the walls are decorated with native paintings by Hopi artist, Fred Kabotie. Colter also designed five other Grand Canyon structures.

> The inner world of the canyon is fascinating, with unexplored side canyons, waterfalls, and hidden grottos.

Inset: Navajo artwork on the ceiling of the Desert View Watchtower

Above: Spider Rock Overlook at Canyon de Chelly

Right (left to right): A California condor in flight; a desert cactus in bloom; The Lookout – gift shop and observation station on the South Rim; awe-inspiring landscape of the Grand Canyon; tourist mesmerized by the grand views

Main: The Grand Canyon from Toroweap Point

THE GREAT ABYSS

GRAND DOESN'T EVEN BEGIN TO DO THIS CANYON JUSTICE. Carved by the mighty Colorado River and shaped by millennia of wind and rain, the Grand Canyon is an awe-inspiring natural work of art. From the South Rim, overwhelming vistas open up in every direction, stretching 15 miles (24 km) to the North Rim. Down below, the multihued rock walls descend over 5,000 ft (1,524 m) to a green ribbon of river on the canyon floor. At sunset, a hush settles over the throngs of visitors gathered along the Rim, mesmerized by the majestic play of light and color across the craggy rock formations.

The inner world of the canyon is even more fascinating, with unexplored side canyons, waterfalls, and hidden grottos where a lush, emerald-green world of plants is fed by trickling ground water. The few trails into the canyon twist as they descend through the strata of the ages, leading past weathered, red rock walls and towering spires of

Above: Tourists exploring the canyon on mules

JAN

FEB

MAR

APR

MAY

JUN

JUL

AUG

SEP

OCT

DAY 1

DAYS
2–4

DAYS
5–7

DAY 8

NOV

DEC

CANYON DIARY

October is an excellent time to visit the Grand Canyon, as the summer crowds are gone and the weather is pleasant. Five days are enough to drive to the national park and explore the inner depths of the canyon by foot or mule. If you have eight days, include a side trip to Canyon de Chelly and Monument Valley.

Eight Awe-Inspiring Days

Arrive in Las Vegas, explore the casino fantasyland, and dine at one of the city's restaurants.

On your first day of exploration around the canyon, get an early start and drive to the South Rim for the awesome view. Take a shuttle to the Information Plaza and arrive at Hopi Point in time for the sunset.

The next day, head to the corral for a two-day mule trip, or grab your backpack and go to the trailhead for an overnight hike.

Alternatively, take a short hike into the canyon and return to the village for lunch. After browsing the galleries and shops, take the shuttle to Hermit's Rest and walk the Rim Trail to Yaki Point.

Take a one-day mule trip into the canyon or drive to Desert View Watchtower for superb views, and explore the museum to learn about the canyon's Native Americans. Then, watch the sunset from Lipan Point.

Head farther east to Canyon de Chelly and take the South Rim drive to Spider Rock Overlook. Then drive out to Massacre Cave Overlook.

Hire a guide to see the ancient ruins up close. Later, hike the steep trail for views of the Whitehouse Ruins.

Take the unpaved 17-mile (27-km) loop drive along the plateau above the valley. Later, hire a Navajo guide and ride horseback through Monument Valley.

On your last day, head south through Oak Creek Canyon into the red rock country surrounding Sedona.

Dos and Don'ts

- ✗ Don't forget to book at least a year ahead for mule trips into the canyon, raft trips down the Colorado River, and backcountry camping permits.

- ✓ Dress in layers, wear sturdy hiking boots, and carry plenty of water and food when hiking.

- ✓ Find a time and place where you can be alone to soak in the serene beauty of the canyon.

- ✗ Don't miss views of the sunset over the canyon.

stone in hues of pink, buff, violet, and gray. The tapestry of life in the canyon is rich and conducive to hardy plant life; chipmunks scurry looking for food, gopher snakes glide across rocks, and overhead, the great California condor soars on the rising thermals.

The heart of the canyon is the Colorado River, where raging rapids challenge those who venture into its powerful torrents by canoe, kayak, and raft. Hikers descend to camp beside the river and each year, thousands mount sturdy mules to ride deep into the canyon to spend the night at the celebrated Phantom Ranch. On the canyon floor, the voice of the river dominates, with the constant sound of rushing rapids echoing off the walls.

Beyond the canyon's grandeur, other natural wonders await. At Canyon de Chelly, natives take visitors into their spiritual home to see the multistoried cliff dwellings built by Ancestral Puebloans 2,000 years ago. A half-day away lie the rock formations of Monument Valley, where you can wrap up your visit by exploring less-frequented corners by horseback or four-wheel-drive.

GETTING THERE
See map p318, B2

Balloon Fiesta Park is located in North Albuquerque, west of I-25, approximately 12 miles (19 km) north of Albuquerque Sunport, the state's only major airport.

GETTING AROUND
With little by way of public transport, visitors rely on rental cars. Two interstate highways pass through Albuquerque: the I-40 goes east-west, while the I-25 goes north-south.

WEATHER
The Balloon Fiesta is held when the weather is cool and crisp. Temperatures in the morning are around 40°F (4°C), warming up to about 70°F (21°C) in the afternoon.

ACCOMMODATIONS
Hotel Albuquerque in Old Town offers doubles from US$150; www.hhandr.com

The Hyatt Place Albuquerque/Uptown provides comfortable lodgings; doubles from US$150; www.hyatt.com

The Albuquerque Marriott Pyramid North is situated near Balloon Fiesta Park; doubles from US$200; www.marriott.com

EATING OUT
You'll find food at Balloon Fiesta Park, but for a real taste of New Mexico cuisine at US$15 a head, try eateries such as Little Anita's, or Perea's and Sadie's, both famous for the use of fiery green chilis in their culinary creations.

PRICE FOR TWO
About US$350 per day, including food, accommodation, and entertainment.

FURTHER INFORMATION
www.balloonfiesta.com

Let the Ballooning Begin...

One of the most interesting aspects of the world's largest balloon event is its rather unimpressive start. In 1972, to celebrate the 50th birthday of local radio station KOB, its manager planned the world's biggest congregation of hot-air balloons. He received a go-ahead from 21 pilots, but bad weather limited the turnout to just 13 balloons. Nevertheless, on April 8, 1972, 20,000 people gathered at a parking lot for the very first Balloon Fiesta. The number of registered balloons touched 1,019 in 2000, but has since been capped at 750 to ease aerial congestion.

Above (left and right): The Old Town Cat House, one of the city's most charming stores; Downtown Albuquerque aglow during late evening
Main: Preparing the balloon for the spectacular take-off known as Mass Ascension

Above: The Sandias, named for their watermelon colors at sunset

JAN
FEB
MAR
APR
MAY
JUN
JUL
AUG
SEP
OCT
FRI
SAT
SUN
NOV
DEC

UP, UP, AND AWAY!

IT'S A ROMANTIC PICTURE – a single hot-air balloon sailing gracefully and silently across the sky, floating with the clouds wherever the wind goes. There's something enchanting about ballooning, as the huge colorful orb just hangs in air as if by magic. If one balloon is magical, seeing hundreds of them dotting the sky in an endless canvas of abstract shapes and vivid colors is beyond words. But this is just what happens once every year at the thrilling Albuquerque International Balloon Fiesta, the largest convention of hot-air balloons in the world and also according to many, the world's most photographed event.

Held across nine days in early October, well past the sweltering conditions of summer, the fiesta is also the perfect time to enjoy New Mexico's natural beauty. Albuquerque, the state capital, pulls out all the stops, welcoming both visitors and participants from all over the world. From building-sized liquor bottles to mythical creatures and cartoon characters, balloons in shapes previously unimagined fill the barren desert sky as the crowds gaze in amazement from below.

Those hoping to catch the best of the action rise at the crack of dawn, when more than 700 balloons lift off simultaneously. Roughly the size of 54 football fields, the Balloon Fiesta Park accommodates the huge crowds the festival draws with absolute ease. When you're not staring up at the spectacle, weave your way through countless docked balloons, chat with pilots, capture breathtaking photographs, and sample traditional New Mexican fare, such as warm, puffy Navajo fry bread and steaming tortilla soup. Enjoy a live musical performance as you eat. At night, stand in awe of the Balloon Glow, as hundreds of balloons on the ground light up all at once from the glow of their burners. Once the field clears, a lively fireworks display wraps up the evening with a bang.

> If one balloon is magical, seeing hundreds of them dotting the sky in an endless canvas of shapes and colors is beyond words.

Inset: Balloons in the sky: dabs of color on a clear, blue canvas
Below (left to right): Balloon Fiesta Park in the thick of activity; Balloon Glow, a magical nocturnal event

NEW MEXICO DIARY

Easily the state's largest festival, the Balloon Fiesta is held every October, when tourists flood Albuquerque and surrounding regions, leaving hotels and restaurants overbooked. If the crowds prove too much, you can always escape north to Santa Fe (see pp184–5), a lovely city known for its history and beauty.

A Weekend in Albuquerque

FRI Ease into the weekend by exploring Albuquerque's Old Town, stopping at shops selling authentic Native American and southwestern wares. Chow down the city's most beloved burger at Bob's, known for its hot green-chili sauce. At sundown, head to the fiesta for Balloon Glow, as grounded balloons glow in the light of their propane burners. Finish off with a bite and a brew at Monte Vista Fire Station, a relaxed hangout housed in a converted Depression-era firehouse.

SAT Rise early to watch the Dawn Patrol, which begins around 6am. Soon thereafter, the Mass Ascension begins. Stroll the grounds as you munch on fresh New Mexican fry bread. Around noon, beat the crowds and explore the area around Albuquerque. If time and the weather are on your side, drive along the 52-mile (84-km) "Turquoise Trail" on the east side of the picturesque Sandia Mountains.

SUN Kickstart your day with a balloon ride, offered by Rainbow Ryders. Then head outside the grounds and visit the Anderson-Abruzzo Albuquerque International Balloon Museum (free on Sunday mornings). Later, enjoy first-rate Texas barbecue and great views of the city as you fill up at County Line BBQ. Be sure to stop by the Bien Mur Indian Market Center for Native American jewelry, pottery, and folk art to take back home.

Dos and Don'ts

✓ Before heading out for the day, check the television or the Internet for the "balloon report." Each year, at least one day of the fiesta is usually called off due to inclement weather.

✓ Brace yourself for the weekend crowds – waiting lines, parking, and traffic can be quite trying on the nerves.

✗ Don't forget to carry enough supplies for your camera – you'll likely end up snapping more photos than expected.

✓ If you're at the fiesta at night, carry a flashlight; traversing the grounds (and finding your car) may prove difficult.

✓ Dress warmly – pre-dawn conditions can be chilly.

GETTING THERE   See map p331, C8

International flights land at Chile's capital Santiago. From there fly south to Punta Arenas, the departure point for your cruise aboard the *Mare Australis* cruise ship.

GETTING AROUND

Each day of the cruise features onshore excursions which include forest hikes, wildlife observation, and glacier visits. The Argentine city of Ushuaia is easily explored on foot.

WEATHER

In October expect temperatures of 41–59°F (5–15°C) with rain. Cabo de Hornos and Canal Beagle are prone to rough winds.

ACCOMMODATIONS

In Punta Arenas, Hotel Nogueira is a restored century-old mansion; doubles from US$190; www.hotelnogueira.com

The stylish Hotel Cabo de Hornos has rooms with views of the Magellan Strait; doubles from US$200; www.hoteles-australis.com

The *Mare Australis* cruise ship has three cabin categories with most cabins falling within the highest price band, so book well in advance for scarcer cheaper options.

EATING OUT

Seafood is the specialty in Punta Arenas and Ushuaia. Onboard, meals are lavish four-course affairs accompanied by Chilean wines.

PRICE FOR TWO

A seven-night cruise, including food, accommodation, and Zodiac excursions costs about US$5,000 per couple.

FURTHER INFORMATION

www.australis.com

Domestic Bliss in the Wild

Mid-October is nesting season for Magellanic penguins, which migrate here. During a 40-day incubation period these monogamous birds are models of dual parenting. The male and female incubate eggs in shifts, each spending 15–20 days at sea to feed. Once the eggs hatch, the parents share duties. This cycle is repeated the next year. The male arrives first to reclaim the same burrow. Then the female follows, calling out to her mate. If one of the birds perishes while migrating, it takes the other up to two years to find a new partner.

> In this magnificent natural theater, great vertical rock faces rise from the sea, and gushing waterfalls plunge into deep channels.

Main: A cruise ship glides past a wall of glaciers in southern Patagonia

DRAMA IN ICE

SAILING THE SOUTH PATAGONIAN FJORDS, you glide slowly toward the bottom of the world, drifting past one stunning scene after another. In this magnificent natural theater, great vertical rock faces rise from the sea, gushing waterfalls plunge into deep channels, and winds howl off massive blue-white glaciers which spill majestically into crystalline blue bays. Elephant seals and Magellanic penguins converge noisily on rugged shorelines, under the watchful gaze of predatory marine birds that dive and soar in search of prey.

Weaving a labyrinthine course through a network of channels, islets, and inlets, and navigating fabled straits, the luxury liners that cruise the fjords of southern Patagonia take you up close to breathtaking scenery and marine wildlife. Cruises start at the city of Punta Arenas in southern Chile and voyage southward toward Cape Horn (Cabo de Hornos), the wind-lashed outcrop that marks the end of the Americas, beyond which lies only Antarctica.

Above: A full moon over the town of Punta Arenas

Inset: A natural glacier bridge

Left (left to right): Glaciar Balmaceda; boats anchored at Ushuaia; Glaciar Pía; tourists at a monument at Cabo de Hornos

Right: Cabo de Hornos lighthouse

ICEBOUND DIARY

October is springtime in the southern hemisphere, which means longer daylight hours and magnificent light and scenery. A seven-night cruise of the southern Patagonian fjords combines a four-night trip south and east and then a three-night sail back, starting and ending in Punta Arenas.

Eight Days in the Fjords

DAY 1 Walk the streets of Punta Arenas before you depart to cross the Estrecho de Magallanes (Strait of Magellan).

DAY 2 Cruise the Seno Almirantazgo to Bahía Ainsworth. In the shadow of the Glaciar Marinelli, disembark to see an elephant seal colony. Then take a Zodiac excursion to the Islote Tucker shores, a haven for colonies of Magellanic penguins, sea lions, and cormorants.

DAY 3 Crossing the Seno Pía, the roar of breaking ice heralds your arrival at Glaciar Pía. Back on ship, sail Canal Beagle (Beagle Channel), passing "Glacier Avenue," and watch as glaciers fall from the Cordillera Darwin.

DAY 4 Drink in the view at the end of the world – Cabo de Hornos. Return northward and stroll the ruins of a native settlement at historic Bahía Wulaia.

DAY 5 Arrive at Ushuaia, the world's southernmost city and visit the Museo Marítimo, Argentina's Alcatraz.

DAY 6 The second leg of the cruise starts by revisiting Cabo de Hornos and Bahía Wulaia. At the Cape view a monument to fallen sailors. From the bay hike through virgin Magellanic forest.

DAY 7 Cruise through narrow channels with more glacial vistas. At night, enjoy the Captain's farewell dinner.

DAY 8 Before returning to Punta Arenas, sail Canal Gabriel to Isla Magdalena, home to a breeding colony of Magellanic penguins.

Dos and Don'ts

✓ Head to top deck around midnight for dreamy views of peaks and glaciers illuminated by the moon and stars.

✗ Don't expect stuffy formality on this cruise. The onboard atmosphere is relaxed and dress code is informal. However, do bring smart clothes for the farewell dinner.

✓ Be prepared for seasickness; rounding Cape Horn, the going can be very rough.

✓ Try the *centolla* (king crab) in Ushuaia, a regional specialty.

✓ Bring high-factor sunblock. The ozone layer is paper-thin and disappears almost completely in October–March.

JAN
FEB
MAR
APR
MAY
JUN
JUL
AUG
SEP
OCT
NOV
DEC

As you sail, Zodiac excursions offer vistas of the fjords from water level. You can even venture onshore to observe the stunning flora and fauna. In the playful company of pods of dolphins, your boat skirts the shorelines of small islets and coves where colonies of elephant seals and sea lions congregate in October to breed. Onshore hikes reveal lush forests and sheltered beaches with nesting colonies of cormorants and Magellanic penguins. Other excursions capture the thrilling drama of the Patagonian Fjords. Close to the great Glaciar Pía, in the shadow of jagged-white peaks, one huge chunk of ice after another breaks away from the glacier's towering front wall to tumble into the frigid waters of Bahía Pía in a concerto of thunderous cracks and booms.

After four days of navigating sheltered waters you reach the desolately beautiful Cape Horn. Here, looking out across the Cape to where the Atlantic and Pacific oceans collide, the sensation is one of utter remoteness. Tiny ice floes pepper the powerful sea and fierce, howling winds that once thwarted many an expedition lash against steep, ragged cliffs. Antarctica and the end of the Earth are just 500 miles (800 km) away.

GETTING THERE   See map p320, A3
The closest large airport is in Portland, served by most major airlines. Rent a car here and follow the Columbia River northwest to Astoria along scenic Route 30 (a 2-hour trip).

GETTING AROUND
Driving is the only option for the coastal route.

WEATHER
October highs range between 50 and 60°F (10 and 15°C) , with lows in the mid-40s (around 7°C). Rain is always a possibility.

ACCOMMODATIONS
Ecola Beach Lodge in Cannon Beach offers rooms and suites near the beach; doubles from US$72; www.cannonbeachlodge.com

The Ester Lee in Lincoln City rents basic but charming seaview cottages with fireplaces from US$55 a night; www.esterlee.com

Ireland's Rustic Lodge in Gold Beach has oceanfront suites from US$99 a night; www.irelandsrusticlodges.com

EATING OUT
Eat your fill of fresh seafood: razor clams, Dungeness crab, and Yaquina Bay oysters are local favorites. Mo's, in Cannon Beach, and elsewhere along the coast, is renowned for its clam chowder and oyster stew. Stephanie Inn in Cannon Beach serves the finest food on the coast, on a US$49 prix-fixe dinner menu.

PRICE FOR TWO
Allow around US$300 per day, including accommodation, car rental, gas, food, and any entry fees.

FURTHER INFORMATION
ww.visittheoregoncoast.com

The Haunted Lighthouse

Tall tales of buried pirate treasure and phantom galleons abound on the mist-shrouded Oregon coast, and a favorite is that of the ghost of Rue, the wife of a 19th-century lighthouse keeper at Heceta Head. One day (so the story goes) Rue sent her daughter out to play, and the child never returned, believed lost to the waves crashing against the cliffs far below the lighthouse. Silver-haired Rue, wearing a black dress, apparently still awaits her daughter's return, and is seen peering out of the lighthouse windows and heard opening and closing doors.

Above (left to right): Cape Kiwanda State Park; fall colors on the coastal road; Haystack Rock, Cannon Beach
Main: Horseback riding on Bandon Beach

Above: Ecola State Park

JAN
FEB
MAR
APR
MAY
JUN
JUL
AUG
SEP
OCT
NOV
DEC

DAY 1
DAY 2
DAY 3
DAY 4

OREGON EXPLORATIONS

"Ocean in view, oh the joy," the explorer William Clark enthused into his diary in 1805 upon first sighting the Pacific Ocean crashing into the Oregon coast. This is one of America's most scenic coastlines and evokes similar excitement in many a modern-day traveler. Every bend in the road along the 350-mile (563-km) length of Highway 101 seems to reveal yet another natural wonder – the waves breaking against the cliffs of Cape Kiwanda, the 40-mile-long (65-km) expanse of sand dunes south of Florence, the heights of Cape Perpetua carpeted in old-growth rain forests, sea stacks rising from the sea off the coast at Bandon, to mention but a few. A drive along this stretch of coast involves pulling over at dozens of viewpoints and scenic lookouts simply to admire a view. It is equally tempting to stop and explore the beaches and forest trails along the way – a walk along the Umpqua Scenic Dunes Trail south of Florence and into the Pacific on a narrow spit of lava at Yaquina Head Outstanding Natural Area, where you'll get to keep company with sea lions, are among the possibilities. In places, the coastline seems utterly remote, with nothing in sight but surf, sand, and forests growing right to the edge of the sea. It's easy to envisage the past, when the galleons of Sir Francis Drake and Juan de Fuca sailed past these headlands and Lewis and Clark built a fort at the end of their momentous transcontinental journey. The realization that these timeless landscapes have fascinated the great explorers add all the more zest to your own discovery of this magical coastline.

A journey along the Oregon coastline is loaded with sensory experiences – the scent of evergreens in Ecola State Park mingling with the tang of sea brine, the roar of surf drowning out the screech of gulls at Cape Meares, and the spectacle of sea lions sunning on the rocks beneath the lighthouse at Heceta Head. All make for one amazing and memorable road trip.

> In places, the coastline seems utterly remote, with nothing in sight but surf, sand, and forests growing right to the edge of the sea.

Inset: Green anemones and starfish in a tidepool
Below (left and right): Fishing boats, Yaquina Bay; Highway 101 at Cape Sebastian

COASTAL DIARY

Many diversions await you along the Oregon coast, so allow four days for the 350-mile (563-km) drive. At this time of year, you can enjoy near-deserted beaches and hike in forests where vine maples and other deciduous trees are putting on a brilliant show of fall color.

Four Days on the Road

Arrive in Astoria, where the Columbia River Maritime Museum chronicles the region's seagoing past. Just south of town, in Fort Clatsop National Memorial, is an authentic recreation of the stockade where 19th-century American explorers Lewis and Clark passed the winter of 1805–6. Pull into Cannon Beach in time for a sunset walk along the beach to Haystack Rock.

Spend the morning hiking the trails that crisscross Ecola State Park, a 1,100-ft (335-m) headland that is often shrouded in mist. Continue south through Tillamook, famous for cheddar cheese, and along the Three Capes Scenic Route (Capes Kiwanda, Meares, and Lookout), where viewpoints are perched high above the crashing surf, to Lincoln City.

Begin the day with a climb through the rain forests and maritime prairies of Cascade Head Preserve. Then head south through the fishing port of Depoe Bay, where at Devil's Punchbowl the thundering sea blasts through rocky channels and erupts in geysers. Stop in Newport for visits to the Oregon Coast Aquarium and Yaquina Head, and plan to arrive in Yachats in time for sunset.

Round Cape Perpetua, the highest coastal viewpoint, to Heceta Head State Park, where trails overlook a lighthouse. From Florence, sand dunes stretch south for 40 miles (65 km), and at Bandon, craggy sea stacks rise out of the surf. The route rounds Cape Blanco, the westernmost point in the western United States, and passes through forests before coming to Gold Beach, where the Rogue River flows into the sea.

Dos and Don'ts

✓ Indulge in the coast's culinary delights. These include fresh bounty such as oysters, Dungeness crabs, and salmon, as well as rich cheddar cheese from the Tillamook County Creamery and saltwater taffy made up and down the coast.

✗ Don't disturb starfish, sea urchins, and other sea life that you will encounter around tidal pools.

✓ Bring a sweater, because sea breezes can be brisk.

✓ Be careful of sneaker waves (which rush in unexpectedly).

✓ Bring binoculars to catch a glimpse of sea lions and other creatures.

✓ Wear waterproof shoes on beach walks.

GARDEN ISLAND

FOR SUCH A TINY SPECK OF AN ISLAND, Kaua'i holds a breathtaking diversity of landscapes. No other place in Hawai'i so perfectly fulfils dreams of a pristine Polynesian paradise as this island, where Pacific surf rolls on to golden beaches fringed by palm trees and backed by densely forested valleys and spectacular, rugged mountains. Exploring Kaua'i is not so much about soaking in the views as immersing yourself in its ravishing wildernesses.

Kaua'i's finest hike, the tough 11-mile (18-km) Kalalau Trail, threads its way along the Nā Pali cliffs, on the northern coast. From the moment the trail climbs away from the alluring Kē'ē Beach, 7 miles (11 km) beyond Hanalei, you feel you're leaving civilization behind. Barefoot warriors once ran this path to bring news to chiefs, while the platforms of lava boulders below mark where hula was

Main: Waipoo Falls in Waimea Canyon

The Birds of Kaua'i

Having emerged from the ocean as barren lava thousands of miles from land, Hawai'i has evolved its own unique wildlife. Before human contact, new species evolved every 100,000 years. Most of Hawai'i's indigenous birds are now extinct, due to hunting and the arrival of new predators and diseases. Kaua'i's upland wildernesses, though, are still rich in native birds. Eagle-eyed hikers in Kōke'e State Park may spot such rare species as the 'i'iwi, a scarlet honey-creeper, the red and black 'apapane (*above*), and the tiny, greenish-yellow 'anianiau.

Left (left and right): Diver observing green sea turtles; beauty in bloom – another common sight in flora-rich Kaua'i

Right: Snorkelers at Lumaha'i Beach

danced for the first time. Each turn opens up new vistas of the precipitous, furrowed cliffs that lie ahead, pleated in gigantic folds and topped by eroded pinnacles so sheer that only velvet moss can cling to them. As you pick your way across waterfalls that cascade from the slopes, white tropic-birds soar overhead. The trail drops back to sea level after a point, where you wade a rapid stream to reach Hanakāpī'ai Beach. In its last few miles, the trail is nerve-wracking at times, consisting of a groove worn into the sloping cliff face. Most day-hikers turn back after exploring Hanakāpī'ai Valley, but if you have a permit – and a head for heights – proceed to camp in Kalalau Valley.

It's possible to drive to the highest peak above Kalalau Valley, but it's only accessible from the south side of the island. Follow the road to the top of Waimea Canyon – an awe-inspiring chasm that nearly splits Kaua'i in two – and you're in Kōke'e State Park, where two overlooks command stunning views over Kalalau Valley, a truly wild and rugged Garden of Eden.

Above: Giant roots of a fig tree at Allerton Garden

Below: A hiker on the verdant Kalalau Trail

Above: The Nā Pali cliffs on Kaua'i

ALOHA DIARY

If you stay less than a week in Kaua'i, you'll regret it – especially in October, when the crowds have gone. The Nā Pali cliffs are a must-see from every angle – on foot, along the Kalalau Trail, from Kōke'e State Park, and by boat. No one can resist the beaches, so keep a few days aside to simply stretch out on the sands.

Seven Days in Kaua'i

DAY 1 Fly in to Līhu'e airport, drive a rental car to your hotel, and enjoy a fine Pacific Rim dinner.

DAY 2 Take a leisurely drive along the North Shore, stopping at beaches like Secret Beach, Lumaha'i, and Kē'ē, with a break for lunch and shopping in funky Hanalei.

DAY 3 Park early at Kē'ē Beach for a full day's hike along the Kalalau Trail. With a permit from the State Parks Office in Līhu'e, you can go beyond the spectacular Hanakāpī'ai Beach, either inland to the waterfalls or farther along the cliff face.

DAY 4 Take a half-day boat trip on the coast of Nā Pali, ideally starting at Hanalei and including a long snorkel stop.

DAY 5 Drive round to the West Shore and up Waimea Canyon. At the top of Kōke'e State Park, swoon at the mile-high views of Kalalau Valley, before hiking the boardwalk of the Alaka'i Swamp Trail, deep into the island's interior.

DAY 6 Drive up Waimea Canyon once more, so you can hike through the rain forest along the Awa'awapuhi Trail, which leads to a staggering overlook of the sinuous Awa'awapuhi ("slippery eel") Valley.

DAY 7 Take an early-morning helicopter ride for spectacular views of the island. Then, spend the day on South Shore, combining a few hours on Po'ipū Beach with a tour of the lush, orchid-laden Allerton Garden in the lovely Lāwa'i Valley.

Dos and Don'ts

✗ Don't take a Nā Pali boat tour from the West Shore if boats are running from Hanalei.

✓ Bite the bullet and pay for a helicopter tour – it's the best way to see much of Kaua'i's most stupendous scenery.

✗ Don't leave too little time to hike in Kōke'e State Park; allow a full day for the expedition to the top of Waimea Canyon and back.

✓ Wear sturdy hiking boots on the Kalalau Trail; the going is muddy and rough.

JAN
FEB
MAR
APR
MAY
JUN
JUL
AUG
SEP
OCT
NOV
DEC

GETTING THERE   See map p321, B3, C5

Los Angeles, San Diego, and San Francisco international airports are served by scores of domestic and international flights.

GETTING AROUND

Car rental is the only practical and affordable way to visit the various wineries, but whoever drives should drink as little as possible.

WEATHER

October is one of the sunniest times of the year, with temperatures above 82°F (28°C) in the wine valleys. The vines are turned out in their gold and crimson fall colors.

ACCOMMODATIONS

Southwestern decor and a golf course setting at Temecula Creek Inn, Temecula; doubles from US$149; www.temeculacreekinn.com

The Cozy Wine Valley Inn in Solvang is close to many wine-tasting rooms; doubles from US$89; www.winevalleyinn.com

Romantic Inn at Depot Hill, Capitola is close to the Santa Cruz wine district; doubles from US$189; www.innatdepothill.com

EATING OUT

California has a world-famous reputation for its food, including nouvelle cuisine. A great meal will cost about US$50 for two.

PRICE FOR TWO

US$350–400 per day includes food, accommodation, car rental, and sightseeing.

FURTHER INFORMATION

www.scmwa.com
www.sbcountywines.com
www.winecountry.com

California Cuisine

The roots of sophisticated cuisine in California go back to the launch of *Sunset* magazine in 1898. The publication embraced the state's multi-ethnic traditions and popularized the use of fresh products from one's own kitchen garden. By the 1970s, these products fused with a search for pure flavors in cooking. Innovative and laboriously prepared according to French traditions, a typical meal might include oyster and caviar on pearl tapioca custard and duck *ragoût* with red wine and pancetta, carrots, turnips, pearl onions, and mushrooms.

California is a wine-lover's haven – numerous wineries are sprinkled through the Golden State, like clusters of grapes on a rambling vine.

Main: The sun sets over a Napa Valley vineyard

LAND OF PLENTY

As if California weren't blessed enough, the state's passion for viticulture is given a helping hand by nature; a range of microclimates and soil conditions result in wines that are renowned all over the world. With so many distinct regions to choose from, California is a wine-lover's heaven unparalleled except, perhaps, by the famed traditional wine regions of France, Spain, and Italy. The number of wineries continues to bloom: over 750 wineries are sprinkled throughout the Golden State like clusters of grapes on a rambling vine.

Napa and Sonoma Valleys are so popular with wine-lovers that weekends bring more traffic than stomping feet in a winery crush. The popularity has led to a Disney effect, with some wineries perhaps becoming a touch too glitzy. More reason, therefore, to escape the well-trodden path and venture into unsung wine districts specializing in grape varieties that make the most of the specific geography and climate of particular regions. The unusual

Above: Grapes in a vineyard in Napa Valley

WINE-LOVER'S DIARY

Fall is when California wine country is at its best. The vines explode with color and the weather is often at its warmest without a cloud in sight. And the wineries are busy crushing or bottling, making a visit engrossing. Eight days is a minimum for enjoying the state's best wine-growing regions, including upcoming areas.

Eight Days on a Tasting Tour

DAY 1
After a day or two enjoying LA, drive south to Temecula, an evolving wine district at 1,500 ft (460 m). Try the Bella Vista Winery, the region's first commercial vineyard.

DAYS 2–3
Journey up the coast to Santa Barbara, a lively beach town. Inland, the Santa Ynez Valley has more than 40 wineries, most scattered along US101. Be sure to visit the charming towns of Solvang and Los Olivos to browse antiques. Rise early next day for a scenic balloon ride over the valley before exploring some more wineries.

DAYS 4–5
Take in the stunning coastal scenery along Hwy 1. Arrive in Santa Cruz by mid-afternoon, allowing for time to savor the vineyards and wineries of Soquel. One place not to be missed is the family-run Bargetto Winery. Cross the Coast Range mountains the next day and drop by San Mateo to visit the Thomas Fogarty Winery, located on a mountaintop.

DAYS 6–7
The twin valleys of Napa and Sonoma await you. You're spoiled for choice, with scores of fine wineries to tempt your palate. High on your list in Napa include the Hess Collection Winery for its remarkable art, Francis Ford Coppola's Rubicon Estate, and the new and outstanding Villa Ca'toga. For a lovely picnic, stop at Sattui for cheeses and cold cuts. In Sonoma, between winery visits, see the historic sites, such as Sonoma Barracks.

DAY 8
Travel north to the Russian River region, where Korbel Champagne Cellars provides an insight into the art of making sparkling wines.

Dos and Don'ts

✓ Read up on the art and science of wine-tasting before you set out. A little education will help you gain far more from your experience.

✗ Don't restrict yourself to just one region. California's wines are amazingly diverse.

✓ Do be cautious about how much you drink. Pace yourself and drink plenty of water.

✓ Splurge on a great meal. Some of the best restaurants in California are in wine country.

JAN
FEB
MAR
APR
MAY
JUN
JUL
AUG
SEP
OCT
NOV
DEC

Inset: A lush vineyard seen through a glass of wine

Left (left to right): A hot-air balloon gliding over vineyards; colorful houses in Danish-influenced Solvang; wine barrels in the cellar at Opus One Winery, Napa Valley

Right (left to right): Grape vines clad in fall colors in Santa Barbara wine country; rolling fields of Hilly Vineyards in Esparto county

east-west orientation of the coastal mountains around Santa Barbara permits the flow of ocean fog and cool breezes perfect for the cultivation of Pinot Noir. The mountain vineyards of the Sierra foothills are ideal for grape varieties such as Syrah, Zinfandel, and Sauvignon Blanc. For oenophiles, as for everybody else, the superb juxtaposition of valleys and mountains is a bonus.

A leisurely drive through the region allows you to enjoy the wine-making experience while appreciating distinct appellations and the dazzling colors during fall harvest. Most wineries have tasting rooms, some offer guided tours, while others are known as much for their spectacular art as for their labels. Smaller wineries may require an appointment, but the person pouring the wine may be the wine-maker himself. And almost all wineries host events, from tastings to dinners.

Plan on visiting four to five wineries each day, with overnight stays in country inns. For a comprehensive wine adventure, a recommended stretch is from the southernmost wineries of Temecula, south of the Los Angeles sprawl, to the ocean-cooled valleys of the Russian River and Mendocino north of Napa, with their world-class Rieslings.

GETTING THERE   See map p323, F6
Oaxaca is in Mexico, 250 miles (400 km) southeast of the capital, Mexico City. Oaxaca's airport has a few international flights from the US, but travelers usually arrive via a domestic flight from Mexico City. Taxis and minibuses cover the 6.5 km (4 miles) between airport and city.

GETTING AROUND
Taxis, *colectivos* (shared taxis), and crowded, stop-anywhere buses run out to the villages and archeological sites outside the city.

WEATHER
By late October, summer rains are more or less over. Temperatures reach a pleasant 77°F (25°C) by day, cooling to around 57°F (14°C) at night.

ACCOMMODATIONS
Hotel Las Golondrinas is a lovely little hotel; doubles from US$100; tel. (951) 514 3298.

Hostal de la Noria, is a converted colonial mansion in the heart of Oaxaca; doubles from US$100; www.hostaldelanoria.com

Misión de los Angeles is a roomy hotel; family suites from US$180; www.hotelesmision.com.mx

EATING OUT
Specialties include the city's famed seven *moles* (sauces), grasshopper, and even the corn mold called *huitlacoche*. Try the Restaurante Los Danzantes, which offers innovative dishes from US$10 in an avant-garde setting.

PRICE FOR A FAMILY OF FOUR
US$300–400 per day including accommodation, food, local travel, and admissions.

FURTHER INFORMATION
www.visitmexico.com

DAY OF THE DEAD

THIS MOST MEXICAN OF FIESTAS IS A TRULY SUPERNATURAL EVENT where the dead return to earth to commune with their living relatives. In the colonial city of Oaxaca, full of beautiful churches and mansions built by the Spanish colonists, and surrounded by indigenous villages where even more ancient beliefs still thrive, the celebrations are at their most vivid.

Mexicans generally consider death to be a continuity, a transition into another realm, rather than an ending. And, happily, the dead come back to visit their nearest and dearest every year on All Souls' Day (November 2) – more commonly referred to as *Dia de los Muertos* (Day of the Dead). In Oaxaca the deceased are believed to arrive back at 3pm on November 1

> In the gorgeous colonial city of Oaxaca … surrounded by indigenous villages where ancient beliefs still thrive, the celebrations are at their most vivid.

and they stay for 24 hours. The preceding 24 hours are for the return of those who died as children, known as *angelitos* (little angels).

The reunion between the living and the dead is at least as joyful as it is poignant, and the atmosphere in homes and cemeteries can be amazingly animated and happy. To welcome their dead, families create elaborate "altars of the dead" in their homes. A table is set under an arch of palm leaves, flowers, and fruits, and is adorned with photos of the dead, saints' images, candles, flowers, favorite foods, drinks, even cigarettes, for the deceased to enjoy. And just to help returnees know they've found the right house, there'll be chocolate or sugar skulls, often inscribed with their names, and miniature skeletons engaged in the kind of things the deceased used to do – dancing, playing soccer, riding a bicycle.

Families also decorate loved ones' graves – with more flowers, candles, photos, drinks, and miniature skulls and skeletons – and will spend hours in graveyards communing with the dead on the afternoon and evening of November 1, even staying for night-long vigils and sharing food and drink with friends and relatives. The magical sight of a cemetery glittering with hundreds of candles, the buzz of talk among the crowds of excited, often joyful people, and the music and dancing that accompany these reunions, lingers in the memory.

Main: Traditional papier-mâché skeleton colorfully decorated with animals and plants
Inset: Zapotec architecture at Monte Albán near Oaxaca
Below (left and right): Carpet of colored sand; costume parade in the Zócalo

Cults of the Dead

All of Mexico's many pre-Hispanic civilizations – the Aztecs, the Maya, the Zapotecs, the Mixtecs and others – believed in forms of afterlife and performed rituals in honour of the dead, often involving feasts and offerings to the departed. Spanish colonial missionaries were able to reinterpret these activities under the umbrella of All Souls' Day, when Catholics pray for departed souls – hence the November 2 date for the Day of the Dead. However, strong elements of the pre-Hispanic ritual beliefs still remain in the way the fiesta is celebrated.

JAN

FEB

MAR

APR

MAY

JUN

JUL

AUG

SEP

OCT

NOV

DEC

Above: Child wrapped in local textiles at a market in Oaxaca

FIESTA DIARY

Oaxaca is the best place to see the Day of the Dead celebrations. Activities run from October 31 to November 2; if you give yourself six days you can experience the essence of this unique event and explore the city and its fascinating surroundings, or extend your trip by visiting Yucatán (*see pp70–71*).

Six Days with the Spirits

Soak up the atmosphere in the Zócalo, the city's leafy central square. Stroll up Calle Alcalá to the lavish Santo Domingo church. See the Market of the Dead, where special flowers, foods, papier-mâché skeletons, and chocolate and candy skulls are sold.

OCT 29

For a different perspective on the Day of the Dead Markets, head out of Oaxaca to one of the local villages. The biggest markets include those at Zaachila, Ocotlán, and Tlacolula – but check what day they are held on as it does vary from place to place.

OCT 30

Back in town, the fascinating Museum of Oaxacan Cultures is worth a look, and take in any Day of the Dead dancing or theater in the evening.

See the altars of the dead in your hotel and in local restaurants. After dark, visit the nearby village cemeteries of Santa Cruz Xoxocatlán and Santa María Atzompa – aglow with candles and full of people.

OCT 31

Experience the city's main cemetery, Panteón General, as people gather to decorate graves and celebrate. Later, enjoy the vibrant costume parade at the Zócalo.

NOV 1

To explore the area's fascinating history, head to the spectacular ruins of Monte Albán, the ancient Zapotec capital dating from around 200 BC–AD 700, which has a superb hilltop site. If you want to visit another cemetery in the evening, try the one in San Felipe del Agua.

NOV 2

Oaxaca has a fantastically vibrant indigenous crafts scene, so spend your final day shopping for souvenirs or head out of town to see more of the area.

NOV 3

Dos and Don'ts

✓ Though the atmosphere in graveyards and around altars may be surprisingly happy and light-hearted, always maintain due respect as this is also a serious event.

✗ Don't take photos without asking, or unless you have been told it's okay by a guide or someone with authority.

✓ Join a class in altar-decoration or Day of the Dead cooking for a unique insight.

✓ Local agencies offer tours to cemeteries and markets, and a good guide will make everything more accessible.

NOVEMBER

Where to Go: **November**

November is a great month for winter sports fans. The Rocky Mountains are gearing up for ski season while the desert states bask in crisp sunshine. Central America's rainy season is drawing to a close and the crowds have yet to arrive, so it's a good time to visit the ancient sites and colonial cities. With the worst of the hurricane season over, winterphobes can head off to the Caribbean, either on a cruise or to bask on a paradise island. November is also the best month for wildlife watching in Argentina's Península Valdés, while the extraordinary natural wonders of Parque Nacional Torres del Paine, Chile, are at their peak and spring brings long, sunny days. Below you will find all the destinations in this chapter and some extra suggestions to provide a little inspiration.

FESTIVALS AND CULTURE

PANAMA CITY Colorful colonial buildings in Casco Viejo

UNFORGETTABLE JOURNEYS

GUATEMALA Women in traditional woven blouses

NATURAL WONDERS

ISLA MARGARITA Baby green turtles

PANAMA CITY
PANAMA

A cosmopolitan colonial port and its famous canal

Wander the charming Old Quarter in this sultry city and take a boat excursion through the locks of the world's largest commercial waterway.
See pp266–7

PALENQUE
MEXICO

One of Mexico's finest Mayan sites

Atmospheric Palenque is home to some of the most beautiful Mayan architecture in existence, including a unique palace, and pyramid tomb.
www.visitmexico.com

GUATEMALA
CENTRAL AMERICA

Explore this land of temples, rain forests, and mountains

Marvel at Tikal, the Mayan city hidden in the forest, stroll around pretty colonial Antigua, and gaze upon the Pacaya volcano lava flow.
See pp262–3

"Leave behind Tikal's lush tropical forest for the exhilarating highland scenery of western Guatemala."

ISLA MARGARITA
VENEZUELA

Perfect for snorkeling, watersports, and nature

Fine sandy beaches, a verdant and mountainous interior, and a fabulous mangrove national park teeming with wildlife.
See pp260–61

BANFF
ALBERTA, CANADA

Join the fun at Winterstart to welcome the new ski season

Banff comes alive with a week-long celebration at the start of winter. Join in the winter sports and festivities, then bathe in hot springs.
See pp274–5

THE TELEFÉRICO, SANTIAGO
CHILE

Fly – without a plane

Take to the air in a spectacular *teleférico* cable car, with the snow-capped peaks of the high Andes close to hand.
www.funicular.cl

BOSQUE DEL APACHE
NEW MEXICO, USA

Ornithological winter wonderland

One of North America's best birding sites, attracting tens of thousands of birds during winter.
www.fws.gov/southwest/refuges/newmex/bosque

OLD SALEM
NORTH CAROLINA, USA

Monument to North Carolina's Moravian pioneers

Historic Old Salem town comprises a living museum of beautifully preserved houses and gardens built by the earliest European settlers.
www.oldsalem.org

LAGO DE COATEPEQUE
EL SALVADOR

Volcanic highland lake

Hike around the stunning crater lake of Lago de Coatepeque, which is ringed by a trio of volcanic peaks.
en.wikipedia.org/wiki/Lake_Coatepeque

HIGH ROAD FROM SANTA FE TO TAOS
NEW MEXICO, USA

Historic mountain drive

Drive this scenic road through the pine-covered Sangre de Cristo Mountains past Native American pueblos and Spanish-style towns.
www.byways.org/explore

REDWOOD NATIONAL PARK
CALIFORNIA, USA

Towering trees

This coastal park has some of the world's tallest trees, including a 367-ft- (112-m-) tall leviathan. Bear and elk are a common sight.
www.nps.gov/redw

CENOTES, YUCATÁN
MEXICO

A unique underwater, subterranean world

The world's largest underwater caves, these cathedral-like caverns beneath the Yucatán are unforgettable places to dive.
www.visitmexico.com

LA DIABLADA
PUNO, PERU

It's time to have some devilishly good fun

Held on the shores of Lake Titicaca, La Diablada features a spectacular parade of locals wearing demonic costumes and a week-long party.
www.perucontact.com/en/conozca

MISSISSIPPI CRUISE
LOUISIANA, USA

Take a paddlesteamer up the great river to the US heartland

Travel in a genuine "floating palace" from New Orleans past stately antebellum houses, historic plantations, and Civil War sites.
www.steamboatnatchez.com

LAGO DE ATITLÁN
GUATEMALA

Central America's deepest lake perched in the highlands

This breathtaking lake lies a mile (1.6 km) above sea level, surrounded by volcanic peaks and colorful Mayan villages.
www.lake-atitlan.com

Previous page: Lenticular clouds over Parque Nacional Torres del Paine, Chile

Weather Watch

❶ Banff, Canada November temperatures are appropriately chilly in this skiing hotspot – daytime highs can reach 23°F (-5°C), while nights are a teethchattering 15°F (-9°C). Snow, of course, is practically guaranteed.

❷ Tucson, USA This is a glorious time to visit Southwestern states, with plenty of sunshine, dry, warm days, and cool, clear nights.

❸ Guatemala Though the wet season is over in Guatemala and the sun is shining, you'll be lucky to avoid the odd afternoon rainshower. The tropical forests are very humid, while the western highlands get chilly after dark.

❹ Bahamas The Bahamas are just settling into winter – which means daytime temperatures of around 75°F (24°C), and a decrease in humidity. Tropical storms are a possibility.

❺ Venezuela At the northernmost reach of South America, Venezuela's coast is hot throughout the year, though cooled by pleasant sea breezes. The rainy season in the rest of the country is abating and summer is on its way.

❻ Argentina The Península Valdés in the south Atlantic is warm and dry in summer, with long hours of daylight, though evenings can be cold. Buenos Aires is warm and humid.

LUXURY AND ROMANCE

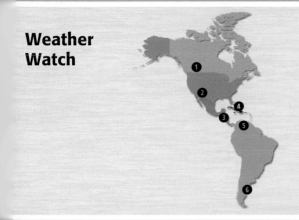

TUCSON Pretty flower-filled courtyard at Tucson Botanical Gardens

BÚZIOS
BRAZIL

Chic Mediterranean-style coastal resort

Stylish Buzios near Rio de Janeiro was put on the map by Brigitte Bardot, and now its cool lifestyle attracts Rio's rich and famous.
www.buziosturismo.com

TUCSON
ARIZONA, USA

A desert retreat imbued with a Wild West atmosphere

Hide out in the arid hills outside this desert city and spend a few days pampering yourself in luxurious sports and health resorts.
See pp258–9

MAR DEL PLATA
ARGENTINA

Sample the scene in the chicest resort in the south

Argentina's vacation season starts here, in this stylish town with dynamic nightlife and long, beautiful beaches.
www.argentinaturistica.com

BARBADOS
CARIBBEAN

Brilliant sunshine and a rather cozy charm

Cricket, golf, driving on the right – it's like a little piece of England with Caribbean beaches and a buzzing nightlife.
www.visitbarbados.org

ISLAND CRUISE
CARIBBEAN

Sail the trade winds on a sail-powered cruiser

Shiver me timbers! This feels like pirate territory. The pirates have left but the beautiful corals, beaches, and forests remain.
See pp272–3

ACTIVE ADVENTURES

PARQUE NACIONAL TORRES DEL PAINE A gaucho on his horse

PARQUE NACIONAL TORRES DEL PAINE
CHILE

Trek beside glaciers and lakes

In a beautiful but harsh landscape, shaped by the wind and the ice, trek this legendary landscape and see incredible sights you'll never forget.
See pp264–5

> "Kayak in an iceberg-choked lagoon or gallop on horseback over wild moors in the shadow of the Paine massif."

LAGUNA SAN RAFAEL
CHILE

Icebergs, glaciers, and penguins

Kayak in the iceberg-studded waters of this spectacular lagoon at the foot of the San Rafael Glacier, and spot penguins and sea-lions.
www.turismochile.com/guide

HIKING IN THE FITZ ROY MASSIF
ARGENTINA

Spectacular Andean range

Hike amidst dozens of razor-sharp rock needles surrounding Monte Fitz Roy, one of the most dramatic peaks in South America.
www.ripioturismo.com.ar

ECUADOR
SOUTH AMERICA

Bike, hike and raft in this paradise for fresh-air fiends

Ecuador is packed with options for active types, from hiking in the Amazon and biking in the Andes, to rafting the fast-flowing rivers.
www.ecuador.com

ORINOCO DELTA
VENEZUELA

Explore the mouth of South America's third-largest river

Ride the waterways of this great wetland wilderness, with its tangled labyrinth of wildlife-rich rain forest and swamp.
www.orinocodelta.com

FAMILY GETAWAYS

THE BAHAMAS Floating above the reef in this snorkelers' paradise

THE BAHAMAS
CARIBBEAN

Sun and fun are guaranteed at this island paradise

The Bahamas is like a vast natural theme park, with safe sandy beaches, warm waters, top-notch hotels, and pirate hide-outs.
See pp268–9

RIO GRANDE VALLEY
TEXAS, USA

Family holiday hotspot in the deep south

On the border between Texas and Mexico, this region offers fishing, birding, dolphin spotting, and diving opportunities.
www.valleychamber.com

COSTA RICA
CENTRAL AMERICA

The most family-friendly destination in Central America

This enticing little country has activities to suit all: turtle-watching, wildlife spotting, jungle treks, rafting, or lazing on the beach.
www.costarica.com

> "To experience nature at its most glorious, rent bikes, gallop horses on the beach, or snorkel in the clear Atlantic waters."

PENÍNSULA VALDÉS
ARGENTINA

Whale watching at the chilly southern tip of the continent

Head for Patagonia and float alongside southern right whales, see mighty seals do battle, and admire tiny Magellan penguin chicks.
See pp270–71

PLYMOUTH
MASSACHUSETTS, USA

First landing site of the Pilgrim Fathers

Mark Thanksgiving where it all began – watch the parade, eat at the Pilgrim Village, and visit the reproduction Mayflower.
www.plimoth.org

GETTING THERE   See map p321, F6
The drive from Tucson International Airport to downtown takes 20 minutes. Taxis and airport shuttles are available, and some hotels and resorts provide transportation for their guests.

GETTING AROUND
Rental cars are the most convenient option for exploring Tucson, although downtown is fun to navigate on foot. The surrounding mountains provide numerous hiking, biking, and horse trails.

WEATHER
Autumn is delightful with sunny, mild, usually rain-free days, and highs of 74–86°F (23–29°C) and lows of 44–55°F (8–14°C).

ACCOMMODATIONS
Hacienda del Sol Guest Ranch Resort was a retreat for Katharine Hepburn and Spencer Tracy; doubles from US$175; www.haciendadelsol.com

Two golf courses, tennis, and a spa are offered at Loews Ventana Canyon Resort; doubles from US$299; loewshotels.com

JW Marriott Star Pass Resort and Spa has a 27-hole golf course; doubles from US$329; www.jwmarriottstarrpass.com

EATING OUT
Feast on mesquite-grilled meats, tasty salsas, and sizzling fajitas. Don't miss a meal at El Charro Café (311 N. Court Ave.), family-owned since 1922.

PRICE FOR TWO
US$600 per day including accommodation, car rental, food and drink, and optional activities.

FURTHER INFORMATION
www.visittucson.org

A Thorny Masterpiece

Rising from the Sonoran Desert floor are the majestic saguaros. Pronounced "sah-wah-roh," these intriguingly shaped, tree-like cacti with multiple arms average 30 ft (9 m) tall and live for up to 200 years. A slow grower, the saguaro spurts less than 2 inches (51 mm) during its first eight years of life. Indeed, one side arm can take up to 50–75 years to develop. It is well worth the wait. The saguaro's white blossoms, which are Arizona's state flower, appear in spring and only open at night, remaining on display until the following day.

Top: Courtyard at Tucson Botanical Gardens

Below (top and bottom): Downtown Tucson at dusk; rock art in Saguaro National Park

Right panel (top to bottom): The painted dome ceiling of Mission San Xavier del Bac; ornate door handle at Mission San Xavier del Bac; cowboy hats

Main: Saguaro cacti silhouetted in the sunset

DESERT HIDEAWAY

SHADES OF VIOLET, DUSTY SAGE, AND COBALT BLUE PAINT TUCSON'S SUNRISES AND SUNSETS, mountain vistas, and desert oases. Imbued with the spirits of Native Americans, Spanish missionaries, lawmen Wyatt Earp and Doc Holliday, black-hat banditos, and sultry saloon queens, Tucson segues between its bygone-days atmosphere and status as an ultra-luxurious playground. Surrounded by the rugged Santa Catalina Mountains and the hauntingly beautiful Sonoran Desert, the city is home to some of the world's most opulent sports and health resorts.

Tucson was founded in 1775 and is a thriving metropolis with a major university, yet it continues to embrace its early heritage. Oozing with colorful character, historic downtown (the "Old Pueblo") hosts a thriving contemporary arts district that features long-standing landmarks, such as the 1934 Hotel Congress where infamous bank robber John Dillinger lived, and El Charro Café, which as been owned by the same family since 1922. Wander the streets in

JAN

FEB

MAR

APR

MAY

JUN

JUL

AUG

SEP

OCT

NOV

DAY 1

DAY 2

DAY 3

DAY 4

DAY 5

DEC

Above: Hot-air balloons floating in a blue Arizona sky

WESTERN DIARY

Autumn is the perfect season for a splurge in Tucson. Days are bathed in warm sun, evenings are basked in starlight, and you can choose from an extensive list of activities and attractions. Five days will allow you to enjoy your favorite sport, spend down time in a spa, visit historic sights, and tour the wine trail.

Five Indulgent Days

Rent a bike or a horse, or take a hike and explore the diverse beauty of the Santa Catalina Mountains or marvel at the prehistoric rock art in the Saguaro National Park. At the end of the day, savor the magical sunset with a margarita in hand.

Hit the golf course or the tennis courts at one of Tucson's luxury resorts, and then be soothed and pampered in one of its lavish spas. Try out desert-inspired treatments and rituals. Couples can arrange for simultaneous sessions in private treatment rooms.

Start the day floating above the mountains and desert on a champagne hot-air balloon ride. Explore downtown Tucson, dubbed the "Old Pueblo," and its ten surrounding historic districts. Among the highlights are the 1934 Hotel Congress, 1775 Presidio San Agustín de Tucson, and the thriving arts district. Stop for lunch or dinner at El Charro Café.

Take another day to enjoy your favorite activity, relax by the pool, or soak in a hot tub surrounded by spectacular mountain vistas. Celebrate another sunset and watch myriad stars emerge from the darkening sky, or view the skies through a telescope at the University of Arizona's Flandrau Science Center and Planetarium.

Visit the Arizona-Sonora Desert Museum, an all-in-one zoo, natural history museum, and botanical garden, or linger in the Tucson Botanical Gardens. Afterwards, head to dazzling white Mission San Xavier del Bac (1783–97) and marvel at its architectural styles and intricate paintings.

Dos and Don'ts

- ☑ Ask permission before taking photos of Native Americans, especially at ceremonies.
- ☒ When walking in the desert, watch your step lest you tread on a snake.
- ☑ Don't venture into the desert or mountains without maps and information about weather and road conditions.
- ☑ Bring a good pair of binoculars in order to view some of the 250 bird species that inhabit the local area.

the downtown area and you will be intoxicated by the scents of mesquite-grills, zesty salsas, juicy chili peppers, and other succulent Southwestern culinary treats.

The hills around Tucson hide other treasures. Looming over the Santa Cruz Valley is the striking "White Dove of the Desert," Mission San Xavier del Bac, a welcoming beacon of elegant domes and arches in a blend of Moorish, Byzantine, and late-Mexican Renaissance architecture. Inside, gaze heavenward at the so-called "Sistine Chapel of North America" with its intricate paintings on the walls and ceiling. About an hour's drive south of Tucson, amid rolling grasslands and tree-covered hills, are a smattering of vineyards that produce Mediterranean and Spanish varietals and invite visitors to stop for tours and tasting. Early frontier life can be experienced by staying on an authentic dude ranch where you can rest up in a comfortable *casita* (guestroom) and soak in a hot tub after a day of horse-riding, hiking, birding, and cookouts. Alternatively, treat yourself to one of the pampering resorts featuring championship golf courses, tennis facilities, and lavish spas and be as active or relaxed as you wish in this picturesque paradise.

GETTING THERE　　　　See map 325, H6
Isla Margarita is 14 miles (23 km) north of the Venezuelan coast. Flights from Caracas, Venezuela's international airport, take around 45 minutes.

GETTING AROUND
Roads are good on the island and rental car is an excellent way to explore. Boat trips are available from most beaches and harbors to visit some of the offshore sights and islands.

WEATHER
Isla Margarita enjoys an average temperature of 81°F (27°C), with a gentle sea breeze.

ACCOMMODATIONS
The colonial-style Hotel Costa Linda Beach is near El Agua beach; doubles from US$50; www.hotelcostalinda.com

Luxurious Hesperia Playa El Agua is a modern complex on the beach; doubles from US$130; www.hesperiaislamargarita.com

The Hilton Margarita has a lovely large swimming pool; doubles from US$259; www1.hilton.com

EATING OUT
Tuna, snapper, and lobster are typical local fare, as are tropical fruits. Look out for the national dish, *Pabellón Crollo* – shredded beef with black beans and fried plantains.

PRICE FOR TWO
US$190–400 per day, depending on accommodation, including food, car rental and gas, trips and activities.

FURTHER INFORMATION
www.islamargarita.com

Historical Margarita

The island has been the setting for many notable events in South American history. Christopher Columbus himself happened upon the island paradise in 1498, and the inhabitants inevitably became slaves to the conquering Spaniards. In 1814 it became the first territory in Venezuela to rid itself of Spanish rule, and it was here that Simón Bolívar, famous liberator of the continent, was confirmed Commander-in-Chief of the new republic. Traces of Spanish influence can be seen throughout the island in the typical Spanish-style architecture in the towns.

COLLAR OF ISLANDS

FLYING OVER THE CARIBBEAN FROM MAINLAND VENEZUELA, you will see a collar of islands, their lush, green interiors ringed by the whitish-yellow of their beaches and an outer circle of light turquoise where the sand is visible through the shallow waters of the sea. Isla Margarita is the largest of the Minor Antilles, although at its longest it stretches a mere 39 miles (62 km), and is a bustling, diverse, and beautiful place to spend an unforgettable vacation.

Mountainous and subtropical, the island is divided into two regions. Its eastern section is developed and populous; Porlamar is a thriving commercial city, and its status as a duty-free port draws in Venezuelan tourists who enjoy its nightlife, casinos, restaurants, and cheap shopping.

You can explore the labyrinthine channels that meander through the tangled roots of the mangroves, a dense green canopy blocking out the sun from overhead.

The west of the island, in contrast, is quiet and unspoiled. The Macanao is an expansive, arid peninsula, with shrubs and cacti peppering the landscape and wild hare darting across the path of your jeep. A string of verdant mountains makes up the interior, encircled by wide, deserted beaches and dunes, with crashing surf and picture-book palms. Often the only people you will see here are local fishermen, rigging their hooks and setting off in search of tuna and red snapper which you can sample, freshly grilled, in one of the small restaurants in town.

The narrow isthmus that connects these two regions is a sand spit that forms part of the Restinga National Park, an area of mangrove swamps filled with bountiful wildlife. Aboard a small wooden *peñero* – a traditional local fishing boat – you can explore the labyrinthine channels that meander through the tangled roots of the mangroves, a dense green canopy blocking out the sun from overhead. The crystal-clear waters are a window onto some spectacular marine life, including green and leatherback turtles and the enormous oysters that cling to the underwater mangrove roots. For visitors wishing to prolong their experience of totally unspoiled Venezuelan sea-life, trips can be made out to the coral reefs of Los Roques, an amazing National Park of sandy beaches and waters that teem with colorful fish, swimming amongst some of the best-preserved reefs in the world.

Main: Aerial view of the coral reefs at Los Roques, Venezuela
Inset: Parrotfish, a common sight in the waters around Isla Margarita
Below (left to right): Nueva Esparta; Playa el Agua; baby green turtles

Above: A flock of scarlet ibis in a tree

JAN

FEB

MAR

APR

MAY

JUN

JUL

AUG

SEP

OCT

NOV

DAY 1

DAY 2

DAY 3

DAY 4

DAY 5

DAY 6

DAY 7

DEC

ISLAND DIARY

November should bring clear skies, warm temperatures, and a refreshing offshore breeze. The island is a manageable size for a week's stay, with enough time to kick back and relax, view the wildlife, and enjoy the nightlife as well. Visitors can extend their trip by visiting the Angel Falls *(see pp292–3)* on the mainland.

A Week of Tropical Treasures

Flights from Caracas arrive just outside Porlamar, so you can begin your trip visiting the duty-free port.

Spend the afternoon relaxing in the warm waters at El Agua beach and have a cocktail at a beachfront bar.

Take a day to explore Macanao, the unspoiled beaches of the eastern region, then drive to Manzanillo on the peninsula's northeastern tip and watch the local fishermen unload their catch.

Try your hand at some water sports: the beach at El Yaque has some excellent windsurfing, while the tides and swell at Parguito make it good for surfing.

Take one of the daily boat trips from Margarita Island to the islands of Coche and Cubagua. The former is a quiet fishing village with white sand beaches, and Cubagua has some excellent diving.

Visit the archipelago of Los Roques, a group of 42 coral reefs and beautiful sandy beaches. Observe the amazing variety of wildlife and try your hand at bonefishing with the locals.

Board a *peñero* to explore the mangroves of the Restinga National Park. Colorful sea- and bird-life and beautiful natural scenery make this one of the undoubted highlights of a trip to Margarita Island.

Take the short flight back to Caracas to connect with your onward flight.

Dos and Don'ts

✓   Be careful of strong currents and tides. Some beaches are dangerous, even for strong swimmers; make sure you know the situation before you take the plunge.

✗   Don't underestimate the sun – a light sea breeze takes the edge off the heat, but the tropical sun is still very powerful.

✓   Get off the beaten track – the island still has many quiet corners and deserted beaches. Rent a car to explore, and you will be rewarded.

✗   Don't miss out on the tax-free bargains in Porlamar.

GETTING THERE
See map p324, B2

International flights to Guatemala land at La Aurora Airport, 4 miles (6 km) south of the capital, Guatemala City. Transfer to the domestic terminal for the short flight to Flores. From here, Tikal is around an hour by taxi.

GETTING AROUND

Bus tours and shuttle buses are useful for getting to most major attractions, but you can take a taxi (US$30) from Guatemala City to Antigua, which can be explored on foot.

WEATHER

Tikal is humid, warm, and sunny, with an average high of 74°F (23°C) and maybe the odd shower.

ACCOMMODATIONS

Jungle Lodge Hotel provides bungalow accommodation in Tikal; doubles at US$130 per night; www.junglelodge.guate.com

Hotel Villa del Lago in Flores has doubles for US$40 a night; www.hotelvilladelago.com.gt

The Cloister in Antigua has well-furnished doubles from US$120; www.cloister.com

La Casa del Mundo on Lake Atitlán offers swimming, kayaking, hiking, and bicycle tours; US$61 per night; www.lacasadelmundo.com

EATING OUT

Specialties include *pollo en pepián* (chicken in a spicy sauce) and *tamales dulces* – corn cakes with fruit baked in plantain leaves.

PRICE FOR TWO

Around US$220 a day with accommodation, food, excursions, admissions, and activities.

FURTHER INFORMATION

www.visitguatemala.com

The Grand Ceiba

With a straight, gray trunk and flat-topped canopy, Guatemala's national tree – the ceiba – can grow to over 100 ft (30 m) in height, while its branches span up to 150 ft (46 m) across. To the Mayans, the ceiba was the "World Tree," connecting the earth to the heavens and the underworld. From its limbs hang epiphytes – moss-like plants that nurture orchids, ferns, and bromeliads. It also shelters hummingbirds, iguanas, and anteaters; bats pollinate its flowers and rest beneath its buttressed roots, while harpy eagles roost in the leaf canopy.

Main: The magnificent ruins of Tikal's Great Plaza, now swathed in forest

TALES OF TIKAL

IT'S BARELY FIVE IN THE MORNING and an eerie silence looms over the rain forest as you tread your path in pitch darkness, when all of a sudden, the air erupts with the raucous call of hordes of howler monkeys as they awaken. Soon after, as you climb the broken steps of the pyramid known to archeologists as Temple IV, day is all set to break and, as the mist clears, the towering ruins of a great civilization come into view.

Once the most powerful and prosperous of Mayan cities, Tikal is now emerging to reclaim its place in history as a national park rich in both natural and man-made beauty. As your guide leads you expertly through the stupendous remains of temples, palaces, and plazas, he describes the astonishing variety of flora and fauna found here – majestic ceiba and sapodilla trees as well as spider monkeys, silver foxes, tarantulas, keel-billed toucans, and oropendulas, as well as the elusive jaguar, held sacred by the Mayans.

Left (left to right): Antigua's Santa Catarina Arch aglow at dusk; black howler monkey in the rain forest; Pacayá Volcano spewing lava; Maximón, the "smoking deity"; the clear and calm waters of Lake Atitlán

Below: Chichicastenango Market's colorful array of fruits and vegetables

Inset: Tapestry work at a market in Antigua

Main: Women wearing traditional, woven blouses

Once the most powerful and prosperous of Mayan cities, Tikal is now emerging to reclaim its place in history.

JAN
FEB
MAR
APR
MAY
JUN
JUL
AUG
SEP
OCT
NOV
DAY 1
DAY 2
DAYS 3–4
DAY 5
DAY 6
DEC

GUATEMALAN DIARY

Six days are sufficient for you to become acquainted with this multifaceted country. At this time of year, unbroken sunshine is the norm, which is why locals refer to the dry season as "summer." You will also be arriving before peak tourist season, an important consideration when visiting Tikal, where crowds are common.

Six Days of Color and Culture

Be up before dawn in Tikal for the dramatic awakening of the rain forest. Spend the day exploring the ruins and following scenic nature trails. Later, head to Flores in time for a swim in Lake Petén Itzá as the sun sinks dramatically over the horizon. Dine at a terrace restaurant, on freshly caught fish from the lake.

Fly to Guatemala City and take a taxi to the charming colonial town of Antigua. Spend the morning at the Centro La Azotea, a museum devoted to Mayan culture, around 1 mile (2 km) north of Antigua. Return to the town center to explore its ruined churches.

Join a tour to the active Pacayá Volcano. Climb to within 984 ft (300 m) of the summit to photograph the glowing lava that snakes down the mountainside. On your return trip, ride part of the way on horseback.

Ride a mini shuttle to Lake Atitlán. After lunch in Panajachel, jump on a motor launch to El Jaibalito and check in at La Casa del Mundo. Bathe in the lake and then take a pre-dinner stroll to the village. Return later to see the changing hues of the lake at sunset.

Go kayaking on the lake, followed by a motor-launch ride to the Mayan village of Santiago Atitlán. Ask a guide to show you the wooden statue of Maximón (San Simón), a Mayan deity who "smokes" a cigar.

Visit Chichicastenango and its market (Thursdays and Sundays). Wander the cobbled streets of this attractive town, home to the Kaqchikel people. Here, admire their weaving skills and colorful folk costumes.

Dos and Don'ts

☑ Stay the night at Tikal to compare the stunning views of the ruins at sunset and at sunrise, as the mist rises.

☑ Flores has no banks or cash points. If you run out of money, take the *tuc-tuc* (scooter taxi) to Santa Elena, on the other side of the causeway from the island.

☑ Dress warmly when you visit the western highlands, where it will feel cooler. Do also pack a flashlight, a camera, mosquito repellent, sunscreen, and headwear.

☒ While in Guatemala, don't stray too far from established tourist routes without a guide or checking with your hotel.

Leave behind Tikal's lush tropical forest for the exhilarating highland scenery of western Guatemala; waiting to greet you is a magical lake, formed 85,000 years ago by a volcanic eruption 30 times greater than Pompeii – the stunningly radiant Atitlán Lake.

With its placid surface ruffled only by the afternoon breeze and motor launches that serve shoreline settlements, Atitlán Lake is over 5,000 ft (1,524 m) above sea level and surrounded by mountains and volcanoes. Most people here still speak the Mayan languages of their ancestors and wear traditional clothes, such as *huipiles* – colorful, hand-embroidered traditional blouses – which can be found in Chichicastenango, home to Central America's largest native market.

A short drive from Lake Atitlán is the sensitively restored colonial town of Antigua. The colonial capital of Guatemala, this architectural gem has earned a place on UNESCO's World Heritage list for its old-world charm, photogenic squares and cobbled streets, and picturesque ruins of churches and convents damaged by earthquakes in the 18th century.

GETTING THERE   See map p331, C7
Take a flight from Santiago to Punta Arenas. From here, travel 249 miles (400 km) by road to Parque Nacional Torres del Paine.

GETTING AROUND
Explore trekking circuits independently or on guided hikes. The southern area's *hosterías* (small hotels) run shuttles between trail-heads; boats cross the Grey and Pehoé lakes.

WEATHER
In October, temperatures range from near-freezing to 64°F (18°C), but the windchill factor can make it seem colder. Conditions veer from high winds and rain to sunshine.

ACCOMMODATIONS
Spread along trails are privately-run *refugios* (huts with dorm beds) and camping grounds, which rent out tents and sleeping bags.

Hostería Lago Grey, on the shore of a lake, has doubles from US$215; www.lagogrey.cl

Hostería Las Torres offers great views; doubles from US$350; www.lastorres.com

Hotel Salto Chico overlooks Lago Pehoé; doubles from US$2,500; www.explora.com

EATING OUT
Regional dishes include barbecued meats, freshwater salmon, and organically sourced salads. Wash it down with Pisco, the national drink, chilled with cubes of glacial ice.

PRICE FOR TWO
About US$500 per day, with transfers, food, accommodation, and adventure sports.

FURTHER INFORMATION
www.torresdelpaine.com

What's in a Name?

The origin of the name Torres del Paine is open to debate. The word Paine means "pale blue" in the tongue of the Tehuelche natives, who are thought to have been inspired by the area's turquoise lakes. Yet, Patagonian names traditionally pay tribute to early explorers who made historic discoveries in the region, and any quick glance at a map of Torres will throw up the surnames of many European pioneers. According to this more prosaic theory, Paine derives from the name of an early Welsh climber. Romance or revisionism? You decide.

Above (left to right): Glacier climber traversing a frozen stream; a gaucho on his horse; hikers on Glaciar Grey
Main: Kayakers near icebergs on Lago Grey

Above: Camper at Lago Pehoé

JAN
FEB
MAR
APR
MAY
JUN
JUL
AUG
SEP
OCT
NOV
DEC

CONQUERING THE PAINE

AFTER WALKING THROUGH LUSH FORESTS OF SOUTHERN BEECH running with tumbling glacial streams, you break the treeline. Suddenly you're exposed to the clear light and unhindered views of extraordinary glacial peaks. As you surge ahead, you unexpectedly find yourself beside a jade-colored lagoon. From the water's far shore three great granite towers, tinged pink in the dawn sun, soar magnificently, piercing the blood-orange skyline with jagged, snow-capped peaks. From the base of the towers, glaciers spill dramatically downwards to empty meltwater into the lagoon. This is Parque Nacional Torres del Paine; renowned trekking destination and natural wonderland.

The majestic Torres del Paine spires lend their name to the national park and form part of the greater Paine massif, whose wild, ice-capped summits lord over a landscape of shimmering glacial lakes, mighty glaciers, powerful rivers, thunderous waterfalls, and verdant forests. World-class trekking circuits traverse the park in its entirety, venturing deep into the forested, mountainous interior of the Paine massif and encircling the lakes and glaciers that mark its outer limits. Trails that hike the perimeter of the massif reveal the intensely turquoise Lago Pehoé and wind westwards towards the immense blue ice mass of Glaciar Grey. Look east from here and the jet-black peaks of the Cuernos del Paine rise above you, draped with glaciers that calve huge chunks of ice into lagoons of brilliant blue-green. Turn to the west and the whirling, dizzyingly beautiful panorama of rock, ice, and water is completed by Cerro Paine Grande, the national park's highest summit.

On every side, you'll find not just breathtaking beauty, but also the potential for adrenaline-charged adventure. Kayak an iceberg-choked lagoon; gallop on horseback over wild moors or experience the heady rush of scaling Glaciar Grey's ice crevasses. Wherever you look, the possibility of adventure and thrills beckons.

> Kayak an iceberg-
> choked lagoon or
> gallop on horseback
> over wild moors in
> the shadow of
> the Paine massif.

Inset: Icebergs afloat on a lake in Torres del Paine
Below (left and right): Patagonian puma; the three granite towers of Torres

BLUE LAKE DIARY

October is springtime in Patagonia, so you'll have longer days and lots of time to explore Torres del Paine. There are two main circuits: the W Circuit (4–5 days) and the Paine Circuit (8–10 days). "Do the W," followed by two days of kayaking and horse-riding. Factor in another two days for transfers.

Eight Days Among Glaciers

Fly to Punta Arenas and complete a 5-hour road transfer across open plains to the national park. Dine under the stars at a Torres del Paine *hostería*.

DAY 1

"Do the W". Start by trekking to the mighty Torres. Then lunch at the base, on the shore of the lagoon.

Hike west along the north shore of Lago Nordenskjöld, splashing across forest streams and trekking through woodland to the base of the Cuernos del Paine.

DAYS 2–5

Trek into Valle Francés and drink in the vistas of the Torres and the Cuernos, Lago Pehoé, and Cerro Paine Grande, whose eastern face is draped by Glaciar Francés. Watch as ice blocks tear themselves off the glacier and crash into the lagoon below.

Take the gentle hike from Valle Francés to Lago Grey. After lunch, take on an ice-climbing excursion.

Congratulations, you've done the W! Now hop on a boat to the scenic Ultima Esperanza Sound, located in the park's most southerly sector. Spend the afternoon riding horseback across the moors.

DAY 6

Round out your adventure by kayaking across one of the Sound's iceberg-peppered lagoons.

DAY 7

Return to Punta Arenas and visit the historical heart of this picturesque town before flying back to Santiago.

DAY 8

Dos and Don'ts

✓ Look out for stunning wildlife. More than 40 mammals inhabit the park, including *guanaco* (a type of llama), the Patagonian gray fox, and the extremely shy puma. Bird species include the condor, the ostrich-like *ñandú*, swans, flamingos, and torrent ducks. Colorful Magellanic woodpeckers are also easily spotted in the forests.

✓ Book accommodation in advance if you are not camping – especially for *refugios*, which fill up quickly.

✗ Don't light open fires in the park. The threat of bush blazes means they are prohibited.

✓ Stop at rivers or streams to stock up on chilled glacial water.

Left (left to right): Independence Square, Casco Viejo (Old City); Panama City's high-rise buildings

Right (left to right): Inside a lock; Miraflores Lock's viewing platform; aerial view of the canal, Miraflores Locks

Below: Wall decoration in Casco Viejo (Old City)

Inset: *Rojos diablos* buses at Chorilla Bus Terminal, Panama City

GETTING THERE

See map p324, H6

Panama City is on the Central American isthmus. Flights arrive at Tocumen International Airport, 15 miles (24 km) east of the city center.

GETTING AROUND

Diablos rojos ("red devils") – gaily painted buses – ply the main routes in and around town, but not to the airport. A tourist taxi from the airport costs about US$25.

WEATHER

By late fall, the rainy season is coming to a close, although humidity remains high. In November, the temperature has cooled to a daytime average of 79°F (26°C).

ACCOMMODATIONS

The luxurious high-rise International Miramar has modern amenities; doubles from US$267; www.miramarpanama.com

The ritzy Hotel Bristol has deluxe rooms, stylish bar, and fine dining; doubles from US$215; www.thebristol.com

Escape the hubbub at the intimate B&B La Estancia; doubles from US$55; www.bedandbreakfastpanama.com

EATING OUT

Panama City offers cosmopolitan dining. Expect to pay US$25–35 per person at better restaurants. Try Eurasia for exquisite French-Asian dishes, and Chef Clara Icaza's hip nouvelle dishes at Limoncillo.

PRICE FOR TWO

US$140–350 per day including hotel, food, local transport, and entrance charges.

FURTHER INFORMATION

www.visitpanama.com

Quaint colonial port and high-rise modernity juxtaposed in dramatic counterpoint.

Main: A cruise ship heading into the waterway that leads to the Panama Canal locks

Engineering Feat

A genius of human triumph over nature, the Panama Canal was carved through the isthmus at its narrowest point to connect the Caribbean Sea and Pacific Ocean. Completed in 1914 after an eight-year endeavor that claimed 5,609 lives (20,000 died during an earlier French effort), the 50-mile (80-km) -long canal runs north to south and features three sets of locks that raise and lower vessels 85 ft (26 m). The lock chambers are paired to permit two-way traffic. Ships sail through the locks while tethered to *mulas* – electric locomotives.

A GLORIOUS PORT

P ANAMA CITY CAUSES A DOUBLE-TAKE; QUAINT COLONIAL PORT AND HIGH-RISE MODERNITY are juxtaposed in dramatic counterpoint. The ghosts of pirates past seem to walk beside you as you stroll the venerable plazas of Casco Viejo, the colonial core of this sultry port city at the southern mouth of the Panama Canal. And there's a special thrill if you take a small boat excursion through the locks of the world's largest watery highway of commerce as massive cruise and cargo ships loom overhead.

Casco Viejo, founded in 1673, simmers with sentimental allure. Though a fire in 1878 destroyed much of the colonial quarter, this ancient district has arisen like a Phoenix that prizes its colorful past. The leafy plazas teem with historic museums and colonial churches and now, too, with trendy restaurants, jazz clubs, and boutique hotels. A 19th-century French effort to carve a canal lent Casco Viejo its Parisian airs: strolling its cobbled streets is

Above: Casco Viejo, Panama City and the white towers of the Cathedral

JAN

FEB

MAR

APR

MAY

JUN

JUL

AUG

SEP

OCT

NOV

DAY 1

DAY 2

DAY 3

DAY 4

DEC

CANAL DIARY

November is a great month to explore Panama's capital city because the weather is usually temperate and rain-free. There's lots to see and do: four days is enough to see the main sights before striking out to outlying regions, but you could easily spend another day or two immersing yourself in Casco Viejo.

Four Days in Panama City

Start with a walking tour of Casco Viejo, the colonial core of the city. From Plaza de Francia follow a clockwise route that takes in Plaza de la Independencia, the main square and site of the Catedral Metropolitana and Museo del Canal Interoceánico, telling the tale of the canal's construction. After lunch at Manolo Caracol, view the Baroque gold altar in Iglesia de San José, then stroll around Plaza Bolívar and finish with a tour of the Palacio Presidencial (you'll need to book in advance). Later, enjoy Mediterranean cuisine and live jazz at S'Cena.

Get a handle on Panama's past with a guided walking tour of Panama Viejo. Wander the ruins of the original city (destroyed by pirate Henry Morgan), and linger in the excellent Museo de Sitio de Panama Viejo, which displays pre-Columbian and colonial artifacts. You'll want to browse the Mercado Nacional de Artesanías, where Kuna Indians sell their fabulous crafts. Later, take in a classical concert at the Teatro Nacional.

Art lovers will enjoy the fine pieces in the Museo de Arte Contemporáneo; nearby, Mi Pueblito recreates villages that replicate those of Panama's diverse cultures. Lunch at Niko's Café before exploring Balboa and Ancón, the old US canal administrative zone where the Administration Building features fantastic murals.

Take to the water on a boat excursion of the Panama Canal. This half-day tour puts you up close and personal inside the lock chambers. After, stop at the Miraflores Locks Visitor Center, with its superb museum, then head across the road to Fondo Peregrino Panama, where you can handle a tame harpy eagle.

Dos and Don'ts

- ☑ Do take a sightseeing boat excursion on the canal. It's the best way to gain a perspective of the immensity of the locks.

- ☑ Visit the real tailor of Panama at La Fortuna, on Vía España, and measure up for a *guayabera* – a traditional men's shirt – or even a suit.

- ☒ Don't go to the Chorrillo area west of Casco Viejo.

- ☑ Do be cautious crossing the road; Panama City's pell-mell traffic (including its garishly painted *rojos diablos* buses) doesn't give way.

a special pleasure as you wander past elegant façades and wrought-iron balconies that generate a sense of déjà vu for visitors familiar with New Orleans' French Quarter.

The other side of the coin is the cosmopolitan, contemporary city – a center for international finance that thrums with modernity – where skyscrapers needle the skyline. Towering marble hotels replete with casinos sparkle in the El Cangrejo district. Adjacent middle-class Bella Vista and Marbella offer a parade of ritzy restaurants and swinging nightclubs. To chill a little, wander along Avenida Balboa, with its monument to the Spanish *conquistador* who first saw the Pacific.

Panama City was thrust into an important world position by the completion, in 1914, of the canal, and ships anchor offshore by the dozen. The leafy enclaves of Balboa and Ancón – former US administrative headquarters for the canal – offer delightful escapes. From the lush rain forests that surround the city and feed the canal with fresh water, comes a cacophony of wildlife. This can be seen in Parque Nacional Soberanía and in Parque Natural Metropolitano close to the city's heart.

GETTING THERE
See map p325, D2

The Bahamas is a chain of some 700 islands spread over 100,000 sq miles (259,000 sq km) in the western Atlantic, southeast of Florida. Nassau has the main airport, but flights from North America also serve Bimini, Eleuthera, and Grand Bahama.

GETTING AROUND
Taxis and minivans operate on most islands, and car rental is available on major islands. Water-taxis run between the cays of Abacos.

WEATHER
November is sunny, with cooling trade winds and temperatures of around 79°F (26°C).

ACCOMMODATIONS
Abaco Beach Resort has family-sized doubles from US$280; www.abacobeachresort.com

Nassau's Sheraton Cable Beach Hotel has children's programs; family-sized doubles start at US$300; www.starwoodhotels.com

Atlantis Paradise Island offers family-sized doubles from US$320; www.atlantis.com

EATING OUT
Dining in the Bahamas is expensive. The clam-like conch is the local staple, often served marinated raw as a ceviche.

PRICE FOR A FAMILY OF FOUR
Between US$650–900 per day including food, accommodation, entertainment, and local transportation.

FURTHER INFORMATION
www.bahamas.com
www.seaworldtours.com
www.dolphinencounters.com

Pirates of the Caribbean

By the 1690s, Nassau's harbor had evolved as a center for pirates, including "privateers," licensed to prey on Spanish ships. In 1703, they proclaimed a "Privateers Republic" – and the notorious Edward "Blackbeard" Teach was the magistrate. Employing hit-and-run tactics, they preyed on merchant shipping that plied nearby trade routes. In 1718, the English Crown offered a "pardon or death," an ultimatum for the pirates to cease their activities. The hair-raising tales of pillage and plunder are revealed in the superb Pirates of Nassau Museum.

Above (left to right): Colorful sails on Treasure Island, Abacos; down under with a friendly dolphin; the Bahamas – a snorkeler's paradise
Main: Underwater plexiglass tunnel at Predators Lagoon on Paradise Island

Above: The Dig at Atlantis – the largest saltwater aquarium in the world

PLEASURE ISLANDS

CLEAR WATERS, GORGEOUS BEACHES, and exciting encounters with wildlife – welcome to the Bahamas, the most-visited destination in the Caribbean, and for good reason. Every colorful island here boasts gorgeous beaches of cotton-white (or pink) sands and bathtub-warm shallow waters in electrifying shades of turquoise and blue.

But there's so much more to the Bahamas, too. The historic capital city of Nassau was once an infamous lair of pirates, but these days it buzzes with water sports and a sizzling nightlife. Head to the famous Cable Beach to lounge, explore the city's fortresses, and visit Junkanoo Expo so your kids can learn about the unique and colorful cultural heritage of the Bahamas. At Blue Lagoon Island near Nassau, you can even swim with trained dolphins or feed stingrays by hand.

Next to Nassau, Paradise Island is the setting for the renowned Atlantis Resort – a fantastical family-focused hotel resembling a set from *Indiana Jones and the Temple of Doom*. Its amazing fish-filled lagoons, waterslides, and interactive Discovery Channel Camp keep both children and adults enthralled from dawn to dusk. The pillow-soft sands of the island also offer water sports, from aqua-biking to parasailing.

The farther you travel from Nassau, the more traditional and relaxed the islands become. The distant Out Islands are known as the Family Islands for their traditional sense of community and laid-back ease. In Abacos, the Loyalist Cays whisk you back in time, with their twee churches, artists' studios, and Victorian gingerbread homes. Green Turtle Cay, with its pastel-colored historic inns, is the perfect spot for a bit of snorkeling in gin-clear waters or paddling a kayak through mangroves and sheltered lagoons teeming with birds and marine life…a perfect prelude to days spent doing nothing but relaxing on talcum-soft sands and drying off under the Bahamian sun.

Every colorful island here boasts gorgeous beaches of cotton-white (or pink) sands and bathtub-warm shallow waters in many shades of blue.

Inset: Atlantis Resort on Paradise Island – a fun-filled and magical family haven
Below (left and right): Typical Bahamian architecture; masks at Straw Market

BAHAMIAN DIARY

November is the ideal time to visit the Bahamas, when the weather is delightfully balmy, rainfall is low, the hurricane season is nearly over, and the teal-blue seas are bathtub warm. Five days are sufficient to enjoy the best of Nassau, with time for a foray to one of the peaceful yet fun-filled Family Islands.

Five Days of Fun in the Sun

DAY 1 Take a day out to enjoy the water park at Atlantis on Paradise Island. The waterslides here provide an adrenaline rush to remember, while the plexiglass tunnel and walls bring you closer to sharks and turtles than ever before. A video games center keeps kids amused, while teenagers get their own disco.

DAY 2 In the morning, go on a horse-drawn carriage ride through downtown Nassau and visit the Pirates of Nassau Museum, with its realistic enactments. After lunch, spend the afternoon enjoying the costumes and exhibits at Junkanoo Expo before heading to Straw Market for some shopping.

DAY 3 Experience an underwater voyage on the *Seaworld Explorer* submarine to view the coral reef. Later, head by boat to Blue Lagoon Island for lunch and to swim with dolphins, watch the sea lion show, or hand-feed stingrays. Spend the rest of the day lazing on the soft sand while the kids wade in shallow waters.

DAY 4 Powerboat around Paradise Island before landing at Blackbeard's Cay for half a day on the beach. In the afternoon, fly to Marsh Harbor and transfer to Green Turtle Cay. Balance off the afternoon with a walk through the colonial village, including a visit to Vert Lowe's Model Ship Shoppe.

DAY 5 Join a full-day "Family Adventure" with Brendal's Dive Center – a chance to hand-feed stingrays, snorkel, ride in a glass-bottomed boat, or sail on the Sea of Abaco. Spend another night in an intimate historic hotel before returning to Nassau the next day.

Dos and Don'ts

✓ Watch the children while they're playing in the ocean and teach them to shuffle their feet to disturb any stingrays that may be hidden in the sands.

✗ Don't overdo the powerful Bahamian cocktails! In any event, be sure to drink plenty of water.

✓ Do plan on a spot of snorkeling or another activity that enables you to tour the stunning underwater world.

JAN FEB MAR APR MAY JUN JUL AUG SEP OCT **NOV** DEC

GETTING THERE   See map p331, D4
Puerto Madryn has a regional airport 6 miles (10 km) from the town center.

GETTING AROUND
The entrance to Reserva Provincial Península Valdés is located at Istmo Ameghino, an isthmus 50 miles (80 km) northeast of Puerto Madryn. You will need a car to explore the peninsula, which you can rent at the airport.

WEATHER
The average daytime temperature is 72°F (22°C) and rain is rarely an issue. Bring a sweater and windbreaker though, as even in high summer there is a cool wind in the evenings.

ACCOMMODATIONS
Las Bardas Apart Hotel in Puerto Madryn has apartment-style rooms; doubles from US$110; www.lasbardas.com

Faro Punta Delgada is a remote old coastal lighthouse at the tip of the peninsula; doubles from US$168; www.puntadelgada.com

A new upscale hotel in Puerto Pirámides, Las Restingas has triples from US$350; www.lasrestingas.com

EATING OUT
Local dishes use a lot of meat and fish. Try Patagonia lamb at Faro Punta Delgada or fresh seafood at the ocean's edge at Punta Ballena Restaurant in Puerto Pirámides.

PRICE FOR A FAMILY OF FOUR
US$750 per day including accommodation, gasoline, food, whale-watching, activities, and protected area fees.

FURTHER INFORMATION
www.peninsulavaldes.org.ar

Killer Whales

The orca whales in the waters off the Valdés Peninsula have developed a hunting technique seen nowhere else on earth. These sleek black-and-white cetaceans stealthily cruise below the surf line beside the beaches where the sea lions and elephant seals give birth. The rising tide brings the orcas ever closer and whenever a pup forgets to move farther up the beach, the orcas are there to take advantage. They swim hard at the shoreline, slide up the pebbly sand to beach themselves and snag a pup in their jaws, then wriggle back into the ocean.

Main: A group of Magellanic penguins waddling along one of the peninsula's pebbly beaches

ANIMAL MAGIC

DEEP IN ARGENTINA'S SOUTHERN PATAGONIA PROVINCE, the Península Valdés juts out into the South Atlantic, connected to the mainland by only a long thin isthmus. The two broad shallow bays which flank the isthmus – Golfo San José and Golfo Nuevo – are favored birthing grounds of the endangered southern right whale. Hundreds of these behemoths arrive here to give birth and nurse their new calves and by November, the newborns are almost ready to set off on their first migration. A trip out to see them is one of the highlights of a visit to the peninsula. Board an inflatable zodiac boat and speed out into the broad calm waters of Golfo Nuevo, where the whales gather. These huge, gentle creatures seem to have no fear of man, often allowing the boats to drift close by.

Back on land, you can drive the gravel roads that run around the peninsula's plateau and cliff tops to see numerous other species that dwell in this wildlife haven. From August to April, the beaches at Valdés are crowded with tens of

Left (left to right): Female southern right whale and calf; red fox; guanacos, Patagonian llamas; young male elephant seal pups fighting for dominance

Below: Whale watching boat tour getting close to southern right whales

Inset: The lighthouse at Faro Punta Delgada

Above: Sheer cliffs lining the peninsula

To experience nature at its most glorious, rent bikes, gallop horses on the beaches, or snorkel in the clear waters of the southern Atlantic.

JAN
FEB
MAR
APR
MAY
JUN
JUL
AUG
SEP
OCT
NOV
DEC

ANIMAL LOVERS' DIARY

As the rich marine fauna is the chief reason for visiting the Valdés Peninsula, it's best to coordinate your visit with that of the wildlife. November is a particularly good month to come here, as nearly all the large charismatic species are present in force. Four days is enough time to circumnavigate the peninsula.

Four Days on the Isthmus

DAY 1

Pick up your vehicle at Puerto Madryn airport and head for the peninsula. When you arrive at the isthmus, stop at the visitor center for up-to-date information about the penguins, whales, seals, and sea lions. Drive the 3 miles (5 km) to Isla de los Pájaros (Island of Birds) and marvel at the sheer density of avian life in this sea colony. Continue on to the tiny village of Puerto Pirámides, where you can stroll the cliff tops at sunset looking for whales in the Golfo Nuevo.

DAY 2

Head out on the water on a whale-watching trip. If you are lucky, you might encounter southern right whales in the sheltered waters of Golfo Nuevo. Back on land, spend the afternoon touring by mountain bike along the tops of the towering cliffs that overlook the ocean.

DAY 3

Drive north, keeping an eye out for lesser rheas, guanacos (a kind of Patagonian llama), maras (a Patagonian rodent analogous to a hare), and their predators, foxes. Continue to Punta Norte, where sea lions raise their young, and packs of orcas try to make a meal of the young pups. Then head south along the cliff top to Punta Calor to see the elephant seal colony. Finish off the day with a meal and a bed at Faro Punta Delgada, an old lighthouse converted into a lodge.

DAY 4

Cruise the cliff tops above the penguin colonies. Stop at the salt pan, located an extraordinary 130 ft (40 m) below sea level. Then head back to Puerto Madryn and round off your trip dining on a fine supper of Atlantic fish or seafood plucked fresh from the ocean.

Dos and Don'ts

✓ Stop in at the Visitor Information Center at Istmo Ameghino to pick up a map and the latest information about the animals you might see that day.

✗ Don't forget to fill up on gasoline in Puerto Pirámides, the only place on the peninsula with a service station. A full circuit is close to 186 miles (300 km).

✓ Flop around on the sea lion beach like a new-born pup, but not while there are orcas around.

✓ Remember to bring along a good light pair of binoculars. You will be thankful for them when you are out spotting wildlife.

thousands of roly-poly Magellanic penguins. The penguin couples come to build a nest, lay a pair of eggs, and care for a growing clutch of young. In November, you can observe the big black-and-white seabirds and their newly hatched chicks from vantage points above the rookeries. Naturalists are on hand to provide binoculars and share educational stories about the penguins. The north tip of the isthmus provides a breeding ground and nursery for the hulking grey southern elephant seal. The males, which grow up to 16 ft (5 m) long and weigh up to 4 tons, arrive at Valdés in October and fight each other for control of beachfront and thus of breeding females. By November, the beaches are thick with seals. From the safety of a cliff-top observation point, you can watch as male elephant seals preen, charge, and batter each other for dominance. You could continue your journey around the peninsula by car, spotting the endless dramas played out in the animal kingdom along the way, but to really experience nature at its most glorious, leave the car behind and rent mountain bikes, gallop horses on the beaches, or snorkel in the clear waters of the southern Atlantic.

Above (left and right): Unwinding in the hot tub on board; relaxing on deck

GETTING THERE
See map p325, I5
The starting point of the Windstar and Star Clipper ships, Bridgetown, in Barbados, can be reached by air from the UK and North America.

GETTING AROUND
Grantley Adams Airport is 8 miles (13 km) from Bridgetown. Island excursions ashore are offered and dockside taxis await custom.

WEATHER
November is delightful, with sunshine, steady trade winds, and daytime temperatures averaging 81°F (27°C). Hurricane season is all but over, and rainfall is limited.

ACCOMMODATIONS
En suite cabins on the ships offer a choice of elegant staterooms or wood-paneled suites.

Bridgetown's secluded, all-suite Cobblers Cove offers country-house sophistication; doubles from US$490; www.cobblerscove.com

Sandy Lane in Bridgetown offers pampered luxury and a colonial ambience; doubles from US$1,100; www.sandylane.com

EATING OUT
Excellent meals are served on board, but do sample local fare. Try pepperpot stew and a pan-fried flying fish sandwich at Bridgetown's Waterfront Café. In Speightstown, Mango's by the Sea is famous for fresh seafood (US$10).

PRICE FOR TWO
Caribbean voyages cost US$600–1,100 per day, including full board. Add sightseeing, airport transfers, and a night ashore.

FURTHER INFORMATION
www.windstarcruises.com
www.starclippers.co.uk

Split Personality

Half French, half Dutch, the island of Saint Maarten/Saint-Martin (and nine more spelling variants) is as schizophrenic as its name suggests. Though they share gorgeous beaches and scrubby terrain, the two halves – there is no border post – are distinctly different. The Dutch capital, Philipsburg, is known for casinos and duty-free shopping, while Marigot, on the French side, is famous for its fort (*see below*), nude beaches, chic hotels, and fine dining.

TREASURE ISLES CRUISE

IT'S DAWN IN THE CARIBBEAN and roseate sunlight glitters upon glassy waters silhouetting emerald isles rising sheer from seas of impossible blues and greens. Coral reefs edge up to frosted sands that coruscate like diamonds washed ashore from a Spanish treasure ship and the colors seem to pulsate in the Caribbean light.

A voyage aboard a modern tall-masted ship inspired by the grand age of sail is different from your typical cruise experience, offering an intimacy that mega-cruiseliners can't deliver. These ships operate Caribbean cruises from November through March, plying the isles of the eastern Caribbean, from the Virgin Islands to Barbados. Itineraries vary, as there are so many islands to choose from and most cruising is done at night to maximize the time you have ashore. Towering, computer-operated sails define the sleek modern vessels, with their casual yet elegant atmosphere.

Gliding from isle to isle and anchoring in pristine bays, cruising reveals the exquisite landscapes that make the Caribbean unique. The colorful Caribbean cultures, influenced by the French, Dutch and English, are as distinct as your thumbprint. Just the printed itinerary seems to conjure up the shrieking of parrots and pirates.

While on board, you can laze on deck to savor the beauty of the passing isles, while spas offer relaxing treatments. Donning snorkel mask and flippers, you'll discover a world more beautiful than a casket of gems. Cloaked in deepest verdure, magnificent mountains rise grandly behind quaint villages of gaily painted wooden houses edged with gingerbread trim. Steel bands welcome you ashore to explore markets piled high with tropical fruits. Well-planned excursions will take you on city tours, into the rain forests, kayaking, or even to the crater of a simmering volcano. Sun on palm-lined beaches, dive with dolphins, or possibly thrill to humpback whales cavorting in bathtub-warm waters. Mother Nature melds with history at colonial-era towns, fortresses and plantations: Basseterre and Wingfield Plantation on St. Kitts, St. Lucia, and Marigot town and St. Louis fort on St-Martin/St. Maarten. Sailing before the wind to these pearls teeming with wildlife and colonial intrigue only adds to the romance of cruising.

Main: Sailing under blue skies
Below (left and right): St. Lucia and the Pitons; colorful sarongs billowing in the Barbados trade winds

Above: Palm-fringed beach in St. Barts

JAN
FEB
MAR
APR
MAY
JUN
JUL
AUG
SEP
OCT
NOV
DEC

TRADE WINDS DIARY

The Windward and Leeward islands are perfect in balmy November weather. Cruising is the way to go, and nothing can quite compare to the romantic thrill of a voyage aboard a tall-masted sailing ship, each with its unique itinerary. Explore ashore, and in the evenings don your tux (or not) and enjoy the good life.

Eight Days Under Sail

Arrive in, and explore, quaint colonial Bridgetown before boarding your vessel for a midnight departure.	**DAY 1**
Shake off the workday routine on your first full day at sea and relax with a good book and spa treatment.	**DAY 2**
Put ashore at Basseterre, St. Kitts, where Georgian architecture nestles against lush foliage. Back on board, continue to neighboring Nevis – another gem with dramatic architecture and mountains.	**DAY 3**
Anchor at St-Martin/St. Maarten and take a shore excursion to compare chic Marigot – a kind of St. Tropez of the Caribbean – with Philipsburg, offering excellent duty-free shopping. Next morning, laze on any of the island's 37 white-sand beaches before departing for picture-perfect St. Bart's. Explore by open air Jeep or "mini-moke."	**DAYS 4–5**
Guadeloupe is home to the enchanting Deshaies Botanical Gardens, sugar estates, and rum plantations. Take the Planter's Experience excursion, and then it's on to quaint Îles des Saintes to explore on your own.	**DAY 6**
Admire the spectacular scenery as you approach St. Lucia. There, cruise by catamaran to Soufrière Volcano, or ride the cable car into the rain forest.	**DAY 7**
After berthing back in Bridgetown, either fly home or spend a day or two exploring this welcoming island.	**DAY 8**

Dos and Don'ts

✓ Pack sunscreen, a shade hat, and comfy walking shoes.

✗ Don't fail to spend time in Barbados before or after your cruise. It's a lovely island, with lots to see and do.

✓ Take advantage of the shore excursions offered on board. They make experiencing each island's highlights easy.

✓ Research prices for electronic goods, perfumes, and other duty-free items, as they aren't always bargains ashore.

PARADE OF WINTER WONDERS

GETTING THERE   See map p313, E6

GETTING THERE
Banff is 78 miles (130 km) west of Calgary. Banff Airporter buses depart Calgary Airport for Banff every two hours. Greyhound buses depart from downtown Calgary.

GETTING AROUND
The best way to travel is by car. Avis and National have agencies in Banff and at Calgary Airport. Banff's Budget Rent a Car is often a cheaper alternative.

WEATHER
Daytime temperatures in November average 23°F (-5°C). At night the mercury drops to about 16°F (-9°C). Expect 14 inches (35 cm) of snow with flurries every third day.

ACCOMMODATIONS
Post Hotel, Lake Louise; doubles from US$300; www.posthotel.com

Château Lake Louise on Lake Louise shores; doubles from US$400; www.fairmont.com

The historic Banff Springs Hotel is one of the nicest in Canada; doubles from US$450; www.fairmont.com/banffsprings

EATING OUT
Eat roadside burgers for US$5 or dine at high-end restaurants serving tasty cuisine for US$75 a head. Try the Buffalo Mountain Lodge or Melissa's Restaurant and Bar.

PRICE FOR TWO
US$600–700 for accommodation, food, car rental, and lift passes per day.

FURTHER INFORMATION
www.banff.ca
www.skibanff.com

The Hot Springs of History

Banff was settled in the early 1880s, after the transcontinental Canadian Pacific Railway (CPR) was built through Bow Valley. In 1883, three CPR workers stumbled across a natural hot spring on the side of Sulphur Mountain. A dispute over ownership of the hot springs led the young Canadian government to intervene in 1885 and create a national park, the third in the world at the time, named simply Rocky Mountain Park.

THERE ARE PARTS OF THE WORLD where the onset of winter is greeted with gray resignation, but those places are far from Banff. Located in a perfect U-shaped glacial valley, Banff is an icy fairyland. With razor-sharp ridges flanking the valley walls and majestic peaks on every horizon, Banff transforms come winter from a verdant playground to a wonderland of snow.

The city and surrounding Bow Valley celebrates this transformation with Winterstart, a week-long festival of events welcoming the winter season. The festival begins with a twinkling parade of lights through the streets, followed by an exhibition of snowboard acrobatics called a Rail Jam, where amateurs and professionals work a snowy ramp and horizontal rail, showing off jumps, twists, and flips of awesome skill. Farther up the Bow Valley at the Lake Louise ski area, witness the most

Main: The Santa Claus Parade of Lights kickstarting Winterstart

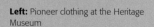
Left: Pioneer clothing at the Heritage Museum

Right (left and right): Sled dogs ready for a run; skiers enjoying the fine powder snow above Lake Louise

prestigious spectacle of Winterstart, the Women's Downhill Races. Thousands of fans ride up on the gondola and line the race course to watch and beat cowbells and wave flags as the world's top-ranked women downhillers scream past at speeds that turn them into blurs.

Between these events, experience the wonders of a Bow Valley winter. On the first Saturday of Winterstart, carve the runs at either Sunshine or Lake Louise, paying a token fee for a lift pass, or hike through snow-draped forests of lodgepole pine and balsam fir. The north wind, Boreas, permitting, strap on skates and glide over the frozen surface of Lake Louise. And perhaps best of all, simply drive along the Bow Valley Parkway, each curve and rise in the roadway offering a majestic vista of frozen lake or tree-clad hillside. Along the parkway there are several spots to pull over and watch the sunshine play across the crystal surface of a white meadow – a chance to glory in the virginal whiteness unique to snow during those first few days when it is still untouched.

Above: Bare branches clad in snow at Banff National Park

SNOWBOUND DIARY

The Winterstart Festival marks the advent of the ski season. Held at the end of November and in the first few days of December, Winterstart offers a parade of lights, snowboard competitions, and the first World Cup ski race of the season. Five days are enough to enjoy the events and explore the region's natural wonders.

Five Days in the Rockies

DAY 1 Drive from Calgary up to Banff. When you arrive in Banff, go for a walk and enjoy the mountain air. Stop at the Whyte Museum of the Canadian Rockies for a deeper understanding of the mountains. In the afternoon, head up to Banff Upper Hot Springs to soak up some local history, but be sure to be back on Banff's main street by evening, to witness the Santa Claus Parade of Lights that kicks off Winterstart.

DAY 2 Experience the snow for yourself at Sunshine, one of three ski mountains that make Banff a winter sports paradise. Be back in town by afternoon to watch the incredible snowboard acrobatics of the CP Rail Jam.

DAY 3 Take a leisurely drive on the stunning Bow Valley Parkway. Stop at the Buffalo Nations Luxton Museum to learn about the First Nations people of the area. Visit Lake Louise and go up the mountain by mid-morning to see the incredible spectacle of speed and control that is World Cup Women's Downhill Races, the first stop on the women's world tour.

DAY 4 Ski at Lake Louise for the day and see how you compare with the world's top-ranked women. In the evening, see one of the mountain films showing in town as part of the Winterstart festivities.

DAY 5 Enjoy the view out over Lake Louise. Don skates and glide across the Lake Louise ice. Alternatively, try some true Canadian culture and set out dog-sledding. Enjoy the beautiful drive back down the valley to Banff and Calgary.

Dos and Don'ts

✓ Keep an eye out for elk as you drive the Bow Valley Parkway. They're prettier in the bush than they are on your bumper.

✓ Bring your skates and say a prayer for cold weather.

✗ Don't forget the scarf and gloves.

✓ Splurge one night on a really top-quality meal; Banff has cuisine to match any in Canada.

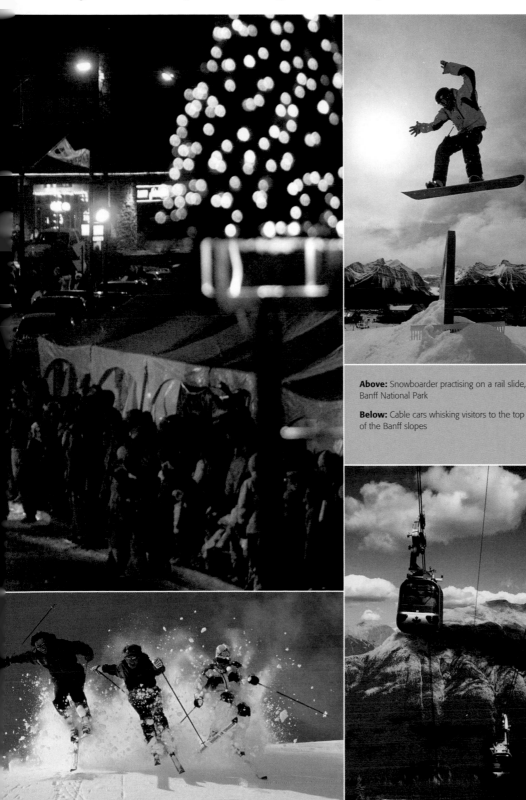

Above: Snowboarder practising on a rail slide, Banff National Park

Below: Cable cars whisking visitors to the top of the Banff slopes

JAN
FEB
MAR
APR
MAY
JUN
JUL
AUG
SEP
OCT
NOV
DEC

DECEMBER

Where to Go: **December**

From the beginning of the month, most of North America is consumed by Christmas fever. Chill temperatures are compensated for by the warmth of colonial-style decorations and steaming mulled wine. Hispanic San Antonio, Texas drapes its pretty River Walk with lights and has carolers sing from boats. Hot on the heels of Christmas comes New Year – Pasadena, in southern California, offers a big parade and balmy temperatures. Canada, meanwhile, comes into its own in December, with vast swathes of pristine skiing territory. Tropical Hawai′i offers a tantalizingly warmer alternative, while much of Central America is dry and sunny, and South America enjoys a sultry summer. Below you will find all the destinations in this chapter and some extra suggestions to provide inspiration.

FESTIVALS AND CULTURE

RIO DE JANEIRO Colorful performers at a samba club

UNFORGETTABLE JOURNEYS

COPPER CANYON Locomotive crossing the canyon on Temoris Bridge

NATURAL WONDERS

ANGEL FALLS A *tepuy* swathed in cloud

RIO DE JANEIRO
BRAZIL

This is a New Year's party like you've never seen before

New Year's celebrations on Copacabana Beach in Rio are an unbeatable mix of hedonism, music, fireworks, and potent cocktails.
See pp302–3

CHICHICASTENANGO
GUATEMALA

Crafts and curios in handicraft heaven

The pretty little town of Chichi hosts a spectacular market, with colorful clothes, crafts, and curios.
www.enjoyguatemala.com/ chichicastenango.htm

COPPER CANYON
MEXICO

The daddy of all canyons, with a railway running through it

The railway is a phenomenal feat of engineering through a natural wonder – the largest canyon in the world.
See pp294–5

CHILOÉ
CHILE

Beautiful islands off the Chilean coast

Ride the ferry from Puerto Montt to the windswept and unspoilt archipelago of Chiloé.
www.chilediscover.com/ chiloeisland.htm

ANGEL FALLS
VENEZUELA

Explore a magical "lost world" and a waterfall

Visit a Permon Indian village and travel upriver in a dug-out canoe to see the world's highest falls in their beautiful rain forest setting.
See pp292–3

NORTHERN LIGHTS
ALASKA/NORTHERN CANADA

Head north in search of the remarkable aurora borealis.

These unforgettable lighting effects are a common sight in Alaska and northern Canada from October through March.
www.alaska.com

BALTIMORE
MARYLAND, USA

One of the east coast's most engaging cities.

Off-beat Baltimore musters an absorbing mix of attractions and an attractively restored waterfront.
www.baltimore.org

DEATH VALLEY
CALIFORNIA, USA

One of the hottest places on Earth

Death Valley National Park is a place of legend, and this desert presents nature at its most extreme and unforgiving.
www.nps.gov/deva

OLD PATAGONIAN EXPRESS
ARGENTINA

Journey Esquel to el Maiten

Hop on this traditional steam-drawn railway, which runs across the endless Patagonian Cordillera.
www.patagonia-argentina.com/i/ andina/esquel/trochita.htm

"Isolated at the bottom of the world, the Falklands make for one of the Americas' most breathtaking stops."

FALKLAND ISLANDS
SOUTH ATLANTIC

Islands at the end of the world – a nature lover's paradise

Set in splendid isolation, the wildlife here (including five types of penguin) has little fear of man, so you'll see it close-up.
See pp298–9

PASADENA
CALIFORNIA, USA

See in the New Year at the Tournament of Roses Parade

This extravanganza featuring rose-adorned floats and marching bands is an all-American way to celebrate New Year's.
See pp300–1

LAGUNA VERDE
CHILE

Surreal volcanic lake high in the Andes

The strangely colored waters of Laguna Verde ringed by towering volcanoes including the soaring Ojos de Salado.
www.visitchile.com

JUNKANOO
BAHAMAS

The biggest party in the Bahamas

Nassau is taken over by competing "crews" and their spectacular floats amidst a riot of music, color, and dancers in fabulous costumes.
www.junkanoo.com

FROZEN ALASKA
ALASKA, USA

Get to the heart of the Arctic winter

Drive a 4WD through frozen woods from Anchorage to Fairbanks and back, and, with luck, you'll see the aurora borealis.
www.alaskatours.com

SAN BLAS ISLANDS
PANAMA

Explore the customs and landscape of Native America

Remote islands that are home to the Kuna Indians, who guide visitors to the abundant wildlife with intimate knowledge.
www.explorepanama.com

Weather Watch

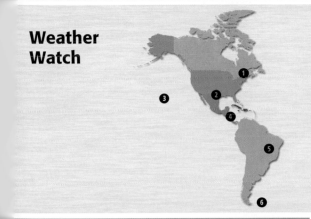

❶ **Laurentians, Canada** Snow falls in luxurious abundance in December, with a flurry at least once every few days. Daytime temperatures are low, but the bright sunshine keeps things cheery.

❷ **San Antonio, USA** San Antonio tends to be warm, sunny, and dry, though temperatures can plummet from one day to the next, and nights are far cooler.

❸ **Hawai'i, USA** If you're beach-bound, you can expect some nice warm weather; up at the crater of the Kilauea volcano, temperatures can drop. Sunshine in the coastal resorts is pretty much guaranteed.

❹ **Costa Rica** The wet season is over in the Nicoya peninsula, where hot, sunny days and balmy breezes are the norm and downpours are a distant memory.

❺ **Brazil** Summer is in full flight in Brazil; it's hot and humid in Rio. South of the city the humidity increases, tempered by rain showers. Rain is generally heaviest south of the Amazon.

❻ **Falkland Islands** Famously changeable, the Falkland Islands are well into their summer, which brings sunny days and pleasant temperatures. There is always the possibility of wind and rain, however, and it can get cool.

LUXURY AND ROMANCE

ANGUILLA A picture-perfect beach

ACTIVE ADVENTURES

CAYMAN ISLANDS Diving around a wreck

FAMILY GETAWAYS

SAN ANTONIO Decorated candle-holders

ANGUILLA
CARIBBEAN

A secluded haven for you and a loved one to enjoy

As well as idyllic white-sand beaches, Anguilla, with its small size, few visitors, and great lodgings has massive romantic charm.
See pp290–91

MANZANILLO
MEXICO

Vibrant yet laid-back resort on the Pacific coast

The busy port of Manzanillo is surrounded by plush resorts and sandy beaches, with plenty of outdoor fun, too.
www.gomanzanillo.com

TORTOLA
BRITISH VIRGIN ISLANDS, CARIBBEAN

An island paradise

Simply enjoy the talcum-soft sand and crystal-clear waters for swimming, freshly caught seafood, and fruity cocktails.
www.bvitourism.com

NICOYA PENINSULA
COSTA RICA

Miles of sun-kissed coastline backed by thick forest

With Pacific coast surf, good weather, beautiful beaches, jungle adventures, and wildlife, the Nicoya peninsula is the hot place to visit.
See pp288–9

> "The mountainous interior forms a rugged backdrop to sensational beaches in every shade, from taupe to gold. "

TELLURIDE
COLORADO, USA

Winter sports with a very fashionable buzz

Every winter sport can be tried in the Rockies' most fashionable resort, or you can just enjoy the stunning view from a luxurious suite.
www.thepeaksresort.com

CAYMAN ISLANDS
CARIBBEAN

A tropical paradise with some of the world's best dive sites

The crystal clear waters of these magical islands are perfect for diving, snorkeling, or paddling with gentle stingrays.
See pp296–7

SIAN KA'AN BIOSPHERE RESERVE, YUCATÁN
MEXICO

Mangroves and history

Go walking or boating through this pristine coastal preserve, dotted with Mayan ruins.
www.cesiak.org

QUÉBEC AND THE LAURENTIANS
QUÉBEC, CANADA

Ski and explore a city

The spectacular Laurentians offer the best skiing east of the Rockies, and all just 30 minutes from fascinating Québec City.
See pp282–3

DOMINICA
CARIBBEAN

This pristine ocean rain forest is a great active destination

Go hiking, scuba diving, or horseback riding and fully experience this wonderful natural wilderness.
www.dominica.dm

THE EXUMAS
THE BAHAMAS

Sea-kayak through the Bahamas

The Exumas' 365 tiny islands and cays are perfect for paddling, with shallow waters and hundreds of deserted sandy beaches.
www.kayakbahamas.com

SAN ANTONIO
TEXAS, USA

Get in the Christmas spirit along the River Walk

Near the historic site of the Alamo, Paseo del Rio in San Antonio puts on a fabulous display of Christmas cheer.
See pp280–81

MOUNT TREMBLANT
QUÉBEC, CANADA

Family-friendly skiing near Montréal

At the highest point of the Laurentian Mountains, this purpose-built, family-friendly ski resort has facilities for all ages.
www.tremblant.ca

WILLIAMSBURG
VIRGINIA, USA

Christmas flavors of 18th-century colonial life

This authentic recreation of the historic capital of Virginia comes alive at Christmas with quaint traditions and festive decorations.
See pp286–7

ACAPULCO
MEXICO

Playas aplenty and a family-fun atmosphere

Fringing one of the most beautiful bays on Mexico's Pacific coast, Acapulco is the country's most famous resort.
www.acapulco.com

> "Hawai'i is not just a smorgasbord of astounding geographical features, but is also home to friendly island communities."

HAWAI'I
HAWAI'I, USA

Also known as "Big Island," it packs a lot in for its size

Famous for its beaches, Hawai'i offers more besides. Explore volcanoes and rain forests and lap up the warm welcome.
See pp284–5

GETTING THERE
See map p318, E5

San Antonio is in south Texas, served by the San Antonio International Airport, 8 miles (13 km) north of downtown. Cars can be rented at the airport. There is a shuttle service into the city.

GETTING AROUND
In the Downtown area most attractions are within walking distance or on the VIA Streetcar route. However, there is also taxi and VIA Bus service. A car is the best way to explore farther.

WEATHER
December is generally sunny and pleasant, with low humidity. Temperature range from 41–64°F (5–18°C) and cooler nights of 41°F (5°C).

ACCOMMODATIONS
Hyatt Regency San Antonio has a section of the River Walk running through it; rooms start at US$175; www.sanantonioregency.hyatt.com

Menger Hotel is a favorite choice; rooms from US$200; www.mengerhotel.com

Amerisuites Riverwalk offers Riverwalk location and rooms with kitchenettes from US$235; www.amerisuites.com

EATING OUT
Local favorites include mildly spicy TexMex, smoke-cooked barbeque, steak, and local wild game. Southwestern and International cuisines is available at upscale restaurants.

PRICE FOR TWO
US$600 per day including hotel, food, admissions, and local travel.

FURTHER INFORMATION
www.sanantoniocvb.com

"Remember the Alamo!"

This popular rallying cry for defenders of freedom derives from the battle in which 189 Texas/American defenders, and more than 600 Mexican soldiers fought called the Battle of the Alamo. Although the first of five Spanish Missions was built along the San Antonio River in the early 18th century, by the Texas Revolution in 1836 the old mission had been used as a military outpost for years. Today, the Alamo is seen as a symbol of bravery, and a shrine honors those who died.

Main: River Walk, a yearly festive celebration of song and good cheer

RIVER OF LIGHTS AND MUSIC

EVERY WEEKEND IN DECEMBER, THE PATHWAYS OF SAN ANTONIO'S historic Paseo del Rio attract thousands of families to enjoy its celebration of Christmas. San Antonio is a small, unpretentious city with a warm heart, especially at this time, when the focus is on genuine festive fun. Here the beautifully landscaped walkways are softly illuminated by thousands of glowing candles that line the river's edge. Overhead, a myriad of tiny glimmering lights hang in festoons from the branches of century-old trees. Strolling musicians play seasonal music as happy crowds fill the walkways, restaurants, and gaily lit bridges that arch gracefully over the river.

Along the River Walk, the joyful melodies of familiar Christmas carols fill the air as boats laden with singing carolers slowly float by, their songs echoed by diners joining in from riverside cafés. The marvelous scents of slow-roasted wild turkey, Mexican fajitas, and hot apple pie waft on the night air, emanating from dozens of riverside

SAN ANTONIO TEXAS, USA   **281**

JAN
FEB
MAR
APR
MAY
JUN
JUL
AUG
SEP
OCT
NOV
DEC

Top: Boy hitting a festive *pinata* (lantern) to break out the candy

Above: Three wise kings in procession

Below: Religious candle-holders

Bottom: Mexican dancer

Above: Store front in La Villita

SAN ANTONIO DIARY

Although the River Walk is festooned with glittering lights for all of December, the first half of the month is particularly enthralling. Three days allows enough time to explore the Alamo and major attractions, and still have time to shop at Market Square and the boutique shops while listening to caroling choirs.

Three Days of Christmas Magic

Head over to San Fernando Cathedral. During the Battle of the Alamo, this is where Mexican General Santa Anna flew the red flag of no mercy. Explore the Spanish Governor's Palace and then go to Market Square for lunch; afterwards, shop in the huge Mexican marketplace.

Drive to the McNay Art Museum where masterpieces by Gauguin, Picasso, O'Keeffe, Hopper, Renoir, and many more are presented in a stunning Spanish Colonial Mansion. Explore the nearby Lucille Halsell Conservatory at the San Antonio Botanical Garden and wander through lush indoor jungles. Or, visit San Antonio Zoo with its 3,500 animals from around the world. Have dinner along the vibrant River Walk.

DAY 1

Walk south along the River Walk to the end of the King Williams District for breakfast, or lunch at Guenther House and visit the museum there. Stroll past the mansions in the King Williams District, and check out La Villita's historic buildings, boutique shops, and galleries. Walk over to the Alamo and visit the shrine.

DAY 2

Wander back to the River Walk, take a boat cruise and have dinner in an outdoor cafe. Meander along the River Walk, admire the festoons of lights, sing along with the carolers, and visit The Landing for live music.

Drive to nearby Missions National Historic Park for the day, and tour the four 18th-century missions standing majestically along the Mission Trail. Head back to the major malls for some last-minute Christmas shopping.

DAY 3

Dos and Don'ts

✓ Make reservations early for accommodations along the River Walk – they become booked up far in advance.

✓ Before booking hotels, check the December schedule for the dates of Bazar Sábado (Saturday Bazaar), which features Mexican folk art, and San Fernando Cathedral's *La Gran Posada*, a re-enactment of the Christmas story.

✓ Splurge and attend a holiday performance at the Lila Cockrell Theatre or in the lavish Majestic Theatre, surrounded by ornate 1920s vaudeville style decor under a simulated night sky.

✗ Don't miss the lobby in the famous Menger Hotel where Theodore Roosevelt stayed in 1898.

restaurants. The lobbies of historic buildings and gleaming hotels all along the river are decked out in appropriate garb, vying with each other to present the prettiest displays of fresh greenery, red poinsettias, and brightly decorated Christmas trees. Take a peek into the magnificent Victorian lobby of the elegant, famous Menger Hotel where Theodore Roosevelt stayed while recruiting Rough Riders during the Spanish-American War.

Around the river, the boutique shops, hotels, and gracious churches of old San Antonio are also decorated with numerous candles and colored lights. Along Alamo Street, the shop windows showcase animated displays of elves and crackling Christmas hearths, and Alamo Plaza has a huge festive tree with lights. Residents and visitors alike enter the Alamo shrine and remember those young men who fought bravely in 1836. A few blocks away, at San Fernando Cathedral in the heart of old San Antonio, the essence of Christmas is celebrated by the annual re-enactment of Joseph and Mary looking for shelter, and visitors and San Antonians join together to rejoice in this historic city's most joyful season.

GETTING THERE
See map p314, E6

The ski areas of Mont Sainte-Anne, Le Massif, and Stoneham are a 30-minute drive north of Québec City. Jean Lesage International Airport is 7 miles (11 km) south of the city.

GETTING AROUND
Québec City's downtown is a lovely place to stroll, even in winter. The Winter Shuttle (US$25) runs 40-minute trips from downtown to the ski areas.

WEATHER
Lack of snow is never a problem as some 30 in (75 cm) of snow falls on average in December. Daytime temperatures hover around 14°F (-10°C).

ACCOMMODATIONS
A smaller antique hotel in the Old City, Hotel Château Bellevue has doubles from US$115; www.oldquebec.com/en/bellevue

Château Mont Sainte-Anne, a four-star hotel, offers doubles at US$290 and discounted five-day packages; www.chateaumsa.com

Fairmont Le Château Frontenac overlooks the river in downtown Québec City. Doubles are US$500; www.fairmont.com/Frontenac

EATING OUT
Enjoy top French cuisine (US$150–200 for two, excluding wine) in the Old City, and Québécois cuisine at Laurie Raphael. You can find good hearty fare for much less as well.

PRICE FOR TWO
US$460 per day covers accommodation, meals, and lift tickets, or a five-day package at Château Mont Sainte-Anne is US$1,400.

FURTHER INFORMATION
www.quebecregion.com/e

Montmorency Falls

A visit to Montmorency Falls is one of the oldest wintertime excursions from Québec City, recorded in oil paintings from before the fall of New France in 1759 (see p186). Named by Samuel de Champlain for his patron Henry II, Duke of Montmorency, and formed where the Montmorency River plunges into the St. Lawrence, the Montmorency Falls are a towering 276 ft (84 m) high, taller even than Niagara. In winter, the spray freezes into a crystalline tower of ice that can reach 98 ft (30 m) in height, known as the *pain de sucre*, or sugarloaf.

Above (left and right): Powder skiing at Le Massif; cross-country skiers heading past a cabin on Stoneham Mountain
Main: Climber on the half-frozen Montmorency Falls

Above: Québec City's Château Frontenac dominating the town

JAN
FEB
MAR
APR
MAY
JUN
JUL
AUG
SEP
OCT
NOV
DEC
DAY 1
DAY 2
DAY 3
DAY 4
DAY 5

SKI TRAILS AND CHATEAUS

"A FEW ACRES OF SNOW" was Voltaire's disparaging assessment of the intrinsic value of Québec, in the years when France was losing its New World empire to the English. Turns out it was closer to a few thousand – 2,841 acres (1,150 ha) of skiable terrain, divvied up among three of the largest and most modern ski resorts in eastern North America: Mont Sainte-Anne, Le Massif, and Stoneham. The three stand close to each other on the north bank of the St. Lawrence River, just upriver from the city that was the heart of New France.

Voltaire may have got the acreage and intrinsic value wrong, but he was right about the white stuff. Positioned on the Gulf of St. Lawrence, the mountains get almost 118 in (300 cm) of natural snow a year, beginning in October and falling every fourth day until March. Due to its high water content, the snow quickly compresses into a fast, firm surface known as "eastern hardpack." Though well endowed with beginner and intermediate runs, Mont Sainte-Anne is known for its black diamond trails: steep straight chutes down the mountain, eastern hardwoods to either side, and icy, fast eastern hardpack underfoot. The relentless carving of countless skiers quickly turns these trails into a cornucopia of moguls (snow mounds) – steep, deep, and icy. Less blessed in elevation than Mont Sainte-Anne, Stoneham specializes as a snowboarders' destination, with three different terrain parks, from a gentle learners' area to a radical half-pipe with 23-ft (7-m) high walls, the equivalent of boarding up the side of a two-story house.

Wherever you've spent your day, in the evening you get to explore Québec City, one of the oldest in North America. Chuck snowballs or dodge the snowflakes on the Dufferin Terrace, then take the funicular down to the brightly lit streets of the Lower City. When the chill sets in, duck into a candlelit restaurant for something warm, filling, and French, preferably with a fine Bordeaux.

> Acres of skiable terrain, divvied up among three of the largest and most modern ski resorts in eastern North America.

Inset: Exhilarating trails on Mont Sainte-Anne. **Below (left and right):** Row of decorated stone houses in Québec City; a French restaurant in the Old City

DEEP SNOW DIARY

The gorgeous walled Québec City (see pp186–7) sits on the heights above the St. Lawrence River, just half an hour's drive from three of the best ski resorts in the Laurentians: Mont Sainte-Anne, Stoneham, and Le Massif. December in Québec brings colored street lights and Yuletide cheer, plus lots and lots of snow.

Five Days of Mountain Sport

Head out early for Mont Sainte-Anne, one of the tallest and most extensive ski areas in eastern North America, to experience the mountains of natural snow. Don't forget to pause and enjoy the breathtaking view of the St. Lawrence River from the summit.

Spend a second day exploring the extensive trails at Mont Sainte-Anne. With three sides of the mountain developed, the skiable terrain never ends. In the evening, enjoy a leisurely dinner at one of the fine French restaurants in the Lower City.

For something different, strap on a snowboard and head for the snowboard park at Stoneham Mountain, Mont Sainte-Anne's smaller neighbor. In the evening, stroll around in the Old City as far as the city walls.

Get up early and make the slightly longer trip to Le Massif, Mont Sainte-Anne's new Laurentian rival. Have dinner at a French restaurant on Grande Allée. If it's snowing, walk on the Dufferin Terrace watching the big, heavy flakes float down and settle.

Return to Mont Sainte-Anne, but for a change of pace head to the cross-country skiing area, the largest selection of groomed cross-country trails in North America. Or strap on snowshoes and explore the terrain on foot. On the final afternoon, take a last stroll around the historic Old City, replete with antique stone houses.

Dos and Don'ts

✓ Brush up on your French before you go. In the sensitive world of francophone Québec, even the smallest effort *en français* is much appreciated.

✗ Don't miss out on maple syrup. In Québec, they slather it on breakfasts of pancakes, sausage, and beans, serve it as dessert in maple sugar and maple toffee, and if that's not enough, you can even have your tree sap with a kick, in the form of maple syrup liqueur.

✓ Take a box lunch to get in a full day of skiing during the short daylight hours, and in the evenings, take advantage of the sightseeing and fine dining Québec City offers.

AN ISLAND OF CONTRASTS

GETTING THERE   See map p322, H7, I7
Flights from mainland USA and other Hawaiian islands land at Kona International Airport on the west side of the Big Island and at Hilo International Airport on the east.

GETTING AROUND
This island is best explored by car; rentals are available at the international airports.

WEATHER
December temperatures average 71–77°F (22–25°C) at sea level and around 57–63°F (14–17°C) at the 4,000-ft (1,219-m) Volcanoes National Park.

ACCOMMODATIONS
Most resorts and hotels are on the Kona and Kohala coasts on the west side.

Near Volcanoes National Park, Volcano Inn offers rustic accommodation; family room from US$95; www.volcanoinnhawaii.com

Casual Outrigger Kanaloa at Kona offers apartments with kitchens; two-bedroom units from US$220; www.outrigger.com

Further north, luxury resort Hilton Waikoloa Village has a dolphin pool; doubles from US$240; www.hiltonwaikoloavillage.com

EATING OUT
Most restaurants serve Pacific Rim and Hawaiian food. Café meals are under US$10; restaurant dinners cost US$35–50.

PRICE FOR A FAMILY OF FOUR
US$750 per day for accommodation, food, and activities described.

FURTHER INFORMATION
www.bigisland.org

HAWAI'I, KNOWN TO HAWAIIANS JUST AS THE "BIG ISLAND," IS ONE BIG BLAST – literally. Comprising five volcanoes, the island presents startling climatic and dramatic diversity, from beneath its coral-fringed sea to the top of the snow-capped Mauna Kea and Mauna Loa peaks. The Big Island's attractions include black- and white-sand beaches, calm inlets and wild surf, humpback whales and basking sea turtles, thundering waterfalls and molten lava deserts, thousands of petroglyphs, and working cattle ranches. Mingling with these stunning images are rare native flora. The aromas of freshly roasted Kona coffee, crunchy macadamia nuts, chocolates, vanilla, and honey waft in the air.

Soaring overhead are flocks of kaleidoscopic birds, including Hawai'i's national bird, the endangered *nene* (Hawaiian goose). And towering over the island is the steep, hard-to-get-to Mauna

The Hawaiian Wild West

Big Island cowboy culture can be traced to 1798, when Captain George Vancouver gifted King Kamehameha some longhorn cattle. Later, horses were introduced, followed by the arrival of rancher John Palmer Parker, who hired Mexican *vaqueros*. Dubbed *paniolo* or Español, these men brought along a hard-working albeit flamboyant lifestyle. Hawaiian women also took to horses. Lei-wreathed and elaborately dressed, the Pau riders created a sort of "hula on horseback," which is still performed at festivals and international parades.

Main: Tourists photographing a humpback whale

Left: Thurston Lava Tube at Kīlauea Volcano

Right (left to right): Fourspot butterfly fish; a Hawaiian *luau*

Right panel (top to bottom):
A crowd of people watching the lava spewing forth at the Volcanoes National Park; Hawai'i's national bird, the endangered *nene*; Mauna Kea Observatory; the black volcanic sands of Punalu'u Beach

JAN

FEB

MAR

APR

MAY

JUN

JUL

AUG

SEP

OCT

NOV

DEC

DAY 1

DAY 2

DAY 3

DAY 4

DAY 5

DAYS 6–7

Kea, which at 13,796 ft (4,200 m) is Hawai'i's highest point. In fact, Mauna Kea rises approximately 32,000 ft (9,754 m) from the ocean floor to its summit, making it reputedly the tallest mountain on the planet. Great for stargazing, this peak is home to world-renowned observatories. It is possible to drive to the Mauna Loa summit, but it can be treacherous and is best undertaken with a tour operator and 4WD vehicle.

The Volcanoes National Park, the volcanic wonderland to the southeast, is home to still-active volcanoes Mauna Loa and Kīlauea. Although there's no guarantee of an eruption (it all depends on the mood of the Volcano Goddess, Pele), there are superb drives and hikes through this landscape of lava tubes and rain forests. Hawai'i is also home to friendly island communities. These include resort towns, sleepy fishing villages, and the "old Hawai'i," Hilo Town. The Big Island encompasses a big 'ohana (family) that welcomes all with a heartfelt aloha.

Above: Rainbow Falls

HAWAIIAN DIARY

December is an ideal time to visit the Big Island with your family and go on a *holoholo* (pleasure trip). The island offers a range of activities, from whale watching to stargazing beneath snowy peaks or simply going on leisurely drives. Extend your stay by visiting Maui (*see pp26–7*) or Kaui (*see pp248–9*).

A Week of 'Ohana

Settle into a relaxed first day and soak up some Hawaiian culture at a traditional *luau*.

From Kona, head to the beach. Family favorites include Spencer and Kahalu'u beach parks, good spots to view green sea turtles. In the evening, stroll in Kailua-Kona.

Drive north to the tip of the Kohala Coast. Along the way see the Kalāhuipua'a Fishponds, the Puakō Petroglyphs, and the birthplace of warrior-king Kamehameha the Great. Venture inland from arty Hawi, through *paniolo* (cowboy) country, to Waimea. Explore Parker Ranch on horseback or in an all-terrain vehicle.

From Kona aim south, stopping at the Captain Cook Monument and the black-sand beach of Punalu'u. Continue to the Hawai'i Volcanoes National Park and Kīlauea Visitor Center. Drive the Crater Rim Drive, which circuits rain forests, Thurston Lava Tube, and the Jaeger Museum. Spend the night at a local inn.

Rise early to catch a rainbow at misty Rainbow Falls and the ancient pools known as Boiling Pots. Enjoy the exhibits at Imiloa Astronomy Center in Hilo. Head north along the east coast, admiring the awe-inspiring Akaka Falls before driving back to Kona.

Spend another day at the beach. Go snorkeling or take a submarine excursion. View migrating humpback whales and other marine life aboard a cruise. On your last day, wake up and smell the Kona coffee with a coffee-farm tour.

Dos and Don'ts

✓ At Volcanoes National Park, always check with park rangers regarding road and trail closures and stay on marked trails.

✗ Don't feed or otherwise tamper with the *nene* (Hawaiian goose) and be careful not to hit one on the road!

✗ Don't stock up on coffee, nuts, orchids, and other agricultural products without making sure whether they can be brought back into your home country.

✓ Make inquiries before diving into the water – even the loveliest of beaches may have dangerous rip currents.

GETTING THERE   See map p316, F7
Williamsburg is in southeast Virginia, 20 minutes from Newport News International Airport, and 50 minutes from Richmond and Norfolk's larger international airports. The town is well connected by buses and trains.

GETTING AROUND
Take advantage of free parking at the Visitors Center and use the shuttle bus to get around. Taxis and local buses are available for traveling outside the historic area.

WEATHER
December is brisk, with an average temperature of 45°F (7°C), dropping to around 37°F (3°C) at night.

ACCOMMODATIONS
Stay at one of the five official hotels close to the historic area. Guests receive preferred reservations for dining and activities.

Williamsburg Woodlands Hotel and Suites offers convenience and a swimming pool; family rooms from US$155.

Williamsburg Lodge was recently renovated; family rooms from US$280.

Providence Hall Guesthouses are serene and spacious; family rooms from US$340.

EATING OUT
Dining options are abundant, but do make reservations, and have a meal in a historic tavern (from US$25, with kids' menus).

PRICE FOR A FAMILY OF FOUR
US$700 per day, including food, local travel, accommodation, and admissions.

FURTHER INFORMATION
www.colonialwilliamsburg.com/christmas

Fifes and Drums

The Fifes and Drums were a key component of the colonial-era army, playing spirited tunes with a steady rhythm to urge marching soldiers into battle. These musicians were boys between 10 and 18, who served with the enlisted men. Today, the Colonial Williamsburg Fifes and Drums carry on the tradition, appearing in more than 700 performances each year. Young boys and girls begin at age 10, performing till they graduate from high school. They also answer visitors' questions and share stories about 18th-century military music.

Main: Visitors and costumed enactors outside the historic area's recreated traditional shops

SPIRIT OF CHRISTMAS PAST

EVERY DECEMBER THE HISTORIC STREETS OF WILLIAMSBURG come alive with the sights and sounds of a colonial Christmas brought to life by the costumed enactors who live and work in the meticulously recreated capital city of Virginia. Here, the trill of fifes and a rhythmic rat-a-tat-tat drumbeat fill the air as the Fifes and Drums Corps marches down the cobbled streets. The tantalizing spicy aromas of mulled apple cider and gingerbread fill the air, and long pine garlands or fir wreaths decorated with real fruits, nuts, and berries adorn homes and public buildings. At dusk, candles and lanterns appear in windows throughout the village.

This is Christmas on the eve of America's independence, when the heated topic of the day is whether Virginia and the Colonies should break away from British rule. Scattered among the village's Christmas tableaus, the voices of Thomas Jefferson, Patrick Henry, and George Washington – three of the architects of democracy for Virginia,

JAN

FEB

MAR

APR

MAY

JUN

JUL

AUG

SEP

OCT

NOV

DEC

FRI

SAT

SUN

Above: Cobbler by candlelight in his shop

Above: Display at a colonial-era general store

Below (top and bottom): Woman preparing a Christmas feast; fruit and berries decorate a wreath

JAMES CRAIG JEWELLER
Engraving Silver Work
Done in the best manner

FESTIVE DIARY

Williamsburg is captivating in December, when the buildings are decorated and the historical area wears a festive air. A long weekend allows enough time to engage in colonial life and take part in the special events for kids. Families often return home with colonial decorations and traditions to use in their own celebration.

A Weekend of Christmas Cheer

Begin at the Visitors Center, where you can take advantage of the Kids' Holiday Weekend, and buy tickets. View the short movie *Williamsburg: The Story of a Patriot*. Enter the living history world of Williamsburg, speak with the costumed enactors, and stroll along the cobbled streets lined with homes and shops.

Head to Market Square for lunch and browse through the boutiques. Be sure to join the early evening parade of the Fifes and Drums as they march through the historic district.

Take part in the Breakfast with Santa Claus that includes lots of holiday fun for kids, or have Breakfast with the Chefs and learn about making colonial pastries. Or, wait till early afternoon and have a proper Holiday Tea. In any case, make reservations early.

Visit the Capitol where Thomas Jefferson and Patrick Henry orated, head over to the Courthouse, and then stop in at the kids' favorite, the Public Gaol. Visit the trade shops and watch colonial blacksmiths, wigmakers, milliners, bookbinders, carpenters, coopers, and shoemakers at work.

Attend an evening event, perhaps the Holiday Theatre at the Kimball, a Capitol evening of dance, or a concert at the Governor's Palace.

Head over to Burton Parish Church for a service, or take a guided Christmas decorations walking tour. Participate in a workshop and learn how to make your own Williamsburg-style holiday decorations. Finally, visit the Governor's Palace, mingle with costumed enactors, and then revisit any favorite places before leaving.

Dos and Don'ts

☑ Dress in layers, with hats, mittens, and heavy jackets available for chilly evenings, as many favorite activities are held, or involve walking, outside.

☒ Don't forget to check the online detailed holiday schedule available from late August and make reservations early for accommodations and special events.

☑ Participate in the free candlelight illumination tours and performances held in the evenings.

and indeed the USA – can be heard in the Capitol and the taverns late into the night.

It's easy to get into the spirit of historic Williamsburg by renting colonial garb complete with a bonnet or tricorn hat. Join the villagers to eat sweets, play with colonial toys, and make Christmas decorations. The sound of Christmas carols fills the streets as wandering carolers stroll, carrying handheld lanterns to light their way. Soft sweet music from hammered dulcimers, Celtic harps, and flutes provides entertainment at candlelit concerts. Lavishly dressed women in long flowing gowns and dapper men wearing fancy wigs dance reels and minuets in the ballroom. Laughter spills into the cold night air as theater performers entertain on the stage.

Christmas is the season to feast on venison at Groaning Board dinners, where diners are entertained by balladeers and madrigal singers. Afternoon high tea is a great time to sample dainty delicacies and learn the latest gossip. Best of all is dinner at the tavern, eating traditional fare, such as savory crab cakes, Gloucester chicken, and southern spoon bread with friends beside a crackling fire and singing folk songs before walking home through the lantern-lit night.

GETTING THERE   See map p324, D6

Major North American airlines fly to Liberia's Daniel Oduber International Airport, near the beaches. Many people also prefer to fly to San José, the capital, and drive to Nicoya, with a cruise to Tortuga Island on the way.

GETTING AROUND

The numerous beaches are accessed via a network of roads, many unpaved. Rent a four-wheel-drive car for the potholed roads.

WEATHER

December is the perfect time to visit, as the rainy season has ended. The weather is clear, with temperatures averaging 82°F (28°C).

ACCOMMODATIONS

Hotel Puerta del Sol, at the Playas del Coco, has a delightful aesthetic and an Italian restaurant, with doubles from US$60.

Intimate and colorful Hotel Bula Bula, at Playa Grande, offers fine dining with doubles from US$95; www.hotelbulabula.com

Enjoy luxury at the Four Seasons Papagayo, with its own golf course; doubles from US$470; www.fourseasons.com/costarica

EATING OUT

All types of cuisine are available, but local seafood is the way to go. Start with *ceviche*, followed by *corvina al ajillo* (garlic sea bass).

PRICE FOR TWO

US$370–400 per day including food, car rental, accommodation, and fuel – assuming a mix of luxury and economy hotels.

FURTHER INFORMATION

www.visitcostarica.com

Turtle Invasion

Ridleys are unique among the world's six species of marine turtles. Instead of nesting singly and at night, they come ashore en masse during the day. Tens of thousands of Ridleys storm select beaches together to dig nests and lay eggs in unison. *Arribadas* (arrivals) are timed to coincide with a waxing full moon and occur on only about a dozen beaches worldwide, two of which – Ostional and Playa Nancite – are in Costa Rica.

Above: Bathroom with a view at the Four Seasons Papagayo

Above (left and right): Peaceful bays near Nicoya; Playa Flamingo at sunset
Main: Boats setting off from the sandy beach at Tortuga Island

MARINE JEWEL

IF YOU'VE EVER IMAGINED YOURSELF AS AN INDIANA JONES, Nicoya is just the place to live out those dreams – glide through the forest on a canopy zipline, whiz around on an ATV, or rent a Jeep for an off-road adventure. Or, if dreaming is the only activity you had in mind, Nicoya is also a prime spot to laze in a hammock. Once a snoozy backwater beloved mostly by backpacking surfers, Nicoya has been thrust into the spotlight by the opening of Liberia airport in the late 1990s. Nearby Bahía Culebra, a vast bay, is now the center of Costa Rica's deluxe resort development and today the region boasts almost three-quarters of the country's hotels, with something for every budget and mood, no matter how sophisticated or adventurous.

Although no longer remote, Nicoya is still wild. This broad rectangular peninsula in northwest Costa Rica shows off the potential of the Central American tropics to full effect. Its mountainous interior forms a rugged backdrop to sensational beaches in every shade, from taupe to gold. Crafty capuchin monkeys scamper along the sands, where marine turtles can be seen at predictable times of year and, at Playa Ostional, in astounding profusion. Like a modern-day Garden of Eden, the wildlife is all around you. Howler monkeys hang by many a hotel pool, like paying guests. Toucans

may land at your breakfast table to beg for fruit tidbits, while high overhead, frigate birds hang in the sky like kites on invisible strings. In the warm seas, scuba divers are in awe of pelagics – big fish – and you won't find a sportfisher who disagrees!

Tamarindo, a surf and sportfishing haven midway down the coast, is the main resort and makes a good base for exploring. The northerly beaches are backed by sun-scorched dry forests that explode in Monet colors with the rains. Southward, verdant rain forests spill down steep mountain slopes to meet the Pacific. Coastal resorts such as Malpaís and Santa Teresa may no longer be tiny, sleepy fishing hamlets, but the beaches just keep getting better as you keep heading south, and, for Indiana Jones types, the winding coastal drive and river crossings will supply plenty of thrills and excitement.

The mountainous interior forms a rugged backdrop to sensational beaches in every shade, from taupe to gold.

Inset: White-faced capuchin monkeys lazing on a tree branch
Below (left to right). Palm-fringed Playa Carrillo near Sámara; an inviting poolside, perfect for a siesta; colorful village church along the road to Sámara

PENINSULA DIARY

December is the ideal time for a trip down the coast. The sun blazes, but fresh breezes keep temperatures within reason. Despite Nicoya's compact size, the dirt roads can be a challenge, turning a seemingly short drive into an adventure the farther south you go. Allow a week to explore the west coast without rushing.

Seven Adventurous Days

DAY 1
Arrive in Liberia and drive the short distance to Playa del Coco if you're on a budget, or Bahía Culebra for the Four Seasons if you're feeling flush. In the afternoon, whiz through the treetops on a zip-line during the Witch's Rock Canopy Tour.

DAYS 2–3
In the morning, laze on the beach as the prelude to an afternoon of sportfishing or scuba diving. Guests at the Four Seasons might enjoy the hotel's golf course. Indulge in a massage or spa treatment before dinner at Playa Hermosa. Next day, follow the "Monkey Trail" (with a river fording) to Playa Flamingo and continue via Huacas to Tamarindo. Walk on the beach, surf, or dine at a beachfront café. Register with a ranger station at Playa Grande to view leatherback turtles at night.

DAY 4
Follow the dirt coast road south past a string of surfing beaches to arrive at Playa Ostional. You'll want to linger if the Ridley turtles are nesting. Otherwise, ford the Río Montaña to reach Nosara and relax on Playa Guiones.

DAY 5
It's a fun drive south to Sámara, perhaps stopping en route at Flying Crocodile Lodge for an Ultralight flight. Surf, stroll along the beach, or hang loose in a hammock until it's time to check out the local nightlife.

DAYS 6–7
A challenging drive today to Islita. Linger at the Open-Air Contemporary Museum, then check out the ibis and pelicans at Puerto Bejuco. Visit the Jungle Butterfly Farm. Have fun fording rivers to arrive in Malpaís. (If the rivers are impassable, the mountain route will add several hours to your journey).

Dos and Don'ts

✗ Don't disturb the newborn turtles you find on the beach. Let them crawl to the sea on their own.

✓ When fording rivers, drive slowly to avoid swamping the engine. Consider wading the river to see how deep it is. Don't forget to calculate for the height of the doorsills!

✗ Don't leave any belongings in your parked car. Theft from cars is a major problem at beaches.

✓ Use caution when swimming. Riptides are a danger on beaches where surf breaks ashore. If caught in a riptide, swim parallel to the shore.

JAN
FEB
MAR
APR
MAY
JUN
JUL
AUG
SEP
OCT
NOV
DEC
DAY 1
DAYS 2–3
DAY 4
DAY 5
DAYS 6–7

CARIBBEAN
SEA

Anguilla ● **THE VALLEY**

St-Martin

St. Maarten

GETTING THERE See map p325, H4
There are no direct long-distance flights but you can fly via Puerto Rico, St. Maarten, Antigua, St. Thomas, or St. Kitts to Wallblake Airport. There is also a ferry from St-Martin.

GETTING AROUND
This tiny island is only 16 miles (26 km) long and 3 miles (5 km) at its widest but it is worth renting a car to explore. Buy a local driver's license (US$20) and drive on the left.

WEATHER
Anguilla is a dry island with little seasonal variation and an average temperature of 80°F (26°C). There is usually a cooling breeze.

ACCOMMODATIONS
Anguilla Great House, Rendezvous Bay, offers "gingerbread" cottages on the beach, many activities, and Caribbean cuisine; doubles from US$310; www.anguillagreathouse.com

Cuisinart Resort and Spa has 93 luxurious accommodations, restaurant, hydroponic farm, organic gardens, and activities; doubles from US$485; www.cuisinartresort.com

EATING OUT
Altamer Restaurant, Shoal Bay West, offers French and Caribbean fusion cuisine and a glass wall to view the chef (from US$50). Enjoy waterside dining in the gardens of a traditional West Indian house at intimate Hibernia, serving innovative French cuisine with touches of the Far East (from US$55).

PRICE FOR TWO
US$625 per day includes accommodation, food, transport, and local trips.

FURTHER INFORMATION
www.anguilla-vacation.com

The First Visitors

Native Americans traveled from South America in dug-out canoes, 4,000 years ago, to settle in Anguilla. They were farmers and fishermen with a religion based on the sun, moon, and the sacred caverns from where they believed humans came, and so they built their worship sites inside caves. Evidence of this can be seen in Big Springs at Island Harbour and The Fountain at Shoal Bay, large sites with carvings, etchings, offering bowls, and artifacts. You can tour Big Springs but The Fountain is being developed by the Anguilla National Trust.

Main: Innovatively designed, Moorish-influenced villas at Cap Juluca resort **Far right (top to bottom):** Pristine beach seen through palm fronds; verandah at Rendezvous Bay; a macaw perching by the pool; fishing boats near Little Harbour

TROPICAL HAVEN

WITH ITS WHITE-SAND BEACHES, clear warm waters, and even warmer locals, Anguilla is a perfect getaway. This idyllic island, one of the most northerly of the Leeward Islands in the Lesser Antilles, rarely gets crowded and has a pace of life which leaves no option but to slow down, relax, and enjoy yourself.

Despite its small size, there are endless ways to unwind. There are 33 beautiful beaches, sunset horseback rides, tropical bird watching opportunities, and a whole magical underwater world to be explored either through snorkeling or diving. If it is a romantic beach picnic you are after, then Elsie Bay, just east of Little Harbour on the southern coast, is just the spot. This quiet little natural beach has a pretty view of neighbouring St-Martin, and although somewhat hard to find, is worth the effort. Farther north, Shoal Bay East, an almost mile-long stretch of pure white sand, is perfect for swimming and snorkeling – for a more secluded experience, walk to the eastern end

JAN
FEB
MAR
APR
MAY
JUN
JUL
AUG
SEP
OCT
NOV
DEC

Above: Fine dining by candlelight on the beach

RELAXATION DIARY

Anguilla is one of the ultimate romantic destinations, because of its luxury resorts, fabulous food, sublime sunsets, and uncrowded beaches. Aside from all this, however, there is also a rich history and culture to enjoy. Rest assured, four December days in Anguilla will provide a lifetime of memories.

Four Serene Days

DAY 1

Relax for a couple of hours and unwind on the beach. Enjoy lunch and then head for Cap Juluca Spa, which offers a number of special treatments for couples. Then settle back, totally relaxed, with a long, cold drink to watch a fabulous sunset. That will set you in the right mood for a very romantic dinner.

DAY 2

Explore The Valley, the sprawling main settlement. Visit Anguilla Museum to learn about the island's past, take in the artistic talent on show at the Savannah Gallery, and tour Wallblake House, the island's oldest and only surviving plantation home, built in 1787. You will still be back in time for a swim and another perfect sunset.

DAY 3

Take the ferry to another Caribbean island delight, St-Martin *(see pp272–3)*. It leaves every 30 minutes from Blowing Point for the 20-minute crossing to Marigot on the French side of the island. Visit the excellent St-Martin Museum to learn more about the region's history and enjoy a leisurely lunch at one of the many fine French restaurants. In the afternoon take a taxi to Philipsburg in St. Maarten, the Dutch side of the island, for some of the best duty-free shopping available in the Caribbean.

DAY 4

Pack a picnic lunch and head for Big Springs National Park at Island Harbour, where you can visit the cave site with its centuries-old carvings. Then find your own deserted beach for a peaceful afternoon after a picnic by the clear, blue water.

Dos and Don'ts

✓ Explore the art galleries on the island. There is some extraordinary talent here.

✓ Take a trip to St-Martin/St. Maarten. This fascinating little island has been peacefully partitioned between two different nations – the French and the Dutch – for almost 350 years.

✗ Don't spend too much time in the sun until you have acclimatized. There is usually a cool breeze that can make you forget how strong the sun really is.

✓ Be careful when driving. The roads are not busy but you never know when a goat may decide to cross in front of you.

of the beach. If the gentle island breezes, quiet beaches, sublime swimming conditions, and stunning sunsets are not enough to chill you out, then treat yourself to a visit to one of the island's many spas and enjoy a program of treatments specially created for couples.

If you tire of perfect beaches, visit some of the 15 galleries and working studios on the island. The Loblolly in Lower Valley is a cooperative of artists and features original works, while the Savannah Gallery, also in Lower Valley, showcases contemporary art from throughout the Caribbean. The works of internationally acclaimed artist, sculptor, and potter Courtney Devonish can be seen at the Devonish Gallery in George Hill on the main West End road. Finally, a ferry trip to St. Martin adds to the romance as you while a day away over lunch in the French Quarter.

There are also many memorable dinners to be had on Anguilla. Visitors to this island are spoiled for choice with intimate waterside restaurants serving all manner of delicious dishes. The standard of cuisine is very high and is matched by quality wine lists. The best way to end a perfect day is, of course, a moonlit stroll along a nearby beach – you can't get more romantic than that.

GETTING THERE   See map p326, G4
The base camp for trips to Angel Falls is the settlement of Canaima, located inside Canaima National Park. Canaima can only be reached by air – daily flights from Caracas with Avior airlines (www.avior.com.ve).

GETTING AROUND
The falls can be viewed by small plane or helicopter, but the best view is obtained by traveling up the Churun river by *curiaras* (canoes), then hiking to the base of the falls.

WEATHER
Daytime temperatures are hot – from 68°F to 86°F (20°C–30°C). Although often sunny in December, there is always the possibility of rain and fog.

ACCOMMODATIONS
Jungle Rudy Campamento is located a short boat ride from Canaima, above Ucaima Falls; US$150 per person per day; Angel Falls trips US$450 per person; www.junglerudy.com.

Angel Adventures offers 3-day/2-night expeditions to the falls, with accommodation in jungle camps and hammocks; US$200 per person; www.salto-angel.com

EATING OUT
Meals are provided either by your lodge or your tour operator.

PRICE FOR TWO
From around US$400 per day, including overnight expedition, food, and one night's accommodation in a jungle lodge. Flights from Caracas US$300 per person.

FURTHER INFORMATION
www.salto-angel.com

Jimmie Angel's Falls

Angel Falls are named not for their seraphic beauty, but for the American bush pilot, Jimmie Crawford Angel, who happened to fly over the falls in 1933 while on a search for gold. Angel returned in 1937, but crashed his plane while attempting to land on the flat-topped tepuy above the falls. He and his three companions were forced to descend the falls on foot – an 11-day journey through the trackless interior. News of their ordeal spread, and as a result the falls were named in his honor.

Above (left and right): A colorful keel-billed toucan; a *tepuy*, or flat-topped mountain, swathed in cloud

A LOST WORLD

THE ROLLING HIGH SAVANNAH LAND OF SOUTHERN VENEZUELA is the natural home of the *tepuy*, a kind of rugged, eerie, flat-topped mountain, draped in rain forest green. *Tepuys* are some of the last holdouts from the Cretaceous era, stubborn rock extrusions that held firm while the weaker stone around them wore away, leaving each *tepuy*-top an isolated little island in the clouds. Sherlock Holmes' creator, Sir Arthur Conan Doyle, postulated that the *tepuys* might provide a refuge to living creatures from that long-lost epoch. In his 1912 novel *The Lost World*, the shrouded *tepuy* tops were a place where pterodactyls and brontosaurs still roamed…

Dinosaurs may no longer exist, but mysteries and unknowns around the falls persisted. Two decades after Conan Doyle, an American bush pilot named Jimmie Angel came back with an incredible tale of the world's highest waterfall – a ribbon of white water falling from a *tepuy* so tall that its peak was hidden in the clouds. It was not until 1949 that the National Geographic Society firmly fixed the newly christened Angel Falls' exact height at 3,212 ft (979 m) – 15 times the height of Niagara.

A visit to Angel Falls is still a journey into the unknown. Canaima, the small Pemon Indian village that serves as base camp, is a place of beauty set on the edge of a dark lagoon fringed by pink-sand beaches. The journey upriver by *curiara* (a dugout wooden canoe) passes several smaller falls and rapids on the way. Passing Orchid Island you pull in to the river landing and trek uphill through the jungle. As you climb, small glimpses of the misty white ribbon that is Angel Falls peek here and there through the rain forest canopy, and the air grows cool and damp, the rocks underfoot slick with moisture. The isolated environments of the *tepuys*' flat plateaus are home to species found nowhere else on earth, many of them as yet undescribed. At the base of the falls, you gaze up through a sheer fine mist, like an eternal spring rain. The sound is curiously calm, even muted. Unlike Niagara or Victoria, Angel Falls doesn't come roaring over its precipice, but spills relentlessly and gently into the ominously named Devil's Canyon below.

Main: The mighty cascade of Angel Falls
Below (left and right): A *curiara* (dugout canoe); Canaima Lagoon waterfall

Above: A view of Sapo Falls

JAN

FEB

MAR

APR

MAY

JUN

JUL

AUG

SEP

OCT

NOV

DEC

CASCADE DIARY

Angel Falls is at its best in early December at the end of the rainy season, when clear skies offer the best visibility but the flow of water is still impressive, and the rivers leading to the falls can still be navigated by canoe. The journey from Canaima includes a night in a hammock at the foot of the falls.

Three Adventurous Days

Flights from Caracas arrive mid-morning. After a transfer to your lodge, take a guided trek to gushing Ara-meru falls where you can swim in the deep natural pools and wander over the natural jade formations. After an outdoor lunch, hike to Sapo Falls, with its fabulous white curtain of water. Keep an eye on the gallery forests by the river's edge for toucans and howler monkeys, particularly later in the day.

DAY 1

Set out early to travel up the Carrao river by *curiaras* (dugout canoe) to Isla Orquídea (Orchid Island), where most tours make a stop to admire the orchids and have some breakfast. Then it's back into the canoes, this time on the smaller Churun river, snaking up the Cañón del Diablo (Devil's Canyon) to a small island at the base of the falls called Isla Ratoncito (Little Mouse Island). From here it's another hour's hike uphill through the forest to the pools at the foot of Angel Falls. Time to relax and stare in awe, and then plunge in for a swim. Relax by the falls until late afternoon, then hike back down and return to the camp on Ratoncito for a meal and a night in a comfortable hammock.

DAY 2

After another early start, hike back up the forest in the early morning light for a last lingering gaze at the high clear stream of Angel Falls. For those brave enough to withstand the bracing waters, this is also the opportunity for another refreshing plunge in the pools at the foot of the falls. Then it's back through the rainforest to the landing point for the canoe-ride back downstream to Canaima.

DAY 3

Dos and Don'ts

✓ Read the book before you go. *The Lost World*, written by Sir Arthur Conan Doyle, is a rollicking good adventure yarn (though alas with no Sherlock Holmes).

✓ Book tours well ahead of your trip. Spots in December are limited and highly sought-after.

✗ Don't forget that on flight-seeing tours, you pay full fare whether or not the falls are shrouded in mist and cloud.

✓ Bring some US dollars in cash. There's a premium on US dollars on the parallel market, which can add on anything from 20 to 40 percent.

USA
Chihuahua
COPPER CANYON
Los Mochis
GULF OF MEXICO
MEXICO
Guadalajara
Mexico City
PACIFIC OCEAN

GETTING THERE   See map p323, C3
The Chihuahua al Pacífico railroad from Los Mochis to Chihuahua cuts through Copper Canyon. Regular flights connect these towns to Mexico City and the USA.

GETTING AROUND
After the journey by train, the best way to explore Creel is on foot or horseback, and there are buses to Batopilas.

WEATHER
Daytime temperatures on the canyon rim drop to 40°F (4°C) and to freezing at night. The floor is warmer at 57–75°F (14–24°C).

ACCOMMODATIONS
Hotel Villa Mexicana offers log cabins and a colorfully painted public area; family rooms from US$65; www.vmcoppercanyon.com

The Lodge at Creel is a comfortable faux-rustic chain hotel set in woodlands just outside the town; family rooms from US$110; www.thelodgeatcreel.com

Riverside Lodge is a 19th-century hacienda at Batopilas, in the heart of the canyon. Doubles are from US$140 for a two-night minimum stay, and children under 12 are not allowed; www.coppercanyonlodges.com

EATING OUT
The area was once mining country and food is traditionally hearty campfire fare. Tamales, quesadillas, and burritos are also available.

PRICE FOR TWO
US$150 per day covers accommodation and food. Add another US$200 for rail fare.

FURTHER INFORMATION
www.visitmexico.com

CANYON JOURNEY

OVER MILLIONS OF YEARS, northern Mexico's Sierra Tarahumara mountains have been lashed by rain and wind and scored by icy-blue, fast-flowing rivers to form one of the western hemisphere's most dramatic landscapes. Rocky crags and snowy mountains look out over folds of hills swathed in pine forest and cut by plunging gorges and canyons. The mountainous canyon walls are capped with snow, yet their sheltered, subtropical depths are home to palm trees and cactus. The most impressive of all is Copper Canyon, or Barrancas del Cobre – a series of vertigo-inducing valleys twice as wide and twice as deep as the Grand Canyon, and far wilder.

The best way to see Copper Canyon is to take the Chihuahua al Pacífico railroad. This was cut and grafted into the mountains in the 19th century, before the Panama Canal provided a less strenuous

The Tarahumara Indians

The Tarahumara (or Rarámuri in their language) are among the few North American peoples who have preserved their pre-Columbian heritage. They greet each other in Tarahumara by saying "as the dove that warbles, I wish you health and happiness with your loved ones." They still wear colorful garments, belts, and headscarves, create wooden and woven handicrafts, and practice traditional music and shamanic rituals. There are 70,000 Rarámuri in the Chihuahua and Copper Canyon region – 14,000 sq miles (36,260 sq km), or half their original territory.

Main: Stunning view over Copper Canyon from El Divisadero

Left: Traditional Tarahumara Indian grass basketweaver near Creel

Right (left to right): Hiker enjoying the mountain view; the mission church of Santa María de los Angeles (also known as the "Lost Cathedral"), Satevó

JAN

FEB

MAR

APR

MAY

JUN

JUL

AUG

SEP

OCT

NOV

DEC

Pacific-Atlantic trade route. Locomotives still creak and shudder up the mountains from Los Mochis, before plunging almost 6,000 ft (1,830 m) through a series of jaw-dropping switchbacks into Copper Canyon. The train climbs steeply as it leaves the town of San Rafael for the lookout at Los Ojitos, before turning back a full 360 degrees on itself at the hair-raising Lazo loop. It stops briefly at the tiny settlement of El Divisadero for a breathtaking view over the contours and crags of Copper Canyon, before grinding to a halt in the sleepy former mining town of Creel.

This pretty, pocket-sized town is perfumed by pines and woodsmoke and busy with Tarahumara Indians, who wander in to sell their wares. It's the best base for further excursions, as jeep, walking, and horseback tours leave for the little village of Batopilas in the depths of the canyon. From here it's possible simply to wander for an afternoon, visit sights such as the eerie abandoned Jesuit church at nearby Satevó, or hike the three-day Batopilas to Urique guided trail.

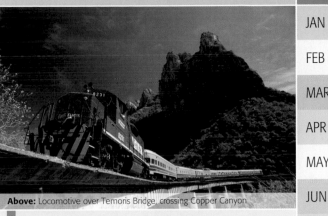
Above: Locomotive over Temoris Bridge, crossing Copper Canyon

RAILROAD DIARY

Hardy adventurers could spend weeks in the canyons, hiking through the forests and hills, visiting tiny colonial villages like Batopilas, and becoming familiar with the Tarahumara culture. But most visitors opt for the highlights – taking the train from the coast and exploring the hills and canyons around Creel.

Three Scenic Days

Begin your journey around 6am in Los Mochis, equipped with plenty of water and snacks for the journey and some warm clothing. After 3 hours, the train reaches the town of El Fuerte and the dramatic scenery begins to unfold, with the first of many towering bridges and rocky tunnels. Eventually, it starts to zigzag its way dizzily up the craggy sides, finally stopping at San Rafael, in the heart of the canyon.

DAY 1

From San Rafael, it's a 90-minute journey to Creel, with further stops at Posadas Barranca and El Divisadero, both of which have hotels and spectacular views. There is just enough time to take pictures.

After an 8-hour journey, and enjoying the breathtaking scenery, check into your hotel in Creel, eat dinner, and collapse into bed.

Spend the day taking a walk or a horseback ride into the canyon. Lunch in the pretty colonial village of Batopilas and be sure to visit the Hacienda San Miguel – a vast, overgrown adobe palace once owned by Alexander Shepherd, Governor of Washington, D.C.

DAY 2

You can either take the early-morning train back to Los Mochis for your flight home, or continue the journey across the desert on to Chihuahua. Returning to Los Mochis will give you another chance to appreciate the beauty of Copper Canyon. When the train stops at San Rafael, take advantage of your last chance to buy some Tarahumara Indian handicrafts.

DAY 3

Dos and Don'ts

✓ Travel from Los Mochis to Chihuahua and stop at Creel. If you make the journey in the opposite direction starting from Chihuahua, you could wind up passing through Copper Canyon at night.

✗ Don't buy a one-way ticket if you plan to come back to Los Mochis from Creel. Seats are impossible to secure from Creel to Los Mochis, so buy a return ticket.

✓ Be sure to sit on the right-hand side of the train for the best views on your way to Chihuahua.

✓ Book your ticket in advance through www.chepe.com.mx or a tour operator in Los Mochis.

Above: Hacienda-style Hotel Mirador above Copper Canyon at Posadas Barranca

Below: Satevó Mission near Batopilas, a relic of the region's colonial heritage

CARIBBEAN SEA

Cayman
Brac

Little
Cayman

Grand
Cayman

● GEORGE TOWN

GETTING THERE　　　See map p325, B4
The international airport on Grand Cayman
is the main arrival point, but another serves
Cayman Brac. Little Cayman has daily inter-
island flights. Cruise ships call regularly.

GETTING AROUND
Rental cars, motorbikes, and bicycles are
available on Grand Cayman and Cayman
Brac; bicycles and four-wheel-drive vehicles
on Little Cayman. Taxis are plentiful.

WEATHER
Highs average 83°F (28°C), night-time lows
around 75°F (24°C), with clear skies and
little rain. December is not hurricane season.

ACCOMMODATIONS
Eldemire's Tropical Island Inn is a family-run
hotel near George Town and Seven Mile Beach;
doubles from US$109; www.eldemire.com

Comfort Suites and Resort is smoke-free and has
its own scuba center; suites with kitchenettes
from US$145; www.caymancomfort.com

Courtyard by Marriott Grand Cayman offers
a wide range of activities; doubles from
US$155; www.marriott.com/gcmcy

EATING OUT
Food is typically Caribbean, with exotic fruits
and vegetables, spicy seasonings, and plenty
of seafood, especially conch.

PRICE FOR TWO
US$600 per day, including accommodation,
food, taxis, an island-hop, and all activities
(including three dives).

FURTHER INFORMATION
www.caymanislands.ky

Cayman Homes

Traditional Cayman homes are built cabin-style,
with a separate kitchen out back. Known as the
"cook-rum" (cooking room), it is set a little way from
the house. That way, if the open fire, over which
food was traditionally cooked, should burn down
the cook-rum, the main house at least would be
safe. The houses themselves are built of wattle and
daub (strips of wood and lime plaster). Many stand
on ironwood posts, to provide ventilation beneath
the building and protect the house from floods.

DIVING INTO THE BLUE

Below (top to bottom): Brac Reef Beach Resort; offshore fishing, wreck diving in Grand Cayman

THE COBALT-BLUE WATERS FRAMING THE CAYMAN ISLANDS in the western Caribbean conceal a breathtaking underwater world studded with flashing shoals of brightly colored fish, dazzling coral reef formations, and eerie shipwrecks. This is a scuba diver's paradise. Warm waters, crystal-clear visibility, stunning marine life, and the sheer number and diversity of sights draw dive enthusiasts back here year after year. The dramatic, submerged landscape around the islands hosts more than 150 superb dive spots, each with its own distinct character, and catering to all levels of ability. You can do night dives, day dives, wreck dives, or cave dives. The choice is dizzying.

Cayman Brac, the farthest east of the three main islands, is home to one of the Caribbean's most sensational dive spots. Here, the famed North Wall drops away to an astonishing 14,000 ft (4,250 m), while the steeper and more awesome South Wall drops away farther still, into the velvet blackness of the precipice below. The walls are alive with sponges, finger corals, sea fans, and an incredible diversity

JAN

FEB

MAR

APR

MAY

JUN

JUL

AUG

SEP

OCT

NOV

DEC

of marine life, which includes moray eels, parrotfish, stingrays, and green sea turtles. Less intrepid divers might prefer to opt for the excellent shallow dives nearby, which lead divers through caves and tunnels, and out across canyons and sublime swathes of coral reef, where, on particularly clear days, the visibility can reach up to 150 ft (46 m).

Aside from the world-class diving, visitors come to the Cayman Islands to relax on the fabulous beaches, enjoy a wealth of other water- and land-based sports, and explore the sights. There are areas of strong swell for windsurfing and surfing, sheltered coves for swimming and snorkeling, and spectacular terrain perfect for golf, hiking, and horse-riding. Must-visit places include one of the region's finest stretches of beach, Seven Mile Beach on Grand Cayman, with its luxury resorts, galleries, and shopping malls; George Town, the islands' tiny, characterful capital; the village of Hell (if only to get your postcards stamped with the name at the post office); the spectacular ridge and caves of Cayman Brac; and the island of Little Cayman, which has more iguanas than people and is a paradise for bird-watching opportunities and, of course, first-rate diving.

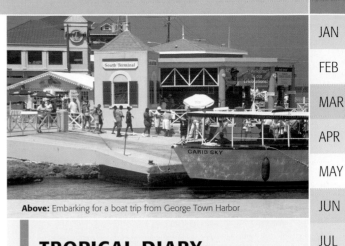

Above: Embarking for a boat trip from George Town Harbor

TROPICAL DIARY

The Cayman Islands are simply the perfect Caribbean adventure playground. They offer world-class diving and sports fishing and a wealth of other water sports, as well as a wide range of dry-land activities. In five days you can pack in all manner of active adventures and still find time to do a little exploring and lazing in the sun.

Five Days in the Islands

Explore George Town and visit the Cayman Island National Museum in the Old Court House to learn about its colorful history. Check out some of the traditional cabin-style houses on the outskirts of town. Take a voyage in the *Atlantis* submarine which visits the Cayman Wall and the wreck of the *Kirk Pride*, that lies in 780 ft (238 m) of water.

DAY 1

Spend the whole day diving and/or snorkeling at the location of your choice. If you are in the mood for a leisurely afternoon, take the trip to Stingray City Sandbar where, in only a few feet of water, you'll be surrounded by dozens of gentle, inquisitive stingrays You can dive, snorkel, or simply stand among them.

DAY 2

Take an early morning flight to visit delightful Little Cayman. Hire a bicycle and spend the day exploring, snorkeling and swimming. Stop at one of the dive resorts for lunch but don't be late for your return flight.

DAY 3

If you are fit, explore the eastern end of Grand Cayman by bicycle (it is flat), or you could drive. Visit Bodden Town and the Queen Elizabeth Botanic Park to discover the wealth of flora and fauna on the island, and then enjoy lunch at one of the many lively beachside restaurants along the coast. Be back by late afternoon to get ready for a spectacular night dive.

DAY 4

Go to Hell and back. Visit this strangely-named village and then perhaps saddle up for a horseback ride along the beach before enjoying another magical sunset and a leisurely last night's dinner.

DAY 5

Main: Divers swimming with stingrays at Stingray City Sandbar

Above (top to bottom): Queen Elizabeth Botanic Park; Devil's Hangout giftshop in Hell

Below: Iguana on a Little Cayman beach

Dos and Don'ts

✓ Visit the reefs, whether you scuba, snorkel, or go by glass-bottomed boat. They are fabulous.

✓ Try to visit the islands – each is different in its own way – and do go to Hell!

✗ Don't forget that they drive on the left here – be extra careful when crossing the road, cycling, or driving.

✗ Don't leave unattended items on the beach or on open view in your car.

ATLANTIC OCEAN

West Island
East Island
STANLEY ®
FALKLAND ISLANDS

GETTING THERE   See map p331, F8
The Falklands lie off the southern tip of South America, 311 miles (500 km) from the mainland. Weekly flights to the islands depart from Santiago, Chile, stopping en route at Puerto Montt and Punta Arenas. The Falklands' Mount Pleasant Airport is 37 miles (60 km) from Stanley, an hour away by taxi.

GETTING AROUND
To visit places near Stanley, hire a driver-guide with an off-road vehicle. Light aircraft fly between airstrips around the islands.

WEATHER
The average nighttime temperature is 43°F (6°C), while the average daytime high is 59°F (15°C). Expect sunshine and long day-light hours but high winds in coastal areas.

ACCOMMODATIONS
Kay's B&B in Stanley offers harbor views; doubles from US$72; tel. (500) 21071

Stanley's Malvina House Hotel boasts spacious rooms and a sauna; doubles from US$260; www.malvinahousehotel.com

Stone House Cottage on Saunders Island has self-catered lodgings and nature tours; doubles from US$440; tel. (500) 41298.

EATING OUT
Mussels, oysters, scallops, and crabs are delicious options. Do also try upland goose pâté, a local delicacy.

PRICE FOR TWO
US$550 per day with lodging, internal flights, 4WD tours, airport transfers, and food.

FURTHER INFORMATION
www.visitorfalklands.com

PENGUIN PARADISE

Main: Stretching out to unwind – a king penguin on the Falkland Islands

I SOLATED AT THE BOTTOM OF THE WORLD and engulfed by the South Atlantic Ocean, the Falklands may appear an unforgiving destination. Yet, they make for one of the Americas' most breathtaking stops, edged by spectacular virgin coastline that draws wildlife enthusiasts for its rare marine fauna.

The experience begins in Stanley, the capital of an island archipelago comprising two main islands – the East and the West – and hundreds of smaller ones. With its colorful cottages and quaint pubs, Stanley reminds you of an English village. Off-road excursions nearby reveal dramatic shorelines of jagged cliffs and white-sand beaches teeming with marine life. Thousands upon thousands of penguins – the islands shelter five different species – waddle along the shore, looking irresistibly cute. Ocean-bashed rocks shelter sea lions, and giant petrels and cormorants soar above in search of food.

Flying High in the Falklands

The black-browed albatross is the seabird highlight on most visits to the Falklands. Every October, some 80 percent of the world's population of this beautiful species migrates to the archipelago to form nesting colonies on precipitous cliffs. Come December, adults are observed with their young. The enormous adult seems ungainly on land, with its large, flat webbed feet, but in flight it is a magnificent sight, when its 8-ft (2-m) wingspan is silhouetted beautifully against the crystal-blue sky.

Left: Stanley, a quaint and colorful capital

Right (left to right): Time for a swim – pod of dolphins in a cove; hefty South American sea lion bull; rockhopper penguins climbing the cliff face

Visits to the offshore islands reveal even wilder scenery. A gentle hike along the ocean-battered cliffs on Saunders Island ends at a colony of black-browed albatrosses, trusting birds that wander over as you sit silently nearby. Sea Lion Island comes alive with rockhopper penguins leaping out of the emerald sea to waddle up cliffs, while elephant seals laze on bleached-white sands and Commerson's dolphins bask in pounding surf. The magical scene is capped by the sight of killer whales patrolling the shoreline, hoping to surprise a sea-lion pup frolicking at the water's edge.

It's fascinating drama, and as you sit on the beach amid its cacophony of roars, barks, and cries, you suddenly realize that the wildlife here in the Falklands has little fear of humans. Each time an inquisitive gentoo penguin waddles up to you or – during a small-boat excursion – a sea lion surfaces within touching distance, its inky-black eyes the size of saucers, the sensation is one of experiencing wildlife at its most uninhibited.

Above: A haven of natural beauty and exotic fauna

Above: Gentoo penguins riding the surf

Below: Magellanic penguin near its burrow

ATLANTIC DIARY

A trip to the Falklands is the journey of a lifetime, so allow yourself at least a week to explore the islands. December is midsummer here, so the days are long and the light is magnificent. Between nature trips, explore Stanley and the various haunting sites of the main battles fought during the 1982 Falklands War.

Eight Days of Rare Wildlife

Arrive in Stanley and hike the stretch of coast at Gypsy Cove, where Commerson's dolphins bask in the surf and millions of birds congregate.	**DAY 1**
Fly to Saunders Island to observe large concentrations of gentoo and Magellanic penguins. At sunrise, make the memorable hike to a nesting colony of black-browed albatrosses. Sit amid the birds and wait for them to approach you. Later, take a hilltop walk for breathtaking vistas. Then head to the ruins of a historic garrison at Port Egmont.	**DAYS 2–3**
Fly to Sea Lion Island in the southeast of the archipelago for two days of wildlife watching. Observe rockhopper and rare macaroni penguins, colonies of giant petrels and cormorants, and killer whales. Watch the large harems of elephant seals and sea lions and wait for the brutal territorial fights between the males of the two species.	**DAYS 4–5**
Fly back to Stanley and visit the ruins of Goose Green, a site of fierce fighting in the Falklands War between Great Britain and Argentina.	**DAY 6**
Your final nature tour takes you to Volunteer Point for a close encounter with majestic king penguins, the archipelago's biggest penguin species.	**DAY 7**
Do some last-minute shopping in Stanley before you hop on your return flight.	**DAY 8**

Dos and Don'ts

- ✓ Bring good-quality sunglasses and high-factor sunblock; the hole in the ozone layer sits right above the Falklands.
- ✗ Don't go too close to elephant seals. These blubbery hulks are aggressive and surprisingly quick on land.
- ✓ Browse shops in Stanley for locally made soft woollens.
- ✓ Pack binoculars, waterproof clothing, and plenty of memory cards for your camera – the wildlife here is spectacular.
- ✓ Brush up on different species, so you can easily recognize a rockhopper from a macaroni or a sea lion from a fur seal.

JAN
FEB
MAR
APR
MAY
JUN
JUL
AUG
SEP
OCT
NOV
DEC

GETTING THERE
See map p321, C5

Pasadena is a 40-minute drive northeast from Los Angeles International airport. Domestic carriers serve Bob Hope Airport in Burbank, which is a 20-minute drive from Pasadena.

GETTING AROUND
Rent a car at the airport or take the metro, which is a cheap, easy way to get around Pasadena. Taxis are widely available.

WEATHER
The average high in January is 68ºF (20ºC); the average low is 50ºF (10ºC). Rain is a rarity.

ACCOMMODATIONS
Holiday Inn Express has doubles from US$110; www.ichotelsgroup.com

Stylish The Westin Pasadena is a block from the Rose Bowl parade route; doubles from US$189; www.starwoodhotels.com

Set on 23 acres, The Langham is a 1906 estate-like landmark; doubles from US$250; pasadena.langhamhotels.com

EATING OUT
Pasadena offers everything from casual outdoor cafés to swanky restaurants serving innovative cuisine. Sample fine fare prepared by budding Le Cordon Bleu chefs at the California School of Culinary Arts, 561 E. Green St.

PRICE FOR TWO
US$420 per day including food, car rental, accommodation, tickets, and sightseeing.

FURTHER INFORMATION
www.pasadenacal.com
www.tournamentofroses.com

The Birth of the Bungalow

Heavily influenced by the British-born Arts and Crafts movement that began in the 1860s, American Craftsman-style bungalows began to take shape in the early 1900s as part of a design-reform movement. Influential brother architects Charles Sumner Greene (1868–1957) and Henry Mather Greene (1870–1954) built a number of Pasadena's bungalows including the masterful 1908 Gamble House. With Japanese and Swiss-chalet influences on its exterior, this National Historic Landmark contains a treasure of fine cabinetry, carved woods, and stained glass.

JAN

FEB

MAR

APR

MAY

JUN

JUL

AUG

SEP

OCT

NOV

DEC

DEC 29

DEC 30

DEC 31

JAN 1

JAN 2

JAN 3

JAN 4

Above (left to right): Huntington Botanical Gardens; Trojans player at the Rose Bowl Stadium; Pasadena at dusk
Main: A spectacular floral float at the Tournament of Roses

Above: A dazzling rider at Equestfest

CARNIVAL OF ROSES

FORGET THE GLITZY COUNTDOWNS AND LAVISH FIREWORKS that dominate most New Year's Eve celebrations: in Pasadena at New Year, the streets are literally coming up roses. The world-renowned Tournament of Roses Parade has grown from a simple display of flower-festooned horse-drawn carriages in the 1890s to a theme-driven extravaganza of elaborate floats covered in a riot of roses and other botanical bounties. Included in the mix is a lengthy roster of high-stepping equestrians, well-tuned marching bands, a Rose Queen and her court, and a celebrity Grand Marshal. Approximately 40 million viewers watch the spectacle on television, while an estimated one million visitors head to Pasadena to witness the dazzling sights that can only be truly appreciated in person.

Reserve a seat in the grandstand, or join the locals partying at the curbside overnight to claim the much-coveted space along the nearly 6-mile (10-km) route. Wherever you sit you will be treated to a lavish spectacle. Come early for a tour of the heavenly scented floats or to catch a football game at the Rose Bowl Stadium before the parade pageantry begins. If the festivities become overwhelming, take some time out to explore some of the city's other attractions.

Set at the base of the San Gabriel Mountains, Pasadena is luxuriously laidback, low-key, and compact, with hip restaurants, boutiques, and Mediterranean-style piazzas. Don't miss the Norton Simon Museum, which holds one of the world's finest private art collections. Tour Gamble House, a perfectly preserved American Craftsman-style bungalow and one of the city's architectural gems, to get a close look at Greene and Greene artistry. Finally, make time to visit nearby San Marino, where an entire day can be spent at the Huntington Library, Art Collections, and Botanical Gardens to view one of the world's most important collections of 18th-century British and French art, the legacy of pioneer railroad tycoon Henry Huntington.

> The Tournament of Roses Parade is a theme-driven extravaganza of floats covered in a riot of roses.

Inset: An ornate fountain at the Huntington Library
Below (left and right): The Rose Queen and her royal court; *Star Wars* stormtroopers parading at the Tournament of Roses

NEW-YEAR DIARY

For five magical days in late December and early January immerse yourself in the action at one of the world's most exciting and spectacular New Year's celebrations. Then spend two more days visiting the area's trove of world-famous art and architecture, and taking in a play at the city's theater.

A Week of Celebrations

DEC 29 Spend the afternoon at Equestfest, strolling the stables, chatting with the riders, and watching the show horses as they perform dances and other demonstrations.

DEC 30 Take in the early show of Bandfest and tap your toes to prize-winning bands. Then visit the Rose Bowl Stadium where volunteers busy themselves putting the finishing touches to the floral floats.

DEC 31 Get into the spirit of the festival at the high-energy Kickoff Luncheon, which features the Rose Bowl Hall of Fame induction ceremony, celebrity sportscasters, athletes, and university coaches. Come evening, Pasadena turns into one big party.

JAN 1 Be in your grandstand seat early for the parade kick-off at 8am. In the afternoon, make a beeline for the Rose Bowl Game to cheer for your favorite team and join the contagious excitement.

JAN 2 View the floats in all their elaborate detail at the Post Parade Showcase of Floats. Later, visit the Norton Simon Museum to view its superb art collections.

JAN 3 Join a tour of the landmark Gamble House, Pasadena's supreme Craftsman-style dwelling. In the evening, take in a play at intimate Pasadena Playhouse, the starting point for many top-name actors.

JAN 4 Spend the day in San Marino exploring The Huntington's expansive library, art collections, and botanical gardens, taking a break in the Rose Garden Tea Room.

Dos and Don'ts

✓ Consider booking a package that includes accommodations, reserved grandstand seats, Rose Bowl game tickets, some meals, motorcoach transportation, and other perks.

✗ Don't be shocked when hugged by strangers upon first meeting – it's a Californian custom.

✓ Research the city's many museums in advance so you won't miss the collections that are of the most interest to you. Don't try to see everything in one visit.

✓ Dress stylishly if you want to get beyond the velvet rope at Pasadena's swanky bars and nightclubs.

DECEMBER

GETTING THERE   See map p329, G4
A major transport hub in South America, Rio de Janeiro is connected by direct flights to cities in Europe, Canada, and the USA. Flights are costlier during Christmas and New Year.

GETTING AROUND
Rio has an excellent subway system, but it's not safe to use after 9pm. The best way to get from Ipanema to Copacabana is by cab.

WEATHER
In December, Rio's daytime temperature range is 77–104°F (25–40°C), which drops to a minimum of 60°F (16°C) at night.

ACCOMMODATIONS
During Réveillon, most hotels offer four night packages at much higher rates than usual.

Arpoador Inn on Ipanema Beach has expansive views, and packages from US$800; www.arpoadorinn.com.br

Ipanema Beach House offers packages from US$880; www.ipanemahouse.com

At the luxurious Fasano a four-day package costs from US$6,000; www.fasano.com.br

EATING OUT
Restaurants such as Roberta Sudbrack are pioneers in Brazilian fusion cooking. There are plenty of cheap restaurants and juice bars, too, offering *prato feito* (dish of the day) or a tropical fruit drink and snack.

PRICE FOR TWO
Around US$360–400 a day with food, tours, accommodation, and local transportation.

FURTHER INFORMATION
www.brazilmax.com

Iemanjá's Day

For African Brazilians practicing the religion of Candomblé, New Year's Eve is significant as Dia de Iemanjá, or Iemanjá's Day, a day spent thanking the goddess of the sea for the goodness she has brought during the year. All day and night, and especially at dawn, gifts, offerings, and messages of gratitude are put in tiny wicker baskets, which are then floated out to sea. "Magic" circles drawn into the sand are lit with candles, and devotees chant and sing to Iemanjá and other *orixá* (goddeses).

FESTIVITY AND FIREWORKS

I F YOU THOUGHT THE CARNIVAL WAS THE BIGGEST FESTIVAL of the Brazilian year, think again. The title goes to the overwhelming spectacle known as Réveillon, the annual New Year's Eve celebrations in Rio. Days before the big occasion, convoys arrive on Avenida Atlântica – the broad highway running the full length of Copacabana – to unload the tubes and boards that are ultimately transformed into vast sound stages. Banners unfurl to announce star-studded shows, visitors rush in from all over, and the beach gets even more crowded with bikini-clad women, men with toned torsos, old ladies with poodles, toddlers, and teenagers. On the day itself, as the afternoon's sun rays turn the talcum-white sands of Copacabana to a deep golden

> As the party fever hots up, the bands get louder and the dancing more frenetic, and just as it appears to reach its climax, the fireworks erupt, shooting into the sky in a cacophony of violets, greens, and peacock blues.

honey, the crowds start to leave, and for a while, all is quiet. Then, as the sun sinks behind the glorious statue of Christ on Corcovado, Copacabana comes alive again – Rio returns, all dressed to party. Bands plug in and the rhythmic beats of the samba, *forró*, and *pagode* dances pound through the air. Steadily, the beach fills up with millions of partygoers until the crowds spill out on to the streets. By night, every inch of Copacabana's sandy 4-mile (6-km) crescent is carpeted by dancers, and the smell of the surf is overpowered by sweat, perfume, and the fragrance of corn on the cob, coconuts, and ice-cold beer sold at stalls.

As the party fever hots up, the bands get louder and the dancing more frenetic, and just as it appears to reach its climax, the fireworks erupt, shooting into the sky in a cacophony of violets, greens, and peacock blues. The crowd roars, the drumbeats rise, and then suddenly, it's midnight. All is quiet for a while, until hundreds of streaming Roman candles and Catherine wheels pour brilliantly crackling gunpowder, phosphorus, and magnesium off the precipitous sides of a towering skyscraper, showering it with an iridescent waterfall of flame.

When dawn breaks, the crowds begin to disperse and leave the sand to the Candomblé priestesses, clad in billowy white robes. As they chant to Iemanjá, the goddess of the sea, the sun drenches the beach in a golden light, warmly heralding the first day of a brand-new year.

Main: Kaleidoscopic shower in the sky – New Year's Eve in Rio
Below (left and right): Ipanema Beach and the mountains beyond; lively samba-club performers
Inset: Ritualistic Rio – "magic" circles of sand, aglow with candlelight

JAN
FEB
MAR
APR
MAY
JUN
JUL
AUG
SEP
OCT
NOV
DEC

Above: Christ the Redeemer, watching over Rio

BEACH PARTY DIARY

For the biggest New Year party, Rio is the place to be. About two million people from all over the world meet up to join in the celebrations and witness a spectacular display of fireworks. Three days will give you time to see a little of the city itself as well as soak in Rio's exuberant, end-of-the-year party spirit (see p307).

New Year's Eve in Rio

The best way to get straight into holiday mode is to hit the beach. Once you arrive, check into the hotel, head to the stylish shops on Rua Visconde de Pirajá in Ipanema, and buy some Brazilian-cut swimwear.

Following a light lunch, spend a few hours simply chilling out on the beach and then sipping some refreshing coconut water in one of the beachside kiosks. In the evening, eat out in a fashionable restaurant in Leblon or the Lagoa and follow this with drinks overlooking the beach.

At 11pm or later, head to one of Lapa's vibrant samba clubs and sip on a *caipirinha* – practically the national drink of Brazil – before returning to the hotel to sleep.

DEC 30

Wake up late and gorge on a hearty Rio breakfast of French bread rolls, strong coffee, and tropical fruit juice – Suco de Açai is the best for energy. Do little for the rest of the day other than take a tour to the Christ the Redeemer statue on Corcovado. Return to the hotel to shower and put on light casuals, put some notes in your pocket but leave your wallet in the safe, and head out to the festival.

DEC 31

This is rest and recuperation day, and there's no better place to spend it than on Ipanema Beach. If you have the energy, visit Tijuca National Park, a rain forest in the heart of Rio, or take a cruise on Guanabara Bay.

JAN 1

Spend your morning on the Sugar Loaf, arriving at 8am to catch the first cable car to the top and beat the crowds. Spend the afternoon in the Botanical Gardens. Then either catch an evening flight out of Rio or spend a few more days in the city before heading home.

JAN 2

Dos and Don'ts

✓ Book a hotel at least six months in advance for New Year.

✗ Don't expect to get by without any Portuguese.

✓ Stay in Ipanema or Copacabana, the hubs of the festival.

✗ Don't display your wallet and camera openly when you're walking around the city.

January – June: **Festivals**

JAMAICA Maroon people gathering under the "kindah tree," Accompong

CANADA Snow sculpture being carved at Winterlude, Ottawa

GUATEMALA Colorful procession during Semana Santa

CANADA

Daaquam River International Dog Sled Race
Saint-Just-de-Breteneires, Québec
January 18–20
Biggest dog sled race in the world with 1,700 dogs taking part.
www.daaquam.qc.ca

International Festival of Animated Objects
Calgary, Alberta
January 23–February 1
Biennial festival celebrating puppets, the art of puppetry, and masks in all their forms.
www.animatedobjects.ca

USA

Mummer's Parade
Philadelphia
January 1
Parade with string bands, comic groups, and costumed revelers.
www.mummers.com

Tournament of Roses Parade
Pasadena, California
January 1
Parade with hundreds of elaborate floats, marching bands, and high-stepping horses.
www.tournamentofroses.com
(See pp300–1)

Sundance Film Festival
Park City, Salt Lake City, and Sundance, Utah
January 17–27
Renowned showcase for independent cinema with Q&As given by leading international film-makers.
www.sundance.org

Miami Art Deco Weekend
Ocean Drive, South Beach, Miami, Florida
January 18–20
Event highlighting Miami's Art Deco buildings with big band jazz, vintage car parades, and classic cinema screenings.
www.mdpl.org

CARIBBEAN

Accompong Maroon Festival
Accompong, Jamaica
January 6
Traditional independence celebration of the Maroon people.
www.visitjamaica.com

MEXICO AND CENTRAL AMERICA

San Sebastian
Chiapa de Corzo, Chiapas, Mexico
January 15–23
Religious festival with a dancing parade between churches.
www.visitmexico.com

SOUTH AMERICA

Festival de Doma y Folklore
Jesus Maria, Córdoba, Argentina
January 4–13
Horse fair with rodeo contests and displays of horsemanship.
www.festival.org.ar

La Procession de La Divina Pastora (The Procession of the Divine Shepherdess)
Barquisimeto, Venezuela
January 14
Religious and folkloric parade. Worshipers and musicians accompany the statue en-route.
www.think-venezuela.net

Feria de Alasitas
La Paz, Bolivia
January 24
Stalls sell miniatures of consumer goods to honor Ekeko, the Aymara god of abundance.
www.boliviaweb.com

Hay Literary Festival
Cartagena, Colombia
January 24–27
Tropical offshoot of the famous Hay-on-Wye literary festival in a beautiful walled city.
www.hayfestival.com
(See pp16–7)

CANADA

Winterlude
Ottawa, Ontario
February 1–14
Wintery fun. Huge skating park and snow playground.
www.canadascapital.gc.ca
(See pp34–5)

Québec City Winter Carnival
Québec City, Québec
February 1–17
Winter party with parades, dog sled races, and ice sculptures.
www.carnaval.qc.ca

Festival du Voyageur
Winnipeg, Manitoba
February 15–24
Winter festival celebrating French-Canadian heritage.
www.festivalvoyageur.mb.ca

USA

Groundhog Day
Punxsutawney, Pennsylvania
February 2
Mike the groundhog informs visitors when spring will begin.
www.groundhog.org

National Toboggan Championships
Camden, Maine
February 8–10
Fun, games, and a thrilling 400 ft (122 m) toboggan chute.
www.camdensnowbowl.com

Mardi Gras
New Orleans, Louisiana
Movable date, 47 days before Easter
Carnival with parades, live street music, and non-stop partying.
www.neworleansonline.com

CARIBBEAN

Feria Internacional del Libro
Havana, Cuba
February 14–24
Important Latin American literary affair.
www.cubaliteraria.com

Fi wi Sinting
Portland, Jamaica
February 17
Family event marking the island's African roots.
www.fiwisinting.com

Holders Season
St. James, Barbados
February 23–March 15
Glamorous arts festival held in the grounds of a 17th-century plantation house.
www.holders.net

Carnival
Port of Spain, Trinidad (and smaller towns in Trinidad and Tobago)
Moveable date, week before Lent
A frenzied few days of costumed parades, soca music, and dancing in the streets.
www.ncctt.org

MEXICO AND CENTRAL AMERICA

Día de la Candelaria (Candlemass)
Tlacotalpan, Veracruz, Mexico
February 2
Tlacotalpan marks the end of the Christmas season with bull fighting and parades.
www.veracruz.com.mx/mes

Fiesta de Virgen de Suyapa
Tegucigalpa, Honduras
February 3
The tiny statue of Honduras' patron saint is venerated by worshipers who make their way to her grand Basilica home.
www.honduras.com

SOUTH AMERICA

Carnaval
Salvador (various sites), Brazil
Moveable date, week before Lent
Carnaval is celebrated in the city of Salvador with a spectacular street festival.
www.bahia-online.net
(See pp50–1)

CANADA

Beauceron Maple Festival
Saint-Georges, Québec
March 12–16
Celebrating one of Canada's major exports – maple syrup. Stands selling pancakes with the ubiquitous sauce are abundant.
www.festivalbeaucerondelerable.com

Caribou Carnival
Frame Lake, Yellowknife, Northwest Territories
March 20–29
Famous International Dog Derby, a three-day dog-sled race on Great Slave Lake. Standard carnival fare alongside more eccentric activities such as ugly truck and bear-growing contests.
www.cariboucarnival.com

USA

Daytona Bike Week
Daytona Beach, Florida
February 29–March 9
Ten-day motorcycle event with speedway, dirt track racing, stunt bike shows, biker weddings, and a blessing of bikes ceremony.
www.officialbikeweek.com

South by Southwest
Austin, Texas
March 6–7
Indie music showcase. Emerging bands perform, with new media and film festivals alongside.
www.sxsw.com

Calle Ocho
Little Havana, Miami, Florida
March 16
Street party hosts the region's best performers on outdoor stages. Local food and drink stalls and a huge conga line as finale.
www.calle8.com

St. Patrick's Day Parade
New York and cities all over the USA, particularly Boston and Chicago
March 17
Irish parade with bagpipes, marching bands, and ubiquitous green costumes and decorations.
www.nyc-st-patrick-day-parade.org
(See pp62–3)

CARIBBEAN

Oistins Fish Festival
Oistins, Barbados
March 22–24
Community festival. Fish-boning and net-throwing competitions, cook-offs, and local calypso and reggae music.
www.oistins.org

British Virgin Islands Spring Regatta and Sailing Festival
Nanny Cay, Tortola, BVI
March 31–April 6
World-class sailing competition with day-time races and after-sundown partying.
www.bvispringregatta.org

MEXICO AND CENTRAL AMERICA

Semana Santa (Holy Week)
Antigua, Guatemala (and many other parts)
Moveable date, Easter
Bejeweled statues of Christ and the Virgin Mary are taken through the streets. Sacred music, clouds of incense, and wailing believers add to the heady atmosphere.
www.aroundantigua.com

SOUTH AMERICA

Vendimia
Mendoza, Argentina
First weekend in March
Grape harvest festival with Blessing of the Grapes ceremony, parades, and lots of red wine.
www.vendimia.mendoza.gov.ar

Festival Iberoamericano de Teatro de Colombia
Bogotá, Colombia
March 7–23
Theater festival which takes place every two years. Theater premieres, fringe plays, street shows, puppetry, and much more.
www.festivaldeteatro.com.co

APRIL

MAY

JUNE

LOUISIANA, USA Musicians at Festival International de Louisiane

PERU Dancers in elaborate masks, Qoyllur Rit'i festival

PERU Locals dressed in warrior costume, Inti Raymi festival, Cusco

CANADA

Empire Shakedown
Saint-Sauveur, Québec
April 4–5
Snowboarding festival with lifestyle exhibits, contests, and 35 professional riders competing alongside 80 amateurs.
www.shakedown.ca

Toonik Tyme
Iqaluit, Nunavut
April 16–20
The beginning of spring in the Arctic with Inuit folklore, throat singing, igloo building, and snow-mobile racing.
www.tooniktyme.com

USA

Alaska Folk Festival
Juneau, Alaska
April 7–13
Week-long folk music festival with accordian and fiddle music, square dancing, and open performance spots.
www.akfolkfest.org

French Quarter Festival
New Orleans, Louisiana
April 11–13
Jazz music flavors this musical street party. Cajun food, patio tours, and a world champion oyster-eating contest.
www.fqfi.org

Kentucky Derby Festival
Louisville, Kentucky
April 12–26
Partner to the famous Kentucky Derby horse races. Huge firework display over the Ohio river, parades, and all things equine.
www.kdf.org

Festival International de Louisiane
Lafayette, Louisiana
April 23–27
Celebration of French cultural heritage in southern Lousiana. Free outdoor music and dance events are highlights.
www.festivalinternational.com
(See pp98–9)

CARIBBEAN

Trelawney Yam Festival
Albert Town, Jamaica
Moveable date, Easter Monday
Community festival with cooking competitions, best-dressed goat, and throbbing sound systems.
www.stea.net

Buccoo Goat Race
Buccoo, Tobago
Moveable date, Easter Tuesday
Hilarious annual goat race conducted with much pomp and ceremony. Prize steeds are trained for months in advance and at the event commentators pick out potential winners at a pre-match paddock parade. Often accompanied by crab racing.
www.tobagowi.com

MEXICO AND CENTRAL AMERICA

Fiesta de Centro Historico
Mexico City, Mexico
April 10–27
Diverse and long-established arts and cultural festival in the atmospheric old center of the capital. Profits go to restoring the crumbling buildings in the area.
www.festival.org.mx

Feria de San Marcos
Aguascalientes, Mexico
April 19–May 18
Three weeks of Mexican partying in the heartland of the country. Mariachi bands, cock fights, fortune telling, and some of the best bullfighting talent in the world.
www.feriadesanmarcos.com

SOUTH AMERICA

Rupunani Rodeo
Lethem, Guyana
Easter weekend
Popular rodeo festival with cultural activities. Traditional Guyanese cowboy culture includes the energetic *faha* dance, similar to Brazilian *forro*.
www.guyana-tourism.com

CANADA

Festival Mutek
Montréal, Québec
May 28–June 1
Workshops, performances, and showcases of electronic music and digital creativity.
www.mutek.org

Bard on the Beach
Vancouver, British Columbia
May 29–September 27
Three-month Shakespeare festival with open-air performances in the spectacular riverside setting of Vanier Park.
www.bardonthebeach.org

USA

Sweet Auburn Springfest
Auburn, Atlanta, Georgia
May 9–11
Street festival celebrating Afro-American culture with markets, workshops, and craft displays.
www.sweetauburn.com

Spoleto Festival
Charleston, South Carolina
May 23–June 8
Upscale arts festival with classical music concerts, opera, jazz, ballet, and theater.
www.spoletousa.org

Indianapolis 500 Festival
Indianapolis, Indiana
May 25
Historic car race with an adrenalin-fueled atmosphere.
www.indy500.com

Portland Rose Festival
Portland, Oregon
May 29–June 8
Festival includes floral floats, tall ships, and a children's fair.
www.rosefestival.org

Memphis in May
Memphis, Tennessee
May
This event includes a music festival, performances by the Memphis Symphony Orchestra, and the renowned World Barbecue Championships.
www.memphisinmay.org
(See pp104–5)

CARIBBEAN

St. Lucia Jazz Festival
Pigeon Island, St. Lucia
May 2–11
Jazz festival with an emphasis on Afro-Caribbean performers.
www.stluciajazz.org
(See pp122–3)

Calabash International Literary Festival
Treasure Beach, Jamaica
May 23–25
Free literary event. Readings, seminars, and discussions.
www.calabashfestival.org

Crop Over
Barbados
May 23–June 8
Celebrating the end of the sugar cane harvest. Calypso music, parades, parties, and the Pic-O-De-Crop contest.
www.cropoverfestival.bb

SOUTH AMERICA

Día de las Glorias Navales
Valparaiso, Chile
May 21
Speeches and processions to celebrate Chile's naval success at the Battle of Iquique.
www.sernatur.cl

La Diablada
Puno, Peru
May 23
Drinking, dancing, and devilish costumes in a day of parades and water fighting.
www.peru-explorer.com

Qoyllur Rit'i
Cusco, Peru
Moveable date, begins a week before Corpus Christi
Traditional festival sees pilgrims heading up to an icy glacier to camp out under the stars.
www.cuscoperu.com

CANADA

Montréal Jazz Festival
Montréal, Québec
June 26–July 6
Largest jazz festival in the world with over 3,000 artists and 450 tree concerts. Book tickets for headlining acts well in advance.
www.montrealjazzfest.com

Yarmouth and Acadian Shores Lobster Festival
Yarmouth, Nova Scotia
June 27–29
Lobster fishing communities celebrate their livelihood with three days of lobster eating competitions, live traditional music, and driftwood art.
www.novascotia.com

USA

Chicago Blues Festival
Grant Park, Chicago
June 5–8
The largest free outdoors blues music event in the world with six stages and 90 performers.
www.chicagobluesfestival.org
(See pp130–1)

Country Music Association Festival
Nashville, Tennessee
June 5–8
"Country music's biggest party" with hundreds of great performers and an emphasis on artist/fan interaction.
www.cmafest.com

International Festival of Arts and Ideas
New Haven, Connecticut
June 14–28
Arts festival with thinkers and philosophers as well as stars of opera, dance, jazz, classical music, and experimental performances.
www.artidea.org

Telluride Bluegrass Festival
Telluride, Colorado
June 19–22
Accessible and intimate folk festival with songwriting contests and jamming sessions in picturesque mountain town.
www.bluegrass.com/telluride

CARIBBEAN

Noche de San Juan
San Juan, Puerto Rico
June 23
Celebration of midsummer and John the Baptist's saint's day with beach parties, bonfires, and numerous superstitious activities – principally running backwards into the sea which is supposed to bring good luck.
www.gotopuertorico.com

Vincy Mas
Kingstown, St. Vincent
June 27–July 8
Summer carnival fun in St. Vincent and its smaller islands, the Grenadines, with colorful parades, soca music, and costumed revelers.
www.carnivalsvg.com

SOUTH AMERICA

Bumba Meu Boi
São Luis, Maranhão, Brazil
June 13–30
Bizarre festival where animal costumes are donned to recreate the folk story of an ox which dies and then comes back to life. Noisy percussion accompanies the dance-drama.
www.maria-brazil.org

Inti Raymi Festival of the Sun
Cusco, Peru
June 24
Important Inca festival of the Sun performed by costumed actors in Cusco in the Peruvian Andes.
www.cuscoperu.com

Tango Festival
Tacuarembo, Uruguay
Week of June 24
The birthplace of Carlos Gardel, the most famous composer of tango music, comes alive with dancing and celebration on his birthday.

July – December: **Festivals**

MEXICO Young dancers in the Guelaguetza Festival procession, Oaxaca

CANADA Crowds at the Edmonton Folk Festival

HAWAI'I, USA Floral parade during the Aloha Festivals in Hawai'i

CANADA

Calgary Stampede
Calgary, Alberta
July 4–13
Rodeo competition, chuck wagon races, and blacksmithing contests.
www.calgarystampede.com
(See pp168–9)

Just for Laughs Comedy Festival
Montréal, Québec
July 10–20
Festival of stand-up comedy with the best international humorists.
www.justforlaughs.com

Great Northern Arts Festival
Inuvik, Northwest Territories
July 11–20
Festival with performing artists from the First Nation communities.
www.gnaf.org

Whistler Children's Arts Festival
Whistler, British Columbia
July 12–13
Festival of children's activities with crafts and magic shows.
www.whistlerartscouncil.com

HSBC Celebration of Light
Vancouver, British Columbia
July 23
Fireworks contest. Displays of the latest techniques and materials.
www.celebration-of-light.com

USA

Hopi Festival of Arts and Culture
Flagstaff, Arizona
July 4–6
Native American storytelling, music, dance, and crafts at the Museum of North Arizona.
www.musnaz.org

Cheyenne Frontier Days
Cheyenne, Wyoming
July 18–27
Rodeo competitions, music, and historical re-enactments.
www.cfdrodeo.com

Vectren Dayton Air Show
Vandalia, Ohio
July 19–20
America's largest air show with static planes and aerial stunts.
www.usats.org

Santa Fe Chamber Music Festival
Santa Fe, New Mexico
July 20–August 25
Performances from some of the finest orchestras and musicians.
www.sfcmf.org

CARIBBEAN

Reggae Sumfest
Montego Bay, Jamaica
July 13–19
Reggae festival with international acts and local performers.
www.reggaesumfest.com

Carriacou Regatta
Carriacou, Grenada
July 27–August 4
Yachting festival with locally built "workboats" and entertainment.
www.carriacouregatta.com

Merengue Festival
Santo Domingo, Dominican Republic
Last week of July
Merengue fans gather for a week of celebrations.
www.godominicanrepublic.com
(See pp176–7)

MEXICO AND CENTRAL AMERICA

Guelaguetza
Oaxaca, Mexico
Last two Mondays of July
Prehispanic harvest festival of thanksgiving and prayers.
www.oaxacainfo.com

SOUTH AMERICA

Fiesta de la Virgen del Carmen
La Tirana, Chile
July 12–18
Festival honoring an indigenous woman converting to Catholicism.
www.chipsites.com

CANADA

Edmonton Folk Festival
Edmonton, Alberta
August 7–10
Variety of international folk music in pretty parkland setting.
www.edmontonfolkfest.org

Opaskwayak Indian Days
Opaskwayak, Manitoba
Third Week in August
Festival held by and about the local Cree Indian community.
www.opaskwayak.mb.ca

Winona Peach Festival
Winona, Ontario
August 22–24
Produce fair with children's entertainers and craft stalls.
www.winonapeach.com

USA

Wisconsin State Fair
West Allis, Wisconsin
August 2–12
Festival with pig racing, moo-ing contests, and fairground rides.
www.wsfp.state.wi.us
(See pp182–3)

Newport Folk Festival
Newport, Rhode Island
August 3–5
Folk music galore at this American institution.
www.newportfolk.com

Tennessee Walking Horse National Celebrations
Shelbyville, Tennessee
August 20–30
Comprehensive rodeo contest, blacksmith competition, and barn decorating contest.
www.twhnc.com

Burning Man
Black Rock, Nevada
August 25–September 1
Alternative festival in the desert with giant installations, outlandish costumes, and anything-goes ambience.
www.burningman.com
(See pp204–5)

Bumbershoot
Seattle, Washington
August 30–September 1
Arts festival with music, performance, and visual arts.
www.bumbershoot.org

CARIBBEAN

Festival of Women Cooks
Pointe-á-Pitre, Guadeloupe
August 10
Women cooks parade through the streets with baskets of home-cooked food.
www.antilles-info-tourisme.com

MEXICO AND CENTRAL AMERICA

Fiestas Agostinas
San Salvador, El Salvador
First week of August
Celebrating the country's patron saint, El Salvador del Mundo.
www.elsalvador.com

Crab Soup Festival
Corn Islands, Nicaragua
August 27
Marking the end of slavery with parades and sporting contests.
www.nicaragua.com

Fiesta de los Mariachis
Guadalajara, Jalisco, Mexico
August 30–September 9
Shows by some of the finest performers of mariachi music.
www.mariachi-jalisco.com.mx

SOUTH AMERICA

Anniversario de la Fundacion de Asunción
Asunción, Paraguay
August 15
Demonstrations of local cuisine and traditions.
www.senatur.gov.py

Festa do Peao Boiadeiro
Barretos, São Paulo, Brazil
August 21–31
Rodeo and cowboy festival in the south of the country.
www.independentes.com.br
(See pp202–3)

CANADA

Vancouver Fringe Festival
Vancouver, British Columbia
September 3–14
Ten days of offbeat theater with over 500 different shows as well as workshops and talks.
www.vancouverfringe.com

Toronto International Film Festival
Toronto, Ontario
September 4–13
North America's premier film festival with industry showcases as well as public screenings.
www.tiffg.ca

Ottawa International Animation Festival
Ottawa, Ontario
September 17–21
Festival of animated film with top-notch guest animators, displays of the latest technology, and over 2,000 screenings.
www.ottawa.awn.com

USA

Aloha Festivals
Hawai'i
All September/October
Six weeks of cultural activities on each of Hawai'i's islands in turn with traditional ukelele music and hula dancing.
www.alohafestivals.com

Boardwalk Weekend/Neptune Festival
Virginia Beach, Virginia
September 26–28
Weekend finale of summer festival. Sporting events, sand-sculpting competition, live music, and local produce stalls.
www.neptunefestival.com

MEXICO AND CENTRAL AMERICA

Belize Independence Day
Belize City, Belize
September 2–23
Three weeks of all-night parties, carnival parades, and celebration.
www.septembercelebrations.com

Independence Day
Nationwide, Mexico
September 15 & 16
At 11pm each September 15, the Mexican president rings the liberty bell in Mexico City with a cry of "Mexicanos, viva Mexico." September 16 is a day of speeches, military parades, and general festivities.
www.visitmexico.com

SOUTH AMERICA

Yamor Fiesta
Otavalo, Ecuador
September 1–15
Highland harvest festival with music, processions, fireworks, carnival queens, and much drinking. Yamor is the name of a toxic drink made from seven kinds of corn.
www.exploringecuador.com

CARIBBEAN

Love our Planet Week
Kralendijk, Bonaire, Dutch Antilles
September 20–27
Ocean environment festival with group scuba dives, seminars with Philippe Cousteau, underwater photo workshops, and mass clean-ups of the sea.
www.bonaireinsider.com

SOUTH AMERICA

International Fishing Festival
Caceres, Mato Grosso, Brazil
September 16–24
Huge river fishing competitions on the banks of the river Paraguay. Boat shows, folkloric dancing, local gastronomy, and music add color.
www.fipcaceres.com.br

Circus Festival
Lima, Peru
September 18–30
International festival of circus arts with performances, showcases, workshops, and lectures.
www.festivaldelcirculo.com

NEW MEXICO, USA Balloons fill the sky, Albuquerque Balloon Fiesta

GUATEMALA Traditional horseback race, Dia de Todos Santos

BRAZIL Spectacular New Year's fireworks, Copacabana beach, Rio

CANADA

Yukon International Story Telling Festival
Whitehouse, Yukon
October 3–5
Storytelling from performers from the circumpolar regions with theater, drums, mime, and music.
www.storytelling.yk.net

USA

Albuquerque International Balloon Fiesta
Albuquerque, New Mexico
October 4–12
World's largest balloon event. Special shape competitions, a twilight firing up of the balloons, and serious balloon races.
www.balloonfiesta.com
(See pp242–3)

Big Pig Jig
Vienna, Georgia
October 5–6
Pork cooking contest. Live animals also with hog calling and piggy parades.
www.bigpigjig.com

Northeast Kingdom Fall Foliage Festival
Various towns, Northeast Kingdom, Vermont
First week in October
Festival celebrating spectacular leaf fall in seven Vermont towns.
www.nekfoliage.com

Parke County Covered Bridge Festival
Rockville, Indiana
October 10–19
Daily bus tours over the weekend of nine local communities with covered bridges, arts and crafts vendors, and food stands.
www.parkecounty.com

Fantasy Fest
Key West, Florida
October 17–26
Camp parades, outrageous fancy dress costumes, and rum cocktails characterize this festival.
www.fantasyfest.net

CARIBBEAN

National Warri Festival
St. Johns, Antigua
First week in October
Championships of Antiguan board game which involves shuffling beads around a hollowed out fish-shaped board.
www.antigua-barbuda.org

Dominoes World Championships
Montego Bay, Jamaica
Third week in October
Internationally recognized competition with large cash prizes and teams from all over the Caribbean, the USA, and Canada. Noisy and great fun.
www.worldchampionshipof
dominoes.com

World Creole Music Festival
Roseau, Dominica
October 31–November 2
Three days of pulsating sounds with performers from the Creole speaking world and beyond.
www.festivalmusiquecreole
dominique.com

MEXICO AND CENTRAL AMERICA

Festival of the Black Christ
Portobelo, Panama
October 21
Worshipers from far and wide crawl along the route, some flagellating themselves, to the shrine of the dark-skinned Christ, patron saint of singers. Food and drink stalls line the way.
www.ipat.gob.pa

SOUTH AMERICA

Círio de Nazaré
Belém, Brazil
Second half of October
Belém's Virgin Mary is carted around the town in a grave procession which is followed by a fortnight of drinking and general revelry.
www.ciriodenazare.com.br

CANADA

Canadian Western Agribition
Regina, Saskatchewan
November 24–29
Huge livestock fair with thousands of animals, a rodeo, and country music.
www.agribition.com

Banff Lake Louise Winterstart Festival
Banff, Alberta
November 24–December 9
Two weeks of entertainment in the Canadian Rockies with emphasis on winter sports – snow boarding and skiing. Film screenings, parades, and gigs feature too.
www.banfflakelouise.com
(See pp274–5)

USA

Lady of the Lakes Renaissance Fair
Tavares, Florida
November 7–9
The best of numerous medieval fairs with costumed revelers, jugglers, jousters, and all manner of games.
www.medievalfest.com

Gatlinburg Winter Magic
Gatlinburg, Tennessee
November 7–February 29
The city is lit up with over three million fairy lights. Traditional hay rides and a spectacular parade are both highlights.
www.gatlinburgwintermagic.com

CARIBBEAN

Pirates' Week
George Town, Grand Cayman, Cayman Islands
November 6–16
Boat races, fancy dress competitions, a mock pirate invasion, and more make this week-long celebration of the Cayman Islands' heritage particularly popular with young children.
www.piratesweekfestival.com

Gimistory
Grand Cayman, Cayman Islands
November 23–December 2
Storytelling in island-wide venues with calypso accompaniment and free swank (lemonade) and fishcakes served up to both audience and performers alike.
www.artscayman.com

MEXICO AND CENTRAL AMERICA

Dia de Todos Santos
Todos Santos de Cuchumatanes, Guatemala
November 1
All Saints' Day celebrated in the highlands with an anarchic horse race. Bareback jockeys get drunker and drunker as the day wears on and cling ever tighter to their mounts while they tear through the town. Firecrackers, firewater, and marimba music in abundance.
www.visitguatemala.com

Day of the Dead
Pátzcuaro, Michoacan, Mexico
November 1 & 2
Celebrated all over Mexico, the candle-lit cemetery vigils when the dead are remembered with flowers, sweets, and singing are particularly moving on the lake island of Janitzio.
www.patzcuaromexico.com

Garifuna Settlement Day
Dangriga, Belize
November 19
A celebration of the arrival of the Garifuna, an escaped slave community from St. Vincent who have retained their African roots. The actual landing is re-enacted with small fishing boats, laden with banana leaves and palm fronds, riding the surf into the Belizean shore. Traditional punta rock music, drumming, dancing, and general merriment.
www.belizeans.com

CARIBBEAN

New International Latin American Film Festival
Havana, Cuba
December 2–12
Major Latin American cinema showcase with world premieres and visiting luminaries.
www.beta.habanafilmfestival.com

Junkanoo
Nassau, New Providence, Bahamas
December 26
Carnivalesque parade commemorating slave hero John Canoe, lasting from 2am to 9am.
www.junkanoo.com

MEXICO AND CENTRAL AMERICA

La Purísima
Countrywide, Nicaragua
December 7
The Virgin Mary is honored with a collective cry (La Griteria) on December 7 at 6pm and home-made altars are set up.
www.nicaragua.com

Quema del Diablo (Burning of the Devil)
Guatemala City, Guatemala
December 7
The start of the Christmas season is marked by the burning of household junk on the streets.
www.visitguatemala.com

Día de la Virgen de Guadalupe
Mexico City, Mexico
December 12
Worshipers mark the day of the symbol of Mexico. Some shuffle on their knees to Tepeyac where she was first sighted.
www.virgendeguadalupe.org.mx

Fiesta de San Cristobal de las Casas
San Cristobal de las Casas, Chiapas
December 12–21
Town festival with processions by Tzotzil and Tzetzal Indians.
www.visitmexico.com

Fiesta de Santo Tomas
Chichicastenango, Guatemala
December 21
Festival in Guatemala's highlands. Parades, marimba music, indigenous clothing, fireworks, and lots of local firewater.
www.guatemalaweb.com

Noche de los Rabanos (Night of the Radishes)
Oaxaca, Mexico
December 23
The central square in Oaxaca is set up with stalls displaying radishes carved in all manner of intricate shapes.
www.christmas-in-oaxaca.com

Fiesta de los Diablitos (Festival of the Devils)
San Isidro del General, Costa Rica
December 30–January 2
Festival which recreates a fight to the death between the Indians (the Diablitos) and the Spaniards, represented by a bull. Traditional music provides atmosphere.
www.visitcostarica.com

SOUTH AMERICA

Feria de Cali
Cali, Colombia
December 6–30
Summer festival with an emphasis on salsa dancing. Concerts, parades, and high energy merriment.
www.feriadecali.com

Surifesta
Paramaribo, Suriname
December 14–January 6
Several weeks of street parties in December, including New Year's Eve.
www.surifesta.com

Reveillon/New Year's Eve
Rio de Janeiro, Brazil
December 31
Celebrations on Copacabana Beach with party-goers dressed head to toe in white, for purity and new beginnings.
www.brazilmax.com
(See pp302–3)

Travel and the Environment

GETTING THERE
The impact of air travel and tourism on the global environment has been well publicized but there are ways to limit the damaging effects of your own travels. Consider trains and ships as alternatives to flying. If flights are unavoidable, look at carbon offsetting or the trips offered by Better World, Responsible Travel, and other ecologically aware operators.

CARBON OFFSETTING SCHEMES
These enable you to "offset" the effects of carbon emissions by planting sustainable forests or contributing to biodiversity schemes that notionally "match" the amount of CO_2 you've generated. Organizations like Better World, Carbon Neutral, and Climate Care offer assistance on making an offset contribution.

HIGH- AND LOW-IMPACT TOURISM
Tourism also directly affects the ecology and local economy of the destination countries. Major resort complexes can damage the landscape and local infrastructure. Not all resorts are the same but don't be afraid to ask questions, such as: how is waste disposed of? Where does their energy come from?

Locally run hotels and tour operations often have a more positive impact, especially if they use zero-impact bathrooms and other environmentally friendly features. The best will work with local communities and guides so that locals have alternatives to harmful practices like deforestation and strip-farming.

Trips to see wildlife and into remote areas should be made in small groups, with local guides, not in big bus tours. It is not only the environment that gains by this – it will also give you a far more memorable experience.

Better World Club
www.betterworldclub.com
Carbon Neutral
www.carbonneutral.com
Climate Care
www.climatecare.org
Responsible Travel
www.responsibletravel.com

Think Global, Shop Local

Spread the financial benefits of tourism by shopping for souvenirs in local shops and markets, instead of hotel stores and large malls. A little research on the customs of the country you're visiting and a few courteous questions will reduce any language barriers. Do not assume that everything you buy should be very cheap because you're in a poor country: people have a right to be paid for their work. And – avoiding the cheapest, shabbiest places – eat in local restaurants rather than those set aside for tourists. The food will usually be more interesting.

Above (left to right): ATM machine in Orlando, Florida; taxis on a New York street; hiking a trail on O'ahu, Hawai'i

TRAVEL INFORMATION

W EBSITES, ONLINE BOOKING, and all the other developments in modern travel and communications, have made every part of the Americas more accessible than ever before. But, to make the most of your trip, you should attend to certain details before you set off – border formalities, insurance, how you're going to travel around, and so on. By doing a little planning you can save yourself money and minimize the chances of something going wrong.

USA & CANADA

HEALTH AND MEDICAL INSURANCE

MD Travel Health www.mdtravelhealth.com

It is essential to have comprehensive travel and medical insurance. Health facilities are excellent but extremely expensive (Canada slightly less so). If you plan to do any sports (especially winter sports, adventure sports, or scuba diving), you should check that these are covered too.

PERSONAL SECURITY

Foreign & Commonwealth Office www.fco.gov.uk
US State Department www.travel.state.gov

Avoid dark or deserted streets; keep valuables hidden; don't use ATMs at night; and don't leave items visible in cars. Carry photocopies of important documents; leave the originals in your hotel safe. If you are a victim of crime, report it to the police immediately and keep a copy of the statement for your insurance claim. Report missing passports to your country's consulate.

PASSPORTS AND VISAS

Canada Government www.canadainternational.gc.ca
US State Department www.travel.state.gov

Citizens of many western countries can enter the USA without a visa under the Visa Waiver Program (VWP), with a machine-readable passport (with a biometric chip if issued after October 26, 2006). Anyone else must obtain the correct visa in advance. VWP entry is for 90 days only – for longer trips a visa must be obtained in advance. Citizens of many countries can also enter Canada without a visa. Check government websites for details.

MONEY AND COMMUNICATIONS

Travelex www.travelex.com

A major credit or debit card is needed for transactions such as renting a car. There's usually a fee for withdrawing cash from ATMs. Bring some currency and dollar travelers' checks as back-up.

Internet cafés are common, and many hotels have internet access. Tri- or quad-band cell (mobile) phones work in North America.

GETTING AROUND

There are hundreds of airports in North America, with budget airlines for internal flights. The All-America Airpass offers discounts with certain airlines throughout North and South America to visitors from Europe, Australasia, South Africa, and Asia. It must be purchased in advance.

Buses are the cheapest alternative to air travel. Greyhound has the largest long-distance network, and offers an unlimited-travel Discovery Pass. Various regional bus routes also operate throughout North America.

Trains are the best overland option, operated in the USA by Amtrak and by Via Rail in Canada. Unlimited travel passes are available from each, covering one or both countries.

In many parts of North America a car is indispensable. Rental rates are better if you book ahead via a reputable website. Many nations' driving licenses are valid in the USA and Canada, but for Canada an International Driving License, available from drivers' organizations, is recommended. To take a vehicle across the US-Canadian border, you must show an insurance certificate. Vehicles rented in the USA may not be taken into Mexico.

THE WESTERN HEMISPHERE TRAVEL INITIATIVE (WHTI)

The WHTI, fully in force from June 2009, is a system for regulating travel between the USA and its neighbors (except Haiti and Cuba). Under the WHTI, full passports are obligatory for air travel between the participant countries. For land or sea borders, however, a full passport or other WHTI-compliant document (such as the US Passport Card and the US-Canadian NEXUS card) are permitted. For the full list of acceptable documents, see government websites.

MEXICO, CENTRAL, AND SOUTH AMERICA

HEALTH AND MEDICAL INSURANCE

MD Travel Health www.mdtravelhealth.com

Full travel and medical insurance is essential, with additional cover for adventure sports. In most cities and tourist areas there are high-quality private clinics, nearly always with English-speaking staff. Elsewhere, facilities are scarce. Many countries have public health clinics which can provide basic emergency treatment, but your insurance should cover evacuation to a fully equipped hospital, or repatriation.

Check current health guidelines before you travel. You should at least be immunized again hepatitis A and B, typhoid, tetanus, and diptheria. In tropical forest areas there may be a risk of yellow fever and/or malaria, and insect repellent is vital. In the High Andes, altitude sickness is a risk. The most common problems, though, are stomach ailments. Drink bottled water and pack anti-diarrhea medications, along with bite lotion, antiseptic cream and wipes, and dressings for cuts and scratches.

PERSONAL SECURITY

Foreign & Commonwealth Office www.fco.gov.uk
US State Department www.travel.state.gov

Apply the same rules as for North America, but be even more vigilant. There are high levels of crime in many cities, and bag-snatching is common. Extra caution is needed, especially on public transport. If you are a victim of crime, report it to the police straight away and keep a copy of the statement for your insurance. Report missing passports to your country's consulate.

PASSPORTS AND VISAS

Foreign & Commonwealth Office www.fco.gov.uk
US State Department www.travel.state.gov

North American citizens can enter Mexico by land or sea (including from cruise ships) with a birth certificate and photo ID, but to re-enter, from June 2009, a passport or other WHTI-compliant document is needed. A full passport is needed to travel by air. A Mexican Tourist Card (FMT), marked at immigration with the length of your permitted stay, is required by some North American visitors in some circumstances. Check government websites for details. Citizens of many countries do not need a visa to enter Mexico, but must have full passports and an FMT card.

For many travelers, a visa is not needed for stays of up to 90 days in most other Latin American countries, just a full passport valid for at least six months after the date of entry. Citizens of the USA, Canada, and Australia must get visas in advance to visit Brazil or Paraguay, and US citizens need visas to enter Bolivia. Americans must also have visas to visit Chile, obtained on arrival. For details of entry requirements, check the website of the embassy of the relevant country before traveling.

MONEY AND COMMUNICATIONS

Travelex www.travelex.com

A major credit or debit card is useful. ATMs are common in Latin America, even in small towns, but the efficiency of the network varies; and not all cards are accepted by all machines. Carry some dollars or euros and US travelers' checks as back-up. In remote areas you may need to take enough local currency for the whole trip, but keep it in a money belt, out of sight. Use cards only for payments to larger businesses, such as car rental agencies. It is essential to notify your card company that you are traveling to Latin America. Concerns about fraud and money-laundering mean that unauthorized use might result in your account being frozen.

Internet cafés are common, and pay-phone cards are usually sold at convenience stores. Phone offices, where the number is dialed for you, are cheaper for long-distance calls. Most cell (mobile) phones in Latin America work on similar frequencies to those used in North America.

DIRECTORY OF USEFUL CONTACTS

USA & CANADA

The Adventure Directory
www.directoryadventure.com
Links to sites for every type of active sport, worldwide

Adventure Sports Online
www.adventuresportsonline.com
Directory of worldwide adventure travel options

Adventure Travel Trade Association
www.adventuretravel.biz
Adventure travel trade website

All America Airpass
www.allairpass.com
Available only in Europe, Australasia, South Africa, and Asia

Amtrak
www.amtrak.com

Australian Department of Foreign Affairs and Trade
www.smartraveller.gov.au
Information for travelers

The Away Network/GORP
http://gorp.away.com
Information and resources for active vacations worldwide

Better World Club
www.betterworldclub.com
Environmentally friendly travel services, such as carbon offsetting

BootsnAll
www.bootsnall.com
A wide range of resources for independent travelers

Budget Airline Guide
www.budgetairlineguide.com
Guide to low-cost airlines in the USA and Canada

The Bus Station
www.busstation.net
A country-by-country guide to bus services worldwide

Canada Travel
www.canada.travel.
Official tourist information site

Canadian Department of Foreign Affairs and International Trade
www.dfait-maeci.gc.ca
Travel advice and consulate details

Centers for Disease Control & Prevention (CDC)
www.cdc.gov/travel
Health information for travelers including lists of travel health clinics throughout the USA

Coach America
www.coachamerica.com
Bus services in western and southern USA

Coach USA; Coach Canada
www.coachusa.com
Bus routes in northeast and mid-west US, Ontario, and Québec

Dogtag Worldwide Assistance
www.dogtag.co.uk
UK-based sports and adventure-travel insurance specialists

Greyhound Bus Company
www.greyhound.com

GSM World
www.gsmworld.com.
Cellphone information and worldwide frequency guide

International Association for Medical Assistance to Travellers
www.iamat.org
Non-profit-making organization and a good information source

Jiwire
www.jiwire.com
Comprehensive guide to WiFi and hotspots around the world

Magellan's Travel Supplies
www.magellans.com
Travel clothing and equipment

The Man in Seat 61
www.seat61.com
A worldwide guide to rail and other alternatives to air travel

MD Travel Health
www.mdtravelhealth.com
User-friendly worldwide travel health information and resources

Motor Coach Canada
www.motorcoachcanada.com.
Local bus routes across Canada

Nomad Travel
www.nomadtravel.co.uk
UK-based travel health advice and on-site vaccination clinics

Official Airline Guide
www.oag.com
Worldwide flight and airport information

Responsible Travel
www.responsibletravel.com
One of the world's largest agents for eco- and socially-aware travel

Scuba Spots Diving Directory
www.scubaspots.com
Diving operators, courses, and facilities worldwide

Travel Insurance Center
www.worldtravelcenter.com
Worldwide travel insurance

UK Foreign & Commonwealth Office
www.fco.gov.uk
Travel advice and warnings

US National Hurricane Center
www.nhc.noaa.gov

US State Department
www.travel.state.gov

Via Rail Canada
www.viarail.ca

World Nomads
www.worldnomads.com
Insurance for independent and adventure travelers worldwide

Worldtravellers
www.worldtravellers.net
Directory of information on all kinds of travel worldwide

MEXICO, CENTRAL & SOUTH AMERICA

Adventure Mexican Insurance
www.mexadventure.com
Insurance for US and Canadian vehicles, and boats, in Mexico

Exito Travel
www.exitotravel.com
Latin American travel specialists

Latin American Travel Association
www.lata.org
Trade organization of UK-based Latin-America tour companies

Latin Guides
www.latinguides.com
Travel information for Latin America and the Caribbean

Mexico Online
www.mexonline.com
Guide to traveling in Mexico

Planeta
www.planeta.com
Information on eco-tourism in Mexico and elsewhere

THE CARIBBEAN

Caribbean Guide
www.caribbean-guide.info
Informative guide to all aspects of travel in the Caribbean

Caribbean-On-Line
www.caribbean-on-line.com
Comprehensive guide

Jamaica Travel Guide
www.jamaicatravelpages.com
Independent travel guide

Leeward Airlines Air Transport
www.liatairline.com
Inter-island flights throughout the eastern Caribbean

PRACTICAL TRAVEL

Above (left to right): Train to Macchu Picchu at Aguas Calientes, Peru; Internet café in Cancún, Mexico; cruise ship entering the harbor of Castries, St. Lucia

GETTING AROUND

Domestic and regional flights can be expensive. The All-America Airpass (see p324) is the most comprehensive discount ticket, but is for non-Americans only and must be purchased in advance. Regional passes available in the USA and Canada include Mexipass, for Mexico and parts of Central America, and the Mercosur Airpass.

Argentina, Bolivia, Peru, and Ecuador still have sizeable railroad networks, but elsewhere in Latin America services are scarce, and there are few long-distance trains. Buses are the main form of land transport, with services even to the smallest village.

There are stringent restrictions on driving your own vehicle in Mexico, including import permits, a bond to prevent selling, and local insurance. Most other Latin American countries have their own temporary import procedures, so check carefully.

Cars rented in the USA or Canada cannot usually be taken into Mexico, but there are plenty of rental agencies on the spot. Local agencies in Latin America often give better rates than the international franchises, so shop around. Due to chaotic traffic it's inadvisable (and slow) to drive in many cities, but a vehicle is often a must for exploring villages, beaches, and pre-Hispanic ruins. In remote and mountainous areas, it may be better to rent a car with a driver, or to take advantage of the many small-group tours offered by local agencies.

THE CARIBBEAN

HEALTH AND MEDICAL INSURANCE

MD Travel Health www.mdtravelhealth.com

Comprehensive travel and medical insurance is essential. Most Caribbean countries have good-standard public or private hospitals in main towns, but foreigners must pay for treatment. Few are equipped to deal with serious injuries, so your insurance must cover air evacuation to the USA or your home country. Foreigners using the Cuban health service must pay in hard currency, not Cuban pesos.

Check current inoculation and health advice for your destination. The only problems most travelers have to deal with are stomach upsets and insect bites (see p325).

PERSONAL SECURITY

Foreign & Commonwealth Office www.fco.gov.uk
US State Department www.travel.state.gov

Be on your guard against petty street and car crime (see p325). Tourist areas attract opportunist criminals who rob from villas and beaches, and some cities have high levels of crime.

If you are a victim of crime, report it to the police immediately and keep a copy of the police statement for an insurance claim. Report lost or stolen passports to your country's consulate.

PASSPORTS AND VISAS

Foreign & Commonwealth Office www.fco.gov.uk
US State Department www.travel.state.gov

For citizens of most western countries, no visa is required for stays of up to 90 days in most Caribbean states.

US and Canadian nationals need a passport to enter by air, but can travel to, and return from, many Caribbean countries by sea with any WHTI-compliant document (see p324). However, the State Department recommends a full passport to avoid confusion. Non-US citizens who travel via the USA must meet US entry requirements (see p324).

All visitors to Cuba must have a visa. This can usually be obtained for a small fee from the travel company arranging your trip. US citizens are currently not allowed to visit Cuba except under special circumstances.

MONEY AND COMMUNICATIONS

Travelex www.travelex.com

Local currencies are often linked to the US dollar, but French islands use the euro. A major credit or debit card is useful. ATMs are scarce on some islands, but you can withdraw cash against a card at bank counters. Bring some cash and travelers' checks as back-up, nearly always in US dollars.

For Cuba, avoid US-related cards, cash, and traveler's checks. There are currently few ATMs, and the street economy is cash-only. Many traders prefer to be paid in hard currency (sterling or euros) rather than pesos.

Internet cafés are common except in Cuba, where hotels are the likeliest place to find Internet access. Most countries, including Cuba, sell pay-phone cards; cell (mobile) phone coverage is extensive across the islands, and restrictions in Cuba have now been lifted by Raoul Castro.

GETTING AROUND

The Caribbean's main hub airports are in Jamaica, the Dominican Republic, Puerto Rico, Antigua, and Trinidad, from where local airlines link to other islands. Many accept the All-America Airpass (see p324). Check for local discount deals before traveling. Cuba has direct flights from many countries; the quickest and cheapest route is from Cancún.

Ferry services link many islands, but there is no ferry guide for the whole region. Each island has bus services, and most have agencies offering rental transport, often with some restrictions. In former British territories, vehicles drive on the left.

HURRICANE SEASON

The North Atlantic hurricane season officially runs from June to November, and affects the whole of the Caribbean, Central America, the Gulf of Mexico, and the eastern seaboard of the United States. During the season the timing, strength, and route of storms cannot be predicted more than a few days in advance, but some major storms are likely each year. The best source of information on everything to do with hurricanes and tropical storms, including the progress of a storm if you think it is likely to threaten your trip or your destination, is the US National Hurricane Center.

Atlas of the Americas

The map references given
for all entries in the book refer
to the maps in this section.

312

322

313

314

315

320 319 316

321

318

323 317 325

325

324

326

328

327 327

330

329

331

KEY TO SCALES

Small scale maps above 1:14,000,000

Medium scale maps 1:8,000,000 to 1:14,000,000

Large scale maps below 1:8,000,000

322

INDEX OF MAPS

KEY TO SYMBOLS

═	Highway	■	Capital city
─	Major road	⊙	Provincial / state capital
─	Other road	✦	Airport
┈	Railroad	△	Peak
━	International border	⬙	Volcano
─	Province / state border		

▶▶

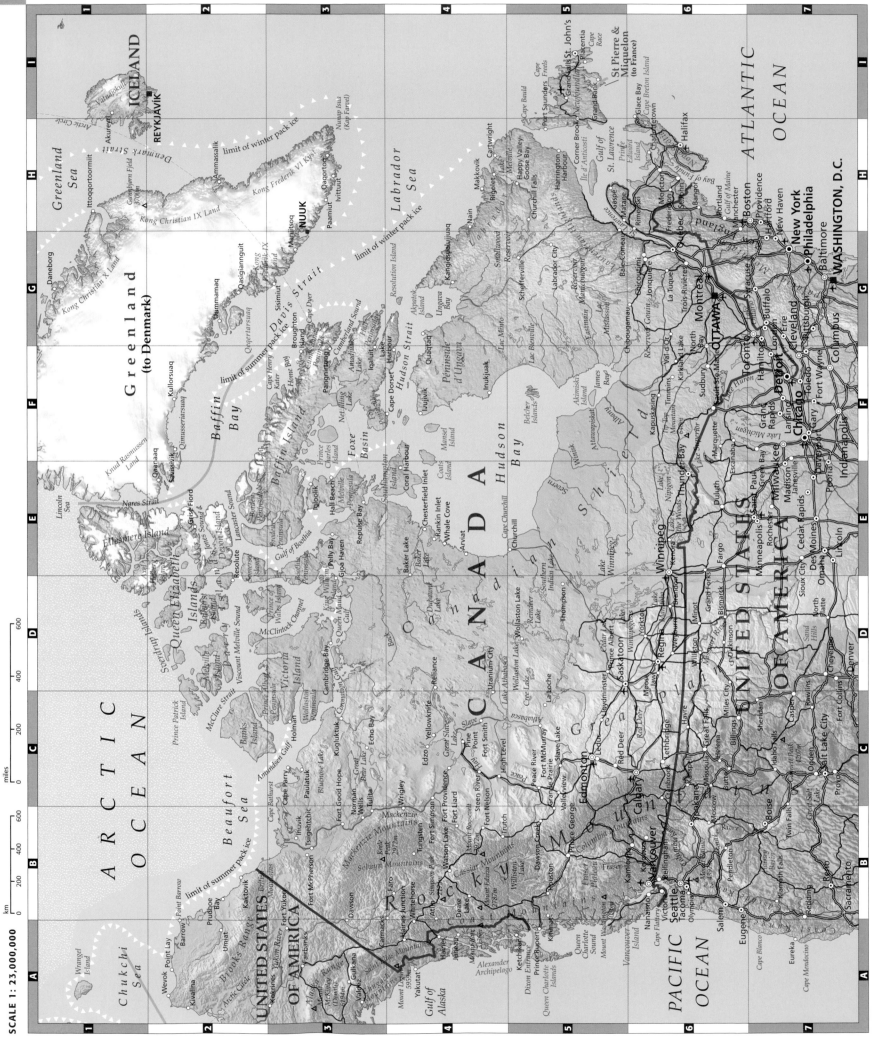

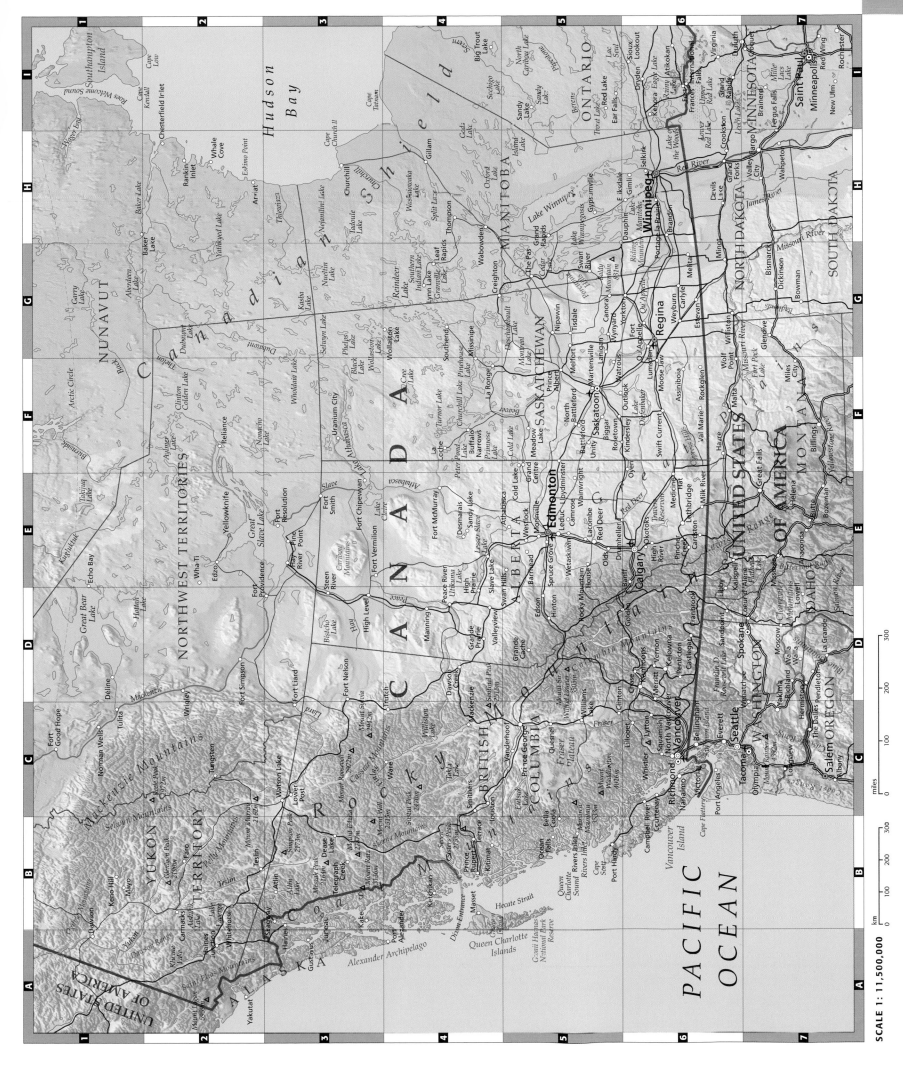

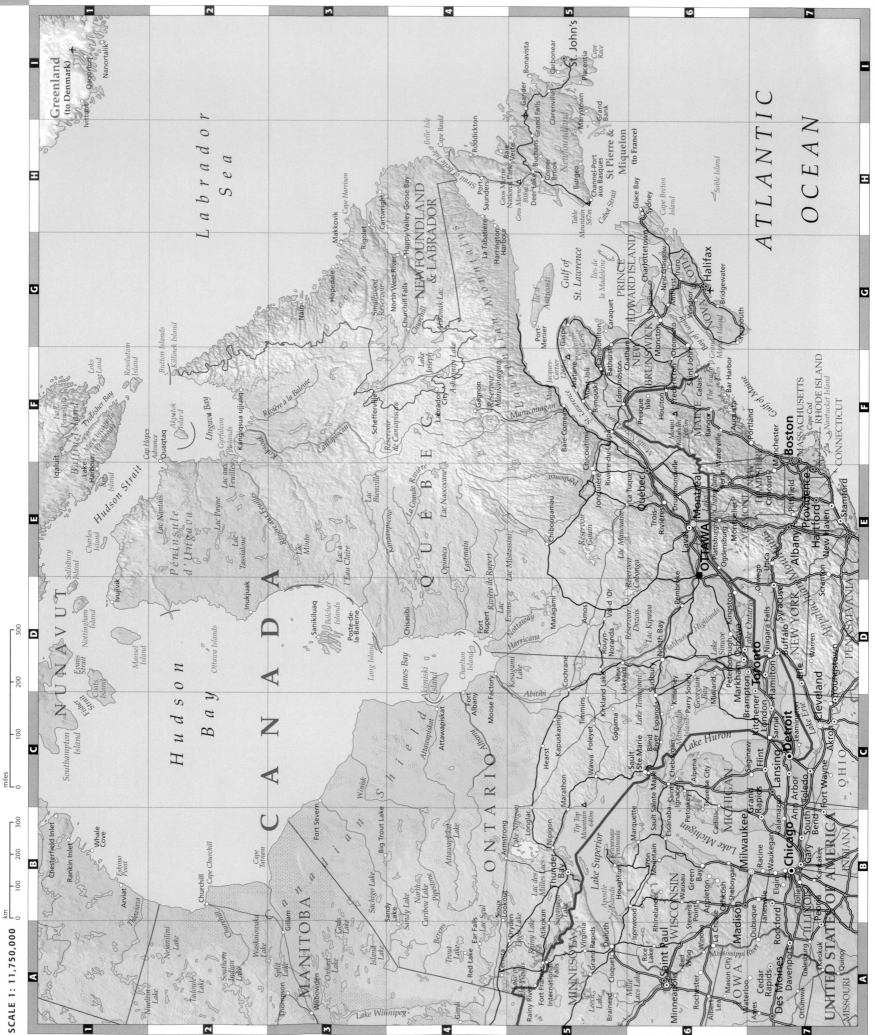

GREENLAND
(to Denmark)

ATLANTIC

OCEAN

Labrador

Sea

NUNAVUT

Hudson

Bay

CANADA

QUEBEC

NEWFOUNDLAND & LABRADOR

MANITOBA

ONTARIO

MICHIGAN

WISCONSIN

MINNESOTA

UNITED STATES OF AMERICA

NEW BRUNSWICK

PRINCE EDWARD ISLAND

NOVA SCOTIA

MAINE

NEW YORK

PENNSYLVANIA

OHIO

Gulf of

St. Lawrence

Lake Superior

Lake Huron

Lake Michigan

Lake Erie

Lake Ontario

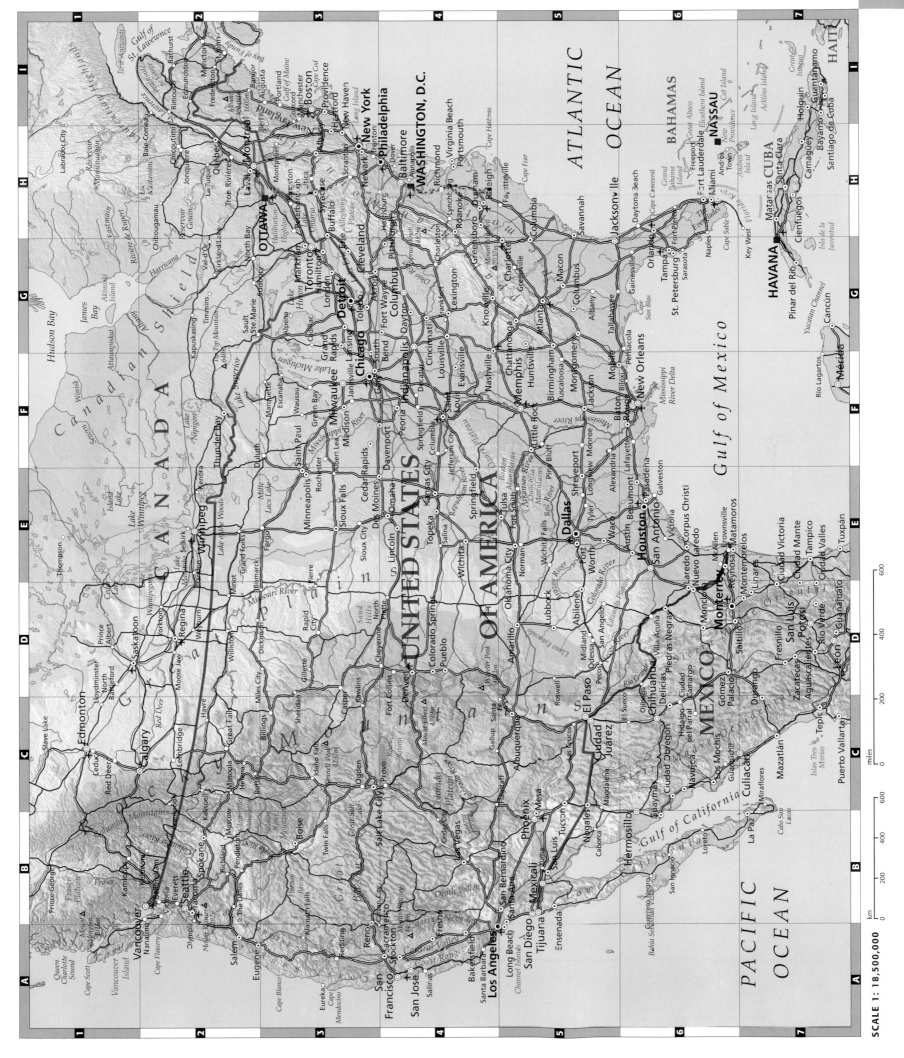

SCALE 1: 18,500,000

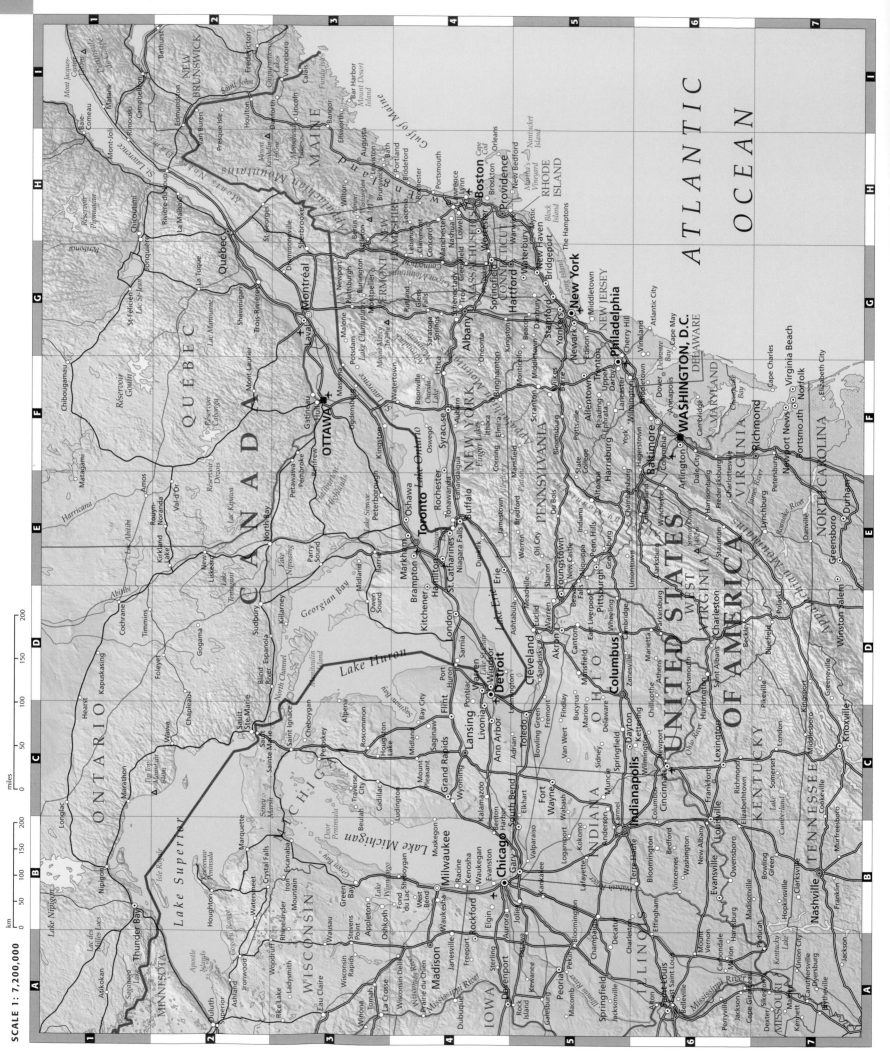

ATLANTIC OCEAN

CANADA

QUÉBEC

ONTARIO

UNITED STATES OF AMERICA

MAINE

NEW BRUNSWICK

NEW HAMPSHIRE

VERMONT

NEW YORK

MASSACHUSETTS

CONNECTICUT

RHODE ISLAND

NEW JERSEY

PENNSYLVANIA

MARYLAND

DELAWARE

VIRGINIA

WEST VIRGINIA

OHIO

MICHIGAN

INDIANA

ILLINOIS

WISCONSIN

MINNESOTA

IOWA

MISSOURI

KENTUCKY

TENNESSEE

NORTH CAROLINA

Lake Superior

Lake Michigan

Lake Huron

Lake Erie

Lake Ontario

Georgian Bay

Gulf of Maine

Washington, D.C.

Boston

New York

Philadelphia

Baltimore

Chicago

Detroit

Cleveland

Columbus

Indianapolis

Toronto

Ottawa

Montréal

Québec

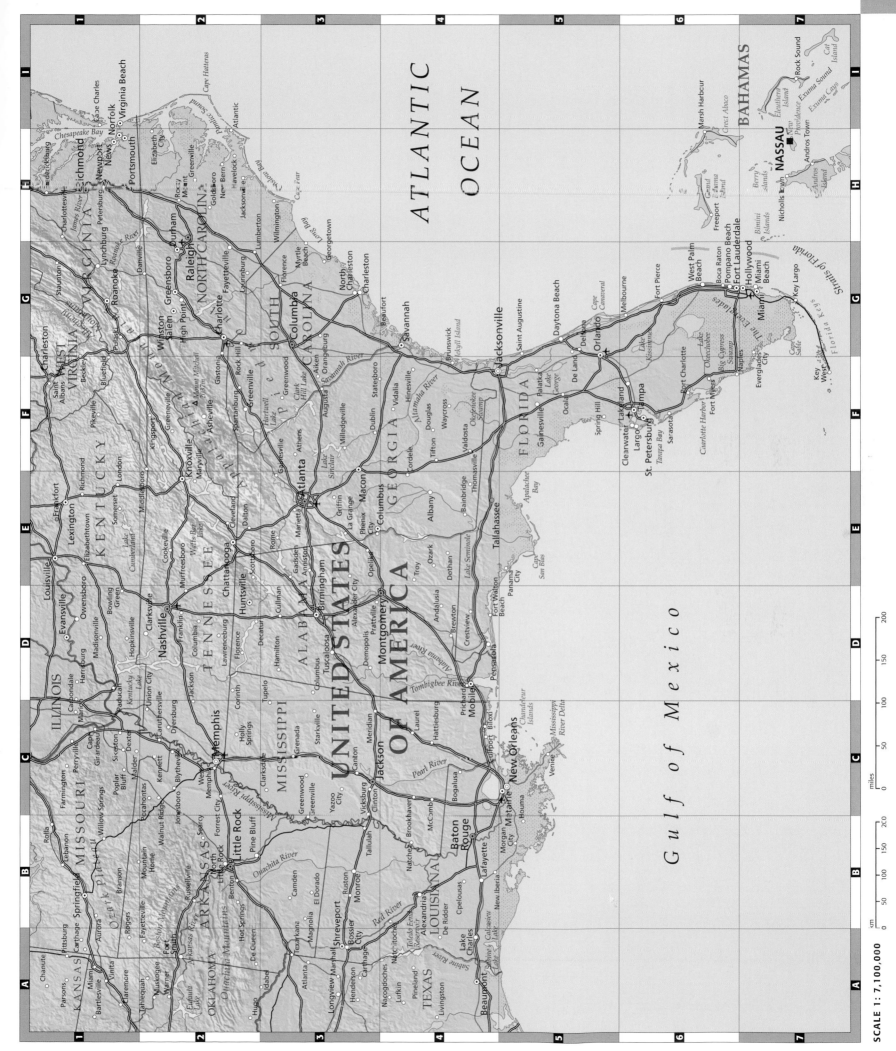

ATLANTIC

OCEAN

Gulf of Mexico

BAHAMAS

NASSAU

WEST VIRGINIA

VIRGINIA

KENTUCKY

TENNESSEE

NORTH CAROLINA

SOUTH CAROLINA

GEORGIA

ALABAMA

MISSISSIPPI

LOUISIANA

ARKANSAS

MISSOURI

KANSAS

OKLAHOMA

TEXAS

ILLINOIS

FLORIDA

UNITED STATES

OF AMERICA

SCALE 1: 7,100,000

miles

km

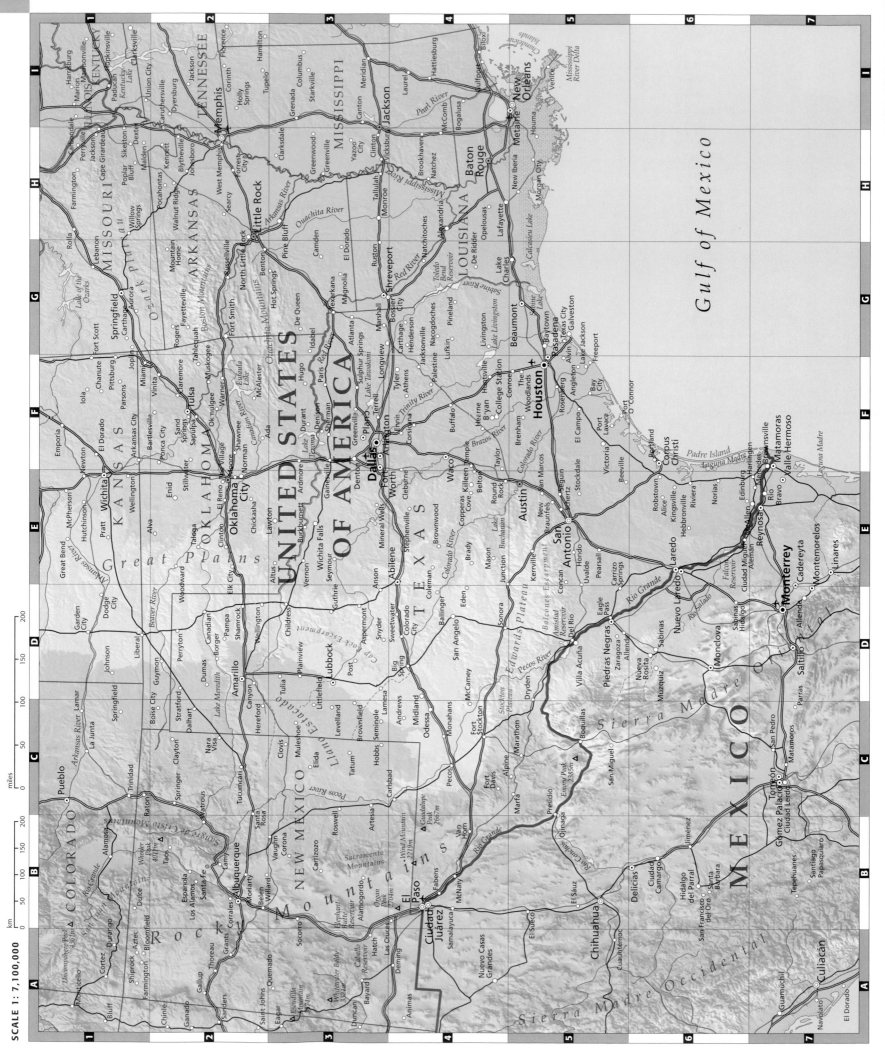

SCALE 1 : 7,100,000

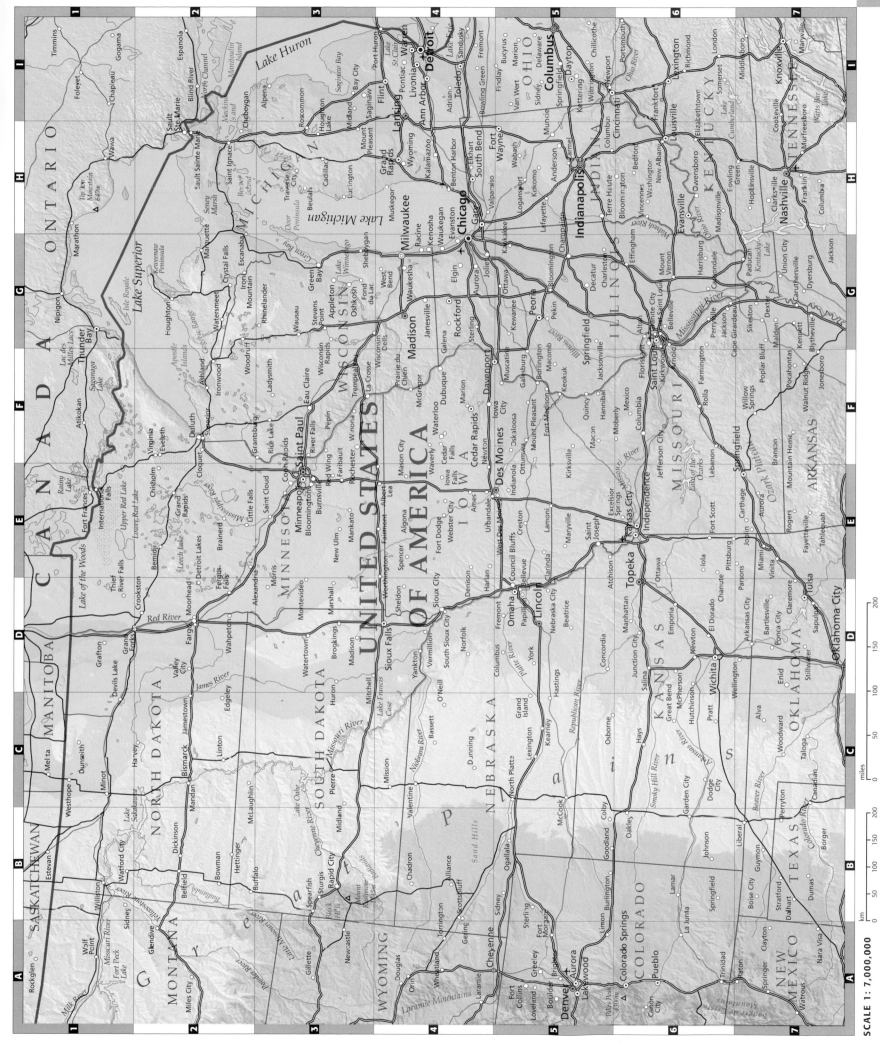

Timmins
Foleyet
Chapleau
Gogama
Espanola

Lake Huron

ONTARIO

CANADA

Wawa

Marathon

Nipigon

Thunder Bay

Lake Superior

Isle Royale

SASKATCHEWAN

MANITOBA

Estevan
Melita
Westhope

MONTANA

Glendive
Miles City
Wolf Point
Rockglen

NORTH DAKOTA

Bismarck
Dickinson
Minot

SOUTH DAKOTA

Pierre
Rapid City

WYOMING

Cheyenne
Casper

COLORADO

Denver
Lakewood
Aurora
Pueblo
Colorado Springs

NEBRASKA

Lincoln
Omaha

KANSAS

Topeka
Wichita

OKLAHOMA

Oklahoma City
Tulsa

NEW MEXICO

TEXAS

MINNESOTA

Saint Paul
Minneapolis
Duluth

WISCONSIN

Madison
Milwaukee
Green Bay

MICHIGAN

Detroit
Lansing
Grand Rapids
Sault Ste. Marie

Lake Michigan

ILLINOIS

Chicago
Springfield
Peoria
Rockford

IOWA

Des Moines
Cedar Rapids
Davenport

MISSOURI

Saint Louis
Kansas City
Springfield

ARKANSAS

INDIANA

Indianapolis
Fort Wayne

OHIO

Columbus
Cincinnati
Toledo

KENTUCKY

Louisville
Lexington
Frankfort

TENNESSEE

Nashville
Knoxville

UNITED STATES
OF AMERICA

Mississippi River

Missouri River

Great Plains

SCALE 1 : 7,000,000

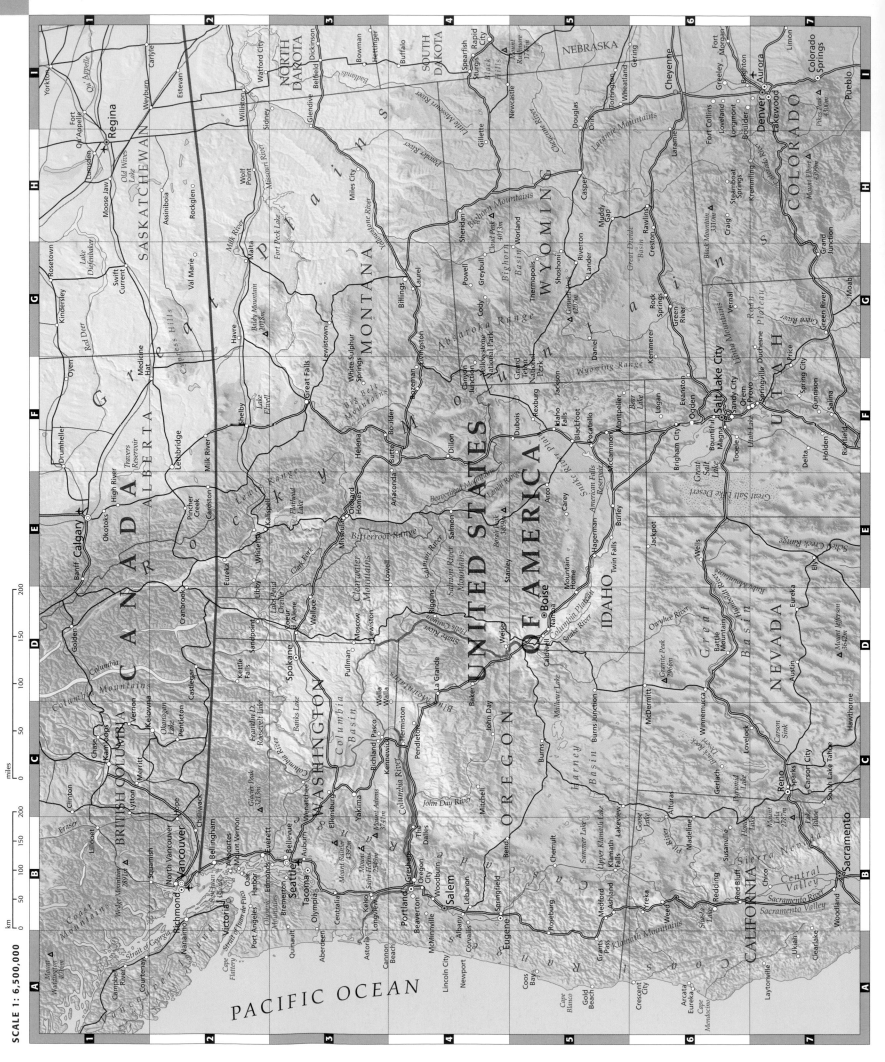

SCALE 1 : 6,500,000

PACIFIC OCEAN

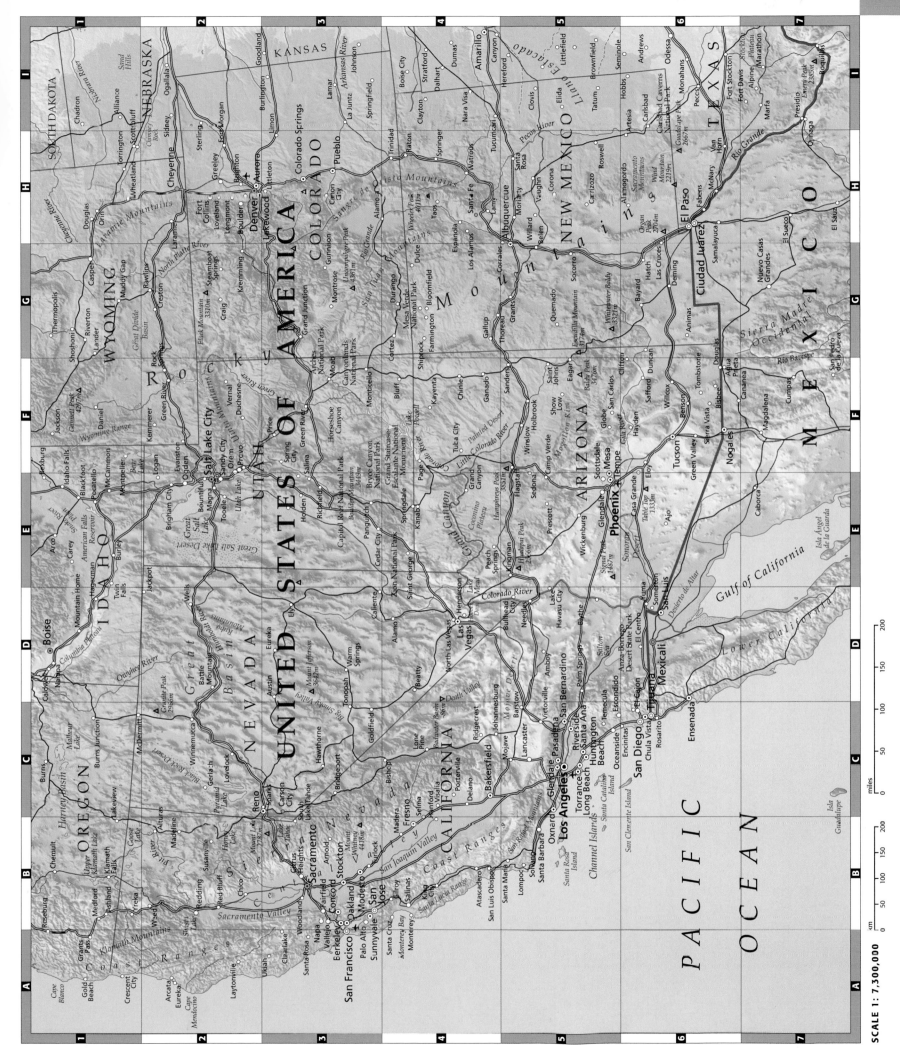

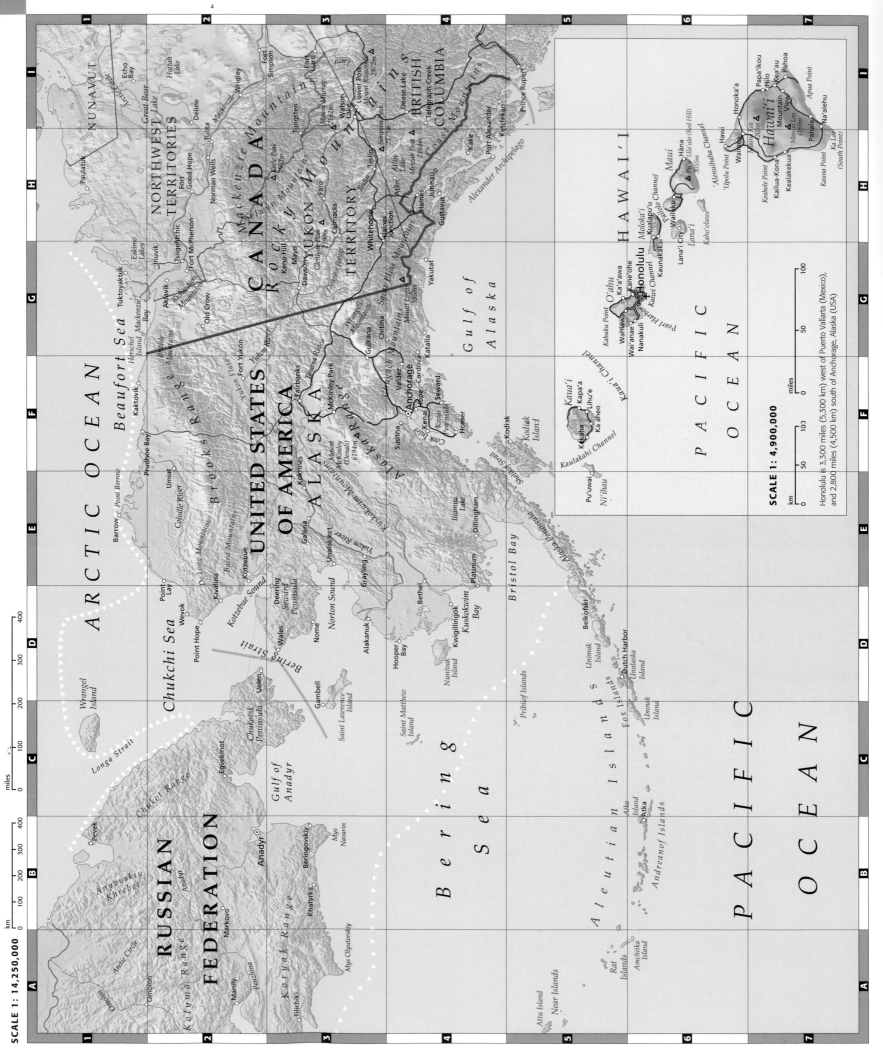

SCALE 1: 14,250,000

ARCTIC OCEAN

NUNAVUT

NORTHWEST TERRITORIES

CANADA

Beaufort Sea

Echo Bay
Great Bear Lake
Arctic Circle
Déline
Fort Simpson
Fort Liard
Liard
Hoiliah Lake

Paulatuk
Tuktoyaktuk
Mackenzie Bay
Herschel Island
Eskimo Lakes
Inuvik
Aklavik
Fort McPherson
Tsiigehtchic
Norman Wells
Good Hope
Fort

Kaktovik
Barrow
Point Barrow
Prudhoe Bay
Brooks Range
De Long Mountains
Umiat
Colville River
Old Crow

Mackenzie Mountains
Rocky Mountains
Selwyn Mts
Keele Peak 2912m
Mount Murray 2162m
Simpson Peak 2775m
Keno Hill
Mayo
Dawson
Glenlyon Range
Pelly Mountains
Keno
Mesitin Peak 2123m
Watson Lake
Lower Post
Mount Roosevelt 2972m
Dease Lake
Telegraph Creek

BRITISH COLUMBIA

Teslin Range 2190m
Teslin Lake
Carmacks
Whitehorse
Faro
Ross River
Teslin
Atlin
Atlin Lake

YUKON TERRITORY

Haines Junction
Haines
Gustavus
Juneau
Alexander Archipelago
Port Alexander
Kake
Port Alexander
Ketchikan
Prince Rupert

Point Lay
Wainwright
Wevok
Point Hope
Kivalina

Baird Mountains
Kobuk
Kotzebue
Kotzebue Sound
Noatak
Deering
Seward Peninsula

Tsigehtchic
Fort Yukon
Yukon Flats
Yukon River
Galena
Fairbanks

UNITED STATES OF AMERICA

ALASKA

Mount McKinley (Denali) 6194m
McKinley Park
Cantwell

Alaska Range
Wrangell Mountains
Chitina
Gulkana
Glennallen
Mount Logan 5959m
Saint Elias Mountains
Yakutat

Chugach Mountains
Valdez
Cordova
Katalla

Gulf of Alaska

Anchorage
Hope
Seward
Kenai Peninsula
Kenai
Soldotna
Homer
Cook Inlet
Susitna

Nome
Norton Sound
Seward Peninsula
Wales
Uelen
Bering Strait

Kwethluk
Bethel
Grayling
Unalakleet
Kuskokwim Mountains
Kuskokwim River
Alakanuk
Hooper Bay
Nunivak Island

Iliamna Lake
Dillingham
Platinum
Kwigillingok
Kuskokwim Bay

Kodiak
Kodiak Island
Shelikof Strait
Alaska Peninsula
Bristol Bay

Gambell
Saint Lawrence Island
Saint Matthew Island
Pribilof Islands

Bering Sea

Belkofski
Unimak Island
Dutch Harbor
Unalaska
Unalaska Island
Umnak Island

Fox Islands
Aleutian Islands
Andreanof Islands
Atka
Atka Island
Amchitka Island
Rat Islands
Attu Island
Near Islands

PACIFIC OCEAN

RUSSIAN FEDERATION

Omolon
Markovo
Anyuyskiy Khrebet
Arctic Circle
Pevek
Egvekinot
Chukot Range
Chukchi Peninsula
Kolyma Range
Chukchi Sea
Longa Strait
Wrangel Island

Gulf of Anadyr
Anadyr
Beringovsky
Khatyrka
Mys Navarin
Mys Olyutorskiy
Koryak Range
Tilichiki
Manily
Pauzhna

SCALE 1: 4,900,000

HAWAI'I

Kaua'i
Kapa'a
Kekaha
Lihu'e
Ka aheo
Kaulakahi Channel
Pu'uwai
Ni'ihau

O'ahu
Kahuku Point
Wahiawa
Wai'anae
Nanakuli
Ka'a'awa
Kane'ohe
Honolulu
Pearl Harbor
Kaiwi Channel

Moloka'i
Kualapu'u
Kaunakakai
Lana'i City
Lana'i
Kaho'olawe

Maui
Wailuku
Wailea
Hana
Kahului
Pailolo Channel
'Alenuihaha Channel
Pu'u 'Ula'ula (Red Hill) 3055m

Kahoolawe Channel

Honoka'a
Waimea
Hawi
Kohala
'Upolu Point
Kawaihae
Kailua-Kona
Kealakekua
Keahole Point
Mauna Kea 4205m
Mauna Loa 4169m
Hilo
Papa'ikou
Kea'au
Pahoa
Apua Point
Pahala
Na'alehu
Ka Lae (South Point)

Hawai'i

PACIFIC OCEAN

Honolulu is 3,300 miles (5,300 km) west of Puerto Vallarta (Mexico), and 2,800 miles (4,500 km) south of Anchorage, Alaska (USA).

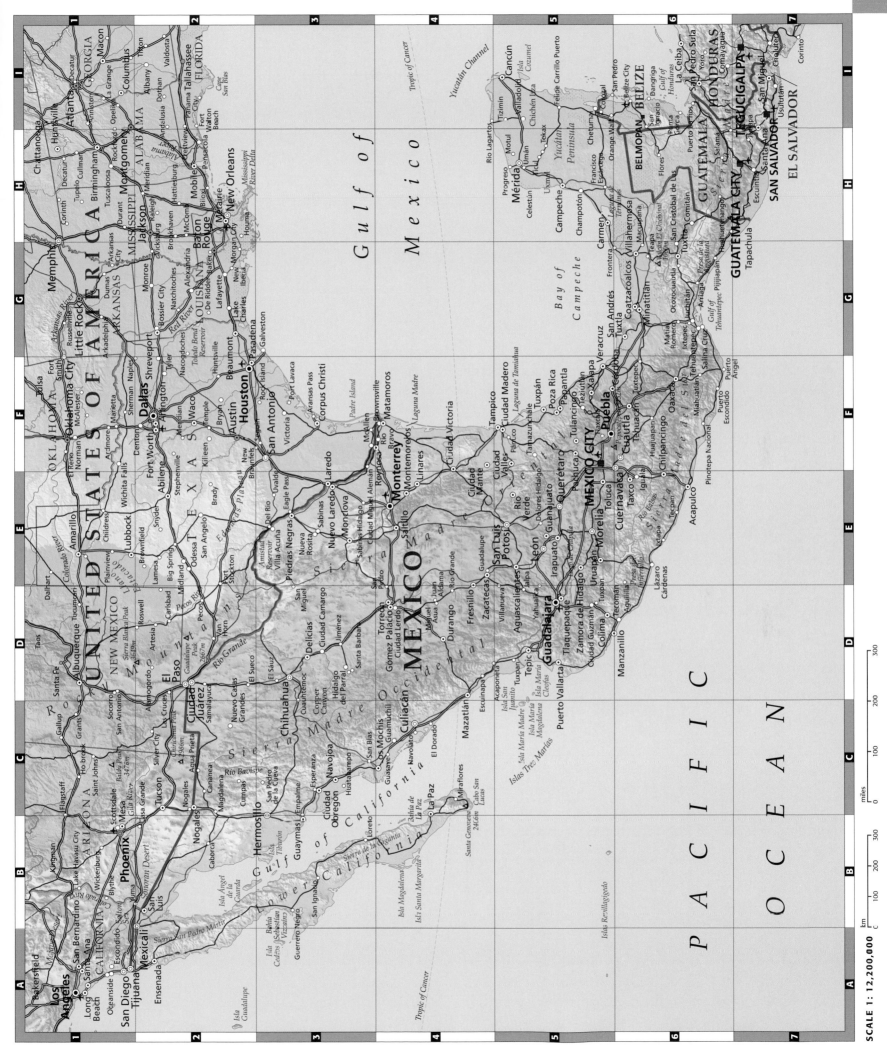

SCALE 1: 12,200,000

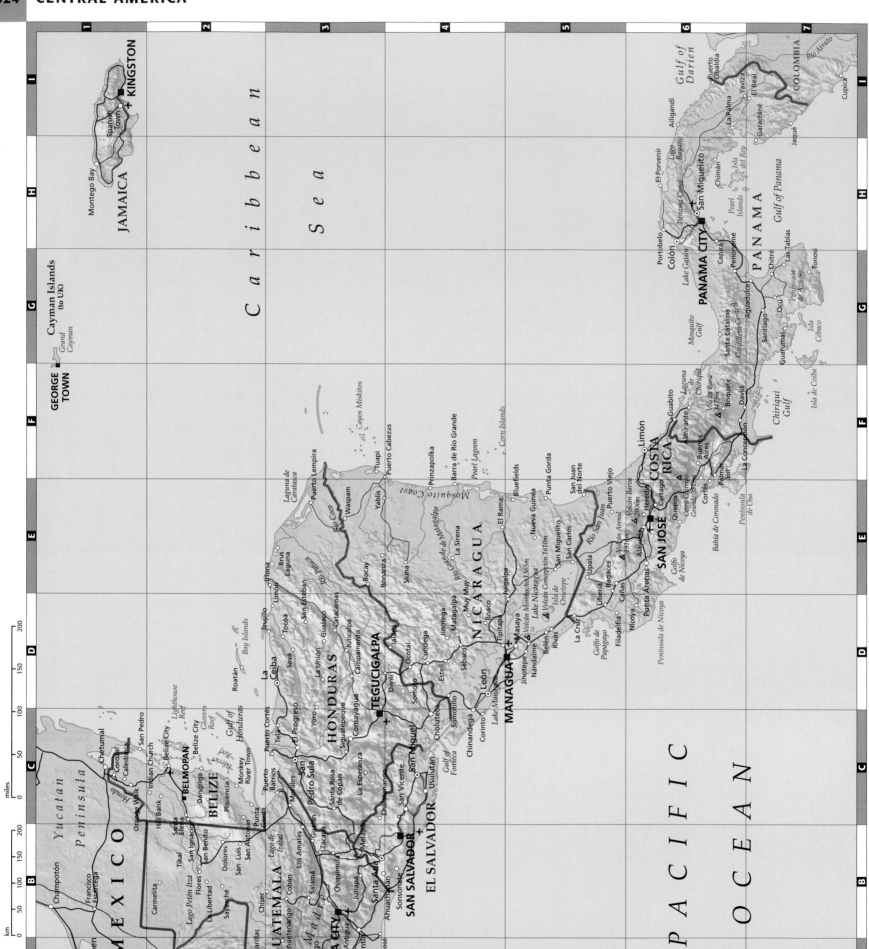

SCALE 1: 7,100,000

JAMAICA

Montego Bay
Spanish Town
+ KINGSTON

C a r i b b e a n   S e a

Cayman Islands
(to UK)
Grand Cayman

GEORGE TOWN

Gulf of Darien

COLOMBIA

Río Atrato

Puerto Obaldia
Yavisa
La Palma
El Real
Garachiné
Jaqué
Cupica

Aligandi
Chimán
Isla del Rey
Pearl Islands

El Porvenir
Panama Canal
San Miguelito

PANAMA CITY
Portobelo
Colón
Lake Gatún
Capira
Penonomé
Chitré
Las Tablas
Tonosi

PANAMA

Gulf of Panama
Peninsula de Azuero

Santa Catalina
Cordillera Central
Aguadulce
Santiago
Guararé
Ocú
Guabito
Laguna de Chiriquí
Volcán Barú
3475m
Boquete
David
La Concepción
Almirante
Buenos Aires
Palmar
Sur
Cortés

Isla de Coiba
Isla Cébaco

Chiriquí Gulf

Mosquito Gulf

Limón
COSTA RICA
Cartago
Heredia
SAN JOSÉ
Alajuela
Volcán Barva
2906m
Volcán Arenal
1911m
Upala
Bagaces
Liberia
Cañas
Filadelfia
Nicoya
Quepos
Cerro Chirripó
3819m
Grande
Bahía de Coronado
Peninsula de Osa

Puerto Cabezas
Cayos Miskitos
Tuapi
Prinzapolka
Barra de Río Grande
Pearl Lagoon
Corn Islands

Puerto Lempira
Laguna de Caratasca
Río Coco
Waspam
Yabils
Bocay
Bonanza
Siuna
La Sirena

Laguna
Brus
Bruna
Trujillo
La Ceiba
Savá
Tocoa
San Esteban
Catacamas
Juticalpa
Campamento

Bay Islands
Roatán

Lighthouse Reef
Glovers Reef

Gulf of Honduras

HONDURAS
TEGUCIGALPA
Danli
El Progreso
Yoro
La Unión
Gualaco
Comayagua
Siguatepeque
Ocotal
Sebaco
Estelí
Somoto
Condega

NICARAGUA
El Rama
Nueva Guinea
Bluefields
Punta Gorda
San Juan del Norte
Río San Juan
San Carlos
Puerto Viejo
Muy Muy
Matagalpa
Jinotega
Boaco
Juigalpa
San Miguelito
Lake Nicaragua
Isla de Ometepe
Volcán Concepción 1610m
Volcán Mombacho 1365m
León
MANAGUA
Masaya
Jinotepe
Nandaime
Belén
Rivas
La Cruz
Golfo de Papagayo
Golfo de Nicoya
Peninsula de Nicoya
Tipitapa
Corinto
Chinandega
Lake Managua

Puntarenas

Chetumal
Corozal
Caledonia
San Pedro
Orange Walk
Belize City
Indian Church
Hill Bank
San Antonio
BELMOPAN
Dangriga
Belize City
Placencia
Monkey River Town
Punta Gorda

BELIZE

Barrier Reef

Puerto Cortés
Puerto Barrios
Morales
Zacapa
La Ceiba
San Pedro Sula
Tela
Santa Rosa de Copán

MEXICO

Yucatan Peninsula

Champotón
Francisco Escárcega
Laguna de Términos
Frontera
Carmen
Villahermosa
Macuspana

Carmelita
Tikal
Flores
La Libertad
San Benito
San Luis
Sayaxché
Dolores
San José
Barillas
Chisec
Cobán
Salamá
Los Amates
Guatán
Jutiapa
Esquipulas

Lago Petén Itzá

GUATEMALA
GUATEMALA CITY
Antigua
Escuintla
Huehuetenango
Quetzaltenango
Jacaltenango
San Cristóbal de Las
Comitán
Presa de la Angostura
Volcán Tajumulco 4093m
Huixtla
Tapachula
Champerico

Sierra Madre

Santa Ana
Ahuachapán
Sonsonate
Chalchuapa
SAN SALVADOR
San Vicente
San Miguel
Usulután
EL SALVADOR
La Esperanza
La Unión
Gulf of Fonseca
Choluteca
Chiquimula
Metapán

P A C I F I C   O C E A N

miles
km
0   50   100   150   200

COLOMBIA

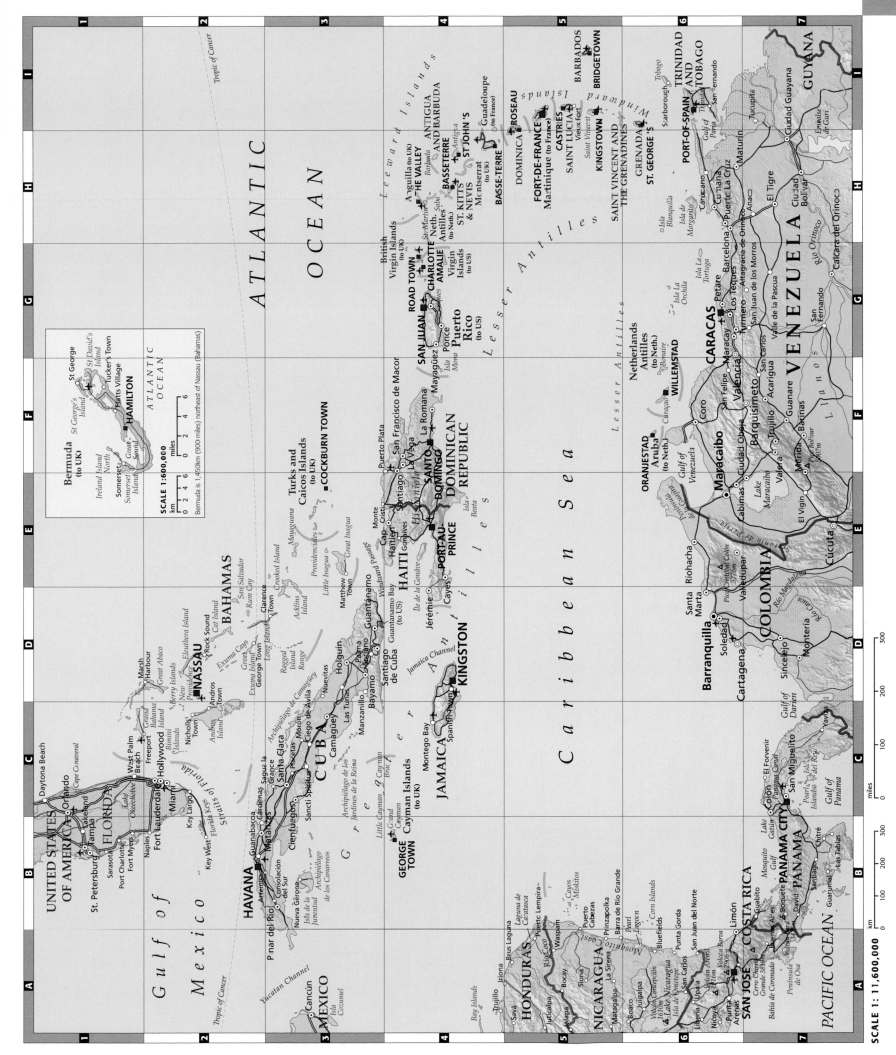

1 2 3 4 5 6 7

I

H

G

F

E

D

C

B

A

CARIBBEAN AND BERMUDA

UNITED STATES OF AMERICA

Daytona Beach
Orlando
Cape Canaveral
St. Petersburg
Tampa
Lakeland
Sarasota
Lake Okeechobee
West Palm Beach
Hollywood
FLORIDA
Port Charlotte
Fort Myers
Naples
Fort Lauderdale
Miami

Gulf of Mexico

Tropic of Cancer

Key West
Florida Keys
Straits of Florida

Key Largo

MEXICO
Cancún
Isla Cozumel

ATLANTIC OCEAN

Bermuda (to UK)

St George
St George's Island
St David's Island
Tucker's Town
Ireland Island North
Somerset Island
Somerset
HAMILTON
Great Sound
Hatts Village

ATLANTIC OCEAN

SCALE 1:600,000
km 0 2 4 6
miles 0 2 4 6
Bermuda is 1,450km (900 miles) northeast of Nassau (Bahamas)

BAHAMAS

Marsh Harbour
Grand Bahama Island
Freeport
Great Abaco
Bimini Islands
Berry Islands
New Providence
Nicholl's Town
Andros Town
NASSAU
Eleuthera Island
Rock Sound
Cat Island
San Salvador
Rum Cay
Andros Island
Exuma Cays
Great Exuma Island
George Town
Long Island
Crooked Island
Acklins Island
Clarence Town
Ragged Island Range
Little Inagua
Matthew Town
Great Inagua
Mayaguana
Providenciales

Turks and Caicos Islands (to UK)
COCKBURN TOWN

HAVANA
Artemisa
Pinar del Río
Consolación del Sur
Nueva Gerona
Isla de la Juventud
Archipiélago de los Canarreos
Guanabacoa
Cárdenas
Matanzas
Santa Clara
Cienfuegos
Sancti Spíritus
Archipiélago de Camagüey
Morón
Ciego de Ávila
Nuevitas
Camagüey
CUBA
Las Tunas
Holguín
Bayamo
Palma Soriano
Manzanillo
Santiago de Cuba
Guantánamo

Archipiélago de los Jardines de la Reina

Cayman Islands (to UK)
Little Cayman Cayman Brac
Grand Cayman
GEORGE TOWN

JAMAICA
Montego Bay
Spanish Town
KINGSTON

Caribbean Sea

Windward Passage
Guantánamo Bay (to US)

HAITI
Cap-Haïtien
Gonaïves
Jérémie
PORT-AU-PRINCE
Cayes
Île de la Gonâve
Île à Vache

DOMINICAN REPUBLIC
Monte Cristi
Puerto Plata
Santiago
La Vega
San Francisco de Macorís
La Romana
SANTO DOMINGO
Hispaniola
Isla Beata

Mona Passage
Isla Mona

Puerto Rico (to US)
Mayagüez
Ponce
SAN JUAN

Virgin Islands (to US)
CHARLOTTE AMALIE

British Virgin Islands (to UK)
ROAD TOWN

Anguilla (to UK)
THE VALLEY

St-Martin
St-Martin/Sint Maarten
Saba
Sint Eustatius
Neth. Antilles (to Neth.)

ST. KITTS & NEVIS
BASSETERRE

ANTIGUA AND BARBUDA
Barbuda
Antigua
ST. JOHN'S

Montserrat (to UK)

Guadeloupe (to France)
BASSE-TERRE

Leeward Islands

DOMINICA
ROSEAU

Martinique (to France)
FORT-DE-FRANCE

SAINT LUCIA
CASTRIES
Vieux Fort

BARBADOS
BRIDGETOWN

SAINT VINCENT AND THE GRENADINES
KINGSTOWN
Saint Vincent

GRENADA
ST. GEORGE'S

Windward Islands

Tobago
Scarborough
TRINIDAD AND TOBAGO
PORT-OF-SPAIN
San Fernando
Gulf of Paria

Lesser Antilles

Netherlands Antilles (to Neth.)
Bonaire
Curaçao
WILLEMSTAD

Aruba (to Neth.)
ORANJESTAD

Isla La Orchila
Isla La Tortuga
Isla de Margarita
Isla Blanquilla

VENEZUELA
CARACAS
Petare
Los Teques
Maracay
Valencia
San Felipe
Barquisimeto
Coro
Maracaibo
Lake Maracaibo
Cabimas
Ciudad Ojeda
Mérida
Trujillo
Valera
Guanare
Barinas
San Carlos
Acarigua
San Cristóbal
San Juan de los Morros
San Fernando
El Tigre
Ciudad Bolívar
Ciudad Guayana
Maturín
Cumaná
Barcelona
Puerto La Cruz
Carúpano
Güiria
Tucupita

Llanos
Río Orinoco
Catara del Orinoco
Embalse de Guri

GUYANA

COLOMBIA
Cúcuta
Barranquilla
Cartagena
Soledad
Santa Marta
Riohacha
Valledupar
Sincelejo
Montería

Gulf of Venezuela
Gulf of Darién

PANAMA
PANAMA CITY
Colón
El Porvenir
Panama Canal
Chitré
Santiago
David
Boquete

COSTA RICA
SAN JOSÉ
Limón
Puntarenas

NICARAGUA
Managua
MANAGUA
Lake Nicaragua
Bluefields
Corn Islands
Puerto Cabezas

HONDURAS
TEGUCIGALPA
Bay Islands
Trujillo

Caribbean Sea

PACIFIC OCEAN

SCALE 1: 11,600,000

km 0 100 200 300
miles 0 100 200 300

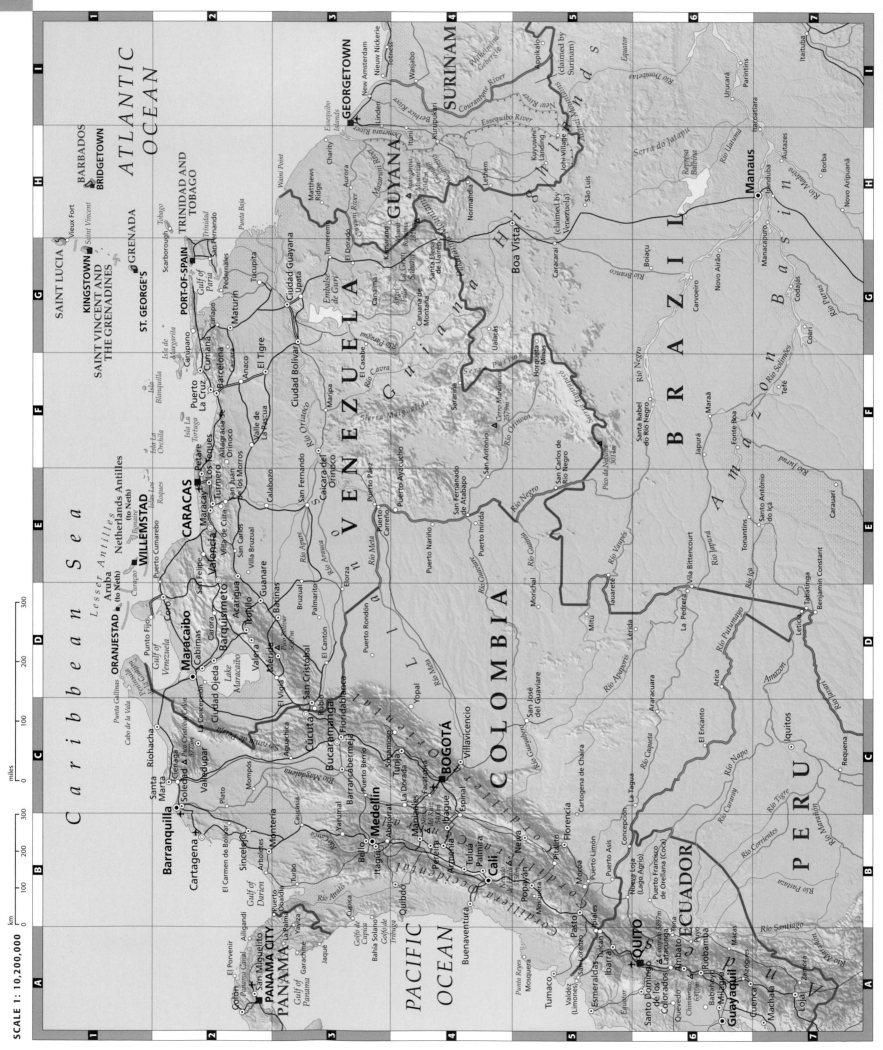

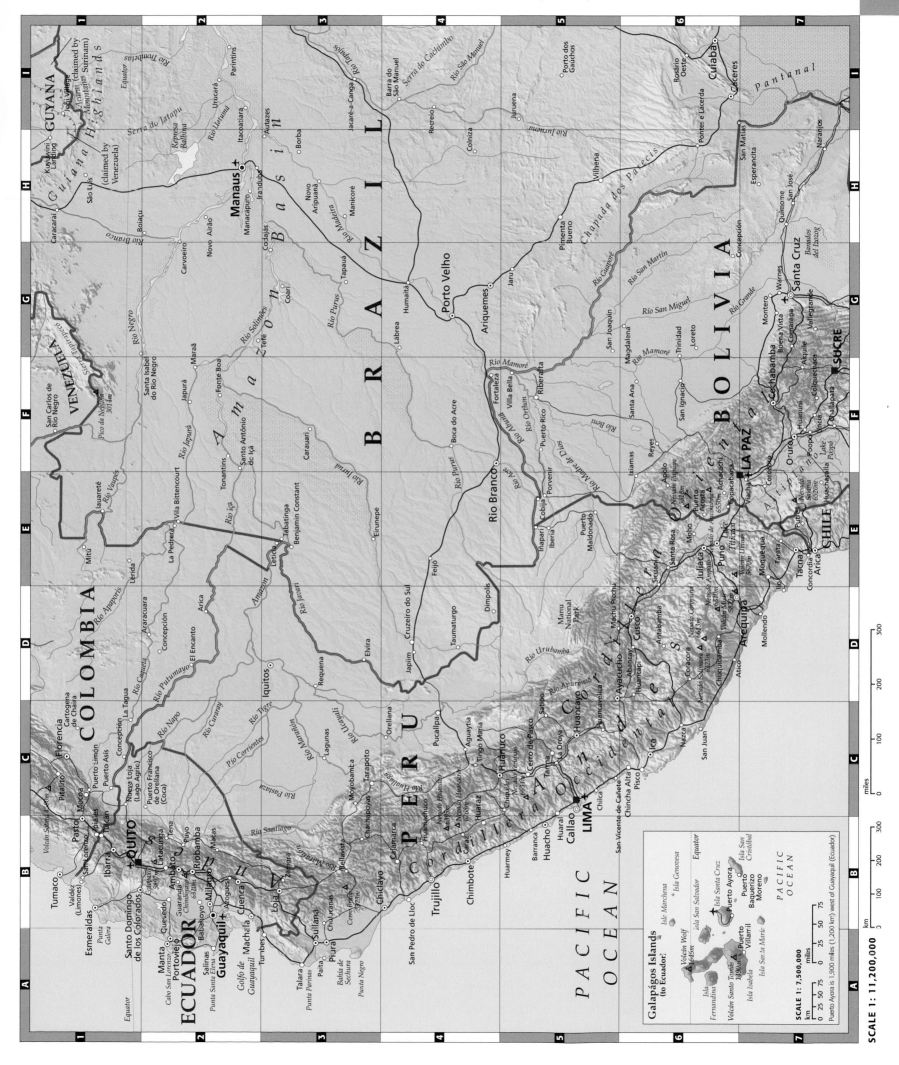

GUYANA

Kaiwini
Landing

Guiana Highlands

Acarai (claimed by Surinam)
Mountains (claimed by Venezuela)

Equator

Caracaraí

Torr Village

São Luís

Boiaçu

VENEZUELA

San Carlos de Río Negro

Pico da Neblina
3014m

Río Branco

Rio Trombetas

Serra do Jatapu

Represa Balbina

Parintins

Urucará

Itacoatiara

Autazes

MANAUS

Manacapuru

Iranduba

Novo Airão

Novo
Aripuanã

Borba

Manicoré

COLOMBIA

Mitú

Iauareté

Río Vaupés

Lérida

Santa Isabel
do Rio Negro

Carvoeiro

Coari

Tefé

Codajás

Rio Negro

Río Içá

Santo Antônio
do Içá

Caruari

Río Juruá

Eirunepé

A m a z o n   B a s i n

B R A Z I L

Rio Tapajós

Barra do
São Manuel

Jacaré-a-Canga

Sucundurí

Serra do Cachimbo

Barra do
São Manuel

Rio São Manuel

Porto dos
Gauchos

Rio Juruena

Recreio

Coliza

Juruena

Chapada dos Parecis

Vilhena

Pimenta
Bueno

Pantanal

Rosário
Oeste

Pontes e Lacerda

Cuiabá

Cáceres

San Matías

Esperancita

Quimome

San José

Naranjos

San Carlos de
Río Negro

PERU

Iquitos

Requena

Río Napo

Río Curaray

Río Tigre

Río Marañón

Río Ucayali

Lagunas

Orellana

Pucallpa

Aguaytía

Río Apurímac

Río Urubamba

Cruzeiro do Sul

Japiim

Taumaturgo

Dímpolis

Feijó

Río Branco

Porto Velho

Ariquemes

Jaru

Humaitá

Lábrea

Tapauá

Manicoré

BOLIVIA

La Paz

Sucre

SCALE 1 : 11,200,000

ATLANTIC

OCEAN

GUYANA

GEORGETOWN

PARAMARIBO

SURINAM

CAYENNE

French
Guiana
(to France)

Guiana Highlands

RORAIMA
(claimed by
Venezuela)

Equator

Mouths of the Amazon

Ilha de Marajó

Belém

Macapá

Manaus

A m a z o n

B a s i n

B R A Z I L

Santarém

São Luís

Fortaleza

Natal

João Pessoa

Olinda

Recife

Maceió

Aracaju

Salvador

Teresina

Palmas do Tocantins

Campina
Grande

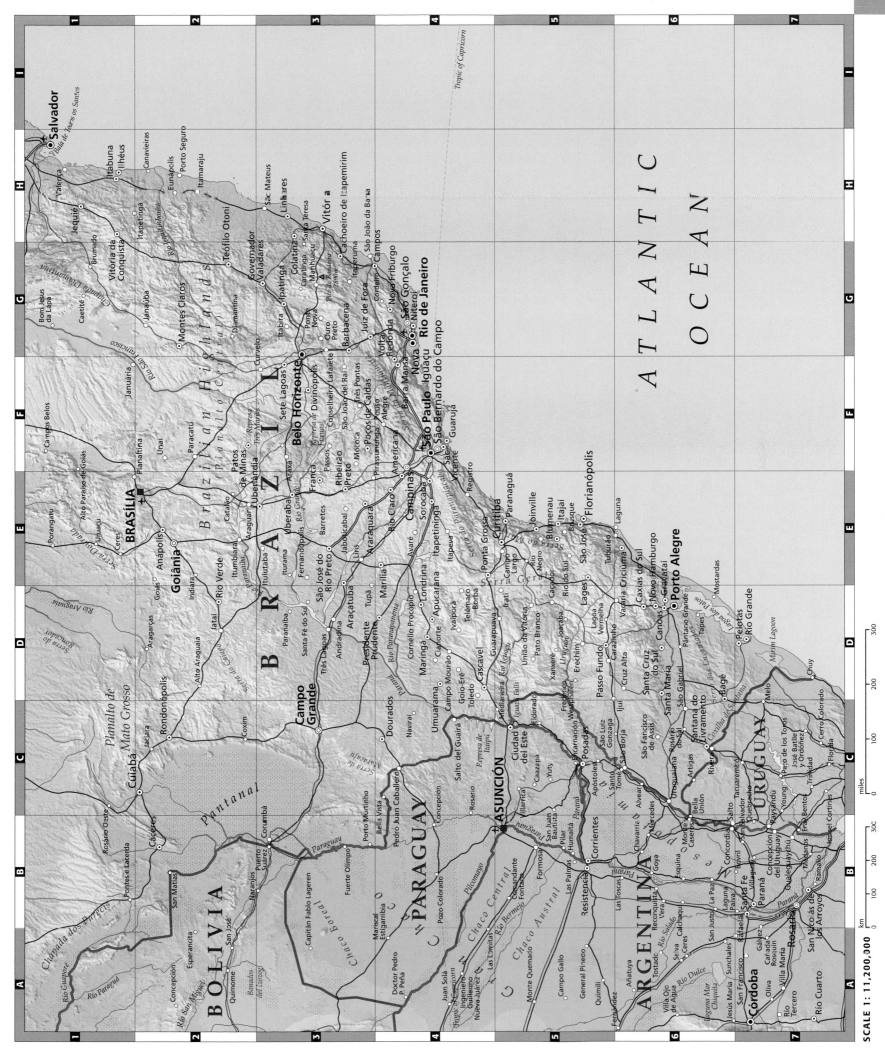

SCALE 1: 11,200,000

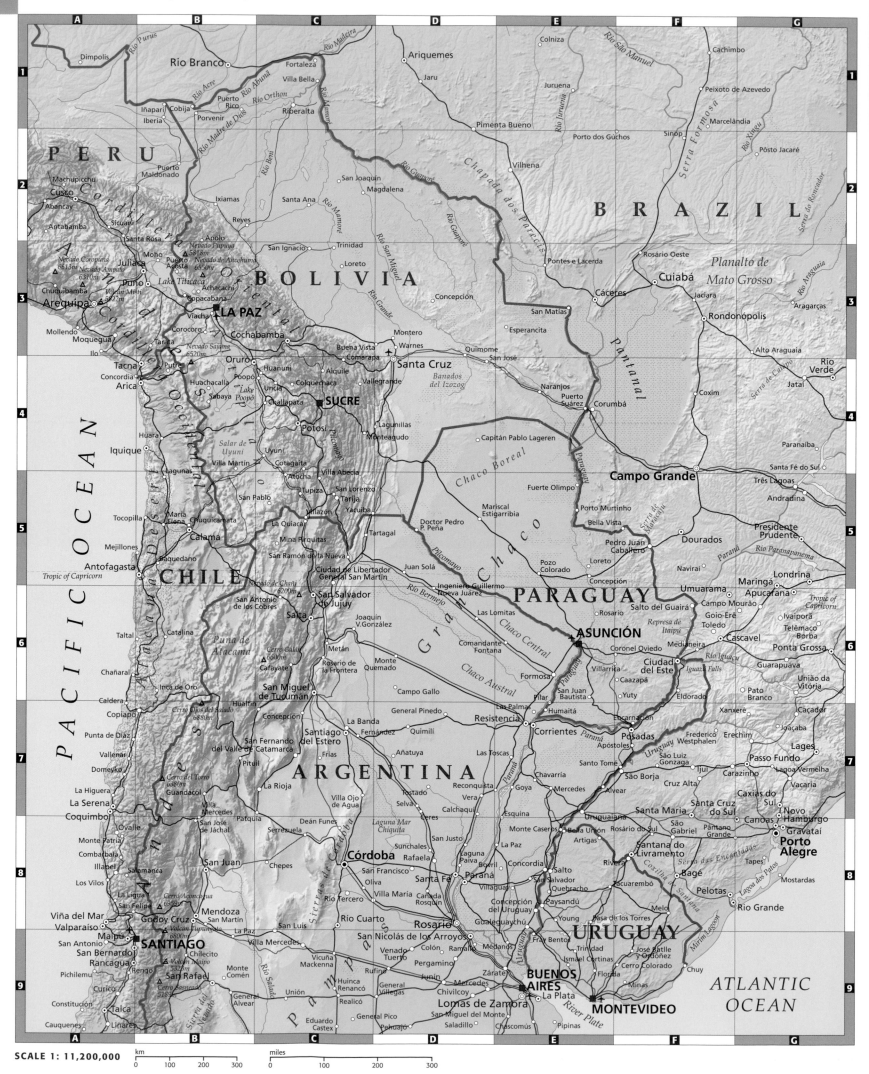

SCALE 1: 11,200,000

km
0   100   200   300

miles
0   100   200   300

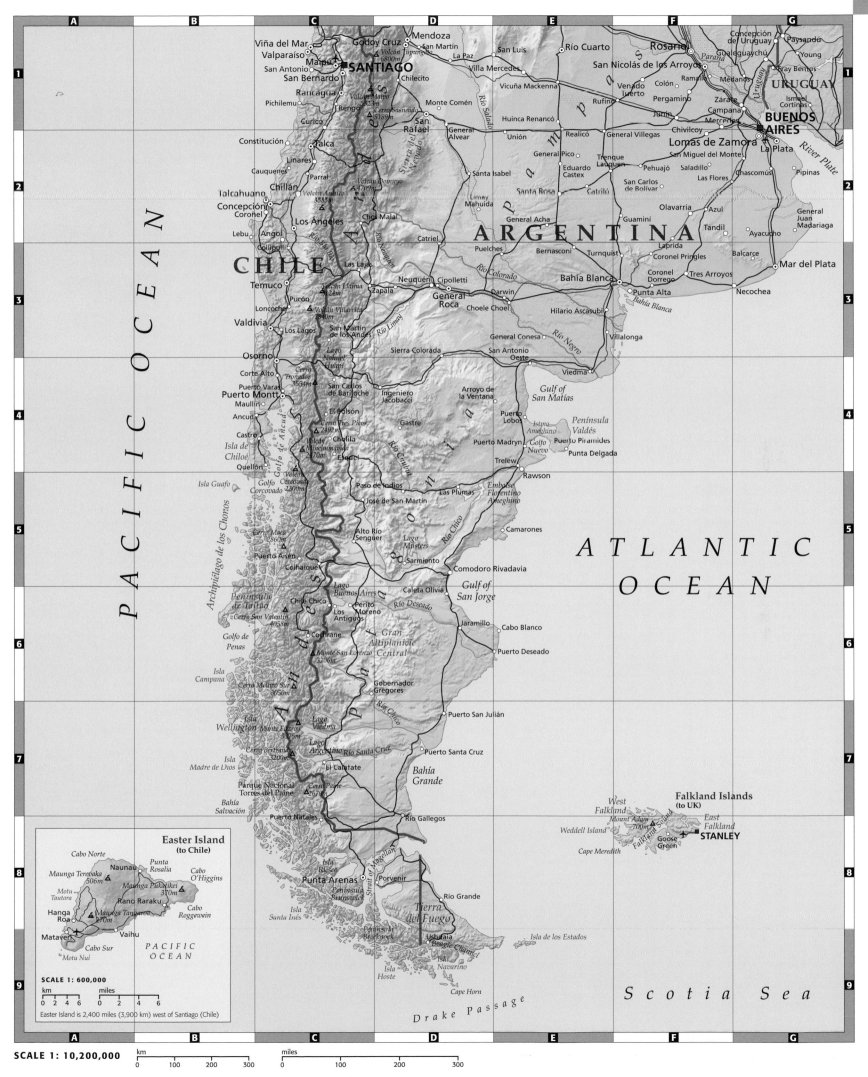

PACIFIC OCEAN

ATLANTIC
OCEAN

ARGENTINA

CHILE

URUGUAY

Easter Island
(to Chile)

Cabo Norte
Maunga Terevaka
506m
Naunau
Punta
Rosalia
Cabo
O'Higgins
Motu
Tautara
Maunga Pukatikei
370m
Rano Raraku
Hanga
Roa
Maunga Tangaroa
270m
Cabo
Roggewein
Mataven
Vaihu
Cabo Sur
Motu Nui

PACIFIC
OCEAN

SCALE 1 : 600,000
km
0   2   4   6
miles
0   2   4   6
Easter Island is 2,400 miles (3,900 km) west of Santiago (Chile)

Falkland Islands
(to UK)
West
Falkland
Mount Adam
700m
East
Falkland
Weddell Island
Falkland Sound
Goose
Green
STANLEY
Cape Meredith

Scotia Sea

Drake Passage

Cape Horn

SCALE 1 : 10,200,000
km
0   100   200   300
miles
0   100   200   300

Index

Page numbers in **bold** indicate main references

Acknowledgments

The publisher would like to thank the following for their contributions and help (in alphabetical order): J.P. Anderson, Christopher Baker, Eleanor Berman, Shawn Blore, Stephen Brewer, Samantha Cook, Kelsey Eliasson, Paul Franklin, Geoff Groesbeck, Eric Grossman, Andrew Hempstead, Marael Johnson, Declan McGarvey, Nancy Mikula, Laura Paquet, Don Philpott, Christopher Rice, Melanie Rice, Nick Rider, Alex Robinson, Polly Rodger Brown, Deanna Swaney, Gavin Thomas, Greg Ward, Sarah Woods.

Picture Credits

The publisher would like to thank the following for their kind permission to reproduce their photographs:

Key: a–above; b–below/bottom; c–centre; f–far; l–left; r–right; t–top

4Corners Images: Cozzi Guido 89tc, 102tl, 104-105, 105bc, 120bc, 171bc, 171bl, 208tc, 228bc, 228br, 283bl; Borchi Massimo 55tr, 70-71, 109bl, 155ca, 164bl, 174bl; SIME/Reinhard Schmid 11tr, 19bl, 19br, 256tc, 260bl, 260bc, 263tr, 289bl; SIME 25tc; SIME/Bernhart Udo 29tr, 128tl, 130br 163cl, 191ca, 221bl; SIME/Biscaro Alberto 142-143; SIME/Damm Fridmar 41tc, 140c, 224-225; SIME/Frances Stephane 70bl; SIME/Giampiccolo Angelo 106bc; SIME/Giovanni Simeone 12r, 88cb, 106clb, 117bc, 117tl, 136bc, 263ca, 288r, 289br; SIME/Gräfenhain Günter 46tc, 50tc, 96cla, 97br, 122clb, 221bc, 269cl, 302bc; SIME/Hans-Peter Huber 14-5, 18br, 52-3, 103tl, 116clb, 227tr; SIME/Johanna Huber 14br, 15fbr, 291ca; SIME/Kaos02 148tc; SIME/Kaos03 18-19, 121bc; SIME/Pavan Aldo 299tr; SIME/ Rinaldi Roberto 268r; SIME/Ripani Massimo 189tr, 214ca, 232tr, 241cl, 256tl, 266ca, 266tc, 267tl; Amantini Stefano 113ca, 116r, 117bl, 129tr, 136tl, 136-137c, 240cr.

akg-images: Arco Petersen.net 196cdb, 197tr; Rubens Abboud 142cb, 236br; All Canada Images/Ron Erwin 193tc; All Canada Photos/Barrett & MacKay 211tr; All Canada Photos/Rolf Hicker 173cr; Alt-6/David Babcock 229crb, 142clb; Arcaid/Mark Fiennes 300cdb; Anthony Arendt 59c; Martin Arpon 96cl; Mary Liz Austin 170bl; AWPhoto 148tr, 149tl; Ryan Ayre 161bl; Walter Bibikow 77tl, 84bl, 85br, 153tl, 171cl; Royer Blickwinkel 95br, 189tl; Steve Bloom Images 233tc, 234ca, 234cb; Steve Bly 23lil, 139cl, 214dlb; Tibor Bognar 219ca; Brandon Cole Marine Photography 88ca, 107bc; Bill Brooks 173tr, 211bc; Bryan & Cherry Alexander Photography 234-235; Buzzshotz 183bc; Andrew Cawley 191bl; Charles O. Cecil 131br; Cephas Picture Library/Andy Christodolo 217bc, 217bl; Cephas Picture Library/Kevin Judd 216r; China Span/Keren Su 305tr; Loetscher Chlaus 149cbl; Shaughn F. Clements 113bc; Jim Cole, Photography 131bl; ColsQuebec 283br; Gary Cook 17br, 87tc; TS Corrigan 112-113; Tony Craddock 19bc; Chris A Crumley 124bl; culliganphoto 62tr; Danita Delimont/Jerry and Marcy Monkman 237bc; Danita Delimont/Walter Bibikow 105ca, 185tc, 222tc, 274bc; Danita Delimont/Cindy Miller Hopkins 36bc; Danita Delimont/Doug Moler 10tl, 17tc; Danita Delimont/Greg Johnston 48br, 144ca; Danita Delimont/Joanne Wells 120bl; Danita Delimont/Keith and Rebecca Snell 294bc; Danita Delimont/Kristin Piljay 165cb; Danita Delimont/Nik Wheeler 143cb, 176-177; Danita Delimont/Russell Gordon 61br; Carlos Davila 35br; Danita Delimont 135br; Daniel Dempster Photography 211tl; Reinhard Dirscheel 176c; Douglas Peebles Photography 27bc; John Earnshaw 46tl; Chuck Eckert 183br; Chad Ehlers 307tl; John Elk III 22rca; eStock Photo/Claudia Uribe Touri 244ca; Javier Etcheverry 190-191; Alissa Everett 285bc; Michele Falzone 51tr; FAN Stock/Katja Kreder 14bc; FAN Travelstock/Rainer Grosskopf 69bc; Steven Folino 92bc; Lee Foster 90br; Tracey Foster 171ftl; Fisher Fotos 84cla; franzfoto.com 188tc; Dennis Frates 257tl, 258tc; S Friberg 1; Robin Frowley 145br; Mark Goodreau 193ftr; Gordon M. Grant 195bl; Jeff Greenberg 85cra; Judith Haden 252cdb; Dennis Hallinan 147bc; Blaine Harrington III 18bc, 18c, 90bc, 239bl; Vince Harris 158bc; Martin Harvey 85tl; Bill Heinsohn 16c; Bill Helsel 212br; Hughes News.fr/ Hughes Herve 63tc; Zach Holmes 125bc, 166-167; Cindy Miller Hopkins 234cr; Jeremy Horner 17cl; Chris Howarth 244c; Chris Howes/Wild Places Photography 137tr; D. Hurst 117cl; Image Source Aurora 209tc, 215tr; imagebroker/Oliver Gerhard 11clb, 256cd, 274br; INTERFOTO Pressebildagentur 172cr; Andy Jackson 284clb; Jacques Jangoux 47tl; Andre Jenny 45cl, 93br, 146clb, 147bl, 154clb, 194bc, 194cb, 195bc; Jerry and Marcy nkman/EcoPhotography.com 210-211; Wendy Johnson 291c; Jon Arnold Images 3 Ltd/John Coletti 229bl; Jon Arnold Images Ltd/Walter Bibikow 45bc, 258clb; Norma Joseph 298bc; Wolfgang Kaehler 115c; Kim Karpeles 134cr, 135ca, 180bc, 182cdb, 183bl, 183cd; Paul Kingsley 148cdb; Erich Kuchling 180tr, 188tr; Douglas Lander 160clb; Yadid Levy 204tr; LHB Photo 170tr, 175bc; Randy Lincks 95tl; James Lipman 159bl; Lynne Siler Photography 92-93; David Lyons 68r, 69br; Manor Photography/Robert Slade 285c; Oyvind Martinsen 43ca; Junior Marx 157cl, 274bl; Neil McAllister 88tc; Jon McLean 176cb; Michael DeFreitas Underwater 47cl; John Mitchell 70br; Gail Mooney-Kelly 244cr, 287c; Mountain Light /Galen Rowell 165bc; Mountain Light/Galen Rowell 219tr; Donald Nausbaum 291cb; Royalty Free/Ian Nellist 159ca; Ron Niebrugge 258c; Dale O'Dell 240ca; M. Timothy O'Keefe 18ca, 105bc, 196ca, 196tc; Sean O'Neill 193tl; PCL 187tc, 222-223, 266tr, 301cl; Chuck Pefley 243cl; Mike Perry 63tc; Chuck Place 58br, 250cb; Porky Pies Photography 128bc, 148tl; James Quine 17tr, 43cb, 200ca; travelstock44 15br, 82tc, 278tl, 282tl; Thibaleye Images/J Marshall 141br; Genevieve Vallee 200tc; Greg Vaughn 23c, 111bc, 259ca; Michael Ventura 279tl, 291tc; Visions of America, LLC 134-135t; VisionStock 259tr; Visual Arts Library (London) 124bl; Richard Wainscoat 285cb; John & Gail Walter 244clb; Brent Ward 128tr, 133br; Nik Wheeler 78bc; A. T. Willett 259tc; Marek Zuk 258ca.

Alaskaphotographics.com: Patrick J. Endres 198cdb, 198r, 199bc, 199bl, 199tr.
Alberta Tourism, Parks, Recreation & Culture: 168bc, 168ca.
Albuquerque International Balloon Fiesta, Inc.: 242clb.
Bryan and Cherry Alexander Photography: 234clb.
AllCanadaPhotos.com: 156bl.
Andrew Hempstead/Escapecentral.com: 173cl.

Ardea: John Cancalosi 240c; Bill Coster 248clb; Francois Gohier 261tr, 271tr; Tom and Pat Leon 292tc; Duncan Usher 142ca; Adrian Warren 278tr, 292tr.
Jon Arnold: FAN Photo Agency 176cr; Gavin Hellier 144cdb, 144-145.
The Art Archive: Dagli Orti 14clb.
Axiom Photographic Agency: Jenny Acheson 61bc; Timothy Allen 118cb; Conor Caffrey 61bl, 221tr; Chris Coe 157fl; Guy Marks 140cb; James Sparshatt 87br.
Tom Bean Photography: 69tr, 177cl.
Branson CVB: 80bl.
BrazilPhotos: Delfim Martins 202br; Olhar/Catherine Krulik 203bc, 203ca; Pulsar/Mauricio Simonetti 203tr.
The Bridgeman Art Library: 186cdb; Private Collection, Peter Newark Historical Pictures 194bl.
Michel Burger: 164br, 165bl.
Calgary Stampede: 169tr.
Camera Press: Mattia Zopellaro 130bc.
Canada Press Images: Edmonton Sun/ Brendon Dlouhy 306tc.
Cherry Crest Farm: 163c.
K. Ciappa: 221ftr.
Coast Mountain Photography: Andrew Doran 57bl.
Colonial Williamsburg Foundation: 286cdb, 286-287, 287cdb, 287tc, 287tr.
Corbis: 87cl, 110clb, 266clb; James L. Amos 147tl; Dave Bartruff 62clb; Bettmann 138cdb, 224bl; John Conrad 87tl; Richard Cummins 301tr; Reinhard Eisele 117tr; EPA/Caetano Barreira 180tl, 202bc; Macduff Everton 55tc, 72cr; Macduff Everton/ 123br; Sandy Felsenthal 281ca; Robert Frerck 253tr; Philip Gould 305tl; Lindsay Hebberd 13bc, 252-253; Hemis/Franck Guiziou 158-159; Jon Hicks 226-7tr; Kit Houghton 211tc; Dave G. Houser 122tc; George H. H. Huey 29tl; Hulton-Deutsch Collection 222cdb; Icon SMI/ Jeff Zelevansky 221tc; William Henry Jackson 188clb; JAI/Peter Adams 152tc, 159tr; JAI/Walter Bibikow 197tc; K J Historical 226tl; Wolfgang Kaehler 122tl; Kelly-Mooney Photography 69tl; Layne Kennedy 118br; Bob Krist 85bc, 150-1, 162-163, 221cl; Lake County Museum 147cl; Robert Landau 246r; Frans Lanting 178-9, 201tr; Danny Lehman 267tl; Michael Lewis 209tl, 217tl; Eduardo Longoni 216cdb; Marilyn Angel Wynn/Nativestock Pictures 228-229; Dennis Marsico 68cdb; Buddy Mays 29bl; Stephanie Maze 50cdb; MedioImages 251tr; David Mercado/Reuters 149tc; Momatiuk - Eastcott 254-5; Tom Myers 233cl, 251c; Kazuyoshi Nomachi 158bl; Richard T. Nowitz 115tr, 304tc; Charles O'Rear 250ca, 250cr; Douglas Peebles 285br; Neil Rabinowitz 236bl; Reuters/Charles W Luzier 119bl; Robert Harding World Imagery/Mark Chivers 159cb; Galen Rowell 11tl, 25tl; Royalty Free/Perry Mastrovito 187bl; San Francisco Chronicle/Kat Wade 33tc, 36bl, 36cr; Kevin Schafer 201tc, 260-1; Phil Schermeister 45tr, 45tc; Paul Seheult 260fbl; Scott T. Smith 206-7; Paul Souders 297bc; Hubert Stadler 217tc; Keren Su 140clb; Rudy Sulgan 118ca; Steve Terril 247bl; Craig Tuttle 247ftr; Underwood & Underwood 228clb; Pablo Corral Vega 25bc; Onne van der Wal 174c, 174-175; Patrick Ward 96-97; Stuart Westmorland 247cl, 296-297; Inge Yspeert 51c; Zefa/Frank Krahmer 2-3; Zefa/Fridmar Damm 245tr; Zefa/Serge Kozak 6-7; Zefa/Theo Allofs 29bc; Zefa/Svenja-Fotoefa 51br.
Corbis Malaysia: Atlantide Phototravel/ Stefano Amantini 48bc; Atlantide Phototravel/Guido Cozzi 90-91, 273tr; Atlantide Phototravel/ Massimo Borchi 71bl, 262-263; Tom Bean 240cdb; Beateworks/Dency Kane 92br; Bettmann 98cb; Tibor Bognar 184-185, 283tr; Brandon D. Cole 167cdb; Guido Cozzi 295tc; Richard Cummins 184ca, 243tl, 269ftl; Momatiuk - Eastcott 299bl; Macduff Everton 88tr, 268ftr, 294-295; Gerald French 278tc, 295tr; Stephen Frink 67cr; Raymond Gehman 161tl; Grand Tour/Massimo Ripani 91tr; Gunter Marx Photography 240-241clb; Blaine Harrington III 32tr, 43tl, 48tr, 48-49, 184tc; Robert Holmes 249tc; Jan Butchofsky-Houser 241cr; Gavriel Jecan 32tr, 42tl; Diane Cook & Len Jenshel 290-291; Ann Johansson 61tc; Wolfgang Kaehler 289cl; Catherine Karnow 49br, 54tr, 59bl; David Keaton 58-59; Kelly-Mooney Photography 143ca; Layne Kennedy 290db; Bob Krist 181tr, 185tr; Frans Lanting 45tc, 249bc; Danny Lehman 243tr; Frank Lukasseck 264bl; Buddy Mays 93bc, 294br; Will & Deni McIntyre 93bl; MedioImages 272bl; Amos Nachoum 106-107b; Richard T. Nowitz 35cr; O. Alamany & E. Vicens/Oriol Alamany 90clb; Carl & Ann Purcell 143ftr; Neil Rabinowitz 153c, 161tr; Jose Fuste Raga 71c; Roger Ressmeyer 24bc; Andy Rouse 298clb; Galen Rowell 153tc, 164-165; San Francisco Chronicle/Paul Chinn 212cr; Kevin Schafer 42-43, 47br; Phil Schermeister 238tr; Scott T. Smith 59br; Carl Van Vechten 184cdb; Ron Watts 35ca, 240-241tl; Michele Westmorland 77tc, 95bl; Stuart Westmorland 55cb, 67cl; Michael S. Yamashita 132-133t; Zefa/ Andy Rouse 81bl; Zefa/Kevin Schafer 47ca.
Richard Cummins: 11tc, 21bc, 21bl, 21br, 21tl, 21tr.
Ron Dahlquist Photography: 26-7, 27cl.
Danita Delimont Stock Photography: Ancient Art & Architecture 224tr; Walter Bibikow 83rc; Gayle Harper 145tc, 161bl; Cindy Miller Hopkins 120cb; Greg Johnston 77cb, 89br; Stuart Westmorland 239ftl.
Joeff Davis: 131c, 131ca.
DDB Stock Photography: Alex OCampo/Photoworks 72cdb.
De Agostini Editore: fcl.
DK Images: 308tc; Max Alexander 41cl; Demetrio Carrasco 82ca, 82-83, 83br, 310tc; Joeff Davis 131bc; Eric Grossman 62ca, 62tc; Nigel Hicks 308tr, 310tr; Magnus Rew 308tl; Rough Guides/Angus Osborn 154br; Rough Guides/Demetrio Carrasco 176clb; Rough Guides/Enrique Uranga 118bc, 118db; Scott Suchman 158bl; Linda Whitwam 308clb, 310tl; Peter Wilson 267tc.
Dolly Parton's Dixie Stampede Dinner Attraction: 80br.
Craig Douce: 274-275.
Dutch Wonderland Family Entertainment Complex: 163tr.
Michele Falzone: 10bl, 13br, 54bl, 61tl.
Festival International de Louisiane: Philip Gould 98c.
FLPA: Reinhard Dirscheel 95tc; David Hosking 86bl; Imagebroker/ Florian Kopp 76tr, 82tr; Frans Lanting 200c, 200-201; Hiroya Minakuchi 270-271clb; Minden Pictures/ Flip Nicklin/115cb, 235tr; Minden Pictures/GERRY ELLIS 106clb; Minden Pictures/Hiroya Minakuchi 298blc; Minden Pictures/Michael & Patricia Fogden 42clb;Minden Pictures/ Thomas Mangelsen 199tr; Minden Pictures/Tom Vezo 40clb; Minden Pictures/Yva Momatiuk & John Eastcott 199ftl; Minden Pictures/Yva Momatiuk/John Eastcott 193bc; Minden Pictures/ZSSD 58bl; Mark Newman 229tr.
fotolia: stsefoto 267tc.
Fotostock Uruguay - Aguaclara: 97cl, 97cr.
Four Seasons Resorts: Michael Calderwood 289tl; Robb Gordon 289tr.
Frank Borges LLosa/Frankly.com: 22bl.
Paul Franklin: 78clb, 171ftr, 184c, 185c, 192clb, 193cl, 193tr, 280-281, 281cdb.
Franz Marc Frei: 41tc, 117cl.
Getty Images: AFP/HECTOR MATA/Staff 205ca; All Canada Photos/Chris Cheadle 157tr; altrendo nature 258-259; Nigel Atherton 144c; Steve Bly 139bl; Frederick M. Brown 301bl; Julien Capmeil 96cr;

Angelo Cavalli 50ca; Diane Cook and Len Jenshel 266cb; Kevin Cooley 223tc; De Agostini Picture Library 136-137tc; Discovery Channel Images/Jeff Foott 236ca; Grant Dixon 140ca; Stephen Dunn 301tc; Paul Edmondson 60r; Neil Emmerson 38br; Grant Faint 140cr; First Light/Peter Mintz 119bc; Jeff Foott 270clb; Stephen Frink 256tr, 260br; Mitchell Funk 195tr; Andre Gallant 222tr; Henry Georgi 275c; Tim Graham 96bl; Corey Hendrickson 20r; Hulton Archive 18bl; Jeff Hunter 284br; Image Bank/Jorg Greuel 100-1; Image Bank/Grant Faint 118-119; The Image Bank/IC Productions 11tca; The Image Bank/Micheal Melford 174br, 175tr; The Image Bank/Steve Dunwell 175bl; Frans Lemmens 115ca; Holger Leue 159tl; Yves Marcoux 172-3; Scott Markewitz 56clb; Will & Deni McIntyre 154bc; Michael Melford 111tl, 214-5; Minden Pictures/Tim Fitzharris 236clb, 236-237; National Geographic/Ira Block 137bc; National Geographic/Martin Gray 305tc; National Geographic/Michael Melford 223tl; National Geographic/ Raymond K. Gehman 275tr; National Geographic/Stephen Alvarez 28r; National Geographic/Steve Winter 124-125; Flip Nicklin 284-285; Michael Ochs Archives 38cdb; Panoramic Images 279tr, 281c; Photodisc/Daryl Benson 223tr; Photodisc/Stuart Gregory 129tl, 145tc; Photographer's Choice/Gerald French 250cl; Photographer's Choice/Darrell Gulin 8-9, 230-231; Photographer's Choice/Jerry Kobalenko 192r; Photographer's Choice/Michael Melford 236c; Photographer's Choice/Walter Bibikow 41tr; Mike Powell 57tl, 57tr; Reportage/Christopher Pillitz 202clb; Lorne Resnick 39br; Roger Ressmeyer 188c; Vincent Ricardel 155c; Riser/Jason Todd 80tr; Norbert Rosing 172ca; Tui De Roy 270tr; Mario Ruiz/Time Life Pictures 194ca; Nicolas Russell 181bl, 191bc; Evaristo Sa/AFP 114br; Sybil Sassoon 87bl; Scott S. Warren/Aurora 137c; Ron Sherman 134-135b; Stephen Simpson 250-251; Jon Spaull 128tc, 135c; Stone/Donovan Reese 80tc; Stone/Gary Vestal 247tl; Stone/Stuart Westmorland 232tc, 246cb; Taxi/Walter Bibikow 25cl, 25fbr; Michael Taylor 191cb; The Image Bank 214tc; Michael Townsend 188ca; Cassio Vasconcellos 50c; Greg Vaughn 285ca, 285tr; Aaron Black Veer 56r; Ron Watts 172c; Stuart Westmorland 36l; Rich Wheatear 214c; Darwin Wiggett 172cb.
Getty Images/Visage Media Services: Aurora/Corey Rich 165tr; Aurora/David Nevala 79ca; Aurora/Kevin Moloney 298-299; Aurora/Peter Essick 165tr; Axiom Photographic Agency/Chris Caldicott 291tr; De Agostini Picture Library/DEA/M.SEEMULLER 70cb; Miles Ertman 133tc; Fred Felleman 152tr, 166clb; First Light/Ron Watts 161tc; First Light/Yves Marcoux 143br, 279c, 283tc; Gallo Images/Martin Harvey 265tr; Hulton Archive/William England 132clb; Hans-Peter Merten 132-133c; National Geographic/Bill Curtsinger 288cdb; National Geographic/Stephen St. John 239tcl; Donald Nausbaum 82cb; Stone/David Hiser 71ca; Norbert Wu 95cl.
Glenbow Museum: 226clb.
Philip Gould: 98tl, 98-99, 99br, 99ca, 99tr.
Hemispheres Images: Patrick Frilet 13tl; Ludovic Maisant 12clb, 13cl; Jean-Baptiste Rabouan 17bc, 17bl, 17tl, 33tl, 41bl, 41br, 41tl; Jean du Boisber Ranger 293tr; Philippe Renault 168clb, 209br, 223cb; Emilio Suetone 304tr.
Houserstock: Ellen Barone 300tr, 301ftr; Steve Bly 129tc, 138r, 139bc, 139tc, 139ftr; Jan Butchofsky-Houser 294cb, 297tc, 297tr; Rankin Harvey 112br, 295bl; Dave G. Houser 211tc, 234c, 272bc.
Hue & Eye: Doug Hickok 78bl.
Fred Hurteau: 125bl.
Imagem Brasil: Gentil Barreira 203cdb.
imagequestmarine.com: V&W/Mark Conlin 37br; V&W/T.Burnett-K. Palmer 74-75.
Impact Photos: Michael Mirecki 50-1.
Insight Photography: 57bc, 57cl, 57tc.
iStockphoto.com: 217cl; Steve Dibblee 72cla.
John Warburton-Lee Photography: Mark Hannaford 263tc.
jupiterimages: Howard Pyle V 66cla.
Wolfgang Kaehler Photography: 197c.
Rusty Kennedy: 220r.
Gabe Kirchheimer: 204tc, 204tl, 204-205, 205cb, 205tl, 205tr.
The Kobal Collection: New Line Cinema 16cb.
Bob Krist: 209tr, 221tl.
Lakes Region Association: Gunstock Mountain Resort 45tl; Inns at Mil Falls 45bl.
Peter Langer/Associated Media Group: 190bc.
Laurence Parent Photography Inc: 68tl.
Jean-Gut Lavoie: 187tr.
Le Massif: 283tl.
James Lemass: 62c.
Holger Leue Photography: 188-189, 189tc, 272br, 272-273.
Kyle Little: 66cb.
Lonely Planet Images Australia: Ann Cecil 249bl; Richard Cummins 46tr; Grant Dixon 165ca; Hanan Isachar 121br; Mark Newman 83tc.
Lonely Planet Images: Olivier Cirendini 99b; Tom Cockrem 32clb, 38bc; Richard Cummins 13c, 281tr; Mark Daffey 141c; Krzysztof Dydinski 96cr; John Elk III 81br; Rhonda Gutenberg 39bl; Richard I'Anson 155bc, 162ca; Lou Jones 62-3c; Ray Laskowitz 141tc; Holger Leue 113br; Cheyenne Rouse 21cl; Witold Skrypczak 233tr, 252bc.
Courtesy Longwood Gardens: L.Albee 162d.
Lucid Images: Mark Downey 247tc.
Marine Scenes: Steve Simonsen 55tl, 64bc, 64bl, 64br, 64tl, 64tr, 64-65, 94r, 95bc.
Gunter Marx - Stock Photos: 57br.
Masterfile: Daryl Benson 161cl; Garry Black 33tr, 34clb, 34-35c, 34-35t, 35cl, 248-249; Frank Krahmer 71br; J. A. Kraulis 243bc; Gail Mooney 34rc; Greg Stott 132tl; Lloyd Sutton 92clb; Jeremy Woodhouse 34cl, 46-47, 262tl, 263cb.
Masterfile: J. David Andrews 171tl; Bill Brooks 210tl, 210tr; Gloria H. Chomica 168-169; Kevin Dodge 112bc; Bill Frymire 115bl; John Gertz 267ftl; Scott Gilchrist 60bl; Chris Hendrickson 235c; J. A. Kraulis 157ftr, 180tc, 193bc, 211ca; Peter Lavery 139bc; Mike Macri 235cl; Zoran Milich 102tc, 115bl; Gail Mooney 104bc, 117tc, 117tr; Roy Ooms 105br; Alec Pytlowany 275bl; Rommel 119bc; Lloyd Sutton 76tc; Mark Tomalty 168c; Marc Vaughn 20cb; Dale Wilson 173c; Jeremy Woodhouse 114-115.
Courtesy Memphis Convention & Visitors Bureau: 104br.
Robert and Linda Mitchell: 280cb.
Mont-Sainte-Anne, Stoneham and QTCQ: Christian Tremblay 283tc.
Courtesy of National Park Service, Lewis and Clark National Historic Trail: 10tr, 29tc, 29tr.
National Geographic Image Collection: STEPHEN ALVAREZ 106br; Skip Brown 295bc; NICOLE DUPLAIX 69clb; RAYMOND GEHMAN 212bl; Bobby Haas 203ftr; RALPH LEE HOPKINS 32tc, 47cb; Vlad Kharitonov 124clb; Tim Laman 262tc; Winfield Parks 94clb; Richard Reid 58bc; Rich Reid Photography.com 59bc; Joe Scherschel 263tl; Steve Winter 242r.
naturepl.com: Christophe Courteau 76cr, 87tr; Pete Oxford 200tr; T.J.

RICH 299ca; Peter Scoones 210tc; Tom Walmsley 33c, 36-7; Solvin Zankl 299cb.
Newport Music Festival: 174clb.
George Oze: 181tl, 194br.
PA Photos: AP Photo/Andres Mata Foundation 292bl; AP Photo/Angela Rowlings 63br; AP Photo/Collin Reid 304tl; AP Photo/Jim Cole 44cdb; AP Photo/Michael Dwyer 54tl, 63tl; AP Photo/Damian Dovarganes 278bc, 301bc; AP Photo/Natacha Pisarenko 190cdb; Andre Luis Mello 307tr; Alexandre Meneghini 203c; Andre Penner 202-203.
Photographers Direct: Fotoscopio Latin American Stock Photo Agency 72c; Magical Andes Photography 103tc, 108bc, 108bl, 108br, 109bc, 109br, 109c, 149cdb, 191tr.
Photolibrary: 84cl, 183tr; Peter Adams 30-1; AlaskaStock 102bc, 110r, 111bl, 111br, 111cl, 111tc, 111tr; Animals Animals/Alan Fortune 45tr; Bill Bachman 126-7; Bill Beatty 125ftr; Walter Bibikow 239tl, 296bl; Cephas Picture Library/R & K Muschenetz 24r; Ron Dahlquist 27bl; Perrine Doug 87bc; Chad Ehlers 103tr, 113cb; Neil Emmerson 39cb; Flirt Collection/Owaki-Kulla 233tl, 236bc; Flirt Collection/Susan G Drinker 237tr; Mickey Gibson 125br; Vaughn Greg 247bc; Robert Harding 144cb; Index Stock 182r; Index Stock Imagery/Barry Winiker 183tc; Index Stock Imagery/Bob Burch 4-5; Index Stock Imagery/Bruce Leighty 183tl; Jon Arnold Travel/Peter Adams 108-109; Mark Jones 86r; JTB Photo 13bl, 117br; Rafael Macia 194-195; Timothy OKeefe 296c; Oxford Scientific (OSF) 158br; Oxford Scientific/Berndt Fischer 244clb; Pacific Stock/David Fleetham 27br; Pacific Stock/William Waterfall 10tc, 26bc; Photononstop/F.Soreau 276-277; Robert Harding Travel/Ellen Rooney 26bc; Mike Rock 122tc, 147br; Royalty-Free/Index Stock Imagery/Everett Johnson 174bc; Royalty Free/Dennis Welsh 22-3; Gerard Soury 270tl; The Travel Library 122tr; Steve Vidler 104clb; Barry Winiker 124bc.
Photolibrary India: AlaskaStock.com 181tc, 199tl; Animals Animals/FRANKLIN VIOLA 257tr, 269tr; Animals Animals/MICHAEL SACCA 167ca; Arcangel Images/Kohi Israel 239ftr; Robert Armstrong 248br; Aurora Photos/Henry Georgi 89tl; Walter Bibikow 239tl, 268cb; Juniors Bildarchiv 82cl; John Brown 43br; John Coletti 218clb; Chad Ehlers 232tl, 243bl; Suetone 169clb; Robert Ginn 121c; Hemis/ Hughes Herve 239ftr; Iconotec/H.FougFre 265bc; Imagestate 269bl; Index Stock Imagery/ Tim Brown 66c; Index Stock Imagery/Angelo Cavalli 106ca; Index Stock Imagery/Barry Winiker 183tc; Index Stock Imagery/NR. Rowan 241tr; Jon Arnold Travel/Peter Adams 238r; JTB Photo 132tr, 185ca, 218-219; JTB Photo/Haga Library 48bl; Duncan Maxwell 78-79; Merten Merten 219tc; Wendell Metzen 79c; Oxford Scientific/Carol Farneti Foster 102tr, 107bc; Oxford Scientific/Colin Monteath 265tr; Oxford Scientific/Tui De Roy 46bl, 299bc; Pacific Stock/Allan Seiden 70bc; Pacific Stock/Dave Fleetham 248bl; Pacific Stock/Perrine Doug 88clb; Pacific Stock/Rosenberg Steve 66cr; Photodisc/Ernesto Rios Lanz/Sexto Sol 265cl; Photodisc/Jeremy Woodhouse 76tl, 90t; Robert Harding Travel/Marco Simoni 264r; Frink Stephen 269tl; Paul Thompson 63tr; Jayme Thornton 79bc.
Photoshot: NHPA/Laurie Campbell 265bl; NHPA/T Kitchin & V Hurst 112clb; NHPA/Trevor Mcdonald 260cr; NHPA/KEVIN SCHAFER 164bc; World Pictures 292br.
Pictures Colour Library: Fotoconcept 145cl; Clive Sawyer 11cr, 15bl.
Heinz Plenge: 200clb.
Marc PoKempner: 130-1.
Prairie du Chien Area Chamber of Commerce: 134clb.
Pulsar Imagens: Ricardo Azoury 302-303; Rogério Reis 302clb.
PunchStock: Photographer's Choice Getty Images 247tr; CreatasImages 186r; Radius Images 146r; Stockbyte 292-3.
Rainshadow Photographics: Mark Gardener 167c, 167tc, 167tr.
Redferns: Jan Persson 130bl.
redshoepub.com: 223ca.
Reuters: Mike Blake 13tr; Daniel LeClair 307tc; Lucy Pemoni 306tr; Jorge Silva 48tl; Paulo Whitaker 202bc.
Rex Features: Rob Crandall 155bl, 25br; James D Morgan 25bl; Sipa Press 153tr, 162clb.
Lucas M. Gómez Rios: 271cb.
Robert Harding Picture Library: 292bc; Bruno Barbier 220clb; Angelo Cavalli 40r; Richard Cummins 144cdb; Odyssey/Robert Frerck 208tl, 219cb; G Richardson 79br; Marco Simoni 257tc, 265tl.
Rocky Mountaineer Vacations: 208bc, 226-7c, 227cb, 227tr.
Royal Canadian Pacific: 226tc;
San Francisco Opera: 213tr.
Sanderling Inn: 124br.
Carlos Sastoque: 17tc.
Allen Blake Sheldon: 135cb.
Shutterstock: Sandra A. Dunlap 67br.
Silver Dollar City Attractions: 77tt, 80bc, 80-1.
South American Pictures: 24clb; Ben Box 245clb; Robert Francis 252br; Mike Harding 270tc; Kimball Morrison 217tr; Tony Morrison 114clb, 225tr, 252cr; Frank Nowikowski 271ca, 271tc.
South End Publishing: Francisco Bedeschi 72bl, 72-73, 73br, 73cl, 73cr.
St. Lucia Tourist Board: 122-3, 123ca; Chris Huxley 123cb.
Stewart Harvey & Associates: Stewart Harvey 204cdb.
Strasburg Rail Road: 162cr.
SuperStock: 201tl; age fotostock 259c; Angelo Cavalli 84bc; Richard Cummins 150tl, 300tl; Hemis.fr 296ca; Prisma 222tl, 227tc, 266-267; José Fuste Raga 289tc.
Terra Galleria Photography: 69tc, 103clb, 121b, 136clb, 136tr, 137tl, 229bc, 26br, 120br, 120-121, 249tr.
The Travel Library: Stuart Black 38-39; John Carr 140-141; Rolf Richardson 39ca, 152bl, 176ca.
Travel Ink: David Foreman 16r.
Tyba Photographic Agency: Ciro Mariano 303tr; Rogério Reis 302cr.
Vancouver Folk Music Festival: 156r, 157bl.
VIA Rail Canada: 226tr.
Dennis Welsh: 44r.
Wikimedia Commons: 23br.
Windstar Cruises & Majestic America Line: 257bc, 272tl, 272tr.
Jenny Woodruff: 66-67.
www.bardonthebeach.org: David Blue 152tl, 157bc.
Yves Tessier/Tessima: 187bc, 187tl.

US Jacket

Jacket images: Front: Alamy Images: nagelestock.com br; Michele Falzone: main; Getty Images: Kevin Horgan bl; Gail Shumway fbr. SuperStock: Bruce Dorrier bc. Back: Alamy Images: Charles O. Cecil crb; StockShot/Ian Parnell ftl; Nik Wheeler tr; Alaska Stock: Corbis: Blaine Harrington III tr; Ann Johansson ca; Stuart Westmorland fcrb; Zefa/Serge Kozak ca; De Agostini Editore: crb; Peter Langer/Associated Media Group: fcra; SuperStock: Prisma cb. Spine: Getty Images: Walter Bibikow t; Tim Thompson b.

All other images © Dorling Kindersley
For further information see: www.dkimages.com

CANADA, USA,
CENTRAL AMERICA
& HAWAI'I

Alaska

Inland Passage

Denali
National
Park

Gwaii Haanas
National Park
Reserve

Whistler
Vancouver
San Juan Islands

Banff and
Lake Louise
Calgary

CANADA

Cape
Churchill

The Viking Trail

Avalon
Peninsula

Cape
Breton Island

The Laurentians
Québec City
Montréal
Ottawa

Halifax
Fundy Isles
Mount Desert Island

Mackinac
Island

Lakes Region
Finger
Lakes
Boston
Cape Cod

Toronto
Niagara
Falls

New York
City
The Hamptons

Rhode Island

Oregan
Coast

Stanley

Yellowstone
National
Park
Cody

Jackson Hole

Wisconsin

Chicago

Pennsylvania
Dutch Country

Philadelphia

Washington, D.C.

California Wine
Country

Reno

South
Dakota

USA

Williamsburg

San Francisco

Utah's
National Parklands

Great River
Road

Blue Ridge
Parkway

Outer Banks

Las Vegas

Mesa Verde
National Park

Branson

Los Angeles
Pasadena

Grand Canyon
National Park
Santa Fe

Memphis

Lowcountry

Bermuda

Anza-Borrego
Desert State Park

Albuquerque

Savannah

Tucson

Carlsbad Caverns
National Park

Natchez Trace

Nogales

Lafayette

Orlando

**PACIFIC
OCEAN**

Copper Canyon

San Antonio

Miami

**ATLANTIC
OCEAN**

Baja
California Sur

MEXICO

Mexico
City

Yucatán

Mayan Riviera

CARIBBEAN SEA

Ambergris Caye
Southern Coastal Islands

Oaxaca

BELIZE

GUATEMALA   HONDURAS

EL SALVADOR   NICARAGUA

Nicoya Peninsula

COSTA RICA

PANAMA

Panama City

Kaua'i

HAWAI'I

Maui

Hawai'i